John Murray

A Handbook for Travellers in Devon and Cornwall

John Murray

A Handbook for Travellers in Devon and Cornwall

ISBN/EAN: 9783337211806

Printed in Europe, USA, Canada, Australia, Japan

Cover: Foto ©Andreas Hilbeck / pixelio.de

More available books at **www.hansebooks.com**

A

HANDBOOK FOR TRAVELLERS

IN

DEVON AND CORNWALL.

SIXTH EDITION, REVISED.

WITH MAPS AND PLANS.

LONDON:
JOHN MURRAY, ALBEMARLE STREET.
1865.

CONTENTS.

	Page
INTRODUCTION	vii

Section I.—DEVONSHIRE.

ROUTES.

_{*} The names of places are printed in *italics* only in those routes where the *places* are described.

ROUTE	PAGE
1 London to *Exeter* (Great Western Railway)	2
2 London to *Tiverton* (Great Western Rail); Tiverton to Crediton (Road)	20
3 London to Exeter (S. W. Rail)	23
4 Lyme Regis to Exeter, by (*Seaton*) *Sidmouth*, *B. Salterton*, and *Exmouth*	31
5 Exeter to Exmouth (Rly.)	43
6 Exeter to Launceston, by *Okehampton* (Neighbourhood of Okehampton, *Lidford*, *Brent Tor*)	44
7 Exeter to *Plymouth* (*Dawlish*, *Teignmouth*, *Newton*, *Totnes*, *Ivy Bridge*, and their Neighbourhoods)	53
8 Exeter to *Torquay* (S. Devon Rail). Neighbourhood of Torquay	88
9 Torquay to *Brixham* and *Dartmouth* (Dartmouth and Torbay Rail).—The Coast (*Slapton*, *Torcross*, the *Start*, the *Prawle*, *Salcombe*, the *Bolt*) from Dartmouth to Kingsbridge	95
10 Exeter to Torquay, by *Chudleigh* (*Haldon*)	108

ROUTE	PAGE
11 Exeter to *Ashburton* and *Buckfastleigh* (*Buckland*, *Holne*, *Holne Chace*)	111
12 Exeter to Tavistock, by *Moreton Hampstead* (the *Teign*, *Drewsteignton*, *Chagford*, *Widdecombe*, *Lustleigh Cleave*, *Heytor*, *Dartmoor*)	117
13 Plymouth to *Tavistock* (S. Devon and Tavistock Rail)	142
14 Walk across Dartmoor, from Tavistock to South Zeal, by *Cranmere Pool*	155
15 Plymouth to *Modbury* and *Kingsbridge*. The Coast from Kingsbridge to Plymouth	156
16 Totnes to Plymouth (Road). *Ermington*, *Yealmpton*.	159
17 Exeter to *Barnstaple* and *Bideford*, by *Crediton*—N. Devon Rail. (*S. Molton*; *Torrington*)	160
18 *Lynmouth* and *Lynton* to *Hartland*, by *Combe Martin*, *Ilfracombe* (Barnstaple), and *Clovelly*	172
19 Taunton to Lynmouth and Lynton, by *Watchet*, *Dunster*, and *Porlock*	193
20 Bampton to *Holsworthy*, by South Molton and Torrington	195

Contents

Section II.—CORNWALL.

ROUTES.

ROUTE	PAGE
21 *Launceston* to Truro, by Bodmin. (Road: over the Bodmin and Goss Moors. *Brown Willy* and *Roughtor*; *Huntergantick*, *Dozmare*.)	201
22 Launceston to Truro, by *Camelford*, *Wadebridge*, and *St. Columb*. (The North Coast. *Boscastle*; *Tintagel*; *Delabole Quarries*; *Padstow*; the Vale of *Mawgan*; *Newquay*)	212
23 Plymouth to *Truro*, by *Saltash*, *St. Germans*, *Liskeard* (the *Cheesewring*, *St. Neot's*), *Bodmin*, *Lostwithiel* (*Restormel*), *St. Blazey*, and *St. Austell*. [Cornwall Railway.] (*Perranzabuloe*; *Perran Round*; the *Coast*)	230
24 Plymouth (*Rame Head*) to Falmouth, by *Looe*, *Fowey*, and *St. Austell*. (The *South Coast*.)	261
25 Plymouth to *Bude Haven*, by Saltash, *Callington*, Launceston, and *Stratton*. (The Coast from Bude to Morwenstow.)	270
26 Truro to *Falmouth*, by *Penryn*, (*Falmouth Harbour* and *Inlets*.)	280
27 Truro to *Penzance*, by *Redruth* (*Portreath*, *Carnbrea*), *Camborne*, and *Hayle* (*Lelant*, *Ludgvan*). *Mount's Bay*, *Madron*	285
28 Truro to Penzance, by *Helston* and *Marazion*. The *Lizard*. (The Coast from Helston to Penzance.)	300
29 Excursions from Penzance. (*St. Michael's Mount*, *St. Ives*, *Gurnard's Head*, *Cape Cornwall*, *Land's End*, *Lamorna Cove*, *Scilly Islands*.)	315

Index 353

Plan of Exeter	6
Plan of Exeter Cathedral .. .. to face	8
Plan of Plymouth	70, 71

INTRODUCTION.

	Page			Page
SKELETON TOURS	vii	TRAVELLER'S VIEW		xlv
GEOLOGY	xiv	OLD LANGUAGE		lvii
ANTIQUITIES	xxiii	DUCHY OF CORNWALL		lix
MINES	xxxiii			

SKELETON TOURS.
No. I.—NORTH DEVON.

ROUTE.	CHIEF POINTS OF INTEREST [THE MOST REMARKABLE WITH THE ASTERISK.]
Bridgewater	Altar-piece of St. Mary's. St. John's Church. Tapestry in the Assize Hall. The bore on the river, spring-tides. Manufacture of Bath bricks.
Dunster	Castle. View from Grabhurst Hill*. View from Minehead. Alabaster cliffs of Blue Anchor.
Porlock	Culbone*. Bossington -Hill*. Dunkery Beacon*.
Lynton	Lyndale*. Valley of Rocks*. Glenthorne*. Simonsbath*. Heddon's Mouth*.
Combe Martin	Watermouth. Manor-house of Berrynarbor.
Ilfracombe	The Coast.
Barnstaple.	
Bideford	Pebble Ridge. Manor-house of Wear Gifford. The Hobby*. Clovelly*. Clovelly Court*.
Torrington.	
South Molton	Castle Hill, seat of Earl Fortescue.
Dulverton	Some of the finest scenery in the W. of England. View from Mount Sydenham*. Exmoor. Pixton Park.
Bampton	Limestone quarries on an uncommon scale. Charming Valley.
Wiveliscombe	View from the Bampton road.
Taunton	Church of St. Mary Magdalene.

Note.—In proceeding from the Great Western Railway to Lynton (besides the railway to Watchet, Rte. 19) there are 6 roads for your choice: viz. 1. From Bridgewater, crossing the Quantock Hills near the sea. 2. From Bridgewater, passing the Quantocks to Bishop's Lydeard. 3. From Taunton, running at the foot of the Quantock Hills, from end to end; identical with No. 2 from Bishop's Lydeard, and perhaps a more picturesque road than No. 1. (The railway to Watchet, Rte. 19, runs parallel with this.) 4. From Wellington Road Station, by Milverton, Wiveliscombe, Dulverton, and Simonsbath. 5. From Tiverton Station, by Bampton, Dulverton, and Simonsbath. 6. From Barnstaple Station, Paracombe, or by Ilfracombe and Combe Martin. 4 and 5 are far more beautiful than 1, 2, or 3, but cross-country roads. Coaches run daily during the summer months, on 1 and 6. On 2, 4, and 5 you must travel with your own horses, post, or walk.

No. II.—SOUTH DEVON.

Route.	Chief Points of Interest.
Taunton	Church of St. Mary Magdalene.
Chard	Church. Lace-mills. Views from Snowdon and Rana Hill. Ford Abbey*.
Axminster	Ruins of Shute Manor-house.
Lyme Regis	Pinney Landslips*.
Seaton	Beer. Branscombe Mouth. Coast thence to Sidmouth.
Sidmouth	High Peak. Knowle Cottage. Church of Ottery St. Mary. Bicton.
Budleigh Salterton	The cliff-walk. Pebbles of the beach.
Exmouth	View from the Beacon Walks.
Dawlish	Parson and Clerk Rocks. View from Haldon*.
Teignmouth	View from the Den.
Torquay	Anstis Cove*. Babbacombe*. Watcombe*. Compton Castle. Brixham.
Newton.	
Ashburton	Heytor Rocks*. Buckland*. Auswell Rock, Lover's Leap*. Holne Chace*. Dart-meet. Buckfastleigh.
Totnes	Berry Pomeroy Castle* Dartington Hall. Voyage down the Dart*.
Dartmouth	Church. Castle. Brookhill. Old houses. Coast between the Start Point and Salcombe*.
Salcombe	Coast from Bolt Head to Bolt Tail. Prawle Point*.
Modbury	Spire of church.
Ivy Bridge	The Ivy-bridge. Valley of the Erme*. Coast of Bigbury Bay. Yealm Estuary.
Plympton	Church of Plympton St. Mary.
Plymouth	⎧ Mount Edgcumbe*. Dockyard. Steamyard. Breakwater*. Plymouth Hoe. Royal Albert
Devonport	⎨ Bridge*. Voyage to Weir-head of Tamar*. ⎩ Saltram. Bickleigh Vale*. Valley of the Cad*.
Tavistock	Morwell Rocks*. Double Water. Mis Tor. Wistman's Wood*. Brent Tor. Tavy Cleave. Lidford Cascade*. Lidford Bridge*.
Okehampton	Castle. Yes Tor*. Belstone*. Cawsand Beacon.
Chagford	Gidleigh Park*. Druidic monuments. Spinsters' Rock. Whyddon Park*. Fingle Bridge*.
Moreton Hampstead	Lustleigh Cleave*. Houndtor Coomb*. Becky Fall*. Grimspound. Celtic bridge at Post Bridge*.
Dunsford Bridge	Scenery of the Teign*.
Chudleigh	Chudleigh Rock*.
Exeter	Cathedral.

Introd. *Skeleton Tours.* ix

No. III.—CORNWALL.

Route.	Chief Points of Interest.
Plymouth	(Rte. 7).
Saltash	Royal Albert Bridge*. Trematon Castle.
St. Germans	Church. Port Eliot.
Looe	Scenery of the estuary and coast.
Polperro	Romantic coast.
Fowey	Place House. Scenery of the estuary.
Lostwithiel	Restormel Castle. Lanhydrock House. Glynn. Boconnoc.
St. Blazey	Valley of Carmeirs* and Treffry Viaduct*. Fowey Consols and Par Consols Copper-mines.
St. Austell	Church tower. Carclaze Mine*. China-clay works. Tin stream-works. Mevagissey. Roche Rocks*.
Grampound.	
Probus	Church tower.
Truro	Scenery of the river. St. Piran's church. Perran Round*.
Perran Wharf	Gardens of Carclew.
Falmouth	Pendennis Castle. Falmouth Harbour. Mabe Quarries. Tolmên.
Helston	Looe Pool. Kinance Cove*. Lizard Point*. Devil's Frying Pan.
Penzance	Museum of the Geolog. Society. St. Michael's Mount*. Land's End*. Tol Pedn Penwith*. Logan Rock*. Lamorna Cove. Botallack Mine (submarine)*. Druidic antiquities. Isles of Scilly.
Hayle	Iron-foundries. St. Ives and its bay*.
Redruth	Mines. Carn-brea Hill.
Newquay	Coast scenery.
St. Columb	Vale of Mawgan. Lanherne.
Wadebridge	Padstow. Church of St. Enodoc.
Bodmin	Glynn valley. Hanter-Gantick*.
Liskeard	St. Keyne's Well. Clicker Tor. St. Cleer's Well. Trevethy Stone. Cheesewring*. Kilmarth Tor.
Jamaica Inn	Dozmare Pool. Brown Willy*. Rowtor*.
Camelford	Rowtor*. Devil's Jump. Hanter-Gantick*. Delabole Quarries. Tintagel*. St. Nighton's Keeve. Boscastle*.
Launceston	Castle. Church of St. Mary. Endsleigh*.
Callington	Dupath Well. Cothele*. View from Kit Hill*.
Tavistock	(Rte. 13).
Plymouth	(Rte. 7).

No. IV.—DEVON AND E. CORNWALL.

A *walk* of 9 weeks taken by T. C. P. It comprehends the chief points of interest in Devonshire, and in Cornwall, E. of a line through Liskeard.

Note.—The best arrangement for a pedestrian tour in England is to send your luggage from town to town by the public conveyances—that is, if you can occasionally do without it for a day or two, for of course there are not vans to every spot you may wish to visit. Provide yourself with a pocket compass.

Days.	Route.

1. London to Taunton by rail. Hemyock.
2. Hemyock Castle. Dunkeswell Abbey. Hembury Fort. Honiton.
3. Axminster.
4. Ford Abbey. Return to Axminster. Shute House. Colyton.
5. Seaton (Pinney Landslips should be seen). Beer Quarry. Branscombe Mouth. By coast to Weston Mouth. Salcombe Regis. Sidmouth.
6. At Sidmouth.
7. Coast to Ladram Bay. Otterton. Bicton. Budleigh Salterton.
8. Exmouth. Starcross. Rail to Exeter.
9. Exeter Cathedral, Castle, &c. Rail to Dawlish.
10. Parson and Clerk Rocks. (You should also ascend Haldon.) Teignmouth. Chudleigh.
11. Chudleigh Rock. Bovey Tracey. Excursion to Hennock and Bottor Rock. Bovey Tracey.
12. Heytor Rocks. Rippon Tor. Houndtor Coomb. Becky Fall. Manaton. Moreton Hampstead.
13. Lustleigh Cleave. Grimspound. Return to Moreton Hampstead.
14. Dunsford Bridge. Up the Teign to Fingle Bridge. Drewsteignton.
15. Preston Berry. Cranbrook Castle. Up the Teign to Whyddon Park. Return to Drewsteignton.
16. Spinsters' Rock. Gidleigh and Gidleigh Park. Chagford.
17. Over Dartmoor to the source of the N. Teign. Ascend Cut Hill. Follow the Dart to Post Bridge. Ascend Bel Tor. Ascend Crockern Tor. Two Bridges.
18. Wistman's Wood. Ascend Bairdown. Dart-meet. Newbridge. Ashburton.
19. Ascend Buckland Beacon. Buckland. Lover's Leap. Return to Ashburton.
20. Penn slate-quarry. Buckfastleigh. Totnes.
21. Totnes Castle. Berry Pomeroy Castle. By boat down the Dart to Dartmouth.
22. At Dartmouth.
23. By coast to Brixham. Paignton.
24. Torquay. Anstis Cove. Babbacombe. Return to Torquay.
25. By coach to Dartmouth.
26. By coast to Torcross.
27. By coast to Start Point and Prawle Point. Salcombe.
28. By coast from Bolt Head to Bolt Tail and Hope. Return to Salcombe.
29. Kingsbridge. Modbury.
30. Caton. Ivy Bridge. Harford. Sharpitor. Ascend Western Beacon. Return to Ivy Bridge.
31. Caton. Mothecomb. By coast to Revelstoke Church. Noss. Plymouth.
32. At Plymouth and Devonport.
33. Plympton. Plym Bridge. Cann Quarry. Bickleigh Vale. Jump.

Introd. *Skeleton Tours.* xi

DAYS. ROUTE.
34. Bickleigh. Valley of the Cad. Shaugh.
35. Hoo Meavy. Ascend Sheepstor. Clacywell Pool. Prince's Town.
36. The granite-quarries. Ascend Mis Tor. Over the moor by compass to summit of Yes Tor. Okehampton,
37. Okehampton Castle. Up valley of W. Okement. Ascend to summit of Lake Down. Lidford.
38. Lidford Castle and Bridge. Lidford Cascade. Ascend Brent Tor. Mary Tavy. Huel Friendship. Mis Tor. Tavistock.
39. Lionizing Tavistock and neighbourhood.
40. Morwell Rocks. Ascend Kit Hill. Callington.
41. Dupath Well. Saltash. St. Germans.
42. Looe. Duloe. St. Keyne's Well. Liskeard.
43. St. Cleer. Half-stone. Trevethy Stone. Return to Liskeard,
44. Hurlers. Cheesewring. Kilmarth Tor. Jamaica Inn.
45. Dozmare Pool. Four-hole Cross. Ascend Brown Willy and Rowtor. Camelford.
46. Devil's Jump. Hanter-Gantick. Wadebridge.
47. Padstow. Endellion. Delabole Quarries. Pengelley.
48. Tintagel. Trevena.
49. Bossiney. St. Nighton's Keive. Willapark Point. Boscastle.
50. Crackington Cove. Stratton.
51. Stamford Hill. Bude.
52. Kilkhampton. Morwenstow. Hartland.
53. Hartland Abbey-church. By coast to Hartland Point. Clovelly.
54. Clovelly Court. By the Hobby to Buckish Mill. Bideford.
55. The Pebble Ridge. Appledore. Barnstaple.
56. Braunton. Ilfracombe.
57. Watermouth. Combe Martin.
58. By coast to Trentishoe. Heddon's Mouth. Lynton.
59. Excursing about Lynton. (You should devote another day to Simonsbath.)
60. Glenthorne. Porlock. Minehead.
61. Ascend Dunkery Beacon (usually ascended from Porlock). Culbone. Porlock.
62. Dunster. Williton. Bridgewater.

No. V.—A PEDESTRIAN TOUR IN CORNWALL.

DAYS. ROUTE.
1. London to Devonport by rail or steamboat.
2. Saltash. St. Germans (or by water to St. Germans).
3. To the coast of Whitesand Bay. Looe.
4. Polperro. Sandplace. St. Keyne's Well. Liskeard.
5. Visit Trevethy Stone, Cheesewring, Sharpitor, Kilmarth Tor, Hurlers, Half-stone, St. Cleer. Return to Liskeard.
6. Lostwithiel.
7. Fowey.
8. St. Blazey. St. Austell.
9. Hensbarrow, and Roche Rocks. Return to St. Austell.
10. Mevagissey. By coast to Penare Head. Tregony.
11. Probus. Truro.
12. Carclew. Penryn. Falmouth.

Days.	Route.

13. Mabe Quarries. Tolmên. Helston.
14. Loe Pool. Coast by Kinance Cove to Lizard Town.
15. Coast from Lizard Point to Cadgewith. Helston.
16. Marazion. St. Michael's Mount. Penzance.
17. Lamorna Cove. Logan Rock. Coast to Land's End and Sennen Church-town.
18. Coast to Botallack Mine (descend into this mine). Gurnard's Head. St. Ives.
19. Coast to Portreath. Redruth.
20. Ascend Castle Carn-brea. Visit St. Day and the Gwennap Consolidated Mines. Return to Redruth.
21. Perran Round. Ascend St. Agnes' Beacon. Perran Porth.
22. St. Piran's Church. Newquay.
23. Vale of Mawgan. Coast to Padstow.
24. Wadebridge. Bodmin.
25. Hanter-Gantick. Ascend Rowtor. Camelford.
26. Tintagel.
27. St. Nighton's Keeve. Boscastle.
28. Launceston (procure a ticket for Endsleigh).
29. Endsleigh. Tavistock.
30. Bickleigh Vale. Plymouth.

No. VI.—A WEEK'S TOUR TO LYNTON.

Days.	Route.

1. Bridgewater to Dunster by Bishop's Lydeard, Crowcombe, and Williton. See Cothelstone Manor-house on W. foot of Quantocks; church and ancient crosses at B. Lydeard; pictures and grounds of Crowcombe Court; cross in Crowcombe churchyard.
2. Visit Dunster Castle and its deer-park. Ascend Grabhurst Hill. Excurse to Blue Anchor (superb view and curious cliffs) and Minehead. Ascend the hill above Minehead.
3. Dunster to Porlock. Ascend Bossington Hill, or Dunkery Beacon (both if possible). Visit Culbone. Sleep at Porlock or Minehead.
4. Porlock to Lynton, visit Glenthorne by the way (there is a coast-path from Porlock by Culbone and Glenthorne to Countesbury).
5. Excurse to Waters'-meet, Valley of Rocks, Lee Bay, and Heddon's Mouth.
6. Lynton to Dulverton by Simonsbath.
7. Dulverton to Taunton—or to Tiverton Stat. by Bampton.

No. VII.—A WEEK'S TOUR IN N. DEVON.

Days.	Route.

1. Taunton to Lynton (a coach), a beautiful drive; but you may go through Exeter by rail to Barnstaple, and thence to Lynton.
2. Excurse to Waters'-meet, Valley of Rocks, Lee Bay, and Heddon's Mouth.
3. Excurse to Glenthorne, returning by Brendon and Waters'-meet.
4. Excurse to Simonsbath.
5. Lynton to Bideford.
6. Excurse to Clovelly and Clovelly Court.
7. Bideford to Exeter by rail.

Introd. *Skeleton Tours.* xiii

No. VIII.—A WEEK'S WALK FROM EXETER.

DAYS. ROUTE.
1. Fingle Bridge. Whyddon Park. Chagford.
2. Gidleigh Park. Scorhill Circle. Sittaford Tor. Return to Chagford by Fenworthy.
3. Lustleigh Cleave. Becky Fall. Heytor. Ashburton.
4. Excurse from Ashburton to Buckland, or Holne Chace.
5. Dart-meet. Crockern Tor. Wistman's Wood. Two Bridges.
9. Prince's Town. Mis Tor. Summit of Yes Tor. Okehampton.
7. Spinsters' Rock, Exeter.

No. IX.—A FORTNIGHT'S TOUR FROM EXETER.

DAYS. ROUTE.
1. Chudleigh. Heytor Rocks. Ashburton.
2. Excursion to Buckland, or Holne Chace.
3. Dartington Hall. Berry Pomeroy. Totnes. In the evening by the Dart to Dartmouth.
4. Coast to Salcombe [or by Brixham to Torquay].
5. Coast to Mothecomb. Modbury [or from Torquay to Anstis Cove, Babbacombe, Totnes, and by rail to Ivy Bridge].
6. Ermington. Ivy Bridge. Explore the valley of the Erme.
7. Plymouth (by rail). Dockyard. Breakwater. Mt. Edgcumbe. Albert Bridge.
8. Voyage on the Tamar to Cothele and the Morwell Rocks, returning to Plymouth.
9. Tavistock, visiting Bickleigh Vale and the Valley of the Cad by the way.
10. Okehampton by Brent Tor. Lidford Cascade and Lidford Bridge.
11. Ascend Yes Tor. Return by Belstone to Okehampton.
12. Spinsters' Rock. Gidleigh Park. Scorhill Circle. Chagford.
13. Lustleigh Cleave. Becky Fall. Houndtor Coomb. Moreton Hampstead.
14. Whyddon Park. Fingle Bridge. Exeter.

No. X.—A THREE WEEKS' TOUR IN S. DEVON.

DAYS. ROUTE.
1. London to Taunton by rail (or London to Dorchester by rail).
2. Taunton to Lyme Regis, a coach (or Dorchester to Lyme Regis.)
3. Pinney Landslips. Seaton. Walk to Beer and Branscombe Mouth. Sleep at Seaton.
4. Seaton to Exeter, stopping at Sidmouth on the way.
5. Fingle Bridge. Whyddon Park. Spinsters' Rock. Chagford.
6. Excurse from Chagford to Gidleigh Park, Scorhill Circle, and Sittaford Tor.
7. Lustleigh Cleave. Becky Fall. Houndtor Coomb. Sleep at Moreton Hampstead.
8. Moreton to Okehampton by Gidleigh. Stop at Sticklepath and walk to Taw Marsh.
9. Castle. Ascend Yes Tor. Return by Belstone to Okehampton.

xiv   *Geology.*   Introd:

DAYS.   ROUTE.
10. Lidford Bridge. Lidford Cascade. Brent Tor. Tavy Cleave-Tavistock.
11. Excurse to Mis Tor and Wistman's Wood.
12. Tavistock to Plymouth, visiting Shaugh Bridge and Bickleigh Vale.
13. Dockyard. Breakwater. Mt. Edgcumbe. Albert Bridge.
14. By the Tamar to Cothele and Morwell Rocks. Return to Plymouth.
15. Ivy Bridge (rail). Explore the valley of the Erme.
16. Totnes (rail). Dartington Hall. Dartmouth by the river.
17. Brixham. Torquay.
18. Anstis Cove. Babbacombe. Berry Pomeroy. Ashburton.
19. Excurse to Holne Chace and Lover's Leap.
20. Heytor Rocks. Chudleigh.
21. Over Haldon to Exeter.

GEOLOGY.

Those who are desirous of studying ancient geological formations will find Devonshire and Cornwall well adapted to such a purpose. Their rugged coasts, mainly composed of the older rocks, display a variety of instructive sections, and the mines afford opportunities which rarely occur in other parts of England of descending through the crust of the earth and examining its structure. The geologist may obtain in these counties abundant evidence of physical convulsions which have modified the surface. He may find igneous rocks which have been protruded from great depths; sedimentary deposits rendered crystalline by heat, or contorted by some local disturbance; stanniferous gravel, apparently accumulated by a flood which inundated the country; the remains of forests buried beneath the sand of the shore; beaches raised 40 and 50 ft. above the present level of the sea; and a great part of the country rent by ancient fissures of unknown depth, now filled with a store of mineral treasure.

The formations which appear in the mineral structure of Devon and Cornwall, arranged according to the supposed order of their protrusion or deposition, may be enumerated as—1. *Hornblende* and *micaceous slate;* 2. *Grauwacke,* a comprehensive series, including the Silurian system of Murchison, and corresponding with the superior and inferior transition rocks of Brittany; 3. *Carbonaceous strata;* 4. *Granite;* 5. *New Red Sandstone;* 6. *Chalk;* and 7. *Tertiary deposits.* The county of Cornwall, compared with the rest of Britain, and even with Ireland, is of a very peculiar mineral construction, but it bears a considerable relation to the opposite coast of France. Its geology, however, is very unsettled; and it is only in recent years that the series intermediate between the Carboniferous and Silurian groups has been considered equivalent to the Old Red Sandstone, and the members of this series, so diverse in structure and colour, arranged as a single family under the name of *the Devonian System.* This system includes the S. of Devon and extensive tracts of Cornwall.

1. *Mica Slate* and its associated metamorphic or crystalline rocks occupy but a small part of the district under consideration. In Devon-

shire they form that bold coast between the Start Point and Bolt Tail, and abut upon grauwacke at a short distance from the sea; "the *gneiss* being chiefly observable near the Prawle, and the *mica slate* best seen in the vicinity of the Bolt Head." In Cornwall they are found only at the Lizard promontory, where they pass under serpentine and diallage-rock, which are supposed to have been protruded in a state of fusion subsequently to the formation of the grauwacke. *Tulco-micaceous slate*, intermixed with hornblende slate, occurs at the Old Lizard Head (a mile W. of the lighthouses), but is confined to that locality. The gneiss rocks of the Eddystone are regarded as a connecting link between the slates of the Lizard and the Bolt Head.

Serpentine is a beautifully coloured rock, so named from the waved form of its lines, or the supposed resemblance of its streaks and colours to those of a serpent's skin, and is traversed by veins of steatite, which occasionally contain fragments of serpentine and strings of native copper. With diallage-rock it constitutes the greater part of the Lizard district, where it forms as it were an island, being surrounded on all sides by the sea or hornblende slate. In many places it appears to pass into hornblende slate, as may be seen in Mullion and Pradanack Coves, the Frying-pan near Cadgewith, and under the Balk at Landewednack; but the priority of the hornblende is inferred from the circumstance of its underlying the serpentine, which between the Dranna Point and Porthalla may be seen thrust among the slates with every mark of violence. The correctness of this inference is evidenced at the Nare Head by a grauwacke conglomerate, which, containing detrital fragments of *hornblende slate*, affords no trace of serpentine or diallage, although they occur in mass at a little distance. The *diallage-rock* predominates on the eastern side of this district, and is referred to a period subsequent to that of the serpentine as in various places veins of the former penetrate the latter. These diallage veins may be seen at Coverack Cove, and in the cliffs near Landewednack. Diallage-rock is distinguished from serpentine chiefly by its metallic brilliancy and laminated structure. The *hornblende slate* which bounds the serpentine on the N. abuts in its turn upon grauwacke, and the junction-line may be traced, but not very clearly, from Bellurian Cove near Mullion by Trelowarren to St. Keverne. Beyond this place, however, as the hornblende slate stretches towards the coast, it becomes so intermingled with common greenstones as to be scarcely distinguishable. Both hornblende slate and greenstone are composed of hornblende and felspar, but the one is schistose and the other granular in its structure.

2. The numerous rocks embraced by the term *grauwacke* occupy extensive districts in the N. and S.W. of Devon, and the entire area of Cornwall, with the exception of the Lizard, the carbonaceous district in the N.E., and the large isolated patches of granite; the beds of the series showing much diversity in their composition and colour, but for the most part consisting of sedimentary rocks, which vary in texture from a fine roofing-slate to the coarsest conglomerate. These deposits are associated with limestones and trappean rocks, the latter being

both vesicular and compact, and formed of volcanic ashes and lava originally projected among the mud, sand, and gravel, now consolidated into slates, sandstones, and conglomerates. The grauwacke slates have been separated into two divisions; the first consisting of strata which are metalliferous, and contain many elvans, but few greenstones; the second, of slates which are only sparingly metalliferous, and associated with a number of greenstones, but no elvans. Tin and copper lodes are found among the former rocks, and lead-veins in the latter.

In the N. of Devon the rugged grauwacke country of Lynton and Ilfracombe attains its greatest elevation on Exmoor, and passes under the carbonaceous deposits on a line between Bampton and Fremington, near Barnstaple. It presents some dreary scenery on the coast at Lynmouth, girding the shore with the most barren siliceous sandstones. In the Valley of Rocks its fantastic crags are composed of calciferous and schistose grits; at Combe Martin the strata are argillaceous slates, very beautifully coloured and traversed by veins of argentiferous lead-ore; at Ilfracombe argillaceous slates and schistose grits; at Morthoo dark slates relieved by a white tracery of quartz; and below Woolacombe sands, towards Baggy Point, streaked with manganese and curiously *weathered*. In the S.W. of Devon the beds of this formation are much complicated by *faults*, and by an irregular covering of more modern deposits, but occupy a large area, being bounded by the sea and mica slate of the Bolt on the S., by granite and the carbonaceous deposits on the N., and by new red sandstone on the E.; the boundary-line passing near the towns of Launceston, Tavistock, Ivy Bridge, Ashburton, Newton, and Torquay. The *limestones* are perhaps the most interesting rocks of the series, bearing on their marble surfaces the stamp of a coralline origin, and contorted and rent by intrusive trap, while they soar from woods or the sands of the shore in grey or glossy roseate cliffs. Those of Plymouth, Buckfastleigh, Chudleigh, Brixham, and Torquay are as well known for their beauty as for their value in an economical point of view. Varieties of argillaceous slate, or *killas*, form romantic cliffs in the bays of the Start and Bigbury.

In Cornwall, on the N. coast, between Boscastle and Tintagel, the grauwacke has been forced seaward by the protrusion of the Bodmin granite, and consists of argillaceous slates intimately mixed with schistose and vesicular trap, the latter being much impregnated with carbonate of lime. This *volcanic ash*, in Devonshire known as *honeycomb dun*, may also be found abundantly above the church of St. Clether. At South Petherwin the slates are variously schistose, calciferous, and argillaceous, and interesting as being stored with organic remains. On the E. the banks of the Tamar afford some instructive sections, especially at low water, between Saltash and the coast, where the mode in which the trap rocks are associated with the sedimentary beds may be well seen. N. of Cawsand, in Plymouth Sound, a porphyritic rock has been protruded with every mark of violence, being curiously intermingled towards Redding Point with the broken and contorted slate-beds. Sir Henry De la Beche conjectures that this igneous mass may be referred to the period of the new red sandstone formation, and its date is an interesting question, as connected with the lamination of the grauwacke, as several of the smaller veins which fill the slate cracks are separated by planes of cleavage coincident with those of the grauwacke. In Whitesand Bay, between Trewinnow and Tregantle, calcareous rocks containing fossils are associated with argillaceous slates, and it is thought probable that these beds may be a continuation of the Plymouth limestones. A calciferous patch again occurs at Looe, quartzose rocks N. of Sandplace, and arenaceous beds at Liskeard; the latter being quarried for building-stone. S. of this town serpentine is found on the eminence of Clicker Tor, apparently included among the slates. The schistose cliffs between Looe and Polperro have recently acquired much interest by the discovery of Mr. Couch, of Polperro, who was the first to detect in them remains which, though in a very mutilated condition, were pronounced to be those of certain fish, characteristic of the Silurian system of Murchison; but the later researches of Sedgwick and M'Coy have shown them to be sponges. At Looe the only fossils are bivalve shells, corals, and encrinites; but W. of this place, on the shore of Talland Bay, the sponges make their appearance, and may be seen as far W. as Lantivet Bay, a short distance from Pencarrow Head, where they are succeeded by corals and shells. It is worthy of especial notice that the rocks of the small district containing these remains underlie to the N. or towards the land, while the rest of the S. coast underlies in an opposite direction, or towards the sea; the same easterly dip prevailing in both. This inversion of the strata is first observed in Pottredler Bay, opposite the W. end of Looe Island; it continues westward a short distance beyond Fowey Haven, and may be traced for 2 or 3 m. inland. Mr. Peach, an indefatigable member of the Cornish Geological Society, has devoted much time to the investigation of these remains, and the result may be seen in the Transactions of that institution.

At Pencarrow Head we again find fossiliferous limestone, which stretches across Fowey Haven near Polruan, in apparent continuation of the beds at Looe, supporting red and variegated slates. S. of Turbot Point hard quartz rock makes its appearance, and constitutes the eminence called the Great Carn; and N. of Gorran Haven another patch of limestone associated with slates and some remarkable rocks of a semi-porphyritic character. The sandstones contain several species of orthidæ and trilobites characteristic of the lower Silurian or Sedgwick's Cambrian period. An excellent section—commencing with the micaceous and arenaceous slates of the Deadman—is exhibited in Veryan Bay, where the coast cuts the strike of the beds. A band of limestone, which is considered lower in the series than the calcareous beds of Gorran and Looe, will be seen in this bay. At Penare Head a number of very interesting rocks are intermingled on the cliffs, consisting of greenstones and trappean conglomerates, argillaceous slates, serpentine, and diallage. The great abundance of igneous products at this spot is regarded as evidence of some local volcanic action during the formation of this part of the series, but occurring previously to the protrusion of the Lizard serpentine. Near Falmouth, between Pendennis Castle and the Swan Pool, a good section is obtained at low water of the red and variegated slate-beds which may be observed intermingled with arenaceous rocks. Further W. the country has been so divided by elvans, cross-courses, and lodes, as to offer few facilities for the study of the grauwacke. On the N. coast argillaceous and arenaceous slates extend from Hayle to Portreath, and fossiliferous calcareous slates occur between Newquay and Towan Head. Watergate Bay exhibits a fine section of the red and variegated beds which may be traced inland to Tregoss Moor. At Towan Head trap-dikes can be well studied, as also on the W. of Trevose Head, and higher up the coast between Endellion and Port Isaac, where, on Kellan Head, is an interesting example enclosing fragments of the adjoining slate, which appears to have been altered by the heat of the igneous mass.

3. The *carbonaceous deposits* extend over a great part of central Devon, and occupy a considerable area in the N.E. of Cornwall, and consist chiefly of sandstones, often siliceous, and of slates of various colours, but also include roofing slates and limestones, and near the western and southern boundary are abundantly associated with trappean *ash* and other productions which bear a striking analogy to those of existing volcanos. The general character of the formation is that of drifted matter, including vegetable remains; the principal difference between the carbonaceous deposits and those of the grauwacke being the more frequent occurrence of carbon in the former, although no trace of this substance is to be seen in many of the beds which consist of light-coloured sandstones, slates, and shales. The prevailing soil on these rocks is a cold and ungrateful clay, and the extensive district between Exeter, Okehampton, and the N. coast is notorious as the most sterile and worst cultivated land in Devonshire.

One of the most interesting circumstances connected with this formation is the disturbance to which it has evidently been subjected. The strata are twisted and contorted in a manner which defies all description, but may be seen on every part of the coast between Boscastle and the mouths of the Taw and Torridge. This universal dislocation has given rise to very extraordinary and picturesque cliff-scenery, rendering this portion of the coast one of the most interesting to the artist as well as to the geologist. In the confusion prevailing among the strata, a general northern dip may be distinguished. The boundary-line, commencing at the united embouchure of the Taw and Torridge, runs eastward along the edge of the grauwacke by South Molton and Bampton over the border into Somerset, where it meets the new red sandstone and turns to the S.W., passing great promontories of sandstone, to Tiverton, Exeter, and King's Teignton; there it again encounters the grauwacke, which it skirts in a W. direction to Buckfastleigh, whence it sweeps round Dartmoor to Tavistock, and runs N.W. by Lezant and the downs of Laneast and Wilsey to Boscastle in Cornwall. The highest beds of the formation are the calcareous rocks at Barnstaple; the lowest, the sandstones of the Lynmouth Foreland: those near Bideford are highly carbonaceous, containing a quantity of anthracite. The singular eminence of N. Brent Tor and the great copper-mine of Huel Friendship are both in this system.

4. *Granite* occurs in Devonshire and Cornwall in six distinct patches, constituting the districts of Dartmoor, Brown Willy, Hensbarrow, Carn Menelez, the Land's End, and Islands of Scilly; rising to an elevation of 2050 ft. on Dartmoor, but sinking gradually in its course westward, until in Scilly its highest point is barely 200 ft. above the level of the sea. These six principal bosses are connected with smaller patches, which appear to be mere outlying fragments, or links, which unite the great bosses, and complete a chain extending through the country in a N.E. and S.W. direction. These minor patches are all marked by ruggedness and elevation above the neighbouring slate, and form the eminences of Boringdon Park near Plymouth, Kit Hill and Hingston Down near Callington, Castle-an-Dinas and Belovely Beacon S. of St. Columb, Carn Brea and Carn Marth near Redruth, Tregonning and Godolphin hills W. of Helston, and the far celebrated St. Michael's Mount in the vicinity of Penzance. Another small patch occurs at the Cligga Head, but further removed than those previously noticed from a large boss.

The granite of Dartmoor and Cornwall consists in general of a coarse-grained mixture of quartz, mica, and felspar; the latter mineral sometimes predominating and frequently occurring in large crystals, so as to render the mass porphyritic. Schorl and schorl-rock occur frequently on the S. of Dartmoor, but rarely in the Brown Willy and Scilly granite. They are, however, found in some quantity in the Land's End district, and abundantly in that of [Hensbarrow, being principally confined to the outskirts of the respective bosses. Schorl-rock may be seen on Dartmoor near Ashburton and Tavistock, and in Cornwall on the Roche Rocks, which are entirely composed of it, and at Treryn Castle, the site of the well-known Logan Stone, where it occurs in an interesting manner, being mostly distributed among the joints. In the central parts of the Hensbarrow district the granite is remarkable for its liability to decompose, and often to considerable depths, the mica being frequently replaced by schorl and a talcose or steatitic mineral. Other varieties of granite may be found on the hills of Godolphin and Tregonning. That which occurs in the parishes of Mabe and Constantine is well known for its beautiful grain, a characteristic which renders it so valuable for economical purposes.

In all these masses of granite a peculiar structure will be observed. The rock is apparently separated into horizontal and parallel beds, and these horizontal lines are intersected by a double series of vertical joints, which run generally from N. to S., and from E. to W. By this network of cracks air and moisture insinuate themselves, and, by decomposing the surfaces, separate granite into cubical blocks, and originate those fantastic forms which seem to start up wildly in lonely places to the bewilderment of the traveller. The Cheesewring near Liskeard,

Bowerman's Nose on Hound Tor, and the Pulpit Rock in Scilly illustrate the effects of this structure. Mis Tor near Prince's Town affords a fine example of decomposition in the horizontal joints alone; and those colossal pillars which rise so magnificently from the headlands of Tol Pedn Penwith and Pardenick, and along that coast towards the Land's End, of the weathering of the vertical joints.

The great elevations of granite, including the large district of Dartmoor, have evidently been protruded at the same period, and to this we obtain some approximation by the circumstance of the Dartmoor granite having displaced the carbonaceous beds which abut upon it. De la Beche supposes that the band of granite was erupted along a line of least resistance through a country previously weakened by volcanic action—of which action the numerous trap-dikes and sedimentary accumulations of *ash* afford indisputable proof, and that the present bosses may mark the position of vents from which former igneous products had been discharged. Wherever the grauwacke can be seen in contact with granite, it will be observed to be altered or rendered crystalline, and to be penetrated in various directions by portions of the igneous rock which, decreasing in size after they have entered the slate, and dwindling often to mere lines, show that the granite when injected must have possessed considerable fluidity. These veins may be well studied near Ivy Bridge, and on the cliffs of the Land's End district, especially at Wicca Pool near Zennor, Porthmeer Cove W. of the Gurnard's Head, Pendeen Cove further W., Cape Cornwall, Whitesand Cove N. of the Land's End promontory, and Mousehole. The geologist will also observe, near and at the line of contact, that both formations are traversed by granite veins which, once regarded as evidence of the contemporaneous origin of slate and granite, are now attributed to the cracking of the upper part of the mass in cooling and the injection of fluid granite into the fissures from beneath. Examples may be seen on the N.E. side of St. Michael's Mount.

In addition to these bosses and isolated patches, numerous bands of a granitic rock—provincially termed *elvan*, from the Cornish word *elven*, a spark—traverse the counties, in courses, with one exception, more or less coincident with the strike of the great granite axis. They are chiefly composed of a felspathic or quartzo-felspathic base, containing crystals of felspar and quartz, mixed occasionally with schorl and mica, and vary from an insignificant breadth to an expansion of 400 ft. These elvans cut through both granite and slate, and are to be considered as dikes of the former rock, which have been erupted at a period subsequent to the protrusion of the bosses. The *Roborough stone* quarried near Plymouth, and the *Pentewan stone* of Cornwall, are elvans, and the latter is remarkable for containing fragments of slate, which may be seen in a branch extending along the shore towards the Black Head. There is also an elvan under the Old Pier and Battery at Penzance, and a fine section of another is exhibited on the coast at St. Agnes, where, at the Cligga Point, it may be observed to enter the granite.

In an economical point of view, granite, although regarded with an evil eye by the farmer, is a most valuable substance, and the traveller will be scarcely correct in saying that all is barren on the Cornish moors. It is largely quarried in various districts; and the granite of Luxulian, the Cheesewring, and Penryn, so well known for its beauty and durability, is the material of London and Waterloo Bridges, the Docks of Chatham, the lighthouse and beacon on the Plymouth Breakwater, and the monument on the field of Waterloo.

5. *New Red Sandstone* and its associated rocks rest upon the eastern flank of the carbonaceous deposits, forming between Babbacombe and Seaton an almost uninterrupted line of picturesque cliffs, passing below the chalk formation near the eastern boundary of Devonshire, and extending northwards along the foot of the Black Down Hills into Somerset; the upper beds of the series principally consisting of marls, the middle of sandstones, and the lower of *breccias* or coarse conglomerates coloured blood-red by peroxide of iron. On the W. side the intrusion of igneous rocks is evidence of volcanic action having accompanied the deposit of part of the series, and the conglomerates, composed of rounded fragments of the older strata, show very impressively that water was a powerful agent during the same period. The boundary-line on the W. is exceedingly irregular, passing by Tiverton and Exeter to Torbay, but between those towns making a sweep to the westward as far as Jacobstow near Okehampton. Some outlying patches also occur at great distances from the body of the formation, viz. at Bideford, Hatherleigh, Slapton in Start Bay, and the Thurlestone Rock just W. of the Bolt Tail. The coast from Babbacombe to Culverhole Point near Seaton exhibits a most excellent view of the entire series, beginning at the lowest and ending at the highest bed. In this section conglomerates prevail between Babbacombe and Dawlish, where red sandstone becomes abundant, increasing towards Budleigh Salterton, and predominating between that town and Sidmouth. Beyond Sidmouth the coast ranges eastward in heights of 400 ft. and 500 ft., the sandstones becoming gradually intermingled with red marls, which form the cliffs at Branscombe Mouth, and beyond that place dip below a patch of chalk, but reappear at Seaton. The upper beds of the series are then exhibited between the mouth of the Axe and Culverhole Point, the red marls being succeeded by others of more varied and lighter tints, and these in their turn disappearing from view below the lias of Dorset. The formation is characterised by a scarcity of organic remains and by the extreme fertility of some of its soils.

6. The *greensand* strata of the *Chalk formation* cap the Black Down Hills and the heights near Axminster, Seaton, and Sidmouth, and with beds of *chalk* occupy a depression in the coast at Beer, coming down to the level of the sea at Beer Head. Outlying patches cover the eminences of Haldon and the lower grounds between Chudleigh and Newton, and a small patch occurs on the Black Hill near Exmouth, and another of a few acres near Bideford, above 40 m. distant from the greensand of the Black Downs. This wide-spread diffusion and iso-

lation of fragments support an hypothesis that the greensand of the Black Down and Haldon Hills was once united, forming continuous portions of a great arenaceous deposit, long since broken up by denuding causes, which have not only borne away the connecting sands, but have also scooped deeply into the supporting and older rocks. Further evidence of a former extension of the chalk is afforded by the flints which everywhere cover the surface of the greensand. On the Black Down Hills concretions of the greensand are extensively quarried for scythe-stones.

7. The *Tertiary deposits* occurring in these counties consist of chalk flints and cherty gravel filling the hollows of the cretaceous strata; of clays, sands, and lignite in the greensand valley of the Bovey Heathfield; and of some remarkable beds of sands and clays resting upon the slate of St. Agnes Beacon, on the N. coast of Cornwall.

In this brief review of the Devonian and Cornish strata it has been shown that they exhibit manifest marks of a disturbing force, which at different times has altered the surface of the country; but few of these signs are stamped in such broad and intelligible characters, or are so vividly significant, as those ancient records which bear witness to successive changes in the relative level of land and sea. On many parts of this coast the retreat of the tide lays bare the trunks of trees, and the stems still attached to their roots, standing in their natural position; and the same phenomena have been exposed by excavations at the Pentewan and other tin stream-works. In the Mount's Bay the bed of the sea contains the remains of an hazel wood, among which are found nuts and leaves, and even the elytra of insects which lived upon the trees. Traces of *submarine forests* are also found in Torbay, at the mouth of the Salcombe estuary, at Porthleven near Helston, on Hayle Sands, at Perran Porth, and at the mouth of the Camel. Again, upon the cliffs at various points on the coast, *seabeaches* may be observed at heights varying from a few to 40 or 50 ft. above the present high-water mark. The examples are numerous; but those occurring between the Land's End and Cape Cornwall are the most interesting, on account of the large size of the rounded stones of which they are composed. Raised beaches may be seen also on Hope's Nose near Torquay, at Plymouth, in Gerran's Bay (a fine example), between the harbour of Falmouth and Coverack Cove, on both sides of Cape Cornwall, in St. Ives' Bay, and at the mouths of the Camel, Taw, and Torridge. On the E. of Trewavas Head, and on the E. side of Pendennis Castle, they may be observed below cliffs which have been worn by the action of the sea, although now beyond its reach. The physical changes which these submarine forests and raised beaches record are a considerable subsidence of the land, by which the woods growing on the shore were buried some depth beneath the waves, which gradually covered them with sand, and a subsequent elevation of the coast, in which the submerged trees were brought to their present position, and the beaches raised to the height at which we now find them.

On the N. of Cornwall the traveller will frequently find the shores desolated by sand, which, principally composed of comminuted shells, is piled upon them in *towans* or hillocks. With respect to the origin of these sandy dunes, the old vegetable surfaces which may be traced in their structure afford evidence of a gradual accumulation, and there is reason to suppose that the principal part of the sand was drifted inland from the beach before the coast was raised to its present height. It is curious to observe how effectually a small stream of water will arrest the progress of the sand. The particles carried forward by the wind are seldom raised many inches from the ground, and individually are held suspended for very short distances. No sooner, therefore, are they drifted past the bank of the stream than they fall into the water, and are carried away by the current.

The fullest information upon the geology of these interesting counties is contained in Sir Henry De la Beche's Report on the Geology of Cornwall, Devon, and West Somerset, and in the Transactions of the Royal Geological Society of Cornwall.

ANTIQUITIES.

PRIMÆVAL PERIOD.—No part of England is richer in primæval antiquities than Devonshire and Cornwall. The high land of Dartmoor, and the remote district between Penzance and the Land's End, contain examples of the cromlech, the stone circle, and the primitive hut, which may compete with any in Wales, and which are only exceeded in size and importance by those in Brittany or in Ireland.

The origin and history of these remains are altogether uncertain. Ethnologists are at present inclined to believe that three distinct waves of migration passed over Europe, including the British Islands, before the arrival of the earliest Teutonic settlers;—the first, Turanian, of which the Finnic races in Northern Europe are surviving representatives; the second, Gaelic; and the third, Cymric, represented by the Cornish, the Welsh, and the Bretons. Competent archæologists are strongly disposed to assign many of these stone relics to the first or Turanian period; but this is as yet mere speculation. Nothing has hitherto been discovered in connection with them which enables us to give them, with certainty, to either of these periods. The tourist should be especially warned against all such theories as connect the cromlechs and stone circles with Druidism, and its supposed rites. The rites and the "Druidism" are in most cases as shadowy and unreal as the theories which have been founded on them; and it will be well to remember that a thorough examination of the remains themselves, and a careful comparison of them with similar relics existing in other parts of the world, are the only means by which we can hope to arrive at any certain knowledge of their origin. Such facts as have been discovered in relation to them are noticed in the following general description.

The remains may be thus classified—1. Cromlechs. 2. Stone circles, generally called "sacred" circles. 3. Upright stones disposed in avenues. 4. The single stone, "maen hir," or "long stone." 5. Kistvaens, or "stone chests." 6. Tolmêns, or "holed stones." 7. Logans, or "rocking stones." 8. Rock basins. 9. Huts and pounds, or "walled villages." 10. Caves. 11. Bridges. 12. Cliff castles. 13. Hill castles and camps. 14. Boundary lines. Of these various classes it may be said at once that some (logans and rock basins) are more probably natural than artificial; and that there is no reason why others (pounds or villages, castles and camps) should not be, as they almost certainly are in some cases, of much later date than the great monuments of unwrought stone, such as cromlechs and circles.

1. *Cromlechs.*—These, which consist of a large cap or covering stone raised on three or more supporters, seem to be, in all cases, sepulchral monuments. The name cromlech (*crom*, bowed or bending; *lech*, a stone) does not seem to have been in use before the end of the 16th century; and it is even doubtful whether it is not of much later introduction. In Cornwall, cromlechs are called "quoits." They may be classed as—1. *Three-pillared* cromlechs; such are the Spinster's Rock at Drewsteignton (Rte. 12), the single (but very fine) example of a cromlech in *Devonshire*; and in *Cornwall*, Pendarves or Carwinnen Quoit (Rte. 27) and Lanyon Quoit (Rte. 29, Exc. 3). 2. *Four-pillared* cromlechs; such as Chûn Quoit (Rte. 29, Exc. 3) and Mulfra Quoit (id. id.), in *Cornwall.* 3. *Many-pillared* cromlechs; of which Trevethy Stone (Rte. 23) and Zennor Quoit (Rte. 29, Exc. 2) are the Cornish examples. And 4. *Chamber cromlechs,* of which the Western Counties afford no specimen. Cromlechs belonging to all these classes exist in many parts of Europe; in Circassia and Syria (Dr. Beke describes one on the hills of Gilead, east of the Jordan, as a "perfect Kit's Coity House"—a famous three-pillared cromlech near Aylesford in Kent); in India, and in Algeria, where no less than eighty were found by Mr. Rhind, in a space covering not more than ten or twelve acres. (These were all four-pillared cromlechs; the size of the cap-stone varying from 7 ft. by 4½ to 9 ft. by 7.) It is believed that all these monuments were originally hidden within earthen tumuli, or great carns of stones. In Borlase's time great part of the covering carn remained about Zennor Quoit; and a small second cromlech near Lanyon (Rte. 29, Exc. 3) was only disinterred from its carn in 1790. Many of them were probably opened, in the hope of discovering treasure, in very early times. Hence the complete disappearance of the carns and tumuli.

The relics which have been discovered in such cromlechs as until the present time had remained unviolated within their earthen mounds, belong exclusively to the earliest or "stone" period; a fact which warrants us in assigning a very high antiquity to this class of monument. (In one instance Roman pottery was found beneath a cromlech in Wiltshire—see *Archæologia Cambrensis,* third series, No. 17—but this was to all appearance the remains of a later interment; a case by no means unusual). An account of the sepulchral arrangements discovered within the remarkable chamber cromlechs in Guernsey, first opened in

1837 by Mr. Lukis, will be found in the first volume of the Journal of the Archæological Institute.

2. *Sacred Circles.*—These, of which the use is uncertain, although in many instances they seem to be sepulchral, consist of upright blocks of stone, ranged at intervals in a circular form. The great example in England of this class is Stonehenge. In *Devonshire* there are, on Dartmoor, Scorhill Circle (Rte. 13), the Grey Wethers (Rte. 12), Fernworthy Circle (Rte. 12), and circles at Merrivale Bridge (Rte. 12). In *Cornwall* are the Hurlers (Rte. 23), the Boskednan Circle (Rtc. 29, Exc. 3), the Nine Maidens at Boscawen-ûn (Rte. 29, Exc. 5), Fregeseal Circle (Rte. 29, Exc. 4), and the Dawns Mên, or Merry Maidens (Rte. 29, Exc. 6).

The number of stones in all these circles varies. Whilst some may have served as sepulchral memorials, others may have marked the spots where sacrifice was offered and judgment pronounced; but of this, it must be remembered, there is no distinct proof.

3. *Parellelitha,* or upright stones disposed in avenues.—Of all remains of the primæval period, these are the most mysterious and the least understood. They are formed by two, three, or more parallel rows of stones, generally running in straight lines, but sometimes winding. The most remarkable example, probably in the world, is the great avenue at Carnac, near Quiberon Bay, in Brittany, where five parallel rows of stones, some of them twenty feet high, wind over the heaths for a length of some miles. (The remains at Carnac have been well described and illustrated by Mr. Deane in the twenty-fifth volume of the Archæologia.) But neither in Brittany, nor on Dartmoor, where similar remains on a much smaller scale abound, is there any tradition as to their origin or probable use. They have frequently been called "serpent temples," and have been regarded as relics of an ancient Ophite worship; but this, it need hardly now be said, is the merest speculation, and is not even supported by the form of the remains themselves, which are rarely sinuous, like a snake. On Dartmoor they are found in direct connection with carns, and circles which are probably sepulchral. The most striking examples are near Kestor Rock (Rte. 12), on Challacombe Down (Rte. 12), under Black Tor (Rte. 12), and the finest and most perfect of all at Merrivale Bridge, under Mis Tor (Rte. 12). No very perfect example remains in Cornwall; but some fragments of avenues may be found on the downs near Kilmarth (Rte. 23).

At Callernish, in the Isle of Lewis, is an avenue of cruciform shape, attached to a circle 60 ft. in diameter (see Wilson's 'Prehistoric Annals of Scotland'). "Avenues are also found in other countries; one is said to be near Hit, on the Euphrates, leading to a circle of upright slabs; and in India, besides many ortholithic remains in various places, are avenues at the village of Mushmaie, near Chirra Poonjee, and others leading to the latter place, on the Cossyah, or Kasia Hills."—*Sir Gardner Wilkinson.*

4. *The Single Upright Stone.*—These are almost certainly sepulchral. [*Dev. & Corn.*]

Many examples occur on Dartmoor and in Cornwall, which need not here be enumerated.

5. "*Kistvaens*," or *Stone Chests*.—These generally contained the body, unburnt; but when of smaller size, they held the burnt bones. The best examples on Dartmoor are at the end of the stone avenue near Kestor Rock (Rte. 12), and one on Cawsand Hill. No kistvaen remains in Cornwall.

6. *Tolméns*, or "*Holed Stones*."—The original intention of these is quite unknown. Many superstitions have become connected with them. In Orkney there was a famous perforated stone adjoining the great circle of Stennis, to which a belief was attached which has been commemorated by Sir Walter Scott in the 'Pirate.' The stone is now destroyed. No true tolmên has been found in Devonshire. In Cornwall the best example is the "Crick Stone," near Lanyon (Rte. 29, Exc. 3). The tolmên at Constantine, near Truro (Rte. 28), is not really a pierced stone, although superstitions of the same class are connected with it. The quoit, or covering block, of the great cromlech at Trevethy (Rte. 23), is pierced by a circular hole, which also has its folk-lore.

7. *Logans*, or Rocking-stones.—"Logan" is the Welsh "Llogi," to shake; and "to logg" is still used in the sense of "to rock" in some parts of Devon and Cornwall. That by far the greater part of these stones rock from natural causes, is more than probable. It has been suggested that they were used by the Druids as a kind of ordeal; but this, it need hardly be said, is entirely unsupported by proof. Logan-stones exist in all parts of the world. Pliny describes one at Harpasa in Asia, that could be moved with the finger. "Cautes stat horrenda, uno digito mobilis."—*Hist. Nat.* ii. 96. The most important example in *Devonshire* is the "Rugglestone" at Widdecombe (Rte. 12); and in Cornwall the famous Logan rock at Treryn Dinas, near the Land's End (Rte. 29, Exc. 5).

8. *Rock Basins*.—These are found on the summits of nearly every tor on Dartmoor; and there is scarcely an instance in which it is not at once evident that they have been produced by the natural disintegration of the granite. Rock basins have been found, however, in some parts of the world which are as clearly artificial. On the capstones of the great cromlechs in Northern Africa are some large square basins (the largest 3 ft. square), with shallow troughs leading from one to another, not so deep as the basins, and 4 in. broad (*Sir J. G. Wilkinson*). It need hardly be said that these basins may be of much later date than the cromlechs themselves. On Dartmoor the rock basins are irregularly shaped, but generally approach to a circle. A valuable paper on the Rock Basins of Dartmoor, by Mr. Ormerod, of Chagford, will be found in the Journal of the Geological Soc., vol. xv. (1859).

9. *Huts*; and *Pounds* or *Walled Villages*.—Of these a sufficient description will be found in the routes where the most important examples are noticed. These are: in *Devonshire*, at *Kestor Rock* (Rte. 12); at *Grimspound* (Rte. 12), the best example of a walled village;

and at *Merrivale Bridge* (Rte. 12). There are, however, many very interesting remains of this class scattered over Dartmoor, and noticed, for the most part, in Rte. 12. In *Cornwall*, the most perfect specimen of a beehive-hut which has hitherto been found is at *Bosphrennis*, near Mulfra Quoit (Rte. 29, Exc. 3). The most remarkable village is at *Chysoyster* (Rte. 29, Exc. 3). The huts at *Old Bosullow* (id. id.) and the Crellas at Bodennar (id. id.) should also be mentioned.

These huts and pounds, although agreeing for the most part in plan and construction, may be of various dates. Many of them, there can be little doubt, belong to the British period, when Dartmoor was covered with tin-streamers; and emporia frequented by foreign (Greek) merchants seem to have existed near the mouths of the chief rivers, on the sites afterwards known as Exeter, Totnes, and Plympton. Examples of the same kind of walled town or " pound " have recently been found in Northumberland, at Chesters, Greavesash, and other places; having also, within the area, a number of hut circles, similar in size and construction to those on Dartmoor. Compare also the "stone-built fortresses and habitations occurring to the west of Dingle, County Kerry," carefully described in a paper (with illustrations) by Mr. Du Noyer (Archæol. Journal, vol. xv.).

10. *Caves.*—Of these, no example has hitherto been found in Devonshire. In Cornwall, the most remarkable is the *Fogou* at Trewoofe (Rte. 29, Exc. 6, where a list of the others is given). Their date is altogether uncertain.

11. *Bridges.*—Some of these on Dartmoor, formed of large flat slabs of granite, are of great antiquity. The most striking are Post Bridge, over the Dart (Rte. 12), and a bridge over the North Teign (Rte. 12).

12. *Cliff Castles.*—Many of the Cornish headlands have been cut off by lines of fortification. The most perfect is *Treryn Dinas*, near the Land's End (Rte. 29, Exc. 5, where others are mentioned). Their date is uncertain.

13. *Hill Castles and Camps.*—The most perfect in Devonshire are, *Cadbury* (Rte. 2); *Hembury Fort*, near Honiton (Rte. 3); *Membury* and *Musbury* (Rte. 3); *Sidbury* and *Woodbury* (Rte. 4); *Castle Dike*, near Chudleigh (Rte. 10); *Hembury* (Rte. 11); *Prestonbury*, *Cranbrook*, and *Wooston* (Rte. 12); and *Clovelly Dikes* (Rte. 18). These are all earthworks; and although there is evidence, in many cases, that some of these camps were used at a later period (after the departure of the Romans), there is nothing to show by what race they were originally constructed. In *Cornwall*, besides some large earthworks, there are some remarkable hill castles, in the construction of which stone has been employed, and which, to some extent, resemble the "pounds" of Dartmoor. The most important are, *Castell an Dinas*, near Penzance (Rte. 29, Exc. 2); and *Chûn Castle* (Rte. 29, Exc. 3). They are probably of later date than the earthworks.

14. *Boundary-lines.*—These are frequent on Dartmoor and in Cornwall. On Dartmoor they have sometimes been called "trackways," but they are certainly not roads. They are formed of large blocks of

granite, ranged at intervals in rows, or as they are called in Devonshire "reaves." To what height these lines (which resemble the foundation of a broad wall) originally rose is quite uncertain. One of them, the central trackway referred to in the notice of Grimspound (Rte. 12), ran, in all probability, from Hameldon to Crockern Tor, and thence to Roborough Down, between Plymouth and Tavistock. Thus it divided Dartmoor, and extended from 12 to 14 miles. It ranges E. and W. "Considerable portions of it can still be traced; but a large extent of it rests rather upon the testimony of tradition than upon the evidence of existing remains."—*Rowe* (*Peramb. of Dartmoor*). It is recognised by the moormen as the central track; all above it is called the north; all below it the south country. The peat-cutters are said to come upon it below the surface in some places. In *Cornwall*, the *Giant's Hedge* (Rte. 24) is the most important ancient boundary; but many others exist. A careful examination of them, in both counties, might assist us greatly in tracing the gradual advance of the Saxons westward.

ROMAN PERIOD.—The Romans have left but few traces of their presence in Devonshire and Cornwall. The greater part of both these counties seems to have been wild and covered with wood; and they were chiefly important as containing the tin districts, and the harbours from which the metal was conveyed across to Gaul. The chief Roman road was a continuation of the Fosse and Ikenild ways, which seem to have met on the eastern borders of Devonshire. Passing by Honiton (perhaps the Moridunum of the Itineraries), it ran to Exeter (Isca Danmoniorum), and thence nearly in the line of the Exeter and Plymouth Railway to Totnes (Statio ad Durium) and King's Tamerton (Tamare), where it crossed the Tamar, and proceeded onwards, in all probability, into Cornwall. Its line in that county, however, has not been accurately traced; and the whole road west of Isca seems to have been of comparatively small importance. The Fosse-way is described in many of the later chroniclers as running "from Totnes to Caithness;" an expression used in the Welsh Mabinogion to denote the whole length of the island, from north to south. Besides this principal road, a second of less consequence ran from Exeter to the north coast.

Only one Roman villa has been found in Devonshire, at Uplyme, near Axminster (Rte. 3). The most important Roman relics in the county have been discovered from time to time at Exeter, which was a walled city, and contained numerous temples and public buildings. The Greek and other coins which have been found here (see Exeter, Rte. 1) were imbedded at a considerable depth, under the line of the Roman road, which crossed the city from E. to W., and is in fact the present High Street. The fact proves the very early period at which Exeter served in all probability as the chief emporium for the tin of the moorlands.

Of the Brito-Roman period the chief are *inscribed* (*sepulchral*) *stones*, many of which exist in Devonshire and Cornwall, and are noticed in the routes where they occur.

MEDIÆVAL PERIOD.—*Churches.*—Although Devonshire and Corn-

Introd. *Antiquities.* xxix

wall are not counties of first-rate interest to the ecclesiologist, the churches in both well deserve careful examination. In both the prevailing style is Perpendicular, and it is not easy to account for the great impulse given to churchbuilding in the West of England from the middle of the 14th to the middle of the 15th century. In some parts of North Devon the towers are of the enriched Somersetshire type, and are very fine. (See *post* for the best examples). Richly carved pulpits and chancel-screens of wood are among the chief peculiarities of Devonshire churches. Norfolk and Suffolk are the only English counties which in this respect admit of any comparison with Devon; and it may be remarked that the general designs, and even the patterns, are very similar in these widely separated districts. In Devonshire there is reason to believe that in some parishes the art of wood-carving became hereditary in certain families, and was followed by them for many generations.

The churches best worthy of attention in *Devonshire* are the following. (The most important are marked with an asterisk.)

Norman.—No perfect Norman church remains in Devonshire, but it is clear, from the number of fonts and other fragments, that the county was covered with small churches soon after the Conquest. Besides fonts, Norman *portions* remain at **Exeter* (Rte. 1, transeptal towers of the cathedral), *Sidbury* (Rte. 4), *Chudleigh* (Rte. 10, tower), *South Brent* (Rte. 7, tower), *Ilfracombe* (Rte. 18, tower), and elsewhere.

Early English.—**Sampford Peverell* (Rte. 1), *Brent Tor* (Rte. 6, plain, but interesting from its situation), **Ottery* (Rte. 3, aisles and transeptal towers), *Branscombe* (Rte. 4, parts only), **Aveton Giffard* (Rte. 15), **Ermington* (Rte. 16, tower and spire), **Buckfastleigh* (Rte. 11, tower and chancel), *Lustleigh* (Rte. 12, parts only), **Combe Martin* (Rte. 18, parts), **Berrynarbor* (Rte. 18, parts), *Morthoe* (Rte. 18, parts), **Atherington* (Rte. 17, parts).

Decorated.—**Exeter Cathedral* (Rte. 1, the whole, except the transept towers), *Axminster* (Rte. 3), **Ottery* (Rte. 3, nave, chancel, and Lady chapel), **Haccombe* (Rte. 8, the finest brasses in Devonshire are here), *King's Kerswell* (Rte. 8), *Dartington* (Rte. 7, parts), *Bigbury* (Rte. 15), *South Brent* (Rte. 7), *Plympton St. Mary* (Rte. 7, parts), *Drewsteignton* (Rte. 6), *Beer Ferrers* (Rte. 7, parts), *Egg Buckland* (Rte. 7, parts), *Tawstock* (Rte. 17).

Perpendicular.—**Tiverton* (Rte. 2, *rebuilt*), **Crediton* (Rte. 17), *Bridestow* (Rte. 6), **Cullompton*, with fine screen (Rte. 1), *Plymtree* (good screen, Rte. 1), *Bradninch* (good screen, Rte. 1), *Honiton* (Rte. 3), **Awliscombe* (Rte. 3), **Ottery* (N. aisle, Rte. 3), **Colyton* (Rte. 4), **Clyst St. George* (Rte. 5), **Kenton* (very good screen, Rte. 7), *Ashton* (Rte. 10), *Christow* (Rte. 10), *Bridford* (Rte. 10), **Doddiscombleigh* (with fine stained glass, Rte. 10), *Marldon*, **Paignton* (with stone screen, Rte. 9), **Totnes* (Rte. 7), **Harberton* (stone pulpit and very fine screen, Rte. 7), *Little Hempstone* (Rte. 7), **Dartmouth* (very rich stone pulpit and screen, Rte. 9), *Berry Pomeroy* (Rte. 7), **Modbury* (Rte. 15), **Bovey Tracey* (Rte. 11), **Ashburton* (Rte. 11), **Widdecombe* (Rte. 12), *Chagford* (Rte. 12), **Throwleigh* (fine tower, Rte. 12),

*Tavistock (Rte. 13), *Buckland Monachorum (Rte. 13), Lamerton (Rte. 13), *Kelly (with much old glass, Rte. 13), *Sydenham (old glass, Rte. 13), St. Andrew's, Plymouth (Rte. 7), Tamerton Foliot (Rte. 7), *Cheriton Bishop (Rte. 6), Lapford (Rte. 17), *Coleridge (very fine screen, Rte. 17), *Chulmleigh (very fine tower and good screen, Rte. 17), *Combe Martin (very fine tower, good wood-work, Rte. 18), *Berrynarbor (very fine tower, Rte. 18), Marwood (Rte. 18), *Hartland (fine screen, Rte. 18), *South Molton (fine tower, Rte. 17), *Bishop's Nympton (very fine tower, Rte. 17), North Molton (Rte. 17), *Chittlehampton (finest tower in the county, Rte. 17), *Atherington (very fine roodscreen, Rte. 17).

Two churches which have been admirably rebuilt, and are excellent examples of modern architecture, should be mentioned here: *St. Mary's Church* (Rte. 8), and *Yeulmpton* (Rte. 16).

The *Cornish Churches* are by no means so rich in architectural details as those in Devonshire, but they present some peculiar features; and the "*oratories*," or small churches of the earliest period, are of course of very high interest. Cornwall was first christianized by Irish and Welsh missionaries during the 5th, 6th, and 7th centuries. These missionaries generally built for themselves a cell, with a small oratory or church attached, in which the inhabitant of the cell was usually buried. Such oratories correspond exactly with the "Dhamliags" or churches still found in Ireland, and there universally attributed to the holy men of this period (5th to 7th centuries). (See *Petrie's* 'Essay on the Round Towers,' for many illustrations). "In character they may be briefly described from the oratory of St. Piran (see Rte. 23), the most perfect of them all. In plan they are a simple parallelogram (the breadth being about half of the length), ranging from 20 to 35 feet in length, and from 10 to 17 in breadth. About one-third of the length, the eastern portion, is separated by a low stone step; this is the boundary of the chancel. Within this is a stone altar; and I have invariably found a stone bench running along the base of the wall on the inside, and the floor sunk two or three steps lower than the ground without the edifice. There is always a door on the south side, and a little loophole about 1 foot 6 inches by 1 foot in breadth, and sometimes a doorway also at the N.E. angle. In Ireland there is generally a round tower at this angle, communicating with the interior of the church. As to height, I can only adduce the height of St. Piran's (the other ruins are scarcely more than 6 or 8 feet high at the present time). St. Piran's was 19 or 20 feet to apex of the gable, the side walls about 13½ feet; the church being 25 feet in length internally. There is always a well beside these structures in Cornwall, as in Ireland and in Wales also." (*Rev. W. Haslam*, Trans. of Exeter Dioc. Archit. Soc., vol. ii.)

Besides the oratory of *St. Piran* (Rte. 23), others, in a more or less ruined condition, exist at *St. Enodoc*, near Padstow (Rte. 22; this is, however, buried in the sand); at *St. Gwithian*, near Hayle (Rte. 27); and at *St. Madron* (called the Baptistery, Rte. 28).

Of the *Norman* period, the most important relics in Cornwall are, *St. Germans* (west front and part of nave, Rte. 23), *Blisland* (Rte. 20), *Kilkhampton* (Rte. 25), *Morwenstow* (Rte. 25), *Tintagel* (some portions may be Saxon, Rte. 22), *Mylor*, near Falmouth (Rte. 26), *Lelant* (Rte. 27), *Manaccan* (S. doorway, Rte. 28).

In many Cornish churches the *font* is the only Norman relic which remains. In some instances it is very doubtful whether the apparent Norman work is not in reality an imitation of a much later period.

Early English.—The most perfect E. Eng. church in Cornwall is *St. Anthony in Roseland* (Rte. 26). Portions of the following churches are also of this date. *Blisland* (chancel, Rte. 21), *Camelford* (chancel and tower, Rte. 22), *Advent* (Rte. 22), *Bottreaux* (Rte. 22), *Minster* and *Lesnewth* (both Rte. 22), *Manaccan* (Rte. 28).

Of the *Decorated* period, the most important remains are at *Padstow* (late Dec., restored, Rte. 22), *St.Columb Major* (mainly early Dec., and very good, Rte. 22), *Sheviock* (very good, restored, Rte. 23), *Lostwithiel* (tower and spire early Dec., and unique, Rte. 23), *St. Austell* (chancel, Rte. 23), *Lanteglos* (Rte. 24), *St. Ive's*, near Liskeard (Rte. 25), *Quethiock* (Rte. 25), *St. Cury* (with curious hagioscope, Rte. 28).

As in Devonshire, the great era of churchbuilding in Cornwall was the 15th century. The chief *Perpendicular* churches are *Launceston* (very rich, Rte. 21), *Bodmin* (fine tower, Rte. 23), *Withiel* (Rte. 21), *St. Wenn* (Rte. 21), *Truro* (Rte. 23), *St. Teath* (Rte. 22), *St. Kew* (Rte. 22), *Egloshayle* (Rte. 22), *St. Mawgan* (Rte. 22), *Antony* (Rte. 23), *St. Neot* (with remarkable glass, Rte. 23), *St. Austell* (nave and tower, much enriched, Rte. 23), *Probus* (tower fine, Rte. 23), *Fowey* (Rte. 24), *Botus Fleming* (Rte. 25), *Callington* (Rte. 25), *Linkinhorne* (Rte. 25), *Stratton* (Rte. 25), *Launcells* (Rte. 25), *St. Keverne* (Rte. 28), *St. Just, in Penwith* (Rte. 29, Exc. 4), *St. Levan* (Rte. 29, Exc. 5), *St. Buryan* (Rte. 29, Exc. 5), *Paul* (Rte. 29, Exc. 6).

Almost every church in Cornwall was restored or rebuilt during this (the 15th) century; and "all in the same general character, a peculiar character, so prevailing, that beyond doubt it was intentional and had an object." Cornish churches "are low, and somewhat flat in the pitch of the roof, and without buttresses to break the long plain horizontal lines which are so conspicuous. All these are features of the Perpendicular style, I admit; but not to the extent to which they are carried in Cornwall. Besides this, the general form of a Cornish church is plain; externally, the plan of the larger ones is a parallelogram, divided into three low ridges of roof: there is a porch on the south side; this is the only break in the horizontal line I allude to. The smaller churches have generally but one aisle, and these have a transept also, and sometimes two transepts; but even these do not relieve the plainness of the exterior. This is not the character of one church, or two, or three; but more or less of all. It is their character, and I attribute it to the boisterous nature of the climate in that narrow county, exposed as it is with very little shelter to violent storms from the sea on both sides.

. . . . . . The towers are generally built of granite, and lofty, and seem to rise in defiance of the storms; but they are for the most part plain; their beauty consists more in elegance of proportion than in richness of ornament. The staircase is generally within the tower. There is a class, however, which have a staircase turret at one of the angles, rising from the other pinnacles, and finished with a little spire. These towers are always found in valleys. Some few churches have, instead of a tower, a spire of stone. These are found particularly along the sea-coast. Some have neither tower nor spire, but a campanile on a neighbouring hill. These churches are always situated in a deep valley. There are six of them : St. Feoc, St. Mylor, Gwennap, Gunwalloe, Lamorran, and Jetland."—*Rev. W. Haslam* (Trans. of Exeter Dioc. Arch. Soc., vol. ii.).

Some few of the Cornish church-towers are more richly ornamented. The chief are Truro, Launceston, St. Austell, and Probus. The tower of Probus is essentially of the Somerset type, and would rank among the best in that county.

In the interior, the chief feature is the absence of a chancel arch, which is almost universal. In many of the churches the woodwork deserves notice.

Crosses formed of granite are very common in Devonshire and Cornwall, and rank among the most ancient ecclesiastical remains in England. Their numbers, indeed, have been thinned by the farmer, who has found them of a size convenient for gateposts, but many remain in their original positions,—in the churchyards, by the wayside, in the market-places, and occasionally in wild and solitary spots on the moors. They all agree in being much weathered by the elements, but vary essentially in size and shape. Some are doubtless much older than others, but the greater number are considered to date before the conquest of Cornwall by Athelstan, A.D. 936. Many of these monuments are Greek crosses, that is, formed of four short limbs of equal length, which are sometimes carved on a circular disc, the spaces between the limbs being pierced, as in the Four-Hole Cross near the Jamaica inn. In a few, as in that at Perranzabuloe, the sacred symbol is marked out by four small holes perforating crosswise the head of the stone. In the Land's End district these monuments are about 4 ft. high, occasionally elevated upon steps, and sculptured with a rude representation of the crucified Saviour. In Devonshire and the eastern parts of Cornwall they are often on a much larger scale, 9 or more feet in height, and sometimes bear traces on the shaft of scroll-work and a moulding. (The most remarkable in Devonshire is at *Coplestone*, near Crediton, Rte. 2.) These crosses may have been erected either as boundary-marks of church property or sanctuaries ; or to denote places for public prayer, proclamation, or preaching ; or, by the wayside, to direct the pilgrim to the different churches; or, lastly, as sepulchral monuments, or records of battle or murder.

Some interesting illustrations of the *Cornish* crosses have been published by *Mr. J. T. Blight*, of Penzance.

Castles and Domestic Architecture.—In *Devonshire* the *Castles* to be noticed are, *Hemyock* (Edwardian, few remains, Rte. 1), *Okehampton* (Edwardian, interesting and picturesque, Rte. 6), *Lidford* (Rte. 6), *Exeter* (few remains, Rte. 1), *Compton* (early 15th century, very curious and interesting, Rte. 8), *Totnes* (keep, Hen. III., Rte. 7), *Berry Pomeroy* (Edwardian, and large ruins of a Tudor mansion, Rte. 7), *Plympton* (Hen. III., Rte. 7), *Gidleigh* (14th cent., small remains, Rte. 6).

Domestic Architecture.—*Holcombe Rogus* (Eliz. and earlier Tudor, Rte. 1), *Bradfield* (Eliz., Rte. 1), Gatehouse of *Shute* (Tudor, Rte. 3), *Hayes* (Tudor, only interesting as the birthplace of Sir W. Raleigh, Rte. 4). *Dartington* (14th and 15th cents., very interesting, Rte. 7), *Parsonage at *Little Hempstone* (15th cent., very good, Rte. 7), *Fardell* (Tudor, small remains, Rte. 7), *Kilworthy, Walreddon,* and *Callacombe Barton* (all Tudor, Rte. 12), *Sydenham* (Eliz., Rte. 12), *Old Morwell House* (15th cent., Rte. 7), *Warleigh* (Tudor, Rte. 7), *Wear Gifford* (15th cent., very good, Rte. 17).

Devonshire has few remains of *Monastic Buildings*. The principal are, *Tor Abbey* (Premonstratensian, Rte. 8), *Buckfast Abbey* (Cistercian, Rte. 11), *Tavistock* (Benedictine, Rte. 13), and *Buckland* (Cistercian, Rte. 13). For all particulars concerning the religious houses of Devon and Cornwall, see Dr. *Oliver's* 'Monasticon Diœcesis Exoniensis,' Exeter, 1846.

In *Cornwall*, the chief remains of *Military Architecture* are, *Launceston Castle* (Hen. III., Rte. 21), *Tintagel* (13th cent., Rte. 22), *Trematon* (Hen. III., Rte. 23), *Restormel* (Hen. III., Rte. 23), *Pengersick* (Hen. VIII., Rte. 28), and *St. Michael's Mount* (Perp. and later, Rte. 28).

Domestic Buildings to be noticed are, *Trecarrel* and *Trerice* (both Perp., Rte. 21), *Place*, near Padstow (circ. 1600, Rte. 22), *Lanherne* (1580 and later, Rte. 22), *Lanhydrock* (17th cent., Rte. 23), *Prideaux* (Rte. 23), *Trelawne* (15th cent., Rte. 24), *Place*, near Fowey (Hen. VII., Eliz., Rte. 24), *Cothele* (Hen. VII., Eliz., Rte. 25), *Godolphin* (Perp., Rte. 28).

The remains of the so-called *Stannary Court* at Lostwithiel are temp. Edw. I., and interesting.

There are no remains of *Monastic Buildings* in Cornwall of much interest or importance. St. Germans (Rte. 23) should perhaps be mentioned here; but little exists except the church.

MINES.

The mineral productions of Devonshire and Cornwall, considered as objects of trade and manufacture, are principally two,—tin and copper, for the former of which the metalliferous district between Dartmoor and the Land's End has been celebrated from a very distant period. We learn from ancient authors, both sacred and profane, that tin was known and manufactured many centuries anterior to the Christian epoch. It is mentioned by Homer as one of the metals employed by Vulcan in the construction of the shield of Achilles; the Tyrians prepared from it their celebrated purple dye; and there are frequent allusions to it in the writings of the Old Testament (Isaiah and Ezekiel).

Whether the tin thus mentioned was brought from the north of Spain and Portugal, where it is still found, but in comparatively small quantities, or whether it came from Western Britain, is quite uncertain. But British tin, found exclusively in Cornwall and Devonshire, was spread over Europe from a very early period. The favourite belief has been that Phœnician ships, either from Tyre or from the Phœnician colonies on the coast of Spain, came direct to Britain to fetch it; but this theory, which rests upon no certain evidence, has been attacked with no small power by Sir George Cornewall Lewis, who, in his 'Astronomy of the Ancients,' has shown that the caravan route across Gaul (which was certainly in use when Diodorus wrote, B.C. 40) was in all probability the channel, from the earliest times, for the conveyance of British tin to the shores of the Mediterranean. "The inhabitants," says Diodorus, "carry the tin to a certain island lying on the coast of Britain, called Iktis. During the recess of the tide, *the intermediate space being left dry*, they carry over abundance of tin to this place in their carts. There the merchants buy it of the natives, and transport it into Gaul." This *Iktis* has been frequently regarded as St. Michael's Mount, which is at present accessible at low water. There is reason, however, for believing that this was not always the case; and the claims of "*Vectis*" (the Isle of Wight) to be the island mentioned by Diodorus are far stronger. Wight, it is true, was never accessible at low water; but Diodorus, in the next sentence, tells us that "the other islands" between Britain and Gaul were also thus accessible—a proof that his knowledge of the British coast and of the tin district was by no means accurate. It is probable that many small islands served as emporia for tin, and that the "Iktis" of Diodorus must be accepted as referring to them generally. The very early coins found at Exeter (see Rte. 1) seem to prove that the site of this city was the chief emporium for Devonshire.

When the Romans became masters of Britain, they of course engrossed the whole of the trade. They introduced an improved method of mining, and taught the inhabitants the application of tin to domestic purposes, and the art of incorporating it with other metals. In the unsettled times which followed their departure, the mines are supposed to have been neglected, but it is probable that they continued to supply the Continent with a quantity of their produce. Church-bells first came into use in the 6th and 7th centuries, so it may be presumed there was a demand for tin during the Saxon period. Upon the establishment of the Normans, that industrious people turned their attention to this source of wealth, and great improvements in the regulation of mining matters ensued; and here we leave the doubtful field of tradition and enter on the sure ground of record. In the reign of King John, when Bruges was the chief tin emporium, Devonshire produced more tin than Cornwall, but the trade was inconsiderable, and entirely engrossed by the Jews, whose ancient smelting furnaces exist at this day under the denomination of *Jews' Houses*, the right of working the mines being wholly in the king as Earl of Cornwall. The exports, however, greatly increased under the auspices of his son Richard, Earl of Cornwall and King of the Romans, in consequence of the Spanish mines having stopped working on the invasion of the Moors. In the first Edward's reign the Jews were expelled the country, and the tin-mines fell back into their former state of neglect; but a few years subsequently Edmond Earl of Cornwall granted to the tinners a charter, which conferred the important privilege of holding plea of all actions relating to the mines, those of "lyfe, lymme, and land excepted," and declared that the prisons for offending tinners should be at Lidford and Lostwithiel. In consideration of these privileges the gentlemen tinners bound themselves to pay to the Earl of Cornwall and his successors a certain duty (afterwards fixed at 4s.) upon every hundredweight of tin, and certain towns were appointed to which the blocks of metal should be brought to be *coined* or assayed and kept until the dues were paid. To facilitate these arrangements the miners of Cornwall were separated from those of Devon, whom they had been previously accustomed to meet every seventh or eighth year on Hingston Down, near Callington; and from this time the Stannary parliaments on Crockern Tor—a wild hill in the centre of Dartmoor—are probably to be dated. The charter of Edmond was confirmed by Edw. I. in 1305, and marks an era in Cornish mining, as it was the origin of many of those customs and practices which are peculiar to the Stannaries, such as the right of *bounding,* or selecting portions of waste land for mining to be marked out by pits, which encouraged the search for tin by vesting in the *bounder* a large proportion of the metal found within the described limits. From the period of the Edwards the mines continued to flourish, under the protection of the Crown, until the reign of Mary, when the tide of fortune once more receded, and at the accession of Elizabeth had reached so low an ebb, that that sagacious ruler invited over a number of Germans to assist and instruct her poor "spadiards" of Devon and Cornwall, of whose doleful condition at that time we have a picture by Risdon:—"His apparel is coarse, his diet slender, his lodging hard, his drink water, and for lack of a cup he generally drinketh out of a spade." Under the wise rule of Elizabeth the mines were soon again filled with busy labourers, and in particular those of silver and lead at Combe Martin and Beer Ferrers, which are supposed to have been vigorously worked in this reign. Some improvements had been made in the laws and regulations of the Stannaries. A *warden* was appointed to do justice in law and equity, from whom there was an appeal to the Duke of Cornwall in council, or for want of a Duke of Cornwall, to the Crown. Henry VII. had conferred an important addition to these privileges—that no law relating to the tinners should be enacted without the consent of the *Stannary parliament,* which consists of 24 gentlemen, a certain number chosen by a mayor and council in each of the Stannary divisions. Whatever is enacted by this body must be signed by the stannators, the lord warden, or his deputy the vice-warden, and afterwards by the Duke of Cornwall, or the sovereign, and when thus passed has all the authority, with regard to tin affairs, as an act of the whole legislature. But a necessity for convening these parliaments seldom occurs. The Devonshire stannators were last assembled on Crockern Tor in 1749, the Cornish at Truro in 1752-3. In 1836 the Stannary courts of judicature were remodelled by the act 6 & 7 Will. IV. c. 106. Their jurisdiction was extended to all minerals; the equitable jurisdiction of the vice-wardens, which had long been questioned, was recognised and confirmed; and the courts of equity and common law were united and placed under the presidency of the vice-wardens, one for each county, who were to be barristers of 5 years' standing at the least. From the judgment of these courts an appeal lies to the lord warden, assisted by not less than 3 of the judicial committee of the Privy Council, and finally from the lord warden to the House of Lords. Since the reign of Elizabeth the ancient tin-trade has kept pace with the extension of commerce, but its importance has been eclipsed by that of copper. The supply of tin from these western counties is at this day not half that of copper, yet Cornwall produces 9-10ths of the tin which is annually furnished by Great Britain and the whole continent of Europe.

The history of Cornish copper, now the principal metallic product of the county, is a tale of yesterday compared to that of tin. The sources of this mineral lying deeper in the earth, it required an improved method of mining and drainage to penetrate to them, and such an assistant as the steam-engine to supersede the rude appliances of ancient days. It appears that no notice was taken of this valuable metal until the latter end of the 15th century, and very little attention paid to it until the Revolution, at which period its true value began gradually to unfold itself. It is supposed, however, that no mine was worked exclusively for copper until the year 1700, previously to which some Bristol merchants had largely profited by buying up the casual produce at the rate of 2*l*. 10*s*. to 4*l*. per ton. In 1718 a Mr. Costar gave a great impulse to the trade by draining several of the deeper mines, and instructing the Cornish in an improved method of dressing the ore. From that period the present trade in Cornish copper may be said to date its rise, the annual produce, with some exceptions, having progressively increased. In the year ending June 30, 1856, it amounted to no less than 209,305 tons of ore, which produced 13,275 tons of fine copper, and 1,283,639*l*. in money. In 1851 the mines of Devon and Cornwall together were estimated to furnish one-third of the copper raised throughout other parts of Europe and the British Isles (De la Beche). Upon the first discovery of the yellow ore, which is now so valuable, the miner, to whom its nature was entirely unknown, gave it the name of *poder*, or *dust*; and it will scarcely be credited in these times that he regarded it, not only as useless, but upon its appearance was actually induced to abandon the mine; the common expression upon such occasions being, that *the ore came in and spoilt the tin!* Lead, silver, antimony, iron, arsenic, and manganese are other products of the mines of Devonshire and Cornwall, but of trifling importance compared to tin and copper. Cobalt has also been discovered in small quantities, and grains and nuggets of gold are occasionally found in the alluvial soil of the tin streamworks. The finer grains amount annually to about 4 oz. They are considered perquisites of the miner, who deposits them in a quill, which he sells, when filled, to the goldsmith.

The peroxide of tin and sulphuret and bisulphuret of copper—the only ores of these metals which are of consequence in a mining point of view—are contained in *veins* or *lodes*, which run in an E. and W. direction, through granite as well as slate, and vary in width from an inch to upwards of 30 ft., but the average breadth is from 1 ft. to 4 ft. These are frequently interrupted by *cross-courses*, or veins seldom metalliferous, which maintain a direction from N. to S., and often prove to the miner a source of considerable vexation, for they alter the position of, or *heave* the lodes they intersect, and occasionally in such a manner as to baffle all attempts for their recovery. The veins containing lead pursue a N. and S. course, but are rarely associated with lodes of copper or tin. Indeed, each district is in general characterised by the preponderance of a particular ore. Thus Dartmoor, St. Austell, and St. Agnes are principally stanniferous, the great mining-field of Gwennap, Redruth, and Camborne, cupriferous, while lead is for the most part confined to the N. and E., and manganese and antimony to the N.E. parts of Cornwall. The Tavistock district is, however, of a mixed metalliferous character, and the ores of zinc and iron are largely distributed, but have hitherto been little noticed by the miner. The geological structure of the country is commonly an indication of the ores which may be found in it. Tin, as a general rule, is to be sought in granite, lead in slate, and copper near the junction of these two formations. But copper and tin frequently occur in one and the same lode, or in separate lodes running parallel courses, and so near each other as to be within the bounds of the same mine.

The usual method pursued in a search for lodes is to sink a pit to a certain depth, and then to drive a tunnel or *cross-cut* N. and S. (for tin and copper), so as to meet with every vein in the tract through which it passes. Another, and an ancient mode of discovery, is that termed *shoding*, which is now little practised, but as it is somewhat curious it deserves to be mentioned. The lodes rise to the surface, and by the wear and tear of ages the upper portions have been detached, and removed from the parent bed. If a tin-stone then should be found in turning up the soil, the Cornishman endeavours to ascertain whence it may have been derived, and tries up hill for the *broil*, or head of the vein, from which it has descended. It is seldom, however, that a new mine is opened from the surface, or *grass*, as it is called; the reworking of those which are from time to time abandoned being in general sufficient to engage all the speculators. But, occasionally, when a lode in a particular undertaking has assumed a very promising appearance,—as has lately been the case in S. Caradon and the Phoenix near Liskeard,—a number of mines will be opened in its vicinity, in the hope of participating in the good fortune.

A lode having been found, the licence of the owner of the soil must be obtained before any operations can be commenced—except, indeed, in a search for tin, when the right of *bounding*, if properly exercised, would authorise the discoverer to proceed. The proprietor of the land, having sanctioned the undertaking, is called the *lord*, and receives, as his share or *dish*, about one-eighteenth of the ore raised; the parties who work the mine being termed *adventurers*, and their shares depending upon the original agreement. The licence to the company is for a period of six months or a year, and at the expiration of this time the proprietor is bound to grant a lease, which is generally in the same terms as the licence.

In working a mine three material points are to be considered—the discharge of the water, the removal of the rubbish or *deads*, and the raising of the ore. To assist in the drainage an *adit*, or subterranean passage, is commenced in a neighbouring valley, and *driven* up to the vein, so that the level to which the water is to be pumped may be brought as low as possible. The *shaft*, a well-like aperture, is then sunk in the rock, and a machine called a *whim* erected, to bring up the *deads* and ore. This is a hollow cylinder of wood, or *cage*, which turns on a perpendicular axis, and is worked by horses—or, in a large mine, by a steam-engine. As it revolves, a rope which encircles it winds and unwinds, and raises one bucket or *kibbal* to the surface, whilst the other is descending the mine. The shaft is in general a square-shaped excavation, about 6 feet in breadth by 9 or 12 feet in length, and divided in the centre by a strong wooden partition, which makes it in reality two shafts, one for the use of the miner, the other for raising the ore. The veins or *lodes* which are to be reached by the shaft may be compared to leaning walls enclosed in the solid rock, slanting or *underlying* to the rt. or l., and descending to unknown depths. Where the shaft intersects them, *levels* or galleries, about 6 ft. in height by 4 in width, are *driven* in a horizontal direction along their course, one below the other, at intervals of from 10 to 20 or 30 fathoms; and when extended to a certain distance from the original vertical shaft, it becomes necessary, for the purpose of ventilation, to *sink* another shaft, which is made to intersect all the levels in the same manner as the first. In the interval a communication is also frequently made between two galleries by a partial shaft called a *wins*. More than one lode are generally worked in a mine, and when this is the case levels run parallel to each other at the same depth, and communicate by *cross-cuts*, driven through the intervening rock, or *country*, as it is called. The excavations are principally effected by blasting with gunpowder, and the annual cost of the quantity consumed in the Cornish mines amounts to as much as 18,000*l*. It is not, however, usual to extract all the ore which can be obtained. Certain portions are reserved to meet any run of ill success; these are termed *the eyes of the mine*, and are *picked out* only under pressing circumstances. The surface of the mine is called the *bal*, and every level and shaft has a name. In large adventures it is the practice to devote a proportion of the proceeds to "discovery," and this is sometimes pursued on an astonishing scale. In about 20 years the solid rock or *country* of the Consolidated Mines, Gwennap, was tunnelled for this purpose a distance of 63 m., at a cost of 300,000*l*. Much skill is shown by the miner in his underground work. The cross-cuts are driven by the guidance of a compass, a survey which is called *dialling*, and a shaft is frequently commenced at different depths, and cut with such exactness that the various parts, when completed, coincide, and form one vertical excavation.

A curious circumstance connected with these gloomy recesses is the increase of the heat with the depth, which is after the rate of 1 degree of Fahr. for every 53·5 ft., and has been cited as an argument for the Leibnitz doctrine of a central fire in the interior of the earth. Some, however, have sought to explain it by imperfect ventilation, and the heat generated by the combustion of candles and explosions of gunpowder; and it is worthy of notice that the recent discovery by Sir James Ross of the uniform temperature of the ocean at great depths appears to militate against the hypothesis of a central source of heat. In the deep levels of the Consolidated Mines the mercury rises to 98° Fahr., in those of the United Mines to 110° Fahr. The miners work naked to the waist, and have been known to lose 5 lbs. from perspiration during the spell of 8 hours.

The drainage of the mine is an important consideration, and the magnificent engines by which it is effected are well worthy of the traveller's attention. Before the invention of the steam-engine, the work was performed by horses, men, or water. The pumping machines were then the *water-whim*, in which a horse raised buckets or *kibbals* to the surface; the *rag and chain pump*, which was kept incessantly in motion by parties of men, who relieved each other at intervals of 6 hours; and the *water-wheel and bobs*, a wheel, perhaps 50 ft. in diam., turned by a stream of water, and connected with pumps formerly of wood, but now universally of cast-iron. This apparatus is still used in Cornwall, and is generally employed in Devonshire, where running water is plentiful. In the 18th cent. Newcomen and Savery introduced their atmospheric or *fire-engine*, for which they obtained a patent in 1705. By its aid the mines were deepened, and new sources of wealth made accessible; but the engine was necessarily both clumsy and costly, and consumed about 100 chaldrons of coal per month. In 1778 this engine was giving place to Watt's, in which steam was substituted for the weight of the atmosphere as the power to drive down the piston. The improvement was a great one. The new engine performed more work at a much less expense than one of Newcomen's, and Watt was amply remunerated for the use of his invention by one-third of the coals saved by it. 3 of his engines erected in place of the same number of Newcomen's on Chacewater effected a reduction of 7200*l*. in the annual expenditure of the mine. From the time of Watt the Cornish pumping engines have made rapid strides to that high position which they now occupy among the powers of steam. Hornblower introduced double cylinders, Woolf high pressure, and Trevithick boilers by which steam can be used at high pressure in single cylinders. The engines are now manufactured in Cornwall, and even one of the worst does the duty of 4 of Watt's. They work, with little noise, expansively at high pressure, and are pre-eminent for the ease with which they drain the greatest depths, and for the small relative amount of fuel consumed by them, and although of colossal size and power are so admirably constructed that they may be placed under the control of a boy. The interior is always handsomely fitted, and in general kept as clean and well ventilated as a lady's drawing-room. Upon the main-beam is fixed a counter, which, by recording the number of vibrations made in a given time, shows the amount of work or *duty* performed. This is called *reporting* the engine, the result being published once a month in *duty-papers*, a practice found advantageous as exciting emulation, for since its introduction some 30 years ago the work performed by the best engines has been more than trebled. The duty is ascertained by finding the number of pounds weight which the engine lifts one foot high by the consumption of one bushel of coals. In Austen's engine, on the Fowey Consols, it amounted one year to more than 87 millions. The beam of the engine is connected with a rod which descends through a chain of pumps to the *sump*, or bottom of the mine, where the water collects, and from this well a certain quantity of the water is raised to the surface, and the rest to the *adit*, down which it flows by a gentle descent to a neighbouring valley. In some cases, however, from the level though elevated character of the district, these subterranean channels are extended to a considerable distance ; and the *Great Adit*, which drains many of the principal mines in the parishes of Gwennap and Redruth, is calculated, with its ramifications, to be nearly 30 m. in length. The quantity of water discharged from a single mine occasionally amounts to upwards of 1600 gallons in a minute, and 37 millions of tons have been pumped from the earth by about 60 engines in the course of the year. Some idea of these wonderful machines may be derived from the following statement. Davey's engine on the Consolidated Mines, Gwennap, pumps directly from a depth of 1600 ft. ; the pumping rod is 1740 ft. long, or, in other words, the third of a mile in length, and lifts at every stroke 33½ gallons of water to the adit level, and 45 gallons more to the surface, the weight of the *pit-work* in the shaft being upwards of 500 tons, and its cost for materials alone 5236*l*.

The traveller who is desirous of descending a mine must lay aside every article of his ordinary dress, and array himself in the costume of a miner,—a flannel shirt and trowsers, worn close to the skin in order to absorb the perspiration, a strong pair of shoes, a linen cap, and a stout broad-brimmed hat, intended to serve the purpose of a helmet in warding off blows from the rock. He then has a candle fixed to his hat by a lump of clay, and is equipped for the adventure. The descent offers little difficulty, as the ladders are generally inclined, and stages occur at intervals of about three fathoms. But the ascent from these deep and melancholy vaults entails of course considerable exertion.

The stranger will, however, find little in the interior of a mine to gratify curiosity; for although the levels and their ramifications extend in general many miles, and hundreds of men are busily working in them at the same time, there are no crystalline chambers glittering with ore, nor crowds of miners grim as the Cyclops, nor caverns lighted by a number of torches and echoing the thunder of explosions and the rending of rocks. On the descent the working of the pump-rods and occasional rattle of the metallic buckets against the side of the shaft produce a certain amount of noise, but the *levels* are as silent as the grave, and sometimes so low and narrow as to admit the passage of one person only at a time, and that in a stooping posture. The miner, too, like the mole, is solitary in his operations, and is often discovered alone at the end of a gallery, in a damp and confined space, boring the solid rock, or breaking down the ore, by the feeble light of a candle.

The most interesting mines for the traveller to descend are those near the Land's End, which penetrate beneath the sea; for in these, when the coast is lashed by a swell from the Atlantic, an accompaniment that is seldom wanting, he may hear in the levels the harsh grating of rocks rolling to and fro overhead in the bed of the sea, and the reverberation of the breaking waves; but the enjoyment of such sublime but portentous sounds will require strength of nerve in the visitor, as the noise is often so terrific as to scare the miners from their work. It is a curious circumstance that these submarine mines are in general the driest in the county.

Besides the mines, properly so called, the Cornish valleys, or *bottoms*, contain numerous *stream-works* which produce a quantity of tin. Some of this, called *grain-tin*, is of great purity, and exclusively used by the dyer. A few of these works are very ancient, and it is supposed that all the tin of former days was procured by *streaming*. They derive their name from the manner in which they are worked, which consists in merely washing the alluvial soil by directing a stream of water over it, when the earthy particles are carried away, and the tin-ore procured in a separate form. Their condition or value is significantly denoted by the technical expressions of the miner,—a *living stream, just alive*, and *dead*. The principal stream-works are situated on and near the S. coast of Cornwall, and the greater number in the parishes of St. Austell and Luxulian. The valleys of Dartmoor, although long deserted by the miner, are everywhere scored by the remains of ancient stream-works.

The miners are divided into two great classes—*underground* and *surface men*, the former being three times as numerous as the latter. The underground-men are divided into *tutmen* and *tributers*. Tutmen sink the shafts and drive the levels and adits, executing their work by the piece, which is generally calculated by the fathom, and earning on an average from 40*s*. to 50*s*. a month. Tributers find the ore and raise it to the surface. A party of these men, however numerous, undertaking the excavation of a particular portion of the vein, is denominated a *pair*. This pair is subdivided into three gangs, which, by relieving each other at the end of every *spell* of 8 hours, keep up the work uninterruptedly, except on a Sunday. The expense of sinking shafts and cutting adits is defrayed by the adventurers; but the working of a limited part of the lode, called a *pitch*, is let by auction on *setting-days*, and is taken by the miners for two months at a time on *tribute*, that is, on an agreement to find their own tools, candles, and powder—a certain sum being advanced to them, called '*sist money*—and to open the vein and raise the ore, on condition of receiving a proportion of the proceeds, the amount of their gains being determined by the value of the ore when ready for market, and varying from 6d. to 13s. 4d. in the pound, according to the richness of the lode. Thus the tributers are adventurers, and the fascination of enterprise induces them, not only to tolerate, but to enter with ardour into their unhealthy occupation. The surface-men attend to the machinery and prepare the ore for market, many of the operations being performed by girls and women, whose gay and varied dresses and garrulous tongues enliven these dreary scenes of labour. On a rough calculation, the number of persons directly employed in the mines of Devon and Cornwall may be estimated at 30,000.

As soon as the tin-ore is brought to the surface it is *spalled*, or broken into smaller fragments, and then pounded in the *stamping-mill*, for the purpose of separating the oxide from the hard matrix through which it is disseminated. The *stamping-mill* consists of a number of *lifters*, or piles of wood shod with heavy masses of iron, which are raised and dropped by *cams* arranged on a *barrel* or shaft, moved by a water-wheel or a steam-engine. These lifters pound or *stamp* the ore small enough to pass the holes of an iron grate, through which it is carried by a stream of water into a series of pits, in which the particles are deposited according to their specific gravity. The richer and heavier portions, called the *crop* or *head*, collect in the first pit, and the slime or *tail* in the others. The crop-ores are then taken to the *buddle*, a pit in which they are arranged on an inclined wooden frame called the *jagging-board*, from which they are again washed by a run of water and separated into three or four parcels of different value. The *head* or *crop* of these deposits is next thrown into the *keeve*, a large vat containing water, and further purified by an operation called *tozing* or *tossing*. This consists in stirring the water round by means of a small shovel, with such rapidity as to bring the *tin-stuff* into a state of suspension, when the *tozer* relaxes his efforts, and by frequently striking the keeve with a mallet, the tin, from its greater weight, sinks to the bottom, or is *packed*, while the earth and other impurities circle at the top, and can be separated. The deposit in the keeve is divided into two or three parts, the lowest of which is fit either for *smelting*, or, if associated with *mundic*, a name the miners have given to arsenical and iron pyrites, for *roasting* in the *burning-house*. This is a reverberatory furnace fed with coal, but previous to the beginning of the 18th centy. the dressed tin-stone was carried for smelting direct to a blast furnace, supplied either with turf or charcoal. It was called the *blowing-house*, and was commonly burnt at the end of every 7 or 8 years for the sake of the tin which had been carried up the chimney, and had collected in the thatch of the roof. After roasting, the crop-ores are again *buddled*, *tossed*, and *packed*, until fit for smelting. The various portions separated from the crop-ores, and which come under the heads of *creases*, *skimpings*, and *leavings*, are subjected to a number of similar operations, namely, *sifting*, *dilluing*, *tying*, *jigging*, *trunking*, and *framing*, all of which are conducted with the object of arranging the particles of ore according to their specific gravity and relative value by the aid of water, and are highly interesting on account of the dexterity exhibited in their performance. The tin-ore thus prepared is called *black tin*, and is ready for sale. It contains 75 per cent. of metal; but when first brought to the surface it has frequently no more than 2 per cent. in it. The mode of *dressing* copper-ore is, in many of the operations, similar to that of tin. The ore is first broken up with hammers, and the best part or *prills* divided into fragments about the size of a walnut, by girls called *cobbers*, or crushed separately by cast-iron rollers. The second sort, the *dredge* ore, is crushed, and then treated in a sieve, called the *jigging* machine, which is jerked up and down in a keeve or *hutch* of water. The poorest, termed *halvans*, is either stamped, like the tin ore, or crushed, and then concentrated with the poorer parts and and leavings of the former classes, in *buddles*, either rectangular or round, or *strakes* and *tyes*, according to circumstances; whilst the *slime*, or that which has been reduced to the state of mud, is treated in *trunking buddles*. The various kinds, when sufficiently *clean*, are arranged in heaps on the surface of the mine, and weighed into *doles* or parcels for sale. The ores of tin and copper having been thus prepared are disposed of on *ticketing days*, or periodical sales, which are held twice a month at Redruth or Treloweth for tin, and weekly at Truro, Redruth, or Pool, for copper. The agents for the companies who purchase the ores, having previously taken samples of the different lots and assayed them, meet the mining agents at a dinner provided at the expense of the mines engaged in the transaction, and deliver sealed *tickets* containing the prices which each offers for the various parcels. These tickets are then opened and read aloud, and the highest bidders are pronounced the purchasers. The business is speedily transacted, and ores to the amount of several thousand pounds change hands in an hour or two. The merchants are at the cost of reducing the ores to metal by the operation of *smelting*. For this purpose the copper ore is shipped to Swansea, but the tin ore is smelted in the county. The stranger may therefore witness the entire series of operations to which the latter mineral is subjected, and, as an appropriate conclusion to his investigation, regale himself with a noted, though unpretending Cornish dainty—a beefsteak broiled on a block of the glowing metal which has just issued from the furnace. Previous to the year 1838, the *white tin* was cast in large blocks, for the purpose of being *coined* and stamped by the Duchy authorities. With that object these blocks were sent to one of the *coinage towns*, where the *corner* of each was struck off, and assayed by officers appointed for that duty. If the tin was found of a proper quality, the dues were paid, and the blocks, being stamped with the seal of the Duchy, were so rendered saleable.

The business of a mine is generally managed by a *purser*, and the working of the concern by an agent called a *captain*, who in a large adventure, has other persons under him styled *grass captains* and *underground captains*; the former superintending the operations on the surface, such as the dressing of the ore ; the latter having the immediate inspection of the works underground, and attending to the timbering of the lode, and the pumps. The miners are an intelligent body of men, their wits being sharpened by the system of tribute-work, which renders their gain in a measure dependent upon habits of observation. They are athletic and good-looking, but certainly are not beheld to advantage when emerging from the dark scenes of their labour, begrimed with soot, and red with the ferruginous soil. Too often, also, may be observed in them the fatal mark of pulmonary consumption, which above all others may be called the miners' disease. Of late years, however, the comforts of these men have been more attended to than formerly, and their condition much ameliorated by the humane exertions of individuals. Mr. Pendarves, for so many years a representative of Cornwall, and who might justly be styled the good genius of that county for the many benefits he conferred upon it, introduced *washing-houses* into all the mines over which he had any control. These are supplied with hot water from the engine, and situated in the immediate vicinity of the shaft, and are indeed a blessing to the miner, enabling him to wash the mud from his person and change his dress without the danger of a sudden exposure to cold air. A century ago these men were by no means remarkable for sobriety, but the preaching of Wesley effected an extraordinary change in their habits; teetotalism is now almost universal, and the thirsty traveller may be inconvenienced by its necessary consequence, a scarcity of beer in the houses of public entertainment. The miner, however, cannot so readily divest himself of a lingering superstition fostered by his occupation : he often hears the Pixies or "small men" sporting in the levels, he carefully abstains from *whistling* when underground, and is a firm believer in the efficacy of the *Virgula Divinatoria* or *Divining Rod*. The absurdity of this faith is indeed so palpable, that the stranger will marvel at finding it countenanced by Cornishmen who hold a higher position in society. The magical rod consists merely of a forked stick of willow or hazel, which is to be held in a particular manner, when it is firmly believed to possess the property of bending towards the earth, and of pointing out the invisible course of a mineral vein or lode. Sixty years ago the efficacy of this wand was unquestioned ; and Pryce, a scientific and experienced miner, has recorded his inflexible belief in its extraordinary virtues, and in his Mineralogia Cornubiensis has left us full directions for its construction and use.

The miners distinguish various mineral substances by technical names, many of which, like the prefix of *huel*, a *hole*, are old Cornish words. Thus, rocks with a slaty cleavage are known as *killas*; porphyry is called *elvan*; disintegrated granite, *growan*; a decomposed killas, *flukan*; quartz, in the western parts of Cornwall, *spar*; sulphuret of zinc, *Black Jack*; a brown earthy substance, composed of oxide of iron mixed with argillaceous and other particles, and regarded as an indication of a rich copper vein, *gossan*; a matrix of copper-ore compounded of mixed argillaceous and siliceous substances, *caple*; whilst iron and arsenical pyrites, which often accompany a lode of copper, are confounded under the name of *mundic*. Gossan lies on the *back* of the vein, and frequently reaches so near to the surface as to be exposed by ploughing, and in this way many of the lodes have been discovered in Cornwall.

With respect to the articles required in working a mine, the consumption of timber, candles, gunpowder, &c., in a large concern, far exceeds any estimate that a person unacquainted with mining matters could imagine.. The following statement of the average monthly consumption (year 1847) in the tin-mine of *Balleswidden*, St. Just, will, however, give the reader definite notions on the subject:—

Powder, 4208 lbs.
Fuze coils, 640 lbs.
Candles, 289 cwt.
Coals, 170 tons.
Oil, 30 gals.
Timber, 2000 ft.
Tallow and grease, 4 cwt. 1 qr. 14 lbs.

Iron castings, 4 tons, 8 cwt. 2 qrs. 14 lbs.
Nails, 5½ cwt.
Steel, &c., 3 cwt. 1 qr. 4 lbs.
Wrought and bar iron, 49 cwt. 0 qr. 24 lbs.

In the same year the number of persons employed in this adventure was 362 men and boys underground, 231 men and boys and 49 girls on the surface; and the average monthly expenditure in wages (for labour only) amounted to 1575*l*. 8*s*. 2*d*. But Balleswidden, although an important undertaking, cannot be compared with the *Consolidated Mines* in Gwennap, the largest of the Cornish group. This wonderful work, though now (1858) almost in abeyance, is nearly 2 m. long, and was conducted as one concern, employing upwards of 3000 persons, and yielding copper and tin from a depth equal to five times the height of St. Paul's. In 1836 it produced ore of the value of 145,717*l*. 1*s*. 1*d*., on which the lord's dues were 6071*l*. 10*s*. 6*d*. The total expenses for the year amounted to 102,007*l*. 12*s*. 1*d*.

THE TRAVELLER'S GENERAL VIEW.

If the traveller could obtain a bird's-eye view over the three western counties of England, he would behold in Cornwall and Devon a surface of accumulated hills, rising in certain districts to a considerable elevation, and in Somerset branching into distinct ranges bounding intermediate plains. Nature has therefore in this part of the kingdom laid the groundwork of great scenic beauty, which she has further developed by protruding the rocky strata through the surface, and by girding the favoured land with a magnificent array of cliffs, and an ocean which is in sight from most of the eminences. In Devon the mode of cultivating the ground is in harmony with this picturesque disposition of the surface; while the barren and elevated moors, having hitherto been left intact, delight the eye by wild and imposing prospects. But no sooner has the traveller passed the Cornish boundary of the Tamar than a change comes over the scene. The hills which have hitherto delighted him are now patched with fields, but otherwise as bald and uniform as the ocean waves which they resemble in their undulations, while they are everywhere disfigured by stone *hedges* disposed along them in straight lines with the utmost exactitude. A great part of the barren country has been stripped of the rocks which once imparted interest to the scenery, and the mining districts are rendered hideous by unsightly erections and heaps of rubbish so impregnated with mineral matter that not a blade of grass will vegetate upon them. Striking, however, as is the contrast between Devon and the inland parts of Cornwall, the shores of the latter county present the most beautiful scenes, and the banks of the rivers, and the deep valleys or *bottoms* with which the county is furrowed, are in general well wooded and picturesque. To Devonshire, however, has nature very classically given the *apple*, for she is pre-eminently *the beauty* of the western counties. The district derives its name from the innumerable heights and hollows diversifying the surface, and to the embellishment of which the soil and the climate, and even the labour of man, have contributed. The lanes are steep and narrow, and bordered by tangled hedges, often thirty feet above the road, sheltering even the hills from the rigour of unfriendly blasts. In the deep shadowy *combes* the villages lie nestled, with rosente walls of clay and roofs of thatch, and seldom far from one of those crystal streams which enliven every valley of this rocky county. Even the cliffs of the coast are festooned with creepers, while old weather-worn limekilns crown them like castles, and woods descend to the very brink of the sea. For those who relish less cultivated scenes, Dartmoor presents a waste of rock-capped heights and dark morasses, most truly forlorn and wild. But the tints of the moor are of surpassing beauty, the air most exhilarating, and the grandeur of its lonely hills calculated to impress the most apathetic tourist.

The finest scenery of Devonshire is to be found in the north, between Lynton and Ilfracombe, where the offshoots of Exmoor abut upon the sea, or are based in woods and subalpine ravines; and on the skirts of Dartmoor, which on every side are pierced by deep romantic glens, leading to a desolation, but clothed themselves with golden gorse and oaks. The rivers Teign, Dart, Erme, and Okement flow from the moor through valleys of this description. With respect to the coast, those portions of it most worthy the traveller's attention are the *greensand*

and *red sandstone* cliffs, ranging at elevations of 400 ft. and 500 ft. between Seaton and Sidmouth; the *mica slate* rocks between the Start Point and Bolt Tail; the romantic *grauwacke* shore of Bigbury Bay; the *carbonaceous* wooded slopes of Clovelly; and the *grauwacke* cliffs of Ilfracombe, Combe Martin, and Lynton.

The *South Hams*, a district bounded by the rivers Tamar and Teign, Dartmoor, and the Channel, is called the *garden of Devonshire*, from its fertility, and contains numerous orchards, which annually supply large quantities of *cider*, the average being 10 hogsheads per acre. This beverage is prepared in the following manner. The apples, when gathered, are exposed in the open air for two or three weeks until the *brown rot* has begun, when they are ground to *cheese* in a mill, and in this broken state heaped up with straw under the *press*. A lever is then applied, and in about two days the juice, or *must*, is expressed. The *must* is kept in large open vessels until the *head* rises, when it is drawn off into casks. It is then frequently racked until the tendency to fermentation is removed. The place of manufacture is provincially called the *Poundhouse*. In this part of Devon the valleys are very warm during the summer; but the visitor may, with little difficulty, refresh himself by agreeable changes both of scene and climate. From the cliffs of the coast, when requiring relief from the glare of sun and water, he can hasten to the skirts of the moor, there to wander through shady dells, amid mossy rocks and mossy trees, or along the banks of pellucid streams; or he may explore labyrinthine lanes, and amuse himself with trout-fishing, or by sketching the weather-worn cottages of granite, slate, or *cob*; or, if desirous of more invigorating exercise, he may ascend into Dartmoor, and there brace his sinews in the healthful mountain air, and delight his soul by grand misty views over those lonely hills. The *Devonshire cottage* is truly said, by Mrs. Bray, to be "the sweetest object that the poet, the artist, or the lover of the romantic, could desire to see." The roof is universally of thatch, and the walls generally of *cob*, which is a concrete of mud and pebbles, very warm, and, if kept dry at top and bottom, very durable. A local aphorism says, "good cob, a good hat and shoes and heart last for ever." Both Devonshire and Cornwall are known for their *clouted cream*, their *junkets* and *squab-pie*, though according to an old authority the dainty dish is more properly Cornubian, the spicy liquor Devonian; for

"Cornwall squab-pie, and Devon white-pot brings,"

is the enunciation of King in his 'Art of Cookery.' Junket is a mixture of cream, rennet, spice, and spirits; squab-pie a savoury compound of mutton steaks, onions, and sliced pippins, arranged under the crust in alternate layers, and "adjusted," says Mrs. Glasse, "in the most orderly manner." Clouted cream is thus prepared. The milk is strained into shallow pans, each containing about half a pint of water to prevent the milk adhering. In these it is allowed to remain undisturbed for 12 or 24 hours, according to the weather. It is then scalded by a wood fire or the warm bath. In the former case it is moved slowly towards the fire, so as to become gradually heated, and in about 40 or 50 minutes the cream is formed. This is indicated by bubbles, and takes place at a temp. of 180° Fahr. The milk is then removed from the fire, and skimmed from 12 to 36 hours afterwards.

The *Cornish* excel in cooking potatoes, which form a part of the usual breakfast of all classes. Pies and pasties are, however, the strong points of the Cornish cuisine. The chief are *conger pasty*; *star-gazy pie*, made of pilchards with their heads centred in the outside crust; *leeky pie*, of green tops of leeks, slices of bacon, and scalded cream; *squab-pie*; *crocky stew*, something like Irish stew, but instead of potatoes having slices of a batter pudding, and served in a tall metal dish like a soufflé-pan, but of less diameter; and *veal and parsley pie*, containing veal, chopped parsley, and cream. The pasty of the Cornish labourer might be copied with advantage elsewhere. It consists of potatoes, with a little meat, salt, and pepper, in a turn-over crust. It is easy and clean to carry; and if you are hungry and the pasty is hot, it is a feast for a king. "Metheglin" (wine made from honey), the "mead" of Saxondom, is still to be found in the old farmhouses of both Cornwall and Devon.

With respect to Cornish scenery, there are parts of the coast which are unrivalled by any similar scenes in England. These are the *slate* cliffs between Boscastle and Tintagel, the *serpentine* rocks of the Lizard, dyed in the colours of the rainbow, and that magnificent barrier of *granite* precipices between the Logan Rock and Land's End. The cliff scenery of the latter is the finest in England; and the huge frame of this astonishing rampart, and the hardness of the material, might be regarded as a special provision against the stormy seas which, by the prevailing winds, are particularly directed upon this part of the shore; but the fact is, no doubt, that "all less impediments have been long since surmounted and washed away." The caverns in these cliffs of serpentine and granite should be explored. In the former rock they are remarkable for their varied and beautiful colouring; in the latter, for their cylindrical shapes, and the extreme smoothness and polish of their walls, the surfaces of which are sometimes without a single fracture. These caverns retain their old Cornish names of *hugo* in the Lizard district and *zawn* in that of the Land's End. Every part of the coast is indented by secluded and romantic coves, provincially called *porths*, which, on the N. coast, are fringed by beaches of shelly sand, extensively used throughout the county as a top-dressing to the land. During the autumn some of these coves present, at low-water, very animated scenes, when a number of donkeys are busily employed in carrying bags of this sand to the summit of the cliffs. Three of these measures constitute a *seam*, 100 of which are sold to the farmer for about 18s. or 20s. The bands of strata along that portion of the coast which lies between Boscastle and the mouths of the Taw and Torridge are so narrow and distinctly marked as to give a ribboned appearance to the cliffs, and are heaved and contorted in a manner which defies all description. They are also so loosely bound together as to yield readily to the assaults of the sea. Here, therefore, the coast presents a ruinous appearance, and huge fragments cumber the shore, bearing a resemblance to enormous walls, or to the carcases of ships which have been stranded and converted into stone. Five of the Cornish headlands may be particularised as pre-eminent for grandeur, viz.:—*Tintagel*, the *Gurnard's Head*, *Pardenick*, *Tol Pedn Penwith*, and *Treryn Castle*, the site of the Logan Rock. Three of these are peninsulas connected with the coast by narrow necks of land,—a shape which every projecting cliff must at one time assume, from being exposed to a particular action of the sea which tends to separate it from the shore; for the waves, hurried into the recesses on either side, are straitened as they advance by the converging cliffs, and ultimately discharge the force of their accumulated parts at the head of the bay; and in whatever direction the waves may roll to the shore, they are deflected and ultimately driven to these points.

In exploring the Cornish coast, the traveller may perchance observe, in some secluded nook among the cliffs, a solitary *chough* or red-legged crow, a bird once so common in the county as to have been called the Cornish daw, but which now is confined to the most desolate and lonely retreats. It is this bird's misfortune to be highly esteemed among collectors, and for this reason a price is set upon his head, and he is hunted by the peasants without mercy. His bill, feet, and legs are long, like those of a jackdaw, but of a red colour, and his plumage is black all over. The *cormorant* or *shag*, unlike the chough, has the good fortune to be vulgar and valueless, and in a crowd of his dark-feathered companions escapes the notice of the curious. He is everywhere to be seen revelling in the storm, or sunning himself on the rocks, and is a strong predaceous bird and an adroit fisher, and with his sooty plumage and hoarse croaking voice is in perfect keeping with the wild, black cliffs he frequents. Milton has made Satan personate this bird when sitting on the tree of life, devising death.

If the traveller should delight in wild scenery, he will derive much pleasure from an excursion across the Bodmin Moors; for instance, a walk from Liskeard, by the Jamaica Inn and Brown Willy, to Camelford. The hills of these moors are lower than those of Dartmoor, but are capped in the same manner by fantastic piles of granite, which in Cornwall are called *carns*. The slopes of these eminences are also frequently strewn with detached blocks, a number of which are annually broken up and removed from the surface, and applied to building purposes, or converted into gateposts or implements of husbandry. The method of splitting the *moor-stone* is to drive wedges into a line of holes cut or *pooled* in the surface, at a distance of three or four inches from each other, according to the size or supposed hardness of the block. The valleys are filled with bogs, often of considerable depth, and sometimes composed of alternate layers of peat and disintegrated granite, a structure showing that the channels of the streams which flow through them have been periodically shifted. Some of these deposits contain an enormous quantity of hazel leaves and branches, supposed to be the remains of ancient woods, as there is a tradition that the county was once covered with forests, which were cut down to supply charcoal for smelting the tin-ore. This tradition is further supported by the discovery of oaks and other trees in the tin stream-works, and on the shore below high-water mark on several parts of the coast. The peat of the moor is extensively used as fuel, but the moormen of Devon and Cornwall pursue a different practice in cutting it. In Cornwall they pare off the surface only; in Devonshire the bog-earth—on Dartmoor called *vaggs*—is removed to a depth of four or five feet, and the lowest part is considered the best fuel. In the autumn the dark herbage of these waste lands is relieved by the white feathery seeds of the cotton-rush.

In rambling over Cornwall the traveller may be frequently puzzled by provincial expressions. Thus, for instance, he may ask of a countryman the nearest road to St. Just, and be told to his surprise that he is now in St. Just, although the moor bounds his view on every side. But St. Just means, in Cornwall, the parish of that name: the town is distinguished as the *church-town*; and so is the smallest village which contains a church. Again, a direction to proceed to such a farmhouse, and then turn to the right through the *town-place*, will be as Hebrew to one uninitiated in the lingo of the west; but the stranger will soon learn that the town-place of a farmhouse is the open space, or farmyard, in front of it. In thus wandering through the county the foot-weary pedestrian will greet with a benediction the *stile* which admits him to the churchyard, or links the field path he may be pursuing. Unlike the harassing obstruction in other parts of England, it consists of bars of granite arranged like a gridiron on the ground, and thus, offering no impediment to a man, though lame or feeble, but an effectual barrier to cattle or other animals confined in the fields, might be advantageously adopted by farmers throughout the kingdom.

The following objects are also calculated to strike the attention by their novelty, viz.:—porphyry and granite houses, stone hedges, teetotal inns, and the *arishmows* in which the corn is so heaped in the field as to be proof against rain. In Devonshire the traveller may view with astonishment, and sometimes with apprehension, the *crooks*, which, slung over a packsaddle, are so laden with furze or faggot-wood that it is no easy matter to pass them in the narrow lanes. In the fields he may observe the *slide* or sledge on its low solid wheels; and occasionally the *winstow*, an old method of winnowing the corn by shaking it in sieves, and thus subjecting it to the action of the wind.

The untidy look of the outside of the cottages and villages is common to both the "Principality" (Wales), and the "Duchy;" but although the outward appearance suggests Ireland, the inside may boast of a cleanliness and tidiness unsurpassed in England. The love of excitement, and of preaching, or any sort of oratory, and an utter absence of method in work or business, proclaim the Welsh "Cymry" and the "Cerniwaith" of Cornwall to be of the same blood and race.

The most interesting scenes and objects in the two counties may be briefly enumerated as follows:—

In Devonshire;

Valley of Rocks, Lyndale, and valley of Heddon's Mouth, near *Lynton*. The Hobby, Clovelly, and park of Clovelly Court, near *Bideford*. Yes Tor, and the fine moorland valleys near *Okehampton*. Wistman's Wood, near *Two Bridges*. Dartmoor, and particularly its skirts on every side. Gidleigh Park, near *Chagford*. The Spinsters' Rock, Fingle Bridge, and the banks of the Teign, Lustleigh Cleave, Houndtor Coomb, and Becky Fall, near *Moreton Hampstead*. The coast from Lyme Regis to Sidmouth. Chudleigh Rock. Berry Pomeroy Castle, near *Totnes*. The Dart, from Totnes to its mouth. Dartmouth. Holne Chace, Buckland, and Heytor, near *Ashburton*. Ivy Bridge. The coast from the Start to the Bolt Tail. Mt. Edgcumbe, the Breakwater, the Royal Albert Bridge, the Tamar from Hamoaze to the Weir-head, Bickleigh Vale, and the Valley of the Cad, near *Plymouth*. Brent Tor, Huel Friendship, and the ravine and cascade of Lidford, near *Tavistock*.

In Cornwall:

The coast between Treryn Castle and the Land's End, the Logan Rock, Botallack Mine, St. Michael's Mount, and the circles and cromlechs, near *Penzance*. Kinance Cove, near *Helston*. The mining-field of *Redruth*. Stream-works and Carclaze tin-mine, near *St. Austell*. The Valley of Carmeirs and Treffry Viaduct, near *St. Blazey*. The antiquities and Cheesewring, near *Liskeard*. Rowtor, Brown Willy, and valley of Hanter-Gantick, on the *Bodmin Moors*. The Delabole Quarries, Tintagel, St. Nighton's Keeve, and the coast between Tintagel and Boscastle, near *Camelford*. St. Columb and the valley to the sea. Cothele, near *Callington*.

Both Devon and Cornwall are pleasant counties to travel in, for the hospitality of the West is proverbial, and the people are obliging and courteous to strangers. No pedestrian has ever wandered over their moors, or explored with curious eye the busy scenes of their labour, without having experienced the truth of this observation. They are a broad-shouldered race, above the average in stature, although individuals may fall below the mark—for instance, Jack the Giant-killer, that "pixy" of a man, was a Cornishman. But it is a fact that west country regiments, when drawn up on parade with those of other counties, have covered a greater space of ground, the numbers being equal. Their courage has been often displayed. Lord Exmouth, when Captain Pellew, fought and won one of the most brilliant of single-ship actions with a crew of Cornish miners. At an earlier period it shone forth as conspicuously. In the Great Rebellion the mainstay of the throne was found in the West, where the Cornish generals were called "the wheels of Charles's wain." Indeed the loyalty that was then manifested has been handed down to our own times in the following quaint nursery song:—

"I'll bore a hoale in Crummel's noase,
And therein putt a string,
And laid en up and down the teown,
For murdering Charles our King."

The *fisheries* of Cornwall and Devon deserve the attention of the traveller as the most important on our S.W. coasts, the *seine-fishing* of St. Ives and the *trawling* of Torbay being respectively characteristic of the two counties. Torbay has long supplied London with a quantity of very excellent fish, such as turbots, mullets, soles, and dories. Plymouth and Clovelly are both well known as fishing stations; but the towns of the W. and S. coasts of Cornwall, St. Ives, Penzance, Mevagissey, and others, possess a more novel and lively interest as the stations of the *pilchard fishery*, a fishery so remarkable for the scale of its operations, and for the science and enterprise shown in its pursuit. Among all the fishers of our southern coasts, the Cornish are considered the most hardy and adventurous, being at sea nearly the whole year round in their arduous occupation, and competing with the Irish on their shores during the herring season. Three kinds of fishing are pursued on the Cornish coasts: the *drift-net*, the *seine*, and the *hook-and-line* fishing; mackerel and pilchards are the objects of the first, pilchards alone of the second; and hake, cod, ling, and whiting of the third; a distinct set of boats being required for each. The drift-net and seine-fishing are, however, the grand operations, and in these the annual routine of the fisherman is as follows. He commences about the end of January with the *early mackerel fishing*, off Plymouth. This lasts about six weeks; but the Cornishman follows the shoals in a westerly direction for some time longer. About the middle of June he sails for the N. coast of Ireland, and there engages in the capture of the herring, returning to Cornwall about the end of July, but in time for the commencement of the *summer pilchard season*. This being concluded, he overhauls his boat for the *autumnal mackerel fishery*, which is at its height in October; and, lastly, towards the end of October, he engages in the *winter pilchard fishery*, which sometimes continues through the following month to December. Of all these various fisheries, that of the pilchard is the most calculated to afford entertainment to the stranger. Its operations are conducted on the largest scale, and interests of such magnitude are staked on its success, that it is associated with the mines in the whimsical toast of "tin and fish." It is exclusively pursued on the shores of Cornwall and the S.W. of Devon, and is so curious in its details as to merit a full description.

The pilchard belongs to the genus *Clupea*, and is a sociable, migratory fish, so closely resembling the herring in size and form as to have been called the *gipsy herring*, but differing from it in some essential particulars. "It is a smaller and less compressed fish, and has larger scales, and the dorsal fin placed exactly in the centre of gravity, so that it will balance when suspended by this fin, whereas the herring, when so tried, will dip towards the head." Pilchards derive their principal interest from that instinct which annually induces them to assemble in millions, and to perform a stately march through the sea, generally in the same direction, and within certain determinate limits. They were formerly believed to migrate from the polar regions, and to return to those icy quarters at the end of the season; but Mr. Couch, the author of 'The Fauna of Cornwall,' to whom the reader is indebted for many of the following particulars (see a paper by Mr. Couch, in the Report of the Penzance Nat. Hist. and Antiq. Soc. for 1847), has ascertained that they remain in small numbers on the coast of Cornwall throughout the year, and that the main body retires for the winter into deep water to the westward of the islands of Scilly, and confines its migrations to an area of sea which would be bounded by a line drawn from the Start Point along the northern side of the Bay of Biscay, then northwards through the Atlantic W. of Scilly, then in an easterly direction along the S. coast of Ireland, and lastly in a southerly direction on the W. side of Lundy Island to the N. coast of Cornwall; although a few pilchards are occasionally found beyond these limits, and, indeed, in the English Channel as far east as Brighton and Dover.

About the middle of the spring these fish feel a desire for companionship and change of scene. They rise from the depths of the ocean and consort together in small shoals, which, as the season advances, unite into larger ones, and towards the end of July, or beginning of August, combine in one mighty host, which, under the guidance of the *Pilchard King* and the most powerful of the tribe (see Mr. Couch's memoir), begins that extraordinary migration which is the object of the Cornish fishery. Pursued by predaceous hordes of dog-fish, hake, and cod, and greedy flocks of sea-birds, they advance towards the land in such amazing numbers as actually to impede the passage of vessels, and to discolour the water as far as the eye can reach. They strike the land generally to the N. of Cape Cornwall, where a detachment turns to the N.E. and constitutes the *summer fishery of St. Ives*, but the bulk of the fish passes between Scilly and the Land's End, and entering the British Channel follows the windings of the shore as far as Bigbury Bay and the Start Point. Their course, however, is often changed by the currents or the state of the weather, and of a sudden they will vanish from the view, and then again approach the coast in such compact order and overwhelming force, that numbers will be pushed ashore by the moving hosts in the rear (Mr. Couch). The spectacle of the great fish army passing the Land's End is described as one of the most interesting that it is possible to imagine. In the beginning of October the *north coasters* and *winter fish*, as they are called, make their appearance on the N.E. of Cornwall, and in such force that 12 millions have been captured in a single day. They arrive at St. Ives about the third week of October, pass thence round Cape Cornwall and the Land's End, and occasionally follow in the track of the summer fish along the shore of the English Channel.

The fishery is pursued both by day and by night, but by different methods. Between sunrise and sunset the capture is effected inshore by the *seine*; between sunset and sunrise some miles from the land by the *drift-net*. The latter mode of fishing is principally pursued in the Mount's Bay, the former at St. Ives. In drift-net fishing a string of nets is stretched like a wall through the sea, very often for the length of ¾ of a mile, and a depth of 30 ft., and allowed to drift with the tide, so as to intercept the pilchards as they swim and entangle them by the gills. In this manner as many as 50,000 fish are commonly taken by a driving-boat in a single night. The chief obstacles to this kind of fishing are the light of the moon and the phosphorescence of the water. The latter enables the fisherman to see his net to its full depth "like a brilliant lace-work of fire," and the splendid display very naturally alarms the fish, which diverge to the rt. or l. and thus avoid the snare. The principal entertainment afforded by the drift fishery to the stranger is the daily recurring spectacle of the little fleet on the wing, its red sails all a-flame in the beams of a setting sun.

The *seine-fishing* possesses a more general interest, and, as by this method the fish are enclosed in shoals, it takes precedence of the other as the grand operation in the fishery. The boats which are employed in it are three in number; the *seine-boat*, carrying the great net or *seine;* the *volyer* or *follower*, in which the *thwart* or *stop net* is stowed ; and a smaller boat called the *lurker*, under the guidance of the *master seiner*, whose duty it is to keep a wary eye upon the movements of the fish. When the season has arrived, and the gathering of gulls and other seabirds gives warning of the approach of the pilchards, look-out men called *huers* (*huer*, French verb, *to shout*) are stationed on the cliffs, who watch the sea for the red tinge which indicates the presence of a shoal. No sooner is this descried than they announce the welcome intelligence by shouting *heva, heva, heva!* (*found!*) a cry which is instantly responded to by the inhabitants rushing from their houses, and the boats flying from the shore in pursuit. All is now hurry and excitement. The rowers use their utmost exertions, the *huer* directing their course by signals with a furze-bush. In a few minutes they reach the indicated spot, when the great seine, which is usually 160 fath. in length by 8 or 12 in depth, is cast into the sea by three men as the boat is gently rowed round the shoal, and with such dexterity that the whole of this enormous net is often *shot* in less than 5 min. The volyer has meanwhile kept the net taut at the other end, and no sooner is it fairly in the sea than the extremities are warped towards each other, and the lurker takes its station in the opening, so as to drive back the fish from the only aperture by which they can escape. When the ends are in contact the thwart-net is dropped across, and the seine, being cautiously raised, is quickly tacked together, and if the bottom be free of rocks, and the water not too deep, the capture is then securely effected, and the men proceed at their leisure to calculate the number of their prisoners, and to secure the net in its position by carrying out grapnels on every side, or, where the shore is sandy and shelving, with the assistance of some extra hands called *blowsers*, to draw the seine into shallow water. At low tide another party of men, termed *regular seiners*, proceed to the next operation, which is the most interesting to the stranger, and is called *tucking*. It consists in removing the fish from the seine into a smaller net, called the *tuck-net*, and in lifting them by *flaskets* from the tuck-net into boats which carry them to the shore. This is a tedious process, occasionally occupying nearly a week when 4

Introd. *Traveller's View.* lv

or 5 millions of fish are enclosed in the seine; for they are not taken faster from the preserve than they can be salted. As calm weather is essential for its performance, and as it generally happens on a serene evening or by moonlight, the sight it affords is so extremely beautiful, that no opportunity of witnessing it should be neglected.

The pilchards having been brought to the shore are wheeled in barrows or carried in cowels to the *cellars* to be *cured*, which is performed by girls and women, who heap them edgewise in broad piles—*in bulk*, as it is called—and sprinkle each tier of fish as it is completed with bay salt. They now resemble a series of sandwiches of salt and pilchards, and are allowed to remain undisturbed about 6 weeks, a quantity of oil and dirty pickle draining from them during the process. This, from the inclination of the floor, finds its way to a well, and is afterwards sold to the currier. The fish are next taken from the bulk, and thoroughly washed and cleansed from the filth and coagulated oil which, rising as a scum to the surface, is collected under the name of *garbage*, and disposed of to the soap-boiler. They are then packed in hogsheads, each containing about 2400 fish, and pressed together for the purpose of squeezing out the oil, which amounts to about 3 gallons a hogshead in the summer, and 2 gallons in the winter, and is an important item in the produce of the fishery. The casks, being then *headed up*, are ready for exportation, and are principally shipped to Naples and other Italian ports, and hence the toast of the fisherman, "Long life to the Pope and death to thousands." Many pilchards also find their way into Spain, and there, says old Fuller, "under the name of fumadoes [Anglicè 'Fair Maids'], with oyle and a lemon, they are meat for the mightiest Don." The broken and refuse fish, and those suffocated in the nets, are sold for manure, and when mixed with the calcareous sand of the beach are used throughout Cornwall with very excellent effect.

It is considered that the pilchard fishery gives employment to about 10,000 persons, and that a capital of 250,000*l.* is engaged in it. The yearly produce averages from 20,000 to 30,000 hogsheads, of which about 6000 are retained for home consumption. In 1847, however, the success was unusually great, and the exports amounted to 40,883 hogsheads, containing a quantity of fish which it has been calculated would form a band 6 deep round the world. In 1846, 75 millions of pilchards were enclosed by the seines of St. Ives in a single day; and in 1836 a shoal extended in a compact body from Fowey to the Land's End, a distance of at least 100 m., if we take into consideration the windings of the shore (Mr. Couch). The expense of the St. Ives fishery, supposing no fish to be taken, amounts to 10,000*l.* a year. The price in the foreign trade averages 50*s.* a hogshead for summer fish, and something less for winter fish. The profits in drift-fishing are divided into 8 shares; 1 for the boat, 3 for the nets, and 4 for the men. In seine-fishing the persons employed are commonly paid fixed wages, but have also a small percentage on the captured fish. The wages may be stated as follows:—

Huer	21s.	per week.
Master seiner	12s.	,,
Seine shooters	12s.	,,
Regular seiners	10s.	,,
Ordinary men	10s.	,,
Salters (girls and women)	3d.	per hour.

Pilchards constitute an important article of food to the poorer classes of Cornishmen, and in a successful season are retailed near the coast at the rate of 12 for a penny.

Fly-fishing for salmon, peal, and trout (the last of which are provincially called *shots*, from their rapid motion through the water) is eagerly pursued on all the brooks and rivers of these counties. Mr. Bellamy, in his 'Guide to the Fishmarket,' enumerates the *Red Palmer*, the *Blue Palmer*, the *Woodcock's Feather*, the *Partridge's Feather*, and (in very hot weather) the *Black Fly*, as the *flies* commonly used in the Devonshire rivers.

The *climate* of Devonshire and Cornwall varies much in different localities; the sheltered recesses on the southern coast enjoying a mild and equable temperature, where the sun has rarely sufficient play to ripen the grape, and snow and ice are almost unknown, and where the myrtle, geranium, fuchsia, hydrangea, and other exotics grow in the open air; while the bare hills and elevated moors, which constitute a great portion of Cornwall, are characterised by bleakness. Atlantic storms sweep unchecked over this wild expanse, and the few trees which grow in exposed situations are dwarfish in stature, and bent nearly into a horizontal position. The extreme fury of these gales would scarcely be credited by a stranger, but on a visit to Cornwall he will observe that even the tombstones in the churchyards are supported by masonry as a protection against the wind. "The gale from the west," says Polwhele, "is here no gentle zephyr; instead of wafting perfume on its wings, it often brings devastation." The salt of the sea is borne across the country by the tempest, and this also has a pernicious effect upon vegetation, and after a gale of any continuance the withered appearance of the trees is very striking. Rain is of frequent occurrence, a fact which is conveyed in a popular Cornish adage, that *the supply for the county is a shower on every week-day and two on a Sunday*. It is, however, rarely heavy or lasting, and the days are few indeed on which the sky is not relieved by a sunbeam. To the farmer this prevalence of moisture is a subject of congratulation, as the soil on the high lands is so shallow and porous as to require repeated supplies; but the quantity that falls during the year is but little above the average of other parts of England. The position of Cornwall necessarily exposes it to sea-mists, which, collecting in the solitudes of the Atlantic, are blown towards this shore by westerly winds; but they are of a very different character to the gloomy fogs which infest some of the inland counties. Sweeping over the land in fantastic masses, they impart a certain grandeur to hill and valley, and affect the inhabitants with feelings the reverse of those which the cockney experiences during a London fog. There is another meaning, besides the frequent recurrence of such mists, in the popular saying that a Cornishman is never in spirits but during *drisky* weather. Both Devon and Cornwall have a mean annual temperature about 1°·5 above that of the midland parts of England, but in the summer they are colder than the whole range of country from the S. coast to the 53rd degree of latitude.

OLD LANGUAGE.

The *Old Cornish Language* belonged to the *Cymric* division of Celtic, to which Welsh and Armorican (Bas Breton) also belong. The *Gaelic* division comprises Irish, Gaelic, and Manx. These (Gaelic and Cymric) resemble and differ from each other in about the same proportions as Latin resembles and differs from Greek. " It may be asserted, without hesitation, that the Cymric was separated from the Gaelic before the division into Cornish and Welsh was effected; and the writer is of opinion that the Cornish is the representative of a language once current over all South Britain at least."—*E. Norris.* In the Cymric division, Welsh differs from the two others much as French differs from Spanish. Cornish and Armorican are in closer relation to each other; much as Spanish and Portuguese. The more perfect and fuller grammatical forms of the Gaelic show it to be older than Cymric. In the latter case an amalgamation seems to have taken place with an earlier (pre-Celtic) race—" the men of narrow skulls, whose skeletons, flint weapons, and tools have been frequently dug up in Britain."—*Norris.*

In the reign of Queen Anne, Cornish was confined to the western parts of the county; and in that of George III., Dorothy Pentreath (died 1778, see Rto. 29, Exc. 6) is said to have been the last person who spoke it.

The main help in the study of Cornish is the 'Grammatica Celtica' of *Zeuss* (Leipzig, 1853); *Pryce's* ' Cornish Vocabulary' (1790) is useful ; *Lhuyd's* ' Archæologia Britannica' is of little value. The most important relics of the Cornish dialect known to exist are three dramas or "miracle plays," entitled 'Origo Mundi,' ' Passio Domini Nostri,' and ' Resurrectio Domini Nostri,' edited and translated by *Edwin Norris* (from MS. in the Bodleian), Oxford, 1859. (A sketch of Cornish grammar is added, and an ancient Cornish vocabulary from a MS. in the Brit. Mus., of the 13th cent.) Two other Cornish poems, the ' Creation' and ' Mount Calvary,' were very indifferently edited by Davies Gilbert (1826 and 1827).

It may here be remarked that the names of both Cornwall and Devon belong to this language. " Kernyw," Cornwall, is from " Kern " (cornu), a horn. Devon is probably the Cornish " dufn," deep or dark, from its deep combes or valleys.

In Cornwall itself the old language survives in the names of places and situations, and of a few plants and animals. The broom-plant is " bannal," the mountain ash " cair (berry) tree," a fiddle is a " crowd "

lviii   *Old Language.*   Introd.

(in Welsh "croudd"); a mine-work is still a "bal" (i. e. "*pal*," digging); "crum" is crooked; "clunk," to swallow; "chield vean," a *little* child.

The more common prefixes of names of places, significant in old Cornish, are:—

Tre, town-place or residence.
Pol, a pool, or place above a port.
Pen, head of hill.
Bo or *Bod*, abode, dwelling.
Ros, a moor, any uncultivated ground.
Kil, a sanctuary, or a sheltered place.
Col, a small hill.
Bron, a breast.
Bryn, a mound.
Cal, a holly.
Lan (same as Welsh *Llan*), an enclosure, and principally the *sacred* enclosure or precincts of a church.
Chy, a house.
Ty, a dwelling.

Many names, properly Cornish, have become curiously corrupted. Of these the following are examples:—

Modern Corruption.	Real Name.	Meaning in English.
Brown Queen	Brow gwyn	White mound.
Brown Willy	Bron welli	Look-out hill.
Tre brown	Tre bron	Place on the hill.
Manacles	Maen-eglos	Church stone.
Percent	Bosant	Holy abode.
Potbrane	Bodbrane	Abode of crows, or rookery.
Broadoak	Braddoc	Trenchery (place of).
Pennycross	Pen-y-cros	Head of the cross.
Cold wind	Col wyn	White hillock.
Beacon Park	Bichan Parc	Small field.
Porth Piggan	Porth Bichan	Small port.
Chysoyster	Chysauster	Heap-shaped houses.
Polscone	Polscoe	Pool of the wood.
Castledoor	Castel an dour	Castle on the water.
Grey mare	Grüg-mor	Great heath.
Cattacleuze	Caracleug	Grey rock.
Penquite	Pen coed	Head of wood.
Colquite	Col coed	Hillock of wood.
Cothele	Coed-heyle	Woods by river.
Mellangoose	Melan-coes	Mill in wood.
Millaudraft	Melan-dreath	Mill on sands.
Down derry	Dun-derru	Oak banks.

THE DUCHY OF CORNWALL.

In the early times of our history mines of every description were deemed royal, as yielding the materials for coinage, the right of which was vested solely in the king. Hence the metalliferous moors of Dartmoor and Cornwall had been crown lands for a long series of years, when they were settled by Edw. III. (1333) upon his eldest son the Black Prince, and his heirs, *eldest sons of the kings of England*, for ever. By the charter of this monarch they were consolidated as the Duchy of Cornwall, which included not only the naked wilds of stanniferous bog, but 10 castles, 9 parks, 53 manors, 13 boroughs and towns, 9 hundreds, and a forest abounding in wild deer. The lands, however, which were comprised in this dukedom, were little better than profitless moors previous to the reign of James I., as the authorities had no power of granting definite leases, and the tenure was dependent on the life of the sovereign. But at that time (1622) the parliament took the duchy in hand, and, by remodelling its constitution, empowered tenants to hold farms in perpetuity by renewable leases, and gave encouragement to the outlay of capital in improvements by creating good and indefeasible estates. This system, no doubt, had then its advantages; but the plan of granting leases for lives or in reversion, and of commuting the greater part of the rents for fines, soon reduced the actual income of the duchy to an amount that was no just measure of its fair annual value. From 1783 to 1830 the duchy was administered for the Prince of Wales, afterwards George IV., who received in the above period about 370,000*l.* from the fines taken on the renewal of leases. From 1830 to 1837 the revenues of the duchy were received by William IV.; and in this short term of seven years there seems to have been an unusual number of renewals, as the fines produced 171,343*l.* Up to this time the revenues of the duchy, when there was no Prince of Wales, were appropriated by the Crown. In 1838 a "Council for the Affairs of the Duchy of Cornwall" was appointed under letters patent. It was afterwards mainly under the superintendence of the late Prince Consort, and the powers of the Council expired when the Prince of Wales attained his majority in 1862. During its existence, the revenues of the duchy were not appropriated by the Crown; and a series of great improvements were effected. No leases are now granted for lives; a fixed term of years is in all cases substituted for them, and life leases have been exchanged for holdings on the more certain tenure. The old fines have of course taken the more regular and calculable form of rent. By these means, the report of the Council states, the income of the estates has been established on a sound basis; and Her Majesty has been enabled, "by the investment of a surplus revenue, to provide a large sum for the Privy Purse of the Prince of Wales." The present income of the duchy is 46,000*l.*

HANDBOOK
FOR
DEVONSHIRE AND CORNWALL.

SECTION I.
DEVONSHIRE.

ROUTES.

** The names of places are printed in *italics* only in those routes where the *places* are described.

ROUTE	PAGE
1 London to *Exeter* (Great Western Railway)	2
2 London to *Tiverton* (Great Western Rail); Tiverton to Crediton (Road)	20
3 London to Exeter (S. W. Rail)	23
4 Lyme Regis to Exeter, by (*Seaton*) *Sidmouth*, *B. Salterton*, and *Exmouth*	31
5 Exeter to Exmouth (Rly.)	43
6 Exeter to Launceston, by *Okehampton* (Neighbourhood of Okehampton, *Lidford, Brent Tor*)	44
7 Exeter to *Plymouth* (*Dawlish, Teignmouth, Newton, Totnes, Ivy Bridge*, and their Neighbourhoods)	53
8 Exeter to *Torquay* (S. Devon Rail). Neighbourhood of Torquay	88
9 Torquay to *Brixham* and *Dartmouth* (Dartmouth and Torbay Rail).—The Coast (*Slapton, Torcross*, the *Start*, the *Prawle, Salcombe*, the *Bolt*) from Dartmouth to Kingsbridge	95
10 Exeter to Torquay, by *Chudleigh* (*Haldon*)	108
11 Exeter to *Ashburton* and [*Dev. & Corn.*]	
ROUTE	PAGE
Buckfastleigh (*Buckland, Holne, Holne Chace*)	111
12 Exeter to Tavistock, by *Moreton Hampstead* (the *Teign, Drewsteignton, Chagford, Widdecombe, Lustleigh Cleave, Heytor, Dartmoor*)	117
13 Plymouth to *Tavistock* (S. Devon and Tavistock Rail)	142
14 Walk across Dartmoor, from Tavistock to South Zeal, by *Cranmere Pool*	155
15 Plymouth to *Modbury* and *Kingsbridge*. The Coast from Kingsbridge to Plymouth	156
16 Totnes to Plymouth (Road). *Ermington, Yealmpton*	159
17 Exeter to *Barnstaple* and *Bideford*, by *Crediton*—N. Devon Rail. (*S. Molton; Torrington*)	160
18 *Lynmouth* and *Lynton* to *Hartland*, by *Combe Martin, Ilfracombe* (*Barnstaple*), and *Clovelly*	172
19 Taunton to Lynmouth and Lynton, by *Watchet, Dunster*, and *Porlock*	193
20 *Bampton* to *Holsworthy*, by South Molton and Torrington	195

B

Route 1.—London to Exeter.

The principal conveyances from London into Devonshire and Cornwall are the following, viz.:

1. Trains by the Great Western and Bristol and Exeter; the Tiverton branch; the London and South-Western; the N. Devon; the S. Devon, the Torquay branch; the Cornwall; and the W. Cornwall railways;—Coaches from Bridgewater and Taunton to the N. of Devon.
2. Trains as far as Bristol, and Steamboats from Bristol to Hayle, some calling at Ilfracombe and Padstow.
3. Trains to Southampton, and Steamboats from Southampton to Plymouth and Falmouth, calling off Torquay and Mevagissey.
4. Trains to Plymouth, and Steamboats from Plymouth to Falmouth, calling off Mevagissey.

ROUTE 1.

LONDON TO EXETER.—(GREAT WESTERN RAIL—PADDINGTON STAT.)

The distance from London to Exeter (194 m.) is performed by express trains in 4½ hrs.; by ordinary trains in 7½.

Except some pleasant scenery in the vale of the Thames, a distant view of Windsor Castle, the famous White Horse of Berkshire stretched along its hill-side l., and the Box Tunnel (1¾ m. long, in places 300 ft. below the surface, cost upwards of 500,000*l.*), there is little to be noticed on this line until the traveller reaches Bath. Between Bath and Bristol the country is picturesquely wooded. After passing Bristol, the Clifton Suspension Bridge, across the chasm of the Avon, is seen rt. Other points of interest, before reaching the Devonshire border, are—

Weston-Super-Mare, rt., with the rocky islets of Steepholme and Flatholme, well-known places of retreat to the old Northmen, rising in the bay; Weston has become a fashionable watering-place; — *Burnham*, whence steamers cross to the Welsh coast, and which is seen rt. from Highbridge Stat., where is the junction with the Somerset and Dorset Rly. (with a branch to Wells);—the *Mendip Hills*, and *Glastonbury Tor* (marked by its tower), l.;—*Bridgewater*, the birthplace of Admiral Blake (the Perp. church of St. Mary is the only sight here);—*Taunton*, where the fine Perp. ch., with its tower rebuilt precisely on the old plan, will repay a visit, whilst the famous vale of Taunton Dean, bounded by the Quantock and Blackdown hills, is full of rich and picturesque scenery (from Taunton a branch line runs to the coast at Watchet, passing under the Quantock hills);—and *Wellington*, where the ch. is interesting, but which is chiefly noticeable from its having given title to the Great Duke, who, after the victory of Talavera, was raised to the peerage as Viscount Wellington of Wellington.

3 m. from Wellington the traveller enters Devonshire through *Whiteball Tunnel*, 5 furlongs in length, piercing the high land prolonged from the range of *Black Down*. Before entering the tunnel, however, observe, on the Black Downs, l.—

The *Wellington Monument*, a stone pillar erected by a county subscription to commemorate the victory of Waterloo. The original intention was to crown it with a bronze statue of Wellington, and this design it is now proposed to carry into execution, together with the addition of a small hospital for decayed soldiers,

DEVONSHIRE. *Route* 1.—*Holcombe Rogus.—Hemyock.* 3

who are to serve as custodians of the monument. An annual fair is held here on the 18th of June. The *Black Down Hills* command a fine view of the *Vale of Taunton*, and on the Devon side embosom some secluded valleys and crystal trout-streams, and are intersected by innumerable narrow lanes. They rise to 800 ft. at their highest point; and on the summit, where 2 ancient roads cross, on the boundary line of Devon and Somerset, is a very large barrow called *Symonsborough*, traditionally said to mark the sepulchre of a king. (Qy. Sigmund the Waelsing? who figures in A.-S. legend; see *Simonsbath*, Rte. 18).

As the traveller proceeds from the border towards Tiverton he will observe the *Scythe-stone Quarries* on the N. escarpment of the Black Downs. These stones are concretions of the greensand. They occur in layers at several places on these hills, and are often associated with organic remains in fine preservation. Among the fossils, according to Conybeare, are no less than 150 species of shell-fish. The beds are about 4 ft. thick, and the stone both above and below them is excavated for building. The galleries run for about 1000 ft. into the hill.

Burlescombe ch., l. of the line, has an ancient screen, a good example, lately renewed at the surface by scraping, and repaired. The Ch. is mainly Perp., and was restored throughout in 1842.

[rt. of the line, 2½ m., is *Holcombe Rogus*, so called from the Norman Rogo, whose descendants held it for 8 generations. It subsequently passed to the Bluetts, one of whom built the existing mansion, which is of Tudor character, and worth notice. The Bluetts (1858) sold the mansion and lands to the Rev. W. Rayer. The view through the gateway arch, of the porch tower, with its oriels, is very picturesque. This portion is of earlier date than the hall, which was built by Sir Roger Bluett, temp. Eliz. Adjoining is a good Perp. *ch.*, of very pleasing character, and beautifully placed. The tracery of the E. window in the S. aisle is unusual. The S. porch has a stone groined roof, with heads of Edw. III. and Philippa as corbels of the outer doorway. In the nave and N. aisle is the manorial pew, of vast size, surrounded by a cinquecento screen of wood, with a cornice of medallions well carved in Scripture subjects. The ch. contains 2 Jas. I. monuments (coloured) for members of the Bluett family.

Sampford Peverell, about 3 m. left of the line and somewhat more from the Tiverton Junction Stat., whence it is best approached, has a *ch.* which is mainly E.E., and interesting. There is a shattered monument of a crusader (Hugh Peverell?), circ. 1259, found under the N. aisle of the nave. The S. aisle, originally Perp. (one window alone remains of this character) is said to have been built by Margaret Beaufort, mother of Hen. VII., who lived here for some time. The manor belonged to the house of Somerset; hence Hen. VII. held it by hereditary right.]

179¼ m. *Tiverton Junction Stat.* Here a branch line passes rt. to Tiverton (see Rte. 2). [A road l. leads to Uffculme (3 m., see *post*) and thence (5 m. further) to

Hemyock (pronounced Hemmick), where are some moated ruins of a Norman castle, which anciently belonged to a family named Ifidon, and, in the Rebellion, was garrisoned and used by the Parl. as a prison. It was taken by the Royalists under Lord Poulett, 1642, and was probably dismantled some years later by Cromwell. The flint-built entrance gateway, flanked by towers, is in tolerable preservation. It immediately faces the W. end of the *Ch.*, which has been lately renewed. It has E. Eng. and Dec. portions, and a font of Purbeck stone (a Norm. bowl on Perp. shaft). Hemyock is situated

B 2

on a stream which flows into the Culme. In this parish, and in others adjacent, are great numbers of circular pits, 3 or 4 ft. deep—probably remains of Roman ironworks, since cinders and iron scoriæ have been found near them in such quantities as to be used for roadmending. About 4 m. S. of Hemyock, in a sheltered vale, are some trifling remains of *Dunkeswell Abbey*, founded by William Lord Brewer in the reign of King John, 1201. Part of the abbey site is now occupied by a handsome ch. erected by 6 ladies, members of the Simcoe family of *Wolford Lodge*. The ornamental work, including the stained glass, was the work of their own hands. Many of the tiles were dug from the site. The parish ch. of Dunkeswell (rebuilt 1817) is the head of the Deanery; and a horse's shoe, taken from the old ch. door, is fixed to the new with 10 nails, said to symbolize the 10 churches of the Deanery.]

From this junction the train traverses the pastures of the Culme valley, disturbing many a contemplative "red Devon" in its course, to

181½ m. *Cullompton* (*Inn:* White Hart), an old but (except for its ch.) uninteresting town, situated on the river Culme, and on the Bristol and Exeter railroad, and formerly known for a manufacture of woollen stuffs.

The *Ch.*, dedicated to St. Andrew, is late Perp. The tower, firm and massive, is of the Somersetshire type, with the belfry windows filled with open stone-work. It dates, as an inscription over the entrance asserts, from 1545. The W. front is much enriched. The pillars and capitals of the nave, and the ceiling, with carved wall-plate and angel corbels, deserve notice. A chapel on the S. side of the nave (forming in effect a second S. aisle) was built 1528 by one John Lane, a clothier of this town, and deserves notice for its external ornaments, which represent the machinery employed in the manufacture of cloth. The roof also is very fine, with superb fan tracery groining springing from corbels, with pendents in the centre. An inscription long read by antiquaries, "Wapat. cust. Lanuarii"—"Wapentaki custos Lanuarius"—wool-warden of the Hundred—turns out to be "with a Paternoster and an Ave." The *roodscreen*, which has been re-coloured and gilt, is a gorgeous specimen—one of the finest and most perfect in Devonshire—and a portion of the rude oak Calvary, with skulls, bones, and mortice, in which the rood itself stood, is still to be seen. It is nearly equal to the screen in length, and is a specimen of extreme rarity. The ch. was restored throughout in 1849; when some curious wall-paintings in distemper, representing St. Christopher, St. Michael, and St. Clara, were found beneath the plaster, but were again concealed by a coat of whitewash. The entire building will repay a careful examination.

The springs of the river Culme rise on the Blackdown hills. Besides Cullompton, the river gives name to many places on its course (Columb David, Culmstock, Uffculm, &c.). It joins the Exe about 3 m. from Exeter. "Culme," says old Westcote, "fleeteth, like the waters of Shiloah, with a slow and still current."

In the neighbourhood are several *paper-mills* and *Hillersdon House*, W. C. Grant, Esq.; on the road to Honiton, *The Grange*, E. S. Drewe, Esq.; and, in the adjoining parish of Uffculme, *Bradfield Hall*, B. B. Walrond, Esq., one of the finest Elizabethan mansions in the county, in which this family has been seated since the reign of Henry III. The hall is of 15th centy. The whole was rest. 1861. [*Uffculme* ch., 4 m., rebuilt in part and embellished, is worth a visit. The original building was E. Eng. (arches N. side of nave, and tower, once crowned by a broach spire). The present chancel is Perp. The aisles extend beyond the nave. That N. forms the Walrond chapel, and contains some curious and grotesque monuments of Charles I.'s time. *Culmstock* ch., 2 m. higher up the river, had a good stone screen, which has been converted into a reredos. In it are preserved an ancient embroidered altar-cloth, and the remains of a beautiful cope. (3 m. further is *Hemyock*; see *ante*). In *Kentisbeare* ch., 3½ m. E., which is Perp., there *was* a good *brass* for John Whiting, 1529, and wife. This brass however was stolen in 1858. *Plymtree* ch., 4 m. S.S.E., is Perp. and interesting. It has a very good ancient screen, and on the W. face of the tower a fine niche, with Virgin and Child. There are also niches for figures against the piers of the nave and chancel. The chancel has been thoroughly restored.]

Still following the valley of the Culme, we reach

185¾ m. *Hele Stat*. 1 m. rt. is *Bradninch*. In 1644, during the Rebellion, King Charles was here in person, and slept several nights at the rectory, now called *Bradninch House*, where his bedstead is preserved. The *ch.* (late Perp.) contains a fine screen, dating 1528, and an old painting of the Crucifixion. Remark the figure of the Saviour on the Cross, with golden wings. It was taken from the N. aisle. The N. aisle was built in the reign of Hen. VII. by the fraternity of St. John, or Guild of Cordwainers.

2 m. rt. the line skirts *Killerton Park*, Sir T. D. Acland, Bart. On the high ground is *Dolbury Camp* (see Rte. 2). There is also a modern *chapel* in the park, which deserves notice. l. *Sprydoncote* (T. D. Acland, Esq., M.P., 1865, for N. Devon).

3 m. rt. *Poltimore House*, Lord Poltimore.

The railway accompanies the Culme to its junction with the Exe, where, leaving on the rt. the park of *Pynes House* (Sir Stafford Northcote, Bart., M.P.), it turns in a curve at the junction of the Creedy with the Exe, and enters,

194 m. from London,

EXETER (St. David's Stat.) [*Inns*: New London (best);—Clarence (in the Cathedral-yard; quiet and good);—Bude Haven;—Queen's;— Globe.

A large new stat. was opened here in 1864, for the Great Western (Bristol and Exeter), the S. Devon, and the N. Devon rlys. The stat. for the S. Western and Exmouth rlys. is at the end of Queen-street; but the 2 stats. (St. David's and Queen-street) are connected by rail. Strangers, on arriving at Exeter, are to be reminded that Devonshire cream and Devonshire junket are among the luxuries to be called for at the hotels. The best shop for Devonshire (Honiton) lace is Mrs. Treadwin's, in the Cathedral-yard.]

Exeter, without rival the Queen of the West, is seated on the l. bank of the river Exe, "upon a hill among hills." Its origin is very remote, and its history distinguished by stirring events. The Britons are supposed to have founded it long before the invasion of Cæsar. By them it was known as *Caer Isc*, the "city on the river" (the Celtic *Isc* (Gael. *Uisge*), water, is retained in the names of the rivers Exe and Axe, and occurs frequently elsewhere). Its position, at the head of the estuary, just where the river ceased to be navigable, resembles that of most other Celtic trading towns; and numerous coins of the Greek dynasties of Syria and Egypt, which have been discovered here, no doubt mark Exeter as having been the chief emporium of the western tin-trade from a very early period (see some of these coins figured in Shortt's 'Sylva Antiqua Iscana'). The Roman name of the city was *Isca Damnoniorum* (so *Isca Silurum* was Caer Leon, on the *Usk*,

Route 1.—Exeter. Sect. I.

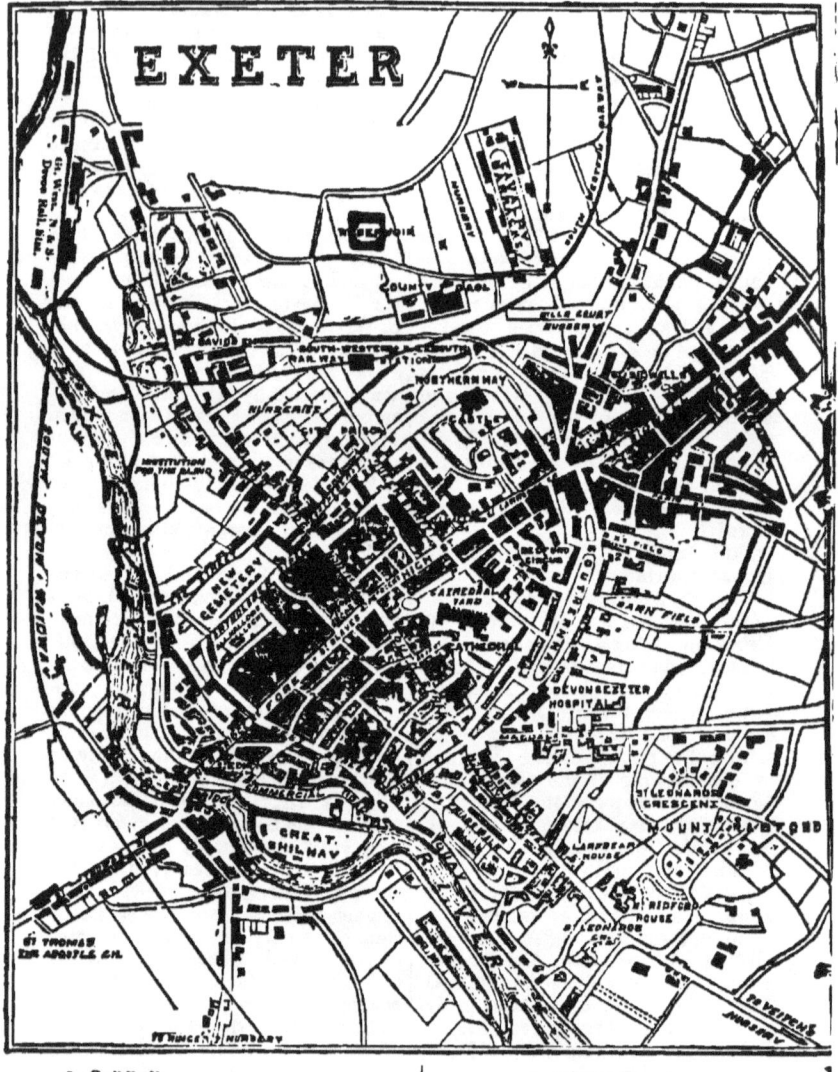

1. Guildhall.
2. Baths.
3. Devon and Exeter Institution.
4. Athenæum.
5. Royal Subscription Room.
6. New London Inn.
7. Clarence Hotel.

in S. Wales); and many coins of Claudius found here prove its early occupation by that people. Under the Saxons, "Exanceaster," the "Chester" or fortified town on the Exe, continued an important mercantile station, still no doubt by reason of its vicinity to the Dartmoor tin-works. "Excestria clara metallis"—Exeter famous for her mines—is the characteristic assigned to her at a later period by Henry of Huntingdon. To the time of Athelstan, however, the Exe had been the boundary of Danmonia, and a portion of Exeter was occupied by the Britons. Athelstan expelled this people, and drove them beyond the Tamar. He surrounded the city with a wall (or repaired the old Roman one), to bridle his newly acquired territory, and to afford protection against the Danes, who wintered in Exeter in the year 876, and repeatedly pillaged it, particularly under Sweyn in 1003. After the Conquest, in 1066, it was besieged by Will. I.; Githa, the mother of Harold, had taken refuge in it, with her daughters, and escaped hence to Bruges. In 1137 it was again besieged by Stephen; unsuccessfully by Perkin Warbeck in 1497 (Hen. VII.); and by the insurgents for the re-establishment of the ancient ritual in 1549 (Edw. VI.). In Sept. 1643, during the Great Rebellion, it was taken by Prince Maurice after an 8 months' siege, and by the Parliamentary forces under Fairfax in April 1646, having in the intermediate period been the head-quarters of the Royalists, and the residence of the queen, who here gave birth to the princess Henrietta, afterwards Duchess of Orleans. In Nov. 1688 the Prince of Orange made his formal entry into this city; and in 1789 it was visited by Geo. III. and his Queen, who were received in great state by the mayor and aldermen—a ceremony which excited the merriment of Peter Pindar, who tells us how

"Mayster May'r, upon my word,
Poked to the king a gert long sword,
Which he poked back agen."

In our days the opening of the railway between London and Exeter, May 1844, has been a memorable event, when the road to the metropolis, in point of time, was at once shortened two-thirds. "Old Quicksilver" accomplished the journey in 17 or 18 hrs. in one unbroken trot of 10 m. to the hour; but the express trains now run the distance in little more than 5 hrs. Great as is the improvement, it appears yet more marvellous if we contrast it with the travelling exploits of the last century. In 1720 a Mrs. Manley published her experiences of 'A Stage Coach Journey from London to Exeter.' The coach started at 3 in the morning, stopped at 10 to dine, and at 3 P.M. was drawn into an inn-yard for the night. The total time on the road was 4 days or 48 hrs., and the pace 4½ m. the hour.

Exeter can boast of many eminent children: *Sir William Morice*, 1602, Secretary of State to Charles II.; *Sir Thomas Bodley*, founder of the Bodleian Library; *Thomas Yalden*, the poet, 1671; *Simon Ockley*, the Orientalist, 1675; *Eustace Budgell*, the friend of Addison, 1685; *William Gandy*, the portrait-painter, buried in St. Paul's ch. in this city, 1729; *Sir Vicary Gibbs*, the lawyer, 1750; *Robert, Lord Gifford*, 1779; and *William Jackson*, the composer, for many years organist of the cath., 1730. *Lord Chancellor King* was also a native of Exeter; and *Richard Hooker*, the divine, born in its immediate neighbourhood, at Heavitree, 1554. Pope's "Modest Foster" was born at Exeter in 1697. This city had one of the earliest presses set up in England, and a translation of the great poem of Tasso was here first printed and published.

Exeter gives the titles of marquis and earl to the Cecil family, and by an act of Parl., enacted in the reign of

Edw. VI., is constituted an independent county.

The principal thoroughfares divide the city into 4 parts; High Street and Fore Street, following the line of the Roman road—the "Ikenild Way," which ran from Exeter into Cornwall—traverse it in a line from E. to W.; North Street and South Street run N. and S., and meet at rt. angles to High Street. Of late years the prevalent building mania has greatly extended its dimensions. The principal streets are continued into *St. Sidwell's* on the E., *Mount Radford* on the S., *St. David's* on the N., and *Exe Island* and a square called *the Quarter* on the S.W. Queen Elizabeth gave the city its present motto, "Semper fidelis," and two "Pegasuses argent" as the supporters for its shield of arms (a castle with a portcullis). A countryman, showing these supporters to a stranger, is said to have observed, "These be the two race-hosses that rinned upon Haldon, wi' names of 'em put under—*Scamper* and *Phillis*."

The **Cathedral* is the chief point of interest in Exeter. The seat of the Devonshire bishopric, which had been established at Crediton towards the beginning of the 10th centy. (circ. 910), was removed to Exeter in 1050 (probably for the increased security of a walled city) by the Confessor. During the greater portion of the intervening period Cornwall had had its separate bishops; but *Leofric*, in whose time the change was made, had received the 2 sees united from his predecessor Living, and they have never since been separated.

Leofric was established in a Saxon ch., which had been that of a monastery. It occupied part of the site of the present cathedral, but no portion remains. A new cathedral was commenced by *Bp. Warelwast* (1107-1136), and was completed by *Bp. Marshall* (1194-1206). In 1136 it was much injured by fire, during Stephen's siege of Exeter. The portions which remain of this *Norman* building are the *transeptal towers*.

Bp. Walter Bronescomb (1258-1280) commenced a series of new works, which led to the gradual removal of the Norman Cathedral and to the erection of the present structure. Part of the Lady chapel was built during his time; but his successor, *Peter Quivil* (1280-1291), seems to have furnished plans for the entire building, which were followed with but little variation by his successors. Bp. Quivil himself constructed the transepts out of Warelwast's Norm. towers, and completed the Lady chapel. *Bp. Stapledon* (1308-1326) commenced the choir, which *Bp. Grandisson* (1327-1369) completed, as well as the nave. *Bp. Brantyngham* (1369-1394) probably added the western screen, with its porches and sculpture. Although it appears from these dates that the greater part of the cathedral was erected during the *later* Dec. (Curvilinear) period, it belongs, nevertheless, in all its details (with the exception of the western screen), to the *earlier* or Geometrical Dec.; an apparent proof that the plans were fully provided by Bp. Quivil, with whose time the details well agree. The building is one of the most interesting and important examples of Dec. in England. Compared with other English cathedrals, the *specialities* of Exeter are its transeptal Norm. towers, and its long unbroken roof, extending throughout nave and choir.

During the Commonwealth the cathedral was divided by a brick wall, erected on the site of the rood-loft; and two eminent preachers took possession of the separated portions, known as "West Peter's" and "East Peter's." They "enjoyed great comfort and quiet" until the Restoration, when they were happily expelled by *Bp. Seth Ward* (1662-1667), who pulled down the "monstrous Babylonish wall" (as it was afterwards called), and "cast out of the temple

PLAN OF EXETER CATHEDRAL.

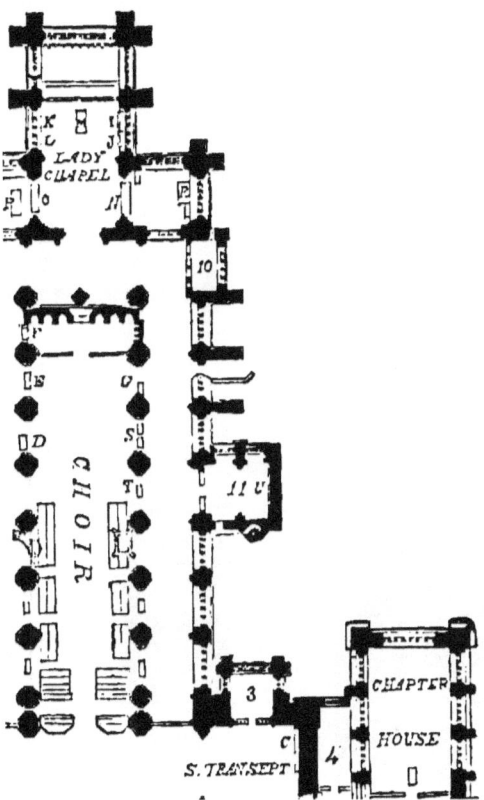

the buyers and sellers who had kept distinct shops in it." The Puritans had pulled down the cloisters, and the Visitors of Edward VI. and Elizabeth had long before worked much havoc among the sculptures and other decorations of the cathedral.

The only good *exterior* view of the cathedral is from the N. side—the only one open. "As we walk round this, we cannot but consider that the cathedral, though far from lofty, and presenting none of the majestic features of several of its sister churches, is nevertheless a fine composition. The aisles of choir and nave, intercepted by the stately Norm. towers, farther broken by the prominence of their chantries, and spanned by flying buttresses richly pinnacled; the large, pure windows, which pierce both aisle and clerestory ; the roof, highly pitched, and finished with crest-tiles, form a decidedly graceful and pleasing whole."—*J. W. Hewett.*

The *W. Front,* probably the work of *Bp. Brantyngham* (1369-1394)—Edw. III.'s Treasurer in Picardy, and more than once Lord High Treasurer of England—is of high interest; and though it cannot compete with those of Wells or Lincoln (both of earlier date), may justly claim great beauty as an architectural composition. In the gable niche is a figure of St. Peter, to whom the cathedral (like the first Saxon ch. here) is dedicated. The screen is pierced by 3 doorways, and surrounded by a series of niches, in which are the statues of kings, warriors, saints, and apostles, guardians, as it were, of the entrance to the sanctuary. These figures are arranged in 3 rows: the lowest are angels, who support shafts with capitals, on which the 2nd row, mostly kings and knights, are placed; in the 3rd row are chiefly saints and apostles. It is scarcely possible to identify any of these figures with certainty. The 2 statues, however, with shields of arms, in niches above the upper row, are those of Athelstane and Edward the Confessor. All are now battered and time-worn; and 2, which crumbled to pieces and fell from their niches, have been replaced by Stevens, a native of Exeter. The whole work is fully entitled to Mr. Cockerell's praise of it, as "remarkable, characteristic, and beautiful sculpture."

The great *W. window* will best be noticed from within. The 3 doorways are much enriched ; remark the moulding of carved foliage round that in the centre. On the central boss of the groining is a representation of the Crucifixion. Within the S. doorway are 2 much-shattered sculptures—" The Appearance of the Angel to Joseph in a dream," and " The Adoration of the Shepherds." Between this doorway and the centre is the *Chantry of St. Radegunde,* constructed by Bp. Grandisson for the place of his own sepulture, and worked into the screen on its completion, by Bp. Brantyngham. On the roof is a figure of the Saviour, in low relief, with the rt. hand raised in benediction. From the holes in the stone, lamps were suspended. The tomb of Grandisson, the most distinguished prelate who ever filled the see, was sacrilegiously violated between 1590 and 1600 (the exact year and the perpetrators are unknown), " the ashes scattered abroad," says Hoker, " and the bones bestowed no man knoweth where."

We now enter the *nave,* 140 ft. in length, and as far as the transepts the work of *Bishop Grandisson* (1327-1369). The walls and roof are of stone from the quarries of Silverton and Beer (see Rte. 4); the clustered pillars of Purbeck marble. Although the view eastward is intercepted by the organ, the general impression is that of great richness and beauty. The roof (owing to the absence of a central tower) is unbroken from end to end, and is exceeded in grace and lightness by no

B 3

other in England. The visitor should remark—

(a) The carved *bosses* of the roof, which retain traces of colour, and represent foliage, grotesque figures, and animals; heads of the Virgin and Saviour, the Passion and Crucifixion; and in the centre of the 2nd bay the murder of Becket. Grandisson wrote a Life of St. Thomas of Canterbury.

(b) The *corbels* between the arches, which support the clustered vaulting shafts. These are peculiar to this cathedral; and the exquisite beauty of the carved foliage calls for especial notice. The easternmost corbels display on the N. side Moses, with his hands supported by Aaron and Hur; and S., the risen Saviour, with cross and banner.

(c) *The Minstrel's Gallery*, in the central bay on the N. side. This is the finest example in England. There is a small gallery at Wells, and the "Tribune" at the end of the nave at Winchester served for the same purpose; but neither equals this. The musical instruments carried by the angels in the niches are worth notice. The two corbelled heads below are possibly those of Edw. III. and Philippa.

(d) The *windows* of the nave, all of the *first* Dec. (geometrical) character, are said to exhibit a greater variety of tracery than can be found in any other building in the kingdom. They are arranged in pairs, on opposite sides of the cathedral, so that no two, side by side, resemble each other. The great W. window is Bp. Brantyngham's (1369-1394) work; and its curvilinear tracery differs from the others. It is a superb example of later Dec. The glass in it (dating from 1766) is quite worthless, and materially injures the beauty of the window.

The fittings of the nave. by which it was adapted for congregational worship, were made in the spring of 1859. Opening from the first bay on the N. side, is the little *chapel of St. Edmund*, of earlier date than the nave, to which it was no doubt united by Bp. Grandisson. It now serves as the Consistory Court. In the fifth bay is the *N. porch*, now disused. The *font*, in the S. side of the nave, was the gift of Archdeacon Bartholomew in 1842, and is a copy of the Perp. font at Beverley Minster. The inscription round it should be read. In the last bay eastward on this side a door opens to the site of the cloisters. There is an inscription against the E. wall not altogether intelligible, and a fine consecration cross between the two first buttresses on the S. side.

On entering the nave the visitor will have been at once attracted by the extraordinary memorial of the 9th (Queen's Royal) Lancers, which covers the wall of the second bay on the N. side. It was erected in 1860 by the officers and men of the regiment to the memory of their comrades who fell in India. Two mounted lancers and two palm-trees figure in bronze on a tablet of grey Sicilian marble. The design, which is utterly without meaning, is by Baron *Marochetti*; and it is much to be hoped that the memorial, which is singularly intrusive and inappropriate, may shortly be replaced by a worthier. On the S. side of the nave is the high tomb with effigies of *Hugh Courtenay* (d. 1377), second Earl of Devon of the house of Courtenay, and of his countess Margaret (d. 1391). On the pavement below is the *brass* of their son, Sir *Peter Courtenay* (d. 1406), standardbearer to Edw. III., and distinguished in the French and Spanish wars under the Black Prince. This brass has been mutilated, but is still fine and interesting. Among the other slabs on the flooring of the nave is that of *John Loosemore*, builder of the noble organ, who d. 1682. He is ranked by Dr. Burney among the first organ-builders of his time.

DEVONSHIRE.   *Route 1.—Exeter—Cathedral.*   11

Passing into the *North Transept,* the visitor should first remark the manner in which Bp. Quivil (1280-1291) formed the transepts out of the Norm. towers of William Warelwast. "The inner side of each (adjoining the nave) was taken down to nearly half its height from the ground, and a vast substantial arch constructed to sustain the upper remaining part." The squareness and narrowness of the transepts are at once apparent. Whether, in the Norm. cathedral, these were the western towers, or, as at present, and as in the church of Ottery St. Mary (see Rte. 3), transeptal towers, is uncertain. The windows N. and S. of the transepts, and the open galleries, which project E. and W., are probably Bp. Quivil's work; as are the chapels of St. Paul and St. John the Baptist, which open E. from the 2 transepts. Adjoining St. Paul's chapel, in the N. transept, is the chantry of *Wm. Silke,* sub-chanter, d. 1508. The inscription above his effigy, an emaciated figure in a shroud, runs—"Sum quod eris, fueram quod es; pro me, precor, ora." A mural painting of the Resurrection, of the same date, has lately been found at the back of this chantry.

The *clock* in this transept is celebrated. It is certain that a clock existed "in boreali turre" of the cathedral in 1317, which was probably the same which yet remains. It has 2 dials, and its construction is referred to the reign of Edw. III. (it is probably older), when the science of astronomy was in its nonage, and the earth regarded as the central point of the universe. The upper disc, which was added in 1760, shows the minutes. The lower disc is divided into 3 parts; the figure of the earth forming the nucleus of the innermost circle, that of the sun traversing the outer space, that of the moon the intermediate one. The sun is stamped with a fleur-de-lis, the upper end pointing to the hour of the day, the lower to the age of the moon; while the figure of the moon is made black on one side, and moved by the clock-work so as to imitate the varying aspect of its inconstant original. Little of the ancient works remain however. The last restoration and gilding took place in 1859. There is a very similar clock in the ch. of Ottery; and one resembling it in Wells cathedral, which is said to have been brought from Glastonbury.

From this transept the N. tower, in which is the great bell, may be ascended. This was brought from Llandaff by Bishop Courtenay (1478-1486), and is the second largest bell in England. It weighs 12,500 lbs. (Great Tom at Oxford weighs 17,000 lbs.) The "Peter" bell, as it is called, was recast in 1676. Its diameter at the mouth is 6 ft. 3 in., its height 4 ft. 8 in. It is never rung—the hours are struck on it by an enormous hammer. From the top of the tower (which was much altered by Bishop Courtenay for the reception of his bell) a superb view of the city, and of the river as far as Exmouth, is commanded.

From the S.W. angle of the *South Transept,* which precisely resembles the N., a door leads into the *Chapel of the Holy Ghost,* a narrow, semicylindrically vaulted building, of E. E. date. The old font, which stands in it, was first used at the baptism of the Princess Henrietta, daughter of Charles I., born at Exeter in 1644. Beyond this chapel is the *Chapter House:* the lower part surrounded by a fine arcade, E.E., and perhaps the work of Bp. Brewer (1224-1244); the upper, with Perp. niches, is assigned to Bp. Lacey (1420-1455). The E. window is given to Bp. Neville (1458-1465); and the ceiling to Bp. Bothe (1465-1478). The Chapter Library, a good collection of about 8000 vols., is preserved here; as are an alabaster model of the tomb of Bp. Carey in the church of Sta. Croce in Florence, where he died 1419; and a sapphire ring, chalice, and paten, found in the tomb of Bp. Bytton, before the high altar.

The *Choir Screen* was possibly the work of *Bp. Brantyngham* (1370-1394). The rose and thistle in the spandrils were barbarously introduced temp. James I.; and the 13 paintings on stone in the small arch above, although sometimes said to be of the 14th centy., are really not earlier than the beginning of the 17th. They are worthless and uninteresting. The parapet above is modern. The *organ*, originally by Loosemore (1665), was rebuilt by Lincoln in 1819, and is among the finest in England. It is said to be the most ancient in actual use. Incledon, the famous singer, born at St. Kevern, in Cornwall, was for some time a chorister here, under Jackson, the composer and organist.

The 4 easternmost bays of the *choir* were the work of *Bp. Walter de Stapledon* (1308-1326). His successor, Bp. Grandisson (1327-1369), completed it, and dedicated the high altar, Dec. 18, 1328. The E. window was inserted by Bishop Brantyngham about 1390. In architectural character the choir differs hardly at all from the nave; remark especially

(*a*) The *roof-bosses* and *corbels*. The latter are even more admirable in design, and more varied in foliage, than those of the nave—maple, oak, ash, the filbert with its clusters of nuts, and the vine with tendrils and fruit, could hardly be reproduced more faithfully.

(*b*) The *sedilia*, with their very rich and fine canopies, the work of Bishop Stapledon.

(*c*) The *misereres* or subsellia, which have been cut down to fit their present places. They are E.E. of Bp. Marshall's time (1194-1206), and are the earliest in the kingdom. Remark the armour of the knights—

their heater shields and flat helmets —and the E. E. character of the foliage.

(*d*) The *Episcopal Throne*, put together without a single nail, and towering almost to the roof. It was the gift of Bp. Bothe (1465-1478). During the rebellion it was taken down and concealed.

(*e*) The *E. window*, early Perp., and filled with stained glass, most of which is ancient and very fine. Much of it dates from the first half of the 14th centy.; and was removed from the earlier window. In the *lowest* row are 9 figures of saints, the three central ones of Brantyngham's time—the others of the first period. In the *middle* row all are Perp. The figure at the extreme l. (looking E.) is St. Sidwell, or Sativola, a British maiden, said to have been contemporary with St. Boniface of Crediton (first half of 8th centy.). She was beheaded by a mower near a well outside the city walls; and the emblems which she holds refer either to this, or make a rebus of her name—"scythe-well." In the *uppermost* row the 3 figures of Abraham, Moses, and Isaiah, are of the first period. The heraldry above is modern. The tone of colour throughout the window is very fine and solemn.

(*f*) The *monuments* to be observed in the choir are—on the N. side, the tomb of *Bp. Marshall*, died 1206; the medallions and E. E. foliage of his tomb, and the ornament round the neck of the cope, should be noticed; and the monument should be compared with those of Bps. Bartholomæus and Simon of Apulia in the Lady Chapel;—and *Bp. Walter de Stapledon*, murdered in 1325 by the citizens of London, who rose on the side of Queen Isabella. The king, Edw. II., had left the city in charge of the Bishop. The body was at first interred in the sand near his own palace, "without Temple Bar;" but six months later was brought to Exeter, and solemnly buried by the Queen's command. The canopy is later than the effigy, and was restored within the present century. Under it, and not visible except from within, is a large figure of the Saviour; and a small figure of a king (Edw. II.) climbs upward at the side towards Him. On the sleeve of the effigy are two keys addorsed—the arms of the see as borne by Bp. Stapledon, who founded Stapledon's Inn at Oxford, now "Exeter College."

Opening from the N. choir aisle is *St. Andrew's Chapel*, of early Dec. character, and possibly the work of Bp. Bronescomb (1257-1280). In a chamber above are preserved the archives of the see, the Fabric rolls, the original of the Exon Domesday, the volume of Saxon poetry bequeathed to the cathedral by Bishop Leofric, and known as the 'Codex Exoniensis,' and the Liber Pontificalis of Bp. Lacey. Remark in this aisle a monument of a knight, cross-legged, probably Sir Richard de Stapledon, an elder brother of Bp. Walter. At the end of the aisle is the *Chantry of St. George*, founded about 1518 by Sir John Speke of White Lackington in Somersetshire. It is a mass of rich carving.

E. of this aisle is *St. Mary Magdalene's* chapel, assigned to Bishop *Bronescomb*, died 1280. The screen between it and the aisle is of Perp. character. A beautiful arcade, much hidden by monuments, runs below the windows. The stained glass in the E. window dates from the 15th centy. Here is a striking Elizabethan monument for Sir Gawain Carew, his wife, and his nephew Sir Peter Carew. It is in 2 stages. The cross-legged figure of Sir Peter is unusual at that period. Both he and Sir Gawain were active in suppressing the Devonshire rising temp. Edw. VI. The monument has been restored, in gold and colours, with very good effect. On the floor is a *brass* for Canon Langton, died 1586. A staircase in the N.E. corner of this chapel leads to the roof of the ambulatory or eastern aisle, commanding the E. window of the choir, through which a very fine view of the interior, looking W., is obtained.

The *E. aisle*, between the choir and Lady Chapel, is Early Dec., and may perhaps be Bp. Bronescomb's work. It served for the circulation of processions. The beautiful effect of the arches which formerly opened at the back of the choir has been destroyed by the heavy modern reredos.

The *Lady Chapel*, now used for early morning service, is the work of Bp. Bronescomb, d. 1280, completed by his successor, Bp. Quivil, d. 1291. The windows oppose each other, as in the nave. The reredos is modern with the exception of the central compartment, which is of Grandisson's time. In the centre of the pavement is the tombstone of Bp. Quivil, with a cross and the inscription, " Petra tegit Petrum, nihil officiat sibi tetrum."

On the S. side are the monuments of *Bp. Bartholomæus Iscanus* (of Exeter), 1159-1184; he shone as one of the two "great lights of the English Church," as this bishop and Bp. Roger of Worcester were called by Pope Alexander III.; remark the beard and moustache worn by the Norman prelate, and the high-peaked mitre like a Norm. helmet;—and *Bp. Simon of Apulia* (1206-1224); the whole of his vestments are richly jewelled; the design resembles that of Bp. Bartholomæus's effigy, but shows much advance in art. On the N. side are the effigies of *Sir John and Lady Doddridge*. Sir John (d. 1628) was one of James I.'s Judges of the King's Bench.

Under the arches opening to the side chantries are the tombs with effigies—S. of *Bp. Bronescomb* (1258-1281), the son of an Exeter citizen, as the inscription, now illegible, recorded:—

"Laudibus immensis jubilat gens Exoniensis, Et chorus et turbæ quod natus in hac fuit urbe."

He did much for the cathedral, as we have seen. His fine effigy is of his own time, but the canopy above is Perp., and was probably constructed at the same time with Bp. Stafford's monument opposite. N. is the effigy of *Bp. Stafford* (1394-1419), brother of Ralph Lord Stafford, twice Lord Chancellor and Keeper of the Great Seal, and the 2nd founder of Exeter College, Oxford, to which he gave its present name. His effigy, very fine in all its details, has been disgracefully used. The tabernacle work above it is rich and beautiful.

St. Gabriel's Chapel, opening S. from the Lady Chapel, resembles that on the N. side, and was Bp. Bronescomb's work. St. Gabriel was his patron saint, and the festival of the Archangel was celebrated here with great magnificence. Against the E. wall is a monument by *Flaxman* to Major-General Simcoe (d. 1806). The Elizabethan high tomb of Sir John and Lady Gilbert, and the medallions of the Rev. John Fursman (1727), his wife and daughter, may be noticed. But the chief object of interest here is *Chantrey's* almost living statue of Northcote the painter, a native of Devonshire.

The chantry opening from the last bay of the S. wall is *Bp. Oldham's* (1514-1519), joint founder, with Bp. Fox of Winchester, of Corpus Christi College, Oxford. It is rich in carving; and in the N.E. corner is the bishop's rebus—an owl with the word "dom" on a label (Old-ham).

In the *S. choir aisle* are the effigies of 2 cross-legged knights, temp. Edw. I. They have been assigned to Sir Humphrey de Bohun, and to a knight of the Chichester family. Opening from the centre of the aisle is the *Chapel of St. James*, Early Dec., and having against the S. wall a very beautiful Dec. monument, said to have been erected as a memorial of Leofric, the first bishop of Exeter.

Of the *exterior* of the Cathedral the visitor should especially remark the *Norm. towers;* that S. is Norm. throughout; that N. was altered by Bp. Courtenay, and its upper stages are Perp.; the leaden fleur-de-lys *cresting* of the roof; the flying buttresses, which derive a very grand effect from the fact that the aisle roofs slope outwards, and not as usual inwards; and the *N.* porch, part of Grandisson's work, and beautiful in details.

The *Episcopal Palace*, almost rebuilt under the present bishop, contains little of interest beyond an E.E. arch of very early character, and a chimneypiece in the hall, erected by Bp. Courtenay, c. 1486.

In the *Deanery*, on the S.W. of the Cathedral, Charles II., William III., and George III. lodged during their visits to Exeter. A house on the N. side of the Close retains a magnificent bay window of Henry VII.'s time, and a fine ceiling of wood, with the arms of Courtenay, the Stafford Knot, &c.

Exeter contains 21 *parish churches*, besides numerous chapels. The following possess some interest for the stranger :—*St. Stephen's* (Highstreet), and *St. John's* (Fore-street), as having ancient crypts, by some reputed Saxon : *St. Lawrence's* (Highstreet), with oak screen, and over the doorway a statue of Queen Eliz., which once adorned a conduit in High-street; the altarpiece (in plaster) was designed by the sculptor Bacon, jun., 1846; the ch. has been well restored : *St. Martin's* (Cath.-yard), believed to date in part from 1065 : *St. Mary Arches* (street of same name), containing old monuments, and so called from its Norman piers (S. Maria de Arcubus): *St. Mary Major's* (Cath.-yard), with Norman and E. Eng. work, and, over the N. entrance, figure of St. Lawrence on a gridiron; the noise

DEVONSHIRE. *Route 1.—Exeter—Rougemont Castle.* 15

of the weathercock surmounting the spire of this ch. so much disturbed the Princess Catherine of Arragon (who, after her first landing at Plymouth in 1501, proceeded thence to Exeter, where she remained 2 nights at the Deanery) that it was taken down: *St. Mary Steps* (West-street); in the tower an antique clock with 3 figures, popularly called Matthew the miller and his 2 sons; the central figure representing Hen. VIII.; the local rhyme respecting these figures runs—

"Adam and Eve would never believe,
That Matthew the miller was dead,
For every hour in Westgate tower
Matthew the miller nods his head."

St. Olave's (Fore-street), very old, given by Will. I. to Battle Abbey, and after the Edict of Nantes to the French Refugees: *St. Paul's* (Paul-street), with painted window and font of black marble: *St. Petrock's* (Cath.-yard), containing among the sacramental plate vessels dated 1572, 1640, and 1692: *St. Sidwell's*, a modern Gothic edifice, but the pillars dividing nave and aisles are part of the original building; the capitals of these pillars are decorated with figures of St. Sidwella and angels, and the pulpit is a rich specimen of carved-work; the tomb and shrine of St. Sidwella (a contemporary of St. Boniface, Winfred of Crediton) were revereuced here before the Reformation.

Rougemont Castle (the site is now occupied by the Devon Sessions House) was the ancient citadel, which, built on an eminence, commanded a view over the town and its approaches. Tradition assigns its foundation (no doubt untruly) to Julius Cæsar in the year 50 B.C., and derives its name (no doubt accurately) from the red colour of the soil and stones. It is built on a patch of red igneous rock, portions of which are observed to rest upon the edges of the older rocks from Broadclyst as far as Exeter. It is clear from the remains, that, whoever had the honour of its foundation, the structure was rebuilt by the Normans. It is generally believed to have been a residence of some of our Saxon kings, and of the dukes of Cornwall. As the citadel of Exeter it has played a conspicuous part in the military history of the county. In 1067 it was taken by the Conqueror, who, having altered its gates as a mark of subjection, bestowed it upon Baldwin de Brioniis, the husband of his niece Albreda, with whose descendants it remained down to the year 1230. Again, during the troubles of Stephen's reign it was captured by the king, when all the outer works were burnt; "the besieged," says an old Chronicler, "being compelled to throw even their supplies of wine upon the flames in order to extinguish them." In the reign of Hen. IV. John Holland, Duke of Exeter, had a fine mansion within its walls, but no traces of that building are now to be seen; and even as early as the reign of Charles I. Rougemont was described as "an old ruyning castle, whose gaping chinks and aged countenance presageth a downfall ere long." Shakspeare represents Richard III. as having visited it, and here felt a presentiment of his approaching fate: haunted by the name of Richmond, the tyrant exclaims—

"Richmond!—when last I was at Exeter,
The mayor in courtesy show'd me the castle,
And call'd it Rouge-mont: at which name
I started,
Because a bard of Ireland told me once
I should not live long after I saw Richmond."

The remains of this castle are now very inconsiderable, consisting only of the gateway, of a portion of the walls, and three of the bastions; but from one part of the rampart the stranger may obtain a peep across the city to distant hills. The pleasure-grounds of *Rougemont Lodge*, R. S. Gard, Esq., M.P. for Exeter (adjoining the castle gate, and where the stranger will be admitted on presenting his card), contain the ivied walls of the ancient entrance, and the most perfect part of the castle mound, which is tastefully laid out as a terrace walk.

Many coins of old Rome, and of the Greek dynasties of Syria and Egypt, have been found in Exeter, from time to time, besides tesselated pavements, fragments of columns, and other relics. The fullest notice of them will be found in Shortt's 'Sylva Antiqua Iscana.'

The promenade called *Northernhay* is under the castle wall, where the sloping bank was first levelled and planted in 1612, and has been improved from time to time. It is a favourite lounge with the inhabitants, and embraces an extensive view. Here are held horticultural shows during the summer, and here are placed 2 guns captured from the Russians. A full-length statue of Sir Thomas Acland, by *Stevens*, a native of Exeter, was placed here in the winter of 1861-2. It represents Sir Thomas, very successfully, " in his habit, as he *lives*." On the granite pedestal in front are the words,— "Presenti tibi maturos largimur honores." On the opposite side runs an inscription—" Erected as a tribute of affectionate respect for private worth and public integrity, and in testimony of admiration for the generous heart and open hand which have been ever ready to protect the weak, to relieve the needy, and to succour the oppressed, of whatever party, race, or creed." Below Northernhay are the *County Gaol and Bridewell*, and the station of the South-Western railway. At the back of the gaol is the *Reservoir* for the supply of the city; where also, close to the road, in the adjoining field, is a small mound dignified with the title of *Danes' Castle*, and supposed to mark the site of an outpost of the Roman garrison. The station of the Exeter Extension line adjoins Northernhay.

The *Devon Assize Hall and Sessionshouse* were built in 1773. The Crown Court contains "The Acquittal of Susannah," a picture presented by the artist, Mr. Brockedon, to his native county.

The Elizabethan façade of the *Guildhall* is the principal ornament of High Street. The Hall was rebuilt (on the site of the original Guildhall of the city) in 1466; and had a chapel, ded. to S. George and S. John the Baptist, in front of it. This was probably pulled down in 1593, when the existing front was built. (About 20 years before the Town-hall of Cologne was refaced in a similar manner.) The hall is ornamented with the armorial bearings of mayors, incorporated trades, and benefactors of Exeter, and contains the following pictures:—Chief Justice Pratt, afterwards Earl Camden, by *Thomas Hudson*; Sir Peter Lely; Sir J. Reynolds; Benjamin Heath (copy), by *Pine*; Gen. Monk, by *Sir Peter Lely* (engraved for Lodge's Portraits); John Rolle Walter, copy from *Sir Joshua*; George II., *Hudson*; Reuben Phillipps, *Sharland*; John Tuckfield, *Hudson*; Princess Henrietta, daughter of Charles I., afterwards Duchess of Orleans (born in Exeter, 1644), *Sir P. Lely*; and Henry Blackall, *Leaky*. In the *Council Chamber* are portraits of Sir Thomas White, one of the founders of St. John's College, Oxford; John Hoker, the Chamberlain (born 1524, d. 1601), the historian of Exeter, and uncle of the "Judicious Hooker;" and some others of interest. High-street is exceedingly cheerful, and contains excellent shops, and many curious old house-fronts.

The *Devon and Exeter Institution* (in the Cathedral Yard), founded in 1813 for the cultivation of the arts and sciences, possesses a valuable library, a few paintings, and some cabinets illustrative of natural history.

In the board-room of the *Devon and*

DEVONSHIRE.   Route 1.—Exeter—Public Buildings.   17

Exeter Hospital (Southernhay) are portraits of John Tuckfield and Ralph Allen by *Thomas Hudson*, and of John Patch, surgeon, by *William Gandy*.

At the E. end of High-street is *St. John's Hospital*, now appropriated to a free grammar-school, a blue-coat and commercial schools. It was founded at a very early time for 5 priests, 9 boys, and 12 almsmen, and suppressed in the reign of Hen. VIII. The structure encloses a quadrangle. Over a doorway on the other side of High-street, opposite the Grammar-school, is a statue of Hen. VII., arrayed as a Roman. It originally stood in a niche over the inner entrance of E. gate, rebuilt in 1511, the old gate having been shattered by the assault of Perkin Warbeck in 1497. The hospital has been perfectly restored by the Church Charity trustees after plans by Mr. Macintosh.

The hall of the *College* (Southstreet), formerly a chantry of the Vicars Choral, dates from the 14th centy., and is hung with antique portraits, supposed to represent certain early bishops of the diocese. It is used as a place of meeting by the *Exeter Diocesan Architectural Society*, and contains models of fonts, rubbings of brasses, and a number of drawings relating to ecclesiology. Here also is an unknown portrait by *Sir Joshua Reynolds*, and one of the Rev. Tobias Langdon by *William Gandy*, native of Exeter. Northcote says that Sir G. Kneller on seeing this picture inquired with astonishment who was the artist capable of painting it, and exclaimed, "Good God! why does he bury his talent in the country?"

Among other buildings and institutions the stranger may be interested by the *Market-houses*, 2 modern erections in Fore-street and Queenstreet;—the *Deaf and Dumb Institution* (in the S.E. suburb, near the banks of the river on the Topsham road), founded in 1826, and open to visitors on Tuesdays and Fridays; —the *Institution for the Blind* (on St. David's Hill, beyond Northstreet), founded in 1838, and shown daily, except on Saturdays and Sundays;— the *Bishop's Palace* and *Gardens* adjoining the Cathedral;— the *Diocesan Training College* and *School* on the Heavitree Road;—and the *Female Reformatory* in Black Bay Road.

Exeter also contains three old chapels, which are connected with almshouses, and may be of interest to the antiquary. They are *St. Wynard's* (in Magdalen-street), date 1436, and admirably restored by its patron Mark Kennaway, Esq.; the chapel of the *Leper's Hospital*, at the foot of Magdalen Hill; and the *Chapel of St. Ann*, a small Perp. building only 15 ft. long, in St. Sidwell Street. In the last hangs the full-length portrait of Sir Edward Seaward, by *William Gandy*, 1702. A house in High-street (at the corner of North-street) supports a colossal wooden figure, which represents St. Peter in the act of treading upon Paganism.

North-street passes down a steep hill to an iron bridge or viaduct of 6 arches, a useful work, erected by the Exeter Improvement Commissioners at a cost of 3500*l*. On the l. side of the street are some remarkable *old houses*, which, with those of Ross in High-st., and Trehane below South-st., are well worth notice. All are of Elizabethan character, except one at the corner of North-street, which is of the 15th centy.

The *Cemetery* is situated to the l. of this street, and comprises about 5 acres of sloping ground, prettily laid out with shrubs and walks.

The *Nursery Grounds* of Exeter have ranked among the largest and most extensive in England, the climate and the nature of the soil being peculiarly favourable to vegetation. That of the Messrs. Veitch, however (which still (1865) contains some very interesting trees and shrubs, including perhaps the largest specimens of *Wellingtonia* to be found in England), was broken up (after the death of the chief proprietor) in 1864-5, and the ground will probably be sold for building purposes. It is on the Heavitree road. At Lucombe and Pince's (on the road to Alphington) there is a remarkable camellia-house, which at the flowering season (Jan. and Feb.) is worth a long journey to see.

Railways to Bristol and London; to Yeovil and Salisbury; to Plymouth and Torquay; to Barnstaple.

Excursions.—Many very delightful spots are within a day's drive of Exeter, even for those who travel after the old fashion; but the railway has brought many of the most beautiful scenes in the county within easy access in point of time. Among the most interesting localities may be mentioned the romantic moorland in the neighbourhood of *Moreton Hampstead*; the *banks of the Teign* from Dunsford Bridge, on the Moreton road, to a point 2 m. above Fingle Bridge; *Chudleigh Rock*; the watering-places of *Sidmouth, Budleigh Salterton,* and *Exmouth*; the *Church of Ottery St. Mary*; the *Dart* from Totnes to its mouth; and the ruins of *Berry Pomeroy Castle.* The Dart and Berry Pomeroy, as well as the towns of Dawlish and Teignmouth, are brought as it were within the environs of Exeter by the South Devon Railway. For a full description of these localities consult the index.

In the immediate vicinity of the town you may make shorter excursions. The park of *Powderham Castle* (Earl of Devon) is no longer accessible to the public. The castle retains little of its old military character, but, according to Polwhele, was built either before the Conquest, to hinder the Danes from sailing up the river to Exeter, or by William de Ou, a Norman baron who came over with the Conqueror. In the reign of Edward I. it belonged to a family named Powderham, from whom it passed to the celebrated Humphrey de Bohun, and in 1377, by marriage, to the Courtenays, Earls of Devon. The park is nearly 10 m. in circumf., and commanded by the *Belvidere*, a tower from which a noble prospect is surveyed in 3 different parts from the 3 windows. Magnificent views are to be obtained from the ridge of *Haldon*, and from *Wattle Down*—locally Waddles Down. To reach the latter eminence you should turn off to the rt. from the old Okehampton road, a short distance beyond the 2nd milestone from Exeter. The banks of the *Ship Canal* afford a pleasant walk to Topsham, or further to the termination of the canal at a place called Turf. And again, those who are interested by vestiges of ancient buildings may pursue a field-path to a farmhouse situated to the l. of the Cullompton road, beyond the turnpike. In this building are some remains of *Polsloe Priory*, one of the 2 religious houses remaining in Exeter at the time of the Dissolution. They were a monastery and nunnery for Benedictines, and Polsloe was the nunnery. The stranger should also know that *Exwick Hill*, N.W., commands a fine view of the city; that *Pennsylvania*, a row of houses on the Tiverton road, looks down the vale of the Exe and the glistening river to its confluence with the sea; and that the delightful grounds of *Fordlands* (E. Walkey, Esq.), 2½ m. W., are often visited (with permission) by parties of pleasure. 2¼ m. E. of Exeter is *Pinhoe* ch. with an ancient screen; and about 4 m. E., *Poltimore House*, a seat of Lord Poltimore, which in 1645 was garrisoned by Fairfax.

At *Heavitree*, 1 m. on the road to Honiton, was the residence of the late *Richard Ford*, who here wrote his celebrated 'Handbook for Spain.' His gardens, adorned with Moorish terraces, and planted with pines and cypresses from the banks of the Xenil and Guadalquiver, display every mark of refined taste. He lies in the neighbouring ch.-yard. By the turnpike-gate stands *Livery Dole*, an old chapel and almshouses, the latter lately rebuilt. The houses were founded in 1591, by Sir Robert Dennis, previously sheriff of Devon; the chapel is of more ancient date. Heavitree is the place where malefactors were formerly executed; we have records of their having been frequently burnt here, and, on digging the foundation for the new almshouses, the workmen discovered an iron ring and chain, supposed to have been used to fasten the unfortunate culprits. The ch. of Heavitree has been rebuilt and enlarged. Near *St. Loyes* (Pitman Jones, Esq.) is the ancient *chapel of St. Eligius* or St. Loyes, now a farm stable.

The *Exeter Ship Canal*, which floats the produce of foreign climes to this ancient city, deserves the notice of the stranger as one of the oldest canals in England. (The only work of the sort which, in this country, exceeds it in antiquity, is *Morton's Leam*, a canal running from near Peterborough to the sea, for about 40 m., and constructed by John Morton, Bp. of Ely, temp. Hen. VII. This was intended for the drainage of the fens as well as for navigation.) In early times the river flowed deep with the tide as high as Exeter; but in 1284 it was closed to salt-water and sea-going vessels at Topsham, by the erection of a weir, the work of Isabella de Redvers, Countess of Devon (whence *Countess Weir*), who thus revenged herself upon the citizens for some affront. Her successor, Hugh Courtenay, added insult to this injury, maltreating the city officers on a quay which he had constructed at his own town of Topsham. The corporation of Exeter ineffectually sought redress. They established at law their right to the navigation of the river, but, with a verdict in their favour, were unable to act until the reign of Hen. VIII., when they procured authority from Parl. to cut a canal from Topsham to Exeter, and this they speedily did, at a cost of about 5000*l*. The city, being thus again connected with the sea, was made a royal port by Charles II. Subsequently, at different times, the canal was enlarged, and in 1826 was extended to a place called Turf, and widened and deepened to its present dimensions. It is now about 5 m. in length, 15 ft. in depth, and 30 ft. in width, so that 2 vessels of considerable size have room to pass each other. At one end it terminates in a lock 120 ft. long, and of the width of the canal; at the other, in a basin opposite the quay at Exeter, 917 ft. in length, 18 ft. in depth, and from 90 to 110 ft. in breadth. The banks of the canal are, as Southey described them, "completely naturalized, and most beautifully clothed with flowers."

The *river Exe*, rising in Somerset, on the barren waste of Exmoor, is one of the most considerable rivers in Devonshire, and, like all the streams of this rocky county, flows in a clear and merry current through wooded and romantic vales. Its course is about 70 m., and in this long journey it is augmented by numerous tributaries. 4 m. below Exeter it is joined by the Clist, when it suddenly expands to more than a mile in width, and becomes navigable for vessels of large size. The shores of this estuary are well wooded and picturesque, but their effect is somewhat injured by the intrusive embankments and long array of poles of the South Devon rail and its telegraph on the W. side, and of the Exeter and Exmouth railway on the E.

ROUTE 2.

LONDON TO TIVERTON, GREAT WESTERN (BRISTOL AND EXETER) RAILWAY.—TIVERTON TO CREDITON, BY ROAD.

For the line from London to 179¼ m. *Tiverton Junction,* see Rte. 1.

A short branch line of 5 m. runs hence to Tiverton. 1¾ m. from the Tiverton Junc. Stat. (rt. of the rail to Tiverton) is the village of *Halberton,* where the tourist will find the ch. (of the 14th centy. restored 1848) worth a visit. The screen, pulpit (of wood, and unusual in form), and the font should be noticed.

5 m. from the Junct., and 184¼ m. from London, we reach

Tiverton (a sister-town to Twyford in Bucks, both signifying Twoford-Town).—*Inns:* Angel; Three Tuns. A well-built place, deriving its name from its position between the rivers Exe and Loman, which here effect a junction, and much of its importance from its connection with Lord Palmerston, who has long (1865) represented this borough in Parliament. Tiverton owes its handsome appearance to a fire which destroyed 298 of the old thatched houses in June 1731. Besides the rly., the town has water communication with Taunton by the *Grand Western Canal,* which is 23 m. long, and was originally planned to connect the two Channels by a line between Taunton and Topsham. The barges are raised from level to level by machinery, without locks. *Hannah Cowley,* the dramatic writer, was born at Tiverton 1743, and died here 1809.

During the disturbances in 1549, a battle was fought at *Cranmore,* near Collipriest, between the insurgents and the king's troops, in which the former were defeated. In the Great Rebellion Tiverton changed hands more than once. In 1643 the troops of the Parliament were driven from its streets. In 1644 it was occupied in force by the King, and Earl of Essex; and in 1645 Massey entered it, and with Fairfax carried its defences by storm.

With the exception of the ch., there is not much to be seen in this town, so that a peep into the Handbook may suffice the traveller. But he need not fear the intricacy of its details, for, if bewildered, he is at the right place for relief. According to the west country saying, all he has to do is to *go to Tiverton and ask Mr. Able.*

The *Castle* was founded about 1100 by Richard de Redvers, but the existing remains are probably not older than 14th centy. It stands on the N. side of the town, and for many years was a residence of the Earls of Devon. As a fortress it was dismantled after its capture by Fairfax in Oct. 1645. The remains consist of the great gateway, and some ivied walls and towers, and are now the property of Sir W. Palk Carew, Bart. The gateway is of the 14th centy., and fine.

The *Ch. of St. Peter,* a beautiful Gothic structure, dates from the 15th centy., but was in great part rebuilt 1853-5; architect, Ashworth of Exeter. On the *exterior,* remark the tower, Greenway's Chapel, and the whole S. front. The *tower,* 99 ft. high, is Perp., of 4 stages, with grotesque figures ornamenting each set-off. All the details deserve notice. The tower belongs to the class of which Chittlehampton (Rte. 17) is the finest example in Devonshire. *Greenway's Chapel,* and S. porch, were erected by John Greenway, a merchant of Tiverton, in 1517. The whole exterior is covered with lavish decorations, consisting of ships, woolpacks, staple-marks, figures of men, children, and horses, inscriptions, merchant adventurers' and drapers' arms. On the corbel line, which runs round the whole of the chapel, are represented in relief 20 of the principal events in the life of our Saviour, beginning with the Flight into Egypt, and ending with the Ascension. These are all minutely carved. The whole S. front was rebuilt by Greenway, and is covered with similar ornaments, characteristic of the coming change from Perp. to "cinquecento."

The *interior* of the ch. is throughout Perp. A Norm. doorway in the N. aisle, however, is a relic of a ch. said to have been dedicated by Leofric, the first bishop of Exeter (1073). The roof of the S. porch (Greenway's work) is enriched in the same manner as the exterior. Above the inner doorway is an Adoration of the Virgin, with figures of John and Joan Greenway kneeling on either side. The oaken door leading into the chapel from this porch, and the stone roof of the chapel itself, should be noticed. On the floor are the *brasses* of John and Joan Greenway, d. 1529.

This ch. was held as a military position against Fairfax, and in the assault the chapel and monuments of the Courtenays were destroyed. Among them was one to Catherine, daughter of Edw. IV. and widow of William Earl of D., and another to the Admiral, Edw. C., third Earl of D., commonly called, "The blind and good Earl"—

"Hoe, hoe ! who lies here?
I, the goode Erle of Devonshere;
With Maud, my wife to mee full dere,
We lyved togeather fyfty-fyve yere.
What wee gave, wee have ;
What wee spent, wee had ;
What wee lefte, wee loste."

The *Almshouses* in Gold-street, founded (for 5 poor men) by John Greenway in 1517, should be visited. The porch and small chapel are partly enriched in the same manner as the S. front of the ch. On the wall of the chapel are the lines—

" Have grace, ye men, and ever pray
For the soul of John and Joan Greenway."

The eagle on a bundle of sticks, which is seen on all these buildings, was probably Greenway's device.

There are also some almshouses in Wellbrook, built 1579, by John Waldron, another Tiverton merchant. The chapel has a good wooden roof.

The *Grammar School*, for 150 boys, was founded 1604 by Peter Blundell, a rich merchant, who in early life was a clothier of Tiverton. The screen separating the higher and lower schools, the timber roof of the schools, and the garden front of the head master's house are well worth examination. The trustees of the charity meet annually on St. Peter's day (29 June) for the election of scholars and exhibitioners.

In August, horse-racing takes place for 2 days in the Castle Meadows.

Lace-making was introduced into Tiverton in 1816, and is now a thriving business. The factory of Messrs. Heathcoat is worth a visit. It employs about 1500 hands. Adjoining it a large *iron-foundry* belonging to the same firm. In the neighbourhood of the town are *Bolham House*, the seat of J. Heathcoat, Esq.; *Collipriest*, — Carew, Esq.; *Worth*, J. Worth, Esq.; and *Knight's Hayes*, Mrs. Walrond.

The stranger should walk by the Cullompton road to the summit of *Newt's Down*, 1½ m., for a view of the vale and town. *Bampton* and *Dulverton* (see Rte. 20), in one of the most beautiful and romantic districts in England, are respectively 7 and 12 m. distant. An omnibus goes once a week during the summer from Tiverton to Bampton. On the road to Exeter is

Silverton Park, Countess of Egremont. The house, which is in the Grecian style, was built by the late Earl, and contains, amongst its pictures, the portrait of *Sir Joshua Reynolds*, which the artist painted for his native town of Plympton. It was sold by the corporation to the 5th Earl of E. for 150*l.* In 1645 Fairfax was quartered at the neighbouring village for 4 days. There are several such names as Silverton in this county, as *Little Silver, Silverhill;* and it is said that these places are one and all situated near some ancient camp. (*Sel,* however, indicating *wood, covert,* is, according to Kemble, one of the roots common to Celt and Saxon.)

The drive from Tiverton to Crediton (12 m.) is a pleasant one. On this road,

3¾ are *Bickleigh* and *Bickleigh Court*, long a seat of the Carews, but now a farmhouse. This was the native place of Bamfylde Moore Carew, the "King of the Beggars," b. 1690, who, near the close of his adventurous life, returned hither and died 1758. He was the son of the rector, Theodore Carew, and was buried in the churchyard. A desecrated chapel attached to the manorhouse is of Norman character.

At Bickleigh Bridge (which the road crosses), where a small stream called the Dart (not that which gives name to Dartmoor) joins the Exe, the scenery is very pleasing.

2¼ l., on an isolated hill, is the camp of *Cadbury Castle*, close to the road. It was occupied by Fairfax's army in Dec. 1645. Across the Exe, in Killerton Park, is another height, called *Dolbury*. There is a saying in the county that

"If Cadburye Castle and Dolbury Hill dolven were,
All England might plough with a golden sheere."

The country people have a legend of a fiery dragon, which has been seen flying by night between these hills, "whereby," says Westcote, "it has been supposed that a great treasure lies hid in each of them, and that the dragon is the trusty treasurer and the sure keeper thereof." There is a Dolberry in Somerset on the range of Mendip. It is an elevated camp above the village of Churchill; and, curiously enough, a similar rhyme belonged to it in Leland's time—

"If Dolberi digged were
Of gold should be the shere."

The Devonshire Cadbury, from which a very wide prospect is commanded,—including the camps of Dolbury, Woodbury, Sidbury, Hembury, Dumpdon, Membury, and Castle Neroche in Dorsetshire,—has a circumference of about 500 yds., and consists of an oval enclosure with a deep fosse, and an additional (perhaps later) entrenchment, semicircular, and ranging E. by S. to W. In the centre of the first area is a pit 6 ft. deep, not a well, but perhaps formed to retain rain-water. It was excavated in 1848, when a curious finger-ring, gold armillæ, and styles for writing were found in it. They are of late Roman character, and are now preserved at *Fursdon House* (between the camp and the Exe river), the residence of the Rev. J. Fursdon. Many Roman coins were found in this neighbourhood in 1830.

Beyond Cadbury the graceful tower of *Stockleigh Pomeroy Ch.* (restored 1862, W. White, architect) is seen l.; and

Passing l. *Shobrook Park* (J. H. Hippisley, Esq.), which contains some noble trees, and from which the views are very picturesque and varied, we reach

6 *Crediton* (*Inn:* the Ship), situated on the small river Creedy. (See Rte. 17.) Crediton is generally approached by the N. Devon Rly.

ROUTE 3.

LONDON TO EXETER. (SOUTH-WESTERN RAILWAY.—WATERLOO STAT.)

The distance is performed by express in 5 hrs.; by ordinary trains in about 6¼.

The rly. passes through a very pleasant country, varied by the meadows, fir woods, and heaths of Surrey, and by the steep, open chalk downs of North Hampshire and Dorsetshire. The ruins of the Holy Ghost Chapel at Basingstoke (rt.—it was the chapel of a guild or fraternity founded in 1525 by the first Lord Sandys); the mound of Old Sarum; the spire of Salisbury cathedral; and the ch. and castle of Sherborne, are the chief objects of interest for the traveller before he reaches the Devonshire border at

147 m. from London *Axminster* (*Inns* : George; Old Bell. An omnibus runs 3 times daily between Axminster and Lyme Regis, 5 m., passing the village of Uplyme. A spring van runs daily between Axminster and Charmouth), a town seated on an eminence above the river Axe in a very pretty country. Its name is widely known in connection with the *carpets* which for many years were manufactured in the *Court House*, close to the ch., and were first made here by a Mr. Whitty, in 1755, who was rewarded for his ingenuity with the medal of the Society of Arts. These celebrated fabrics were far superior to anything of the kind which had been previously produced in England; rather glaring in colour, but for durability considered equal to the carpets brought from Turkey. Their excellence in this respect was due to their being made entirely by hand, like tapestry. The manufacture is now carried on at Wilton, near Salisbury, but the rugs alone are hand-made, the carpets are woven. The factory at this place has been closed since 1835.

Axminster has been the theme of much antiquarian discussion. It is generally believed to have been a British settlement connected with the camps of *Membury* and *Musbury*, which are still in good preservation N. and S. of the town. Some also suppose that this neighbourhood was the scene of the furious battle of *Brunenburgh*, A.D. 937, in which Athelstan defeated a combined host of Danes, Scotch, and Irish; and the Anglo-Saxon name of the town, *Brunenburgh* (?), as well as others in the vicinity, such as *Kingsfield* and *Warlake*, would seem to give support to this opinion. The modern name of Axminster possibly originated about that time, when Athelstan is said to have founded the Minster for 7 priests to celebrate the obits of 7 earls and 5 kings who fell in the battle, which was sung by the minstrel as the greatest triumph gained by the Angles and the Saxons "since they crossed the broad and stormy sea." (See this famous poem in the Saxon Chronicle, *sub anno* 937. The site of Brunenburgh remains quite uncertain; but the tradition which fixed it at Axminster is as ancient as the time of Edw. III., when it is recorded in a register of Newenham Abbey. The battle is there said to have begun "al munt St. Calyxt en Devansyr," and to have ended at Colecroft under Axminster, where the 7 earls were killed.) In the Rebellion Axminster suffered considerably. In 1644 it was occupied by the Royalists during the siege of Lyme, and in one of the many conflicts it was partly burnt. In 1689 the P. of Orange rested some days here on his road to London, at "the Dolphin," which had been a residence of the Yonge family.

The *Minster* is the prominent and only interesting feature of the town. It is a handsome stone structure dedicated to St. Mary, and, in part, unquestionably of early date. It exhibits the 3 styles of Pointed architecture. The lower stage of the tower and a portion of the chancel are E. Eng.; the nave and the greater part of the chancel Dec.; the N. aisle is Perp.; the S. aisle Gothic of the year 1800. The building had formerly transepts, which were called respectively the Yonges' and the Drakes' aisle. In the nave are a triple pulpit of carved oak, 1633, an old but plain font, and on the wall under the organ-loft 2 sculptured figures which belonged to a monument of the Drakes of Ashe. On each side of the chancel is an ancient freestone, but painted, effigy in a niche; the one supposed to represent Alice, the daughter of Lord Brewer and wife of Reginald de Mohun, the other her father's chaplain and first vicar of this ch., Gervase de Prestaller. On the rt. of the altar are 3 sedilia and a piscina under arches; in the S. aisle is a painting of the 12 Apostles by some unknown genius of Axminster; and in the N. aisle a part of the ancient screen. The chancel has an old roof, the nave a modern one perfectly plain. The pillars of the nave are of blue lias, painted grey. The most ancient part of the Minster is a Norm. arch with zigzag moulding at the E. end of the S. aisle, removed there in 1800, but originally forming the S. door of nave. Here is a memorial window to the late Rev. W. J. Conybeare, the geologist, &c.

Dr. Buckland, the eminent geologist, born 1784, was a native of Axminster. His father rests in the churchyard — with his crutches, which are represented on the tombstone. *Micaiah Towgood*, a learned Dissenter, was likewise a native of this place, b. 1700. *John Prince*, author of 'The Worthies of Devon,' was born in the farmhouse at Newenham Abbey, 1643. In the vicinity of the town are *Clocombe House*, built 1732, H. Knight, Esq.; *Sector House*, late James Davidson, Esq.; *Fursbrook House*, S. Northmore, Esq.; *Seacombe House*, J. H. Richards, Esq.; *Castle Hill*, Major N. T. Still; and *Coryton House*, late W. Tucker, Esq., built 1756, and so named from the rivulet *Cory*, which flows through the estate. A farmhouse N. of the mansion was the residence of the Warrens, of whom the property was purchased by the present family 1697. Seaton and Axmouth are each 6 m., Lyme Regis 5 m., and Chard 7 m., from Axminster.

Some pleasant *excursions* can be made from this town, and one which should be the object of every visitor, viz. to *Ford Abbey* (the Knap *Inn;* see *Handbook for Dorset*), situated on the border of the neighbouring county, 7 m. distant. *Thorncombe*, 1½ m. S.E. of Axminster, was the birthplace of *Admiral Hood*, Visc. Bridport, 1728. His father was the vicar. The *ch.* contains a fine brass to Sir Thos. and Lady Brook, 1437. S. of the village is *Sadborough House*, Col. Bragge; and W. the ruins of *Olditch Court*, long a residence of the Brook family, afterwards Lords Cobham. They are probably of the time of Edw. III., and now partly incorporated with a farm-house.

The ch. of *Uplyme*, 4 m. from Axminster on the road to Lyme Regis (the omnibus to which passes it), is beautifully situated in a landlocked valley, immediately within the range of cliffs. It has Dec. portions, and has been well cared for by the present rector. In 1850 a beautiful tesselated pavement was discovered here, marking the site of a villa on the Ikenild Way. This is the only Roman villa which has been found in Devonshire.

Other objects of interest are some trifling remains of *Newenham Abbey*, ¼ m. S. of Axminster on the road to Seaton, founded for Cistercian monks by Reginald de Mohun in the reign of Hen. III., 1246, and colonized from Beaulieu in Hampshire, whence the future abbot, 12 monks, and 4 lay brethren proceeded on foot, taking 4 days for the journey. The ruins are to be found in the orchard of Mr. Swain's farm, rt. of the road, by a path through 5 fields. The E. window of the abbey ch. and some of the arches are standing. The ch. was a noble building, resembling (as far as can be judged from fragments dug up on the site) Salisbury Cathedral in its architecture. Many of the Mohuns and Bonvilles were interred in it.—*Ashe* (2 m. on the same road towards Musbury and Seaton), the birthplace of the great *Duke of Marlborough*, now a farmhouse, but with the original kitchen, and some other old rooms long believed to be haunted by their ancient lords, whose effigies may be seen in the ch. of Musbury (otherwise of little interest), 1 m. distant. John Churchill, the illustrious warrior, "Conqueror of the Bourbons" at Blenheim, Ramillies, Malplaquet, and Oudenarde,—

"The man to distant ages known, Who shook the Gallic, fix'd the Austrian throne,"—

was born here on the 5th of July, 1650. His father, says Alison, was Sir Winston Churchill, a gallant cavalier, who had drawn his sword on behalf of Charles I., and had in consequence been deprived of fortune and driven into exile by Cromwell. His mother was Elizabeth Drake, collaterally connected with the descendants of the great navigator. The Drakes were seated here from 1526 to 1782.—To resume our list:—*Membury* and *Musbury*, single-ditch entrenchments on lofty hills, respectively N. and S. of the town, 3 m.; *Hawksdown Hill*, over Axmouth, the site of another camp; all three commanding very extensive prospects:—the *cliff scenery W. of Seaton*; —and lastly the *Pinney Landslips* on the coast between Axmouth and Lyme Regis. (*See* Rte. 4.) From

[*Dev. & Corn.*]

Musbury no less than 12 hill forts are in view, border fortresses of the Danmonii and Morini, between which tribes the Axe here formed the boundary.

The river Axe (Celtic, *Isc*, water), which is crossed at Axminster, rises in Dorsetshire, on the high ground near Crewkerne, which forms the watershed of the district; the river Parrett, which also rises there, taking the opposite course, toward Bridgewater Bay.

The road to Chard passes in 1 m. *Weycroft Bridge*, where, on a height overlooking the river, are some traces in a farmhouse of an ancient seat of the Brooks. ¾ m. further is *Coaxden*, an old mansion, birthplace of *Sir Symonds D'Ewes*, the puritan and antiquary, 1602. *Coaxdon Mill* on the river is picturesque.

Proceeding on our route:—
1 m. from Axminster the river *Yart*, descending from the eastern border of the Blackdown Hills, is crossed, and the rly. then follows the valley of the Cory rivulet, winding round Shute Hill, to
Colyton Stat. (An omnibus runs from this stat. through the village of Colyton, 2 m. (Rte. 4), to the little watering-place of *Seaton* (Rte. 4) 2½ m. farther. The road is pleasant, with picturesque peeps of the sea. A branch rly. is in progress (1865) from the Colyton Stat. to Seaton.)

Close above the Colyton Stat. is seen the gatehouse of *Shute*, the ancient seat of the Bonvilles, and in which the Poles, who purchased the property 1787, have resided from the reign of Q. Mary. It is an interesting Tudor ruin embowered among trees. The present mansion (Sir J. G. R. Pole, Bart.), built 1787-8, commands a view of the sea, and contains pictures occasionally shown to strangers. Nearer Colyton are the ruins of *Colcombe*, another old seat of this family. · (*See Colyton*, Rte. 4.) In the *Ch.* of Shute, a mossy Dec. and Perp. building overshadowed by an enormous yew-tree, are the monuments of the Poles, and among them one to *Sir Will. Pole*, 1741, who is represented in his court dress, as Master of the Household to Queen Anne. On Shute Hill, ½ m. N., is an ancient beacon-house in excellent preservation.

The old deer-park of Shute, stretching toward the village of Kilmington, is a wild tract of broken ground, shaded by thickets and venerable oaks. On Kilmington Hill grows *lobelia urens*, said to be peculiar to this locality.

After leaving the stat., the village of Colyton with its ch. (Rte. 4) is seen l., and, somewhat farther, *Widworthy Hill* and *Widworthy Court* (Sir E. Marwood Elton, Bart.). The former is a beautiful eminence; near the summit is a small Dec. ch., with a mailed effigy in the N. transept, possibly Sir Robert Denham, temp. Edward I. In the S. transept is a monument by *Bacon* for James Marwood, 1767. The Marwoods have been seated in Devonshire from the earliest period of the county history. In 1830 Sir E. M. Elton assumed the name, by royal licence, as representative of this ancient family.

Through a rich country the rail, which follows nearly the line of the old high road, reaches

Honiton Stat. The old ch. and parsonage are on the hill, l.; rt. is seen the town, lying picturesquely in the valley of the Otter, and backed by steep hills, some of which are crested with wood, and belong to the same range on which are the camps of Hembury and Dumpdon (see *post*).

From the Honiton Stat. there is a coach daily to Sidmouth (7 m., Rte. 4).

Honiton. (Inns: Dolphin; Golden Lion, said to have been a residence of the Abbot of Dunkeswell. The name Honiton seems connected with those of "Honeyditch," "Hen-naborough," ancient camps in the county.) Honiton is well known for its lace, made by hand on the *pillow*, a beautiful fabric, but of late years in a measure supplanted by bobbin-net, a cheaper and inferior article worked by machinery. The manufacture of lace was introduced into Devonshire by the Flemish immigrants in the reign of Elizabeth. The best point lace was then made exclusively of Antwerp thread. Scarcely any lace is now made at Honiton. Beer and the villages on the coast (see Rte. 4) are now the chief places in which it is manufactured. (For the history of Devonshire lace see Mrs. Bury Palliser's 'Hist. of Lace,' London, 1865.) The *Vale of Honiton* is as famous for its butter as the town for its lace, and, with the Vale of Exeter, forms the principal dairy district of the county, and one of the richest in the kingdom.

The *Old Church* stands in a commanding position on the hillside S. of the town, and, contains an oak screen, exceedingly light and elegant, but unfortunately painted. This screen is late Perp., and, like the greater part of the church, was probably the work of Bishop Courtenay (1477-1487). The aisles were added by John and Joan Tassel, before 1529. By the E. door is the black marble tomb of *Thomas Marwood*, "who practised physic 75 years, and died at the age of 105, physician to Queen Elizabeth." Marwood rose to this eminence by means of a cure which he effected on the person of the Earl of Essex, for which special service he was presented by Elizabeth with an estate near Honiton. His son and grandson were also of the medical profession, and the former built the house still standing in Honiton, and but little altered, in which Charles I. passed the night of 25th July, 1644. Observe the grotesque heads on the ceiling of the ch. The churchyard

DEVONSHIRE. *Route 3.—Hembury Fort.—Awliscombe.* 27

commands a view of the vale; of Tracey House, on St. Cyas Hill, opposite; of *Hembury Fort*, further to the N.W.; and of the round-backed eminence of *Dumpdon Hill*, 2 m. N. of Honiton. Dumpdon is 879 ft. high, and has a large oval camp on its summit.

St. Paul's Church (1837) is more conveniently situated in the centre of the town. It contains a copy of Raphael's "Transfiguration," and monuments to the memory of the Rev. R. Lewis, and J. Marwood, Esq., the great-grandfather of Sir E. M. Elton, Bart.

About ¼ m. from the town, on the Exeter road, is the *Hospital of St. Margaret*, originally founded for lepers early in the 14th centy; but renewed and greatly benefited by Thomas Chard, the last abbot of Ford, who was born at Tracy, in the adjoining parish of Awliscombe. It is now a hospital for 9 poor persons. There is a small chapel, which, together with part of the hospital itself, may belong to the original foundation, although the Perp. E. window of the chapel is of Chard's time. Dr. Pring (*Memoir of Thomas Chard*) has suggested that the ex-abbot may have been buried here; and at any rate a sepulchral stone from which the brass had been removed, was formerly used for securing the W. door.

The *river Otter*, above which Honiton stands, so named from the otters which once frequented it, has a high reputation among anglers.

[*Hembury Fort* may be visited from Honiton, from which it is distant 3½ m. It is a fine specimen of an ancient camp, crowning a bold spur of elevated land about 4 m. N.W., and commanding on 3 sides a vast prospect over the vale of the Otter to the sea, and beyond Exeter to the heights of Haldon and Dartmoor. It consists of an oval area, about 380 yds. in length by 130 broad, encircled by 3 lofty ramparts in excellent preservation, and is divided into 2 parts by a double agger, between which, on the W., one of the gateways leads obliquely through the entrenchments. Several Roman coins, and an iron "lar" representing a female figure 3 in. high, have been found here. There can be little doubt but that Hembury Fort is the *Moridunum* of Antonine's 'Itinerary,' there described as 15 m. from Exeter and 36 m. from Dorchester. The Fosseway and the Ikenild passed close to it on their way to Exeter. On *Blackborough Down*, N.W. of Hembury, and about 10 m. from Honiton, are *whetstone quarries*, from which scythestones are sent to all parts of England. The down is also distinguished for the beauty and extent of the view.

Awliscombe ch., 2 m. on the road from Honiton to Hembury Fort, is very good Perp. and deserves a visit. The S. porch (erected by Thomas Chard, last abbot of Ford) is in the angle between the S. wall and the transept, with 2 outer doorways. The exterior niches, the deep mouldings of the arches, and the groining, should be noticed. In the S. aisle is a beautiful Perp. window, also the work of Thomas Chard, who founded a chantry in this aisle. He built much at Ford Abbey, where his initials are visible. The screen is (unusual in Devonshire) of stone, with angels projecting from the spring of the arches. (An interesting memoir of Abbot Chard, who was many years suffragan bishop, has been written by Dr. Pring, of Taunton : London, 1864.) The ch. of *Broadhembury*, 1¼ m. N.W. of Hembury Fort, is Perp. with a good W. tower, said to be coeval with that of Broadclyst. "The master built Broadhembury, the men Broadclyst." The W. window is very good.

The remains of *Dunkeswell Abbey* (Cistercian, founded 1201 by William Lord Brewer) are situated in a secluded vale, 5½ m. N. of

c 2

Honiton (but they are not worth seeing). A tower called the *Basket House*, and the surrounding woods of *Offwell* (a seat of the late Dr. Coplestone, Bp. of Llandaff), on the summit of Honiton Hill, are objects for another excursion. Among the seats in the neighbourhood may be noticed *Manor House*, Visct. Sidmouth, near the village of Upottery, 5 m., containing a full-length portrait, and bust by *Roubiliac*, of the first Lord Sidmouth; *Netherton Hall* (date Eliz.), Sir E. S. Prideaux, Bart., about 3 m. S., under *Chinehead*, which has a single-ditch entrenchment called *Furzey Castle*; and *Deer Park* (W. M. Smythe, Esq.). *Sheafhayne House*, on the border of the county, near Yarcombe, about 8 m. from Honiton, is an old mansion belonging to Sir T. T. F. E. Drake, Bart., a descendant of the illustrious "warrior Drake." (The terminations "hayne" and "hayes," which are very common in this part of Devon, are plural forms of the A.-S. *haga*, a hedge, — and mark early enclosures. Hallam has remarked that some hedges are amongst the most ancient remains in England. A field shut up for hay is still said in Devonshire to be "hained up." Is not the word "hay" itself from this root?)]

2 m. from Honiton the ch. of *Gittesham* (mainly Perp. and of no great interest) is seen l. in a village pleasantly situated. The river Otter, which rises on the Blackdown hills, is crossed, and the train reaches

Ottery Road Stat. Hence an omnibus runs 4 times daily to *Ottery St. Mary* (1 m.), and once a day to *Sidmouth* (6 m., Rte. 4). Sidmouth is more easily reached from this stat. than from elsewhere; and a rly. is in progress (1865) hence to that watering place, passing Ottery in its way. A branch will run to Budleigh Salterton.

Ottery St. Mary (*Inns:* King's Arms; Red Lion; London Hotel) is

3 m. (by road) from Honiton, the road to it passing *Hunter's Lodge*, a halfway house; and, opposite this inn, a block of stone, of which marvellous stories are told. It is said to roll away in the dead of night, and descend into a neighbouring valley to drink, and to derive this power of locomotion from human blood which has been shed on it; for, according to the wild legend, it was originally a sacrificial stone on which the witches immolated their victims. Ottery St. Mary, situated in a broad pastoral vale, is celebrated for the beauty of its ch. (which, after the cathedral, is the most interesting in the county), and connected with some historic incidents. The traveller is shown the *Convention-Room of Oliver Cromwell*, who (says the local story) came to Ottery for the purpose of raising men and money, but, failing in that object, gave the run of the ch. to his destructive followers, who decapitated a number of the old monumental figures (they probably also broke the stained glass in the church). Fairfax subsequently made the town headquarters for about a month. In the reign of Elizabeth Sir Walter Raleigh resided in Mill Street; but the ruinous turret, which was long pointed out as the remains of his house, has been destroyed. Ottery was once noted for the manufacture of serges, a business now supplanted by silk-spinning and lace-making. It was the birthplace of the poet *Coleridge*, whose father was master of the grammar-school.

The manor of Ottery was granted by Edward the Confessor to the Church of Rouen: but there is no evidence that any ch. existed on it until *Bp. Bronescombe* dedicated one in 1260. *Bp. Grandisson* in 1335 bought the manor from the Chapter of Rouen, erected the parish ch. into a collegiate establishment, and granted the manor and advowson to his new college, which was otherwise richly endowed. It consisted of 40 members, under 4 principal officers —warden, minister, precentor, and sacristan. Alexander Barclay, author of the 'Ship of Fools,' was a prebendary here about 1500, and wrote (or translated) his book here. The 8 minor canons of Ottery were, he says, "right worthy" of places on board.

The *Church, which stands in a valley, surrounded by trees, and is only well seen near at hand, consists of nave and aisles, with a large chapel added on the N. side; of a transept formed by 2 towers; of a chancel and aisles with a small chapel on each side; and of an eastern Lady chapel. Its great peculiarity is the transept—formed from the towers, and in this respect resembling Exeter cathedral—the only two instances of transeptal towers in the kingdom.

The *aisles* and transeptal *towers* are E. Eng.; the *nave*, *chancel*, and *Lady chapel*, Dec.; and the *aisle* or *chapel* N. of the nave, Perp. The E. Eng. portions were no doubt part of the ch. dedicated by Bp. Bronescombe; the Dec. are Grandisson's work; and the Perp. chapel was built by Cicily, Countess of Stafford, (died circ. 1530), only daughter and heiress of William, Lord Bouville,—under Bps. Courtenay and Vesey, whose arms appear on the roof. (These are the dates usually assigned to the different portions of the ch., but it has also been suggested that the entire building (with the exception of the N. aisle, and perhaps part of the towers) dates from the latter half of the 14th centy., and that the lancets of the chancel and transepts are instances of the use of an earlier style, just as in Exeter Cathedral, Bp. Grandisson adopted the *first* (geometrical) Dec., instead of the later (curvilinear), which was the contemporary architecture.)

The *restoration* of the entire ch. was commenced in 1849, under extreme difficulties, the "corporation" (in whom, unhappily, Henry VIII. vested the fabric) offering, as usual in such cases, all possible opposition. It was carried through mainly by the exertions of the Coleridge family, and especially by the aid and influence of the Right Hon. Sir John Coleridge. The architect was Butterfield. Galleries and pews have been swept away; the stone work has been restored when necessary; stained glass and colour have been introduced; and the whole ch. is now a "pattern and ornament to the entire county."

On the *exterior* the general effect "is that of boldness and simplicity rather than richness; the grouping of the towers with the projecting chapels and porches, and the variety of style shown by the lancet windows of the aisles and transept, by the singular windows of the clerestory, and the Perp. work of the N. chapel, impart a picturesque character." *Within* the ch. a similar effect of solemn dignity is produced, mainly by the light falling from the clerestory. Here remark the difference between the groining of the aisles (E. Eng., or at all events of that character) and that of the nave (Dec.); the unusual form of the clerestory windows, rather Perp. than Dec., as they really are (these windows have been filled with stained glass; the subjects from the life of our Lord); the richly moulded piers substituted for the N. wall when the Perp. chapel was built; and the rich fan tracery of the chapel ceiling. Between the arches and the clerestory is a series of *niches*, of which those in the nave were badly restored before the general restoration; those in the chancel are in effect new, the old ones having been found quite shattered, under the plaster. In the transepts there were no doubt altars under the 5-light lancet windows, E.; since the 3 centre lights are shorter than the rest. The chancel greatly resembles the nave. From the chancel aisles (E. Eng.) an E. Eng. chapel opens on either side, with a chamber above each, containing a chimney. These chapels (ded. to St. Stephen and St. Catherine) have been restored as "oratories, or places for meditation." The stained glass is by Hardman, from Pugin's designs. The *reredos* was restored (not too well) by Mr. Blore from the original, much defaced, discovered behind the wainscoting, by which it had been hidden, probably by Q. Eliz.'s commissioners in 1561. The arms on the cornice are those of Grandisson, Montacute, Courtenay, England and France, and the Earl of March. On the S. side of the altar are 3 very good sedilia. A very beautiful stone gallery (roodloft?) separates the Lady chapel from the ambulatory. The Lady chapel itself deserves special notice for the excellence of its design and workmanship. It was restored from the designs of Mr. Woodyer.

In the vaulting of the ch. are more than 100 small apertures, probably intended for the suspension of lights or "coronæ." (There are 50 such apertures in the aisles of Exeter Cathedral, and 40 at Winchester, in the nave alone.)

Of the *stained glass*, the 5-light E. window in the N. transept, representing the "worship of the Lamb by the whole Church" (Rev. xiv.), is by *Hardman*, from Pugin's design. There are many windows by *Warrington*, of which the great W. window is the best. The best of *Wailes'* windows is the W. of the N. chapel, representing the 12 Apostles. Throughout the glass has the usual defect of want of unity of design. *Colour* has been used largely on the roof, but slightly elsewhere; the reredos, the parcloses, and the font, bring it to the ground. The font is new, from Butterfield's design, and of Devon and Cornish marbles.

Of the *monuments*, observe, N. and S. of the nave, the high tombs, with effigies, of *Sir Otho Grandisson,* brother of the Bp.; and of Beatrice his wife, dau. of Nicholas Malmayns. The knight's armour is an excellent example of the middle of Edward III.'s reign. The canopies of these tombs, and the mingled shields and foliage which form the borders of the arches, are very good and striking. (They have been restored with exact fidelity.) In the N. aisle is also the effigy of John Coke of Thorne, 1632; who according to a wild but groundless tradition was murdered for his inheritance by his brother. According to popular belief this effigy descends from its niche at night and walks about the ch. At the end of the S. chancel aisle are epitaphs for John Sherman (1617) and Gideon Sherman (1618). Southey suggested that they are probably by William Browne, author of 'Britannia's Pastorals,' who was long resident in Ottery, and died here in 1645.

Ottery St. Mary is 6 m. by a hilly road from Sidmouth. In the neighbourhood of the town (1 m. rt. of the Ottery Road stat.) are *Escot House* (Sir J. Kennaway, Bart.; here in 1755 died Sir William Yonge, well known to the readers of Pope and Walpole); *Cadhay*, 1¼ m. N., an Eliz. mansion, now the property of Sir Thomas Hare, Bart., of Stow Hall, co. Norfolk; *Gosford House* (Sir H. A. Farrington, Bart.); *Heath's Court* (Rt. Hon. Sir John Taylor Coleridge); and *Salston House* (Mrs. Wm. Coleridge). *Bishop's Court,* the property of J. Garratt, Esq., is reputed to have been a residence of Bp. Grandisson. The house (which has been restored) contains some portions of early character; and a small chapel is perhaps of Grandisson's time. The ch. of *Sowton* (in which parish Bishop's Court stands) was entirely rebuilt 1844-5, at the sole expense of J. Garratt, Esq.; Hayward of Exeter, architect. The style is Perp., and there is much stained glass, most of it by Willement. It should be seen.

DEVONSHIRE.   *Route 4.—Lyme Regis to Exeter.*   31

[*Feniton ch.*, 2½ m. N.E. the Ottery Road stat., of Perp. and debased character, has an ancient screen, and in the chancel a highly decorated altar-tomb, with effigy of an emaciated figure, probably of the 15th centy. In *Payhembury ch.* (about   m. N.) is a good screen and parclose, painted and gilt.]

Passing the stats. at *Whimple* and *Broad Clyst* (on Whimple Hill is the *Country Hotel*, commanding a fine view of Dartmoor; this is the old "half-way house" between Exeter and Honiton, 8 m. from each; opposite is *Strete Raleigh Manor House*, W. W. Buller, Esq.; l. lies Woodbury Hill), the line turns S., and through some deep cuttings reaches

Exeter (see Rte. 1), *Queen's Street Stat.* This is the stat. for the S. Western and the Exmouth railways. A short line connects it with the *St. David's Stat.* for the Bristol and Exeter, the S. and N. Devon railways. Between the two stats. a striking view of the river Exe opens rt. and l. after passing through a short tunnel.

ROUTE 4.

LYME REGIS TO EXETER, BY (SEATON) SIDMOUTH, B. SALTERTON, AND EXMOUTH.

Lyme Regis (*Inns*: Cups; Lion). (*Handbook for Dorset.*)

The coast W. of this town, as far as Culverhole Point near the mouth of the Axe, has been the theatre of remarkable disturbances, similar to those which have produced such striking effects in the Isle of Wight. But the *Pinney Landslips*, unlike that once romantic region the Undercliff, are wild and solitary, and bear only the impress of the convulsions to which the district has been subjected. They comprise the cliffs of Pinney, Whitlands, Rowsedown, Dowlands, Bendon, and Haven; but the most remarkable scene is on the estate of Dowlands, where a chasm 250 ft. in width, and 150 ft. in depth, extends parallel with the shore a distance of ¾ m. This was caused by a great landslip which occurred at Christmas 1839, and devastated upwards of 40 acres belonging to the farms of Bendon and Dowlands. The catastrophe, however, was not attended by any sudden convulsion; but nature seemed to deliberate as she formed the craggy pinnacles and buttresses which now so astonish the beholder. For a week previously cracks had been observed on the brow of the hill, but on the night of Christmas Eve the land began slowly to subside, while crevices extended in every direction. This disturbance continued on the following day, and at midnight a party of the coastguard were witness to the commencement of the great chasm by the opening of fissures, which produced a noise like the rending of cloth. This was the most eventful period; and by the evening of the following day the down had regained its stability, but it presented, for a long distance, a wild scene of ruin. In the ensuing February another landslip occurred at Whitlands, near the centre of the district. This was, however, on a much smaller scale; but it originated some delightful crag-scenery, which is now richly embellished with wood.

Those who are in the humour for exercise may scramble all the way from Lyme to the great chasm by the undercliff; but every visitor to Lyme should make a point of exploring the coast for the first mile westward, which presents little difficulty. The grand scene of ruin is, however, on the estate of Dowlands, and to reach this by road you must proceed to the farmhouse of Dowlands (3 m., where you will be compelled to pay 6d. for your inspection of the landslip), and then by a field-path to the summit of the cliff, from which a cart-road descends to the undercliff. The whole landslip is covered with trees, of which many went down in the debacle; some were killed, and their withered arms now wave in the wind above the crags and chasms, but an orchard thus roughly transplanted still flourishes and bears fruit. Two cottages descended with like good fortune. They were afterwards pulled down, but one has been since rebuilt on the original site, and with the original materials. It is inhabited by farm-servants of Dowlands, and commands an excellent view of the mural precipice, the great feature of the landslip, and from which Mistress Echo will return you some wild music, if you shout to her. Travellers should come provided with the knowledge that the finest views are to be obtained from the brink of the cliffs overhanging the landslip, from the cottage, from the knolls near the sea, and from the E. end of the great chasm, which is situated just W. of the mural precipice. The great chasm itself will probably disappoint; it too much resembles a gravel-pit; but the view from the E. end of it is wonderfully fine, and the old hedges which cross it, disjointed by the fall, are interesting. The features of the scene are much changed since the landslip occurred. They are, in fact, continually changing, and many curiosities, such as the beaches heaved up on the shore, and the *havens* which were formed in it, have long since disappeared. A decided path runs E. for about 1 m., and, though intruding on the privacy of the rabbits, you are advised to explore it. A variety of wild flowers (among them the wild larkspur) grow in great luxuriance over every part of the landslip.

5 The village of *Axmouth* is about 1 m. to the l. under *Hawksdown Hill*. (See *post*.) The Ch. is worth a visit. The S. aisle and a doorway on the N. side of nave are Norm.; the nave E. Eng. and Perp.; the chancel E. Dec., with the effigy of a priest in stole and chasuble on a recessed monument on the N. side. The tower is Perp., and has some curious gargoyles. Axmouth Ch. was granted by Rd. de Redvers to the Benedictine Abbey of St. Mary of Montbourg (Diocese of Coutances). Lodres Priory in Dorsetshire was a cell of this abbey, and Axmouth ch. was served by monks from Lodres. *Stedcombe House*, formerly the family mansion of the Halletts, and built 1695, on the site of one destroyed by the Royalists, 1644, is situated on the N. side of Hawksdown. At the time of the Rebellion it belonged to Sir Walter Erle, an active Parliamentary leader.

Axmouth is a station of the Survey made in 1837 to ascertain the difference of level between the Bristol and British Channels, and to establish marks by which any future movement of the land may be detected. For this purpose a copper bolt has been fixed in the wall of Axmouth ch., and another in a granite block on the grounds of Mr. Hallett. The line of the Survey extends from Bridgewater to the mouth of the Axe, passing Ilminster and Chard, and many years ago was selected by Telford for the ship canal with which it was proposed to connect the two seas.

1 *Colyford*, a very ancient hamlet, birthplace of *Sir Thomas Gates*, appointed Governor of Virginia by James I. He was shipwrecked on his voyage to that colony on the Bermudas, in company with Sir

George Somers, after whom these islands were at first called the Somers Islands. A road on the l. leads to

Seaton, 2 m. (*Inns:* Pole Arms; Golden Lion), a small watering-place situated at the mouth of the valley of the Axe. It consists of little more than a single street, built at right angles to the shore of a small bay, which is bounded on the E. by Culverhole Point, and on the W. by *Beer Head*, an ivy-hung cliff of the lower chalk, and the last chalk promontory in England. Seaton is one of 3 localities which claim to be the site of the *Moridunum* of Antoninus, an important Roman station, which some antiquaries (and almost with certainty, see Rte. 3) place at Hembury Fort near Honiton, and others at High Peak on the shore at Sidmouth. There was an entrenchment on *Hanna Hill*, adjoining this town (rt. of the road to Beer), known by the name of *Honey Ditches*, but now destroyed by the plough: in conjunction with Hawksdown on the opposite side of the Axe (see *post*) it commanded the opening of the river Axe to the sea—thought to be the 'Almni Ostia' of Ptolemy.

The principal features of the shore are the valley boundaries abutting on the sea, viz. on the W. *White Cliff*, a bluff picturesque headland; on the E. *Haven Cliff*, a lofty height towering above a mansion of the same name, the residence and property of J. H. Hallett, Esq. Between Seaton and Haven Cliff is a great bank of shingle, mentioned by Leland as " A mighty rigge and barre of pible stones," and stretched across the mouth of the valley like a dam. At its E. end is a ferry to a road running to Axmouth (distant 1 m.), and to a diminutive quay and pier at the embouchure of the river, which is a shifting opening little broader than the vessels which enter it, and sometimes completely barred by an easterly wind. The view from this little pier is most charming; Culverhole Point is the furthest land eastward; Beer Head, called by the fishermen Berry Wold, to the westward. The cliffs of Seaton are remarkable for their colouring. In the centre of the bay they are of bright red sandstone capped by grass; and as red and green are complementary colours, and therefore heightened in tone by juxta-position, the effect is very brilliant. Haven Cliff is red sandstone surmounted by chalk; and White Cliff, chalk based on brown, red, and amber grey strata, which, by their dip, give the buttresses of this remarkable headland the appearance of leaning towards the sea.

The *church* (of no great interest) is chiefly of the transition date between Dec. and Perp.; but of an earlier time are parts of the chancel, with 2 hagioscopes and a piscina.

The nearest railway stat. to Seaton is Colyton, 4 m. The distance to Axminster is 6 m., Chard 14 m., Lyme Regis 8 m., but for one afoot only 6 m. over the ferry.

The objects of interest in the neighbourhood are the *Pinney Landslips* (just E. of Culverhole Point), 1½ m. E. over the ferry, and by horse-path to Dowlands up Haven Cliff Hill (passing the farmhouse of *Bendon*), but about 6 m. by road through Colyford; the villages of *Beer* and *Branscombe*, W.; *Hawksdown* and *Musbury* camps, the *valley of the Axe* and town of *Colyton*, N.; and the *cliffs from Seaton to Sidmouth*, so remarkable for their altitude. They are geologically composed of chalk, greensand, and red sandstone, and average from 400 to 600 ft. in height. They are particularly fine between Branscombe and Sidmouth.

Axmouth is 1 m. from the opposite side of the ferry, but 2½ m. from Seaton by road It is situated under *Hawksdown*, which is crowned by an ancient camp formed by a triple vallum with a fosse, enclosing an irregular oblong area. It was possibly a frontier camp of the Morini, who inhabited this part of Dorsetshire. The Axe separated them from the Danmonii of Devon. There is a pretty walk to Axmouth along the crest of the hillside from Haven Cliff, with fine view of the bay, and of the valley, which, however, is sadly deficient in wood. The entrenchment of *Musbury* is rt. of the Axminster road, near the village of Musbury, 3 m. from Seaton. Axmouth ch. (p. 32) is of some interest, and ¼ m. beyond it is *Stedcombe House*, property of Mr. Hallett, commanding a fine view of the valley. A lane runs from Axmouth to Dowlands, the scene of the great landslip in 1839. Another leads to the farmhouse of *Bendon*, which still retains the interesting features of a manorhouse of the 16th cent. It was long a seat of a branch of the Erles, now represented by Thomas Erle Drax, Esq., and from whom Mr. Justice Erle is lineally descended. Sir Walter Erle, a distinguished officer on the side of the Parliament, resided here. Bendon is about ¾ m. both from Axmouth and the ferry at Seaton. It lies l. of the road from Haven Cliff to Dowlands, and nearly opposite the great chasm of the landslip.

The pedestrian can take the following delightful walk from Seaton to Sidmouth:—

He will proceed across *White Cliff*, by a path, to

Beer, 1½ m., a rare subject for the pencil, and in times past a nest of the most incorrigible smugglers, among whom was Jack Rattenbury, whose name was long a byword in the county. It is now a complete fishing village, and will recall some of the best descriptions of Kingsley. The traveller will be charmed with this romantic village on his descent from the cliffs. It is situated in a little glen, and a stream runs merrily through it, leaping to the sea in a cascade. The cove is a rugged recess, bounded on the W. by *Beer Head*, remarkable for its two natural towers of chalk. The chalk cliffs at this point are pierced by some of the most picturesque caverns imaginable; and the artist should make a point of passing into them in a boat, which he can do at high water. The forms of the rocks and openings are singularly wild and fantastic. From this village the stranger may visit the celebrated *Beer Quarry*, about 1 m. up the road. It is entered by a gloomy archway, and extends about ¼ m. under-ground, at a depth of about 300 ft. from the surface. Its caverns are therefore both dark and wet, and, as they branch in every direction, form so perfect a labyrinth, that it would be very rash to enter them without a guide. A shout at the entrance will, however, generally bring a quarryman from one of their recesses, who, candle in hand, will conduct the traveller to the scene of his labour, and show him the massive pillars left for the support of the roof, and strange nooks in which the smugglers were accustomed to conceal their tubs of spirit. The freestone consists of beds which lie at the junction of the chalk with the greensand, and is principally composed of carbonate of lime, being easy to work when first extracted, but gradually hardening on exposure, from the evaporation of the water it had contained. The quarry has been worked for ages, and supplied some of the stone employed in the decoration of Exeter Cathedral. The Chapel of Beer contains Dec. portions, but has been added to at various times, and in singular fashions. The burial-ground is said to have remained unbroken since the great plague, which was very destructive here. A path leads from the quarry over the fields (about 1 m.) to *Branscombe Mouth*; and from Beer another (from the lane running W.) will conduct you to the coastguard station on Beer Head, and then by an abrupt descent, with a glorious cliff-view, to the same destination. The view from Beer Head is one of the finest on the southern coast; and a sunset here will never be forgotten. It embraces the whole of the great W. bay from Portland to the Start; and the long line of Dartmoor, with the twin peaks of Heytor conspicuous, stretches away rt. The headland is broken into cliffs and spires of rock, evidently formed by ancient landslips. It should be thoroughly explored.

About 1 m. N.W. of Beer stands *Bovey House*, seat for many generations of a younger branch of the Walronds of Bradfield Hall, near Cullompton. In 1790 Polwhele described it as an antique mansion, with a rookery, a mossy pavement to the court, and a raven in the porch. It is in the Eliz. style, and the approach to it is formed by an avenue of limes. The entrance arch bears the shield of Walrond—*argent*, 3 bulls' faces, *sable*, horned, with a crescent for difference.

Branscombe is a straggling village, beautifully situated in a wide but irregular basin, at the junction of three valleys, and as many streams which flow to the sea at *Branscombe Mouth*. The sides of these valleys form a perfect jumble of picturesque hills, one of which, on the S., gives a character to the scene. It rises abruptly with a load of old trees, to the height of 600 ft., and there meets with the precipice which forms the other side of the hill, and descends at once to the shore. The traveller should visit the beach at the Mouth, where calcedonies are numerous among the shingle, and the white towers of Beer Head are seen to much advantage. On *Southdown*, of which Beer Head forms the point, a landslip of about 10 acres occurred in 1789. The manufacture of *pillow-lace* is busily pursued both at Branscombe and Beer, and Mr. Tucker, of this place, is one of the principal lace-merchants in the county, employing several hundred hands. In 1839 his workpeople made the Queen's wedding-dress, and in 1851 exhibited in the Crystal Palace a marvellous specimen of their art, valued at no less than 3000*l*. *Petrifying springs* are numerous in the neighbourhood.

The *ch.*, dedicated to St. Winfred is cruciform, with a central tower. The chancel is apparently E. Dec., with a Perp. E. window inserted. Under the W. light of the last window, N. and S., a seat with splayed sides is formed, in an unusual manner. The transepts and central tower seem E. Eng. A monument with 2 kneeling effigies in the N. transept is assigned to the Wadhams, who dwelt at *Edge*, N. of Branscombe, from the reign of Edw. III. to that of James I., when Nicholas W., the founder of Wadham Coll., Oxford, and whose monument is in Ilminster ch., Somerset, bequeathed the property to the families of Wyndham and Strangways. In the churchyard lies an ancient stone coffin, and against the S. wall of the ch. rests the gravestone of Joseph Braddick, 1673, on which the inscription begins thus:—

"Strong and in labour,
Suddenly he reels
Death came behind him,
And struck up his heels."

A house called *the Clergy* adjoining the ch. is a curious building full of hiding-places, and is said by the villagers to have another house under it. *Berry*, on the N. side of the Sidmouth road, just beyond Branscombe, is likewise interesting for antiquity, and has also its legend. It is reputed to be haunted by the ghost of an old-fashioned woman who a long time ago was murdered in it. *Edge* or *Egge*, in a valley N. of the ch., was the residence of the De Branscombe family to the reign of Edw. III., and from that period to 1609 of the Wadhams.

From Branscombe Mouth the pedestrian will pursue his walk along the cliffs as far as Weston Mouth, 3 m. The coast is everywhere lofty and extremely beautiful, rising from the sea in slopes or precipices, and occasionally varied by an undercliff of small extent, a rude kind of terrace which here and there affords space for a little orchard or corn-field. The rocks are festooned with ivy and other creeping plants, and the cliffs command the coast from Portland to the Start. In this extended prospect the *Heytor Rocks* are conspicuous, but the grand red *cliffs of Sidmouth* will excite the most admiration.

Weston Mouth, a coastguard station at the opening of a glen, bounded on the W. by *Dunscombe Cliff*, alt. 351 ft. Near the summit of this cliff are a layer of shells which have been converted into calcedony, and a bed of rolled chalk-flints. A path winds up the hollow through a wood to the ruinous old mansion of Dunscombe, and to a road which leads to

Salcombe Regis, the *Salt Vale* (1½ m. from Weston Mouth), a group of cottages in another dell which opens to the sea. Here there was once a fort, which was the last in the county to hold out for King Charles, and from that circumstance added *Regis* to the name of the village. The ch. is prettily situated; the chancel late E. Eng. The tower has the demi-octagonal turret so often seen in Devonshire. In the vicinity of the village are quarries of a freestone similar to that of Beer. *Thorn*, now a farmhouse, was formerly seat of the Mitchells, whose monuments are in the ch.

From Salcombe the road crosses *Salcombe Down*, from which the traveller descends, with a noble prospect extended before him, into the vaunted vale of *Sidmouth* (2 m.).

———

Returning to Colyford, the point at which we left the high road (p. 32), 1 m. to the rt. is

Colyton (Inns : Dolphin; Commercial Hotel), a town prettily situated. It is approached from Seaton by 2 roads, of which the higher is the more interesting, as commanding a fine view of the valley of the Axe, and of the bold ridge which stretches from Axminster to the sea, and upon which are the Roman camps of *Musbury* and *Hawksdown*.

At Colyton you will find a *paper-mill*, and a busy manufacture of *pillow-lace*. The *Church* is interesting, and deserves a visit. It consists of nave, transepts, central tower, chancel, and chantries, S. and N. The nave was rebuilt circ. 1750, but the original W. window was retained. This is Perp., and must have been very rich before the foliation of the lights was destroyed. It is crossed by 3 transoms, and a square-headed W. door runs up to the first transom, having lights on either side. The central tower was originally E. Eng., but it has been much altered. It is crowned by a large octagonal turret, of late Dec. character. The chancel is very good Perp. The pier arches and the original windows should be noticed. The stained glass in the E. window is chiefly modern and bad. Against the N. wall is the tomb, with effigy, of Margaret, daughter of the 9th Earl of Devon, by Katherine, youngest daughter of Edward IV. She died at Colcombe Castle, 1512, choked by a fish-bone, and her effigy is generally known as the "little choakabone." N. is the Yonge chantry, now used as a vestry; and S. the Pole chantry, with some curious monuments of the Pole family. Here is buried Sir W. Pole, the Devonshire antiquary. In the S. transept is an inscription for John Wilkins, d. 1667, the Nonconformist minister, who was deprived in 1662. He continued to preach at his own house in the town. The inscription runs thus:—

" Such pillars laid aside,
How can the church abide?

Hee left his pulpit, hee,
In Patmos God to see.
This shining light can have
No place to preach but 's grave."

It is curious to find this shining light granting a licence to Sir John Yonge (temp. Cromwell) to eat flesh in Lent. The licence is recorded in the register. This is one of the best preserved in Devonshire, beginning at the earliest possible date, 1535. The vicarage-house, rebuilt by a Dr. Brerewood in 1529, is also worth seeing. Above the porch window is inscribed " Meditatio totum : Peditatio totum," or motum? the meaning of which is not clear. A fragment of the same inscription in stained glass is fixed in one of the drawing-room windows. The remains of *Colcombe Castle* are ½ m. from the town, on the l. of the Axminster road, and now partly converted into a farmhouse. The mansion was first erected by the Earl of Devon in the reign of Edw. 1., but rebuilt about 1600 by Sir William Pole, the county historian, who occupied it until his death, 1635, when it was abandoned for the neighbouring manor-house of Shute, and fell into decay. A well covered with masonry, in a field to the N., is still in good preservation. The *Great House*, another farmhouse at Colyton, was the principal residence of the Yonge family, who settled in Devonshire temp. Henry VII., and were baronets from 1661 to 1812, but are now extinct. The wainscoting of one of the bedrooms is curiously carved, and in the garden is an antique picturesque summer-house. Nearer Axminster is the ancient gatehouse of *Shute*, mentioned in Rte. 3. *Yardbury*, for many generations a seat of a branch of the Drakes, was destroyed by fire 1853. About 5 m. W. is *Wiscombe Park*, C. Gordon, Esq.

Proceeding on our route from Colyford,—

2 A road on the l. to *Beer*, 2 m.
5 *Sulcombe Regis*.

2 *Sidmouth* (*Inns:* Royal Bedford Hotel ; Royal York Hotel ; both on the Esplanade ;—London Hotel). This watering-place occupies the mouth of one of the main valleys, which, like the small dell of Salcombe, run nearly at right angles to the coast. This valley is enclosed by lofty hills, which terminate towards the sea in the cliffs of *Salcombe* and *High Peak*, sheer precipices of about 500 ft. Meadows and woods diversify the landscape, and the rural *Sid* brightly glistens among the fields, and forms a pool dammed up by shingle before it joins the sea. The view from the beach is of more than usual interest, on account of the position of the town in the centre of that great bay which is bounded on the E. by the Isle of Portland, and on the W. by the Start. It therefore includes a semicircle of cliffs which stretch in perspective to those distant points, while huge red promontories occupy the foreground. It is an opinion of the inhabitants, based upon tradition, that the coast W. of Sidmouth once extended much farther into the sea, so as to render their bay a secure anchorage ; and that such was the case appears more than probable, from the many large rocks which emerge westward at low water, and the remains of houses which have been discovered beneath the shingle of the shore. Further evidence in support of the tradition is afforded by the early coins and relics, which are so frequently washed up by the sea, that it is a common practice with the " mud-larks " of the place to search for them after storms. Roman coins have been found on the beach ; and in 1841 a remarkable figure (Chiron with Achilles and a dog), probably the head of a Roman ensign, was found here. (It perhaps belonged to the 2nd Legion of Carausius, of which a centaur was the device.) There are traces of an ancient fortification on High Peak. Sidmouth is cele-

brated for its *pebbles*, which consist of *calcedonies, green, yellow,* and *red jaspers, moss agates,* and *agatized wood,* and are often so hard as to require a diamond in the working. They are derived from the greensand, and are not found far W. of this town, even the shingle of Sidmouth being succeeded at Budleigh Salterton by flat oval stones of a very different character. The neighbourhood abounds with petrifying springs which flow down the cliffs and encrust the mosses growing on them. The stranger will of course visit the esplanade, and the mouth of the river Sid, which forms a pretty scene where it filters through the shingle to the sea. It is spanned by a rustic foot-bridge, and on the slope of the hill are a zigzag walk and seats. A geologist should also inspect the cliff beyond, where two faults are visible. The strata, says Mr. Hutchinson, "rise in steps towards the W.—that is, towards the uplifting cause, the granite of Dartmoor." On the beach are the flat-bottomed boats which convey coal from the colliers to the town; for all vessels, to land cargoes at Sidmouth, must employ boats for the purpose, or lie ashore and hazard the chances of the weather. In 1827 a project was entertained of running out a pier on a reef of rocks at the W. end of the bay, and a tunnel was actually excavated as a roadway for the transport of the stone; but the undertaking was ultimately abandoned, on account of a clashing of opinions and interests. With respect to the climate of Sidmouth, the air is remarkable for its purity and mildness, but moist and relaxing, The temperature, on the average of the year, is about 2° warmer than that of London.

The characteristic feature of the sea-view are the blood-red cliffs, which rise to a height of about 500 ft. above the beach. They exhibit a section of 3 distinct formations: the lower portion is new red sandstone, the middle red clay or marl, the upper greensand.

The objects of interest in the town and its immediate neighbourhood are—the *Ch. of St. Nicholas,* dedicated to St. Giles by Bronescombe, Bishop of Exeter, 1259, but the greater part of it appears to have been rebuilt early in the 15th centy., probably in the reign of Henry VII.; it has been restored; Wm. White, architect;—the *Esplanade,* protected by a wall 1700 ft. in length, constructed 1838, to stop the encroachment of the sea, which in 1824 swept away a great part of the beach, and inundated the town;—and *Salcombe Hill* and *High Peak,* respectively rising from the shore E. and W. 497 and 511 ft.

Many delightful excursions may be made among the hills and valleys of the neighbourhood; viz. to any of the places previously mentioned in this route, particularly to *Weston Mouth* and *Dunscombe,* either by walk over Salcombe Hill, or by boat to the Mouth:—

—To *Bulverton Hill,* the N. extremity of the high land of Peak Hill, 1½ m., and further N. to the pretty dells of *Harpford* (pronounced *Harford*) *Wood.*

—To *Sidford,* 2 m., passing 1. *Manstone,* a very ancient farmhouse. Sidford has an ivy-mantled bridge, and several picturesque tenements of the 17th cent. In one called *Porch House,* at least so says tradition, Charles II. slept the night after his narrow escape from Charmouth (see *Hdbk. for Dorset*). It has a hiding-place to the rt. of the stairs, and the date 1574 on one of the chimneys.

—To *Sidbury,* 3 m., where there is another old bridge over the river, and 1½ m. W. of the village a camp upon *Sidbury Hill.* The *ch.* is interesting, and contains examples of all periods from E. Norm. to Perp. The W. tower (Norm.), which had become unsafe, was rebuilt in 1846, but precisely as before, leaving the

Perp. insertions, as well as the striking 2-light Norm. belfry windows, and corbel table. 2 ancient sculptures, found in the old walls, are iuserted. The broach is restored in wood, shingled. The nave is Trans. Norm.; the chancel originally E. Eng. A tablet in the chancel bears a puzzling inscription, of which the following is a translation:—"1650. Here lies Henry, the son of Robert Parsonius, who died in the second-first climacteric year of his age." Adjoining the village are *Cotford*, W. R. Bayley, Esq., and *Court Hall*, R. Hunt, Esq., and in the latter some remains of an Eliz. mansion, including a "haunted chamber," in which a human skull was discovered below the floor. *Sand*, further N.E., and now a farmhouse, has been the seat of the Sand, Tremayle, Ashley, and Huyshe families, and retains some shields in painted glass and stone and other vestiges of its ancient dignity. It was built 1594. W. of the village rises *Sidbury Castle*; a camp of the British period on a spur of *East Ottery Hill*. According to the legend a store of gold lies buried within it, and a heap of stones among the trees on the rapid slope to the E. is known as "the Treasury." The position is strong and well supplied with water by springs. On each side of the camp (which is nearly oval) there is a sort of semicircular platform attached to the agger, perhaps for beacon fires. A branch of the Ikenild Way passed towards Exeter about 1 mi. S. of this camp. *Ottery East Hill*, stretching northward to *Chineway Head*, offers a breezy expanse for a more extended ramble, and another fine point of view in *Beacon Hill*, which dips directly to the Vale of the Otter. In the far W. the angular granite rocks of *Heytor* loom on the horizon.

—Through *Newton Poppleford* (*i.e. Pepple-ford*), 4½ m., so called from the oval pebbles found in the soil, to the British or Saxon camp of *Woodbury Castle*, situated upon the lofty hills between Newton Poppleford and Topsham. The camp was originally oval, but enlarged by considerable outworks supposed to have been constructed during the Devonshire rebellion of Edw. VI.'s reign, when Lord Russell defeated the insurgents near this place. A very extensive view is commanded from Woodbury camp, which was occupied by a park of artillery during the French wars, 1798-1803, when camps were formed on Woodbury common.

—To the camp of *Blackbury Castle*, 6 m., l. of the road to Lyme. N. of the entrenchment is *Broad Down*, and on its W. declivity, near a group of barrows, a romantic hollow called *Roncumbe Gate*.

—To *Ottery St. Mary* (Rte. 3).

—Over High Peak to the cliffs of *Ladram Bay*, *Otterton*, and the beautiful gardens of *Bicton* (Lady Rolle), a walk which may be extended to *Hayes Barton* (p. 41) and *Budleigh Salterton*. The botanist will observe *Anchusa sempervirens* and a rich variety of ferns in the lanes, and *Arenaria rubra* (*marina*) on the face of the cliffs.

High Peak is the greatest ornament of Sidmouth, and, for *beauty* of shape and colour (the Prawle for *grandeur*), perhaps the most noted cliff on the coast of Devon. A path leads over its summit to *Ladram Bay*, where the red sandstone is much caverned, and the sea rolls though an archway detached from the shore. High Peak slopes rapidly landward, and on the top may still be traced the segment of an earthwork, which doubtless encircled the summit at a time when the headland extended much farther into the sea. High Peak is Mr. Hutchinson's candidate for the honour of the ancient *Moridunum*, which others have placed at Hembury Fort. Directly N. of it rises *Pin Beacon*, and in the hollow below lies Pin farmhouse, a gabled building bearing the date 1587, and formerly residence of a family named De Penne.

In the neighbourhood of Sidmouth are *Peak House* (E. Lousada, Esq.), the finest place at Sidmouth; *Woolbrook Glen*, at the end of the esplanade, (Mrs. Gen. Baynes)—the late Duke of Kent died in this house, 1820; *Witheby* (James Cunningham, Esq.); *Cotmaton Hall* (J. Carslake, Esq.).

For the angler, there are trout in the *Sid* and *Otter*. The latter river may be fished between Newton Poppleford and Otterton, but permission must be first obtained at Bicton.

The road by Ottery to Exeter is called 18 m. It passes within 1 m. of the old encampment of *Woodbury Castle*, and joins the Honiton road on *Fairmile Hill*. Sidmouth, however, is now best reached from either the Honiton or Ottery Road stat. on the S.W. rly. From both places it is distant about 7 m.

Proceeding on our route towards Budleigh Salterton—

4 *Otterton*, a village as red as the soil, consisting of rude *cob* cottages, in which the manufacture of pillow-lace is busily pursued. It is a place of some size and of great antiquity. The *Ch.* was partly restored by the late Lord Rolle, and adjoins the remains of a religious house, a priory for 4 monks, which, founded soon after the Conquest, belonged, together with the manor of Otterton, to the wealthy abbey of Mont St. Michel, on the coast of Normandy. Henry V. attached Otterton to his foundation of Sion House. The Ch. is of no great interest. Beyond the bridge over the Otter is a path on the rt., which leads in ½ m. to

Bicton Ch., an elegant edifice, recently erected through the munificence of Lady Rolle, and standing on a site somewhat in advance of the old parish ch., a part of which has been converted into a mausoleum, and connected by a cloister with the ancient tower, which is allowed to retain possession of the spot which it has occupied for ages. The new Ch. (Hayward, arch.) was completed in 1850. It is Dec. in character. The heads terminating the window labels (exterior) form a series of kings and queens of England from Edw. I. to Victoria (beginning from S. porch and proceeding E.). The corbels supporting the roof-timbers represent 18 Anglican "doctors," beginning with Wickliffe. The 20 windows are filled with stained glass by Warrington. This group of buildings is separated by a light iron railing from the beautiful gardens of *Bicton* (Lady Rolle), with their terraces, temple, fountains, lawns, and statues. The view of this terrestrial paradise from the road is extremely charming, but it gives no idea of the horticultural treasures which enrich it. Of these the *Arboretum* must be singled out for notice, since it contains representatives of every hardy family of tree and shrub, systematically arranged, and so conspicuously labelled that the visitor may "read as he runs" along the broad turf drive which extends from one end of it to the other. For size, selection, and arrangement, this collection may challenge comparison with any in the kingdom. *The Pinetum* and evergreens are little if at all inferior, in extent and beauty of growth, to those at Elvaston, the seat of the Earl of Harrington. The park contains an avenue of *araucaria imbricata*, and oak and beech, which are perfect giants of their kind. The late Mr. Loudon has recorded his opinion of the Bicton Gardens in the following words: "We never before saw culture, order, and neatness carried to such a high degree of perfection in so many departments on so large a scale. From the commonest kitchen crop, and the mushrooms in the sheds, up to the pine-apples, the heaths, and the orchideæ, everything seemed to be alike healthy and vigorous." The gardens of Bicton can only be seen on application by letter *direct* to Lady Rolle. Only *four* persons are admitted in one party, and only a certain number of parties are admitted on the same day.

An ancient *cross*, raised aloft on a brick pediment a century old, stands ½ m. W. of Bicton, at the intersection of 4 roads. On the pedestal are appropriate verses from Scripture referring to the rough and smooth roads we travel in life.

1½ *East Budleigh*, a true Devonshire village, with its *cob* cottages. 1¼ m. to the rt. is *Hayes Barton*, the birthplace of *Sir Walter Raleigh*, 1552, now a farmhouse belonging to Lady Rolle. It is in the picturesque style of Eliz., with thatched and gabled roof, mullioned windows, and projecting porch; but, with the exception of its heavy door and wooden frieze, it has not much the appearance of antiquity. In the interior an oaken table is the principal relic; but they show a room in which Sir Walter is said to have been born. Raleigh was the son of a 2nd marriage, and his mother a daughter of Sir Philip Champernowne, of Modbury. His father resided at Fardell, an estate near Cornwood, but was also the proprietor (in copyhold) of Hayes. The neighbouring ch. contains the Raleighs' pew, dated 1537; and, in the pavement of the nave, a sepulchral slab to the memory of Joan, the 1st wife of Walter Raleigh, and beneath which, according to the local tradition (unsupported), the head of the unfortunate statesman was buried. The inscription is reversed, the words reading from rt. to l. *Hayes Wood* is often visited by picnic parties from Sidmouth and Exmouth.

2½ *Budleigh Salterton*. (*Inn:* the Rolle Arms.) This is a delightful little watering-place, of recent origin, just W. of the mouth of the *Otter*, a river well known to the angler, and whose waters, "rolling musically," have awakened an echo in the breast of the poet :—

"Mine eyes
I never shut amid the sunny ray,
But straight with all their tints thy waters rise,
Thy crossing plank, thy marge with willows gray,
And bedded sand that, vein'd with various dyes,
Gleam'd through thy bright transparence!—
Coleridge.

B. Salterton is situated in a narrow dell, which runs obliquely to the shore, while a swift sparkling stream, accompanying the road, skirts the villas and their gardens, which are entered by bridges. The locality is very warm and sheltered, and a perfect bower of myrtles. Here you should notice the flat oval stones which are confined to a strip of beach between the Otter and the cliff called the West Down Beacon. Differing from the common shingle, they appear to have no propensity to travel along the shore, although the opportunity is frequently afforded them, for in gales of wind they are washed away, but always return. Observe particularly the beauty and variety of their colours and patterns when the stones are wet with the breaking wave. The short excursions from this place are to *Ladram Bay* on the other side of the Otter (which may be crossed by a timber bridge ¼ m. from the sea), to *Budleigh* and *Hayes Barton*, and to *West Down Beacon*. The latter, a short distance W., is an eminence by the shore commanding the estuary of the Teign and a grand sweep of coast and hills, and approached by a delightful cliff-walk provided with seats. The stones on the beach in its vicinity merit notice for their colours, which will appear singularly beautiful to a bather who opens his eyes under water and observes them through that medium. Near the top of the cliffs may be observed the *nidus* of the flat pebbles of Budleigh Salterton.

An omnibus runs three times a day from Budleigh Salterton to Exmouth, so as to meet the trains.

Those who are fond of walking can proceed from the Beacon to Exmouth by the secluded village of *Littleham*, where there is a carved screen (not very good) in the ch. The distance is about the same as that by the road.

5 *Exmouth*. (*Inns*: Royal Beacon Hotel; — Globe Hotel; — Clarence Hotel.) This town is well known for its high rank among the watering-places of the county, but differs much from the others in point of situation. The best part of Exmouth stands on a hill falling abruptly to the mouth of the sandy estuary of the Exe, and commands the scenery of a coast, a river, a cultivated country, and barren elevated moors. The grand feature in the landscape is the great ridge of *Haldon*, ranging as a background N.N.W. and S.S.E. about 8 m., at almost a uniform elevation of 800 ft. By sunset it has quite a mountainous appearance, and with the long vista of the river in the one direction, of the coast in the other, with the woods of Powderham in the middle distance, and the bright broad sands and glistening waves in the foreground, forms a picture of which the inhabitants may well be proud. This view from the *Beacon* (or rather from the Beacon Walks) is the principal thing to be seen at Exmouth. The *Beacon Walks* are cut on the slope of the hill, and in a hanging shrubbery, planted for public use by the late Lord Rolle. They form a delightful promenade, and add not a little to the beauty of the prospect, by framing it, as it were, in trees. Another walk and drive extend for a distance of 1800 ft. along the *Strand*, which is bounded by a very substantial sea-wall, and was the munificent gift of the late Lord Rolle. From these walks the stranger may notice the sand-bank called the *Warren*, which straitens the mouth of the estuary, and is connected with a *bar* which has only a depth of 8 ft. of water over it at low tide. These sands appear to have accumulated in modern times, for in the reign of Edw. III. Exmouth was a port of some consequence, contributing 10 ships to the fleet which assembled before Calais. In the year 1001 it was burnt by the Danes.

Among the seats and villas in the neighbourhood may be noticed *Bystock* (E. Divett, Esq., M.P. for Exeter); *Courtlands*, on the shore of the estuary (W. F. Spicer, Esq.); *St. John's Cottage* (C. Sanders, Esq.); *Bassett Park* (C. Wheaton, Esq.), encircled by the most beautiful grounds; and *A-la-Ronde* (Miss Parminter), a house as fanciful in construction as in name, the rooms being arranged around a central octagon hall, and fitted with sliding-shutters instead of doors. In its vicinity an almshouse founded for 4 poor old maids by the late Mrs. Parminter; it is called *Point-in-view*, and bears the motto "Some point in view we all pursue."

The *excursions* from Exmouth are numerous. The visitor can cross the ferry to *Dawlish, Teignmouth, Powderham Castle, Haldon,* &c. On this side of the water he can wander to *Orcomb Point;—to Littleham* (a Dec. wooden ch. screen) and *Budleigh Salterton;* —to the pretty village of *Withycombe,* and the dilapidated *Ch. of St. John in the Wilderness*, about 2½ m. N.E., which is the mother ch. of the neighbourhood, and said to have been called the Chapel of St. Michael in the reign of Hen. VIII.; and from this spot — where there is a noble old yew in the chyard—he can proceed to *Woodbury Common,* and its camp. From Exmouth it is a pleasant drive to Exeter, but the usual way of reaching that city is by rly. (Exeter and Exmouth line—see the next route). The tourist may also pass the river to Starcross, and there take the S. Devon rail. Another agreeable mode of proceeding as far as Topsham is by boat.

ROUTE 5.

EXETER TO EXMOUTH.—LONDON AND
S. W. RAILWAY.— BRANCH LINE,
QUEEN-STREET STATION, EXETER.

This rly., 10¾ m. in length, follows throughout its course the l. bank of the estuary of the Exe. Fine views are commanded of the opposite bank, with the heights of Haldon rising behind it.

Between Exeter and Topsham is seen l. *Weir House*, the seat of the Duckworths. On the pillars of the park-gate are 2 of the stone shot which struck the Royal George in the passage of the Dardanelles, 1807. One weighs 590 lbs. Another shot, which fell into the sea, swept every man from a gun, killing 3, wounding 27 and the first-lieutenant. But the Windsor Castle was struck by a more terrific missile. It was a stone shot, as the others, but of enormous size. In diam. it measured 27½ inches, and it weighed 850 lbs.

5½ m. *Topsham* Stat. Here the rly. crosses the river *Clyst*, which at this point joins the Exe. It rises, from many springs, on the high ground, of which the hill of Hembury Fort (near Honiton) forms a portion, and which is the watershed of that division of the county.

The town of *Topsham* (Topa's ham or home.—*Inns:* Salutation ; Globe), before the completion of the ship canal in 1544, was the only port of Exeter, and had a larger trade with Newfoundland than any other town in the kingdom. In very early times the river is said to have been navigable as far as Exeter; and there is a tradition that Isabella de Redvers, Countess of Devon, to revenge herself upon that city for an affront, cut down the trees which were growing near Powderham, and, throwing them into the river, so choked the channel. In 1643 the Earl of Warwick attempted to land a force at Topsham for the relief of Exeter, which was besieged by the royalists. But after pouring shot from his ships with little effect for 3 or 4 hours, the tide fell, and he was forced to retire and abandon 3 of his vessels which had taken the ground. In 1645 Topsham was made head-quarters by Fairfax, before he removed to Ottery. The stranger should notice the views from the *Strand* and the *Ch.* This building, which has been restored, but is of little interest, contains 2 monuments by *Chantrey*, in memory of the gallant Admiral Sir J. T. Duckworth, Bart., G.C.B., and of his son, Colonel George Duckworth, who fell at Albuera.

[1¼ m. N.E. of Topsham is *Clyst St. George*, an interesting Perp. ch., which has been thoroughly restored by the Rev. H. C. Ellacombe, one of the most ardent Campanologists in the country. There is much stained glass; the soffete of the chancel arch has been inlaid with serpentine and various marbles. The modern schools adjoining are picturesque and good in design.

Clyst Heath, in the parish of *Clyst St. Mary*, N. of Clyst St. George, was the scene of the defeat of the rebels by Lord Russell in the reign of Edward VI. Adjoining the village is *Winslade House*, H. Porter, Esq. The ch. of Clyst St. Mary is entirely without interest.]

Still coasting the estuary, the line reaches 7 m. *Woodbury road Station.* The village is distant 2 m., and Woodbury Castle (see Rte. 4) somewhat farther.

l. is seen *Nutwell Court* (Sir T. T. F. E. Drake, Bart.). Here there is a portrait of the "old warrior," Sir Francis Drake, wearing a miniature of Queen Elizabeth, which was given to Drake by the queen herself. This very miniature, the work of Vicentio Vicentini, is in the possession of Sir Trayton Drake, with other relics.

8½ m. *Lympstone.* The village is famous for its oysters, and whitebait may be eaten here in its season. The *Church* is Perp., with a good west tower.

10¾ m. *Exmouth.* The stat. is close to the town; an omnibus runs hence twice a day to Budleigh Salterton, 5 m. distant.

From the station there is a very striking view across the Exe to Haldon; at sunset it is magnificent.

For Exmouth see Rte. 4.

ROUTE 6.

EXETER TO LAUNCESTON, BY OKEHAMPTON. (NEIGHBOURHOOD OF OKEHAMPTON, LIDFORD, BRENT TOR.)

(A branch rly. is in progress (1865) from the Yeoford Stat., on the N. Devon Rly., to Okehampton. From Okehampton it will be continued to Lidford, where it joins the rly. (also in progress) from Tavistock to Launceston. This will be, when the rlys. are completed, the shortest and most convenient way of approaching Okehampton, Launceston, and Tavistock from Exeter; and it will also afford a shorter (and very picturesque) line from Exeter to Plymouth, than by the S. Devon Rly.

There will also be branch lines in connection with the Okehampton Rly. by Hatherleigh and Holsworthy to Bude Haven; and by Hatherleigh to Torrington and Bideford, where the line will join the N. Devon Rly.) The existing turnpike-road from Exeter to Okehampton takes the following route.

The road leaves Exeter by its western suburb, crossing the Exe by St. Thomas's Bridge. From the banks of the river it gradually rises so as to command one of the finest views of Exeter, and then descends very sharply, by a deep cutting, into the vale of Ide, which, with its green hillsides and flourishing orchards, forms a pleasant introduction into Devonshire.

9 About 1 m. to the l. *Fulford House* (B. Fulford, Esq., but not at present inhabited by him), dating from the reign of Eliz., and situated in a picturesque park, in which is a beautiful *beech avenue* well worth the artist's attention. The estate has been the seat of the Fulfords since the time of Rich. I. In the Rebellion the house was garrisoned for the king, but taken by Fairfax Dec. 1645. It is now in a sad state of decay, but still contains family portraits and a full-length of Charles I. The Fulford monuments are in the neighbouring ch. of *Dunsford*, the most interesting being for Sir Thomas Fulford, 1610. This monument has been restored and freshly coloured. The ch. contains Perp. (nave) and Dec. (chancel) portions, and a very good Perp. font. It has been well and judiciously restored, stained glass inserted, &c.

1 At a distance of ½ m. to the rt. the Perp. tower and ch. of *Cheriton Bishop*. The tower is fine, and one of the best in the district. There are some fragments of old glass in the ch. and good modern windows by *Hardman*. The E. window is early Dec., and there are some in the N. aisle of the same date. On the road is *Cheriton Cross*, a granite fragment by the wayside, and an innkeeper bearing the singular geological patronymic of "Lias."

Passing the hamlet of *Crockern Well*, where is a large and rough but conveniently situated *Inn*,—

1½ A lane on the l. leads to *Drewsteignton* (1 m.), and *Fingle Bridge.* (Rte. 12.) rt. *Fuidge House*, seat of J. Norris, Esq., and *Spreyton*, with its weird old oak-tree 40 ft. in circumf.

1½ About 2 m. on the l., and close to the road from Moreton to Okehampton, is the *cromlech* called the

Spinsters' Rock. (See Rte. 12.) 4 m. beyond we reach the village of *Sticklepath* (i. e. steep road, A.-S. *stigele,* steep. *Stickle* is the west country word for a *rapid.* Stickles and ranges are respectively the rough shallows and smooth reaches of a stream). Rt. is the village of S. Tawton (on the Taw river), with a good Perp. ch. At Sticklepath there is an inn, where the traveller should rest and consult the Handbook; for this village is a good starting-point for the ascent of *Cawsand Beacon,* or *Cosdon* (its old name). There are some antiquities, too, in the neighbourhood, and fine moorland scenes near *Belstone* and in the gorge from which the Taw issues. (Even if the tourist proceed at once to Okehampton, 4 m. further, he will find Sticklepath one of the best points from which to ascend Cawsand.)

Ascent of Cawsand Beacon. At the W. end of the village, l. of the road, is a granite *cross,* rudely sculptured, and from that ancient guide-post a path will lead the traveller along the river-bank to *Taw Marsh,* where the peculiar scenery of the border is displayed in perfection. The swampy vale is wildly decked with grey stones; *clatters,* or the débris of rocks, stream down the neighbouring slopes; whilst aloft in the blue air stand the giant tors. From this valley (whose peaty soil entombs the oak and the birch) the pedestrian can steer direct for the summit of Cosdon, which commands an amazing view. On a clear day the Bristol Channel may be seen; but the English Channel from Teignmouth to the Start is commonly visible. Dartmoor is, however, the most impressive feature of the prospect. Far and wide stretch its desolate hills, the ancient haunt of wolves and wild deer, and barbarians as untamed; a solitary wondrous region, everywhere darkened by morasses, but piled with fantastic rocks and glowing with innumerable tints. To the W. will be seen Yes Tor, the highest hill in the South of England; to the S. the rocks of Heytor; and to the S.W. the grand central wilderness of deeply-fissured bog, in which lie concealed the mysterious pool of *Cranmere,* and the fountains of the rivers Dart, Taw, Teign, Okement, and Tavy. On the summit of Cosdon is an enormous *cairn,* on which beacon-fires are supposed to have been formerly kindled. There are some remains, too, of *kistvaens,* and a small circular *pound;* and on the slope of the hill, nearly opposite Belstone Tor, a number of *hut circles.* The village of *Throwleigh* will be observed below Cawsand Beacon on the E. Its lofty Perp. ch. tower is perhaps the finest in the district. The ch. itself (entirely Perp.) has been (1862) restored, but contains nothing of special interest (except an unusually enriched priest's door S. of the chancel). W. of Throwleigh church about ½ m. is *Shelstone Pound,* in the midst of the site of a British village. This enclosure is in a very perfect state, and formed by a ring of stones, about 7 ft. thick and 3 ft. high.

4 m. *Okehampton,* commonly called *Ockington (Inn:* White Hart). This little town is conveniently placed for excursions on the moor, lying immediately under the N. flank of Yes Tor, within an easy distance of wild and rugged scenery, and upon the conflux of the 2 heads of the *Okement river,* well known, like most of the streams of this county, for their excellent though small trout. The town lies in a valley, and is a place of about 2000 Inhab., disfranchised by the Reform Bill. It presents nothing of interest, except perhaps its *Chapel of Ease,* with a granite tower of Perp. date, and some fragments of carved seats within. The *Parish Ch.* stands on a height to the N.W. It was burnt down 1842, but has been well rebuilt—Hayward of Exeter architect. The Vicarage, adjoining the Ch., is very picturesquely placed.

The *Castle* is situated 1 m. S.W., in the W. Okement valley, close to the Launceston road. It occupies the summit and eastern slope of a tongue of rock, isolated by an artificial cut on the W. side, by a natural ravine on the N., and by the valley of the Okement on the S. side. Its position is very strong, and the view from it of the dell of the brawling river—and of the skirt of Dartmoor, once the Castle Park or Chace, is extremely wild and beautiful. The loftiest part of the ruin is a small quadrangular keep, of which a fragment resembles some time-worn crag, and is inclined from the S.W. as if bent by the prevailing winds. It is prettily tinted, and in one of the adjoining walls is a curious recess or oratory. Below are the remains of the great hall, which will be distinguished by the huge old chimney, and of numerous chambers, including part of a chapel, with a piscina. The keep may be Norm. The lower buildings seem to range between E. Dec. and Perp. The ruins form a picturesque and interesting group.

The reputed founder of this border castle was Baldwin de Brionis, created Earl of Devon by the Conqueror. It afterwards, with other estates, came to Richard de Redvers, or Rivers, and from him by inheritance to the Courtenays, who held it with a forfeiture under Edw. IV., and a restoration under Henry VII., and a second forfeiture in the person of Henry Courtenay under Hen. VIII., and a second restoration under Mary, until, in the reign of Charles I., it descended by marriage to the Mohuns, who became Barons of Okehampton, and failed in 1712. Long before that period the castle had ceased to be a residence of its lord. In the reign of Henry VIII. it was dismantled, and the chace disparked, and from that time to the present the bats and owls have been the only occupants of the ruin, which has recently been purchased by Sir R. R. Vyvyan, Bart. A *cross-course*, containing lead and silver, is worked on the bank of the river below the castle.

A weekly *Market* is held at Okehampton on Saturdays, and, from the circumstance of the oat being the principal grain which is grown on the high or poor land in the neighbourhood, the supply of this article is very abundant, and the price unusually low. S. of the town the Okement flows through the woods of *Okelands* (— Holley, Esq.).

Those who take delight in moorland scenery should make the ascent of *Yes Tor* (probably a corruption of *East* Tor), the highest hill on Dartmoor (and in England south of Skiddaw), and 2050 ft. above the level of the sea. The summit is about 5 m. from Okehampton, and best reached by the valley of the W. Okement (rt. bank), which for the first 3 m. is of considerable width, its sloping declivities presenting happy contrasts of wildness and cultivation. After a short ascent from the town the traveller will enter *Okehampton Park*, a rough hillside, which still preserves in its name the memory of the barons' chace, and where enormous furze-bushes, old hawthorns, and hollies, remain as memorials of former times; and where, on the brow of the hill, is *Fitz's Well*, a spring, it is said, of marvellous virtues, and to which it was once the custom for young persons to resort on the morning of Easter-day. The castle will be observed on the bank of the river, and a little beyond it a view is obtained of the old ruin in the foreground, the town in the middle distance, and woods and blue hills filling in the background. Okehampton Park is the scene of the nightly penance of Lady Howard. (See *Tavistock*, Rte. 13.) At a distance of about 3 m. the valley contracts to a glen, and a turn in the path opens to view the mossy water-wheel of *Meldon Quarry*, a huge and deep excavation in limestone, which you should cross the stream to examine. On the l. the hills are divided by a rough moorland cavity, remarkable for a white granite of peculiar character, of which a specimen may be seen in London, in the Museum of Practical Geology (Piccadilly). It is of so fine a texture, and so pure a white, that it has been employed in the sculpture of chimneypieces. ¼ m. beyond the quarry, look back at the view. In another ¼ m. the glen divides, and at a solitary cottage (where a search has been unsuccessfully made for ore) the traveller leaves the Okement, and turns to the l. up a deep hollow, which is abruptly closed by a steep acclivity. When this is surmounted he finds himself upon the upland of Yes Tor, a wilderness of bog and granite, through which he may at will direct his steps towards the summit, which is now visible, and marked by piles of stones; but he is advised to diverge a little to the rt., to some rocks called *Great Black Tor*, and to look down upon the course of the W. Okement, where the scene may remind him of some of the Highland glens. The summit of Yes Tor commands an extraordinary prospect. On the one side lies extended the hazy area of N. Devon and a great part of Cornwall, sunset defining by darker tints the mountainous region of Brown Willy: on the other, an expanse so wild and desolate as almost to defy description. The traveller looks into the heart of Dartmoor, and sees lengthening before him gloomy ridges which stretch for miles, and are so entirely covered with bog as to be inaccessible for many months in the year. The morasses occupy the summits as well as the slopes, and are everywhere rent by deep black chasms, which, intersecting each other, cover the hills like a net. To the E. (at a distance of about 4 m.) is the hillside of *Cawsand Beacon*, which will excite astonishment by the extent of its surface : to the S.W., beyond the intervening gorge of the W. Okement, the summit of *Great Links* (or Lynx; Lynnick, *Corn.* marshy?) *Tor*, resembling the ruins of walls. The S. side of Yes Tor is scored with long lines or *streams* of granite stones,—such as Creswick loves to paint,—which important items of a wild scene, from the remoteness of the locality, have hitherto escaped the quarryman. From the valley on this flank of Yes Tor may be observed some rocks which bear a whimsical resemblance to works of art, viz. on a low eminence (E. side), a tor which will undoubtedly be mistaken for the ruins of a tower; and on the hill-top (W. side) an isolated mass of granite, so true in outline to the figure of a huge recumbent animal, that it might be supposed to have originated the name of Great Lynx Tor. These chance resemblances are best seen from the S. end of the valley. Those who desire a more intimate acquaintance with the moor may trace the W. Okement to its source in *Cranmere Pool*, called "the mother of rivers," under the popular idea that it contains the fountains of the Taw, the Dart, the Tavy, and the E. and W. Okement; but, in fact, these rivers, with the exception of the W. Okement, flow from morasses which cover the neighbouring hills. The miraculous pool was never above 220 yds. in circumf., and is now partially, if not entirely, drained by the removal of peat from its banks. It is invested with a certain mystery, which has probably arisen from its isolation in the midst of such desolate bogs, and from the many fruitless attempts made by travellers to discover it. The name occurs in other parts of England (for instance, in Woolmer Forest, Hants), and, according to De Luc, signifies the *lake of cranes*. Should the traveller fancy this bold adventure of tracing the W. Okement to its fountain-head, let him move obedient to the following directions, which may prevent his being checkmated at the confluence of the tributaries with the main stream. We suppose him under the N. side of Yes Tor on the bank of the river. At the 1st confluence the W. Okement is the stream on the rt., at the 2nd on the l., 3rd on the l., 4th on the rt., 5th on the rt., 6th on the rt., 7th on the rt., 8th on the l. Another bold walk may be taken across the moor to *Prince's Town* or *Two Bridges*, the traveller steering by compass, or following the course of the streams, if provided with a good map; but such excursions are attended with hazard in unsettled weather, as this elevated region is frequently enveloped in mist for a week or a fortnight at a time.

The visitor to Okehampton should also ascend *Cawsand Beacon*, alt. 1792 ft., and explore the valley of the E. Okement, which is rich in wild rocky scenery, particularly about the village of *Belstone*, 2 m. distant. The river comes roaring down *Belstone Cleave* over a solid floor of granite, and in the glen of *St. Michael of Halstock*, near Belstone, meets the *Blackaven* from the uplands of Yes Tor. Here is *Chapel Ford*, which preserves in its name the memory of the ancient shrine of St. Michael, of which there is no other vestige. Belstone Tor is rather more than a mile above Chapel Ford; and on the W. side of this hill is a sacred circle called *the Nine Stones*, but consisting of 17, the highest of which is barely 2½ ft. above the ground. The tradition common to such monuments belongs to them, that they were human beings converted into stone for merrymaking on the Sabbath. They are said to dance every day at noon, and, though a pity to mar so pretty a fancy, it may be easily explained. Currents of air then rise from the heated surface of the moor, and give an appearance of a tremulous motion to objects near the ground. Belstone *ch*. contains Norman work, and is traditionally said to have been built by Baldwin de Brionüs. The tower is singularly low.

Between Okehampton and Tavistock are three of the most remarkable objects in the county, viz. *Lidford Bridge*, *Lidford Cascade*, and *Brent Tor*. The village of Lidford is 9 m. from Okehampton, and the road to it runs over elevated ground under the escarpment of Dartmoor. In 6 m. the traveller reaches a few cottages, collectively known by the name of *Lake*, where, l. of the road, in a deep gully, is a small copper-mine called *Tor Wood*, deserving notice for its water-wheel and picturesque locality; and on the neighbouring heights *Granate Tor*, very beautifully covered with snow-white lichens, which show that the rock is not granite, although the name would seem to imply it. About 2 m. from Lake the road crosses *Vale Down*, a projection from Dartmoor, beyond which a lane on the rt. leads in ½ m. to

Lidford. (The only house deserving the name of *Inn* is the Dartmoor Arms on the high road, 1 m. from the village.) The stranger will learn with surprise that before the Conquest this group of "ragged cottages, cold, treeless, and unprotected," was one of the principal towns in Devonshire, and the seat of a mint, which, however, was worked only for a short time, and principally through the reign of Ethelred II. In the Domesday Book it is described as taxed in the same manner as London itself; and Sir William Pole mentions it as "the principal town of the stannary." Edw. II. conferred the manor and castle of Lidford upon his favourite, Piers de Gaveston. At the present day the chief interest of the place is derived from its position, as it stands in full view of the western front of Dartmoor. It belongs to the duchy of Cornwall, and the parish includes the entire forest of Dartmoor—53,900 acres—with a Pop. of only 933. The objects of curiosity are the ruin of a *castle*, an old weather-beaten *church*, and a *bridge* which is one of the wonders of the county.

The *Castle*, however, scarcely merits notice, except as a feature in a distant view of the village, being merely the shell of a square tower on a mound by the roadside. It is of evil notoriety as an ancient prison of the Stannary Court, and in 1512 was described in an act of Parl. as " one of the most heinous, contagious, and detestable places in the realm." The Stannary Court, which was held in it until late in the last centy., was of no better repute, for its proceedings are said to have been so arbitrary in their character that "hang first and try afterwards" was the fundamental maxim of "Lydford law." Accordingly Browne the poet, a native of Tavistock, has given us the following humorous description :—

" I've ofttimes heard of Lydford law,
How in the morn they hang and draw,
And sit in judgment after ;
At first I wonder'd at it much,
But since, I've found the matter such
That it deserves no laughter.
They have a castle on a hill ;
I took it for an old windmill,
The vanes blown off by weather.
To lie therein one night 'tis guess'd
'Twere better to be stoned or press'd,
Or hang'd, ere you come hither."

Some have derived "Lydford law" from "the strange acts of tyranny" committed by Sir Richard Grenville (Charles I.) when governor of the castle, but the phrase had a much earlier origin, as it occurs in the curious poem on the deposition of Richard II., edited by Mr. Wright. The Stannary Courts had great privileges, and their customs were no doubt of extreme antiquity; hence, except among the miners, they were in no very good repute. The infamous Jeffreys presided as judge at Lidford, and the inhabitants affirm that his ghost to this day occasionally visits the old court-room in the shape of a black pig. The castle was founded at a period subsequent to the Conquest, and by charter of Edw. I. was made the Stannary Prison for Devonshire. In 1650 it was dilapidated. There is a tradition of a subterranean passage leading from it to the neighbouring ravine.

The *Ch.* (in the style of the 15th centy., and containing a primitive font) is close to the castle, and commands a magnificent view, particularly of the long front of Dartmoor with its giant tors. In the churchyard the stranger will notice an old tombstone resembling a cromlech, and the following curious specimen of sepulchral wit inscribed on a tomb by the porch.

"Here lies in horizontal position the outside case of George Routleigh, watchmaker; whose abilities in that line were an honour to his profession. Integrity was the mainspring, and prudence the regulator, of all the actions of his life. Humane, generous, and liberal, his hand never stopped till he had relieved distress. So nicely regulated were all his motions that he never went wrong, except when set a going by people who did not know his key. Even then he was easily set right again. He had the art of disposing his time so well, that his hours glided away in one continual round of pleasure and delight, till an unlucky minute put a period to his existence. He departed this life Nov. 4, 1802, aged 57, wound up in hopes of being taken in hand by his Maker, and of being thoroughly cleaned and repaired and set a going in the world to come."

A short descent leads from the ch. to *Lidford Bridge*, which in point of situation much resembles that of the Pont y Monach, or Devil's Bridge, in Cardiganshire. It consists of a single arch, which is thrown across a frightful cleft or ravine; the country in its vicinity, though open and bleak, being cultivated and disposed in such gentle undulations, that the traveller would never suspect the vicinity of such a chasm. Many persons have in fact passed over the bridge without being aware that it was an object of curiosity. The river Lyd, rising on Dartmoor, here worms its way through a cleft about 70 ft. deep, but not more than a few yards in breadth, and so narrow towards the bottom that the struggling stream can be scarcely discerned in noonday. To obtain a good view of the singular scene, it is necessary to scramble as far as practicable down the rocks. The visitor should also ascend the course of the river (about 1 m.) to *Kitt's Fall*, a small cascade named (says tradition) from the circumstance of a young woman called Catherine, or Kitty, having been drowned near it in attempting to cross the stream when swollen by rain; and, if an antiquary, 1½ m. farther, to the basement of an *ancient hut*, of which both the form and construction are uncommon It is situated on the river-bank, below *Doe Tor*. The shape is rectangular, and the stones set face to face.

A story is told of a person who arrived at Lidford from Tavistock late one night, and much to the astonishment of the inhabitants, as the bridge had been lately broken town. The traveller, however, had remarked nothing more than that his horse had made a sudden spring. Upon being afterwards shown the fearful chasm which he had thus unconsciously passed, it may be imagined with what mingled sensations he contemplated the danger he had so narrowly escaped. Another incident connected with this bridge is related of a Captain Williams, who, having determined upon destroying himself, rode at night from Exeter to Lidford Bridge, and, as was afterwards discovered by the marks on the road, endeavoured to spur his horse over the parapet. The horse, however, refused the leap, for he was the next day found loose on the road; but the saddle and bridle were discovered entangled among the trees, and it is supposed that Captain Williams, in the vain hope of concealing the wilfulness of his desperate act, threw them into the ravine before he sprung into it himself. In the reign of Charles I. Lidford glen would have often afforded subjects for the pencil of a Salvator—savage rocks, wild woods, and outlaws, for the neighbourhood was the favourite haunt of Roger Rowle, the Robin Hood of the West. He was the leader of the *Gubbins*, a gang of broken men, with the like of whom the remoter parts of England were then greatly infested. "Gubbins' land," says old Fuller, "is a Scythia within England, and they pure heathens therein. Their language is the drosse of the dregs of the vulgar Devonian. They hold together like burrs; offend one, and all will revenge his quarrel."

At Lidford the traveller has entered the *mining-field* which lies between Dartmoor and the Tamar, and several mines of copper, manganese, and lead are scattered over the country in the vicinity of this village and Brent Tor.

Lidford Cascade is situated immediately rt. of the Tavistock road, 1½ m. from Lidford. It is in one of the prettiest spots imaginable, although the seclusion has been materially injured by the Tavistock and Launceston rly., which runs through this wooded glen. A small stream which has its source on *Blackdown* here slides about 110 ft. down a darkcoloured schistose slope to join the Lyd in its deep ravine. The adjoining ledges are mantled with trees, and the scene of so soft and tranquil a character as to contrast delightfully with the rough moorland views from the higher grounds. A zigzag walk has been cut to the foot of the cascade; and a miller, who lives hard by, keeps the key of this approach, and a certain quantity of water ponded back, which, by the magic of sixpence, may be made to spring over the fall, to which it gives

Route 6.—Brent Tor.

an imposing volume and impetuosity. Observe the view from the top of the winding descent, where the village and castle of Lidford are seen in connection with the wild front of Dartmoor, the lower parts of the picture being occupied by the wooded ravine of the Lyd. "The fall of the river," says Gilpin, "is the least considerable part of the scenery."

Brent Tor, or the *Burnt Tor* (2½ m. beyond Lidford Cascade, on the road to Tavistock, and in alt. 1100 ft.), is an outlying peak of the great Dartmoor range, from which it is now further separated by cultivation. It is truly a most singular eminence; it is capped by a church, and when seen from a distance, grouped with other Dartmoor hills, resembles in shape a flame starting upwards from the earth. This conical form and its mineral formation have excited much discussion among geologists. Some have seen in Brent Tor the crater of an extinct volcano (*red jasper* may be found in blocks on the N. side of the hill), and there is but little doubt that its substance is of igneous origin, and identical with other rocks intermixed with the carbonaceous deposits, and termed *volcanic ash* by De la Beche. The name of the hill is thus singularly appropriate; but it doubtless originated in beacon-fires, which anciently "flamed amazement" from this frontier summit. It is an obsolete word, used by Spenser and other old writers, and derived from the Saxon *brennan*, to burn. The ch., called *St. Michael de Rupe* in old records (of which one dates as early as 1283), is a curious little weather-worn structure, about 40 ft. in length by 14 in breadth, with a roof of oak, and lighted by 3 small windows. The building is very plain, but is apparently E. Eng., as the low western tower (32 ft. high) certainly is. It was attached to the great Benedictine Abbey of Tavistock. It stands on the verge of a precipice, and in a diminutive churchyard, containing a few mouldering gravestones. An erroneous idea has been very generally entertained, that in digging burial-places at this spot the rock is found to be so saturated with moisture that the excavation is in a short time filled with water. The fact is, however, the ground is as dry here as in other churchyards; and the notion doubtless originated in an incident which occurred after a heavy fall of rain, when, a coffin being brought for interment, the grave was found partly filled with water, which had been directed into it by the shoot from the roof of the ch. There is, however, no lack of water on the hill; as on its eastern side a spring gushes forth which has been never known to fail; and the village of N. Brentor is supplied by wells, some of which are 10 fath. deep. To return to the little ch., which bears every mark of antiquity and the weather, to which it is so exposed. Its erection is attributed by tradition to a merchant, who, overtaken by a storm at sea, resorted to the expedient of bribing the interference of a saint by the promise of a ch., which he vowed to build upon the first point of land which should appear in sight. This happened to be the lofty peak of Brent Tor, and here, accordingly, he founded his ch. But there is another version of the story, which places the building originally at the foot of the hill, and attributes its removal to that busybody the Devil, who, being "prince of the powers of the air," carried the ch. to the summit, which lay in his own dominions. No sooner, however, had the edifice been dedicated to St. Michael, than the archangel ousted the enemy, and, tumbling him down hill, sent a huge rock flying at his heels, and this, it is said, may be seen to this day at the base of the tor. There is a similarity in the situation of this building and those of the chapels on the *mounts* of St. Michael on the coasts of Cornwall and Normandy. The 3 churches are dedicated to St. Michael; such elevated sites being often selected as significant of the archangel's position at the head of the angelic hierarchy. In ancient times the abbots of Tavistock held an annual Michaelmas fair on Brent Tor. Observe a curious monumental stone on the exterior of the ch. On the single bell is a curious inscription—" Gallus vocor ego, solus super omne sono." The view of the moor from this elevated spot is truly delightful. When the sun shines brightly, the spectral appearance and delicate tints of these barren hills are remarkable. The most conspicuous summits of this, the western, front of Dartmoor are *Great Links Tor* in the N., capped by masses of granite, resembling the walls of a fortress; *Hare Tor* nearly opposite, distinguished by the beauty of its conical form; and *Great Mis Tor*, one of the most imposing of the Dartmoor hills, about 4 m. farther S. In the direction of Hare Tor the traveller looks up the valley of the Tavy, or *Tavy Cleave*, and upon a cloud of miners' huts, marking the site of the great copper-mine of

Huel Friendship. This mine is well worth a visit, and is no great distance from Brent Tor. It is highly remunerative to the adventurers, and curious as being entirely worked by water. The machinery kept in action by this motive-power is on the largest scale; and the manner in which the element is economised and made to traverse every part of the surface, so as to turn a number of colossal wheels, and to perform other labours, shows great ingenuity. The mine is provided with a steam-engine, as a precaution against a drought; but the supply of water is seldom deficient. The high road from Tavistock to Exeter passes through the works.

The valley of the Tavy (see *Tavistock*, Rte. 13) abounds in picturesque scenery. The stream is of a very beautiful character, the limpid water flowing over schistose rocks, which occupy its bed in masses. If inclined for a wild excursion, you may ascend the river to the source of its northern branch on Dartmoor, passing under the escarpment of Hare Tor. It lies on a boggy platform, immediately above the valley previously described as on the southern flank of Yes Tor (p. 46). You can then ascend Yes Tor, and pass down the valley of the W. Okement to Okehampton. Another walk may be taken over the moor by *Cranmere Pool* (Rte. 14) to Okehampton, or by Great Mis Tor to Prince's Town.

Having returned to Okehampton after this long digression, and proceeding again towards Launceston,—

The road passes the Castle on the l., and, skirting Dartmoor for some distance, commands the numerous tors which crown the detached summits.

4 From *Sourton Down* a road branches off on the l. to Lidford and Tavistock.

2½ *Bridestow.* The churchyard has a curious gateway, formed from a Norm. arch removed from an earlier ch. The present ch. dates about 1450, and contains a good roodscreen of wood, surmounted by the royal arms, which fill up the chancel arch. It is dedicated to St. Bridget (St. Bride), hence the name of the parish. On the l. is *Leawood House* (S. C. Hamlyn, Esq.); and beyond the village, on the rt., and situated in a pretty valley, *Millaton*, the house of J. G. Newton, Esq., which contains a *collection of stuffed birds*, including the following rare specimens, procured on Dartmoor, or in its immediate vicinity—the merlin, grey shrike, golden oriole, hawfinch, parrot crossbill, great black woodpecker, wryneck, red-legged partridge, little egret, and little crake. Further towards Lifton, on rt., is *Haine Castle* (Mrs. Harris).

DEVONSHIRE. *Route 7.—Exeter to Plymouth.* 53

8½ *Lifton.* The Ch. is Perp., with a good Norm. font. In this neighbourhood the Lyd and two other trout-streams effect a junction. About 3 m. S. are *Kelly House* (A. Kelly, Esq.), and *ch.* with good ancient stained glass, and *Bradstone Manor-house*, an old Tudor building approached through a gatehouse. The latter was formerly a seat of the Cloberry family, but is now tenanted by a farmer.

l. *Lifton Park* (H. Blagrove, Esq.), an ancient possession of the Arundel family, whose quarterings are suspended in the village.

1½ *Poulston.* Here the traveller will cross the Tamar, although "there passeth a pleasant tradition," says Fuller, "how there standeth on Poulston Bridge a man of great strength and stature, with a black bill in his hand, ready to knock down all the *lawyers* that should offer to plant themselves in the county of Cornwall." In about 2 m., however, whether lawyer or not, he will in these days reach the old town of *Launceston.* (Rte. 21.)

ROUTE 7.

EXETER TO PLYMOUTH.—(DAWLISH, TEIGNMOUTH, NEWTON, TOTNES, IVY BRIDGE, AND THEIR NEIGHBOURHOODS.)

South Devon Rly. (St. David's Stat.—*see* Rte. 1—Exeter).

The S. Devon Railway, an interesting line to travel over, from its vicinity to the sea, and one of the most picturesque in England, was originally laid down as an atmospheric line, and the numerous engine-houses, designed with much taste, still remain as monuments of an experiment which cost the company 364,000*l.*, total loss.

Leaving the *St. David's Station*, the line crosses by a low timber bridge to the rt. bank of the Exe. l. is seen the line of railway connecting St. David's stat. with that in Queen-street (S. Western, and Exmouth rlwys.), and on rising ground a part of the suburbs of Exeter; above, on a higher hill, are the lofty trees and buildings of the castle and the old walls of the town. Winding round the high ground on which Exeter is built, we reach *St. Thomas' Stat.*, communicating with the W. end of the city.

The line next traverses the marshes, leaving close on the rt. the red tower (Perp. and turreted) of *Alphington Ch.*, known for its Norman font with carved bowl, of early date. The carving is said to represent St. Michael and the dragon. The font was copied for the Temple ch., London. The chancel-screen is late (circ. 1672?) and of no interest. The ch. is generally fine, and well placed; the ancient shield and supporters of the Courtenays may be traced on the porch. Near the ch. is a very pretty valley and trout-stream, and opposite Alphington, on the l., the embankment of the *Exeter Ship Canal.*

3 rt. close to the road the *Devon County Lunatic Asylum*, long under the excellent management of Dr. Bucknill.

5 rt. *Exminster.* The ch. is Perp., with a good screen.—l., across the river, the town of *Topsham*, with its white houses, ch., and shipping.

[2½ m. rt. is *Kenn* ch., Perp., in which is a good carved screen]. In this neighbourhood are limestone-quarries, and contortions of the strata which may be observed in the cuttings of the road. *Peamore House*, a fine old mansion, is the seat of S. T. Kekewich, Esq., M.P.

2 The line approaches *Powderham* (Earl of Devon). First is seen the *Belvidere*, a prospect-tower, erected on an eminence near the castle, and commanding delightful views.

Next the *Ch.*, a Perp. building, with triple chancel, or aisles of equal projection, a common arrangement in the west. It dates from about 1470, but is of no very high interest. In the S. aisle is the monument, with effigy of Isabella de Fortibus (?), Countess of Devon temp. Hen. III. There are also modern monuments and memorial windows for Harriet Countess of Devon, d. 1839; and the Hon. T. P. Courtenay. Much has been done for this ch. of late years; and an E. E. chapel at Cofton in this parish, long in ruins, has been restored by the Courtenay family. Finally, the *Park* and *Castle* appear. The park covers a large tract of undulating ground, and its woods of oak stretch their branches to the very brink of the estuary. The Castle is well seen, but will probably disappoint, as the walls look so fresh in their coats of plaster, that it is difficult to believe they have formed the seat of the "imperial family" for the last 500 years, and before that of the Bohuns, the maternal ancestors of the Courtenays. Powderham is, in truth, one of the oldest places in the county. It was founded at the distant period of the Conquest (by William Count of Eu, who also built the castle of Hastings), and has belonged to the Courtenays since the year 1377. In the Rebellion it was garrisoned and armed, and captured more than once by the contending parties. Among the *pictures* here are Courtenay Earl of Devon temp. Eliz., 3-quarter—engraved in Lodge; General Monk, 3-quarter; Lady Honywood and child, and Lady Courtenay, by *Sir Joshua Reynolds;* Dr. Markham; and Cyril Jackson. There are some pleasant gardens at a short distance from the castle.

On the opposite shore are the woods of *Nutwell Court*, and the pretty village or town of *Lympstone*.

[1¼ m. rt. of Powderham is *Kenton*. Here there is a very fine Perp. ch., which will repay a visit. On the exterior, the S. aisle, with porch and parvise chamber, should be noticed. The aisle has butresses with pinnacles. There is a good rood turret. The S. porch is ornamented with a profusion of niches, and is stone groined. The W. tower, 100 ft. high, is fine. *Within*, there is a superb screen, of the same date as the ch.—the base panelled, and painted with figures of saints. The ch. was no doubt built by the Courtenays, who have long been proprietors of the manor. *Oxton House* (Major-Gen. Studd) is 1¼ m. W., at the foot of Great Haldon, on whose dark crest a lowering cloud is sure forerunner of a storm; for

"When Haldon hath a hat,
Kenton may beware a skat."]

9¾ m. from Exeter, *Starcross Stat.*, quite on the water-side, with a little pier attached. Opposite is the town of *Exmouth*, placed precisely, as its name imports, at the mouth of the estuary of the Exe.

Starcross (*Inn:* Courtenay Arms) is a town rising, through the influence of the rail, to the remunerative dignity of a watering-place. A short distance beyond it is the ferry from the *Warren* sand-bank to Exmouth. rt. beyond Starcross, an obelisk comes in view, crowning the wooded heights of *Mamhead*, seat of Sir Robert Newman, who fell at Inkermann, and now of his brother Sir Lydston Newman, Bart.

The line which has hitherto run between the cultivated ground and the water now cuts off a tract of salt marsh and sandhill called the Warren (used for rifle practice); and, turning to the rt., passes through *Langstone Cliff* to the shore, upon which, piercing occasional headlands, it remains as far as Teignmouth.

3½ *Dawlish Stat.* is upon the beach, with a good view of the Clerk Rock headland.

Dawlish (*Inns:* London Hotel; York Hotel) is a small but fashionable watering-place, of recent origin, exceedingly picturesque, and with peculiar features. It is situated in one of those numerous valleys for which this sheltered and sunny coast has long been celebrated, and is a continuation towards the shore of the old village of Dawlish, which, with the parish ch. and a few villas, stands half a mile from the sea. A sparkling stream flows down the centre of the valley between two rows of houses, which, built on each side of it at the foot of the slopes, are separated from each other by a grassy enclosure, which allows of an uninterrupted view up the valley to the wooded heights of *Luscombe* (Peter Hoare, Esq.). These houses, with a row fronting the sea, form modern Dawlish.

The gardens and grounds of *Luscombe* are fine. Attached to the house is a very beautiful private chapel, built (1862) from the designs of Mr. G. G. Scott. The pillars are of Devonshire marble; and the carved seats of cedar, mostly grown on the estate.

The hills around include the principal eminence of *Little Haldon*, a 2 m. walk from the ch., with a fine view.

The *ch.* of Dawlish was rebuilt in 1825, saving the tower, and, all things considered, there is reason to be grateful that it is no worse. The nave piers and roof appear to be in part from the old edifice. Here, amidst a crowd of monuments to visitors from all parts of the kingdom, are tablets to Sir Wm. Grant, Capt. G. Anson Byron, and Admiral Shanck. There are two monuments by *Flaxman*. The aspect of Dawlish is bright and cheering. The rly. runs across the mouth of the valley. Opinions differ as to its effect upon the appearance of the place; but the taste of the late Mr. Brunel has been shown in a small granite viaduct in a plain Egyptian style, which carries the rail across the brook, and affords a free communication with the shore. The rly. company have also formed a handsome esplanade along the side of the line, and the station-house and building intended for an engine-house are certainly ornamental. The portion of the line seen from the promenade skirts the very edge of the sea, and piercing several headlands has a fine effect, especially when a train is approaching.

Dawlish is considered to be as warm as Torquay. The prices generally are reasonable, and there is good sea-bathing.

The cliffs of the bay, composed of blood-red sandstone, traversed by numerous *faults*, terminate on the W. with the singular rock called the *Parson*, bearing some resemblance to a huge monk with his back against the headland; and on the E. with the *Langstone*, divided by the rail, but still projecting as a fragment on the shore.

With respect to excursions, you should ascend *Little Haldon*, alt. 818 ft., commanding the estuary of the Exe on the one side, and of the Teign on the other. The hill is strewed with blocks of quartziferous porphyry, and marked by an old camp called *Castle Ditch*, a circular work 124 yds. in diam., 2½ m. W. of Dawlish. In a swamp at the head of the valley are the ruins of *Lithwell Chapel* (p. 57). You should also visit the promontory of the *Parson and Clerk*, about 1 m. distant. The Parson sits at the pitch of the headland, but the sea seems to have had little respect for the sanctity of his person. The Clerk rises from the waves in advance, and W. of his master, and cuts a whimsical figure. His head is silvered with *guano* and bristles like a hedgehog, whilst his raiment is of many colours. One fond of cliff-scenery will be gratified by a scramble along the base of the cliff W. of the Clerk. The rock is principally a conglomerate with a magnesio-calcareous cement, and belongs to the new red sandstone, a formation so largely developed on this coast. Observe the size of the concavity opposite the Clerk. The botanist will find *Rubia sylvestris*, or *madder*, in hedge-rows round Dawlish.

Leaving Dawlish, the line crosses the mouth of the valley in which the town is built, allowing of a brief but pretty view, and then dives through 5 short tunnels driven in a soft conglomerate of the new red sandstone. In the intervals between these tunnels the cliffs rise above the traveller, to a height of about 200 ft., in such threatening masses that it was prophesied before the opening of the railway that old Neptune would claim his share before the proprietors could receive their dividend. In Feb. 1853, this prediction was partially verified, when some 4000 tons fell with a crash, carrying rails, and railway, and wall, into the sea. Providentially no train was passing at the time. A 6th tunnel leads to

3 *Teignmouth Stat.*, where the line quits the sea, and ascends the l. bank of the Teign.

Teignmouth (*Inns:* Royal Hotel; Commercial Hotel), with the exception of Torquay, is the largest watering place in the county, and is divided into two parishes, E. and W. Teignmouth, forming one town. It lies at the mouth of the wooded estuary of the Teign, the vista of which terminates grandly in a moorland ridge capped by the rocks of Heytor. The river, which rises in the northern quarter of Dartmoor, discharges its waters by a narrow channel obstructed by a shifting bar, and in the course of ages has accumulated at its mouth a huge bank of sand like the Warren of the Exe. This is called the *Den* (a name possibly connected with the Flemish "Dunes"), and forms a wide esplanade, which is the distinguishing feature of Teignmouth. At the end of it is a quaint little lighthouse, erected in 1844-5, for the direction of vessels approaching the river; and to this spot the stranger should proceed for a view up the Teign. He will observe in the foreground the *bridge*, which is said to be the longest in England. It is on 34 arches, having a swing-bridge at one end, and is 1671 ft. in length. It was constructed in 1825-7, at a cost of about 20,000*l*. On the other side of the river is the village of *Shaldon* and the promontory of the *Ness*. Under the shelter of the latter is the marine villa of Lord Clifford of Chudleigh, who has cut a carriage-drive by tunnel to the shore. Looking E. from the Den, the *Parson and Clerk Rocks* are striking objects, and the Parson from this point really bears some resemblance to the figure of a monk in a cringing attitude. Some rare shells may be found on the sands, such as *Mactra lutraria* and *Nerita glaucina* or *Livid Nerite*. The hills above Shaldon command a bird's-eye view of the town.

The Danes are said to have landed at this place, and to have committed such havoc that the cliffs have ever since been the colour of blood. In the words of the poet—

"With blood they all the shore did staine,
And the gray ocean into purple dy."

(There is probably, however, some confusion with the Northumbrian Tynemouth, where the scene of Ragnar Lodbrok's death is usually placed.) In 1347 Teignmouth, then a fishing village, was burnt by some French marauders, and again in 1690, in the reign of William and Mary, by the French admiral Tourville, after his defeat of the combined English and Dutch squadron, under the Earl of Torrington, off Beachy Head. The Admiral landed in Torbay, and despatched his galleys along the shore. The *port* belongs to that of Exeter, and has a considerable trade with Newfoundland, and an export of china-clay from the parish of King's Teignton, and of granite from the Heytor quarries. In the town, tables and other articles are manufactured from the madrepore marble of the neighbourhood.

The Teignmouth *Churches* are uninteresting. In that of E. Teignmouth, rebuilt 1823, there is a very good font; and a Norm. doorway from the old ch. forms the S. entrance.

The *Public Assembly Room* on the Den is a handsome building, date 1826.

From Teignmouth you can visit the *Parson and Clerk Rocks*, 1¼ m. E., by a pleasant stroll along the beach as far as *Smuggler's Lane*, and can make a longer excursion to *Chudleigh Rock*, 8 m. (see Rte. 10), or about 6½ by true Devonshire lanes, over the shoulder of Little Haldon from King's Teignton, and by the old mansion of *Lyndridge* (in the latter route, however, the stranger should be careful not to be benighted in the labyrinth of lanes);—to *Heytor*, *Becky Fall*, and *Lustleigh Cleave* (Rte. 12); to *Ashburton* and *Buckland* or *Holne Chace* (Rte. 11), and to *Babbacombe* (about 4 m.), *Anstis Cove*, and *Torquay*, all described in Rte. 8,—and a charming walk by the cliffs, passing the romantic cove of *Maidencombe* and the landslip of *Watcombe*. You can also visit the pottery at Bovey Tracey; and make an excursion by high-road, rail, or water, to *Newton* (market-boats ply daily).

The churches of *Bishop's Teignton*, and of *Combe-in-Teignhead*, about 2 m. from Teignmouth, rt. and l. of the river, retain some early Norm. features, although both have been much tampered with. The latter is the more interesting. At Bishop's Teignton, Bp. Grandisson (1327-1369) built a palace, of which the walls of the chapel alone remain.

About 3 m. N.W. are the ruins of *Lithwell Chapel*, in which, runs the legend, some time in the 16th centy. dwelt a villanous priest, who waylaid travellers on a neighbouring heath, despoiled them of their money, hoarded his ill-gotten booty beneath the altar of this chapel, and threw the bodies of his victims into a well. This well may be seen among the ruins covered with a slab of granite.

Bitton House, on the W. cliff, was the seat of the late W. Mackworth Praed, Esq.; the *Hennons*, 1 m. N.W., belongs to W. B. King, Esq.

On leaving the station at Teignmouth you will observe the red promontory of the *Ness* at *Shaldon*, and the long straggling bridge; and higher up the estuary the village of *Coomb in Teignhead*, in a lovely dell. Then *King's Teignton* is passed—birthplace, in 1628, of *Theophilus Gale*, the Nonconformist divine (see Rte. 10)—and the train reaches the confluence of 3 water-channels, where a fine view opens up the course of the river towards *Stover Lodge* (Duke of Somerset), *Heytor*, and other Dartmoor hills. Cross Teign to

5 *Newton Junct. Stat.*, at Newton Abbot and close to Newton Bushel. (*Chudleigh Rock*, *Ugbrooke Park*, and the *Pottery* at *Bovey Tracey*, are distant about 6 m. The ch. is seen on the rt. Here is the junction with the branch line to Torquay (see Rte. 8), and with a line (in progress) up the valley of the Teign to Moreton Hampstead.

6 *Newton* (*Inn:* Globe Hotel, good and cheap; Pop. of parish 4427), a town composed of *Newton Abbot*, once subject to Tor Abbey, and *Newton Bushel*, commemorative of its lord in 1246. It is beautifully situated in a vale, on the Lemon rivulet, which here joins the Teign. The town has been much extended and embellished of late years. Its market is widely known for its abundant supplies. Here William of Orange made his first declaration after landing in Torbay, at a stone still preserved in Woolborough Street, in front of the Chapel. He encamped his army on Milber Down, and established his head-quarters at Ford, and the next day proceeded on his march to Exeter.

D 3

The Dec. tower of the Chapel of St. Leonard stands in the street of *Newton Abbot*. The chapel has been pulled down; it was in the parish of *Woodborough*, the ch. of which stands at some distance, on high ground. It is wholly Perp., with a plain tower. The S. door is set in a square head, with a deep hollow moulding with flowers. The capitals of the nave piers resemble bands, and are coarsely executed. There is a good deal of wood screen-work, late Perp., and in excellent order. It severs the chancel and 2 side chapels or ancient pews. The *font*, of Norman date, has a bowl of a fine red gritstone (Roborough stone), boldly and most effectively ornamented. In the windows, among fragments of good stained glass, are the arms of De Vere quartering Clare, Courtenay, Scrope, &c.; and in the chancel those of Nevil, Montague, and Morthemer. The arms of Sir W. Courtenay, Kt., are carved on the gallery. The arms in the windows are older than the connexion of the Courtenays with this place, and probably have been brought from some other ch. In the chancel is an elaborate marble tomb, with effigies and canopy, to Sir R. Reynell of Ford, and Lucy his wife, date 1633. He built Ford, and he endowed the ch. with a fund for its repairs.

Ford House, close to the railway stat., is the property of the Earl of Devon, but is not occupied by him. It was erected in the reign of James I. by Sir R. Reynell, a maternal ancestor of the Courtenays, who here entertained Charles I., Duke "Steenie," and the rest of the court, on their return from Plymouth, in September, 1625. The King attended Divine service in Wolborough ch. During the Rebellion it was the scene of some memorable actions. Thrice was it taken by either party before Fairfax and Waller finally captured it. Here, too, the P. of Orange slept on his road from Torbay to Exeter, in a room still pointed out. The house has been repaired in good taste. About a mile above the town, at a bend of the valley, is the very curious *Manor-house of Bradley*, with chapel, &c., now used as a sort of farmhouse, but very perfect, and standing in a level mead of peculiar beauty. It is a 15th centy. mansion, and was the seat of the Yardes from the reign of Richard II. to about 1750. It originally formed a quadrangle; but 3 of the sides have been taken down. The chapel and hall remain, and the principal front, with 3 oriel windows projecting from the upper floor. From the *Oywell Rocks*, near Newton, there is a fine view. Between Newton and the coast, on a streamlet tributary to the Teign, are *Haccombe House* and *Haccombe Church*, the former, seat of Sir W. Palk Carew, Bart., whose family has possessed it for many generations. (See Rte. 8.)

After passing Newton, the Plymouth line no longer follows a well-defined valley, but threads its way through a series of combes, many of which are in the limestone, and much resemble in their features some of the upper Dovedale scenery. The steepness of the gradient at several points is proclaimed by the uneasy and measured puffing of the engine, but this immediately ceases, and the train proceeds with sudden velocity, after passing the short *Daignton tunnel* at the summit and reaching a valley tributary to the Dart. The line passes within a mile of the romantic ruins of *Berry Pomeroy Castle* (Duke of Somerset; see the present route, *post*), and then crossing the Dart, in view of *Dartington House* (see *post*), reaches

8½ *Totnes Stat*. Part of Totnes lies low. Its principal features are its 2 churches, and the ivy-covered keep of its Castle on the escarpment of the hill rising (l.) above the rly. The old town of *Totnes (Inns:*

DEVONSHIRE. *Route 7.—Totnes.*

Seven Stars; Seymour Hotel, the latter pleasantly situated on the river bank; Pop. 3409) "from the margin of the river Dart climbs the steep acclivity of a hill, and stretches itself along its brow, commanding a view of the winding stream, and of the country in its vicinity, but sheltered at the same time by higher hills on every side." In Domesday it is called *Totenais*, a name doubtless derived from the Anglo-Saxon *tot, toten*, to project—as in Tothill, Tottenham—and *ness* or *nes*, a 'nose' or headland. (The original "Totnes" may have been either Berry Head or Prawle Point —the most southernly point of land in Devonshire. The whole coast was named from it; and the landing of Brutus of Troy is fixed by Layamon (about 1205) at "Dertemuthe in Totenes." The name became at last confined to the chief town of the district.) The stone on which Brutus is said to have landed is still pointed out in the Fore St., nearly opposite the Mayoralty. His words are said to have been—

"Here I sit, and here I rest,
And this town shall be called Totnes."

The tradition which thus gave the Britons, like their Roman masters, a Trojan origin, was no doubt of Roman invention, but seems to have been readily appropriated. Totnes —no doubt the "Ad Durium" of the Itineraries—was situated upon a Roman road which ran from Exeter to the Tamar, by Ugbrooke, Newton Abbot, Totnes, and Boringdon Park. It is one of the oldest boroughs in the country (the first charter dates 1205) and there are fragments remaining of the *walls* with which it was formerly surrounded. Other proofs of its antiquity are the ruins of the castle, the venerable ch., and some houses in High Street with fronts of slate, with piazzas, and projecting gables. In the 12th and 13th cents. Totnes was one of the chief clothing towns of England; and "hose of fine Totnes" appear in sundry romances, and in the Welsh 'Mabinogion,' where the dress of an important personage is described as especially splendid. The country in the neighbourhood is remarkable for its fertility, and for this reason will be interesting to many travellers. Dartington parish has a fine growth of timber, and also a store of wealth below the surface of the ground, yielding chocolate and madrepore marbles, of which beautiful specimens appeared in the Great Exhibition of 1851. Totnes is connected with its suburb by a bridge built in 1828, at a cost of 12,000*l*. Steps descend from it to a small island, planted by the Duke of Somerset for public use.

Among the natives of this place were *Benjamin Kennicott*, 1718, the Hebrew scholar, and collator of the Hebrew Bible; and the artist *William Brockedon*, distinguished for his literary attainments and fertile invention, and so widely known as an Alpine traveller. Specimens of his skill as a painter may be seen at Exeter and Dartmouth. Sir George Carew, the able commander of Q. Elizabeth's reign, was created *Earl of Totnes*.

The *Castle* stands on the summit of the hill, and is said to have been built by Judhael de Totnais, a Norman baron, on whom the manor was bestowed at the Conquest. The keep is the only part now remaining. It is circular in form and battlemented, a mere ruin of crumbling red stones profusely mantled with ivy, and is probably not earlier than Henry I.'s time. Its position, however, on the first bridge over the Dart rendered it of some importance. It commands a very interesting view of the windings of the river and of the rich surrounding country. The grounds around it are planted, and have been opened to the public by the Duke of Somerset. The honour or barony of Totnes passed from the Norman Judhael to the Nonants, Cantilupes, and Zouches; which last great house long retained it. After sundry changes it came to the Seymours.

The *Ch.*, a noble building, utterly spoiled by its atrocious internal arrangements, is constructed of red sandstone, which, like that of Chester Cathedral, is much abraded by the weather. By an old record, this edifice appears to have been rebuilt about the year 1430. The S. porch is good, and there is a very fine internal rood-turret on the N. side of the chancel. The E. end is wonderful and "classical." The glory of the ch. is its very rich and elaborate *stone* roodscreen (a rare example in Devonshire) and its stone pulpit. There are some monuments, but of little interest. The exterior buttresses and the S. façade should be noticed. The Priory of St. Mary, founded by Judhael de Totnes as a cell to the Benedictine Abbey at Angiers, stood on the N.E. side of the church.

The *Parochial Library* has a good collection of weighty volumes on divinity, published chiefly in the 17th cent. Among them are the works of SS. Augustine, Ambrose, and Gregory, and of "the High and Mighty K. James;" the Homilies of St. Chrysostom, Birkhead's Protestant Evidence, and Walton's Polyglott.

The stranger should be directed to the *Public Walk* below the bridge, whence the steamers set out for Dartmouth, and a path along the banks of the mill-leat from the Seven Stars. The finest view of Totnes is to be obtained from *Sharpham Lodge* on the Dart.

With respect to *excursions*, from Totnes, the principal of these are to Berry Pomeroy, and to Dartmouth by the river.

(A line of rly. is authorised for connecting Totnes with Buckfastleigh and (probably) Ashburton. This line will render the Holne Chase and Buckland scenery (Rte. 11) easily accessible from Totnes. At present Ashburton or Buckfastleigh are the best centres from which to explore it.)

The ruins of *Berry Pomeroy Castle* are situated about 2 m. from Totnes, in a thick wood; and to reach them the traveller will pursue the Torquay road as far as the turnpike, and then turn to the l. towards the village of Berry Pomeroy. Here he will notice the fine ch. built by one of the Pomeroys, and in which lie the remains of *John Prince*, author of the 'Worthies of Devon,' who was vicar here for 42 years. It contains a good screen and pulpit, restored by the late vicar (Rev. W. Cosens); two monuments, with effigies of Pomeroys (one dating 1475); and an elaborate monument for Lord Edward Seymour (son of the "Protector" Duke of Somerset, 1593; his son, Sir Edw. Seymour, 1613, with wife and children. The S. porch and the W. tower should be noticed. The ch. is mainly Perp., but contains E. Eng. and Dec. portions. Beyond the village there are signs of the old ruin in the neighbourhood. An ivy-mantled wall stretches in fragments across the fields, and an aged tree here and there remains as a memorial of the park in which the barons chased the deer. In ½ m. the visitor reaches the entrance of a wood, where the key of the castle must be obtained at the lodge. He is immediately received by noisy acclamations from an ancient rookery, and, having descended a winding road, comes suddenly upon the remains of the once stately mansion of the Seymours. This interesting ruin derives a peculiar charm from its retirement, and from the lofty trees which encompass and have penetrated its deserted halls and courts. But an imperfect idea is obtained of its size and romantic position on the approach, as the whole is so embedded in ivy, and screened by wood, that little more of it can be seen than the great gateway. The stranger should gain an opposite eminence by following the path to the rt. of the gateway, and ascending the hill above the quarry which he will observe on the opposite side of the valley. From that point he will command a small solitary glen, watered by a little rivulet, and thickly wooded, and an excellent view of the ruin rising among the trees. The interior of the castle displays the usual grass-grown courts, mossy walls, old chimneys, broken arches, and crumbling steps descending into so-called dungeons and underground passages. Trees are rooted in every nook and cranny, and ivy hangs the whole with verdurous festoons. The oldest part of the ruin is the great gateway sculptured with the arms of Pomeroy (a lion rampant, gules,—within a border invected, sable,—but these are now concealed behind the ivy), and a circular tower called St. Margaret's, connected with this gateway by a curtain wall. This portion of the building dates from the early part of the 13th centy., and was perhaps the work of Henry de Pomeroy, one of the most powerful barons of the West during the reigns of John and Hen. III. The body of the building is the ruin of a sumptuous mansion, begun by the Protector Somerset. The original castle is said to have been erected by Ralph de la Pomeroy, to whom the manor was given by the Conqueror. The Pomeroys were wealthy and powerful. A fragment of their Norman stronghold still remains in the Çinglais, not far from Falaise. (It is there called "Château Ganne"—Ganelon's Castle.) Henry de Pomeroy fortified his castles of Berry Pomeroy and of St. Michael's Mount in behalf of Prince John; and on Richard's return fled to the latter, where, says the tradition, he "caused himself to be let blood to death." His son was active on the side of Simon de Montfort. The Pomeroys resided in their castle here until the reign of Edward VI., when, Sir Thomas Pomeroy having engaged deeply in the Devonshire rebellion, his estates were confiscated, and granted to "my Lord Protector's Grace." "This family of Seymour," says Prince, in his 'Worthies of Devon,' "built at the N. and E. end of the quadrangle a magnificent structure, at the charges, as fame relates, of upwards of 20,000*l.*, but never brought it to perfection, as the W. side of the quadrangle was never begun. The apartments," he continues, "were very splendid, especially the dining-room, which was adorned, besides paint, with statues and figures cut in alabaster with elaborate art and labour; but the chimneypiece, of polished marble curiously engraven, was of great cost and value. The number of apartments of the whole may be collected hence, if report be true, that it was a good day's work for a servant but to open and shut the casements belonging to them. Notwithstanding which, 'tis now demolished, and all this glory lieth in the dust." According to a tradition, Berry Pomeroy was destroyed by lightning. In the reign of James II. Sir Edward Seymour, the famous leader of the country party, lived here in great splendour, and the ruins still belong, with the manor, to his descendants, and are in the possession of the present Duke of Somerset. *Polypodium semilacerum* has been found in the woods.

Dartington, seat of the Champernownes, 1½ m. from Totnes, and rt. of the Ashburton road, is also an estate of great antiquity, the gift of the Conqueror to the Norman baron William de Falaise. From that distant period it has successively belonged to the families of Martyn, Audley, Vere, Holland, and, for a short time, Courtenay. Dartington House is very interesting as comprising a part of the feudal mansion of the Dukes of Exeter, and in particular the Great Hall and kitchen, the latter ruinous, the former, though unroofed, a most interesting relic, apparently of the time of Rich. II. It is 70 ft. in length by 40 in breadth, and has a huge old fireplace 16 ft. broad, and a porch with groined ceiling bearing the escutcheon of Holland. This is the latest portion of the ancient house. The earliest part of the building remaining is the old hall, on the E. side of the quadrangle at the N.E. corner. This, with the gateway at its S. end, is of very plain work, early in the 14th centy., and has a good wooden roof. The N. and S. sides of the quadrangle are of the middle of the 14th centy. The former has three singular porches, looking like large buttresses; the two eastern ones have each a double inner doorway; all have rooms over them. There is one external staircase.—*J. H. P.* At the end of the pile are some of the original windows, and on the W. side, which was rebuilt in the reign of Elizabeth, a terraced garden. *Dartington Ch.* stands close to the house, and contains some richly coloured glass, the remains of a screen, a fine pulpit of Henry VII.'s time, and, near the altar, a curious monument (dated 1578) in memory of Sir Arthur Champernowne, the first of this family who possessed Dartington. There is also a small effigy in armour. The ch. is Dec. and Perp., has been reseated, and is in excellent order. The surrounding scenery is varied and pleasing. The river sweeps through a wooded vale, and the old town of Totnes terminates the view. Other seats near Totnes are *Sharpham Lodge*, R. Durant, Esq.; *Follaton House*, G. S. Cary, Esq.; *Broomborough*, J. F. P. Phillips, Esq.; and *Tristford,*

Mrs. Pendarves. There is a heronry at Sharpham, one of the few now existing in England.

The stranger may ramble either from Totnes or Ashburton to *Holne Chace* and *Buckland*, described in Rte. 11. On the road from Totnes up the valley of the Dart he should notice the view from *Staverton Bridge*, just beyond Dartington, and the pretty picture formed by *Austin's Bridge* in connection with the ch. of Buckfastleigh. He should also turn off from the road at *Cadover Lane*, before reaching Austin's Bridge. The summit of Cadover Hill is near the spot chosen by Turner for his view of Buckfast Abbey, now in the possession of Mr. Windus of Tottenham. The pastoral valley of the Dart, scattered over with fine trees, lies before the spectator:—

"Meadows trim with daisies pied, Shallow brooks and rivers wide."

Nor is any other feature of the great poet's description wanting. Steep hills close in the valley on either side, and on their slopes lie orchard, and farm, and tower, "bosomed high in tufted trees." Towards the centre of the picture rises Buckfast Abbey, round which the river winds; and, beyond that, the woods of Holne Chace and Buckland, all closed in by the long range of the Dartmoor hills, lifting their granite crests against the sky. *Buckfastleigh* and its neighbourhood (see Rte. 11) are well known for *quarries of black marble*.—To the old gateway and remains of the chapel of *Cornworthy Priory* (about 4 m. S. of Totnes, on the farm of Court Prior), an Augustinian nunnery founded in the 14th centy. by the Zouches, lords of Totnes.—To *Harberton Ch.*, (about 3 m. on the road to Kingsbridge), one of the most interesting in the county, a fine specimen of Perp. date, containing a sculptured stone pulpit, gilt and coloured, its niches filled with figures; it deserves careful study. There is also a fine screen, painted and gilt, with perfect roodloft. The S. porch is good. Near it at Harbertonford is a *shovel and reaping-hook manufactory.*—To Little Hempstone or *Hempstone Arundell* (2 m. N.E. of Totnes), where there is an interesting Perp. ch., with a good screen, and some fine glass in the N. chancel window. In the 3 window recesses of the S. aisle are 3 effigies—a Crusader (cross-legged), much defaced, perhaps Sir John Arundell (the Arundells were lords of this manor from Hen. I.'s time); a knight in plate armour; and a lady. The *old parsonage* is a curious small house of the 15th centy., built round a square court. The hall, which remains perfect, is on the S. side, with buttresses at the W. end. From the corner of the hall a circular staircase ascends to the solar on the S. side of the court. It is exactly the priest's house of Chaucer's time.—To *Dean Prior* and the *Vale of Dean Burn,* by a road on l. beyond Dartington, climbing by steep lanes to the village of *Rattery,* where a glorious prospect bursts upon the view.

The most pleasant excursion from Totnes is a *trip down the river to Dartmouth.* Steamers leave Totnes every day when the tide permits (N.B. the river is unsightly at low water), and make the voyage to Darmouth, 12 m., in 1¼ hr. The return fare is 2s. The river pursues a course among shelving hills and woods, but the great charm of the scenery lies in the vagaries of the stream, which is whimsically deflected, and twists and doubles as if determined to push a passage where nature had denied one. Hence, the river has the appearance of a string of lakes, an illusory effect well seen from a hill at *Sharpham,* from which no less than 10 distinct sheets of water are in view, each apparently isolated and land-locked.

The voyager, having started from Totnes, glides swiftly with the stream, soon sweeping to the l. in full view of (rt.) *Sharpham* (R. Durant, Esq.), where the hills lie intermingled, as if to oppose a farther progress, and the river begins its beautiful convolutions. The traveller has barely time for an admiring glance backward at the ch. tower of Totnes, before a sudden turn to the rt. displays one of the most striking reaches of the river, apparently closed at the further end by dense masses of wood (Sharpham). The hills, however, soon open on the l., and the boat enters another glistening sheet of water, bounded on the rt. by a crescent of trees (Sharpham) so grand in its proportions as to claim an interesting place in the traveller's reminiscences. It is farther remarkable as containing one of the largest heronries in the county, and as haunted by an echo, which the stranger must not fail to salute. From this reach the voyager again turns to the rt., and then to the L., opening a long vista of the river, which expands at the end to a spacious basin, presenting at high water the appearance of a bay. In this reach will be observed on the l. the village of *Stoke Gabriel,* the woods of *Maisonette* (H. Carew Hunt, Esq.), (l.) *Sandridge* (Lord Cranstoun), and *Waddeton Court* (H. Studdy, Esq.). At the edge of the rt. bank, nearly opposite Sandridge, the liveliest echo on the river will be found among some trees. In the next reach, which bends to the rt., the stream contracts, and lofty ridges bound it on each side, the village of *Dittisham* (rt.), famous for plums (in the ch. is a good stone pulpit), and the woods of *Greenway* (l., — Harvey, Esq.), once a seat of Sir Walter Raleigh, adorning the shores. At the narrowest part, in the middle of the stream, a rock called the *Anchor Stone* is visible at low water, and rises abruptly from a depth of more than 10 fathoms. It was on this rock, according to the legend, that Raleigh was in the habit of smoking his pipe.

Route 7.—Ivy Bridge. Sect. I.

At the present day a railway company have contemplated throwing a bridge across the river by its aid. The voyager, having passed the Anchor Stone, feels the breeze of the sea, and, skirting the slopes of *Mount Boone* (rt., Sir H. P. Seale, Bart.), in a few minutes reaches the haven for which he is bound—
Dartmouth (see Rte. 9).

After leaving Totnes the traveller will remark that the thatch of the neighbouring cottages is coated thickly with white-wash to protect it from the fiery showers of the passing engine. A short tunnel brings the train to
7 *South Brent Stat.* To the rt. are the tors and the wild vale of *Dean Burn*.

South Brent is a small town on the Avon, and below that striking eminence *South Brent Tor* (or *Beacon*). Here you should notice the wild river-bed at the bridge, and the old ch., which has a tower of very early Norm. character, and some good Flamboyant windows—there are also the remains of a good screen; and stretch your sinews by a walk to the top of the Beacon. Micaceous iron-ore, called *Devonshire Sand*, and used for sanding writings, is procured in this neighbourhood.

A rly. has been authorised for connecting the S. Devon Rly. (from S. Brent Stat.) with Kingsbridge, but it is not yet begun.

The line has here reached Dartmoor, and from this point it runs at a considerable elevation, skirting like a terrace the southern headlands of the high country, and affording one of the most beautiful rly. rides in the kingdom. A viaduct carries it into

2 *Kingsbridge Road Stat.* (where there is a tolerable Inn, and whence an omnibus runs daily to Kingsbridge, meeting certain of the trains). Beyond this place the *Western Beacon* rises on the rt., and l. stretches a far extending landscape. The rly. crosses several deep and broad valleys, spanning them by viaducts of iron and timber on tall piers of masonry. A short but lofty work of this description bears the line in a curve across the romantic valley of the Erme to

3¼ *Ivy Bridge Stat.*
Ivy Bridge (*Inn*: Mallet's Hotel, near the old Ivy Bridge). This village, though not very picturesque in itself, is justly a favourite, being situated at the mouth of a romantic valley, in close proximity to Dartmoor. It derives its name from the old *Ivy-bridge*, once embowered as its name imports, and traversed by the high-road, but now somewhat denuded by a winter's flood, and deserted in its old age among a barren company of rocks. This venerable structure is but a few yards in length, yet it stands in 4 parishes—Ugborough, Ermington, Harford, and Cornwood—each of which claims a fourth part of it. The objects of interest here are the *Ivy-bridge*, the *river Erme* and its glen, *British antiquities on Dartmoor, the viaduct of the S. Devon railway, paper-mills,* an embryo *lead-mine,* and the *leaning spire of Ermington.*

The *river Erme*, rising on the hills near Fox Tor, flows through Ivy Bridge, and falls into the sea at Bigbury Bay; and is at times a wild impetuous stream, which leaves its bed of granite, and carries the wreck of the moor over the neighbouring fields. For about 2 m. above Ivy Bridge (as far as *Harford Bridge*), those who enjoy fine scenery should explore this river, which for that distance flows through a romantic solitary glen, filled with old woods and rocks, and just above Ivy Bridge spanned by a *viaduct* of the South Devon Railway, a spider-like fabric of such slender proportions that one wonders it has not long since been blown away into the moor. It resembles at a distance a line of tall chimneys, and consists of a black wooden roadway, which is carried in a curve over ten pair of white granite pillars, each pair being 60 ft. apart, and the most elevated 115 ft. above the valley. Having reached *Harford Bridge*, the stranger should ascend to the village. The Perp. ch. is in a sad state of neglect. The carved roof-ribs and wall-plates deserve notice. The wall-plate on the N. side of the chancel has the inscription "IHS. helpe us. Amen. Walter Hele Pson, 1539." There is a *brass* for Thomas Williams, Speaker in Parliament, 1566; he is in armour; and the inscription records that he "Now in heaven with mighty Jove doth raigne." In the S. aisle is a monumental *brass* for John Prideaux of Stowford, wife, 7 sons, and 3 daughters. The fourth son, in a doctor's gown, was Reg. Prof. of Divinity at Oxford, Rector of Exeter College, and the learned author of the 'Connection of the Old and New Testaments.' This brass was placed here by him. The tourist may look into the churchyard, noting the ages marked on the tombstones, and an old granite monument, which will remind him of the cromlech. On the hill above the village he may, however, find a sepulchre to which these old tombs are but memorials of our own generation, — a *kistvaen*, enclosed within a circle of 9 upright stones, still erect.

From Harford, if he finds a pleasure in rambling through rude and pathless wilds, he should trace the stream towards its source, passing the remains of some ancient rings of stone (refer to Introd.), to the huge flank of *Sharpitor* (rt. 1½ m. from Harford), where he will find growing on the rocky slope some dwarf oak-trees and hawthorns, not so aged as those of Wistman's Wood (Rte. 12), but, like them, remarkable for their small size, contortion by the wind, and golden coats of moss. The scene is wild and solitary, and on the opposite side of the stream there is an abrupt and dreary hill, the haunt of a lazy echo, who, taking time to frame her answers, renders them by that means the more impressive. Having paused to listen to this "spirit of a sound," he should next visit a *cairn*, some 60 yards in circumf., on the top of Sharpitor; and then proceed to *Three Barrow Tor* (the next hill to the N., and 1519 ft. high), which is both crowned with a *cairn* and traversed by an ancient road or *trackway*, in places 16 ft. wide, which runs down the N. slope, towards the N.W. Farther up the river (3 m. from Sharpitor) is *Erme Pound*, another work of the old inhabitants, or tin-workers. *Erme Head* is nearly 2 m. N., and *Yealm Head* 1½ m. S.W. of this pound. *Plym Head* is about 2 m. N.W. of Erme Head. The wanderer, as he returns, can ascend the *Western Beacon* (alt. 1130 ft.), a lofty hill at the entrance of the valley. It commands a fine view, and is crested by barrows; and others may be observed disposed along the moor in a line to the N.E.

Two *paper-mills* are situated on the Erme at Ivy Bridge; and below them, ¼ m. from the hotel, is the entrance of a field-path, which accompanies the river to the pretty hamlet of *Caton*, passing the works of a *lead mine*, the shaft of which is sunk to a depth of 25 fathoms on the opposite side of the stream. From Caton a lane leads to *Ermington* (Fawn Hotel), the ch. of which is known for its *leaning spire*. (See Rte. 16.) From Ermington the pedestrian, if bound for the romantic shores of *Bigbury Bay* (Rte. 15), can follow the stream through the park of *Fleet House* (— Splatt, Esq.), and pass thence at low water along the shore of the estuary to *Mothecomb*; or, if likely to be met by the tide, turn to the rt. after passing the mansion of Fleet House, and proceed to Mothecomb by *Holbeton* (see p. 158).

One of the most beautiful of Creswick's pictures, and which gained the prize at the British Instit., was painted in the lane between Ivy Bridge and Caton.

Adjoining Ivy Bridge is *Highland House*, long the residence of the late Wm. Cotton, Esq., well known for his labours on the Life of Sir Joshua Reynolds, and for his munificent donation of the "Cottonian Library" to Plymouth.

On the skirts of the moor near Ivy Bridge are *Blachford* (Sir F. Rogers, Bart.), containing pictures; *Slade* (Mrs. Pode); and the old farmhouses of *Furdell* and *Cholwich Town*, the former anciently the seat of the family of Sir Walter Raleigh, the latter of Cholwich. Raleigh's father removed from Fardell to Hayes near Budleigh Salterton, where the statesman was born. There are considerable remains of the old mansion at Fardell, including portions of the chapel. In the lane between Ivy Bridge and Fardell was an inscribed stone of the Roman-British period, which has been removed to the Brit. Mus. It has Ogham characters along the edges,—the only example hitherto found in Devon, and is probably a record of some early Christian who may have been taught by missionaries from Ireland, if the stone does not record the Irish teacher himself.

2¼ m. N.W. of Ivy Bridge is *Cornwood*, commonly called *Cross*, a village on the Yealm, about 4 m. from its fountain-head. The ch. is of little interest. There are lofty tors and antiquities in the moorland valley of this river. *Pen Beacon*, 2 m. N. of Cornwood, is 1570 ft. high; *Shell Top*, or *Pensheil*, 1 m. N. of Pen Beacon, 1600 ft. On the S.W. slope of the latter are numerous *hut circles*, and in the neighbourhood of these hills, on the bank of the river, about 1 m. from *Yealm Head*, the foundations of an oblong building (21 ft. by 16 ft.), which the late Mr. Woollcombe, President of the Plymouth Instit., conjectured had been a hermitage. Near *Tolch Gate*, on Cholwich-town Moor, are remains of a *stone avenue* (partly destroyed by the rly. contractors), and a *circle* (some 5 ft. in diam.), of which 6 stones stand erect. Close to Cornwood are *Goodamoor*, Henry Hele Treby, Esq.; *Delamore*, Mrs. Praed; and *Beechwood*, Lady Seaton. 1 m. S.W., the eminence of *Hemerdon Ball*, on which a large camp was formed when Napoleon was threatening the country with an invasion. In this neighbourhood, too, are the *China-clay Works of Heddon*, *Small Hanger*, and *Morley*. *Hall*, N. of Cornwood, was the residence of Col. Chudleigh, father of the notorious Elizabeth C., afterwards Duchess of Kingston.

Beyond Ivy Bridge the rly. pursues its course along the edge of Dartmoor, and commands on the rt. one of the most charming views on the whole line—that of the valley and woods of *Slade*, and of a great moorland hill which closes in the valley. *Blachford*, seat of Sir F. Rogers, Bart., is next seen rt., and the train then commences a long descent to

6¾ *Plympton Stat.*, near which on the l. is the town and handsome Perp. pinnacled tower of

Plympton St. Mary. The only building deserving notice is the *Ch.*, a remarkably handsome structure, standing in a lawn-like churchyard. It has (1860) been restored in good taste by the incumbent and parishioners. The exterior is beautifully tinted with lichens, and displays a profusion of fanciful ornament. The ch. contains Dec. and Perp. portions; the tower, 108 ft. high, is of the latter period. Observe the E. window, the double row of granite piers in the nave, and the Strode monuments, dated respectively 1460 and 1637. This ch. was formerly attached to a priory of black canons founded by the Norman bishop Warlewast, and adjoining it are some trifling remains of the ancient priory, which was for some time the richest monastic establishment in the county, exceeding even the Benedictine monastery at Tavistock in its yearly revenue. The seal displayed the Blessed Virgin with the Divine Infant seated on her lap, and bearing a hawk, hooded and belled, on her wrist,—a mark of feudal dignity. 2 m. to the rt. are *Plym Bridge* and *Bickleigh Vale* (Rte. 13); and 1 m. to the l.—

Plympton Earl (commemorative of its Norman lords, the *Earls* of Devon), an old Stannary and borough town, which returned M.P.s from the 23rd of Edw. I. to the time of the Reform Bill, but more famous as the birthplace of *Sir Joshua Reynolds*, our greatest portrait-painter, b. 16 July, 1723. It contains the ruin of a *Castle* built by Richard de Redvers, and first dismantled when the second Earl of Devon was defending Exeter against Stephen (see the *Gesta Stephani*, which describes the valley of Plympton as one of the richest in the county). It was soon afterwards restored. There was some skirmishing around it in the time of King John; and—to step at once over 4 centuries—it was the head-quarters of Prince Maurice during the siege of Plymouth, 1643. In the following year it was taken by the Earl of Essex. The extensive site of the ancient building is encompassed by a moat, and now forms an agreeable promenade; a fragment of the circular keep crowning a mound which commands a view of the town and of the neighbouring hills. The antiquary may speculate on a singular hollow, which runs through the wall of the keep, and may remind him of those in the Scottish "duns," or Pictish towers.

Many of the houses in Plympton bear the stamp of age, and some project on arches like those of Totnes.

Plympton House, a large mansion so called, was built by the Rt. Hon. George Treby in the reign of Q. Anne. The venerable *Guildhall* is marked on the front with the date 1696, and was formerly enriched with a portrait of Sir Joshua Reynolds, by himself, now at Silverton. It was presented to the corporation by the artist on his being elected mayor of his native town (a circumstance, says Cotton, which he declared gave him more pleasure than any other honour he had received during his life), and was disgracefully sold by the Reformed Corporation for 150*l.* The *Grammar-School*, of which his father was master, was erected about the year 1664. It is a quaint old building with high roof, portico, and piazza, and well accords with the time-worn granite ch. and castle adjoining it. It was founded and endowed, 1658, by Sergt. Maynard, one of the trustees of estates left to charitable purposes by Elize Hele, Esq., of Fardell. The school-room, 63 ft. long, is lighted E. and W. by large Perp. windows, N. and S. by square-headed windows. 2 shields on the wall bear the arms of Maynard and Hele. Below is the arcade or cloister, with its long range of granite columns, the subject of one of Reynolds's earliest essays as a perspective drawing. The old oaken door which opens to the staircase will be noticed. In another part of the house is the room in which the artist is said to have been born.

The *ch.* is supposed to have been originally a chapel appendant to the ch. of P. St. Mary. It was first dedicated to St. Thomas à Becket and afterwards to St. Maurice.

In the neighbourhood of these 2 towns of Plympton are the seats of *Chaddlewood*, Soltau Symons, Esq.; *Hemerdon House*, Admiral Woollcombe; *Newnham Park*, Sidney Strode, Esq.; and *Elfordleigh*, W. Fox, Esq. The line of a *Roman Road*, the

Route 7.—Plymouth.   Sect. 1.

branch of the Ikenild which passed into Cornwall, is indicated by the names of Darkstreet-lane and Ridgeway. The parish road which runs from the rly. stat. at Plympton to Plym Bridge, and thence to Tamerton, is part of the same ancient way.

Starting again from Plympton, the rly. leaves the hills for a broad flat valley, bounded 1. by the woods of *Saltram* (Earl of Morley, but occupied by — Hartmann, Esq.). It crosses the narrow head of the *Laira Estuary* (perhaps a cousin of the Icelandic "Leiru-vogr" — the "bay of mud" — near Reykjavik. "Leary" in some parts of Devonshire means "empty," *e.g.* "a leary cart:" both words may be connected), and runs along its margin. In the distance is seen the iron *Laira Bridge* of 5 arches, and as this vanishes from the view the line enters a deep cutting, and then passes through a tunnel to the station in the centre of

5 *Plymouth*. As the train rushes through the suburbs, the traveller will observe to the rt. the new cemetery, with its two chapels for Churchmen and Dissenters.

6 PLYMOUTH. *Inns:* 1. Royal Hotel; Globe; Albion Hotel; Chubb's Commercial Hotel, rebuilt 1858 in the Anglo-Italian style, on the site of one of the oldest hostelries in the town: C. O. C. Arthur, architect. 2. A magnificent new hotel (the Duke of Cornwall, joint stock company: C. F. Hayward, architect, 1865). It promises to be the best and most convenient in Plymouth. Pop. in 1861, 62,599.

STONEHOUSE. (*Inn:* Brunswick Hotel.) Pop. in 1861, 14,343.

DEVONPORT. (*Inns:* Royal Hotel; London Hotel.) Pop. (including Stoke) in 1861, 50,440.

The stat. serves for the S. Devon, the Cornwall, and the Plymouth and Tavistock Rlys.

These three maritime towns of the West, situated on the shore of a noble harbour, at a part of the Channel the most convenient for a war-station and for the purposes of commerce, and in a country rich both in minerals and agricultural produce, have long occupied a high place in public estimation, and are among the most thriving of all the towns in Great Britain. So rapid, indeed, has been their growth, especially during the French war, that the three may be now considered as one grand focus of trade and naval and military preparation. They have parted with their individuality, and become the sections of a far more important union. The two extremities are the naval and military stations, and Stonehouse the quarters of the marine corps. For the information of the traveller, we shall describe these three great divisions separately, then conduct him along the shore of the Sound, proceed with him up the river Tamar, and to places worth viewing in the immediate neighbourhood; and then take him to scenes more distant, but of singular beauty and interest.

Plymouth is the first-born of this sisterhood of towns, and is described by Leland as in being in the reign of Hen. II., but only as "a mene thing, an inhabitation of fishars." At that time it appears to have been called *Sutton* or *South Town*, a name by which it was known down to the 15th cent., when it was rechristend as Plymouth. It was then of considerable importance, and had been repeatedly honoured by the undesirable notice of the French, who first attacked it in 1338, but were repulsed by Hugh Courtenay, Earl of Devon. In 1377, however, our restless neighbours succeeded in burning a part of the town; in 1400 they plundered the place; and in 1403 favoured it with another incendiary visit; and it still retains traces of their attacks in the names of its streets; the part destroyed by them being still called

Briton (Breton) side; while "Old Town Street" represents the part which was left uninjured; "New Town," immediately above, is of altogether later growth. Such repeated acts of aggression at length aroused the inhabitants, and suggested the expediency of fortifying their town, which in 1439 was done with the approval of the king, Hen. VI., who, as a set-off to their misfortunes, dignified the citizens as a corporate body. In 1512 an act passed parliament for the further strengthening of these works, and since that time they have increased by a yearly growth, and now present a formidable barrier, bristling with cannon.

Fortifications have (from time to time) been erected on St. Nicholas' Isle and the shores of the Sound; and, in consequence of the Report of Commissioners of Defences, Plymouth will be surrounded by a line of inland forts, much of the ground for which has been already purchased, and the works commenced at various points. The fort at Tregantle is described Rte. 24.

The importance of Plymouth as a harbour increased enormously after the discovery of America. Drake, Raleigh, Cavendish, and many of the adventurers to the "new-found world," sailed from here; and the "Pilgrim Fathers," after leaving Delft and Southampton, finally sailed hence for their new colony, which they named in consequence "New Plymouth." In 1471 Margaret of Anjou landed here; and in 1501 Catherine of Arragon. (The landing here of the Black Prince, with his captive, King John of France, is uncertain, although Walsingham asserts it.) During the civil contests of Charles I. the inhabitants of Plymouth sided with the parliament, and the town was several times besieged, but unsuccessfully, by the royal forces. Capt. Cook sailed from Plymouth in 1768; and again in 1772. Plymouth has contributed many names to the list of eminent men. It was the birthplace of the bold seaman *Sir John Hawkins*, of *Jacob Bryant*, of the poet *Carrington*, and of the artists *Northcote, Haydon, Eastlake,* and *Prout,* who, says Ruskin, "was trained among the rough rocks and simple cottages of Cornwall." The *Citadel* and *Hoe* are here the chief objects of interest; but the following buildings also merit notice.

1. The *Royal Hotel*, a huge structure erected by the corporation of the town between the years 1811-18, at a cost of 60,000*l.* It comprises an inn, a theatre, and assembly-rooms, and is situated in a good position at the end of George-street, and conveniently near the Rly. and the Hoe. The roof and internal framework of the theatre are of iron, owing to which the theatre suffered little when the central mass of building was greatly injured by fire in January, 1863.

The *Athenæum* (close to the Royal Hotel), built in 1818-1819 by the members of the *Plymouth Institution.* It has a valuable library and museum, casts from the Elgin collection in the Brit. Museum, and some pictures, including a portrait of Alderman Facey, said to have been one of the earliest by *Sir Josh. Reynolds*, and one of the late President, Colonel Hamilton Smith. In the hall is hung one of the pieces of tapestry, representing the defeat of the Armada,—the only piece saved from the burning of the Houses of Parliament. The hall of the building is generally used as a lecture-room, but occasionally for the exhibition of paintings and sculpture by native artists. In the museum are the roots of a tree of considerable size, which were found in a bog on Dartmoor. The *Nat. Hist. Soc.* in Union-street has been lately incorporated with the Athenæum.

3. The *Public Library* (Cornwall-street), which now contains the Cottonian collection of books and MSS.,

1. Royal Hotel, Athenæum and Plymouth Institution.
2. Duke of Cornwall Hotel.
3. Public Library.

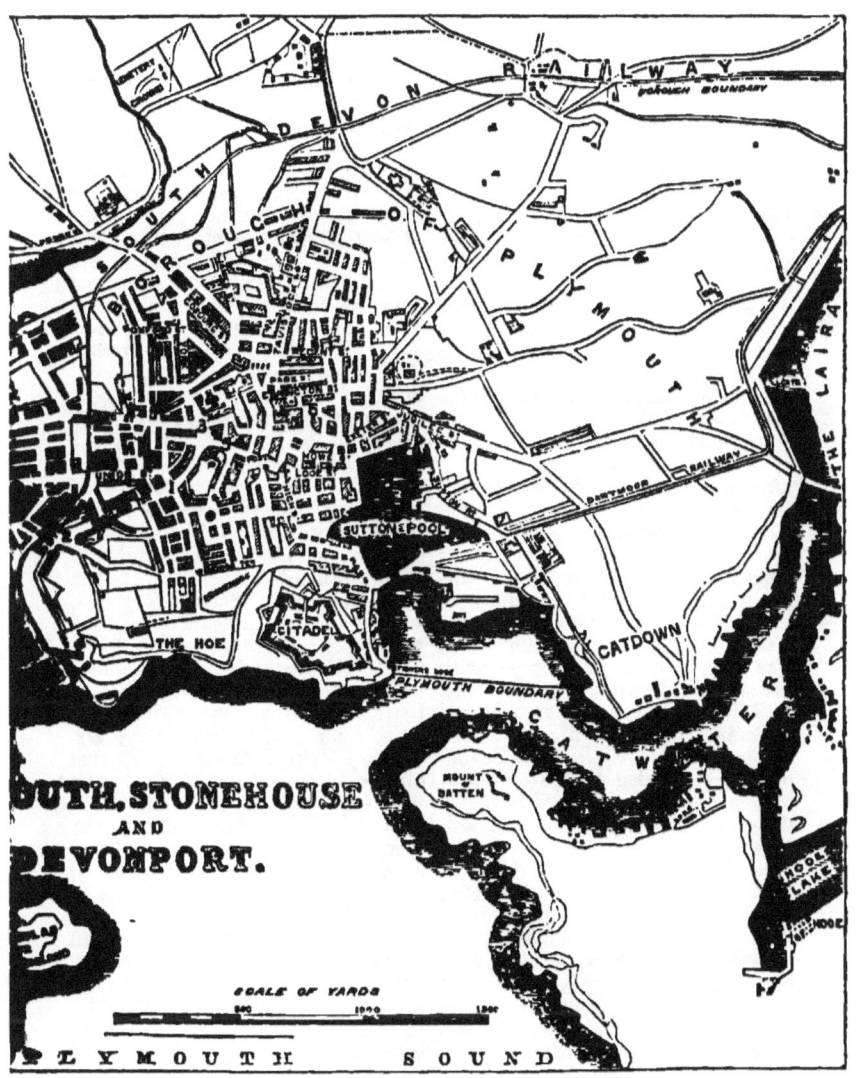

4. Guildhall.
5. St. Andrew's Church.
6. St. Charles's Church.

prints and drawings, paintings, bronzes, and other works of art. These were presented to the town in 1852, by Wm. Cotton, Esq., of Highland House, Ivy Bridge. The drawings include nearly 300 original sketches by the old Italian masters. Among the paintings are 3 portraits by *Reynolds*, viz. 1. of himself; 2. a profile of his father, the Rev. Samuel R., head-master of Plympton grammar-school; and 3. his youngest sister Frances, who for a considerable time presided over her brother's household. The building was erected 1811, and enlarged 1852, for the reception of the Cottonian collection. It is open free to the public every Monday.

The Royal Devon and Cornwall Botanical and Horticultural Society hold their meetings either in Plymouth or Devonport. Both towns have a *Mechanics' Institute*. In private collections are many interesting *specimens of rare birds*, which have been procured on Dartmoor, or in its neighbourhood. Mr. Bolitho, of this town, has the merlin, rough-legged buzzard, long-eared owl, grasshopper warbler, Dartford warbler, Bohemian waxwing, hawfinch, siskin, spoonbill, avocet, and Temminck's stint; Mr. J. B. Rowe, the grasshopper warbler, Bohemian waxwing, Richard's lark and bee-eater; Mr. Tripe, of Devonport, the bearded titmouse, spoonbill, and avocet; Mr. J. Pincombe, the gyrfalcon, rough-legged buzzard, Montagu's harrier, long-eared owl firecrest, and siskin; and the Rev. W. S. Hore, of Stoke, the snowy owl, pied flycatcher, and Richard's lark. With respect to art collections, the following portraits by *Sir Josh. Reynolds* are in the possession of Miss Gwatkin, 21, Princess Square :—Two of Sir Josh. R., viz. the first and last he painted of himself; Mary Palmer, his niece, afterwards Marchioness of Thomond; J. Lovell Gwatkin, Esq.; and Theophila Palmer, on her marriage with Mr. Gwatkin.

4. The *Guildhall*, in Whimple-st., containing some pictures, including a portrait of Geo. IV., when Regent, by *Hoppner*.

5. *St. Andrew's Church*, at the corner of Bedford-street. A ch. was built here at an early period by the Augustinians of Plympton, to whom this part of the town belonged. It was rebuilt, like most of the Devonshire churches, during the Perp. period, and no part of the present structure is older than 1430. The tower was built about 1460, when, says Leland, " one Thomas Yogge, a marchant of Plymmouthe, paid for makynge of the steeple. The towne paid for the stuffe." This tower is fine, and the arrangement of the pinnacles very good. The nave and aisles are lofty, and extend to the E. end, producing the usual west-country triple chancel. Much has been done to this ch. of late years, but the interior is not satisfactory. Into this ch., during service, the news was brought of the return of Sir Francis Drake from his voyage round the world, when all the congregation hastened to the pier to welcome him. Here Chas. II. touched for the king's evil; and here Dr. Johnson in 1762 listened to a sermon written expressly for his edification by Dr. Zachary Mudge. *Chantrey's* fine bust of this vicar of St. Andrew's, who was eulogized by Johnson as "a man equally eminent for his virtues and abilities, at once beloved as a companion, and reverenced as a pastor," is at the end of the S. aisle. The bust was taken from a portrait by Reynolds. The body of Blake (who died in the harbour, 1656) was embalmed at Plymouth, and his heart buried in this ch. " by the Mayor's seat doore." Among other monuments, remark those of Sir John Skelton, Lieut.-Governor of Plymouth, 1672; Dr. Woolcombe, d. 1822, by *Westmacott*; Mrs. Rosdew, by *Chantrey*; and a tablet in

the S. aisle for Charles Matthews, the comedian, who died at Plymouth in 1835. Under the chancel is a crypt, which is said to communicate with a 15th centy. building on the S. side of the ch., called "the Abbey." Of its history nothing is known. It may have been connected with Plympton Priory, to which St. Andrew's belonged. Since 1640 the parish has been divided, and a part of it appended to

6. *Charles' Church*, erected 1646-58, and consecrated by Bp. Seth Ward, in 1664, in the name of King "Charles the Martyr." It has a light and elegant spire, and is a remarkably good building for its time.

Sutton Pool, the harbour of Plymouth, is the property of the Duchy of Cornwall, but leased to a company. The entrance is 90 ft. wide, between 2 piers called the *Barbican*, erected in 1791-9. There is a lighthouse on the W. pier.

Plymouth Hoe (Sax. high ground—a place for watching or observation. So "Hawley's Hoe" at Dartmouth, Rte. 9) is justly celebrated as one of the most beautiful promenades in the kingdom. It consists of a high ridge of land, stretching from Mill Bay to the entrance of Sutton Pool, and constituting the sea-front of Plymouth. The view from it is unrivalled for variety. By aid of the map the spectator may hence distinguish by name the many interesting features of the Sound (see *post*), and on a clear day may look for the Eddystone Lighthouse in the waste of waters to the S.W. Plymouth Hoe has some legendary and historic associations. It is mentioned by the poet as the spot where Corineus, the companion of Brute of Troy, fought with the gigantic aborigines:—

"The Western Hogh, besprinkled with the gore
Of mighty Goëmot, whom in stout fray
Corineus conquer'd."
Spenser, book II. c. 10.

Corineus was the ancestor of all [*Dev. & Corn.*]

Cornishmen. A "pourtrayture of 2 men with clubbes in their hands" was cut on the turf of the Hoe in commemoration of this fight, and the steps by which Corineus, after his victory, dragged the body of Goëmot to the edge of the cliff, whence he flung it into the sea, were pointed out very recently. Mr. Rowe, in his 'Perambulation of Dartmoor,' has hazarded a conjecture that the Hoe (or St. Nicholas Island below it) was the *Iktis* of Diodorus Siculus, from which tin was anciently shipped. With more certainty it was the point of the English coast from which the Armada was first descried (the tradition runs that Sir Francis Drake and the other sea captains were playing bowls here when the news of the great fleet's approach was brought to them); and on the anniversary of that day it was long the custom for the mayor and corporation of Plymouth to wear their "scarlet," and to treat their visitors with cake and wine. It was from the Hoe too that Smeaton watched the progress and the safety of his lighthouse on the Eddystone. "After a rough night at sea his sole thought was of his lighthouse . . . . There were still many who persisted in asserting that no building erected of stone could possibly stand upon the Eddystone; and again and again the engineer, in the dim grey of the morning, would come out and peer through his telescope at his deep-sea lamp-post. Sometimes he had to wait long, until he could see a tall white pillar of spray shoot up into the air. Thank God! it was still safe. Then, as the light grew, he could discern his building, temporary house and all, standing firm amidst the waters; and thus far satisfied, he could proceed to his workshops, his mind relieved for the day."—*Smiles' Lives of the Engineers,* i. 43.

The *Citadel*, with its formidable works, occupies the eastern end of the Hoe, and commands the entrance of the *Catwater* and *Sutton Pool*.

This fortress was erected in the reign of Charles II., on the site of a more ancient building, and consists of three regular bastions, with two intermediate ones, and the necessary works and ravelins. The entrance is by two sculptured gateways with drawbridges, which admit the stranger to a spacious esplanade, adorned by a bronze statue of Geo. II. in the costume of a Roman warrior. The most interesting part of the citadel is the walk round the ramparts, for hence are obtained delightful and varied views, with a foreground of embrasures, massive walls, and cannon.

Mill Bay, on the W. of Plymouth Hoe, is a larger harbour than Sutton Pool, and so deep that vessels of 3000 tons may lie close to the pier at low water. The *Great Western Dock Company* purchased both pier and harbour, and constructed, at the head of the bay, the *Great Western Docks*, of which the basin has an area of 14 acres and a depth of 22 ft., and iron gates 80 ft. in width. Within this basin is a graving dock 379 ft. by 96 ft. These docks are connected with the station of the S. Devon and Cornwall railways.

·Of *ancient buildings* in Plymouth, beside the churches, there are few relics. In the Ch. of the Carmelites, in Briton side (of which an arch and a few low walls only remain), the sittings of the Commissioners were held during the "Scrope and Grosvenor" controversy in 1387. *Palace Court* in Catte-street shows the quadrangle of what must have been a fine 15th centy. house. It was built by John Painter, 4 times mayor; and in it the Princess Catherine of Arragon was received on her first landing at Plymouth in 1501. There are some good Elizabethan houses in Notte-street. *Hoe Gate*, at the head of Hoe-street, the single surviving relic of the ancient fortifications, was pulled down in January 1863.

Plymouth and Devonport are supplied with excellent water by *leets*, or streams, conveyed by artificial channels from Dartmoor. The Plymouth leet winds along the hills, at a gentle inclination, a course of about 30 m., and flows into a reservoir in the northern suburb, from which it is distributed. The inhabitants owe this important benefit to the munificence of Sir Francis Drake, who, when representative for Plymouth, obtained an act of parliament authorising him to bring the stream through private property. The completion of the work was attended with public rejoicings, and the stream, on its arrival, welcomed by the firing of cannon; the mayor and members of the corporation, attired in full dress, going out to meet it, and accompanying it in procession as it flowed into the town. The country-people; however, give another version of its first introduction; for they say that the inhabitants, or rather the laundresses, being sorely distressed for water, Sir Francis Drake called for his horse, and, riding into Dartmoor, searched about until he had found a very fine spring, when he bewitched it with magical words, and, starting away on the gallop, the stream followed his horse's heels into the town. Plymouth leet is derived from the river Meavy, about a mile above Sheepstor bridge; that of Devonport from springs N. of Prince's Town. It is to be regretted that more care is not bestowed upon these good gifts. The channels are exposed to many sources of impurity; and the difference is very sensible between the stream at Dartmoor and at the entrance to Plymouth. New reservoirs have however been constructed at Knackersknowle and on Hartley Hill. It was before the construction of the Devonport leet that Dr. Johnson, during his Plymouth visit in 1762, exclaimed, "No, no, I'm against the *Dockers*. I'm a Plymouth man. Rogues! let them die of thirst. They shall not have a drop." The "Dockers" had begged for a supply from the Plymouth leet.

Stonehouse is comparatively of modern date, and derives its name from Joel de Stonehouse, who held the manor in the reign of Hen. III. It contains those important government establishments, the Victualling Yard, the Naval Hospital, and the Marine Barracks.

The *Royal William Victualling Yard*, designed by the late Mr. Rennie, occupies a tongue of land at the mouth of the Tamar, and was completed in 1835 at a cost of 1,500,000*l*. It is estimated to extend over 14 acres, 6 of which were recovered from the sea, and consists of a quadrangular pile of buildings, and of spacious quays or terraces, fronted by a sea-wall 1500 ft. in length. The plan of the structure may be understood at once from the adjoining hill, on the summit of which is a stone reservoir, supplied with water from the Plymouth leet, and calculated to contain 6000 tuns. To provide against the failure of the leet, a second reservoir has been excavated at Long Room, in its vicinity; and a third at Bovisand, opposite the eastern end of the Breakwater. The building presents a triple frontage, of which the most imposing is that facing Mount Wise. This consists of a central pile, surmounted by a clock-tower, and of two detached wings, each garnished with a lofty chimney; the entire range of buildings being constructed of granite and limestone, and roofed with a framework of iron. The rt. wing of this frontage is appropriated to the corn and baking department, the l. to the cooperage, and the central part to the purposes of a general storehouse. The abundance of the articles here in waiting for consumers may be imagined when it is stated that the salted beef and pork alone amount to several thousand tierces, each tierce containing 80 pieces of meat of 8 lbs. each. The buildings opposite Mt. Edgcumbe are called the Clarence stores; and on this side, at *Devil's Point*, are the government stairs. The front facing Stonehouse is adorned by a bold and sculptured archway, surmounted by a colossal statue of William IV.

With respect to the interior, it is impossible to enumerate all its wonderful contents. Steam, that great *ouvrier* of the present day, is in every department the mainspring of incessant manufacture and conversion. In one, this versatile spirit does the work of a thousand bakers, and exhibits such rapid and delicate manipulation as to excite the admiration of the beholder. The following departments may be mentioned as most deserving of notice:—The *Bakehouse*, in which 2 engines of 40-horse power grind the corn, knead the dough, and spread it ready to be cut into biscuits, and where a sack of flour is prepared for removal to the oven in $2\frac{1}{2}$ minutes.—The *Cooperage*, in which casks and water-tanks are constructed, and kept by thousands in readiness to be shipped.—The *Stores* of provisions, bedding, clothes, books, &c., where the stranger will acquire definite notions with regard to the expense of supporting a large body of men.—The *Slaughterhouse*, so contrived that the *coup-de-grace* may on an emergency be given at once to 70 or 80 head of cattle, but in which 12 bullocks per diem is the average number sacrificed on the 4 days of the week to which the business is limited. Contiguous to the slaughterhouse are the *Weighing-house*, the *Beef-house*, and a *Store of Vegetables*. —The *Quays*, which are furnished with cranes of enormous power, where vessels load with water, which is discharged into them at the rate of 80 tons weight in 20 minutes, and transferred from these small vessels to ships in the Sound or Hamoaze at the rate of 3 tons in 2 minutes. Near the Victualling Yard is the headland of Western King, on which a fort, called the *Prince of Wales's Redoubt*, was erected 1849.

The *Royal Naval Hospital* is a large building, conspicuous in the N. of Stonehouse, and occupies an area of 24 acres. It dates from the French war (1762), and can accommodate 1200 patients.

The *Royal Marine Barracks* are situated near the shore of Mill Bay, and built around a spacious parade. They are capable of containing a thousand men.

Devonport is the youngest of the 3 great towns. The principal part of it is of recent growth, but the heart of the place dates from the reign of Will. III., when the dockyard was first established. To the year 1824 it was called Plymouth Dock, but at that period it repudiated the vassalage implied by that name, and assumed the title which now designates it as the leading maritime town in Devonshire. It is situated on much higher ground than either Stonehouse or Plymouth, and is the head-quarters of the military and naval authorities. To the passing stranger its great attraction (independent of Mt. Edgcumbe, the Breakwater, the Tamar, and the many objects of interest in the neighbourhood) is

The * *Dockyard* (hours of admittance are the working hours of the yard: observing that the yard is closed from 12 to 1 in winter, and from 12 to ½ past 1 in summer). This vast manufactory of war-ships, and all their complicated gear, dates its origin in the reign of Will. III., from which time it has advanced by slow but certain steps to the rank it now holds as one of the finest arsenals in the world. It affords employment in time of peace to some 2600 persons, and covers an extent of ground along the shore of Hamoaze of about 96 acres, which on the land side is protected by a high wall. All persons, except foreigners (who must obtain an order from the Admiralty), are allowed, under the guidance of a policeman, to make the tour of the establishment. The visitor, having entered the gates, has the *Police Offices* on his rt., the *Chapel*, *Guardhouse*, and *Pay Office* in front, and the *Surgery* on his l. He is immediately conducted down a paved avenue, and turning to the l. passes along the *Row* (the residences of the dockyard authorities) to a flight of steps which lead at once into the busy parts of the yard. His attention will there find ample employment in contemplating on every side the most colossal works and ingenious processes. The principal curiosities may be classed under the following heads:— The *New North Dock*, excavated from the solid rock in 1789, for the reception of vessels with their masts standing; its dimensions being, length 234 ft., width of entrance 64 ft., depth over sill at high water 20 ft. Adjoining it are a smithery, and workshops of plumbers, stonemasons, and bricklayers.—The *Engineer*, *Millwright*, and *Sawing-mills Department*, in which metal is worked by steam-power with almost as much facility as wood. Here are lathes for turning iron, and machines for shaping it into screws and bolts; and for planing, punching, shearing, and drilling it. Among those for cutting wood are circular and segment saws, turning-lathes, and an instrument for cutting trenails. In the same department a machine is employed in plaiting signal halliards, with a continual "wheel about and turn about" motion, from which it has received the name of a "*Jim Crow*."—The *Mast-house and Basins*, where the masts and spars (so astonishing to landsmen) of ships laid up "in ordinary" are stowed or kept afloat. In their vicinity are the North Dock—originally 197 ft. long, and reconstructed on an enlarged scale in 1854, to accommodate the largest men-of-war then known; owing to the alteration in the build of vessels, it is now too short for the larger class of frigates — the Admiral's

Stairs, the Double Dock (on the site of which a new Dock is being constructed), and the Basin; the last, originally constructed in the reign of Will. III., was appropriated to the boats belonging to the arsenal, and communicates at the upper end with a dock for the reception of frigates. The Basin was reconstructed in 1854, and is now used for fitting, &c., vessels of a large size. Here also are kilns, in which planks to be curved are steam-boiled; and vast stores of rigging and sails: and here also the visitor should give a share of his attention to the sea-wall. Beyond the N. Dock is the Camber, a canal 60 ft. wide, running far up the yard, and adjoining the Anchor Wharf. This canal is used for the purpose of discharging stores from the vessels in which they are brought to the yard; to expedite which, hydraulic cranes (Armstrong's) are being (1862) fitted along it. At the end of it is an incline, on which boats are hauled up for repair; and above the canal, at the higher end, is a large boat-store, in which boats of all sizes are stored, being lifted from the water into the store through a trap door in the floor, and carried to their allotted berths by travelling cranes. Here also may be seen boats stored with Clifford's and Kynaston's apparatus, by which they may be safely and instantly lowered from a ship's side in the roughest weather.

Near the boat-shed are the new *Smithery* and *Saw-mills*, the former containing every facility for the working of iron (anchors are no longer made here), and the latter some beautiful machinery for sawing wood.

On the site of the *Double Dock* (built 1717 and 1753 for the reception of line-of-battle ships) there is being constructed one *long dock* to accommodate the largest class of war-ships now known, deep enough to allow of their being docked every day in the year. Some idea of the difference between the vessels known as "men-of-war" 100 years since and now, may be gathered from the fact that the new dock will be longer than the united length of the 2 former docks, each of which has accommodated line-of-battle ships.

The *Rope-houses*, two buildings, each 1200 ft. long, in which the largest rope cables are made. All kinds of rope and line are made here, from the smallest fishing-line to the largest cable. The yarn is at present hard-spun, with the assistance of machinery. The ropes are all laid up by steam-power.—The *Mould Loft* (to be seen only by express permission), where plans are prepared of ships intended to be built.—*King's Hill*, an oasis in this hard-featured scene, and preserved from being levelled like the ground around it at the wish of Geo. III., who was pleased with its commanding position when he visited Devonport.—Lastly, the 5 great *Building Slips*, protected from the weather by enormous sheds. Here may generally be seen some first-rate ships in different stages of their growth; and it is truly interesting to gaze from the interior of one, of which the framework is open to view, at the timbers huge and ponderous which are destined to be floated about the world, and rocked to and fro by the waves.

The *Gun Wharf* is situated to the N. of the dockyard, and is the depôt for munitions of war. Cannon and other destructive engines are here grouped in formidable array, and a large store of small-arms is artistically arranged in the various buildings. To complete his survey of the arsenal, the stranger should also visit

Keyham Yard, which forms, in fact, an integral portion of the Dockyard, though from some unintelligible cause (probably an ill-judged and very costly economy) it is separated from it by the Ordnance Stores, the town fortifications, and part of the towns of Devonport and New Passage. The inconvenience arising from this has to a small extent been obviated by the construction at a great cost of a tunnel nearly ¾ m. long, connecting the 2 establishments.

Keyham Yard contains the steam-factory, now used for the repair of steam machinery and the construction and repair of boilers; and employing ordinarily from 600 to 700 men. It is, however, as yet in its infancy, and could conveniently afford space and machinery for the employment of many times that number. The Steam-Docks here are by far the most extensive in the kingdom, being one-third larger than those at Woolwich. Altogether, the large floating basin, and great amount of dock accommodation for the larger class of vessels, besides the convenience arising from the vicinity of the steam factory, make this the most important portion of the dockyard. The sides of the basin and dock are furnished with steam and hydraulic cranes and capstans of immense power for lifting boilers and other heavy weights into and out of ships, and for facilitating the docking and undocking of ships.

The factory is well supplied with machinery of the best description, which is being added to year by year as improvements in mechanical science occur.

The next object within the limits of the town most worthy the attention of the stranger is

Mount Wise—so called from a family of that name formerly lords of the manor of Stoke Damerell. Devonport is essentially a military station, containing barracks for 2000 men, and protected on the land side (since the reign of Geo. II.) by lines of defence, and seaward by a chain of batteries; and Mount Wise is the arena on which its defenders are occasionally marshalled in review. This hill is, however, principally noted for the beauty of the prospect, and its excellence as a promenade. On the summit is a telegraph, which communicates with the guard-ship by signboards, and with the Admiralty by electricity; and the stranger will generally have the opportunity of beholding its pictorial language hung forth and shifted for the direction of some bark in the offing. By the side of the parade are the residences of the Lieutenant-Governor of the garrison and the Port Admiral; and at its eastern end a large brazen cannon, taken from the Turks by Sir John Duckworth. Near the Semaphore is a camera obscura, in which the visitor may study the surrounding scenery in miniature; and below, by the waterside, the *Royal Clarence Baths*, by which a pleasant walk leads round the base of the hill by Stonehouse Pool. Mount Wise bristles with cannon commanding the entrance of Hamoaze.

Among the *public buildings* of Devonport the following deserve notice. The *Town Hall* (date 1821-2) containing portraits of Geo. I., II., III., Will. IV., Queens Charlotte and Caroline, and Sir Edw. Codrington, the first M.P. for the borough;—the *Column*, a Doric pillar of granite 125 ft. in height, erected in 1824, at a cost of 2750*l.*, to commemorate the change in the name of the town;—the *Public Library* (in Ker-street) of 4000 vols., and a cabinet of minerals, presented to this institution by the late Sir J. St. Aubyn, Bart.;—the Rom. Cath. *Ch. of SS. Mary and Boniface* (the "Cathedral" of the R. C. bishopric of Plymouth), built 1856-8, in the E. Engl style, of unhewn limestone; Messrs. Hansom, of Clifton, architects: it has piers of polished limestone in the choir, and of polished granite in the nave, a tower of 4 stages, and a spire of 200 ft.;—*Mount Zion Chapel*, a Calvinist meetinghouse, b. 1823-4, in imitation of the Hindoo style of architecture;—lastly, the *Military Hospital* near Stoke Ch.

DEVONSHIRE. *Route 7.—Plymouth—The Sound.* 79

Stoke Ch. itself is of little interest. St. Stephen's Ch., George-street, Devonport; St. Mary's Ch., James-street; and St. James's Ch., Keyham, are new churches, all of good design.

The most agreeable and fashionable residences are in *Higher Stoke*, and the stranger should make a point of visiting the summit of Stoke Hill, where the old Blockhouse stands. The view from it is very delightful, and embraces every object of interest in the surrounding country.

Such is a brief account of the 3 great towns of the West. With respect to the *excursions* which should be taken in their neighbourhood, proper objects for them are to be found in every direction; but those worthy of the front rank, to which we must confine ourselves, may be enumerated as follows:—

The Breakwater and Bovisand; Mount Edgcumbe; the Royal Albert Bridge (Rte. 23); the Tamar to the Weir-head; the Oreston Quarries; Bickleigh Vale; Cann Quarry; and the Valley of the Cad.

The visitor to Plymouth should, however, be first made acquainted with

(a) *The Sound.* This magnificent roadstead, so well known as a station for our navy, has been often described as the most beautiful estuary on the English coast; and the stranger entering it from the Channel on a sunny serene day will probably acknowledge that there are grounds for the eulogy. Here "the land," says Risdon, "shrinketh back to give way for the ocean's entertainment, of Tamar, which cometh galloping to meet her, almost from the Severn Sea." The shores rise in hills of from 100 to 400 ft. in height, and are varied by woods and villages, and margined with rocks. On the N. are the towns of Plymouth, Stonehouse, and Devonport, with some minor bays and creeks, and the fine harbours of Hamoaze and Catwater; and the eye ranges from those busy scenes and watery vistas over hill and dale to the heights of Dartmoor. The Sound is about 3 m. in width and the same in length, and covers at high water an area of 4500 acres. At its mouth it is bounded by *Penlee Point* (W.), and *Wembury Point* and the shaggy Mewstone (E.); or, further seaward by the *Rame Head* (W.) and *Stoke Point* (E.); the distance between the 2 last-mentioned headlands being 8½ m. It receives the tribute of 3 rivers, the Tamar, Laira, and Plym; the estuary of the first forming the harbour of Hamoaze, and that of the others the Catwater, both of these estuaries branching into a watery labyrinth of creeks and inlets. The *Isle of St. Nicholas*, or *Drake's Island*, a bold pyramidal rock, strongly fortified and garrisoned, stands at the entrance of the Tamar [here the republican General Lambert ended his days a prisoner (1683), having been confined on the island since 1667]; and the *Mewstone* gives a finish to the eastern horn of the bay. The most striking feature, however, in a general view of the Sound, is the park of *Mount Edgcumbe*, the seat of the noble family of that name, which, comprising the lofty hills on the western shore, presents a varied expanse of foliage descending to the water's edge.

As a roadstead, Plymouth Sound was long found inconvenient, from its exposure to southerly gales; but this is now remedied by the erection of an outlying barrier, which, breaking the force of the waves as they are driven in from the Channel, converts the entire Sound into a harbour. This outlying barrier is the well-known

(b) *Breakwater*, a work which originated in the suggestion of our great Admiral, Earl St. Vincent. It dates

Route 7.—*Plymouth—Breakwater.* Sect. I.

its rise from 1806, when Earl Grey was First Lord of the Admiralty. The late Mr. Rennie, being then instructed to survey the Sound, and report upon the best means of rendering it a secure anchorage, advised that a detached mole should be formed at the mouth of the Sound, where nature pointed out the site for such an erection by a string of shoals called the Panther, Tinker, Shovel, and St. Carlos Rocks, on each side of which the channel was deep and sufficiently wide to afford a safe passage for vessels. As to the mode of construction, he proposed that *rubble*, or rough angular blocks of stone, from 2 to 10 tons weight and upwards, mixed with smaller materials, should be cast into the sea, when the waves would arrange them in the shape best calculated to resist the action of the breakers. In fact, the shoals were to be raised to a height sufficient to arrest the undulation of the sea. The mole was to consist of 3 arms, or *kants*, inclining towards each other at an angle of 120°; thus giving the structure a curved form, which it was considered would prevent the too great accumulation of the waves on the outside, and offer the least impediment to the current. The total length was to be 1700 yds., and the whole was to be raised to the level of half-tide. The estimated cost was 1,055,200*l*., and the quantity of stone that would be required 2,000,000 tons. It was suggested also that a subsidiary pier should be thrown out from the shore. Mr. Rennie's proposal, however, lay dormant for several years, and other plans were, in the interim, offered to the Admiralty : such as to construct piers at different points ; to moor 117 triangular floating frames in the desired direction; to sink on the shoals 140 wooden towers with stones in a double line (Gen. Bentham's); or to connect these cones with a superstructure, so as to form an open-arched mole, similar to those of Tyre and Athens. Valid objections were, however, found to all these proposed works, and it was finally determined to adopt the plan of Mr. Rennie, who received the order for carrying it into execution in June, 1811. A lease of 25 acres of limestone, at Oreston on the Catwater, was purchased for 10,000*l*. of the Duke of Bedford; and in March, 1812, operations commenced by opening the quarries, laying rails, building wharves, and making other preparations for the transport of the stone. The flotilla to be engaged in this work consisted of 10 vessels, each of 80 tons, provided with a line of rails on the deck and in the hold, and of 45 sloops of smaller size. On the 12th of Aug. the first and centre stone was laid on the Shovel Rock ; and on the 30th of March of the following year the work made its appearance above the level of low-water spring tides, 43,789 tons of stone having been deposited. By August following it had advanced so far that labourers could be employed upon it; and in March, 1814, it stood the trial of a storm, and resisted successfully the heavy southerly seas, a large French three-decker riding out the gale in safety under its lee. In this year the original plan was modified, and it was determined to raise the structure to the level of 2 ft. above high-water mark, spring tides. In 1816 the largest annual amount of stone was deposited, viz. 332,407 tons. In the winter of the following year a furious hurricane displaced 200 yds. of the upper rubble, removing it from the sea-slope to the northern side. The effect, however, was to increase the stability of the work, the waves having thus formed their own slope, or the angle of repose at which the blocks would lie undisturbed by storms. It is to be remarked that this action of the waves was exerted only from the level of low-water upwards. The original slope had been 3 ft. horiz. to 1 perp., and it was now flattened to 5 to 1, or

Route 7.—Plymouth—Breakwater.

11°, an alteration recommended by Mr. Rennie when it was resolved to raise the height of the structure. Upon this occasion the Jasper sloop of war and Telegraph schooner, which had anchored outside the protection of the Breakwater, were driven ashore and wrecked with a melancholy loss of life.

In 1821 Mr. Rennie died, and the Admiralty consulted his son Sir John Rennie and three other engineers upon the best mode of completing the work; who advised that the sea and land slopes should be respectively at angles of 11° and 26°; that the sea-slope should be strengthened by dovetailed courses of granite, and the top paved, reduced in width, curved, and its central line removed 36 ft. further inland. Upon the plan thus amended the work was carried on; but such difficulties were experienced in its progress towards the west, where the water was deep, and the roll of the sea more impetuous, that Sir John Rennie proposed that a *foreshore*, or platform of rubble, should be raised in advance of the sea-slope to the level of 2 ft. above low-water mark; this foreshore to be 50 ft. wide at the western end, and to decrease to 30 ft. at its eastern termination. To this the Admiralty acceded, and the foreshore has proved a complete protection, tripping up the heavy seas before they can reach the slope. The plan of the western arm was also at this time amended. Its head was to be circular, and of solid dovetailed masonry; and in the heart of the pile was to be rooted the base of a lighthouse, to consist of an inverted arch filled with solid courses, and resting on masonry equally compact. In 1838 this foundation had been nearly completed, when the work was delayed by a severe storm, which carried blocks of 12 and 14 tons weight from the sea to the land slope. Finally, this important arm, after being additionally strengthened, was completed in 1840. In the following year the first stone of the lighthouse, designed by Messrs. Walker and Burges, the engineers of the Trinity House, was laid, and the structure finished in 1844. It consists of a circular tower, 126 ft. in height from the base of the Breakwater, 71 ft. above high-water mark, and 18 ft. diam. over all at its broadest part. It is constructed of the finest white granite from the quarries of Luxulian in Cornwall. The floors are of stone and arched, but differ from those of the Eddystone in forming at their outer ends a part of the wall. By this mode of construction there is no lateral pressure, and some other advantages are obtained. It is divided into five stories, the highest of which is the lantern with a floor of polished slate. The light is on the dioptric or French principle, having a range of 8 m., and, as an auxiliary, a large bell, which, suspended on the outside, is tolled by clockwork during foggy weather. The E. end of the Breakwater is constructed with a circular head, and of solid masonry, like the W., and supports a pyramidal beacon of beautiful white granite, 25 ft. in height from the top of the Breakwater, and of 20 ft. diam. at its base. It is divided into 12 steps, and crowned by a pole of African oak 17 ft. high, supporting a hollow globe of gun-metal, in which the shipwrecked mariner may take refuge. This beacon was begun and finished in the year 1845.

Such is a brief account of Plymouth Breakwater. Its efficacy in resisting storms has been fully demonstrated, and the thick coating of seaweed which now covers the rubble shows the perfect repose of its angular stones. The depth of water in which the structure has been raised varies from 18 to 45 ft.; the quantity of rubble deposited up to June, 1847, amounted to 3,620,444 tons, and at that time it was presumed that 50,000 tons more would be required. The total cost on the completion of the work is estimated at 1,500,000l. A comparison has been frequently instituted between the Plymouth Breakwater and its sister-work of our neighbours at Cherbourg. The sections of the structure are dissimilar. The construction of the latter has, moreover, been attended by very melancholy casualties, which have been attributed by our engineers to the small size of the rubble employed. The *Digue of Cherbourg* is, however, more than double the length, as will appear by the following comparative admeasurement in yards:—

	Length.	Breadth.	Height.
Digue	4111	90	75 ft. *
Breakwater	1760	120 at base	50 „ †

A new fort (in connection with the defences of Plymouth) is erecting just inside the Breakwater. It is on piles; the first body of which, which had taken 6 months in constructing, was carried away by the sea in August 1862.

After visiting the Breakwater you should land at *Borisand*, the watering-place of her Majesty's ships at anchor in the Sound. Here is a granite battery, mounting heavy guns on revolving platforms (more important fortifications are (1862) in course of construction); and, at a distance of ¾ m. from the shore, a reservoir capable of containing 12,000 tuns of water, which is tapped at the surface by an ingenious contrivance, and conveyed through iron pipes to the Pier at Staddon Point, another work by the late Mr. Rennie. Here also is a picturesque vale, from which the Breakwater is seen in perspective, with a blue patch of sea, framed as it were by the acclivities on each side of the valley. It is a pleasant walk along the adjacent *Staddon Heights* (near *Radford*, H. B. Harris, Esq.)

* To top of parapet.
† To top of breakwater.

to *Mount Batten* at the mouth of the Catwater, which you can cross by boat to Plymouth. Mount Batten is a picturesque old tower, the scene of repeated skirmishes during the sieges of Plymouth by the Royalists. The doorway is so high above the ground as to be entered by a ladder.

(c) There are few more interesting spots in England than **Mount Edgcumbe* (Earl of Mount Edgcumbe), which occupies the western shore of the Sound; and for the splendour of its prospects, for the variety of its surface, for its groves and tasteful gardens, has been long the boast of the county. The Countess of Ossory observed that "Mount Edgcumbe has the beauties of all other places added to peculiar beauties of its own." On the approach to it from a voyage it is seen to peculiar advantage. Contrast then adds a charm; and it is easy to understand the feeling of the admiral of the "Invincible Armada," who is said to have resolved that Mount Edgcumbe should be his in the anticipated division of the kingdom. By the liberality of the noble owner, the park is open to the public every Monday during the summer; and the stranger, by applying at the Manor Office, E. Emma Place, Stonehouse, can procure admittance on other days, but he must be then accompanied by a guide. The ferry across the water is from the Admiral's-hard, Stonehouse, to Cremill. Those who are not able to walk may send over a carriage beforehand by ferry. The house is a castellated building, erected in the reign of Queen Mary, with a hall which, says Fuller, "yeildeth a stately sound as one entereth it." The E. front commands a view of the sea through a vista of trees, and the rooms contain several family portraits—by *Lely*, the 1st Earl of Sandwich, killed in the action of Sole Bay; his countess; his daughter Lady Anne, and her husband Sir Rich. E.;—by *Reynolds*, the Hon.

Richard E.; George, the 1st Lord E., and his wife; Captain E.; and Richard, Lord E., painted when the artist was a boy at Plympton. There are full-lengths of Charles II., James II., Prince Rupert, and Will. III., heads of Charles I. and the Duke of Monmouth, and a small collection by Dutch and Italian masters. But the park and pleasure-grounds are the principal attraction, and in these the visitor should direct his attention to the following objects:—The Italian, French, and English *Gardens*: the first, with its delightful terrace, orangery, and conservatory, and its walks converging to a point at a marble fountain; the second, with its basin and jet-d'eau, prim parterres, and octagon room opening into conservatories; the third, with its pavilion and noble trees, including the red cedar (the largest in England) and cork-tree, and exemplifying rather the picturesque and irregular grouping of nature than the skill of the gardener. In the vicinity of these gardens is the *Blockhouse*, an old fort on the shore of Barnpool, dating from the reign of Elizabeth; *Thomson's Seat*; the *Temple of Milton*; and the *Amphitheatre*, a recess in the woods.—The *White Seat*, near the summit of the park, an alcove commanding a rare prospect.—The *Ruin*, artificial, but happily placed.—The *Cottage*, embowered in creeping plants, with a rustic verandah.—The *Arch*, adjoining a stone seat on the edge of a precipice overlooking the Sound.—The *Zigzag Walks*, leading down the cliffs among rocks and woods, and affording delicious glimpses of the surrounding scenery. —*Redding Point*, where an unbounded expanse of ocean bursts upon the sight.—*Picklecoombe*, a secluded dell, but with a formidable battery; and, lastly, the *Valley of Hoe Lake*, and the *Keeper's Lodge*, hung with trophies of the chace. The stranger should also make an excursion by boat along the shore of the park for a view of the rocks. He can extend it to *Cawsand*, walk thence to the *Rame Head*, and indulge himself with a prospect over Whitesand Bay and a long range of the Cornish coast. (See CORNWALL, Rte. 24.) He will find a boat on *Cremill beach*, where, according to the story, Reynolds painted his first portrait on an old sail, and with the materials of a shipwright. (On the side of the hill above Cawsand, a new fort is being thrown up (1862), which will completely command the western entrance to Plymouth and Devonport.)

Drake's or *St. Nicholas' Island* is another good point for a view of the Sound. It was once crowned by a chapel dedicated to St. Michael, but has long been a fortress, and one of the principal defences of Devonport. The largest battery mounts 19 guns, ranging from 32 to 68 pounders. In 1667 Lambert, "the arch-rebel," was brought here a prisoner, and here he died 1683. A ledge of rocks, called *the Bridge*, connects the island with the shore of Mount Edgcumbe.

(*d*) *The Tamar*. This beautiful river rises in the parish of Welcombe, on the extreme border of the county, near the shore of the Bristol Channel, 59 m. from the sea into which it ultimately falls. A trip by water to the *Weirhead* (22 m. from the Sound) should be an object with every visitor to this neighbourhood. It can be easily accomplished in a rowing-boat, on a summer's day, with the advantage of the tide. A steamer plies as far as Calstock, and occasionally extends her voyage to Morwellham; but those who have time for the full enjoyment of the excursion should select a less rapid and noisy mode of conveyance. Upon leaving Devonport you launch at once into *Hamoaze*, the celebrated anchorage of her Majesty's ships "in ordinary," extending from Mt. Edgcumbe to Saltash, a distance of 4 m. The rt. bank here offers in succession, the creeks of *Millbrook* and *St. John's Lake*, the town of *Torpoint*, the woods of *Gravesend* and *Thankes* (seats of Lord Graves), and of *Antony House* (W. H. Pole Carew, Esq., M.P.), and the *Lynher*, a creek which flows to St. Germans. The l. bank, the *Victualling-yard*, *Dockyard*, *Morice Town*, *New Passage*, *Keyham Steam-yard*, and an inlet reaching to Tamerton. The wonderful tubes of the *Albert Bridge* then span the river at a height of 170 ft. above the surface, and *Saltash* greets you. The view is extremely picturesque. The old crazy houses, with their balconies and balustrades, rise one above the other from a steep slope; and the place is often invested by an atmosphere so clear and bright as to remind the traveller of the sunny south. Above Saltash the river expands so considerably as to assume the appearance of a lake; and here, on the l. bank, the Tavy joins the stream amid the woods of *Warleigh* (Rev. W. Radcliffe), and a distant view of Dartmoor—particularly of Mis Tor—enhances the beauty of the neighbouring shore. On the rt. bank is the *Ch. of Landulph* (CORN., Rte. 25), standing at the mouth of a creek, which is overhung by the trees of *Moditonham* (— Carpenter, Esq.), a house in which the Commissioners of the Prince of Orange treated with the Earl of Bath for the surrender of the castles of Pendennis and Plymouth. The voyager now reaches a sharp turn of the river, and, upon rounding the corner at the village of *Hall's Hole* (famous for cherries), suddenly beholds *Pentillie Castle* (CORN., Rte. 25) and its crescent of wooded hills. Through scenery of this description the boat glides onward, passing the village of *Beer Alston*—once a borough, disfranchised by the Reform Bill—to *Cothele* (CORN., Rte. 25), where it will be necessary to disembark and foot it to the old mansion of the lords of Mount-Edgcumbe. The river-scene is delightful; the limpid water is margined by rocks, and clearly reflects the green foresters overhead: while, at a bend of the stream, the wood recedes into the glen of *Danescombe*, which is so called from a tradition that the Danes landed in it previous to their defeat on Hingston Down by Egbert, in the year 835. Above Cothele is the village of *Calstock*; beyond that place a wooded crescent skirts the river, which, winding round the demesne of *Harewood House* (Reginald Trelawny, Esq.), so lingers in the vicinity of Calstock, that the best course is to proceed through the grounds of Harewood and meet the boat at the ferry opposite *Morwellham*. Here there is an inn, to which you can return after continuing the voyage to the *Weir-head*; but this should be done, as above Morwellham the river is girt on either bank by elevated hills, which, on the l. shore, are faced by the superb crags called the *Morwell Rocks*. These will excite the admiration of the beholder, rising in shaggy pinnacles to au immense height. From *Morwellham* you should walk up the inclined plane of the Tavistock canal, to the summit of the rocks. (See p. 149.) The ch. of

Calstock (*Inn*: Naval and Commercial) crowns an opposite hill. It is built of Cornish granite, and contains the vault of the Edgcumbes, built in 1788, and monuments to Pierce Edgcombe, and the Countess of Sandwich, widow of that earl who was killed in the furious action with De Ruyter, 1672. In the vicinity of Calstock, near Harewood, are quarries of the porphyritic elvan called *Roborough stone*.

(c) Shorter excursions can be taken on this river; viz. to *Trematon Castle*, *Antony House* (pictures), *St. Germans*, *Tamerton Foliot*, &c. (*See* Rte. 23.) It is a pleasure to be floated by the tide along *Tamerton Creek*, when its woods and venerable *Warleigh Tor* are lighted by a summer's sun.

Tamerton Foliot, the bourn of such a voyage, is an interesting village, placed at the meeting of 3 valleys, with an old church approached by steps hewn from the rocky ground. In this ch. (Perp., with a good tower) are the tombs of the Foliots and Coplestones, and effigies of Roger de Gorges and his lady, of the time of Hen. V. (a fine specimen, the heads supported by angels). Near the churchyard wall was *the Coplestone Oak*, the "fatal oak" of 'Warleigh,' that tale of Mrs. Bray's, so rich in word-paintings of the scenery of this neighbourhood. This picturesque old tree was blown down some years since. It was at its foot that the "godson" of John Coplestone, of Warleigh (temp. Eliz.), fell dead. He had much "angered" his godfather, and after a long absence presented himself in Tamerton ch., where Coplestone was present. Seeing his godfather's "fierce looks," he hastened out of ch. after the service, but was followed by Coplestone, who threw his dagger after him and killed him on the spot. Coplestone's pardon, says Prince, "was hardly obtained at the cost of about 13 manors in Cornwall." Adjoining Tamerton, on the shore of the Tavy, is the mansion of

Warleigh (Rev. Walter Radcliffe), inhabited by Sampson Foliot, lord of the manor of Tamerton, in the reign of Stephen. The present house, however, dates from those of Hen. VII. and VIII. Here is a *great hall* hung with family portraits, among which may be seen those of Gertrude Coplestone and her husband Sir William Bastard, who assisted old John Arundell in the defence of Pendennis Castle. There is also a large family-piece by *Hudson*, the master of Sir Joshua Reynolds. The hall is lighted by windows of stained glass, bearing the arms of Foliot, Radcliffe, and Coplestone. In the grounds are avenues, terraces, and gardens. The park (but with slender foundation) has been sometimes fixed on as the scene of Ethelwold's murder by Edgar. (This has also been fixed at Harewood, the seat of the Trelawneys. But Harewood forest in Hampshire (near Andover) has the best claim to this distinction. A spot called from time immemorial the "Dead Man's Plack," is there pointed out as that on which Ethelwold fell.)

(*f.*) The *Oreston Quarries* and *Saltram* will contribute to another day's pleasure. They lie just E. of Plymouth, and are most agreeably reached by boating it up the Catwater. The Oreston Quarries have furnished all the limestone employed in the Breakwater; and the extent of ground there cumbered by broken cliffs and the ruins of the land is astonishing. During the progress of the excavation the workmen discovered in certain fissures the bones of hyænas, elephants, rhinoceroses, wolves, deer, and other animals now foreign to the country; remains curiously intermixed, but supposed to have been brought together by animals *falling into cracks*, which in time became filled by loam, sand, and the fragments detached from their sides. A good example of the junction and alternation of the limestone with the slate may be seen near the

Laira Bridge, an elegant cast-iron structure, built 1824-7, at the expense of the late Earl of Morley, by the late J. M. Rendel, who was then only 25 years of age, and received for his account of it the Telford medal. It is on 5 elliptical arches, and at the time of its erection was the largest structure of the kind in the country, excepting that of Southwark. Adjoining it is the terminus of the railway from Dartmoor, heaped with a ponderous load of granite. At this bridge the estuary of the Plym changes its name of Catwater to the *Laira*, and at high water spreads over a broad and sedgy channel, of which 175 acres were reclaimed from the water by the late earl at a cost of 9000*l*. The embankment is 2910 ft. long and 16 high. The woods of

Saltram skirt the E. shore its entire length. This seat of the Earl of Morley is justly admired for its picturesque beauties, and was purchased in 1712 by Geo. Parker, Esq., ancestor of the present Earl. The mansion, erected by Lady Cath. Parker early in the last centy., is the largest in the county, and well known for the *Saltram Gallery*, a very interesting collection, formed chiefly by Sir Josh. Reynolds for the first Lord Boringdon. It contains the following portraits by this eminent artist:—

Hon. Mrs. Parker, whole-length, engr. Watson.
John, E. of Morley, and his sister, whole-length, engr. S. W. Reynolds.
Hon. Mrs. Parker and her son, whole-length, engr. S. W. R.
John, Lord Boringdon, small whole-length, engr. S. W. R.
Theresa, daughter of Lord B.
Montague Edmund Parker, Esq.
Walter Radcliffe, Esq., of Warleigh.
Sir Thomas Acland, Bart.
Sir John Chichester, Bart.
Sir John Davis, Bart.
William, Marquis of Lansdowne.
Commodore Harrison.
Bartolozzi, the engraver, 1771.
Kitty Fisher, as Cleopatra dissolving the pearl, a most beautiful face, engr. Houston and S. W. R.
Mrs. Abinger, as Miss Prue, engr. S.W.R.
Miss Fordyce (Mrs. Greenwood), engr. S.W.R.

The library contains a portrait of Sir Joshua by *Angelica Kauffman*, painted 1768, but, says Cotton in his 'Life of Sir J. R.,' "it has all the look of a real matter-of-fact likeness, very different from the fine pictorial heads he painted of himself, with bushy hair, and a loose robe thrown over the shoulders." Of the other pictures may be mentioned—

Lady Catherine Parker, whole-length. . . . *T. Hudson.*
Cattle . . . . . . *Cuyp.*
Madonna and Child . . *Sassoferrato.*
Flight into Egypt . . . *G. Poussin.*
Marriage of St. Catherine *Correggio.*
Spanish Figures . . . *Palamedes.*
Soldiers in a rocky scene . *Salvator Rosa.*
St. Anthony and Christ . *Caracci.*
St. Catherine . . . . *Guido.*
Tribute Money . . . . *Caravaggio.*
Landscape . . . . . *Wouvermans.*
Adoration of the Shepherds *Carlo Dolce.*
Madonna and Child . . *Andrea del Sarto.*
Landscape . . . . . *Berghem.*
Bolingbroke Family . . *Vandyke.*
Three Female Figures . *Rubens.*
Game . . . . . . *Snyders.*
Holy Family . . . . *Guido.*
Bacchanalians (valued at 3000 guineas) . . . *Titian.*
Sir Thomas Parker . . *Jansen.*
Queen Elizabeth.
Sea-piece . . . . . *Vanderveldc.*
Two small pictures . . *Albano.*
Charles XII.
Apollo and Daphne . . *Albano.*
Phaëton . . . . . . *Stubbs.*
Sigismunda.
Landscape . . . . . *Wilson.*
Decapitation of St. Paul . *Guercino.*
Cattle . . . . . . *Rosa di Tivoli.*
Animals . . . . . *Snyders.*
The Assumption . . . *Sabbatini.*

The ceilings of the saloon and dining-room were painted by Zucchi; and the house contains many other specimens of art, among which is a bust of the Earl of Morley by *Nollekens*, and casts of Psyche, a Faun, and a Hebe by *Canova*. A collection of rare birds killed in the neighbourhood includes the Bohemian wax-wing, Montagu's harrier, short-eared owl, and siskin.

(*g*) *Bickleigh Vale* and the *Valley of the Cad* will be explored by all those who like to seek out Nature in her lonely retreats, and to commune with her in rocky dells and moorland solitudes. They are now best reached by the Plymouth and Tavistock Rly., and are described in Rte. 13.

(*h*) Short excursions may be made from Plymouth to the neighbouring villages; such as *Tamerton Foliot* (see *ante*), *St. Budeaux*, and *Egg Buckland*.

Near Tamerton Foliot is *Warleigh* (Rev. W. Radcliffe); near St. Budeaux, an ivy-mantled tower of the old manor-house of *Budocksheds*; from the ch. tower is a fine view over the Tamar. This is one of the points selected for the line of fortifications which are to surround Plymouth on the land side. The ch. and churchyard here were fortified by the Royalists, and stormed by the Roundheads in 1646. Near Egg Buckland is *Widey Court* (Miss Morshead), the headquarters of Prince Maurice when he besieged Plymouth in 1643, and visited by the king in 1644. The *Ch.* of Egg Buckland (B. by the sea?—Sax. *Egstream*—the *edge*—boundary-stream) is Dec., and has a good S. porch. The tower well deserves attention.

(*k*) The *Eddystone Lighthouse.* Weather permitting, you will probably be tempted to visit this wonderful work, which, erected on a mere point in a stormy sea, affords a beacon and guiding-light to mariners. The Eddystone is a narrow rock of gneiss, situated 14 m. from Plymouth, daily submerged by the tide, and of most mournful celebrity as the scene of repeated disasters. For many years the possibility of raising some structure to mark this hidden danger had been a mooted point with engineers, when, in 1696, Mr. Winstanley succeeded in erecting a lighthouse, which he imagined to be as firmly seated as the rock itself. The building was, however, scarcely complete before a furious storm engulfed it (1703), together with its unfortunate projector. After a lapse of 3 years Mr. Rudyard constructed a second lighthouse, and this was better calculated to resist the watery element, but fell a prey to fire. It was then that Smeaton planned the present structure, taking, it is said, as his model the trunk of an oak, which so seldom succumbs to the tempest. This work was commenced in 1757 and finished in 1759, and the success with which it has braved the storms of 100 winters is sufficient proof of the skill of its projector. The case of the building is formed of granite, and so rooted in the rock by the means of dovetailing, that in fact it forms a part of the Eddystone. The structure is 100 ft. in height and 26 in diameter; and being situated so far from the land, with the strong waves sweeping around it, is truly imposing in its effect. "Were there only a dark rock emerging from the sea in this lonely position, it would command the presence of very unusual feelings in the breast; but when to this is added a graceful building inhabited by man, growing as it were out of the bosom of the deep, the sensation produced is altogether indescribable. We seem transported to a scene in some new kind of existence." Over the door of the lantern, and upon the stone which appears to have been the last fixed, is engraved the date, and the following words of thanksgiving for completion of so arduous an undertaking—"24th Aug. 1759. Laus Deo." A full and most interesting account of the progress and completion of the building will be found in *Smiles' Lives of the Engineers* (vol. ii. Smeaton).

ROUTE 8.

EXETER TO TORQUAY (S. DEVON RAILWAY.) TORQUAY AND ITS NEIGHBOURHOOD.

From Exeter to Newton the line is the same as in Rte. 7.

At Newton a branch passes off on the l. to Torquay and Torbay. At first it coincides with the main line (passing under Milber Down, where is a large ancient camp); but then, diverging, passes the King's Kerswell Stat. (with the ch. rt.), and ascends the valley to a summit at Shiphay, from which it descends to

6½ m. from Newton, *Tor Stat.*, for St. Mary Church, Tor, and Torquay, through Union-street; and

7 m. *Torquay New Stat.*; affording a much prettier approach by Tor Abbey and the Sea Road.

On leaving this stat. the Bay suddenly bursts upon the view in full beauty, *Berry Head* and Brixham on the rt., and the broken cliffs and bright sunny houses of Torquay on the l. The road, a new one, skirts the shore, and leads to an open place about the centre of the town.

Before describing Torquay we may mention the places of interest which adjoin this short line. All are of course within easy distance of Torquay or of Newton; but there is no intermediate stat. except at King's Kerswell.

On the summit of *Milber Down* (1¾ m. E. of Newton) is a celebrated camp, consisting of a rectangular triple entrenchment, probably Roman, begirt at a considerable distance by a circular vallum. A road passes through these ancient works to St. Mary Church. (S.W. of Newton, 3 m., rises *Denbury Down*, which is crowned by an elliptical camp.)

Haccombe House (Sir Walter Carew, Bart.), about 6 m. from Torquay and 3 from Newton (it is on the N. side of Milber Down), was built about 50 years ago on the site of a very ancient Hall. In the time of the Conqueror the property was held by the Haccombes, from whom it passed through the Archdeacons to the Courtenays, and in the 14th centy. to the present family.

Haccombe Ch., which was dedicated to St. Blaise in 1328, contains, notwithstanding, some portions of earlier date; and Dr. Oliver conjectured that the new dedication was rendered necessary by extensive alterations made by Sir Stephen de Haccombe, whose effigy remains in the chancel. This is a fine example, cross-legged, with the armour curiously engraved. In the N. aisle are 2 figures on an altar-tomb —possibly Hugh Courtenay, and Philippa his 2nd wife; and a tomb with recumbent female effigy (14th centy., but unknown). On the chancel floor are 4 interesting *brasses* of the Carews: —Nicholas Carew, 1469; Thomas Carew, 1586; Marie, his wife, 1589; and Elizabeth, wife of John Carew, 1611. These monuments and brasses are among the most interesting in Devonshire, and should be seen by the antiquarian. Much has been done for the ch. of late years. On the door are 2 horse-shoes, placed there (says tradition) to commemorate the wild feat of a Carew, who won the wager of a manor of land by swimming his horse a long distance from the shore into the sea, and back again.

King's Kerswell Stat. (the turnpike road passes through the village, 3 m. from Newton, and there is a rly. stat. here). The *Ch.* has a late Dec. tower, with octagonal staircase turret. In the recessed windows of the N. aisle are 3 effigies—a knight and two ladies, probably Sir John Dinham and wife (temp. Richard II.), and a daughter of Sir Thos. Courtenay, who brought the manor to the Dinhams. The knight and his wife were no doubt removed from a recess in the S.

wall, now converted into a seat. His armour and the lady's very rich dress deserve notice.

7 Torquay. (*Inns*: Royal Hotel; — Queen's Hotel; — London Inn.) Pop. in 1861, 16,419 (including Tor Moham). This watering-place, reputed to possess one of the most equable climates in England, and much resorted to by invalids with delicate lungs, is for the most part of very modern growth. It is built on the northern angle of Torbay, at the confluence of 2 deep valleys with the sea; and while its regular streets, for the most part, occupy the lower levels or terraces, the cliffs and summits are dotted with villas. The general effect of the white houses, the grey limestone cliffs, and the foliage and greensward forming the ground of the whole, is unusually pleasant and picturesque, and calculated to soothe, as far as scenery can soothe, the lassitude and depression of ill-health. Torquay seems first to have been brought into notice as a residence by the families of naval officers, when, during the French war, the Channel fleet under Earl St. Vincent used the bay as an anchorage. Here, as elsewhere, the supply of houses has recently been great, but only a very little, if at all, beyond the demand. The town lies upon a cove or bay, extending from Tor Abbey sands to the quay and tidal basin of the town, while lofty villa-crowned heights overlook it. These are the *Braddons* on the N., *Park Hill* on the E., and *Waldon Hill*, with its wood of firs, on the W. The appearance of the place from the sea is very striking.

With respect to the temperature to which Torquay is so much indebted, the following table and remarks by Mr. E. Vivian were published at the meeting of the Brit. Assoc. in 1856 :—

	Torquay.	England.
	°	°
" Annual mean temp...	50·3	48·3
Max. temp.	76	83
Min. temp.	27	15
Mean daily range	9·9	14·5
Quarterly range	15	46
Days of rain	155	170
Inches of rain	27·8	25·5
Mean humidity	0·76	0·82

The cool summers and mild winters are to be attributed to the equable temp. of the sea. The humidity of the air in summer is diminished by the same cause. The temp. of the sea being frequently below the dew-point of the air, it acts as a condenser, and produces results the reverse of the relaxing character which has been assigned to this district on insufficient data." The mean temp. of the winter months at Torquay is above 46°. The neighbourhood possesses a great variety of both beautiful and sheltered drives and walks, to which, no less than to its climate, the reputation of Torquay is due.

The town has a manufacture to supply the visitor with a memento on quitting it—that of ornamental articles in Devonshire *madrepore*, and *malachite*, which is imported from Russia. At Babbacombe are marble-works, supplied from the Petit-tor quarries. (See *post*.)

The *Ch. of Tor Moham* (a corruption of Tor Mohun) is the parish ch. of Torquay. It is a Perp. building, with large aisles and a good font. It contains some Jacobean monuments of the Carys, and a curious tomb and effigy of about the same date. Both church and churchyard are filled with monuments. St. John's, formerly a Chapel of Ease, has now a district assigned to it; and the ch. is rebuilding from the designs of Mr. Street. The chancel alone is (1865) completed, and in such a manner as to show that the ch., when finished, will be one of the most beautiful in the country. A handsome new ch., St. Luke's, on Waldon Hill, is connected with the original structure. In the vicinity is

Tor Abbey (property of the Carys). It was founded in the reign of Rich. I. (1196), by Wm. Lord Brewer, for Premonstratensian (Norbertine) monks, and was by far the richest of the 32 houses possessed by this order in England. (They were called Premonstratensians, from the mother house, founded by St. Norbert in 1121, in the valley of Premontre, in the diocese of Laon.) It was purchased by the Carys 1662; but this old and loyal family were long seated at Cockington in the neighbourhood of Torbay. Notwithstanding the addition of a mansion with wings, enough of the abbey buildings remain to give a character to the whole. The gatehouse is a striking relic of the 14th centy. Under the vaulting are the arms of the Abbey (a chevron between 3 crosiers), and those of Brewer, Mohun, and Speke. "The roofless chapter-house, the prostrate masses of the central church tower, the refectory converted into a chapel in 1779, and the stately grange, are still interesting." The church measured 200 ft. in length. The chapel (refectory) is of the 14th centy.; the barn (now converted into stables) of the 13th. In the small park are ancient avenues of limes and elms.

Torbay, so well known for its stores of fish, is semicircular in form, about 3½ m. wide at the entrance, and bounded on the N. and S. by the limestone promontories of *Hope's Nose* and *Berry Head*. "On both sides," says Gilpin, "its shores are screened with ramparts of rock, between which, in the centre, the ground forms a vale, declining gently to the water's edge." It is a noted anchorage, protected from the prevalent gales, and affording space for the largest fleets; and, between the years 1792 and 1815, was frequently the refuge of our Channel squadron,

when driven from its cruising-ground. Brixham, near Berry Head, is the station of the fishermen. *Raised beaches* and a *submarine forest* may be observed at various points on the shore; and good examples of the former occur on Hope's Nose, and on the *Thatcher Rock*, just inside that headland. Whilst the Bellerophon lay in Torbay, with Napoleon on board, he observed, "What a beautiful country! How much it resembles Porto Ferrajo, in Elba!"

This beautiful bay has, moreover, an historical interest, as the scene of the landing of the P. of Orange (painted by Northcote), Nov. 5, 1688. But on that memorable occasion it presented an aspect very different from the present. "Its quiet shores," says Macaulay, "were undisturbed by the bustle either of commerce or of pleasure; and the huts of ploughmen and fishermen were thinly scattered over what is now the site of crowded marts and of luxurious pavilions." On Nov. 1 the P. of Orange set sail from Helvoetsluys, and for 12 hrs. stood to the N.W., to divert attention from the scene of his intended operations. Then, changing his course, he bore up for the English Channel before a favouring gale; passed the armament under Lord Dartmouth, wind-bound in the Thames; and, on Nov. 3, reached the Straits of Dover, where his ships extended from one shore to the other, and saluted both Calais and Dover at the same time. On the morning of the 5th of Nov. the land was concealed by a fog, and before the pilots could determine their position the fleet had been carried beyond Torbay, while the gale blew so furiously from the E. that it was impossible to return. Upon the discovery of this misfortune, all was given up for lost; Plymouth was strongly garrisoned, and Lord Dartmouth in full pursuit. But suddenly, it is said, when the calamity seemed irretrievable, the wind abated, the mist dispersed, a gentle breeze sprang up in the S., and the fleet was wafted back to Torbay. The disembarkation was immediately begun. 60 boats conveyed the troops to the shore; the prince himself landing on a desolate beach, which is now the busy quay of Brixham. No sooner, however, had the landing been effected than the wind, the good genius of the prince, came fiercely from the W., and encountering the ships of Lord Dartmouth, drove them for shelter to Portsmouth. To the P. of Orange and his army the welcome gale brought a little discomfort; the ground was soaked with rain; the baggage still on shipboard ; and the prince was fain to pass the night in a miserable hut, from which his flag, with its memorable motto—" God and the Protestant religion"—waved over the thatched roof. On the following day the army commenced its march upon the capital, and towards evening the vanguard reached Newton Abbot, where the Declaration was first publicly read. Here the prince rested a day, and then proceeded towards Exeter, which he entered amid the acclamations of the people on the 8th of Nov. The fleet wintered at Plymouth, and caused a considerable scarcity of provisions in the neighbourhood.

Torquay and its bay have been thus eloquently described by the author of 'Glaucus:'—" Torbay is a place which should be as much endeared to the naturalist as to the patriot and to the artist. We cannot gaze on its blue ring of water, and the great limestone bluffs which bound it to the N. and S., without a glow passing through our hearts, as we remember the terrible and glorious pageant which passed by in the glorious July days of 1588, when the Spanish Armada ventured slowly past Berry Head, with Elizabeth's gallant pack of Devon captains following fast in its wake, and dashing into the midst of the vast line, undismayed by size and numbers, while their kin and friends stood watching and praying on the cliffs, spectators of Britain's Salamis. The white line of houses, too, on the other side of the bay, is Brixham, famed as the landing-place of William of Orange ; the stone on the pier-head, which marks his first footsteps on British ground, is sacred in the eyes of all true English Whigs; and close by stands the castle of the settler of Newfoundland, Sir Humphrey Gilbert, Raleigh's half-brother, most learned of all Elizabeth's admirals in life, most pious and heroic in death. And as for scenery, though it can boast of neither mountain peak nor dark fiord, and would seem tame enough in the eyes of a western Scot or Irishman, yet Torbay surely has a soft beauty of its own. The rounded hills slope gently to the sea, spotted with squares of emerald grass, and rich red fallow fields, and parks full of stately timber trees. Long lines of tall elms, just flushing green in the spring hedges, run down to the very water's edge, their boughs unwarped by any blast; and here and there apple orchards are just bursting into flower in the soft sunshine, and narrow strips of water meadow line the glens, where the red cattle are already lounging knee-deep in richest grass, within ten yards of the rocky pebble beach. The shore is silent now, the tide far out: but six hours hence it will be hurling columns of rosy foam high into the sunlight, and sprinkling passengers, and cattle, and trim gardens which hardly know what frost and snow may be, but see the flowers of autumn meet the flowers of spring, and the old year linger smilingly to twine a garland for the new."

In the town and its immediate vicinity the stranger should direct his attention to the following objects and localities:—

The Museum of the *Torquay Nat. Hist. Society* in Park Street, and the Public Baths and Assembly Rooms on Beacon Hill.—The *Rock Walk*, on the Warren, W. of the harbour, as affording delightful views through the trees.—*Daddy's* (i.e. the Devil's) *Hole*, on Daddy-hole Common, just beyond the easternmost villa on the cliff. It is a limestone chasm, formed by a small landslip, and sheltering some trees and shrubs, and commands an excellent perspective view of the Nose, which is about 2 m. from Torquay. In the opposite direction, nearer the town, is a point called the *Landsend*, and the arched rock known as *London Bridge*. Below the common lies the cove of *Meadfoot*, in which crescents and terraces have risen like mushrooms; and from *Meadfoot Sands* a pretty coomb ascends to Ilsham, an ancient farmhouse, formerly a grange of Tor Abbey, where may be seen a very small Perp. domestic chapel, with upper chamber for the chaplain's residence, and a ground floor, the whole strictly ecclesiastical in character.—*Kent's Hole*, the celebrated ossiferous cavern, rt. of the Babbacombe road, about ¾ m. from the town. Permission to view it must, however, be first obtained from the Curator of the Torquay Nat. Hist. Society, and a guide with a torch will be required. The floor of this limestone cavern was first examined in the year 1824, when it was found, like those of Kirkdale and Yealm Bridge, to be abundantly stored with the fossil bones and teeth of animals now foreign to this country, such as the bear, hyæna, rhinoceros, and elephant. Flint arrow-heads, pottery, and other relics of human occupation, have also been found. The entrance is about 5 ft. high. The interior, which was formerly hung with stalactites, and of which many still remain, ranges from 2 ft. to 70 ft. in breadth, with a maximum height of 18 ft., and may be explored for a distance of 650 ft., when a pool of water presents an impassable barrier. The inner chambers are reached by a squeeze through the *Great* and *Little Oven*, but the passages are wet and muddy, and there is little to repay the fatigue of the adventure. Sir H. De la Beche supposes that Kent's Hole was at first a den of bears, and afterwards the retreat of hyænas, since it contains a quantity of gnawed bones, and the fæcal remains of those animals. (A most interesting memoir of the original opening of this cavern, edited, from the manuscript notes of the late Rev. J. M'Enery, by E. Vivian, Esq., President of the Torquay Nat. Hist. Society, may be obtained of Mr. Cockrem, Torquay.) On the Newton road, close to the Tor rly. station, is *Chapel Hill* or *St. Michael's Mount*, crowned by an old chapel to the archangel. It belonged to Tor Abbey; but no mention occurs of it in the registers or chartularies. It is 36 ft. long, built and roofed with stone, and serves as a sea-mark. Dr. Oliver suggests that the W. end may have been occupied by a hermit. Among the seats in the neighbourhood the site laid out by the late Mr. Brunel is remarkable for the beauty of the grounds.

The following *excursions* can be made from Torquay, but that to *Anstis Cove, Babbacombe*, and *Watcombe* should on no account be passed over.

Looking at the map, it will be seen that Torquay forms part of a small rocky peninsula, which divides Torbay from that far more extensive concavity which includes the coast of Devon hence to Axmouth. A road leads across the root of this peninsula direct to Babbacombe, 2 m., passing the *Public Gardens*, in which is a new Scotch Kirk; or, down a lane to the right near St. Matthias's Ch., close to Kent's Hole and by Austis Cove. But a far pleasanter course is by a path crossing the hill near Hope's Nose (on which may be observed a raised beach and fine examples of trap-rock with contortions of the limestone strata). It winds midway along the ivy-hung cliff, presenting a series of delightful prospects. By this path an easy stroll of about 3 m. brings us to—

Anstis Cove, justly considered one of the most beautiful spots on the coast. It is sheltered from the wind by lofty cliffs very brilliantly coloured and glossy like satin, and based on a beach of white crystalline shingle, derived from the slates in the neighbourhood. The rocks in the centre form buttresses of limestone, which are ivied like a ruin, and screen a little undercliff and tangled wood. The northern horn of the cove is a promontory of limestone, and a busy quarry; a seat on its summit commands, in one direction, a view in which hills and patches of sea are very curiously intermingled; and, in another, the headlands from Teignmouth to Portland stretched out in long succession. On this down, Walls Hill, are the targets and rifle-range of the Torbay Volunteer Rifle Association. On the beach the fossil madrepore is often found. Close to the cove, but on the Babbacombe road, is *Bishopstowe*, the handsome and well-placed Italian villa of Dr. Philpotts, the venerable Bishop of Exeter. ½ m. N. is

Babbacombe (*Inn :* the Cary Arms, close to the beach). A few years ago this pretty village was one of those romantic seclusions which have rendered the coast of Devon such a favourite with the novelist. At a turn of the coast the shore receding forms a tiny bay, in which a group of cottages most fanciful and picturesque lie nestled in a wood.

The bay is little more than a stone's-throw across, and bounded by cliffs of marble and dark red sandstone, rising from a white beach of quartzose pebbles. Far as the eye can reach, the coast stretches eastward, and the eye, ranging along the barrier, may trace the different formations as they appear in the cliffs, from the slate-rocks, which here first abut on the sea, to the chalk of Beer Head. Speculating builders are, however, now effecting a change in Babbacombe. The village is extending inland in ugly houses, and will probably, at no very distant period, amalgamate with Torquay.

On the N. side of this bay is *Petit Tor*, extensively quarried for marble, and exhibiting an interesting geological section, in which a mass of slate is seen to have been thrust up by the action of trap in the form of an arch. It supports a bed of limestone, portions of which have been fairly squeezed into the shales. About ¼ m. distant is *St. Mary Church*, where there are marble-works that will repay a visit. The parish *church*, formerly a plain late Perp. building, has been wholly rebuilt with the exception of the tower (architect S.W. Hugall), and is now one of the most beautiful in the county. The style is Geometrical (Ear. Dec.). The nave is 6 bays in length, divided by moulded piers with shafts of Bath stone and Petit Tor marble. The clerestory is of spherical triangular lights. The font, of Norm. date, and covered with curious carving, is enshrined in a casket of Caen stone and marble. The chancel, the chief point of interest, is simple, though rich in detail, with pietra-dura and carved work. It has a massive oak roof. The screen and reredos, both inlaid in the parish, and with native marbles, were respectively the gift of A. J. Beresford Hope, Esq., and of Miss Burdett Coutts. The organ was given by Mr. Brunel, the celebrated engineer. Including these gifts, the whole cost of the ch. was about 10,000l., the parish having, during the 10 years of rebuilding (1851-1861), contributed by far the larger part of this sum. It is now in contemplation to substitute for the existing tower a spire of the same style as the new ch. 1 m. E., the shore, the romantic landslip of *Watcombe*, broken ground encircled by fantastic red cliffs; and further E. the little dell and cove of *Maidencombe*. It is a delightful walk by the coast from Babbacombe to Teignmouth, a distance of about 4 m.

Another excursion can be made from Torquay, in a westerly direction, to the pretty village of *Cockington*, 2 m., and extended to the remains of *Compton Castle* (an additional 2 m.), once a seat of the family of Pole, but now converted into a farmhouse. This very interesting place should on no account be left unseen by the antiquary. In the reign of Henry II. it belonged to Sir Maurice de la Pole. It went from his descendants to the Comptons, and in the reign of Edw. II. passed by marriage to the Gilberts of Greenway, who sold it about the commencement of the present cent. to the Templers. Behind it are the formal walks of the old garden, or *pleasaunce*. The castle dates from the early part of the 15th centy. "It has no moat, and therefore required other means to be adopted to protect the foot of the wall from being undermined. This object is effected by the great number of projections carried on machicoulis, through the openings of which stones and other missiles could be thrown on the heads of assailants. (That these projections were not garderobes is shown by the fact that a garderobe turret is provided at the back of the same chambers in which they are.) The chapel is tolerably perfect, with a room over it—perhaps the priest's. It had originally a floor in the western part, dividing it into 2 rooms; and there are 2 squints from other rooms toward the altar. The buildings originally surrounded a small quadrangle, and had a square tower at each corner, and were enclosed by a wall 20 ft. high, the greater part of which remains. The postern gate at one end of the front, and the principal entrance in the centre, both had a portcullis. The hall was pulled down when the house was adapted to its present purpose."—*J. H. P.* The strong defences of Compton were rendered necessary from its being so close to the shore, on which landings of the French frequently occurred. Sir Humphrey Gilbert, the discoverer of Newfoundland, and the half-brother of Sir Walter Raleigh, lived for some time at Compton.

The ch. of *Marldon*, in which parish Compton Castle stands, is interesting. The capitals of the Perp. piers have foliage resembling plaited wreaths, which are almost peculiar to Devonshire. Over the entrance door is an inscription. The ch. is said to have been built by the Gilberts, and has been (1862) restored; Wm. White, architect.

A stranger residing any time at Torquay will also visit *Berry Pomeroy Castle*, and *Totnes* (Rte. 7), descend the Dart to *Dartmouth* (Rte. 7; for Dartmouth itself see the following route), and return by *Brixham*, sleeping a night at Totnes or Dartmouth. Or the order of this route may be reversed. *Paignton Ch.* (see the following route) is also worth a visit.

ROUTE 9.

TORQUAY TO BRIXHAM AND DARTMOUTH (DARTMOUTH AND TORBAY RAILWAY). — THE COAST (SLAPTON, TORCROSS, THE START, THE PRAWLE, SALCOMBE, THE BOLT) FROM DARTMOUTH TO KINGSBRIDGE.

From the Torquay Stat., the rly. encircles Torbay, with stations at *Paignton* and *Brixham Road*, and thence crosses the headland to *Kingswear* (opposite Dartmouth — there is a steam ferry across). The distance (performed in less than half an hour) is 8¾ m. Magnificent views of Torbay are commanded along the whole line from Torquay to Brixham Road.

Passing Corbon's Head, with the 3-gun battery of the Torbay Volunteer Artillery, and *Livermead*, where is a good and pleasantly situated lodging-house, the rly. reaches

2 m. *Paignton Stat.* (*Inn*: Crown and Anchor.) This town is at present a little distance from the sea, but it has approached it in villas, and, like Torquay, is rapidly extending in every direction. It is, however, an old place, having formerly, with the manor, belonged to the see of Exeter; and some trifling remains of the *Bishop's Palace* (a crenellated wall, and a tower of the 14th centy.) may be observed at this day adjoining the churchyard. The last tenant of the palace was the celebrated prelate Miles Coverdale. In a newspaper of June, 1809, it is stated that "at Paignton Fair the ancient custom of drawing through the town a plum-pudding of immense size, and afterwards distributing it to the populace, was revived on Tuesday last. It was drawn along the street by a yoke of 8 oxen."

The *Ch.* is ancient (chiefly Perp.), and contains a pulpit (carved and painted wood) worth notice. Observe also the Perp. windows, the shield of Bp. Coverdale on the painted glass of the N. aisle, and the Kirkham chapel, with its tombs, on the S. side of the nave. The stone screenwork here is very fine, but has been mutilated with the utmost barbarism. It is late Perp., and forms a mass of elaborate tabernacle work, with niches and figures. The pinnacles above are crowned with angels bearing shields. The effigies are those of members of the Kirkham family, by whom the screen was erected. On the wall by this chapel is an escutcheon with this inscription:—" Here lyeth the heart and bowels of the most honourable and most worthy and high esteemed John Snellin, Rear-Admiral of Holland and West Friesland, who dyed the xxiiii. of August, MDCXCI." On the exterior of the tower is an arch with a zigzag moulding, like one at Axminster; and, in the churchyard, the steps and shaft of an ancient cross. Paignton is noted for an early *cabbage*, which is sent to all parts of the country. *Kirkham's Hill* (Hall?) here is a 15th centy. house. " The fireplace in the hall is a good example, and in the same apartment is a good water-drain. The outer doorway (of timber) is good."—*J. H. P.*

[Several lanes lead from this town to the shores of the Dart, particularly to *Stoke Gabriel*, a retired and pretty village, remarkable for its yew-tree, said to be the 2nd in England for size and age. Further down the river are *Sandridge* (Lord Cranstoun), an Italian villa, with a double view of the Dart through long vistas of trees — and *Watton* or *Waddeton Court* (H. Studdy, Esq.), a modern building in the Eliz. style. In *Par-*

liament Lane, leading from Stoke Gabriel to Portbridge, a farmhouse is pointed out as the scene of the first council held by the P. of Orange after his landing in Torbay.

On the roadside between Paignton and Totnes the botanist may find *Linum angustifolium*, or narrow-leaved flax.

Berry Pomeroy Castle lies on the road to Totnes].

From
3 m. *Brixham Road Stat.* an omnibus runs to Brixham, meeting some of the trains.

Brixham (*Inns:* London Inn; Bolton Hotel; Globe, at the Quay. Pop. of parish in 1861, 5984). Every intelligent traveller will visit this place, as it is unique of its kind, being the head-quarters of the great Devonshire fishery of Torbay, of which *trawling* is the main feature, whereas *seining* and *driving* are characteristic of the Cornish fisheries. Brixham is divided into the Higher and Lower town, together extending a distance of about a mile up a valley; but the Lower town, or *Brixham Quay*, is the only part deserving notice. A fourth of the manor was purchased many years ago by 12 Brixham fishermen, whose shares have been since divided and subdivided, so that visitors to the pier may generally have the opportunity of cultivating the acquaintance of a "Brixham lord."

About 200 *trawlers* belong to this port, being large decked sloops of from 40 to 50 tons burthen, each generally managed by 3 men and a boy. The trawl-net is about 70 ft. long, in the form of a bag, and provided with a beam, occasionally 40 ft. in length, to keep the mouth open. This net is drawn or *trawled* along the bottom of the sea, and procures flat-fish, gurnards, haddocks, whitings, &c. It is best to visit Brixham on a Saturday, as on that day as many trawlers as can find accommodation enter the harbour, while the rest of the fleet moor off the entrance. Evening on every week-day is the most interesting time, as the fish are then landed, and if the trawlers have been successful the *Quay* presents a lively and picturesque scene; the fish lying in broad piles, a saleswoman disposing of them by auction (knocking down the lots by dropping a stone, the subject of Collins's picture in the possession of the Earl of Essex), men and women engaged in packing them, and vans in attendance to carry the baskets to the rail. In the centre of the quay stood a pillar commemorative of the landing of the Prince of Orange on the 5th of Nov. 1688. It is now removed to the pier, and is said to enclose a part of the stone upon which the prince placed his foot as he stepped from the boat.

Brixham was long celebrated for the ebbing and flowing of the spring *Laywell* (Philos. Trans., vol. vii.), which is situated on the outskirt of the Higher town. This spring is, however, no longer intermittent; the erection of some neighbouring houses having, it is supposed, effected the alteration. The name is evidently a corruption of *Lady-well*.

The *ch.* of Higher Brixham is ancient, and contains several monuments, one to Judge Buller.

The *pier* was built in 1808. At the end of it is inserted in the wall a tablet commemorating the visit of the Duke of Clarence to Brixham in 1823. Upon that occasion the royal duke was presented with a chip from the stone upon which the Prince of Orange is said to have landed, enclosed in a box of heart of oak. The town has a large trade independent of its fishery, and the *tidal harbour*, although tolerably capacious, is found insufficient to accommodate the shipping. A *breakwater*, however, is now in course of construction, the completion of which is expected to render the roadstead a secure anchorage. The Admiralty have an establishment here for watering the navy.

At *Upton*, adjoining the town, an iron-mine is worked with considerable profit.

Berry Head, 1 m. E. of the harbour, should be visited. It is a square-shaped headland of hard limestone, of a flesh-coloured tint, and with a surface glossy like satin. The face of the cliff inside the point is largely quarried, and falls so abruptly to deep water that vessels lie moored alongside, as at a quay. On the summit are the ruins of two large military stations which were used during the French war; and in their vicinity a cavern, in which the bones of hyænas and other extinct animals have been found. Above these were a quantity of human bones and pottery, relics, it is supposed, of the Roman garrison. It is called, from this circumstance, the *Ash Hole*. Another cavern, recently discovered in a quarry above the town, has been very carefully explored by the Geological Society, under the direction of Mr. Pengelley, F.G.S., and some members of the Torquay Natural History Society. The results were considered to prove the very high antiquity of the human race in this district—flint implements, similar to those found in the Drift, having been discovered in the loam at the lowest levels, associated with the remains of hippopotamus, cave lion, hyæna, and other sub-tropical animals. Deeply imbedded in the stalagmitic floor was found a fine pair of antlers of the reindeer, showing a vast change in the climate between these periods.

Should the traveller visit Brixham on his route through the country, and be bent upon thoroughly exploring the southern coast, he will perhaps proceed by the cliffs from Berry Head to Dartmouth. This route, however, is very circuitous

[*Dev. & Corn.*]

(about 7 m.) and laborious. In the space of a mile the path rises many times to an elevation of 300 or 400 ft., and falls as often to the level of the sea, while a series of jutting headlands render it zigzag in a horizontal as well as a vertical plane. There are parts of the shore, however, well worth seeing. About 3 m. W. of Berry Head the quick interchange of hill and valley is remarkable, and gives the advantage of picturesque form to cliffs which are unrivalled for beautiful colouring. They are partly composed of slate, partly of limestone, and include patches of red sandstone; while their colours are crimson, purple, brown, but, beyond all in effect, a delicate blue with a silvery lustre. In this walk from Berry Head to Dartmouth you will pass over fields which are dyed with the red soil of the sandstone formation, while the slate and limestone which lie below it are exhibited in the cliffs. For more than a mile W. of Berry Head the country is divided by formidable stone hedges, rendered quite impassable by ivy. It is therefore advisable to follow a lane to the vicinity of Upton, and there take to the cliffs near *Sharkham Point*.

The high road from Brixham to Dartmouth, 4 m., consists of one long ascent and descent; the view towards Brixham on the ascent meriting notice. The blue waters of the Channel and Torbay occupy the sides of the picture, while the land towards Berry Head rises in the centre in enormous hilly masses; but woods and rocks are wanting in the prospect. On the descent to the Dart, this river opens in a new light to a person who has viewed it only from a boat. The foldings of the hills are beautifully displayed in perspective, and the granite tors of Dartmoor form the background. The river is crossed by a floating-bridge, worked by a horse, occupying 20 min. in the passage.

In the neighbourhood of Brixham are—*Lupton House*, seat of Sir John

F

Yarde Buller, who in 1858, after representing S. Devon for 24 yrs., was raised to the peerage as Baron Churston of Churston Ferrers; the first of the family who lived at Lupton was Judge Buller, the purchaser, 1778; *Upton Lodge*, C. H. Cutler, Esq.; *Nethway House*, on the road to Dartmouth, a mansion visited by Charles II., seat of the Luttrells, also of Dunster Castle, Somerset; *Laywell House*, H. B. Pierrepoint, Esq.; *Churston Court*, Lord Churston; *Galmpton*, also of the Luttrells; and *Greenway*, on the shore of the Dart, and once a seat of the Raleighs, — Harvey, Esq.

From the Brixham Road Stat., crossing the projecting land of which the northern point is Berry Head, we reach

3¾ m. *Kingswear* (see *post* for description), whence there is a ferry to Dartmouth across the river.

Dartmouth (*Inns*: Castle, on the Quay; London Inn. Pop. in 1861, 3330 (including Kingswear), like Totnes, is extremely old, and as interesting for that reason as for the beauty of its position. It is built in terraces upon the shore of a romantic harbour, a lake-like expanse completely land-locked, opening to the sea by a narrow channel, and encompassed by steeply shelving hills of from 300 to 400 ft. in elevation.

The traveller, having disembarked upon the island called *New Ground*, which was reclaimed from the river about a century ago, will observe in the street leading from the quay some of the grotesque old houses for which the town is remarkable. They bear upon their fronts the dates 1625 and 1640, and are truly picturesque, with their wooden framework, rich carving, piazzas, and gables: unfortunately, they are fast giving place to regular London "shop fronts." But the strangest part of Dartmouth lies S. of the New Ground, and consists of two narrow streets, or rather lanes, running parallel with the shore, and along so steep an acclivity, that the pavement of the one is nearly on a level with the roof of the other, while the communication between them is by flights of steps. These streets contain a number of old houses, elaborately carved, and built with overhanging stories, and gables projecting still farther in advance, so that two persons might possibly greet each other by a shake of the hand from opposite windows. The stranger will remark that many of the fronts are supported by brackets, carved in the likeness of a lion, a unicorn, and a griffin.

Dartmouth was first incorporated under the title of Clifton-Dartmouth-Hardness in the reign of Edw. III., 1342, at which time it was evidently a port of great consequence, as it furnished no less than 31 ships to the fleet intended for the siege of Calais, a larger quota than was supplied by any other town in the kingdom, excepting Fowey and Yarmouth. We have also incidental proof of its ancient maritime importance. Chaucer has taken his " shipman" from Dartmouth—

" For aught I know he was of Dertemuthe.
. . . .
By many a storm his berde had been y-blowe."

And we learn that, cotemporary with the poet, there were merchants at this place so wealthy, and possessed of so many ships, that it was said of one Hawley—

" Blow the wind high, or blow it low,
It bloweth fair to Hawley's hoe."

At a more recent period Dartmouth sent some of the first adventurers to the banks of Newfoundland, and largely profited by the fishery. Sir *Humphrey Gilbert*, who took possession of that island for Queen Elizabeth, was born near this town, at Greenway, on the shores of the Dart; and at Sandridge, *Davis*, the bold navigator, who here fitted out the ships with which he penetrated the northern seas to the straits which now bear his name. The town is further distinguished as the birthplace of *Newcomen*, whose name occupies so prominent a place in the history of the steam-engine. He carried on business as an ironmonger in the Butter Row, S. of the New Ground; but was a person of some reading, and particularly acquainted with the projects and writings of his countryman Dr. Hooke. A genius for mechanics, however, directed Newcomen to the path in which he so highly distinguished himself. He was the first to apply the power of steam to the important purpose of draining the Cornish mines, and, in connection with Captain Savery, obtained a patent for his engines in 1705. In the earlier of these machines the steam was condensed by a current of cold water admitted on the outside of the cylinder, the piston being driven down by the weight of the atmosphere. The operation of the engine was therefore slow and attended with a great consumption of fuel, and a boy was required to turn the cocks for the alternate admission of steam and water. Accident, however, suggested two important improvements before Watt took these engines in hand, viz. the condensation of the steam by the injection of water *into* the cylinder, by which means a far more rapid action was obtained, and the connection of the stop-cocks with the beam, by which the engine was made to work itself. The grand improvement of substituting steam for the atmosphere, as the power to drive down the piston, was effected, as is well known, by the genius of Watt.

Dartmouth has many historic associations. A portion of the crusaders' fleet, under Cœur-de-Lion, assembled in its harbour in 1190.

Off the Start Point they encountered a great storm, and were saved by St. Thomas of Canterbury, who descended on the mast of the leading ship burning like fire.—*Hoveden*. In 1347, as above stated, the town contributed a large quota to the armament of Edward III. In 1377, immediately after the death of that monarch, it was destroyed by the French, who in that year swept our shores from Rye to Plymouth. In 1403 it returned the visit of the Frenchmen, when, Du Chastel having a second time destroyed Plymouth, Dartmouth combined with that town in ravaging the coast of France, burning and sinking forty of the enemy's ships. In 1404 the French in their turn sought revenge. Du Chastel again descended upon Dartmouth, but the expedition was this time so roughly received as to be compelled to draw off with the loss of 400 killed and 200 prisoners, including Du Chastel himself. In the wars of the Roses the Lancastrian party used Dartmouth as their port. In the Great Rebellion the town declared for the Parliament; and in 1643 was taken by Prince Maurice, after a siege of a month. The Royalists, however, after an interval of 3 years, were attacked by Fairfax, who carried the place by storm in Jan. 1646. Upon this occasion upwards of 100 pieces of ordnance were captured; and the many old towers and forts, now in ruins on the shore or the heights of Dartmouth, show the formidable number of the works with which the general had to contend.

The objects of interest in the town are: the *old houses* in the Butter Row, particularly Newcomen's, and, on the terrace to the N., a modern house erected by Mr. Holdsworth, the Governor of Dartmouth Castle, in imitation of the old buildings. It is richly ornamented with carving by Dartmouth workmen, after models in the town, and cased curiously with slates, so disposed as to resemble the scales of an armadillo.—The Ch. of St. *Saviour*, date about 1372, in which the stranger should particularly remark the door at the S. entrance, with its curious iron ornament (1631), representing grotesque lions impaled on a tree, which is fashioned with its full complement of roots, branches, and leaves. The *stone pulpit* of St. Saviour's, carved, gilt, and painted, is one of the most remarkable examples in the county, and deserves a special pilgrimage. The same may be said of the *Roodscreen*, which is exceedingly handsome, and rivals even the pulpit in the variety of its tints and the intricacy of its workmanship. In the floor of the chancel is the *brass* of *John Hawley*, founder of the Chancel (1408), in armour; and 2 wives, Joan, whose hand he holds (1394), and Alice (1403). This is a fine example. Hawley was probably the merchant of Dartmouth who, in "1390, waged the navie of shippes of the ports of his own charges, and tooke 34 shippes laden with wyne to the summe of fifteen hundred tunnes."—*Stowe's Annals*. The visitor will also direct his attention to the altarpiece, of "Christ raising the widow's son," by Brockedon, the artist and Alpine traveller, a native of Totnes, a picture which gained the prize of 100 guineas at the British Iustitution. The wainscoting and panels of this curious church are painted, gilded, and emblazoned with coats of arms. Among them may be noticed the lion of Pomeroy, the manche (sleeve) of Mohun, and the badges of FitzStephen, Fleming, and Carew. The Ch. has been restored to some extent.

After a visit to the ch. and a survey of the old houses, the stranger can search for other interesting objects on each side of the harbour, first proceeding S. by the neglected ruin of the *Old Castle*, and the cove and hamlet of *Warfleet*, where stand another crumbling tower called *Para-*

dise Fort and a mill with a waterwheel 50 ft. in diam., to

Dartmouth Castle. This picturesque building is situated at the extreme point of the promontory which bounds the entrance of the harbour, mounting guard at the very edge of a shelving rock of glossy slate, and washed by the sea at high water. It consists of a square and a round tower, the latter of which is the elder, and supposed to date from the reign of Hen. VII. Adjoining this building are 3 platforms for guns, the little ch. of St. Petrox (containing an armorial gallery and a *brass* —son of John Roope, 1609), and the ruins of a more ancient castle, the whole being enclosed by a wall and a ditch. The hill, which rises behind to the height of 300 ft., is crowned by the remains of another fort, which is mentioned by Fairfax in his despatch to the Parliament under the name of *Gallant's Bower*. The round tower of the castle is now a magazine, but formerly no doubt received the iron chain which was stretched as a defence across the mouth of the harbour, and was here drawn tight by a capstan. That this was its use has been made apparent by the discovery, in the wall of the ground-floor, of a large wooden bolster or roller, which was evidently intended to ease the chain as it passed through the wall. On the opposite shore, a groove in the rock clearly was scooped out for the reception of the chain. (Portsmouth, Plymouth, and most of our ancient harbours, were secured in a similar manner.) The best view of the Castle is, in the general opinion, obtained from the sea; but, weather permitting, all strangers should take boat, and decide this question for themselves. From Dartmouth Castle the visitor should return to the *Old Castle*, and cross once more by ferry to the little town of

Kingswear (if he has not examined it on first arriving), which bears every mark of antiquity, and is supposed to be older even than Dartmouth. The ch. stands some height above the shore; and yet higher is a fort of 5 bastions, called by Fairfax "Kingsworth Fort," but now known as *Mount Ridley*, commanding a fine view. A pleasant path leads from the ch. to Brookhill, at the mouth of the harbour. To the rt., on the outskirt of the town, the stranger will notice the old fig-trees in the hedges, affording evidence of a superior cultivation in times long past, and very probably the relics of gardens once belonging to the merchant-lords of Kingswear.

The *Terminus* of the Torquay and Dartmouth *Branch Railway* is at Kingswear, and may be reached by ferry.

At a short distance from Kingswear the path reaches the *Beacon* (A. H. Holdsworth, Esq.), a mansion remarkable for its commanding and beautiful position. In a field about 100 yds. above this house is a terrace, which from time immemorial has been known as the *Butts*, and was, doubtless, the place where the archers formerly practised with the bow: ¼ m. beyond the Beacon is

Brookhill, distinguished for the romantic beauty of the grounds, and the interesting embellishment of the house, and deservedly considered one of the principal ornaments of Dartmouth Harbour. It lies in a wooded cove, so sheltered by hills as to be one of the warmest spots in the county, where oaks and evergreens of remarkable size descend the shelving shore to the very brink of the sea, flourishing strangely on storm-beaten crags amid showers of spray, which are plentifully thrown upon them when the wind is to the S. On the seaward point of this cove are the foundations of a castle which was evidently of importance, and probably corresponded with the ruin on the opposite shore; and below them, at the base of the cliff, among the weed-grown rocks, the traces of a landing-place, and a groove and holes cut in the slate for securing the chain which was formerly stretched across the mouth of the harbour. Close at hand was the guard-room where the men kept watch over the chain, for the cliff has been evidently cut away to form a level space, and on the face of the rock are the holes in which the beams and rafters were inserted. On ascending from the examination of these interesting old marks, the stranger should diverge to the rt. and peep into a romantic recess where large oak-trees grow from the crevices of the cliff, and have been whimsically twisted by their efforts to keep erect. He will then, with permission of its proprietor, pay a visit to the house. In the dining-room the panels of the wainscoting are emblazoned with the arms of the most distinguished families of the county, in illustration of the histories of Devonshire and Dartmouth, which are ingeniously set forth on the ceiling by the following method:—A number of shields, each stamped with the name and the date of a Devon "worthy," are sculptured in a circular order round a single one in the centre, which records one of the principal events in the history of the county and the parish—the landing of the Prince of Orange in Torbay. Other shields, disposed in straight lines on opposite sides of this circle, commemorate the many eminent divines who were natives of Devonshire. On the border of the ceiling the history of Dartmouth is told similarly by shields, inscribed in order with the leading events as they occurred; the whole presenting at one view a tablet of history, which is certainly most novel, ingenious, and comprehensive. The visitor, having taken in this knowledge at a glance, will next turn to the chimney-piece, over which he will observe the carving which was taken from Newcomen's sitting-room, representing Shadrach, Meshach, and Abed-nego before Nebuchadnezzar; parts of the chimney-piece being of black oak, to which an interesting legend attaches. These were brought from Greenway, on the Dart, where they formed a portion of the chimney-nook in which it is said Sir Walter Raleigh indulged himself with the first cigar which was smoked in England. On the opposite wall of the room is an old print of the "Britannia" after Vandevelde, and around it the names of the 4 Devonshire "worthies" who figured in the defeat of the Armada—Raleigh, Gilbert, Drake, and Hawkins, of whom Drake and Gilbert led the fire-ships. Close upon the shore, beyond the grounds of Brookhill, is the ruinous tower of *Kingswear Castle*, so shattered by time as to afford, with its background of sea, an excellent subject for the pencil. The geologist may remark on the cliffs of the neighbourhood that the dip of the strata tends to their preservation.

In 1856 Dartmouth was for a time the station of the mail-packets to the Cape of Good Hope, the Mauritius, Point de Galle, and India. Its harbour has many advantages. It has a convenient depth of water, a sheltering screen of hills, and an entrance independent of the tide.

[The road from Dartmouth to Plymouth passes near some fine old camps at the following points:—
2½ *Woodbury Castle* on the l.
6¼ *Morleigh, Stanborough Camp*, 1 m. on the l.
3 *Blackdown Camp*, about 1 m. on the l.
5 *Modbury*.]

Excursions from Dartmouth: to *Brixham* (ante), to *Slapton Sands*, and the *Start Point* (post), and to *Totnes* by boat up the river (see Rte. 7). The grand and romantic coast of the *Prawle, Bolt Head*, &c., is most agreeably reached by the following delightful walk to Salcombe (which is 18 m. by the old road through Halwell and Kingsbridge, passing *Woodbury Castle* on the l.).

2 *Stoke Fleming*, a retired village, with a ch. so conspicuously placed as to form a useful landmark for Dartmouth harbour. The manor has belonged to the families of Fleming, Mohun, Carew, and Southcote, and in a garden adjoining the ch. are some crumbling masses of red sandstone which formed part of the ancient manor-house. In the ch. is a fine *brass* for John Corp (1361), and his granddaughter Eleanor (1391), with canopy.

1 *Blackpool*, another small village on a secluded little bay of the same name, and perhaps so called as having been fatally mistaken by vessels running for Dartmouth. The beach is composed of an extremely fine shingle. From this place there is a road through the village of *Street*, and a path along the edge of the cliffs, which are of various colours and very lustrous, to

Slapton Sands, now traversed by a carriage-road as far as Torcross. (There is a comfortable hotel at the N. end of the sands.) Here commences a vast bank of regular beach minute pebbles, extremely heavy to walk on, which extends, almost uninterruptedly, to within a short distance of the Start. The accumulation is due to the exposure of the shore to a long range of breakers, and to the circumstance of the shingle being unable to travel so as to escape out of the bay. (The sands are divided by name—there being no real division whatever—into Slapton Sands, Torcross Sands, and Hall Sands. The Sands Hotel is at the N. end; Torcross quite in the centre; and the hamlets of Beasands and Hallsands at the S. end. The whole is 7 m. in extent). From the northern end of the bank of pebbles to Torcross, a distance of 2¼ m., it is separated from the land by a freshwater lake called *Slapton Lea*, which is formed by the water of three small streams, descending from as many valleys, and dammed in by the shingle. The Lea contains some fine pike, perch, and roach, but no trout. In the winter it abounds with wild-fowl. The Dec. ch. of *Slapton* (6 m. from Dartmouth) contains a beautiful screen. To this parish *John Flavel*, an eminent nonconformist, retired from Dartmouth after the passing of the Oxford or Five Mile Act. He found an asylum at *Hudscott*, then a seat of the Rolles (and still the property of that family), where he preached in the great hall at midnight. In the neighbourhood are some remains (an old tower) of *Poole*, W. Paige, Esq., formerly in the possession of the Hawkins family. Poole (erroneously said to have been a priory) was the residence of the Bryans, one of whom, Sir Guy de Bryan, was one of the "prime founders of the Order of the Garter." He established a collegiate chantry adjoining Slapton Ch.

4¼ *Torcross* (near the *Sands Hotel*, on the beach), a secluded little hamlet at the southern end of the Slapton Sands, which are here bounded by argillaceous slate cliffs of a light greenish hue. (There is, however, no break in the cliffs here, and the end of the Slapton Sands is only marked by the carriage-road turning inland towards Kingsbridge.) It is much frequented by the neighbouring gentry as a watering-place, and is the most easterly station of the pilchard fishery; but the shoals rarely pass the point of the Start, and the Torcross fishermen have to proceed as far the Bolt for a chance of success. About 1½ m. inland is the church-town of *Stokenham;* and *Widdecombe* (A. H. Holdsworth, Esq.), a fine estate embracing the Start Point, and that lonely romantic coast between the Start Point and Lannacomb Mill. *Stokely House*, Sir Lydston Newman, Bt., and *Coleridge*, T. Allen, Esq., are other seats in this neighbourhood.

From Torcross a path (which is, however, obscure, and little used—the pedestrian may make his way by the sands) leads westward along the edge of grey slate cliffs, descending again to the sands at a slate-quarry, which opens to the beach by an archway. The traveller is now approaching the termination of Start Bay, and the grand coast of the chlorite and mica slate formation, which, including the promontory of the Start, extends westward as far as the Bolt Tail. Two secluded little fishing hamlets, *Beasands* and *Hallsands*, are passed on the shore, which then sweeps round to the picturesque promontory of

3½ *The Start*. This headland at once shows the stranger that he has entered upon a geological formation differing from the grauwacke slates which he has been traversing from Dartmouth. The ridge stretches boldly to sea, sloped on each side like the roof of a house, and crowned along its entire length by fanciful crags, strangely weathered, and shaggy with moss. Its different sides strikingly illustrate the influence of a stormy sea on the picturesqueness of a coast. On the W., the dark cliff, incessantly assaulted, presents a ruinous appearance; on the E., although moulded from the same material, it descends to the waves in a smooth precipice. The lighthouse is situated at the extreme point, about 100 ft. above the water, and exhibits two lights—a revolving light for the Channel, and a fixed light to direct vessels inshore clear of a shoal called the *Skerries*. Here the traveller has reached a point beyond which the sea is occasionally agitated by a roll from the Atlantic, the *ground swell* of the ocean rarely extending farther eastward than the Start. The name is the Anglo-Saxon *Steort*, a "tail" or promontory (so the bird called a red-*start* from its red tail); but it is commonly explained as the *starting-point* of ships outward bound from the Channel. A few rugged steps and "juts of rock" lead down from the lighthouse to a miniature bay and pebbly beach.

From this promontory those who are fond of cliff-scenery should proceed along the coast to the Prawle and Salcombe, a dist. of about 9 m.; and, bending their steps to the next headland of the *Peartree*, look back at the western face of the Start. The actual *cliff* is not high, but, like that of the Land's End of Cornwall, as dark as Erebus, and an impressive ruin. It is further remarkable for bands of variously coloured *quartz veins*, which, descending vertically to the sea, give the rocks a ribboned appearance. Similar quartz veins produce a happy effect in a little bay just W. of the Peartree, where they cover the slate, as it were, with a network, the beach being almost wholly composed of rolled fragments of white quartz. From the Peartree the stone-crested hills recede from the shore, and, curving as they run westward, enclose a terrace of fields, which is bounded towards the sea by a low cliff of earth resting upon a talus of slate. The traveller may marvel how this apparently feeble barrier can resist the waves; but, on a closer examination, he will perceive that the dip of the strata is directed towards the W., and at such an angle with the plane of the horizon that the sea rolls harmlessly up the slope. This terrace is terminated on the W. by *Lannacomb Mill*, where the craggy belt again sweeps to the coast in a soaring eminence, notched like the edge of a saw. Beyond this point the hills a second time recede, and form a semicircle; but in places they break irregularly, and are disposed as a background to two terraces, one high above the other. The effect of this grouping is extremely beautiful. To this bay succeeds a smaller indentation, near the centre of which the stranger will remark the whimsical station of some fishermen. The sea has formed in the slate a little channel just wide enough to allow the passage of boats to a few square yards of beach, upon which the craft are laid; while the chasms of a conical rock, a short distance from the shore, are converted to the purposes of a sail-room and fish-cellar. This bay is terminated W. by perhaps the finest headland on the S. coast of Devon, the

5 *Prawle Point*, bounding on the E. the entrance to the Salcombe Estuary, which is sheltered on the W. by the more elevated and massive headland of the *Bolt*. These two promontories are the most southerly points of the county; and, when viewed from the sea in connection with the inlet, and the town of Salcombe just peeping through the opening, form by far the most romantic scene on the coast. ("Prol in Anglia," or Prawle Point, is mentioned as one of the stations which guided ships on their way from the North seas, through the Channel, toward the coast of France. Port St. Matthien, on the opposite coast of Britanny [which trends away S. nearly in a line with Prawle Point] was the next station.) The Prawle is principally composed of gneiss rock, which on the western side is weathered like a surface of snow which has been exposed to the sun's rays. It is everywhere broken into crags, and terminated at the point by a singular archway, through which a boat

might sail in calm weather. Many years ago the Crocodile frigate was wrecked upon this headland with a great loss of life. The pedestrian can now continue his way along the ivy-hung cliffs, or strike inland to a lane which will lead him to *Portlemouth*, where he will cross by ferry to

4 *Salcombe* (*Inns*: Victoria Inn; King's Arms; but both of a very humble description). This picturesque town, lying far south of the principal roads, and separated from them by a broad tract of country comparatively uninteresting, is rarely visited by travellers; but the coast in the neighbourhood, comprising the headlands of the Start, the Prawle, and the Bolt, is the grandest on the S. of Devon, and the shores of Bigbury Bay exceedingly romantic, although almost as unknown as those of Kamschatka. The district round Salcombe, bounded on the E. and W. by the Start and Bolt Tail, is composed of the hard rocks of the chlorite and mica slate formation, and for this reason has withstood the assaults of the sea, while in Bigbury Bay, W. of it, many acres have been swallowed by the sea within living memory. Thus it projects into the Channel like a wedge, which is pierced about the centre by the estuary which flows past Salcombe to Kingsbridge. Salcombe lies just within the mouth of this inlet, and is a small retired town, pleasantly situated, and so sheltered by high land as to be one of the warmest in the kingdom. The myrtle and other tender plants clothe the shores; the lemon, orange-tree, and aloe flower in the gardens: but beyond the protecting influence of the ridge on the coast, the country consists of bare bleak hills, where but few trees can grow above the valleys. Salcombe has been called the "Montpellier of the North," and its mean winter temperature is but $2^\circ \cdot 4$ Fahr. below that of Montpellier and of Florence (*Humboldt*).

To descend from the scenery to the produce of Salcombe, the stranger should know that the town is noted for *white ale*, a beverage peculiar to a district which would be bounded by a line drawn between Plymouth and Totnes, along the river Dart and intermediate coast, and first made by some genius of Kingsbridge. It differs essentially, both in composition and colour, from common ale. It is made with a smaller quantity of hops, and contains flour and spices; but some skill is required in its preparation, and many fail in the attempt. When poured into a glass, it has the appearance of tea. It is intended to be drunk quite new, according to the saying, that it is made on the Saturday to be tapped on the Sunday. White ale has, however, much deteriorated of late years, in consequence of the neglect of adding eggs to its ingredients.

The *harbour of Salcombe*, like that of Dartmouth, is sheltered by high land, but it has a bar at low water, and sunken rocks at the mouth, which render its entrance by night hazardous. The rugged foundation of the neighbouring coast is the haunt of crabs and lobsters, which are captured in numbers, and sent to different parts of the country. Adjoining the town are *Ringrone*, Lord Kingsale, and the *Moult*, a villa of the Earl of Devon, but occupied by Lord Justice Turner.

From Salcombe the traveller should visit the *Prawle Point*, about 4 m.; and, weather permitting, make an excursion by boat from the *Bolt Head* to the *Bolt Tail*, a distance of about 5 m., coasting the intermediate range of black cliffs, so remarkable for their massive proportions, altitude, and the dark caverns with which they are pierced. He should also devote a day to the several interesting spots on the summit of the ridge, which he may visit by the following walk:—

He will take a road from the town towards the mouth of the harbour, passing *Woodville* (— Yates, Esq.) and the ruin of *Salcombe Castle*, whose battered old stones tell a tale of the civil war. The castle had been repaired at the commencement of the Rebellion, and placed under the command of Sir Edmund Fortescue, when in 1645 it was invested by Col. Weldon, the Parl. Governor of Plymouth. After Weldon's arrival the retired inlet of Salcombe was a scene of incessant uproar. For a period of 4 months the batteries thundered from each bank of the river, but at the end of that time the garrison capitulated. For this spirited resistance Sir Edmund Fortescue was allowed to march with the honours of war to his mansion of *Fallapit House* (4 m. N.E. by E. of Kingsbridge, W. B. Fortescue, Esq.), where the key of the castle is preserved to this day. The field above this tower is called *Gore*, or *Gutter*, and tradition points it out as the scene of a bloody affray. The summit of the hill is known as *the Bury*, and marked with an old circular entrenchment. The road now descends to a patch of beach (the N. Sands), below which are found the fossil remains of a nut-wood, and then skirts the grounds of the *Moult* to another strip of sand (the S. Sands), which likewise entombs the trees of other days. These relics may also be found in *Mill Bay*, on the opposite shore, where they are exposed when the tide has receded a few feet from high-water mark. The traveller is now at the foot of the promontory of the

Bolt Head, composed of mica slate, and rising 430 ft. from its base. (Bolt was the name of a sort of arrow, the head and feathering of which are represented by the Bolt Head and Tail.) He may observe, in the low cliff to the l., the entrance of a cavern called the *Bull's Hole*, which, the country-people aver, passes obliquely through this high ridge of land, and opens again to the shore in Saw-Mill Bay, which we shall presently visit. They tell also an absurd story of a bull which once entered it and came out at the opposite end with its coat changed from black to white, and it is curious enough to find a similar legend current on the coast of Spain, near Coruña. The mysterious cavern may be visited at low water. The traveller, having ascended to the top of the headland, will see below him, and just within the point, the little cove of *Stair Hole*, a favourite retreat of grey mullet, and perhaps deriving its name from a steep roadway by which seaweed is carried from the beach to a neighbouring farm. The *Salcombe Mew Stone* bounds it on the S. Proceeding along the ridge, he will pass in succession the *Little Goat*, halfway down to the sea; the *Great Goat*, a rock on the summit—their resemblance, if they have any, to the animal in question being distinguishable only from the water; *Steeple Cove*, below a pinnacle of slate; and the *Old Man and his Children*, a whimsical crag, and a number of smaller rocks, which, grouped in a cluster, very probably bear a likeness to a family party when viewed from the sea. A sharp descent now leads into

Saw-Mill Cove (3 m. from Salcombe), terminating a valley, which is the only break in the range from the Bolt Head to the Tail. Here the hills are bold and rocky, and the cliffs, where beaten by the waves, so dark in hue as to give a solemn grandeur to the scene. On the shore is the entrance of *Bull's Hole* cavern, previously noticed, and outside the cove the *Ham Stone*, to which a saying of the Salcombe people attaches. When a young married couple have no child born at the end of 12 months, the gossips assert that the husband should be sent to dig up the Ham Stone with a wooden pickaxe. The cove has probably derived its name from a saw-mill once worked by the stream which here flows to the sea. Further W. we reach

Bolbury Down, the loftiest land between the cove and the Tail, where, just over the edge of the cliff, at the summit of the hill, is a chasm called *Ralph's Hole*, which was long the retreat of a noted smuggler. It is easy of access, but difficult to find without a guide. The botanist will observe that the furze-bushes in its vicinity are thickly mantled with the red filaments of the parasite *Cuscuta Epithymum*, or Lesser Dodder. A short way beyond the head of Bolbury Down a very interesting scene is displayed. The cliff, which is here about 400 ft. in height, has been undermined by the waves, and has fallen headlong in a ruin, the fragments of which appear as if they had been suddenly arrested when bounding towards the sea. They are lodged most curiously one upon another, and the clefts among them are so deep and numerous as to have given the name of *Rotten Pits* to the locality. A little further W. another landslip has occurred, but with such a different result that the stranger must take especial care to look where he goes. The ground has been rent inland some distance in fissures, parallel with the shore, and concealed by furze-bushes; many are little more than a yard in width, but of unknown depth, at first descending vertically, and then slanting at an angle which prevents their being sounded. Others, again, are scarcely larger than chimneys, but just of a size to admit the body of a man. These chasms are called the *Vincent Pits*, and were once railed in for the protection of sheep and, perhaps, strangers. At present, however, there is nothing to warn the traveller of the danger in his path.

From the Vincent Pits the land shelves towards the

Bolt Tail, and is indented at the shore by *Ramillies Cove*, so named as the scene of the disastrous wreck of the Ramillies frigate, 1760. Just inside the Tail, in *Bigbury Bay*, is the wild cove and hamlet of *Hope* (2 m. from Saw-mill Bay), inhabited by a few poor fishermen, who now subsist upon the produce of their nets, but were formerly notorious as some of the most successful smugglers on the coast. Here a benighted traveller may find tolerable accommodation at the Yacht *inn*, or, if proceeding further along the coast, at *Buntham*, a village ½ m. above the mouth of the Avon, and where there is a ferry across the river. The remoteness of this cove of Hope is pleasing to the imagination, while the view from it is suggestive of an unexplored solitude. The eye wanders down the shore of *Bigbury Bay*, a district isolated by rivers, far from busy roads, and rarely visited save by some rambling pedestrian. A striking object in the view is about 1 m. distant, the

Thurlestone, a perforated rock islanded in the sea, and geologically remarkable as an outlying patch of red sandstone. Yet farther in the bay, at the mouth of the Avon (4 m.), is

Burr Island, once crowned with a chapel dedicated to St. Michael, and more recently used as a station for the pilchard fishery. It is about 10 acres in extent, and connected with the mainland at low water. The visitor can now return to Salcombe by a direct road through Marlborough (4½ m.), or retrace his steps, which is the better plan, as the coats in this part of Devon has a monopoly of the picturesque.

From Salcombe we can make for the Plymouth road at *Modbury*; selecting either the high road, which makes a circuit to Kingsbridge by *Marlborough*, or a cross road, which takes a more direct course near the river (4 m.). On foot the distance to Kingsbridge may be still more curtailed by a field-path by *Shabicombe* and *Blank's Mill*.

(For Kingsbridge see Rte. 15).

ROUTE 10.

EXETER TO TORQUAY, BY CHUDLEIGH. (HALDON).

This is the old turnpike-road from Exeter to Newton.

From Exeter our route crosses the *Haldon Hills*, which attain an elevation of 818 ft. above the sea, and are of the same class, geologically speaking, as the Black Down Hills; the *greensand* surface of Little Haldon supporting in places blocks of *quartziferous porphyry* of more than a ton in weight. In every direction these hills are studded with barrows, and the views on all sides are superb. The road, leaving *Shillingford* Ch. (Perp. with a W. tower built by Sir Wm. Huddersfield, whose brass, 1500, with that of his wife Katherine dau. of Sir Wm. Courtenay, in heraldic dresses, is in the chancel), and *Dunchideock*, J. S. Pitman, Esq.,

to the rt. (the ch. of Dunchideock, much neglected, is Dec. with a rich screen), passes, 2 m. off, *Haldon House*, Sir L. Palk, Bart., M.P. (who has a collection of Oriental china). The *Belvidere*, a tower which crowns Pen Hill, west of the house, is a landmark for all this part of Devon. It commands a vast extent of country, looking to the sea in one direction, to N. Devon in another, and to the long range of Dartmoor—with the peaks of Heytor, and the mountainous ridge of Cawsand conspicuous—in a third. Parts of the vallum and fosse of a large entrenchment may be traced on Pen Hill. The road skirts the Exeter racecourse, and then descends towards

10 *Chudleigh* (*Inn:* Clifford Arms), a mean place, now suffering by the removal of traffic to the railroad, and mostly built since 1807, when 166 houses were destroyed by fire. The town at one time belonged to the Bishops of Exeter. The most interesting portions of the ch. are the base of the tower, which if not Sax. is very early Norm., and the font, which is of Trans. character. Chudleigh is noted for cider, and for the far-famed *Chudleigh Rock*, a wild eminence of blue limestone, extensively quarried under the name of *Chudleigh marble*. The objects of curiosity in the vicinity of the town are *Chudleigh Rock, Ugbrooke Park* (the seat of Lord Clifford), and some trifling remains of the *Bishop's Palace*,—in the neighbourhood, the *valley of the Teign, Bovey Tracey*, the *Heytor Rocks*, and the *Bottor Rock* at Hennock (about 3 m. distant). (For the 3 last places see Rte. 12.) *Skat Tor* and the *White Stone* are also of interest, and rise high above the valley of the Teign, the one between Bridford and Christow, the other 1 m. N. of Christow. The country around Chudleigh is intersected by a great number of steep and solitary lanes, which form so perfect a labyrinth

that the traveller involved among them towards nightfall will find no little difficulty in reaching his inn. At the base of the town runs the river Teign, once well stored with food for the fisher, but the fish have been almost destroyed by water from the mines higher up the river. On the Ashburton road a lane on the l. (by the blacksmith's shop), ½ m. from the ch., leads direct to the

Bishop's Palace, or rather its site, which is occupied by an orchard. An old crumbling boundary-wall, and an insignificant fragment, now serving as a cider-room, are the only remains. The palace here was fortified under a licence to the Bp. of Exeter of the 3rd Richard II. Immediately beyond them is *Bishop's Kiln*, and the

Chudleigh Rock, rising on the skirts of Ugbrooke, and presenting naked surfaces of stone, which are seen here and there in the gaps of a wild and irregular wood, and at the summit form platforms, commanding the most delightful views. Within this marble barrier is a glen, where trees grow tangled, and a brawling stream, concealed from sunshine by the foliage, runs murmuring to its mossgrown stones, and, at one point, leaps in a cascade, which is sketched every year by a legion of artists. The rock is bound, as it were, with creepers, and has open spots on the summit, on which wild fennel grows luxuriantly; and midway on the cliff the mouth of a deep cavern (the key must be obtained) which the country people describe as haunted by the Pixies. " At a small distance from a village," says Coleridge, " half way up a wood-covered hill, is an excavation called the Pixies' Parlour. The roots of old trees form its ceiling, and on its sides are innumerable ciphers, among which the author discovered his own and those of his brothers, cut by the hand of their childhood."—Note to the *Songs of the Pixies*.

In Russia, on the shore of the Baltic, is a town of *Chudleigh*, which, in situation, much resembles its namesake in Devon. Erman, in his ' Travels in Siberia,' when describing the Russian Chudleigh, remarks, " The *limestone rock* has here the appearance of a great promontory; for on the east it is bounded by a *deep ravine*, cut by a rapid stream, which falls into the bay."

Ugbrooke Park (Lord Clifford of Chudleigh) is bounded by Chudleigh Rock, and is a large and beautiful demesne, about 6 m. in circumference. On its highest point are the bold mounds of *Castle Dike*, a circular camp, no doubt of the British period. It overlooks a great extent of country toward the N. and W. The Roman road from Exeter into Cornwall (the Ikenild Way) passed a little E. of the camp; and on this side is one of the principal entrances. The house of Ugbrooke is furnished with a collection of pictures, which are sometimes shown to strangers. *Whiteway House*, N. of Chudleigh, is the seat of Mrs. Parker, and *New Canonteign House* of Viscount Exmouth. The former contains one of the earliest of *Reynolds's* portraits, viz. that of Captain Ourry, M.P. for Plympton in 1780, painted for the corporation of that town. The latter is in the valley of the Teign, about 4 m. towards Dunsford Bridge amid beautiful scenery, a stream tumbling in a cascade near the house: from a branch of this the Torquay Waterworks are supplied, at a cost of 50,000*l*., 18 m., by iron pipes. The old mansion of Canonteign, stormed by Fairfax in 1645, is now tenanted by a farmer. The Chudleighs, of which family was Walpole's " Ælia Lelia Chudleigh," the famous Duch. of Kingston, were long seated at *Place* in the adjoining parish of

Ashton, and some remains of their residence may still be seen.

Ashcombe Ch., 2½ m. S. of Chudleigh, is Perp., and has been well restored. [The archæologist should visit the 4 churches of Ashton, Christow, Doddiscombleigh, and Bridford; all in the valley of the Teign, between Chudleigh and Dunsford. (The *Teign Valley* line of rly., just (1865) commenced, will open this country as far as Doddiscombleigh). To *Ashton*, about 5 m., he may proceed along the banks of the river, visiting Canonteign in his way. The ch., dedicated to St. Nectan, is Perp., with a good W. tower. The chief points of interest here are some good carved bench-ends; some paintings in panels at the base of the screen and parclose (the screen itself has been cut away); and some remains of stained glass in the windows. The relics of Place Barton are hardly worth notice.

Christow Ch. (dedicated to St. Christina), 1½ m. on the other side of the Teign, is mainly Perp. (circ. 1538?), but has a Norm. door and font. There are 2 figures in stained glass remaining. The ch. was given to Eton by Henry VI.

Bridford Ch. (dedicated to St. Thomas of Canterbury), 2 m. farther, is, like the others, Perp., with good screen, painted and gilt, with date 1508. The oak seating, and some figures in glass of the S. window of nave, should be noticed.

Doddiscombleigh, on the l. bank of the river, and about 1½ m. from Ashton ch., is the most interesting of the 4. The chancel is early Dec.; the nave and N. aisle Perp.; and in the latter are 4 Perp. 3-light windows containing very fine glass. That in the E. window is the best in the county (except what is in the cathedral). It displays the 7 Sacraments of the Roman Church: in the centre, the Reconciliation of Penitents; rt. the Eucharist, Marriage, and Confirmation; l. Baptism, Ordination, and Extreme Unction. In another window are figures of St. Michael, St. Peter, St. Andrew, St. James, St. Christopher, St. George, with various emblems. The tourist may proceed 3 m. to

Dunsford (Rte. 12), where the ch. is interesting, and where there is a tolerably good roadside inn.]

On the l. bank of the Teign, 1½ m. off the road, before reaching Newton is *Kingsteignton*, where is a large and good Perp. ch. In the S. aisle are many chained books—Fox's 'Martyrs' among them.

6 m. *Newton* (see Rte. 7). From Newton the turnpike road follows nearly the line of the rly., skirting Milber Down, and passing through King's Kerswell. (For these places see Rte. 8). 6½ m. from Newton it reaches

Torquay (see Rte. 8).

ROUTE 11.

EXETER TO ASHBURTON AND BUCK-
FASTLEIGH. (BUCKLAND, HOLNE,
HOLNE CHACE).

(The tourist may make his head-quarters either at Ashburton or Buckfastleigh, either of which places is well situated for exploring the scenery of Holne and Buckland,—among the finest in Devonshire. From Ashburton he may join the South Devon Rly. at the Brent Stat., and proceed to Plymouth.)

From Exeter to Chudleigh the same as Route 10.

2 *Knighton.* Beyond this village the traveller enters the *Bovey Heathfield*, and obtains an uninterrupted view of the barren slopes of Dartmoor. A road on the rt. leads, in 2 m., to

Bovey Tracey (*Inn :* Union Hotel), a village conveniently situated for a visit to the *Heathfield* and an excursion to the *Heytor Rocks, Houndtor Coomb, Becky Fall,* and *Lustleigh Cleave* (Rte. 12). In early times it belonged to the Traceys, barons of Barnstaple, and has a place in history as the scene of Lord Wentworth's discomfiture by Cromwell, who dashed upon the Royalist camp at night, and captured 400 troopers and 7 standards. So complete, it is said, was the surprise, that Wentworth's officers were engaged at cards, and escaped only by throwing their stakes of money out of window among the Roundheads. This, however, is a piece of Puritan scandal, frequently repeated elsewhere. For the real history see Sprigge's 'England's Recovery.' Upon an open space in the village are the shaft and steps of an ancient cross, and in the street above it one of the wayside monuments of the same description, now built into a house, called Cross Cottage from the circumstance. It bears the stamp of a cross, which is a modern addition. The *ch.*, ded. to St. Thomas of Canterbury, which has been renovated through the exertions of the Hon. and Rev. C. L. Courtenay, contains a perfect screen and roodloft, a coloured stone pulpit, and some curious inscriptions to the memory of Archbishop Laud and others, placed there by Forbes, the expelled vicar, after his restoration, temp. Charles II. It is throughout Perp.

The *Bovey Heathfield*, as the neighbouring valley is called, is the lowest land in the county, and remarkable for containing deposits of sands and clays which are used in the manufacture of china. It is supposed to have been originally a lake, in which the decomposed granite brought by the rains from Dartmoor was gradually deposited; nature having thus formed the china-clay in the same manner as it is now artificially prepared in Cornwall. The *Pottery*, estab. 1772, is close to the village, and worth a visit, as the manufacture has greatly improved during the last few years. Adjoining it are the pits of *Bovey coal*, or lignite, a bituminous fuel, used only at the pottery, in the limekilns, and by the poor of the neighbourhood, as it emits a disagreeable odour in burning. It is the Norwegian "surturbrand," the driftwood of ancient forests, chiefly fir, which has accumulated in this valley for a distance of 7 or 8 m. The coniferous trees are sometimes found entire in it, together with lumps of inspissated turpentine, called *bitumy* or *bitumen*, which will burn like a candle. It is evidently a deposit of comparatively modern date, as the bark and internal structure of the wood may be distinguished. A very beautiful *ch.*, in which the daily service is choral, has been built close to the Potteries, for the especial benefit of the workmen.

Bovey is situated at the foot of a great ridge of hills, which is crowned (at the village of *Hennock*, 2 m. E.) with the *Bottor Rock*, an interesting tor of *trap* (its fissures lined with *byssus aurea*), now islanded in cultivation, but overlooking the moor and neighbouring country for miles. The road to Hennock is an excellent specimen of the *Devonshire lane*, frightfully steep in places, and so narrow, particularly where intruded on by the boles of huge trees, as barely to afford room for the *wains* of the country. It will give you rare peeps into valleys; and Hennock itself is exceedingly picturesque, and contains the fragment of an old cross like that at Bovey. A *lead-mine* is worked 2 m. N.E. of Hennock. The *White Stone* and *Skat Tor*, in the same direction, are other rocks often visited from Bovey.

Proceeding again on our route,— the road crosses the *Heytor railroad*, used for the conveyance of granite; then passes on the l. the entrance of *Storer Lodge* (Duke of Somerset); and then, on the l., *Ingsdon* (C. H. Mouro, Esq.). *Baytor*, some distance to the rt., among very picturesque scenery, under Heytor, is a seat of Lord Cranstoun's, and was the birthplace of *Ford* the dramatist, 1586. In its neighbourhood is the village of *Ilsington*, and (near the ch.) ruins of the *Manorhouse of Ilsington*, commenced, but never finished, by Sir Henry Ford, Charles II.'s Secretary for Ireland. In Ilsington ch. some of Lord Wentworth's fugitive troops barricaded themselves, after their flight from Cromwell at Bovey Tracey. They left it, however, on his approach.

7½ *Ashburton* (*Inns*: Golden Lion, best; London Inn), one of the old Stannary towns, situated in a valley on the skirts of Dartmoor, which are here characterised by a grandeur and variety of scenery not surpassed in the county. The places to be visited in this neighbourhood are pre-eminently *Buckland* (a seat of the Bastards), and *Holne Chace* (Sir B. P. Wrey, Bart.), grand wilds of rock and wood on the banks of the Dart. *John Dunning*, solicitor-general in 1767, and *William Gifford* (1756), apprenticed in his early years to a shoemaker, but afterwards known as a translator of Juvenal and the editor of the 'Quarterly,' were natives of this town. In 1782 Dunning was raised to the peerage as Baron Ashburton, a title which became extinct in 1823, but in 1835 was revived in the person of Alexander Baring.

In 1646 Ashburton was taken (without conflict) by Fairfax, who lodged after the exploit at the Mermaid Inn. This is now a shop, but of very venerable appearance. Another old house in West Street, the property of B. Parham, Esq., containing an ancient *oratory* (?), richly decorated with carved oak, is supposed to have been an occasional residence of the Abbots of Buckfast, though without the slightest foundation. The *Town-hall*, constructed entirely of timber, is picturesque and curious. A very curious timber market-house was pulled down some years since.

The ch. (St. Andrew) is a fine cruciform structure of Perp. date (the transepts date from about 1679), but has suffered much from modern "improvements." The screen and pulpit have been removed, and the roof and many of the windows rebuilt. The roof of the N. aisle is ancient, and has carved oak timbers with fine bosses—much decayed. The S. aisle contains a tablet with inscription, by Dr. Johnson, to the memory of the first Lord Ashburton. The tower of the ch. is 110 ft. high, with indifferent parapet and pinnacles.

The excursion through the woods of *Buckland* and back to Ashburton is about 10 m. (The drives are at present (1865) open *for carriages* only on Tuesdays, Thursdays, and Saturdays. Carriages must enter by Holne bridge,—reversing the order in the following description.) You can take the road to the village of *Buckland on the Moor* (3 m.), a continual ascent until close upon the summit of *Buckland Beacon* (rt.), a rocky tor, which should be ascended for a panorama of singular interest. The following objects will present themselves at different points in the picture:—*Rippon Tor*, alt. 1549 ft., close at hand, N.N.E.; *Cut Hill*, that lonely hill of bog, on which the Dartmoor rivers have their source (see Rte. 12), very distant, but marked by a pile of turf, N. of N.W.; *Crockern*, and his brother tors, fringing the horizon in the N.W.; *N. Hessary Tor*, alt. 1730 ft., and *Prince's Town*, N. of W.; *Buckland House* and village ch., W.; the huge dreary ridge of *Holne Moor*, alt. 1785 ft., on which the winter's snows make their first appearance, W.S.W.; the *windings of the Dart*, and woods of Buckland, S.W.; the distant but striking eminence of *South Brent Tor* (which serves the purpose of a barometer to persons in this neighbourhood), S.S.W.; *Auswell* or *Hazel Tor*, rising from a wood of firs on the other side of the road, and often ascended for the sake of the view, S. ; and the little town of *Ashburton*, nestled among its hills, S. of S.S.E. The Beacon consists of a white and close-grained granite. Three low distorted oaks on its western slope will remind the traveller of Wistman's Wood (Rte. 12). Hazel Tor is crowned by a large cairn ; and there is a circle of stones (not a hut circle) on the side of Buckland Beacon.

Having descended from this hill, we enter the little hamlet of Buckland, where most picturesque cottages of old red brick are shut out from sunshine by lofty trees; after passing the ch. we turn into Mr. Bastard's grounds by the first gate on the l., and proceed along a drive which will eventually lead us to Holne Bridge. The road makes at first for the *Webburn*, a stream flowing from the moor by Widdecombe, and then turns and winds through the valley so as to accompany the torrent in its course. Soon an old bridge is passed, leading toward *Spitchwick*, seat of the late Lord Ashburton, on the opposite bank. A stream, which has had the run of mines, then enters the valley, tinging the Webburn with its ferruginous hues. At length, after glancing up a steep-sided vista at one spot, and following the narrow roadway along all its ups and downs and convolutions, we reach the turbulent Dart, and enter a deep and tortuous ravine, where the woods are pierced by rocks, and naked crags crown the hills. And here a turn of the road will open to our view the gem of the Dart scenery,—the *Lover's Leap*, a rough mass of slate rising vertically from the river. Beyond it the heights have quite a mountainous appearance, and soar so boldly that their sombre woods of fir are often capped by the clouds. Having passed the Lover's Leap, we reach, in another mile, the Ashburton road at *Holne Bridge*, and from this spot those who are curious in such deposits may trace up the l. bank a bed of gravel, at an elevation of about 80 ft. above the present course of the river, apparently affording evidence of the stream having once flowed at a higher level than it does at present.

Holne Chace extends about 2 m. into the forest of Dartmoor, and skirts the Dart and Webburn opposite to Buckland. The carriage-drive here winds along the valley at a lower level, and the trees were finer (they have been ruthlessly felled within the last few years) than those of Buckland. The banks of the rushing river are fringed with *Osmunda regalis.*

New Bridge, on the Dart, beyond the mansion of Holne Chace, is another spot which should be visited, as the scene is little inferior to that at the Lover's Leap. The bridge is a lonely, picturesque structure, green with ivy, and the river on each side is hedged in with schistose crags and woods. It is crossed by the road to Two Bridges, which immediately climbs the moor by a most formidable hill (the long ridge of rocks, rt., is *Lonjator*, or the "Raven's Rock"), and again passes the E. Dart at *Dart-meet*, (the confluence of the E. and W. Dart). Those who travel this road will find on *Yartor*, just above the descent to Dartmeet Bridge, a great number of ancient *hut circles* and lines of stones, and from the same spot will enjoy a very delightful prospect in a southerly direction, *Sharpitor*, a height of remarkable beauty, rising l. of the road. Among the remains on Yartor (rt. of the road) is a *rectangular enclosure*, 42 ft. by 11 ft.; nearer the river, a *hut circle*, 38 ft. in diam., with walls 6 ft. thick, and door-jambs 6 ft. high; and a very perfect *kistvaen* surrounded by upright stones. The village was, evidently, of considerable size, and a road appears to have led from it across the river by a bridge, formed of huge blocks of granite, which was standing some years ago. The scene at New Bridge is calculated to give most pleasure to those who come suddenly upon it on descending from the moor, as the confined valley and green woods are a most agreeable change from the long-continued view of naked hills; and the craggy and richly coloured schistose rocks a striking contrast to the grey massive tors of granite. The Dart flows for a long distance in a wild tumultuous stream, and its "cry," in the stillness of night, may be heard far from its banks. It is subject to frequent and sudden inundation. "Dart came down last night" is an expression often in the mouths of the moor-men, and it is said that a year never passes without one person at the least being drowned in the river. Hence the local rhyme:—

" River of Dart, oh, river of Dart,
Every year thou claimest a heart!"

The admirer of wild scenery will do well to find his way along the banks of the Dart from New Bridge to Dart-meet. This will be a laborious pilgrimage, but one that will introduce him to, perhaps, the very finest points on the river. *Benjie Tor*, at all events, must not be left without a visit. It may be reached most conveniently from the village of *Holne*, where a guide should be procured, as there is no road across the moor. The visitor will find himself unexpectedly on the summit of a lofty pile of rocks, which descend in rugged steps to the river. Beyond rise wild "braes" with equal steepness—their sides strewn with moorstone, and mantled with furze and heather; the grey cone of Sharpitor lifts itself above all. To the rt. the eye ranges freely over Dartmoor, and to the l. across a vast extent of cultivated land to a blue fringe of sea, the Isle of Portland being visible in clear weather. Far below, in the river, are 2 still and dark "wells" known as *Hell Pool* and *Bell Pool*. The scene is strikingly Highland.

The little Dec. ch. of *Holne* contains a carved screen, with painted figures of saints, which are curious and worth examination, and were probably the work of the monks of Buckfast, to whom the building belonged. Holne is so named, either from the holly-trees (*holline, holne*) which abound in the chace, and are of very great size, or, more probably, from a Saxon word signifying "deep," "hollow."

The traveller may visit *Dart-meet* by way of New Bridge, passing over Yartor, and return by a road which, skirting *Cumston Tor* (a fine mass of rock on the l.), will bring him to the village of Holne, whence the road

Route 11.—*Buckfastleigh.*

is clear to Ashburton (dist. 3¼ m.). By this route he will enjoy some fine moorland scenery, especially near a curious old structure called *Pucksaddle Bridge*, over a feeder of the Dart.

Another course for a ramble in this neigbbourhood is the road through *Buckland* in the direction of Widdecombe. Buckland we have already visited, but a drive of ½ h. beyond this village will bring the traveller to a scene on the banks of the Webburn where he must draw the rein in admiration.

Close to Ashburton (in the first lane to the l. on the Totnes road) is a gate called *Sounding Gate*, as the spot at which an echo, remarkably clear and loud, may be drawn from a quarry opposite. From this lane another branches off to the *Penn Slate Quarry*, an excavation about 100 ft. deep; and in this neighbourhood also (1½ from Ashburton, l. of the Totnes road) is a limestone cavern on a farm called *Pridhamsleigh*, running an unknown distance underground, quite dark, and containing pools of deep water. From *Whiterock* (to be reached through a lane and some fields, rt., on the road between Ashburton and Buckfastleigh) there is a fine view over the upper valley of the Dart.

Widdecombe in the Moor, the *Heytor Rocks*, *Houndtor Coomb*, and the curiosities in their vicinity (*see* Rte. 12), can be conveniently visited from Ashburton.—*Berry Pomeroy Castle* is more within reach from Totnes (Rte. 7).

Proceeding on our route :—

3 *Buckfastleigh* (*Inn:* King's Arms), a large village, encompassed, like Ashburton, with short steep hills which characterise this part of the county. It has 4 blanket and serge mills, 2 of which are occupied, and employ about 400 hands. The objects worth notice are, the *ch.*, on a commanding eminence, bounded on each side by black marble quarries. It is rendered difficult of access by 140 steps, and capped with a spire, which is uncommon in Devonshire churches. The tower and chancel are E. Eng., the nave Perp. Remark the rude blocks of granite which form the steps of the tower. The tradition common to churches on high ground belongs to this of Buckfastleigh. It is said that the Devil obstructed the builders by removing the stones; and a large block bearing the mark of the "enemy's" finger and thumb is pointed out on a farm about 1 m. distant. The churchyard is darkened by black marble tombstones, and contains the ivied fragment of an old building, "which could never have been very large; but whether baptistery or chantry must be left uncertain. Apparently it is of E. Eng. date. It stands due E. of the ch., with which, however, it was never united. There are remains of a piscina at the S.E. angle." *R. J. K.*—The *black marble quarries* are now worked principally to supply the kilns.—The ruins of the Cistercian *Abbey of Buckfast*, founded in the reign of Hen. II. by Ethelwerd de Pomeroy (but on the site of a Benedictine house of Saxon antiquity), are situated 1 m. N. of the village, on the rt. bank of the Dart. This was the richest Cistercian house in Devonshire. Edw. I. visited it in 1297; and the abbot supplied 100 marks towards the expenses of the Agincourt expedition. It had one learned abbot, William Slade, famous (circ. 1414) at Oxford for his lectures on Aristotle. He "adorned the abbey with fair buildings" after becoming its head. The last abbot, Gabriel Donne, received his promotion as a reward for the share he had in the capture of Tyndale, the reformer, at Antwerp. He was a monk of Stratford-le-Bow. The ruins of this abbey are inconsiderable, consisting of little more than an ivied tower (part of the abbot's lodgings—the garderobe

116 Route 11.—*Vale of Dean Burn.* Sect. I.

tower?) close to the present mansion of *Buckfast Abbey*, and the tithebarn, a building about 100 ft. long, at the Grange. A part of the abbey site is occupied by a large woollen factory. The woollen trade at this place is probably of great antiquity. The Cistercians were all wooltraders; and a green path over the moors towards Plymouth, known to this day as *the Abbot's Way*, is said to have been a "post-road" for the conveyance of the wool of the community. The modern Buckfast Abbey is Strawberry Hill Gothic, but stands on the ancient vaulted foundations, of E. Eng. date. About 2 m. N.W. of the town is *Hembury Castle*, an oblong encampment of about 7 acres. In the neighbourhood is *Rigadon*) — Fleming, Esq.), commanding fine views over the lower valley of the Dart, towards Totnes. On the estate of *Brook* (belonging to the Earl of Macclesfield) is a Jas. I. house of some interest, and some picturesque woodland scenery.

You can make excursions either from Buckfastleigh or Ashburton to the *Vale of Dean Burn*, and to the village and *Beacon* of *South Brent*. You should also see the pretty view of *Austin's Bridge* below Buckfastleigh, on the road to Totnes, and that of the Dart valley from the summit of *Cadover Hill* (turn up Cadover lane, just beyond Austin's Bridge), a point of view selected by Turner for his picture of Buckfast Abbey, now in the gallery of Mr. Windus of Tottenham.

From Buckfastleigh the road to Plymouth (and to the Brent Stat.) abuts on the southern slopes of Dartmoor.

1 rt. the *Vale of Dean Burn*, of which Polwhele remarks, "it unites the terrible and graceful in so striking a manner, that to enter this recess hath the effect of enchantment." Halfway up the glen are some picturesque waterfalls. One tumbles into a deep hollow called the *Hound's*

Pool, of which the following story is told. "There once lived in the hamlet of Dean Combe a weaver of great fame and skill. After long prosperity he died and was buried. But the next day he appeared sitting at the loom in his chamber, working diligently as when he was alive. His son applied to the parson, who went accordingly to the foot of the stairs, and heard the noise of the weaver's shuttle in the room above. 'Knowles,' he said, 'come down; this is no place for thee.' 'I will,' said the weaver, 'as soon as I have worked out my quill' (the shuttle full of wool). 'Nay,' said the vicar, 'thou hast been long enough at thy work; come down at once!' So when the spirit came down, the vicar took a handful of earth from the churchyard, and threw it in its face. And in a moment it became a black hound. 'Follow me,' said the vicar; and it followed him to the gate of the wood. When they came there, it seemed as if all the trees in the wood were 'coming together,' so great was the wind. Then the vicar took a nutshell with a hole in it, and led the hound to the pool below the waterfall. 'Take this shell,' he said; 'and when thou shalt have dipped out the pool with it, thou mayest rest—not before.' At midday or at midnight the hound may still be seen at its work." *R. J. K.*

Dean Prior, once belonging to the Priory of Plympton, was the living of *Herrick* the poet, who wrote most of his Hesperides here, and was buried in the churchyard, 1674. (His interment is duly recorded in the register). He was expelled during the Protectorate; but lived to be reinstated under the Act of Uniformity. His poems contain many hits at his parishioners, whose manners, he says, "were rockie as their ways;" but they are full of the wild flowers—the daffodils and primroses—which abound in the orchards and steep hedge-rows of Dean: and he probably found his "Julias" and "Antheas" in the "fair mistresses" of *Dean Court*, a house built by Sir Edward Giles, temp. Edw. VI. It passed by marriage (which Herrick commemorates) to the Yardes; and is now the property of Lord Churston. At the vicarage of Dean Prior are portraits of William Johnson, when a boy (nephew of Sir Josh. Reynolds), by his aunt Fanny Reynolds, and of Mary Furse (niece to Sir J. R.) by *Sir Josh. Reynolds.* To the l. is *Bigadon* (— Fleming, Esq.).

2½ l. *Marley House* (T. Carew, Esq.)

1½ m. Brent Stat., where the tourist may join the rly. to Plymouth. (For Brent, and the stations between it and Plymouth, see Rte. 7.)

ROUTE 12.

EXETER TO TAVISTOCK, BY MORETON HAMPSTEAD. (THE TEIGN; DREWSTEIGNTON; CHAGFORD; WIDDECOMBE; LUSTLEIGH CLEAVE; HEYTOR; DARTMOOR.)

(The best centres for the tourist throughout this tract of country, the wildest and perhaps the most interesting in Devonshire, are Moreton Hampstead and Chagford for exploring the scenery on the river Teign and the adjoining parts of Dartmoor, and Two Bridges or Prince Town for the central wastes of Dartmoor itself. At all these places there are tolerable inns; those at Moreton and at Prince Town being the best. The line of rly. in progress from Newton to Moreton Hampstead, by Bovey Heathfield, will, when completed, afford the readiest access to all this scenery.)

2½ l. *Fordlands* (J. E. C. Walkey, Esq.).

1¼ l. *Perridge*, or *Cotley Camp*, commanding a fine view of Exeter on the one side, and of the vale of the Teign on the other. The form of the camp is circular, and it is about 320 yds. in circumference.

3 *Dunsford Bridge* (*Inn*: a public-house called the Half-Moon). [Hence a road runs S., in company with the Teign, to Chudleigh, passing rt. *Christow*, where there is one of the most picturesque water-mills in the county; and, in about 5 m. rt., *Canonteign House*, an elegant mansion, erected by the late Viscount Exmouth, near the manor-house of Eliz. date, which in the reign of Charles I. was garrisoned for the king, and taken by Fairfax, Dec. 1645, and is still used as a farmhouse. The ch. of *Doddiscombleigh*, in the hollow E. of Canonteign, has some windows of excellent painted glass. (See Rte. 10.)]

Heltor, or the *White Stone Rock* (see *post*), a striking mass of granite forming a conspicuous landmark for all the country on the N. side of the moor, may be reached from Dunsford Bridge. It is a climb through picturesque woods of about 1½ m.

Dunsford Bridge, encompassed by lofty hills, is the point from which travellers generally ascend the banks of the Teign, a crystal stream abounding with trout, and celebrated for its romantic valley. For a distance of 8 m. the river pursues a swift and tortuous course through a profound dell; its bed strewed with large stones and canopied by trees; its banks rising

118   Route 12.—*Fingle Bridge.*—*Cranbrook Castle.*   Sect. I.

in abrupt masses, thickly covered with copse, and occasionally diversified by a projecting cliff. Scenery of this beautiful character is shifted at every bend of the stream. A good path leads from Dunsford Bridge along the l. bank as far as *Clifford Bridge*, on the old road from Exeter to Moreton, where there is a watermill, singularly picturesque; and midway on a hill which descends in a precipice to the river, *Wooston Castle*, one of the most interesting camps in the neighbourhood, and pronounced to be British. It is an irregular oval, formed by a single ditch and rampart, but connected with other works higher on the hill. On the E. side is a covered way, which leads in one direction to the river, and in the other to an elevated mound, which was probably a fire-beacon used in communicating with the other camps on the Teign.

From Clifford Bridge a road proceeds to Fingle Bridge and Drewsteignton (about 3 m.); but the pedestrian should pursue his way by the side of the water (although a difficult course), as the road is uninteresting, and affords no view of the river until it turns abruptly to the l. at the foot of the ascent to Drewsteignton, and passes down a romantic hollow to

Fingle Bridge (the etymology is quite uncertain). This is generally considered the most beautiful spot on the Teign. The scenery, however, for 2 m. above it, is worthy of equal praise. The bridge is itself a very picturesque old structure, narrow and buttressed, based on rocks, and mantled with ivy. The locality is secluded, and the river shut in by towering hills rising to an immense height. The l. bank soars upward so abruptly as to form precipices and a slide for the debris of the rocks. At its summit is the old camp of *Prestonbury Castle*, in form a parallelogram, the area about 250 ft. from E. to W., and 150 ft. from N. to S. There is a high vallum N.; S., where the hill is precipitous, it is slight. There are many outworks. The entrances were on the N., E., and W. sides. The whole comprised about 25 acres. Prestonbury may be of British origin. This camp is, however, commanded by another, called *Cranbrook Castle*, on the opposite side of the river. This camp is of irregular form, circular towards the N.E. and S.E., but almost square in other quarters; on its S. side it has a high rampart and a deep ditch. On its northern side the steepness of the hill formed the only defence. The mound is composed of fragments of stone mingled with earth; but the antiquary will observe with regret that from this old rampart the material is taken for the repair of the neighbouring roads. The ascent from the bridge towards Cranbrook Castle is by zigzags through a dense coppice, and at one of the angles the wood opens and displays a very beautiful vista of "many-folded hills," the eye glancing up the course of the river through a group of wooded promontories, which alternately project from the opposite sides, and appear as if they had been cut from recesses which front them. A mill is prettily situated a short distance below the bridge, and the miller, who gravely offends by diverting the water from the bed of the stream, provides, in deprecation of the traveller's resentment, a parlour and kitchen, with which parties bringing their own provisions are accommodated.

Mr. Merivale ('Hist. of the Romans under the Empire,' vol. vi., p. 28) " is disposed to regard the strong camps which guard on either side the narrow gorge of the Teign as having witnessed the final struggles between Roman and Danmonian. The scene is at any rate picturesque enough for the last act of the drama; and the antiquary, as he traces the strong lines of Wooston, or struggles upward to the watch-tower of Prestonbury, may please himself with the conjecture that it was during the attack on one of these fortresses that the life of Vespasian was saved by his son Titus, then a novice in arms. The incident occurred, at all events, during this western campaign."—'Quart. Rev.', vol. 105. It should be remarked that these 3 camps—Wooston, Prestonbury, and Cranbrook—defended the main northern pass into the hill country of Dartmoor from enemies which might approach through the valleys of the Exe or of the lower Teign. It is only the approaches to Dartmoor which are protected by such camps as these. On the moor itself there are none.

Drewsteignton stands on high ground about ½ m. from the bridge. This place is supposed to have been the principal seat of the Druids in Devonshire, and has been interpreted the *Druids' Town on the Teign*. The British camps on the river and some other antiquities in the neighbourhood would certainly appear to countenance the idea that this part of the country was thickly peopled in the time of the Britons. Drewsteignton, however, derives its name from Drogo or Drewe de Teignton, who held the manor in the reign of Hen. II., as *King's* Teignton and *Bishop's* Teignton are called after their respective proprietors. The village is provided with some alehouses, of which the Victory is the best. The *Church* has a fine late Dec. tower of granite; the nave Perp.; the chancel modern, and very bad.

From Fingle Bridge there is a good walk cut into the side of the l. bank, at some height above the river, along Piddledon Down. It is reached by a gate l. after crossing the bridge. The views from this walk are superb; but those who can buffet with briers should first scramble up the side of the stream for 2 m. The brake is in places almost impenetrable, but the scenery is of a character to repay any amount of exertion. The l. bank is roughened by some beautiful crags. The first which meets the view is known by the common name of *Sharptor*, or *Sharpitor*. Having passed safely beneath this frowning ruin, you will reach a bend in the river, and beyond this, in the channel of the stream, but close to the bank, lies a reputed *logan-stone*. This great fragment, about 12 ft. in length by 6 in height and width, has evidently fallen from the hill above it, and once, by all accounts, oscillated freely on its point of support. Polwhele informs us that he moved it with one hand in 1797. At present, however, it stands as firmly rooted as the hills around it, and is probably fixed by sand washed under it by the floods. At this spot the wanderer will open to view the mouth of the ravine, formed on the one side by a ruinous crag called *Hunstor*, and on the other by *Whyddon Park* (E. S. Bayley, Esq., but long the seat of the Whyddons), one of the most romantic scenes imaginable, a wild hillside covered with aged oaks and mossy rocks. You should ascend to the top of Hunstor for the best view of this charming scene (and here you may take the path before mentioned, back to Fingle). From this eminence the river has the appearance of flowing up hill from a swampy valley into a rugged defile and the heart of a mountainous country. To the W. the sombre masses of Dartmoor give a magnificent finish to the landscape. About ½ m. beyond the portal of the ravine, the Teign is crossed at Dogamarsh Bridge by the road from Moreton to Okehampton. About 1 m. from this bridge, in the direction of the latter town (or 1½ m. from Drewsteignton), a fine cromlech called the

Spinsters' Rock stands on an eminence of Shilston farm ¼ m. rt. of the road (turn to the rt. through a lodge-gate). This interesting old monument derives its name from a whimsical tradition that 3 spinsters (who were *spinners*) erected it one morning before breakfast; but "may we not," says Mr. Rowe (Peramb. of Dartmoor), "detect in this legend of the 3 fabulous spinners the terrible Valkyriur of the dark mythology of our Northern ancestors — the *Fatal Sisters*, the choosers of the slain, whose dread office was to 'weave the warp and weave the woof of destiny'?" Polwhele informs us that the legend varies, and that for the 3 spinsters some have substituted 3 young men and their father, who brought the stones from the highest part of Dartmoor; and in this phase of the legend has been traced an obscure tradition of Noah and his 3 sons. The Spinsters' Rock consists of a table-stone about 15 ft. in length by 10 in breadth, supported by 3 pillars 7 ft. high, so that most people can walk under it erect. (Many cromlechs exist which have only 3 supports—those at Lanyon and Pendarves in Cornwall for example. See *Introd.*) The hill on which it stands commands an excellent view of *Cawsand Beacon*. The cromlech fell during the spring of 1862. It would probably have remained in its original state had a few yards of greensward been preserved about it; but the plough was driven close round the imposts, and the long-continued rains of the season had saturated the soil. It was, however, replaced in November of the same year, at the expense of the Rev. W. Ponsford, the Rector of Drewsteignton; and the stones occupy, as nearly as possible, their former positions. It was needful to clear away the soil under and about the cromlech to place the machinery for raising the quoit or covering stone (estimated to weigh 16 tons); and the soil did not appear to have been disturbed, and no remains were found. Like other cromlechs, this is no doubt a sepulchral monument. About 100 yds. beyond the cromlech, on the other (N.) side of the lane, is a pond of water, of about 3 acres, called *Bradmere Pool*, prettily situated in a wood. It is said to be unfathomable, and to remain full to the brim during the driest seasons. It is really the result of old mine-works. The country people have a legend of a passage formed of large stones leading underground from Bradmere to the Teign, near the logan-stone. The skirts of Dartmoor in this neighbourhood abound in rugged, romantic scenes, particularly about Gidleigh and Chagford.

Resuming our route from Dunsford Bridge to Moreton Hampstead, we proceed by a road among the hills; but a pedestrian should follow the *old* Moreton road, which turns off l. through the wood.

3 A dark rock to the l. forms part of a tor called the *Black Stone*. The hills now increase in boldness, and the stones which strew their flanks remind the traveller of his approach to the granitic region of Dartmoor, which opens magnificently to view on the descent to Moreton.

2 *Moreton Hampstead*, commonly called Morton, *i.e.* Moor-town (*Inns*: White Hart, comfortable; White Horse). This small place, situated in a wild and beautiful country on the border of Dartmoor, and swept by the purest and most invigorating breezes, is remarkable for its salubrity, which the stranger may infer from the healthful looks of the inhabitants. The *ch.* (Perp.) has been plainly restored. The houses are mean and thatched, and, with the exception of the *poor-house*, which has an arched arcade of the 17th century, there is nothing worth notice in the town save an old cross and elm-tree at the entrance of the churchyard. It

is said that the elm-tree had its branches trained to support a stage for dancing, and that the boughs above afforded a pleasant perch for the fiddler. The scenery in the neighbourhood is of an exquisite cast; the hills wild and rocky, and covered with furze "so thick and splendid that it may be compared to an embroidery of gold on velvet of the richest green."

The following are the most interesting scenes and objects accessible from Moreton:—The valleys of *Lustleigh Cleave* and *Houndtor Coomb*, *Becky Fall*, the *Heytor Rocks*, *Widdecombe Church*, *Fingle Bridge*, the *Spinsters' Rock*, the town of *Chagford* and *Gidleigh Park*; the British camps of *Prestonbury*, *Cranbrook*, and *Wooston Castle*, on the Teign; ancient *stone circles*, near Fenworthy and on Sittaford Tor; and an old British village called *Grimspound*, in the parish of Manaton. Those who make any stay at this town should also visit the

Black Stone (about 2 m. E.), a very interesting tor; the

White Stone or *Heltor* (1 m. N.E. of Black Stone, and the same N. of Bridford), towering like an old castle above the valley of the Teign, and easily reached from Dunsford Bridge. On this tor are some large "rock basins," which some antiquaries regard as artificial and "Druidical," but which result in all probability from the disintegration of the granite. The local legend runs that King Arthur and the "enemy" flung quoits at each other from the tops of these hills, which quoits remain in the shape of the granite that crests them.

Shat Tor (between Bridford and Christow), another feature of the Teign scenery, chiselled by nature in the form of steps, as if for the
[*Dev. & Corn.*]

purpose of an Ascension; the beautiful

Valley of Lustleigh, with its picturesque village (4 m. S.), and *ch.*, with E. Eng. portions in the chancel, a Norman font, and Perp. nave. In the N. aisle are effigies of a knight and lady (temp. Edw. III.?) probably of the Dinham family; and adjoining the S. porch is Sir Wm. Prowse's chapel, with his effigy (temp. Edw. II.) At the threshold of the S. porch is an *inscribed stone* of the Brito-Roman era. The *ch.* has been well restored, and is beautifully situated. The

Bottor Rock, a tor of trap (at Hennock, some 6 m. S.E.), curiously fissured, and commanding a magnificent view.

Near Moreton is *Wray Barton*, a Tudor mansion, belonging to J. Courtier, Esq. *Bridford* ch., 4 m. E., has a fine screen. (See Rte. 10.)

Lustleigh Cleave (about 3½ m. from Moreton, and ½ m. below the village of Manaton) is one of those rough romantic valleys in which granite acts as a scarecrow to improvement, and nature is free to follow the bent of her own sweet fancies. Withal it is so secluded, that were it not for the rocks, which serve the traveller as a landmark, there would be difficulty in finding it. These conspicuous objects roughen the hillside which bounds it, and at the summit of the ridge hang in crags so fancifully shaped as to have acquired names from the peasantry. One, ivy-mantled, and massive as a ruin of old, is called the *Raven's Tower*, being a haunt of these birds. Another, a favourite retreat of Reynard, is distinguished by the name of the *Fox's Yard*. At the entrance of the valley the stream is checked by a singular impediment. The channel is deep, but filled to the brim with masses of granite, so that the water

G

flows as it were underground, but its murmurs are heard as it forces its way through the pores of this natural filter. The stones are called the *Horsham Steps*, after the name of the estate, and from the circumstance of their being crossed by a footpath. The stream flows along the skirts of an old wood which climbs the acclivity of a hill among weed-grown rocks, and altogether the scene is as beautiful as it is curious. At certain seasons of the year these "steps" are passed by salmon; and in the winter frequently buried under a flood, when a woody recess below them, called *Horsham Bay*, is filled with water. The angler should be informed that the *Bovey Brook*, as this limpid rivulet is called, is a notable trout-stream. A little beyond the Horsham Steps the traveller will obtain the best view of the Cleave, and remark the charming irregularity of the hillside on the rt., which presents a sweet interchange of wooded swells and hollows. On the granite ridge to the l. lies a logan stone called the *Nutcrackers*, difficult to find, but situated near the S. end of the ridge, and on the Cleave side of the summit. The mark for it is a spherical mass of granite perched aloft on the top of a conspicuous carn. The Nutcracking Rock lies just below, and S. of this object. It is a small rock, about 5 ft. in length and breadth, resting, as it were, upon a keel, so that a push rolls it from side to side; its progress, at each vibration, being arrested by a stone against which it knocks. Hence it derives its name; for a nut, being inserted at the point of contact, is very thoroughly broken by a stroke of the logan. The block next to it oscillates in a similar manner, and is a larger piece of granite; but the former stone is so perfectly balanced, that it can be moved with the little finger. From this elevated position the traveller may gain a geographical idea of the Cleave and surrounding country; and such knowledge may be useful, as heights and hollows in this beautiful neighbourhood are so irregularly grouped that it is difficult for a stranger to direct his course with certainty. He will observe that 3 valleys meet at the end of the Cleave; viz. the valley of Lustleigh, in which the village of that name is situated; the Cleave; and Houndtor Coomb, which, winding from the moor near Heytor, is joined near Manaton by another valley, which passes that village in its course from Hamilton Down. The view is truly delightful; the Bovey Heathfield is seen to the S., the fantastic rocks and brown moors of Heytor and Houndtor to the W., and the ch. of Manaton just peeping over the boundary of the Cleave. The traveller should next pass from this secluded vale by the Horsham Steps, and ascend the pathway through the wood to the village of

Manaton, which is about 4 m. from Moreton through N. Bovey (a poor public-house is the only accommodation for those who hunger and thirst). The situation of this village is wild and beautiful; woods, rocks, and singularly shaped hills are seen from it in every direction, and a rugged carn rises behind the clergyman's house. The *ch*. is particularly well placed. There are some fragments of stained glass, a good tower, Perp. nave piers, and a fine old yew in the churchyard. In a field to the E. of it, and near the road, you may find a small elliptical *pound*. Opposite to Manaton the granite tors are remarkably imposing. One rock, formed of five layers of stone, and rising to a height of more than 30 ft., resembles a gigantic human figure, and is known by the name of *Bowerman's Nose*; "of which name," says Mr. Burt, in his notes to Carrington's 'Dartmoor,' "there was a person in the Conqueror's time, who lived at Huntor or Houndtor in Manaton." This curious object rises from a clatter about 1 m. S.W. of Manaton, and is viewed to most advantage from the N. When seen from the higher ground on the S. it bears some likeness to a Hindoo idol in a sitting posture—a form which may often be traced in granite piles; for instance, in the Armed Knight, seated among the waves below the cliffs of the Land's End. Snakes, called in Devonshire *long cripples*, are said to be numerous in this parish, and Polwhele tells us of one which so greatly alarmed the neighbourhood, that "fancy, worked upon by fear, had swelled it beyond the size of the human body, had given it legs and wings, and had heard it hiss for miles around." The name Manaton has been explained by Col. Hamilton Smith as *Maen-y-dun*, the fort or enclosure of erect stones. (But query?)

Becky Fall is in the valley of Houndtor Coomb, about 1 m. from Manaton, from which it is approached over a rustic bridge by a field-path from the lane. The small stream of the Becky, after flowing some distance from its source, here tumbles some 80 ft. down an escarpment of granite. The channel is, however, so broad and deep, and heaped with so many rocks, that in summer the water is only heard in its stony bed; yet the spot is at all times romantic and delightful, the ground being wooded, and sloping abruptly to a dell. In the winter the cascade very frequently presents an imposing spectacle, thundering in volume over the steep, while icicles hang from the trees and wave in the wind which is raised by the rushing water. Here the botanist may find some curious mosses, and *Lichen articulatus*, a rare plant. *Beck* is a common term in the N. of England for a hill stream. A new road lately cut through this country passes close to Becky Fall (where there is a cottage belonging to the Earl of Devon). It should be followed to its termination.

The view to be obtained from it of Lustleigh Cleave and the adjoining valleys is very peculiar and striking.

Houndtor (or Hounter) *Coomb* is a good specimen of those wild valleys on the border of Dartmoor, where the farmer has penetrated a short distance, and rocks and bogs are intermingled with oak woods and fields. Its prominent feature is the summit of Houndtor, capped by some remarkable rocks, resembling the pillars of a ruinous old temple, but changing their forms as often as the spectator shifts his position. The stranger will be astonished on beholding from one point a stony mushroom of extraordinary size (like the Cheesewring in Cornwall); and at another a fantastic group bearing some resemblance to a conclave of monsters. Such a wonder will probably tempt him to dispel the illusion by a scramble up the hill, and he may be assured that a nearer view of this strange assembly will repay the exertion. The remains of a *kistvaen* in a circle of stones may be found about a furlong S. of the tor. At the head of the valley the moor is seen in all its grandeur and desolation, and the slopes are covered with granite, which is extensively quarried on the heights. About 2 m. in a southerly direction, or 3 m. from Becky Fall, soar aloft those conspicuous rocks which form the cleft summit of

Heytor or *Hightor*, an eminence, however, some distance from Moreton, and more generally ascended from Chudleigh or Ashburton. The traveller, no doubt, will already be distantly acquainted with its remarkable crown of granite, as its bold and singular shape renders it a striking feature of many views from the eastern parts of the county. Arrived at the dizzy pinnacle, he will find it to consist of 2 tors, which are of little interest in comparison with the superb landscape which opens to the sight, and for the enjoyment of which he should climb the westernmost rock. From that summit he will behold in one view the area of the South Hams, a splendid prospect of woods, rivers, and "the infinite of smiling fields," bounded by the sea. Towards the E. the hills are also cultivated, though crowned with the *Bottor Rock*; but on the N. and W. the face of nature wears a frown, and gloomy moors stretch away into the farthest distance. The grandeur of this lonely region is, however, most impressive, and must forcibly arrest the traveller's attention. There is a solemnity in the deep-toned colouring of the moor, in the stillness which reigns around, and the vastness of the desolate view; while variety and animation are imparted to such scenes by the glancing lights and moving shadows, the purple bloom of the heather, and the changeful tints of the innumerable hills. On Heytor are remains which possess a human interest, and carry the mind back to the most distant times; for on the slope of the tor may be observed a group of *hut circles*, and the ruins of an ancient road, or *trackway*, which traverses the hill from N.W. to S.E. Immediately below the summit, on the eastern side, is the celebrated quarry, well adapted as a foreground for a sketch, and displaying magnificent walls of granite, which can supply the largest blocks. London Bridge, the Fishmongers' Hall, and the columns in the library of the British Museum, are of Heytor granite. The stone is carried down the declivity of the moor on a granite tramroad. It is then shipped on the *Stover Canal*, by which it is conveyed to Teignmouth. About a mile distant on the same side of the hill is the hamlet of *Heytor Town* with a small inn. If determined to see all the curiosities of the neighbourhood, you should now walk to

Rippon Tor (alt. 1549 ft.), situated next to Heytor, in a W. direction, and commanding a view of the romantic vale and hamlet of Widdecombe in the Moor. Upon this rugged eminence are the remains of a *trackway*, and ¼ m. W. of the summit, on the crest of the ridge, the *Nutcrackers*, once a logan-stone, but now immoveably fixed. It is, however, an interesting object—a stone about 16 ft. in length, poised horizontally upon an upright rock, which rises from a wild *clatter* (the true Devonshire word) of granite fragments.

Widdecombe in the Moor marks the frontier of cultivation, but is a very ancient place, as may be seen by the weather-stained walls of the cottages. An old manor-house called *North Hall*, of which no remains are now visible, formerly stood near the churchyard. The almshouses near the ch. are of the 15th centy. The ch., dedicated to St. Pancras, has an excellent Perp. tower—often compared, for its beauty of proportion, to Magdalen Tower, Oxford—which is said to have been voluntarily built by a company of tinners who had worked the neighbouring mines with profit. The edifice has been the scene of a singular disaster. In Oct. 1638, during divine service, a terrible storm burst over the village, and, after some flashes of uncommon brilliancy, a ball of fire dashed through a window of the ch. into the midst of the congregation. At once the pews were overturned, 4 persons were killed, and 62 wounded, many by a pinnacle of the tower which tumbled through the roof, while "the stones," says Prince, "were thrown down from the steeple as fast as if it had been by 100 men." The country people accounted for this awful destruction by a wild tale that "the devil, dressed in black, and mounted on a black horse, inquired his way to the ch. of a woman who kept a little public-house on the moor. He offered her money to become his guide, but she distrusted him on remarking that the liquor went hissing down his throat, and finally had her suspicions confirmed by the glimpse of a cloven foot which he could not conceal by his boot." On the same day Plymouth was pelted by enormous hailstones. The visitor to Widdecombe church should read some edifying verses on a tablet in the N. aisle commemorating the calamity. Schools, and a good chapel, have lately been erected in this parish by Mrs. Larpent, a resident, to whom Widdecombe is greatly indebted.

Widdecombe is locally spoken of as "Widdecombe in the Dartmoors," and occasionally, in a quainter phraseology, as "Widdecombe in the cold country, good Lord!" Its position is a bleak one, on the border of so wild and extensive a moor; and along the S. coast there is a saying when it snows, "that Widdecombe folks are picking their geese." This, however, writes a correspondent of 'Notes and Queries,' may be only an allusion to the sky, which in Devonshire is also called "widdicote," for example in the nursery riddle—

"Widdicote, woddicote, over-cote hang,
Nothing so broad, and nothing so lang,
As widdicote, woddicote, over-cote hang."

Just S. of Widdecombe, on the side of Torrhill (W. of the Ashburton road), are the remains of a *British village*, very curiously partitioned by *track-lines;* and within ½ m. N. of the ch. tower 2 *logan stones*, still moveable; one called the *Rugglestone*, about 5 ft. thick, 22 ft. long, 19 ft. broad, and computed to weigh 110 tons; the other a flatter stone, about 10 ft. in length, and 9 ft. in breadth. The vale of Widdecombe, shut in by lofty and granite-strewn hills, with the fine Perpendicular tower rising in the centre, is of extreme beauty. Ancient sycamores are scattered up and down the slopes, so stately and wide-spreading as to recall the noble lines of Waller:—

"In such green palaces the first kings reign'd,
Slept in their shade, and angels entertain'd:
With such old counsellors they did advise,
And, by frequenting sacred shades, grew wise."

The old monument called *Grimspound* is situated on *Hamilton Down* (alt. 1738 ft.), about 7 m. W. of Moreton, and 3 m. W.N.W. of Manaton. From the former town it may be reached on foot or horseback, by pursuing the Tavistock road 5 m., and then turning to the l. and crossing the moor for about 2 m. in a southerly direction. In a carriage it will be necessary to proceed along the high road 6 m. to a small public-house near *Vitifer Mine* (observe the old stone *cross* where you turn from the high road). Vitifer Mine lies in a valley to the l., and Grimspound is situated high above it, 2 m. E. From Manaton a person on foot should direct his course up the valley to the first farmhouse under Hamilton Down (on which may be seen remains of the central *trackway*, or boundary, vide Introd., and *Berry Pound* on the N.E. declivity), and then turn to the rt. and follow a stream to its source on the summit of the hill. There he will find himself on the naked moor, and, by walking a little distance down the declivity, will open to view the grey stones of Grimspound. This is the most remarkable of the walled villages or "pounds" on Dartmoor. "It has a diameter of 502 ft. by 447 ft., including the walls; and 25 hut circles still remain within its area. The walls, composed of large granite blocks, are between 9 and 10 ft. thick. A stream of water runs through one end of its area; and its position is well chosen to command the passage over the hills, and to intercept the communications through this part of the country. Here, no doubt, the old road passed from the E. side of Dartmoor, traversing this difficult hilly country toward the W.; and the position of the old bridge (at what is now called Post Bridge) shows that it ran in former times directly in the line of Grimspound, and of the valley in which it stands, between the heights of Hamilton and Hooknor Tor. The site has not been chosen without due consideration of its merits in a military point of view. For though we should now consider it to be commanded by the hills on either side, . . . this was no objection in olden times for the position of a fortified town. The strong city of Mycenæ in Greece is more immediately under a lofty hill from which every movement of the garrison could be descried; and the same may be said of Greaves-ash in Northumberland and other places . . . The hut-circles of Grimspound are of the usual size; the doorways generally turned S. The original entrance was on the E. side, about 15 ft. S. of the present passage, which has been forced through the wall, and by which the modern road leads toward Manadon."—*G. Wilkinson*. The etymology of Grimspound is evidently the same as that of the many "Grimsdikes" which occur in different parts of England. In these "Grim" appears to be equivalent to "boundary." Grimspound would therefore signify the pound or enclosure on the "boundary;" and it should be remarked that the central trackway, marking the division between N. and S. Dartmoor (see *Introd.*) passes on Hamilton close by. The locality is wild and desolate, and well calculated to encourage the train of thought which such venerable relics may suggest. The declivity slopes to a barren valley (the site of Vitifer mine); rock-strewn eminences rise on either side, and lonely hills close the view. On *Challacombe Down* a stone avenue (double, or formed by 3 rows of stones) may be traced N. and S. about 80 yards; and on *Hooknor Tor*, just N. of Grimspound, are a number of hut circles. The traveller should ascend this tor so as to look down upon Grimspound. He can then, if bound to Moreton Hampstead, strike over the moor towards the N., when he will shortly reach the high road at about the 5th milestone from his destination. If viewed by sunset this interesting old monument will long linger in the memory.

Chagford (*Inns:* Three Crowns, Globe Hotel) is a picturesque old Stannary town about 4 m. from Moreton. It is situated on elevated ground in the midst of deep dells and half-reclaimed hills of a very beautiful character, and commands a view of Cawsand Beacon, with other mountainous tors, and of the entrance to the gorge of the Teign, near Drewsteignton. It is recommended by physicians for its pure and bracing air, and the scenery in the neighbourhood is also calculated to restore the invalid. "In winter, however," writes a visitor, "Chagford is desolate and almost unapproachable; and if an inhabitant be asked at this season concerning his locality, he calls it, in sad tones, 'Chagford, good Lord!' In summer it is picturesque and accessible, and then the exulting designation is 'Chaggiford, and what d'ye think?'" During the Rebellion the royalists made an attack on this village, when, says Clarendon, "they lost Sidney Godolphin, a young gentleman of incomparable parts. He received a mortal shot by a musket, a little above the knee, of which he died on the instant, leaving the misfortune of his death upon a place which could never otherwise have had a mention in the world." Clarendon, however, it must be remembered, wrote before handbooks were in request, for it is impossible to enumerate all the romantic scenes round Chagford. At all events the stranger will do well to wander about the course of the Teign, and down by the village of Gidleigh along the skirt of the moor. Chagford is justly a favourite retreat of artists, and the Three Crowns, with its thatched roof and ivied porch, was for many years an irresistible bait, but it is now denuded of its ivy and partly modernised. It was formerly the dower house attached to Whyddon Park, and was built by Judge Whyddon in the reign of James I. Godolphin —so runs the local tradition—was killed in the porch. An old watermill at Holy-street, about 1 m. W., is an excellent subject for the pencil although the roof was re-thatched in 1857. It had been previously painted by Creswick in 3 pictures, viz. 1, with the wheel at rest; 2, with the wheel in motion; 3, from another point of view, with the entrance and footway of mossy stones. The botanist in his rambles will notice the profusion of ferns. The *Tasselled Pteris*, the *Cleft Asplenium Trichomanes*, many varieties of *Polypodium*, and strange *Lady Ferns* are found here.

Chagford *Ch.* (ded. to St. Michael) is a fine specimen of a Perp. granite church. The tower is good. There is a parclose screen and an Elizabethan monument to the Whyddons, blocking the chancel window. The interior arrangements are not to be commended. Against the N. wall is a monument for Sidney Godolphin, who, however, is said to have been buried at Oakhampton.

The neighbourhood is rich in antiquities. Within the compass of a walk or ride are the *British camps* above Fingle Bridge; the *cromlech* called the Spinsters' Rock; so-called *Druidical circles* on Scorhill Down, on Sittaford Tor, and near Fernworthy; a *British bridge* on the N. Teign; a *rock pillar* and *hut circles* on Kestor; and the remains of a *castle* at Gidleigh. Chagford is also a convenient starting-place for a hunt after *Cranmere*, " the mother of the Dartmoor rivers," a pool which has been invested with a certain mystery by the extreme wildness of its situation, and the difficulty of traversing the morasses which surround it. Indeed, it is so seldom found by those who go in search of it, that many have ranked this "mother of rivers" with that creation of the fancy the Brown Man of the moors.

The antiquities can be easily seen in 2 days. On the first you may visit Fingle Bridge, Spinsters' Rock, and return to Chagford by Gidleigh. On the second you can proceed by Holy-street and Gidleigh Park to Scorhill Circle; ascend Kestor; follow the stream to Sittaford Tor; inspect the bridge on the Teign, and the circles called the Grey Wethers; and return by the Fernworthy circle to Chagford. You will find these curiosities fully described below.

Holy-street is a romantic hamlet, about 1 m. W., close to the confluence of the N. and S. Teign. The name has given rise to a conjecture that a sacred Druidical road once passed this way from the cromlech at Shilston to the circle on Scorhill Down (but no one need believe this unless he chooses). Here there is a mill most wonderfully picturesque; and ½ m. further W., on the river's S. bank, the *Puckie* or *Puggie Stone*, which commands an excellent view of the wild glen of Gidleigh Park.

Gidleigh Park (Rev. A. Whipham) is well known as a magnificent scene of wood and rock, where the Teign hurries down a declivity, and, in the course of ages, has wormed a deep channel in the granite, which it traverses with a roar which may be heard at a great distance. The slopes are forest wilds, in which birches are interspersed among rocks of granite. A reputed *tolmên*, or holed stone, may be found in the river, close to the N. bank, a little below the confluence of the Wallabrook with the N. Teign, and opposite the end of a stone hedge. (The hole, however, has been formed by the action of

128   Route 12.—Gidleigh.—Kestor Rock.   Sect. I.

water, and not by human agency.) A little above the meeting of the same streams is *Scorhill Circle*, considered the finest example in the county. 26 stones are standing, and 6 fallen, out of about 55; though the spaces vary too much to enable us to arrive at a satisfactory estimate of the real number. The diameter of the circle is 88 ft. The stones are of various sizes, but there is one nearly 8 ft. and another 6 ft. in height. Adjoining this circle, on the Wallabrook, is an ancient bridge, or *clam*, of a single stone, 15 ft. in length. About 1 m. N. of Gidleigh Park is the village of *Gidleigh*, containing a picturesque fragment of a castle, which belonged to the family of Prous from the reign of the Conqueror to that of Edw. II. The remains are of the 14th centy. The lower chamber has a barrel vault, and there are 2 old staircases. *Throwleigh ch.*, 2 m. N. of Gidleigh, has the finest Perp. tower in the district; and on the N. side of the chancel a priest's door (Perp.) of unusual size and ornament. The ch. has been well restored, and the churchyard cared for. The ch. house is a good 15th centy. cottage, with lych-gate of same date.

An excursion is often made from Chagford to the *Castor* or *Kestor Rock*,—" a mortal (i.e. 'great,' Devonicè) place for ravens," say the neighbours—a tor in sight from the village, and about 3 m. W. The road to it is a lane (so designated by courtesy) as far as a most primitive hamlet, called *Teigncoomb* (2 m.), which is the limit of cultivation. Above this place, on the moor, are a number of *hut circles* and lines of stones (refer to Introd.) scattered over a large area. One of the former is uncommonly perfect. The earth has been evidently lowered in the interior, and the stones are on their edges in contact, and form, on one side, a small recess. The slope

towards the Teign is also covered with these interesting remains, among which there is one which differs from the rest, being a circle 106 ft. in diam. enclosing a smaller one of the usual size. This is known by the name of *Roundy Pound*. It is strongly built, the walls being 6 ft. 2 .in. thick, and composed of large blocks. The inner circle is 47 ft. in diameter. "The space between the outer and inner circles has been divided into several spaces by walls radiating towards the centre, similar to those at Greaves-ash in Northumberland, at Chun Castle, and other places, probably intended for securing and penning sheep. The door of the outer circle opens toward the N.W.; that of the inner one S."—*Sir G. Wilkinson.* Further traces of the old Britons may be seen on the next hill to the W., which is scored by a *stone avenue*, or double row of detached upright stones, which are disposed along it like tombstones for a distance of 554 ft. This avenue is 3 ft. 6 in. broad, and is terminated at each end by two large monoliths. At one end of the avenue is a carn, composed of 4 concentric circles. (See *Introd.* for general remarks on stone avenues). On Kestor Rock is the largest "rock basin" on Dartmoor, 8 ft. by 6 ft. 8 in. and 31 in. deep. (Kestor lies, like other tors on which are the most important basins, in a central belt which occupies about 1-3rd of the area of the moor. Along this belt " the granite is for the most part more liable to decomposition than at the harder and more crystalline tors. This is shown by the many rounded tors; and every roadside cutting shows the rapidity of the decay." (See Mr. Ormerod's paper on the Rock Basins of Dartmoor in the Quarterly Journal of the Geological Society, vol. xv. 1859.) S.W. of Kestor, at a distance of 1 m., is the *Longstone*— doubtless, says Mr. Rowe (Peramb. of Dartmoor), a genuine rock pillar, although used as a boundary-stone in modern times. A *stone avenue* runs from it in the direction of Scorhill Circle. This avenue is 473 ft. long; and on the brow of the hill, about 300 ft. beyond it, is another avenue, 382 ft. long, terminating in a cairn, containing a cist or coffin 7 ft. in length. From the Kestor Rock the stranger will gain an insight into the character of Dartmoor, and, if charmed with its heathery hills and bound in a westerly direction, he may trace the N. Teign to its source, which lies between Cut Hill and Sittaford Tor, at a distance of about 4 m.; and from that lonely spot among the bogs he may reach the head of the W. Dart by crossing its E. branch and the opposite hill, and may descend through Wistman's Wood to Two Bridges (an additional 6 m. or thereabout). *Cut Hill* is a great eminence (crowned with a pile of turf) in the central morass of Dartmoor; its sides rent open by the rain, and quite inaccessible in a wet season. Its summit commands a grand desolation—extensive bogs, which contain the fountains of the Dart, Tavy, Teign, Taw, and Okement. These rivers may be said to drain all from one source, but they flow in different directions, and are soon a great distance apart. In the view from Kestor the traveller will observe in the W.N.W., on the distant profile of the moor, a barren eminence fringed with rocks which in outline bear a whimsical resemblance to trees. They may illustrate a remark of the author of 'Modern Painters.' "A tree," says Ruskin, "50 yds. from us, taken as a mass, has a soft outline; but put it 10 m. off against the sky, and its outline will be so sharp that you cannot tell it from a rock." W. by N. of Kestor, at a distance of some 2 m., rises *Watern Tor*, a very interesting pile of granite divided by a cleft, through which it is said a horseman may ride.

No stranger in this neighbourhood should neglect to visit *Whyddon Park*, a romantic hillside at the entrance to the gorge of the Teign, and a short 2 m. walk from Chagford by a path along the river-bank. You will enter the park at the mansion of Whyddon, anciently the seat of the Whyddon family, and now of the Bayleys. Here are huge old Scotch and silver firs to delight you at the threshold; but higher on the hill are scenes and objects magnificently wild—vistas of beech and aged oaks, chaotic *clatters* and piles of granite, herds of deer among the fern and mossy stones, and at a distance the towering tors of Dartmoor.

Sittaford Tor, the site of the Druidical circles called the Grey Wethers, is about 6 m. from Chagford and 3 m. from Kestor, and may be found by pursuing the N. Teign nearly to its source. The tor is situated S. of the river, on the rt. bank. In its vicinity the traveller (if he keeps near the stream) will find one of the most interesting relics on Dartmoor, an ancient *bridge* of 3 openings, spanning the N. Teign. This rude old structure, which is in fine preservation, is about 7 ft. in width and 27 in length, and formed entirely of granite blocks. On the S.E. slope of Sittaford Tor are the *Grey Wethers*, 2 circles of which the circumferences nearly touch, like those of the Hurlers on the Bodmin Moors. Each circle is 120 ft. in diam., and appears to have once consisted of 27 stones; but 9 only are now erect in the one, and 7 in the other. About 2 m. E. is the *sacred circle* near Fernworthy, which is 60 ft. in diam., and formed of 27 stones, which are all erect. They stand about 3 ft. apart, and the highest is 4 ft. above the ground.

Cranmere Pool (Rte. 14) is very difficult to find, and very difficult of approach, but is perhaps more easily reached from Chagford than from any other border town, as it is situated about 2 m. due W. of a conspicuous mark in this neighbourhood, *Watern Tor*. It is merely a pool of water in the midst of deep morasses, which are everywhere rent open by the rain; but as there is some chance of being bewildered among the bogs in a search for it, and as it has been considered the fountain-head of more than one well-known river, the stranger may like to go in quest of it; and if provided with these directions, with a pocket compass, stout legs, and fine weather, his adventure will probably be crowned with success, and he will reach the shore of this dreary *Lake of Cranes*. From Chagford and Watern Tor he may ride as far as *White Horse Hill* (just N. of Sittaford Tor); but there he will enter the *turve-ties* (where they cut peat), and soon the lonely region of the great central wilderness, which is impassable by a pony. Here he may consider the scenery rather dreary; but there are many who will find an indescribable charm in it. Far to the N. and W. stretches an immense morass, coating both hill and valley, and seamed on the slopes by furrows of black earth 8 or 10 ft. deep. But there are voices and visions in this wilderness to cheer the wanderer. The murmurs of the rivulets and the cries of strange birds fall pleasantly on the ear; while the hills are varied by the most beautiful tints, which alternately shine and wane as the lights and shadows play over them. Cranmere Pool is the largest piece of water on Dartmoor, though not above 220 yards in circumf. It has been called "the mother of the Dartmoor rivers," but is, in fact, only the source of the *W. Okement*, which receives many other little streamlets as it trickles towards Yes Tor. Four other rivers, however, rise at short distances from Cranmere,— the *Taw*, ½ m. E.; the *Tavy*, below Great Knecset Tor, 1 m. S.W.; the *Dart*, 1 m. S.; and the *Teign*, near Sittaford Tor, about 2 m. S.E. In the belief of the country people Cranmere is a place of punishment for unhappy spirits, who are frequently to be heard wailing in the morasses which surround it (see Rte. 14).

The ascent of *Cawsand Beacon*, alt. 1792 ft. (see Rte. 6), is another excursion often made from Chagford; you can visit *Gidleigh Castle* and *Shelstone Pound* on the way. From the summit of the Beacon the 2 channels—the Bristol and the English—are (in very clear weather) visible at once.

To resume our route from Moreton Hampstead:—the traveller should prepare for an arduous journey, and we may remind him of an alehouse sign which a few years ago would have greeted his eyes on the border of the moor. It represented a solitary wayfarer battling against a storm, and below was written—

"Before the wild moor you venture to pass, Pray step within and take a glass."

3 *Bector Cross*, at the intersection of the Moreton and Tavistock, and Ashburton and Chagford roads. The old *cross* may be found in an adjoining field.

1 The traveller bids adieu to cultivation, and rises into the elevated wilds of Dartmoor, of which it is now necessary to give some description.

Dartmoor occupies an area of about 130,000 acres, the greater part of which was afforested by King John, under the name of *Dartmoor Forest*, which was granted by Hen. III. to his brother Richard Earl of Cornwall, and in the reign of Edw. III. united to the duchy. The length of the moor from N. to S. is 22 m., the breadth about 20 m., and the mean elevation about 1700 ft. This vast expanse has, in every part, that billowy aspect which Humboldt describes as characteristic of primitive chains. It is entirely of granite, and has been aptly compared to a mountain squeezed down, and in the process split asunder, "till the whole was one hilly wilderness, showing ever and anon strange half-buried shapes striving to uplift themselves towards the sky." "The formation of large roads over the hilly country of Dartmoor has long since altered its ancient character; and deprived it of that appearance of seclusion, and that difficulty of access, for which it was once so remarkable; but any one who, leaving the high road, wanders amidst the hills on either side, may still form an idea of the previous aspect of that inhospitable region, and of its natural strength against hostile intrusion."—*Sir G. Wilkinson.* With the exception of the land surrounding the prisons, and some small farms, on the high road and far from each other, Dartmoor is entirely uncultivated, its gloomy hills and glens being seldom disturbed by other sounds than those of the rushing torrent or howling wind. A coarse grass, heather, reeds, the whortleberry, and moss, are the principal produce of the granitic soil; trees vanish from the view upon entering the moor, and even fern and furze are confined to the deepest valleys; but there is a tradition that Dartmoor was once clothed with a forest, in which deer and wild cattle found a secure asylum, and the trunks of trees often found in the bogs would seem to warrant the legend. In the heart of the wilderness both hill and valley are desolated by an immense morass, deeply furrowed by the rain, inaccessible except after a long continuance of dry weather, and in some places incapable of supporting the lightest animal; and here rise the most celebrated of those numberless streams which give life to the dreary waste, and descend through ravines on the border of the district. The Dart, Teign, Tavy, and Taw all drain from this huge plastic store of peat; the rivers Erme and Yealm, and about 50 smaller streams, from less extensive swamps in other quarters of the moor; all being alike characterised by a beautiful transparency during fine weather, but subject to sudden inundation, when, in the language of Ossian, "red through the stony vale comes down the stream of the hill." "The roaring of these torrents after heavy rain, and when the wind favours its transmission, is sublime to a degree inconceivable by those who have never heard their impressive music in a wild and solitary district." There are two streams on the moor, which indicate by their names the peculiarities of these mountain rivers: *Cherrybrook,* denoting their colour when flooded; and *Blackbrook,* or Blackabrook, having reference to the dark coating of moss on their granite stones.

The most striking features of Dartmoor are the *Tors,* enormous rocks of granite crowning the hills, and remarkable for their whimsical resemblance to ruinous castles, the figures of uncouth animals, and even to "human forms, gigantic in their dimensions, which sometimes seem to start up wildly as the lords and natural denizens of this rugged wilderness." These tors are all distinguished by names, which attach to the hills as well as to their granite crowns, and may afford entertainment to those who are versed in the Welsh or Celtic language. Some, it has been suggested, are derived from the gods of the Druidical worship, as *Hessary* Tor, *Mis* Tor, *Bel* Tor, and *Ham* Tor; respectively from *Hesus,* the God of Battles; *Misor,* the moon; *Bel* or *Belus,* the sun; and *Ham* or *Ammon,* another of the British deities (but as these gods are themselves of very "shadowy" existence, etymologies derived from them are at least uncertain). Others, again, it would seem, have been taken from various animals, as *Lynx* or *Links* Tor, *Hare* Tor, *Fox* Tor, *Hound* Tor, *Sheep's* Tor, and *Dunnagoat* Tor; yet it is not unlikely that they are corruptions, and have had a very different origin. Thus Lynx Tor is probably the Cornish *lynnick*, marshy; Dunnagoat, *dun-a-coet*, answering to the Saxon "underwood;" and many others—such as High Willies and Wallabrook—are perhaps memorials of ancient tin-mines, the Cornish *huels*, which are pronounced *wheels*. Ephraim's Pinch, a high tract N. of Bel Tor, would seem to be indebted for its name to the Jews, who so long farmed the tinworks. The loftiest of these rock-capped hills is *Yes* (East) *Tor*, near Okehampton, 2050 ft. above the sea, and 682 ft. higher than Brown Willy, the summit of Cornwall; but no less than 19 of the Dartmoor tors attain a greater elevation than Brown Willy. Of their number an idea may be conveyed by the statement that 150 are enumerated by name in a note to Carrington's poem of 'Dartmoor;' but some which are therein mentioned are now separated from the moor by cultivation. The principal summits are *Yes Tor*, *Cawsand Beacon*, *Fur Tor*, *Lynx Tor*, and *Rough Tor*, in the N. quarter; *S. Brent Tor*, *West Beacon*, and *Holne Ridge*, in the S. quarter; *Hey Tor*, *Rippon Tor*, *Hound Tor*, and *Hamilton Down*, in the E. quarter; and *Sheep's Tor*, *Lethe Tor*, *N. Hessary Tor*, *Crockern Tor*, *Whiten Tor*, *Great Bairdown*, *Great Mis Tor*, *N. Brent Tor*, and *Hare Tor*, in the W. quarter. These are the most conspicuous eminences, and, with the exception of the two Brent Tors, as wild and rude as mountains, and well calculated to delight all those who can appreciate the grandeur of their desolate scenery. Their hues are ever changing, and indescribably beautiful, depending in a measure upon the altitude of the sun, and the spectator's position with regard to it. On a cloudless day the hills have a spectral appearance from the light tone of their colour, while the delicate shadows add not a little to their sublimity. At all times, however, they exhibit that harmonious combination of tints peculiar to wild districts where nature has been left to herself. She paints the land which is patched with fields and scored with hedgerows; but there her colouring is regulated by the farmer. The artist will find that the tints of the moor, although infinitely varied by distance and the state of the atmosphere, are derived from a few humble plants, viz. heather, a grass with white seeds, a pale green grass, a bright green moss, and a red grass and rushes in the swamps. They are beautifully mingled with the grey of rocks and the blue of streams, and modified by the shadows which fleet over the expanse. By sunset, however, it is a far more difficult task to analyse the colours which shine on these solitary hills. The surfaces of the tors are everywhere much *weathered*, and principally, no doubt, by the abrasion of the rain which is dashed against them, for the fury with which the winds assail these granite heights can be understood only by those who have been exposed to it. The nakedness of the moor much increases the effect of these *aërial shoals*, which cause the wind to rush over their crests with an accelerated velocity, as banks in the bed of the sea quicken the currents which flow over them. The Germans wish a troublesome neighbour on the top of the Brocken. Dartmoor is the Devonshire Brocken, the local rhyme running thus:—

"He that will not merry be,
With a pretty girl by the fire,
I wish he was a-top of Dartemoor
A-stugged in the mire."

Those who have a taste for the wild and the wonderful may glean a rich harvest in the cottages of the peasantry, where a view of the desolate moor will impart a lively interest to such traditions. Before the construction of the present excellent roads, it was not very unusual for travellers to be lost, or *pixy-led*, in the mist, when they often perished either with cold or hunger. At one period robbers defied the law among the inaccessible morasses, and levied toll upon the wayfarer. But, according to the country people, the mishaps on the moor have more generally arisen from evil spirits, whom to this day they believe to haunt the hills, where, they also affirm, " under the cold and chaste light of the moon, or amidst the silent shadows of the dark rocks, the elfin king of the pixy race holds his high court of sovereignty and council."

With respect to the *climate*, the altitude of the moor, the frequent occurrence of rain, and the impervious nature of the subsoil, necessarily render it both cold and moist. The hills are often enveloped in mist for a week at a time, and the clouds assemble with so little warning, that no stranger should wander far from the beaten track without a compass. The streams, however, will generally afford clues of safety. The danger arises from the bogs, which are significantly called the *Dartmoor Stables*; and in winter from snow, which is indeed often fatal to those who have the greatest experience; but at all times " a storm on Dartmoor bears little resemblance to storms in general. It is awful, perilous, astounding, and pitiless; and woe to the stranger who, in a dark night and without a guide, is forced to encounter it!" The *soil* consists of a fine granitic sand, or *growan*, upon which is superimposed a layer of peat of uncertain depth, but occasionally as thick as 25 ft. or 30 ft. The prevailing gloom of the moor and the want of drainage are the principal obstacles to successful cultivation. The vapours swept from the Atlantic by the westerly winds are uniformly condensed by these chilly heights; and so frequent is the rain that it might be imagined, in accordance with a popular rhyme, that clouds hover in the neighbourhood ready to relieve each other as the wind may shift, for thus a poet has sung of the climate of Dartmoor:—

"The west wind always brings wet weather
The east wind wet and cold together;
The south wind surely brings us rain,
The north wind blows it back again."

However, says an old writer, "The ayre is very sweete, wholesome, and temperate, savinge that in the winter seasons the great blustering winds, rowling upon the high craggy hills and open wastes and moores, do make the ayre very cold and sharpe." Those who find pleasure in wild scenery and invigorating exercise may pass a week or more pleasantly at Two Bridges or Prince's Town. The streams abound with trout, the morasses with snipe, and one fond of natural history may observe many a rare bird (as the rock or ring ouzel) and many an interesting moss and lichen (as the Iceland moss, which is made into cakes by the Icelanders) in his rambles. In the summer, if benighted far from the inn, it is no hazardous adventure to pass a night in the open air. A couch of heather may be had for the trouble of gathering it, peat that will burn well may generally be found stacked and sufficiently dried; and, indeed, a companion, a warm plaid, a knife, a tinderbox, a well-stored wallet, and perhaps a pouch of tobacco, are the only essentials for a very pleasant bivouac. The antiquary may derive further amusement from the names of the tors, and the many old British remains which are scattered over the hills. (See *Introd.*) With respect to the *wild animals* which at one time were the denizens of Dartmoor, although uncommon in other parts of England, there now remain only the badger, polecat or fitchet, pine-weasel, and the otter, which frequents all the moorland rivers to the sea, and also the caverns at their mouths. Of *rare birds* there is a greater variety, but some are migratory, and others only casual visitors. Among those which breed upon the moor may be enumerated the marsh harrier or moor buzzard, hen harrier, raven, hooded crow, ring ouzel, water ouzel, missel thrush, song thrush, whinchat, stonechat or stonesmith, black grouse, landrail, golden plover, lapwing, sanderling, curlew, dunlin, moor hen, and coot. Among the visitors the osprey or bald buzzard, peregrine falcon, common buzzard, kite (but becoming rarer every year), hobby falcon, snow bunting, mountain sparrow, mountain finch, grey wagtail, yellow wagtail, great plover, water rail, night heron, little bittern, jack snipe, herring gull, whistling swan, wild goose, white-fronted goose, and bean goose. The honey buzzard or goshawk, kestrel, and great snipe, are very rare, but have been seen.

Many of the surrounding manors have a right of common on Dartmoor, for which they pay a small sum to the Duchy called *venville* or *fen-field* money. The Duchy, however, has the right of stocking the forest, and for this purpose much of the moor is let on lease. The antiquities and natural history of the district have been fully and very pleasantly described by the late Rev. S. Rowe, of Crediton, in his 'Perambulation of Dartmoor,' published 1848. The visitor will also find some valuable information in the notes to Carrington's 'Dartmoor,' and in the poem itself, which may be read to advantage on the misty heights of the tors. It has been compared to certain wines, which can be drunk in perfection only on the spots on which they are grown.

Returning from this digression to our route:—

l (5 m. from Moreton) rt. of the road are the remains of *trackways* connected with a *pound* 80 yards in diameter, enclosing 2 *hut circles*.

1 *Newhouse*, a small inn, and adjoining it a rabbit-warren. Some years ago John Roberts was the landlord, and the following his sign

"John Roberts lives here,
Sells brandy and beer,
Your spirits to cheer;
And should you want meat,
To make up the treat,
There be rabbits to eat."

l. an ancient stone *cross*, and a road to *Vitifer Mine*. About 2 m. E. of this mine is *Grimspound*, described *ante* in the present route.

2 *Post Bridge.* The E. Dart here crosses the road, and the valley is partly cultivated. *Archerton* (J. N. Bennett, Esq.), a *new take*, a name given to portions of land recently enclosed, will be observed on the rt. On the barren hillside l. of the road is *Lakehead Circle*, or *pound*, a ring of stones enclosing about 2 acres, and of a similar character to the British village of Grimspound, but not so large or perfect. The area is studded with a number of *hut circles*, many of which, with 2 *kistvaens*, may be seen on the open moor in its vicinity. (It is much to be regretted that so many of these remains have been injured by the fencers of "new takes" on the moor, who resort to them as their readiest quarry. Such spoliation should be strictly forbidden by the officers of the duchy.) Immediately W. the traveller will observe the bold rocks of *Bel* or *Bellever Tor*, an excellent point for a panoramic view.

Just below Post Bridge is one of the most interesting of all the Celtic remains on Dartmoor — an ancient *bridge* of Cyclopean architecture. (See it figured in Smiles's 'Lives of the Engineers,' vol. i.) It is formed of rough granite blocks and slabs, and consists of three piers and a roadway of table-stones, each about 15 ft. in length, and 6 ft. in width. One of the latter has fallen into the river, but with this exception the bridge is perfect. About 1¼ m. lower down the stream is a smaller but similar structure, of which the central impost is the only part displaced. N. of the high road are some other relics. At Archerton, in a field fronting the house, remains of *kistvaens* and an elliptical *pound*; 1 m. N., opposite *Hartland Tor*, a mutilated but interesting enclosure, smaller, but resembling that of Grimspound; and on *Chittaford Tor* (just W. of Hartland Tor) *a trackway* or road, running a westerly course from the river.

2 rt. by the side of the rivulet are numerous traces of the "old men" who here streamed for tin. Leland mentions the Dartmoor mines, and says " they were wrought by violens of water." The ridge on the rt. at this part of the road is crested by 4 tors, which rise one beyond and above the other nearly in a line. The lowest is *Crockern Tor*, celebrated— the reader will doubtless marvel at the information—as the ancient Stannary House of Parliament. By charter of Edw. I., the tinners of Devonshire were to assemble on this wild and lonely hill, where, seated on their benches of granite, and generally immersed in a cloud-drift, they swore in jurors, and transacted other preliminary matters, when the judge very naturally proposed that the court should be removed to one of the Stannary towns. A meeting of this description was held on the hill as late as 1749. At an earlier period the Earl of Bath, Lord Warden of the Stannaries (son of the well-known Sir Beville Grenville), attended the meeting with a retinue of several hundred persons--his own retainers and gentlemen of the county. At such times the scene about the rude old tor must have resembled some Norwegian or Icelandic Al-thing. Mr.

Polwhele remarks, "I have scarce a doubt that the Stannary Parliaments at this place were a continuation, even to our own times, of the old British courts before the age of Julius Cæsar." "These primitive courts," says Sir R. C. Hoare, "were usually held on artificial mounts, or natural ones adapted to the purpose. The Tinwald Hill in the Isle of Man, the moot hills of Scotland, and the Irish parle, or parling hills, prove the universal practice, adopted, perhaps, from the Gorseddau, or court of judicature among the Britons, which was assembled on a hill within a circle of stones, or an amphitheatre of turf." The three tors which rise above Crockern Tor are called *Little Longaford*, *Great Longaford*, and *White* or *Whiten Tor*, the last crowning the summit of the ridge. They all finely illustrate the structure of granite, and command imposing views of the moor.

2 *Two Bridges*, an inn and a few cottages on the banks of the W. Dart, and convenient head-quarters for the angler or sportsman.

About 1 m. up the stream lies the lonely old *Wood of Wistman*, supposed to be a remnant, and the only remains, of the forest which traditionally once covered Dartmoor; but of so weird an appearance, so stunted and misshapen in its growth, so impenetrable from the nature of the ground, and exhibiting such singular marks of age, that it cannot fail to excite the most lively wonder and astonishment. It is situated in a desolate valley, bounded on the one side by Crockern Tor and its associate hills, on the other by Little and Great Bairdown, the slopes being strewed with blocks of granite, and the vista closed by a barren ridge, upon which will be remarked the isolated rock of Rowtor, which bears no fanciful resemblance to some huge animal reclining on the moor. Pursuing his toilsome way through this rugged hollow, the traveller will soon discover the wood, which, from the opposite height of Bairdown, has the appearance of three patches of a scrubby brake. Arrived at the spot, however, he will find " growing in the midst of gigantic blocks, or starting, as it were, from their interstices, a grove of dwarf oaks," interspersed with mountain ashes, which, with the oaks, are everywhere hung with fern and parasitical plants, and bent to the ground by the winds which sweep up the valley. Many of these trees are wonderfully diminutive, scarcely exceeding the stature of a man, and the average height of the wood is only 10 or 12 feet; but the oaks, at the top, " spread far and wide, and branch and twist in so fantastic and tortuous a manner as to remind one of those strange things called mandrakes." How they are rooted it is impossible to tell; they grow in a dangerous wilderness, "a whist old place," where rocky clefts, swarming with adders, are so concealed by a thorny undergrowth that a person who should rashly enter the wood will be probably precipitated to the chin before he can escape from it. Another curious circumstance is the apparent barren condition of this antiquated family. No young scions are to be found springing up to supply the places of the elders, and not a few of these veterans are already dead, and the greater number withered at the extremities. It would seem, indeed, that this race of vegetable pigmies, although by an ancient record proved to have presented a similar appearance in the reign of the Conqueror, was doomed to a speedy extinction, and that the spot on which it has flourished, where it has so long afforded shelter to the fox and the serpent, must after a few more winters be as desolate as the savage hills which surround it. The numerous parasitical plants have probably hastened the decay of these melancholy old trees. " Their branches are literally festooned with ivy and creeping plants; and their trunks are so thickly embedded in a covering of moss, that at first sight you would imagine them to be of enormous thickness in proportion to their height. But it is only their velvet coats which make them look so bulky. for on examination they are found not to be of any remarkable size. Their whole appearance conveys to you the idea of hoary age in the vegetable world of creation; and on visiting Wistman's Wood it is impossible to do other than think of those 'groves in stony places,' so often mentioned in Scripture as being dedicated to Baal and Astaroth.— *Mrs. Bray.* It is popularly said that Wistman's Wood consists of 500 trees 500 ft. high, or that each tree averages 1 foot in height. The etymology of " Wistman's Wood " is uncertain; but there seems good reason for making it " wise-man ;" *wisc*, or *wish*, being, according to Kemble, a name of the old deity Woden, often found in composition—as *Wish*borough, &c. Woden is still represented on Dartmoor in the shape of the swart " master," who follows the *wish* hounds (hounds of Odin ?) —spectral dogs which hunt over the wastes. "Whistness" in Devonshire is used for any unearthly being. After the Saxon conquest the Britons were driven into Wales and Cornwall, and indiscriminately called Weales, or Welshmen; and doubtless, at that time, a number of the original inhabitants sought an asylum on Dartmoor, where also tin-streamers must have been settled long before. Hence the names of the tors,' and the numerous time-worn remains of British villages and monuments, of which some imperfect specimens may be found in this valley. The traveller will learn with pleasure that the old wood is protected by the Duchy authorities.

Two Bridges is in the neighbourhood of the great central morass, and a company some years since erected works near the inn for the purpose of preparing a patent fuel from the peat, which yields, among other products, peat charcoal, pyroxylic spirit, chloroform, peatine, tar, acetate of lime, and sulphate of ammonia.

Just E. and W. of the hamlet roads branch to Moreton, Ashburton, Plymouth, and Tavistock. 2½ m. on the Ashburton road (l. of it) is *Dennabridge Pound*, formed by a rude stone wall, and now used for the forest "drifts" of cattle. There are some interesting antiquities in the immediate neighbourhood. The *Cowsic* joins the W. Dart at Two Bridges, and on the former, just below Bairdown Farm, is a *British bridge* of 5 openings, 37 ft. long, about 4 ft. broad, but only 3½ ft. above the surface of the water; on the adjoining common, *Bairdown Man* (evidently *maen*, a stone), a *rock pillar* 11 ft. high; and on the Blackabrook, just below the Plymouth road, near Prince's Town, a *British bridge* of 2 openings. (The antiquary should be told that some inscriptions in mysterious characters, on the rocks of the E. Dart, were the work of the Rev. E. A. Bray.)

Panoramic views of the moor are obtained from the summits of Crockern Tor and Bairdown; and the highest tor on the latter is in itself very interesting. This is called *Bairdown Tor*, those to the N. of it being distinguished as *Lidford Tor* and *Devil Tor*.

Prince's Town (a tolerable inn called the Duchy Hotel) lies on the Plymouth road, about 2 m. from Two Bridges, and is one of the most gaunt and dreary places imaginable. It is situated at least 1400 ft. above the level of the sea, at the foot of *N. Hessary Tor* (alt. 1730 ft.), and is surrounded on all sides by the moor, which comes in unbroken wildness to the very door of the inn. With such dismal scenery the hotel is in keeping; its granite walls are grim and cheerless, but the windows command an imposing sweep of the waste, and this will be an attraction to many travellers. It is truly impressive to gaze upon this desolate region when the wind is howling through the lonely village and the moon fitfully shining.

A short distance from the inn is the celebrated *Dartmoor Prison*, erected in 1809 at a cost of 127,000*l*. for the accommodation of French prisoners of war. It occupies no less than 30 acres, and is encircled by a double line of lofty walls, which enclose a military road, nearly a mile in length, and are furnished with sentry-boxes and large bells, which, during the war, were rung when the moor was darkened by mists. The Prison consists of a governor's house and residences for officers, built on each side of a Cyclopean gateway, over which is the motto "Parcere subjectis," a hospital, sheds for exercise in wet weather, and five buildings for prisoners, each 300 ft. long and 50 ft. wide, which at one time held as many as 10,000 prisoners. All the arrangements are contrived with every regard to the comfort and health of the inmates for whom the building was intended; but for many years after the war the prison served no other purpose than a landmark for persons wandering in its lonely neighbourhood. At length it was leased to a company engaged in extracting naphtha from peat; but in 1850 it underwent a rapid change into a prison for the reception of convicts, the motto "*parcere subjectis*" remaining over the gateway. French writers give a curious account of Dartmoor. "For seven months in the year," says a M. Catel, "it is a vraie Sibérie, covered with unmelting snow. When the snows go away, the mists appear. Imagine the tyranny of perfide Albion in sending human beings to such a place!"

Since the introduction of convict labour the experiment of cultivating Dartmoor has proved satisfactory. More than 100 acres around the prison are now under tillage, and produce abundant crops of mangold-wurzel, carrots, barley, oats, flax, and vetches. Many tons of hay are also annually stacked. For the improvement of the land the sewage is collected, and forced into an elevated tank, from which it is distributed over the fields. In the year ending 29th Sept. 1857, the daily average number of prisoners was 1051, the total establishment 178 persons, the net total expenses 37,764*l*. 9*s*. 11*d*., the net annual charge per prisoner 35*l*. 18*s*. 6*d*. In 1852 the value of the convict labour was estimated at 13,000*l*. For *seeing* the interior of the prison, an order (readily procured) from the Home Office is necessary.

Here the stranger should visit the *granite works and quarries* on the W. side of N. Hessary Tor, and about 2 m. from the inn, where he will observe with no little astonishment that the ground upon which he is treading is the most solid compact stone, concealed at the surface by only a thin covering of turf and heather. The quarries are on a large scale, and have derived an impulse from the demand for granite for the completion of the steam basin at Devonport. They swarm with men busily employed in breaking up the ponderous material with their iron instruments, while others are scattered far and wide over the huge side of N. Hessary, protected by reed-covered frames, and preparing the surface blocks for removal. It is impossible, however, to view this wholesale destruction of the picturesque rocks without a feeling of regret, and it is much to be wished that those who have the power would save the tors, at least, from the general havoc. The finest stone can be procured in any quantity below the surface; and all allow that these venerable tors, which are the distinctive features of one of the most beautiful counties in England, are of little value in an economical point of view. But, although comparatively worthless, they are successively reduced to heaps of rubbish by that spirit of wanton destruction which posterity will fruitlessly deplore. About 200 men are engaged in these works, and the moor resounds with the din of iron clashing against granite. From the quarry runs the *Plymouth and Dartmoor Railroad*, winding round *Crip Tor* and *King Tor*, and commanding a succession of magnificent landscapes, and, where it crosses the coach-road, a finely grouped company of tors to the N.E.

Great Mis Tor (alt. 1760 ft.) is distant about a mile to the N. This is one of the grandest hills in the county (particularly as seen from the N.), and is said by some wild antiquaries to have derived its name from the British deity Misor, or the moon, but the *mists* which cling about its crests are more likely responsible for it. The tors on the summit are superb, resembling structures of Cyclopean masonry, and illustrate in a very striking manner the apparent stratification of granite, the horizontal layers being best seen on their western sides. On the summit of the highest rock is a celebrated *rock-basin* called *Mis Tor Pan*, perfectly smooth and circular, about 8 in. in depth, and 3 ft. in diam.; and just S.W. of the principal tor, in the vicinity of an ancient tin stream-work a protuberance of granite called *Little Mis Tor*. Several of the rocks on Great Mis Tor are so whimsically arranged, that the antiquary will very probably attribute their position to human handiwork. An egg-shaped mass is poised almost on a point at the eastern summit; and a group on the N. flank of the hill forms a rude archway, through which a person might crawl. This side of

Mis Tor is perfectly white with surface granite, which will doubtless soon attract the destructive host of quarrymen. The river *Walkham* flows at its base, and the slope which rises from the opposite bank is studded with a number of ancient *hut circles*, and scored by lines of stones. Two of the former are of considerable size, and one consists of a double circle, one within the other. High above this river tower castellated rocks, which, beginning with the northernmost, are called *Rolls Tor, Great Stapletor, Middle Stapletor*, and *Little Stapletor*. The view from Great Mis Tor will alone repay a scramble up the hill. On the one side the eye ranges over sterile bogs, which by sunset afford a grand and solemn prospect; and on the other, by a downward glance, to the vale of the Tavy, and beyond to the heights of the Bodmin Moors.

It is a wild day's walk from Prince's Town, by Great Mis Tor and Yes Tor to Okehampton, Yes Tor being the landmark by which the pedestrian can direct his course. The summit of Great Mis Tor will be the first stage of his journey; and from this eminence Yes Tor is in sight, but so distant that it may not be at once identified. The stranger had better, therefore, direct his attention to *Fur Tor* (2000 ft. high), which occupies a position intermediate between Mis Tor and Yes Tor, and will be easily distinguished as covered with surface granite and pale green grass, and crowned with a rock like a tower, while it stands out in advance of dark-coloured ridges which are covered with morasses. From Mis Tor he will follow the Walkham to its source; and near its head-waters, in a lonely region, will find 11 upright blocks of granite, which he may spend an hour in sketching, as a Druidical monument; but they are probably the pillars which once supported a shed at an old tin stream-work. Opposite Fur Tor he will cross the Tavy and have a good view of Yes Tor, for which he can steer direct. (See OKEHAMPTON.)

1½ m. N. of the prison is *Fice's*, or *Fitz's Well*, protected by rude slabs of granite, bearing the initials I. F., and date 1568. It is said to possess many healing virtues, and to have been first brought into notice by John Fitz of Fitzford, near Tavistock, who accidentally discovered it, when, riding with his lady, he had lost his way on the moor. "After wandering," runs the legend, "in the vain effort to find the right path, they felt so fatigued and thirsty, that it was with extreme delight they discovered a spring of water, whose powers seemed to be miraculous; for no sooner had they satisfied their thirst than they were enabled to find their way through the moor towards home without the least difficulty. In gratitude for this deliverance, and the benefit they had received from the water, John Fitz caused a stone memorial to be placed over the spring, for the advantage of all *pixy-led* travellers." The well is about 3 ft. deep, and lies in a swamp at a short distance from an *ancient bridge*, or *clam*, of a single stone, on the Blackabrook.

If the traveller should be desirous of taking a very delightful, though circuitous, walk from Prince's Town to Plymouth, he can strike across the moor S. by *Classenwell Pool*, long believed to be unfathomable, to *Sheepstor*, the haunt of the pixies, and descend *Bickleigh Vale* to his destination. This route will lead him through one of the most beautiful districts in the county, and is described below as an excursion from Plymouth. (He will find a stat. on the Plymouth and Tavistock rly. at *Bickleigh*. See Rte. 13.) The main road to Plymouth descends from the moor 4 m. from Prince's Town. In its course over the high ground it passes a group of *hut circles*, and (1½ m. from Prince's Town) *Black Tor*, a rocky hill, very interesting in itself, and towering above a British settlement. In the glen below it, on the bank of the stream, are 2 *stone avenues*, running E. and W., and terminating in circles 15 ft. in diam. (these circles are in fact carns, marked by concentric circles of stones); and on the opposite slope numerous *hut circles*, 9 of which are enclosed in a *pound* 360 yds. in circumf. On the W. side of the same hill are remains of habitations and a smaller *pound*.

About 3 m. S.E. of Prince's Town, in a desolate region, is a hill called *Fox Tor*, connected with the following legend. In the reign of Edw. III., John Childe of Plymstock, a gentleman of large fortune, and very fond of hunting, was enjoying his favourite diversion during an inclement season, when he happened to be benighted, and, having lost his way, he perished with the cold, although he had taken the precaution to kill his horse and creep into its bowels for the warmth. The monks of Tavistock, hearing of the mysterious disappearance of Childe, and of his intention to leave his lands to the church in which he should be buried, immediately started for the moor, where they found the lifeless bodies of the hunter and his steed in a morass under Fox Tor; and also the will of the deceased, written with the blood of the horse:

"The fyrste that fyndes and brings me to my grave,
The lands of Plymstoke they shall have."

Upon this they eagerly seized the corpse, but, approaching the edge of the moor, were somewhat disconcerted to learn that the people of Plymstock were waiting at a ford to intercept them. The monks, however, were not to be easily outwitted. They hastily changed their course, and, throwing a bridge, known to this day as *Guile Bridge* (but more commonly called the Abbey Bridge), across the river near the abbey, reached Tavistock in safety, and thus gained possession of the lands. In memory of Childe, a cross was erected on the spot where he died, and was standing 20 years ago, when, a Mr. Windeatt having taken a lease of some land in its vicinity, it was accidentally destroyed by workmen during his absence. The foundations still remain. The story of Childe the hunter probably represents some early Saxon legend,— since Plymstock belonged to the Tavistock Benedictines before the Conquest. Another version of it occurs in the life of St. Dunstan, who ought to have become Archbishop of Canterbury on the death of Odo. But an intruding Elsi, whilst crossing the Alps on his way to Rome for his pall, was frozen to death in spite of having killed and got inside his horse.

Syward's Cross, 3 m. S. of Prince's Town, is an ancient monument, stamped with the words "Syward" on one side and "Bonde" on the other. Like Childe's Cross, it has been overturned and broken, but the late Sir Ralph Lopes had the public spirit to repair and replace it. The letters may be of the 12th or 13th centy. Syward's Cross formed one of the boundary marks of Buckland Abbey. Beyond Syward's Cross the view from *Cramber Tor*, looking across Lethitor to Sheepstor, is strikingly wild and grand.

Proceeding again from Two Bridges, the road passes between N. Hessary Tor and Great Mis Tor to

Merrivale Bridge, another moorland hamlet on the river Walkham. Here (½ m. E.), rt. and l. of the road, is an important group of Celtic remains, consisting of *circles*, *stone avenues*, *cromlechs*, a *rock pillar*, and *foundations of a village* extending a mile along the hillside; the whole overlooked by the huge pile of Mis Tor. "Avenues," says Mr. Rowe, "are the characteristic features." Two run E. and W. distances of 800 and 1143 ft.; their courses parallel, and about 100 yards apart. The real use of these stone avenues is quite uncertain. The Dartmoor tradition bears that they were erected when wolves haunted the valleys, and winged serpents the hills. (See *Introd.*) The longest (on the N.) is connected with 3 *circles*, 1 at each end and 1 in the centre. The shortest (on the S.) passes a *circle* midway, and is 100 yards N. of *another circle* of 10 stones, 67 ft. in diam, and a *rock pillar*, 12 ft. high. Near the avenues stand the supporting stones of a *cromlech*, the quoit of which is dislodged, and measures about 10 ft. by 5 ft. N.E. by N. of the avenues is a *pound* 175 ft. in diam., the wall formed chiefly of upright stones; and 30 ft. from this pound the reputed remains of *another cromlech*. The *hut circles* are numerous and in good preservation, and, according to a tradition, were used as a market when the plague raged at Tavistock in the year 1625, the country-people and the inhabitants of the town in turn depositing in them provisions and money. To this day they are known by the name of the *Potato Market* (for a similar reason a boulder on Cotherston Moor, in the valley of the Tees, has been called the *Butter Stone* since 1636). And here, before leaving Dartmoor, it may be proper to add a few words to what has been already written respecting the date of these ruinous habitations, which are scattered over the district. That many are of British origin cannot be doubted—immediately connected, as they are, with sepulchral and other remains. (For some general remarks on these, see *Introd.*) But Dartmoor has been thickly peopled with a mining population at a comparatively recent period. Some thousands were housed on it in Elizabeth's time; and we would venture to hint—in spite of the wrathful eyes of Celtic antiquaries—that *some* of the rude foundations of buildings may be of later date than has been suspected. In two or three cases (on Holne Moor, for example) remains of square walls are intermixed with those of circular huts; and, universally, the largest villages are found near the abandoned stream-works. We must, however, leave this matter to be decided by the traveller himself; only cautioning him to use his own judgment, and not to be led away by mere assertion, however pleasing to the imagination.

S. of Merrivale Bridge, at the distance of 1 m., is a remarkable rock called *Vixen Tor*, after the female fox. It is well worth a visit, as it commands in perspective the *valley of the Walkham*, whose irregular slopes present a charming landscape of mingled wildness and cultivation, of rock and of wood in loving companionship, of furze-brake and cornfield side by side, as if inseparable friends. The tor consists of 3 distinct piles, which rise from an extensive declivity to a height of 100 ft., and when viewed from different sides present some curious chance resemblances. On the road from Tavistock the resemblance to an Egyptian Sphinx is very remarkable; from a point to the S.E. the granite courses of the tor resemble the walls of a ruinous castle beetling over the river. Should you have time to make a circuit (on foot) to Tavistock, leave the high road at Merrivale Bridge, and take the Walkham as guide to the vale of the Tavy. The stream will prove a lively companion, and will lead you among beautiful scenes, particularly at Ward and Huckworthy bridges.

From Merrivale Bridge the road passes along the flank of *Cock's Tor* (a tor of trap, alt. 1472 ft.), and soon reaches the edge of the moor, 5 m. from Two Bridges, when the far-celebrated *Vale of* the *Tavy* opens suddenly to view, and the traveller descends rapidly to

8 TAVISTOCK. (*Inns*: Bedford Hotel; Queen's Head.) (Rte. 13.)

ROUTE 13.

PLYMOUTH TO TAVISTOCK. (SOUTH DEVON AND TAVISTOCK RAILWAY.)

This line was opened in 1859, and is worked by the South Devon Railway Company, with whose main line it communicates at Laira. The distance from Plymouth to Tavistock by rly. is 16½ m., by road it is only 14.

Joining the S. Devon line a little above Longbridge, the rly. follows the l. bank of the Plym river as far as Plymbridge; here it crosses the river, passes through Cann slate-quarry, and proceeds through Bickleigh Vale to

7¾ m. *Bickleigh Stat.* The ch. is 1 m. rt.

The seclusion of Bickleigh Vale has been greatly injured by the formation of the rly., but the scenery is still wild and romantic. It may be reached either from the stat. at Bickleigh (the first after leaving Plymouth), or by ascending the shore of the Laira to its termination at *Longbridge*, and thence proceeding by road or rail (by walking along it—the Plymouth and Dartmoor Railroad, *not* the Tavistock—which is allowed) to

Plym Bridge (about 3 m. from Plymouth), where the Vale of Bickleigh commences. (rt. lies the rly. to the Leemoor clay-works, and the Plymouth and Tavistock rly.) This is a delightful spot, in spite of the new lines of rly.; and the bridge a mossy old structure, partly hid by foliage, and based among the many-coloured pebbles of a rapid stream. Adjoining it are the ruined arch of a wayside chapel, with a niche for the figure of a saint; a rustic cottage, mantled with the rose and woodbine; and a narrow lane which climbs a hill towards Plympton. You should ascend this hill for ½ m. to enjoy one of the finest bird's-eye views of Plymouth Sound, the estuary of the Laira, Mount Edgcumbe, &c. The best point of view is occupied by *Boringdon House*, now a farmhouse, but anciently the residence of the Parkers, now seated at Saltram and enjoying the earldom of Morley. Boringdon House was built about the middle of the 14th centy.; but there are few remains of the old house. The hall, however (of much later date), is still to be seen, and is a noble room, with a chimney-piece, ornamented with figures emblematical of Peace and Plenty, supporting the royal arms (Charles I.), and date 1640. The views on each side of the lane are of a character to delight the enthusiast for scenery. On the one side the splendid prospect of the Laira and Plymouth Sound; on the other a rude group of hills and highland woods, wild and rough, and perhaps darkened by clouds. From Plym Bridge there is a way on either side the river up the valley; a road

DEVONSHIRE. *Route 13.—Bickleigh.—Valley of the Cad.* 143

on the rt. bank, and the canal, or tramway, rt., through the wood. This latter winds through the wood and valley to

Cann Quarry, a dark blue excavation in slate, finely contrasted by gay foliage, where the stone is drawn from the quarry and the drainage effected by water-machinery. Just beyond it is the *Weir-head*, in the shape of a crescent; and at that spot the wanderer will plunge into the shady recesses of the wood, and pursue his way around the elbow of many a mossy rock, where he may obtain glimpses of rare nooks and seclusions, to

Bickleigh Bridge (about 3 m. N. of Plym Bridge), from which the village of *Bickleigh* (with an *Inn*, the Maristowe Arms) is about 1 m. distant to the l. A beautiful picture is framed by the ivy-clad arch of the bridge; and another fine prospect will greet the traveller over a gate to the rt., where the road turns uphill towards the village. In Bickleigh the *Ch.* (rebuilt by Sir Ralph Lopes, the patron) contains the tomb, helmet, and gauntlet of Sir Nicholas Slanning, with effigies of himself and his wife. His melancholy death forms the catastrophe of Mrs. Bray's novel of 'Fitz of Fitzford.' A descendant of this Slanning was one of those Royalist warriors who were called " the four wheels of Charles's wain ":—

"Grenville, Godolphin, Trevannion, Slanning, slain."

By the churchyard wall is a perfect *cross*, with a modern shaft. The ch. tower is ancient, and deserves notice; the thin buttresses are probably later additions. A church-path leads across the fields to the entrance of the far-famed *Valley of the Cad* at

Shaugh Bridge Stat. This is a singularly wild and romantic spot, where the *Mew* and *Cad* unite their noisy streams among antique oaks and rocks, and take the name of Plym. It highly deserves the attention of artists. Below the bridge are the remains of *Grenofen*, the ancient residence of the Slannings. Tradition has much to tell of the state in which this family lived here; and the mossy barn with its gables, the rough hillside, and glittering river, will probably call the pencil and sketch-book into requisition. Above the bridge tower the crags which guard the entrance to the solitary glen; and a steep road, threading a labyrinth of rocks, winds up the neighbouring hill to the village of *Shaugh*, where granite cottages and granite stones stand elbowing each other. Here there is a small *Inn* (the Thorn Tree), adapted to the wants of an angler or pedestrian, and a venerable weather-beaten *Ch.* The churchyard contains among its mournful memorials one grand old tomb, in which, as the story goes, lie the remains of two sisters, such twins in affection that the decease of the one was the deathblow of the other.

"They grew together,
Two lovely berries moulded on one stem;
So, with two seeming bodies, but one heart."

This is emblematically told by sculpture representing the union of 2 hearts. 100 yds. E. of the ch., in a hedge fronting the end of the lane, is the remnant of a cross. On all sides the ground is cumbered by rocks, and the adjacent *Valley of the Cad* presents one of the wildest scenes imaginable. It is literally covered with granite, and the torrent comes roaring down the glen as though frenzied by the obstruction. The traveller may explore it with the greatest advantage (in a picturesque point of view) by descending the l. bank of the stream from *Cadaford Bridge* (near which is seen a vast sweep of the moor, and Brent Tor in the distance). But although this feat was accomplished by the writer of these directions, it is scarcely practicable. There is not even the ghost of a path; and the brake is so thick, that with the coat and strength of a rhinoceros one might experience some difficulty. By this rough course, however, we obtain the best view of the whimsical rock which rises from the rt. bank in the shape of a pillar, surmounted by a rude capital, and of the mighty *Dewerstone* (now, alas!(1862) being converted into a quarry—a result of the new rly.), a cliff of most elegant proportions and beautiful tints, seamed in the manner peculiar to granite, and apparently bound together by bands of ivy. The summit of this rock was often the resort of a poet whose name will be always associated with the hills of his favourite Dartmoor, and "on one of the flat blocks on the ground above the Dewerstone—at the front, as it were, of the temple where he so often worshipped—is engraved the name of '*Carrington*,' with the date of his death." Visitors are recommended, in the introduction to his poem of 'Dartmoor,' to climb to the summit of this cliff; for "he who has sufficient nerve to gaze from the Dewerstone into the frightful depth beneath, will be amply remunerated for the trouble which may be experienced in ascending. The rocks immediately beneath the view seem as if they had been struck at once by a thousand thunderbolts, and appear only prevented from bursting asunder by chains of ivy. A few wild flowers are sprinkled about in the crevices of the cliff, tufts of broom wave like golden banners in the passing breeze, and these, with here and there a mountain ash clinging half-way down the precipice, impart a wild animation to the spot." Superstition has connected a fantastic legend with the Dewerstone. In a deep snow, it is said, the traces of a cloven hoof and naked human foot were found ascending to the highest summit; and on stormy winter nights the peasant has heard the "whist-hounds" sweeping through the rocky valley, with cry of dogs, winding of horns, and "hoofs thick-beating on the hollow hill." Their unearthly "master" has been sometimes visible—a tall swart figure with a hunting-pole. Dewerstone is probably "*Tiue's-stan*," *the rock of Tiue*, the Saxon deity from whom we derive the name of Tuesday. The laborious descent of the valley is by no means necessary for a view of the Dewerstone, but the rocky features of the glen are seen to advantage by such a course. The granite carn of *Shaugh Beacon* rises close to the ch., and the only act incumbent on the traveller is to cross over this eminence to the Valley of the Cad. A short distance below it he may, perchance, pass in view of some blocks of stone so whimsically arranged as to resemble the figure of a huge warrior stretched at length on the hillside. On the moor, about 2 m. from Shaugh, on the road to Ivy Bridge, those curious in minerals will find the *Lee Moor chinaclay works*, from which a rly. descends to join the S. Devon line at Longbridge. N. of these works is a mutilated granite *cross;* and between them and Shaugh an entrenchment commonly called *the Roman Camp*. It is a rectangular enclosure formed by a lofty mound of earth *thrown up from the inside*, and was therefore more probably a place of meeting or diversion than a camp.

There are some other antiquities in the neighbourhood of Shaugh. About 1 m. E. of Cadaford Bridge, on *Trowlsworthy Tor* (which is of red granite), a *pound* of elliptical form, 90 ft. by 70 ft., and the prostrate stones of a *sacred circle* some 18 ft. in diam.; ¼ m. further E. a *sacred circle* about 70 ft. in diam., consisting of 8 stones, 7 of which are erect, and connected with a stone avenue which runs towards a small stream called the Blackabrook. These British remains are more readily accessible from Plymouth than any others on

Dartmoor; and are very good examples.

The stream of the Cad, says Mr. Rowe (Peramb. of Dartmoor), "is erroneously so called, as its source has from time immemorial been known as *Plym Head*. Cadaford does not necessarily mean ford of the Cad. Cad is a battle-field. Hence it may be conjectured on more satisfactory grounds that this bridge may have been so designated from some unrecorded conflict on the neighbouring moors." It must be admitted, however, that Cad, as the name of a river, occurs in all Celtic districts, and that its recurrence at the mouth of the Laira—the Catwater—would seem to prove it was the old British name. Plym is Saxon.

From Shaugh the excursion should be prolonged (though not on the same day), either by the moor or the *Vale of the Mew* or *Meavy* (skirting Roborough Down), to the villages of *Meavy* and *Sheepstor*. On the approach to the former (by valley) the granite hill of *Sheepstor* is the engrossing object, and when in sunshine quite spectral in its appearance, its light aërial tints being contrasted by the woods and shaded verdure of the foreground. The valley is a wild romantic scene. The stream sings and dances through it, and from among the mosses and the stones rises *Polypodium phegopteris*, a fern which has been likened to the figure of a mendicant imploring charity with outstretched arms. At Meavy there is an inn, favourite head-quarters with the angler, and the *Meavy Oak*, an old giant of the vegetable world, 27 ft. in circumf., but bald at the top, and with a trunk so decayed as to form an archway through which a person may walk erect. It is supposed to have been standing here in the time of King John. The granite churches of Meavy and Sheepstor are of small architectural interest, but their weather-stained walls and towers

[*Dev. & Corn.*]

are in fine keeping with the wild scenery by which they are surrounded. At the end of the village turn to the rt. to the bridge, near which, up the road, is a granite cross, about 9 ft. high, in good preservation. A lane leads from this spot to a farmhouse, called *Knolle*, bearing on its front the date 1610, and situated at the entrance to a romantic glen, in which there is a cascade. A path traverses the neighbouring hill to the rude village of

Sheepstor, which consists of a few cottages round an ancient granite ch. and still older school-house; and from this place you should climb the eminence of *Sheepstor* (or *Shittistor*, as in old records), the fabled haunt of the Devonshire fairies, the Piskies or Pixies, and where, certainly, the crevices in the huge mass of granite, which at the eastern end is precipitous and so fissured (like the rocks of the Cad) as to resemble basaltic columns, would afford a rare seclusion and plenty of accommodation for such shy and tiny folk. The cavity which is said to be their favourite haunt is called the *Pixies' house*, and is formed by two rocks resting in a slanting position against the vertical side of the tor. Mrs. Bray informs us that the peasantry who venture to visit it still drop a pin as an offering to the pixy, and to this day it is considered a critical place for children to enter after sunset. The pixies are described as a race "invisibly small;" yet, in the vulgar belief, they may be heard on dark nights riding the horses of the neighbouring farmers, and "pounding their cider" within this cavern. According to Polwhele, the Pixies' house was selected as a hiding-place by one of the Elford family, who here successfully concealed himself from Cromwell's troopers, and employed his leisure time in painting on the walls. From the summit of the hill a wild and beautiful prospect is unfolded. Close at hand rises a

H

Route 13.—*Horrabridge.*—*Tavistock.* Sect. I.

granitic cone, *Lethitor* by name, and perhaps the most elegantly formed of all the Dartmoor tors, but seen to most advantage from the half-reclaimed valley on the N. side of Sheepstor. If bound to Prince's Town, the traveller may steer direct from Sheepstor for its conspicuous ch.; and if benighted on the moor, as happened to ourselves, may take the pole-star for his guide. About 1 m. N. upon elevated ground, on the rt. side of the valley which extends towards Prince's Town, is *Chicywell* or *Classenvrell Pool*, a small pond of water, long believed to be unfathomable. It is said that no bottom has been found in it with the ch. bellropes of Walkhampton, which tied together made a line of 90 fathoms. However, in 1844, when the Plymouth leet, which runs near it, was at a low ebb, the water was pumped in large quantities from this natural reservoir, and its depth ascertained. It probably occupies the shaft of an old mine, as the moor in its vicinity is much furrowed. Sheepstor is traditionally rich in precious minerals, said to have been stored here by the pixies, who, it would appear, are miserly in their habits:—

"Little pixy, fair and slim,
Without a rag to cover him."

Grains of gold are occasionally found in the streams below the hill. *Longstone*, in this neighbourhood, was the ancient seat of the Elfords.

About 3 m. E. of Sheepstor rises the Plym, at *Plym Head*, in a most desolate region; and ¼ m. W. of this source, in Langcoomb Bottom, on the W. bank of a feeder to the Plym, is a *kistvaen* of more than common interest, as it stands by itself in the midst of wild and lonely hills. The cover has fallen, but the old tomb is otherwise uninjured, and some of the stones which enclose it in a circle are still erect.

1 m. beyond Bickleigh Stat. the line opens upon the valley of the Meavy river. The view rt. is here magnificent. The villages of Shaugh and Meavy, with their churches, are good landmarks. The *Dewerstone* and *Sheepstor*, both favourite spots with visitors, also lie to the rt. of the line, and are within easy distance of the Bickleigh stat. (See *ante.*)

Through a long tunnel under Roborough Down, the train reaches

12 m. *Horrabridge* stat. The village lies a little below the stat. Here the line commands a beautiful view of the Walkham river valley. Opposite winds the turnpike-road to Tavistock. rt. *Grimstone* (Mrs. Collier), and the church and village of *Walkhampton*. (The ch. is Perp. with a good tower.)

A long and lofty timber viaduct carries the line across the Walkham river and valley. Passing *Grenofen House* (— Deacon, Esq.) l., and the pretty village of *Whitchurch* rt., the traveller comes in sight of

16½ m. *Tavistock*. The stat. is elevated considerably above the town, which lies in a valley l.

Tavistock (*Inns*: Bedford Hotel, best; Queen's Head;—Pop. in 1861, 8965) lies in a trough of the hills, on the banks of the Tavy, which is here expanded to a considerable width, but retains its rocky channel, and as much of its moorland transparency as the neighbouring mines will permit, whilst the neighbouring woods and fields agreeably contrast with the heights of Dartmoor rising to the clouds at a little distance. It is a place of considerable antiquity, but has experienced many ups and downs on the wheel of Fortune. At one time its vicar had to petition the parish for a pair of shoes; at another, its clothiers were wealthy and celebrated, and *Tavistock kersey* was sought throughout the kingdom as the best fabric of its kind. Its inhabitants are now chiefly connected with mines. The importance of the town was, however, mainly derived from a magnificent Abbey, which, dedicated to the B. V. Mary and St. Rumon, was founded for Benedictines, about the year 960, by Ordgar, Earl or "Ealdorman" of Devonshire, whose wealth, says Master Geoffry Gaimar, was so great that "from Exeter to Frome" there was not a town or a city which did not call him master. He was the father of Elfrida, famous for the romantic story of her marriage with King Edgar. The abbey was completed and endowed by his son Ordulph. Ethelred granted Tavistock Abbey many privileges, but in 997, 36 years after its foundation, during the lifetime of the 1st abbot, it was burnt to the ground by the Danes, who had ascended the Tavy under their renowned leader Sweyn. It was rebuilt, however, with increased splendour, under the auspices of the 2nd abbot, Livingus, Bp. of Crediton, and the friend of Canute, and had attained a grey old age in the keeping of its ghostly proprietors, when it was confiscated at the Dissolution, and bestowed by Hen. VIII. upon John Lord Russell, whose descendant, the Duke of Bedford, is now the owner of its site and ruins. At that time its yearly revenue amounted to upwards of 900*l.*, which was a large sum in those days. Tavistock was the chief religious house in the 2 western counties; and the wealthiest, except for some time that of the Augustinians at Plympton. The abbot ruled the borough with ample authority, being possessed of the entire jurisdiction of the hundred, and in the early part of the reign of Hen. VIII. was honoured with a mitre and a peerage, and made independent both of the bishop and archbishop by a bull of Pope Leo X. "The great church, with its shrine of St. Rumon (a Cornish bishop of whom nothing is known), whose relics had been the gift of Ordulph, was almost equal in size and importance to the cathedrals of Wells or of Exeter.... The early abbots, like Aldred, who had offered a golden chalice at the Holy Sepulchre, and brought home his palm-branch from the Jordan, and who afterwards, as Abp. of York, consecrated both Harold and the Conqueror, were men of learning and piety. Many of the later functionaries caused no small scandal and disturbance. Two were deposed by the Bp. of Exeter. Abbot John de Courtenay is severely reproved for having

'——loved the deer to track
More than the lines and the letters black'—

and for the total want of discipline in his convent; and Abbot Cullyng not only winked at the private suppers of the monks in their cells, but actually permitted them to flaunt about the streets of Tavistock in secular 'buttoned tunics,' and in boots with pointed 'beaks.'"—Qu. Rev. vol. 105. A part of the abbey was destroyed by Cromwell, Earl of Essex, at the Dissolution; and a portion of the site is now occupied by the Bedford Hotel, which was erected as a residence by one Saunders, "of barbarous memory," as he destroyed the fine old Chapter-house for the purpose.

The remains of the abbey are not very considerable, and, though they show the extent, convey little notion of the splendour of the ancient pile. They consist of the N. or principal gateway, with a room now used as a public library; a small but picturesque tower adjoining this archway; the refectory, now a Unitarian Chapel behind the Bedford; a porch, adorned by 4 lofty pinnacles, at the back of the hotel; the still-house of the monks, and Betsy Grimbal's Tower, both in the grounds of the vicarage (the tower deriving its name from a legend that a young woman was murdered in it); and several ruinous ivied walls and arches. These remains are all of Perp. date, but are not very picturesque. Tavistock Abbey had, it is said—but this is very uncertain—a school for the study of Saxon, and a printing-press, which is said to have been the second set up in England. It was the first in the West country. A copy of Boethius, printed here in 1525, is in the library of Ex. Coll., Oxford.

At the breaking out of the great Rebellion, the inhabitants of Tavistock, influenced by the Duke of Bedford and their representative Pym, declared for the Parliament; but the neighbouring gentry remained true to the throne, and, consequently, many of their houses were besieged and pillaged by the rebels. On the outskirt of the town, by the side of the new Plymouth road, is the interesting old gateway of *Fitzford*, a mansion which was regularly garrisoned for the king, but taken by Lord Essex in 1644. A barn and this gateway are the only remains, and the oak-branch and label ornaments of the latter refer it to the reign of Hen. VII. Fitzford was anciently a seat of the family of Fitz, but belonged, in 1644, to Sir Richard Grenville, one of Charles's generals in the West, who possessed it in right of his wife, the lady Howard, of whom a curious legend is told in the town. She was the daughter and heiress of Sir John Fitz, and, according to the tradition, a mysterious person, who, by some unknown means, had disposed of 3 husbands in succession before she was wooed and won by Sir Richard Grenville. Whatever were her crimes, she is now believed to run nightly as a hound from the old gateway of Fitzford House to the park of Okehampton, between the hours of midnight and cockcrow, and to return to the place whence she started with a single blade of grass in her mouth, and this, it is said, she is to repeat until every blade is picked. In 1645, when Plymouth was invested by the Royalists, Prince Charles paid a visit to Tavistock, where he is said to have been so annoyed by the incessant wet weather, that, ever afterwards, if anybody remarked that it was a fine day, he would reply, that, however fair it might be elsewhere, he felt confident it was raining at Tavistock.

The *Ch.* (St. Eustace), restored 1846, is a handsome building of unusual size, the aisles extending to the extreme end of the chancel. There is a 2nd S. aisle of late date. The rest of the ch. is late Perp., except the base of the tower, which is Dec. The piers and arches within are of granite, and very plain. In the ch. are a fine Elizabethan monument, with effigies, to the great lawyer Sir John Glanville and his lady; monuments to the Bouchiers, Earls of Bath, and families allied to them; a beautifully carved altar; and an E. window by Williment. The *tower*, 106 ft. high, with buttresses, battlemented parapet, and pinnacles, is pierced with arches on all 4 sides, so that it stands on piers. It is thus a true campanile, and was never joined to the ch. In the ch. are preserved some bones of gigantic size, found in a stone coffin among the ruins of the abbey. They are commonly believed to be those of Ordulph (though Professor Owen might perhaps tell a different story), of whose amazing stature and prowess we have such stories as the following:—" Ordulph travelling towards Exeter with King Edward the Confessor, to whom he was related, when they came to the gates of the city they found them locked and barred; and the porter, knowing nothing of their coming, was absent. Upon which, Ordulph, leaping from his horse, took the bars in his hands, and with great apparent ease broke them in pieces, at the same time pulling out part of the wall. Not content with this, he gave a second proof of his strength, for, wrenching the hinges with his foot, he laid the gates open." William of Malmesbury speaks of Ordulph's extraordinary stature, and tells us that the stalwart Saxon would often, for his amusement, bestride a river near his residence, 10 ft. broad, and chop off with his knife the heads of wild animals which were brought to him.

The rooms of the *Tavistock Institution*, a literary and philosophical society, are over the abbey gateway, and contain a small cabinet of Devonshire minerals. The town has 2 large *iron-foundries*.

Many eminent persons have been born in Tavistock and its neighbourhood. At Crowndale (1 m. S.W.), *Sir Francis Drake* (the house no longer exists); at Kilworthy (N. of the town), the ancient seat of the Glanville family, *Sir John Glanville*, who was made serjeant in company with 2 other Devonshire lawyers, Dew and Harris, and of G., D., and H., sayeth Fuller, it was commonly reported that

"One { gained / spent / gave } as much as the other two."

In Tavistock, *Browne*, a poet contemporary with Spenser and Shakspeare, and author of 'Britannia's Pastorals.' (There is, however, no entry of his baptism in the registers of Tavistock ch., although he is generally said to have been born here.) The works of this poet have not obtained that celebrity which they merit, for they are replete with the most beautiful imagery, and deserve to be placed on a shelf below the 'Faerie Queene.' An episode of the 'Loves of the Walla and the Tavy,' in the Pastorals, is the most admired of his productions. To this list of "worthies" who have shed lustre on Tavistock may be added the name of *Mrs. Bray*, the lady of the late incumbent, and so well known to every English reader. She has laid the scene of some of her fictions at Tavistock, and presented us with a clever and entertaining description of 'The Borders of the Tamar and the Tavy.' In her tales of *Fitz of Fitzford, Courtenay of Walreddon, Warleigh, Henry de Pomeroy,* and *Trelawny of Trelawne*, the reader is introduced to many remarkable and romantic places, both in Devonshire and Cornwall. They are sketched from nature, and with the feeling of no ordinary artist.

The traveller should make Tavistock head-quarters for a time, as there is much deserving notice in the neighbourhood, and some celebrated "lions" are within an easy distance. To begin with a favourite spot on the outskirt of the town—

(a) *The Walk*, behind the Bedford. The old abbey wall bounds it on one side, the Tavy flows merrily along a rocky bed on the other, and the wooded *hill of St. John* (which commands a fine view) rises to some height from the opposite margin of the river. A path leads from the Walk to the *Canal*, which was completed in 1817, at a cost of 68,000*l.*, and connects Tavistock with the Tamar at Morwellham Quay. The towing-path leads through some very pleasant scenery, and those fond of sketching will find the drawbridges on the banks, in connection with the distant heights of Dartmoor, well adapted to their purpose. The canal passes *Crowndale*, celebrated as the birthplace of Drake, "the old warrior," as he is called by the country people; and more recently known for a smelting establishment, now abandoned. Beyond Crowndale the subjacent valley unfolds a picturesque scene, the Tavy entering a defile of wooded hills, which are rugged with rocks, and have the engine-house of a mine here and there peeping from the foliage. The canal soon sweeps round the shoulder of a hill, and, passing a deep hollow by an embankment, is joined by a branch from the mining district of the Devon Great Consols (formerly Huel Maria), and enters a tunnel which has been excavated for 1¾ m. through the heart of a hill, and thus runs underground to its termination on the high land above Morwellham. There the little iron barges shift their cargoes of granite or copper-ore to trucks, which are lowered by water-machinery down a steeply inclined railroad to the river-side. The head of the inclined plane is situated on the skirt of a wood, which, traversed by paths, hangs about the beautiful crags known as the

(b) *Morwell Rocks*. In a carriage they are reached by ascending the Callington road as far as the 2nd turnpike; turning rt. down a lane leading to the old Abbey Grange of Morwell. The paths lead to the most striking points of view, and suddenly open upon dizzy platforms, the pinnacles of the rocks, which dive sheer down through the brushwood to the Tamar. From these points the river will be seen glistening far below: the *Weir-head* in the centre of the valley; *Harewood House* (Reginald Trelawny, Esq.), the scene of Mason's drama of 'Elfrida,' to the l.; and to the rt. the mining village of *Gunnislake* climbing the sandy heights of the Cornish shore. A path will conduct you along the entire range of cliffs; at one place it passes the slender water-wheel of a mine called *Chimney Rock*, and will ultimately lead you to the Callington road, which is descending, to cross the Tamar by the picturesque structure of *New Bridge*.

(c) There are several curious houses near Tavistock. *Kilworthy* (1½ m. N.), the ancient seat of the Glanvilles, modernised in the reign of Geo. III., but containing remains of the hall which indicate its former grandeur. About the house are vestiges of the old style of gardening, and in "sweet Ina's Coomb," the *Walla Brook*, interesting to all who have read in 'Britannia's Pastorals' of its love for the Tavy. Near Kilworthy is *Mount Tavy* (Mrs. Carpenter), a modern house situated below *Rowden Wood*, which overhangs the river, and in 1768 was devastated by a remarkable whirlwind. It cut through the wood a passage of about 40 yards in width, tearing up the largest oaks by the roots, and carrying their branches to a considerable distance, and afterwards "rolled up the vale of the Tavy into the forest of Dartmoor, where it had full scope for exhausting itself." *Walreddon House* (W. Courtenay, Esq. 2½ m. S.), dating from the reign of Edw. VI. Mrs. Bray remarks, "a ride through its woods is worth coming miles to enjoy." *Collacombe Burton*, near Lamerton, rebuilt in the reign of Eliz., and long the seat of the Tremayne family, of whom, says Fuller, were Nicholas and Andrew T., two remarkable twins, who could not be distinguished but by their several habits; who felt like pain, though at a distance, and desired to walk, travel, sit, sleep, eat, and drink together, and who were both slain together at Newhaven in France, 1564. In one of the rooms is a window containing 3200 panes of glass. A chimney-piece has the date of 1574. *Sydenham* (J. H. Tremayne, Esq.), about 8 m. N.W., on the banks of the Lyd, another venerable house in the shape of an E, and considered a fine example of the domestic architecture of the Elizabethan age. It contains a noble staircase, portraits of the Wise and Tremayne families, a number of antique cabinets, furniture of the time of Charles I., and a costly suit of harness. One chamber is hung with damask, and the banqueting-hall ornamented with carved oak panels, one of which opens to a secret passage leading to other rooms. This old house was built by Sir Thomas

Wise, who was knighted at the coronation of James I. It was garrisoned for King Charles, and taken by the Parliamentary troops under Colonel Holbourn, Jan. 1645. *Bradstone Manor-house* (near Sydenham), a Tudor building approached through a large gatehouse, and anciently the possession of the Cloberry family.

(*d*) *Buckland Abbey*, a seat of Sir Trayton T. F. E. Drake, Bart., a distinguished soldier and descendant of Sir Francis Drake, is situated on the Tavy about 4 m. from Tavistock. It was dedicated to SS. Mary and Benedict, and founded—(for Cistercians—it was colonized from Quarr Abbey in the Isle of Wight)—in the year 1278, by Amicia, Countess of Baldwin de Redvers, Earl of Devon, and is interesting as the favourite residence of Sir Francis Drake, to whom it was given by Queen Elizabeth. Of the Abbey the remains are but scanty. Its first grantee, Sir Richard Grenfield of Bideford, is said to have pulled down much of it. The existing house, built by Sir Francis Drake, occupies the site of the church, since the 4 large arches of the central tower remain in a garret close under the roof. The ancient belfry, and a noble barn 180 ft. in length, are perfect. The mansion contains a fine portrait by Jansen and some relics of the great circumnavigator, viz. his sword, his shipdrum, and the Bible which he carried with him round the world. Delightful grounds encircle the house, and near it is the abbey orchard, which, according to the tradition, was one of the very first planted in Devonshire. (This, however, must be received " cum grano." It is probably to the zeal of the monks in procuring the choicest grafts from Normandy, and in the careful management of their trees, that the county is indebted for its pre-eminence in the matter of cider; but long before Buckland was founded, the abbots of Montbourg had planted apple-orchards on their manors of Lodres, in Dorset, and Axmouth.) To the N. of this estate is the village of *Buckland Monachorum*, with a ch. remarkable as a fine specimen of Perp. The old seating, the angel corbels of the roof, the west tower with its fine turrets and pinnacles, and the ancient glass in the 5-light Perp. E. window representing (but in fragments) events in the life of St. Andrew, should be noticed. Here is also a very elaborate monument by *Bacon* to the memory of Elliot Lord Heathfield, the defender of Gibraltar. The laboured panegyric should be read. Lord Heathfield (died 1790) married a daughter of Sir Francis Drake, and was himself buried at Heathfield in Sussex. To the S. is the beautiful demesne of *Maristowe* (Sir Massey Lopes, Bart.); and, near the mouth of the Tavy, baronial *Warleigh* (Rev. W. Radcliffe). *Old Morwell House*, near the S. end of the canal tunnel, although now a farmhouse, was once a hunting-seat of the abbots of Tavistock, where the merry monks were wont to regale themselves after chasing the wild deer on Dartmoor. It is a quadrangular stone building, with a gatehouse of the 15th centy. The hall and chapel remain. This house with the abbey lands passed at the Dissolution to the family of Russell, and has been restored by its proprietor, the Duke of Bedford. The far-celebrated *Cothele* (Cornwall, Rte. 23) may be added to this list of curious houses within reach of Tavistock.

(*e*) *Endsleigh*, the villa of the Duke of Bedford, deserves a special visit for the sake of its grounds, and the beauty of its site. It is situated above the Tamar, near *Milton Abbot* (an inn), about 6 m. from Tavistock, on the Launceston road, and may be viewed by strangers who have obtained permission at the steward's office. The house, a cottage, was designed by Sir

Route 13.—*Valley of the Tavy.*   Sect. I.

G. Wyattville (1810), and is only remarkable for its picturesque irregularity; but the woods and the grounds are the attraction, particularly the *Dairy Dell*, the *Alpine Garden* with its Swiss cottage, and the *Terrace* for the extreme beauty of the prospect. The private roads run for many miles through woods on both sides of the river, which winds most capriciously, flowing a long way to the E., and then as far to the W., and nearly encircling the hills which oppose it. It is crossed by means of a floating bridge. The stranger should obtain permission to ride to Endsleigh by the road through *Blanchdown Wood*. Above Endsleigh, near Dunterton, are the remains of a *chantry* at a place called Chapel Field, and a *waterfall* flowing to the Tamar, over a rocky steep 100 ft. in height.

(*f*) No one fond of scenery should leave the neighbourhood of Tavistock before he has explored the *Valley of the Tavy*, and visited, in particular, a romantic spot called *Double Water* (about 4 m. S.), where the Tavy is joined by the Walkham and spanned by a timber bridge. The hills are adorned by woods and cliffs, and the Walkham comes impetuously down the valley of Grenofen, enlivening the dark rocks with its spray and the glen with its music. One of the crags is called the *Raven Rock*, and other wild and picturesque masses overhang the mine and cave of the *Virtuous Lady*, a name said to have been given in honour of Q. Eliz. Rude lanes lead from this mine to Roborough Down and the Morwell Rocks. *Grenofen* (about 1 m. up the Walkham) is the seat of T. Morris, Esq. Above Tavistock the Tavy flows through scenes of a charming character, but its valley is distinguished near the moor by a mixture of the wild with the beautiful, the former predominating in the *Tavy Cleave* and around the romantic hamlets of *Peter Tavy* and *Mary Tavy*

and the copper-mine of *Huel Friendship* (see Index). Mrs. Bray recommends every traveller who comes to Tavistock to see Devonshire scenery "to find his road out to Peter Tavy, crossing *Hertford Bridge* in his way, which is in itself worth seeing; thence to continue on as far as Mr. Bray's mill in Peter Tavy, to ramble to the *Coomb* (a glen by the mill), return back through *Shellands*, and then, if he can get any little boy to become his guide, he may go on to *Mary Tavy Rock* (an insulated crag covered with ivy and lichens) and the *Clam* (a light wooden bridge at a great height above the stream, which, as usual, tumbles over rocks); and if he be a good walker, he may proceed to *Cudlipp Town* and *Hill Bridge* (where the river has a solid floor of granite), and so he will have seen all the sights in that quarter in one round." The Tavy Cleave is closed by the heights of Dartmoor, the ridge of *Stannaton Down* rising immediately to the E., the beautiful hill of *Hare Tor* on the N., and *Lint's Tor*, where the ground is curiously uneven from mole or ant hills, on the S. Below the castellated piles of Hare Tor comes the Tavy hurrying from the naked moor, and those who are in the humour for a supplementary walk may follow the stream some distance towards its source (say to *Fur Tor*, 2000 ft. high, and crowned by a rock tower), or strike boldly over the hills to *Great Mis Tor*, and return to Tavistock by Merrivale Bridge. Tavy is supposed to be derived from *Taw vechan*, little Taw, the river being a tributary of the Tamar, or *Taw-mawr*, the great Taw (or river).

(*g*) *Brent Tor* (4 m.), *Lidford Cascade*, and *Lidford Bridge*, are objects for another excursion in this direction. (See Rte. 6.)

(*h*) The *Valley of the Walkham* abounds in the most romantic scenery, and will well repay those who explore it from Double Water (confluence of the Walkham and Tavy) to Merrivale Bridge on Dartmoor. But at least *Ward Bridge* (4 m. from Tavistock) should be visited. You will proceed by the old Plymouth road over *Whitchurch Down*, which commands one of the finest views of Tavistock, and is bounded on the l. by *Pewtor* (2½ m. from Tavistock), piled with masses of granite, which stand at the 4 cardinal points of the summit, and thus frame as many views of sea and land. *Sampford Spiney*, "a ch. and a house, high up in the air," lies S. of this tor, and between Sampford Spiney and Ward Bridge, the old monument of *Beckamoor Cross*. The ch. of Sampford Spiney (*Spinetum*, a thornbrake) has a Perp. nave and Dec. chancel. The Perp. tower is fine. It belonged to Plympton Priory. At Ward Bridge the banks are covered with oaks and rocks, and the river struggles bravely with a host of impediments. If inclined for a struggle himself, the pedestrian may track the stream through wild moorland scenery to Merrivale Bridge, whence he can return by high road to Tavistock. Ward Bridge is situated between Huckworthy Bridge and Merrivale Bridge.

(*i*). The village of *Lamerton* (3 m.) is said by Devonians to have been the birthplace of *Rowe*, the dramatic poet; but Johnson tells another tale. There is, however, no doubt that the father of the poet was the rector of the place. In the parish are *Venn House* (Rev. W. Gill), and *Ottery Park* (H. Terrell, Esq.). The *Ch.*, which belonged to Tavistock Abbey, is fine. It is Perp., except the tower and E. end of the chancel (where a Perp. window is inserted in a Dec. arch), which are Dec. There are some fragments of good glass, and some finer and better in *S. Sydenham* ch., about 2 m. W. The tower is good. In *Kelly* ch. (about 8 m. from Tavistock, N. of the Launceston road) is a profusion of old Perp. glass,—3 large windows being filled with it. The ch. has been restored.

(*k*) Between Dartmoor and the Tamar the bowels of the earth are the resort of miners, who extract from them the ores of copper, tin, lead, and manganese. Near *Beer Ferrers*, on the shore of the river, is the *Tamar silver-lead mine*, in which a most interesting experiment was made. The riches of this mine are under the bed of the river, 220 fathoms below the surface of the water. The levels had been driven to a point where the miners were obliged to desist from their operations for want of air, the engines being too distant to effect a proper ventilation, and the river overhead rendering it impossible to sink a new shaft in the desired direction. To meet these difficulties, an inclined plane was commenced at a point within 50 fath. of the top of the shaft, and driven at an angle of 37° through all the old workings down to the 160 fath. level, and, at the suggestion of Dr. Spurgin, an engine was erected on the 145 fath. level, in the course of the inclined plane, with the several objects of ventilating the workings, of drawing up the stuff, of sinking a partial shaft through a rich course of ore, of opening new levels, and of lessening the cost. This underground engine fully answered all these purposes, and seemed to have established the important fact that sources of mineral wealth which have long been deemed inaccessible from their depth are now within our reach. *Spurgin's engine* was one of 20-horse power, and worked on a consumption of only half-a-crown's worth of coals in the 24 hrs. It pumped the water from the new shaft, and raised the ore to the 145 fath. level, the smoke from the furnace being conveyed along a flue which ran through the old workings to the surface, a distance of 2 m. A model section of the mine appeared in the Great Exhibition of 1851.

In 1860, however, the water forced its way in from the river, and filled up the mine. Fortunately, at the time it happened, none of the miners were at work.

The richest copper-mine in the county—and one of the richest in the world—the *Devon Great Consols*, formerly known as Huel Maria, is situated in a valley to the rt. of the Callington road, about 4 m. from Tavistock, and, although not so deep as Huel Friendship in Tavy Cleave, is a most profitable concern, and on so large a scale that it has quite the appearance of a village. In one month it has shipped 1200 tons of ore at Morwellham Quay, while in the same time Huel Friendship has yielded only 200 tons. It is drained entirely by water power, the 2 wheels for the purpose each revolving with the force of 140 horses. The wealth of this mine has caused a diligent search to be made in the neighbouring hills, which are clouded with smoke, and bristle with engine-chimneys. The *Mill-hill slate-quarries* are also rt. of the Callington road (1½ m. from Tavistock). About 200 men are employed in these works, which are therefore of such a size as to be worth seeing. The high road in their vicinity ascends Morwell Down, where it commands a view of Dartmoor, of a similar character—to compare small things with great things—as that of the Alps from the Jura. In this fine prospect Brent Tor is the most prominent object, standing out in advance of the main body of hills, and soaring aloft bright and distinct in the shape of a flame.

(*l*) Lastly, in this long catalogue of interesting scenes round Tavistock, the *road to Beer Ferrers* should not be omitted. An archæologist should also be directed to the *church*, which is of Dec. and Perp. character, and very picturesque. It was rebuilt (before 1330) by Sir Wm. de Ferrers, who made it collegiate. His endowment provided for an archpriest, 4 priests, and a deacon. It contains the monument (with effigies) of the founder, Wm. de Ferrariis, and his wife, and another of a knight of the same family, of early date (a Crusader, crosslegged, removed from the earlier ch.). In the E. window *were* the very interesting figures in stained glass of Sir Wm. Ferrers and his wife (see them figured in Lysons). This glass is now in a chest in the vestry (?). There are some very scanty remains of the castle, which John de Ferrers had a licence to crenellate, 14th Edw. III. *Stothard*, the antiquary and artist, was killed here by a fall from a ladder.

[The old turnpike-road from Tavistock to Plymouth commands some fine scenery.

9 *Jump* (*Inn*: Lopes Arms), a small village on the high land of *Roborough Down*, derives interest from the view, which is yet more extensive ½ m. nearer Plymouth. To the E. the *western front of Dartmoor* bristles with a hundred tors; to the W. are the Moors which extend to Bodmin, and the ridge of *Hingston Down* and *Kit Hill*, forming a link between the highlands of Devon and Cornwall; to the S. the Channel, blending with the sky, and Plymouth Sound, with its breakwater and romantic shores, displayed as on a map. The Plymouth and Devonport *leets* run past the village on different sides of the road; the former a swift clear stream abounding with trout; the latter equally swift, but of a red colour, from the character of the soil it has traversed. The *Vale of Bickleigh*, the *Valley of the Cad*, and the *Cann slate-quarry*, are all within a walk of this place; the rocky entrance to the vale of the Cad being very conspicuous in the view of *Dartmoor*.]

(A rly. is in progress—and is nearly completed, 1865—from Tavistock to

Launceston, following the valleys of the Tavy, the Lyd, and some smaller streams. At Lidford it will join the rly. from Okehampton and Yeoford, in connection with the N. Devon line. A very picturesque route from Plymouth to Exeter will thus be opened, and one that will be shorter than that by the S. Devon Rly.)

ROUTE 14.

WALK ACROSS DARTMOOR, FROM TAVISTOCK TO SOUTH ZEAL, BY CRANMERE POOL.

We followed the Okehampton road for about 6 m., and then struck directly across the moor, towards the position of Cranmere Pool, as well as we could conjecture it from the Ordnance Map: our companions a couple of moormen, whom we picked up on the road, both of whom professed much familiarity with the country, but neither had ever been able to find the famous Pool, to which a kind of traditional mystery seems attached. Passed a solitary moorland farm called *Redford*, situated on a brook running S., which here follows the line of junction of the altered rocks with the granite, on which latter we now emerged. Leaving these last enclosures, we made for *Hare Tor*, a very bold pile of rocks, the summit of which we left a little to the l. Hence the narrow gorge of *Tavy Cleave* is visible, and beyond it (S.E., in the direction of Cut Hill) the solitary tree called *Watern Oak*: to the S.W. a wide view over the Tavistock country and Cornwall; thence descended to *Rattle Brook*, which we crossed a little above its junction with the Tavy, and thence across *Amicombe Hill* (2000 ft., De la Beche), making our landmark the height called *Great Kneeset* by the moormen, and in the Ordnance Map; a very high point, reached by a gradual rise over ground becoming more and more boggy and broken. Great Kneeset itself is crowned with the remains of a vallum of turf and loose stones. Hence a fine but exceedingly desolate view over the central region of the moor: Yes Tor rising very boldly to the N.W., yet seeming equalled in elevation by some of the dark undulations nearer us; the only link with the cultivated world, a glimpse far down the valley of the West Okement. At this point the difficulty of the search began: our moormen knowing nothing about the matter, we followed the indication of the Ordnance Map, and proceeded E., keeping Great Kneeset and Links Tor as nearly as possible in a line behind us. We floundered through a mile or more of the worst bog over which it has been our lot to travel: heathy hummocky land, seamed in every direction with rents like *crevasses*, 5 or 6 ft. deep, filled with black soil, to be jumped across if possible, if not, waded through, avoiding the soft and dangerous parts. After this bad travelling we discovered the object of our search, the black bed of a pool of about 2 or 3 acres in extent, almost destitute of water, while from its western extremity oozed the highest spring of the West Okement; a spot remarkable for nothing but the singular desolation and lifelessness of its vicinity. The Mere is the locality of an often-repeated legend: a spirit (Bingie by name) is confined in it by a conjurer, and condemned to the hopeless task of draining it with an oat-sieve; but one day Bingie found a sheepskin on the moor, which he spread across the bottom of his oat-sieve, baled out the water, and drowned Okehampton town. Hence N.E. across the broad morassy plateau, keeping Yes Tor a little to the l. by way of guide; a round hill to our E. (Newlake?) appears to the eye as perhaps the highest point of the moor (only 1925 ft., however, according to De la Beche). The broken bog is on this side a little less extensive, and more traversable than on the other. The abrupt peak of *Steeperton Tor*, and the well-known form of *Cawsand Beacon* beyond it, were soon visible to the N.E., and the latter became our landmark. Crossed the Taw a few hundred yards from its source, which is not in Cranmere Pool according to the common story, nor even in the morass around it, but in a well-defined little amphitheatre of heathy slopes, on the opposite side of which rises the Dart. Hence across difficult and fatiguing ground, passing another brook in a marshy bottom, to *Wild Tor* or *Wills Tor*, a very conspicuous pile of castellated rocks. Near Wild Tor we struck a cart-track, used by the South Zeal folks to convey turf, which we followed for 5 or 6 m. across the eastern shoulder of Cawsand to *South Zeal*, immediately adjoining the northernmost edge of the moor. Time, from the point where we left the Tavistock and Okehampton road to South Zeal, about 6 hrs., stoppages included.

ROUTE 15.

PLYMOUTH TO MODBURY AND KINGSBRIDGE. THE COAST FROM KINGSBRIDGE TO PLYMOUTH.

The tourist may proceed to Modbury from Plymouth, following the old Totnes turnpike-road as far as Ermington, and thence branching rt. to Modbury (2 m.). From Modbury he may take the road by Aveton Gifford to Kingsbridge (7½ m.). The most interesting part of the coast between Kingsbridge and Plymouth is, however, approached by a pleasant walk from Modbury. From Kingsbridge the coast scenery, perhaps the finest in Devonshire (see Rte. 9), between that place and Dartmouth, may be explored.

Kingsbridge itself is most easily reached from Plymouth by taking the rly. as far as the *Kingsbridge Road Stat.*, whence an omnibus runs to the town. A branch-line from the Brent Stat. to Kingsbridge, following the valley of the Avon, and passing by Loddiswell, Gara Bridge, and Curtisknowle, has been authorised, but is not yet (1865) begun.

The drive (7 m.) from the rly. to Kingsbridge is of no great interest.

Kingsbridge (12 m. from Totnes, 14 m. from Dartmouth) (*Inns:* King's Arms; Golden Lion—Pop. in 1861, 1585) is built upon a steep hill at the head of the estuary, and has a modern appearance, although it was a town of some consequence in the year 1460. *Dodbrooke*, with which it is now connected, is more marked by age, and is said to have been the place where *white ale* was first brewed, for which a tithe was anciently paid. The only curiosities in the town are the museum of a *Literary and Scientific Institution;* Pindar

Lodge, at the Quay, as the birthplace of *Dr. Wolcott*, better known under his assumed name of Peter Pindar; and a house in Fore Street, the office of Mr. Weymouth the solicitor, which contains some finely carved wainscoting, and is supposed to have belonged to the monks of Buckfastleigh, whose abbot always spent the season of Lent at Kingsbridge. The *Church* was reseated and restored in 1845, and contains some Norm. portions. The tower is central, with a spire. The land in this neighbourhood is based upon the red and variegated grauwacke slates of De la Beche, and remarkably productive.

About 2 m. from this town, on the high road to S. Brent, and ¼ m. below *Loddiswell*, there is an exceedingly pretty view down the Avon. The valley sides are steep, and studded with wood, wild croft, and meadow; two old bridges span the river, and the tower of Churchstow crowns a hill in the distance.

Proceeding from Kingsbridge to Modbury (a route which will be reversed if the tourist approaches Kingsbridge from the former place), the road takes us direct to this airy village—

2 *Churchstow*, which commands an extensive prospect over a broad tract of country patched with fields, but bare of timber. The distant spire of *Marlborough Ch.* is conspicuous in the direction of the Bolt, and, adjoining Kingsbridge, the ch. tower of *West Allington* (Perp. and fine), with its 4 lofty pinnacles.

2 *Aveton Giffard*, a village prettily situated on the Avon, 2 m. N.E. of *Bigbury*, which now gives its name to the wild bay on the coast, and formerly imparted it to an ancient family who lived in this neighbourhood from the Conquest to the reign of Edw. III. The *ch.* of Bigbury is partly Dec., and contains a fine *brass* for a lady of the Bigbury family, circ. 1440. There is also a brass for Robt. Burton (effigy gone) and wife, Elizabeth de Bigbury, whose first husband was Thos. Arundell, 1460. The ch. is a sea-mark. The *ch.* of Aveton is mainly E. Eng., of very good character. The windows are later insertions. The central tower is Trans. Norm. This ch. deserves a visit. Beyond this village the hills grow bolder, and the country becomes more picturesque as we approach Dartmoor, which forms the background to the different views on the road. The land is exceedingly fertile, and orchards numerous and flourishing.

3½ *Modbury*. (*Inn:* White Hart.) This is an antiquated town, built in 4 streets, which, descending hills from the cardinal points, meet at the bottom of a valley. Many of the houses are blue and ghastly from their fronts of slate, and, on the E., are perched on so steep an acclivity that they look as if they would tumble below and overwhelm the White Hart. Here the family of Champernowne lived in great splendour from the reign of Edw. II. to the beginning of the 18th centy. Modbury Court was their mansion, and stood on the hill W. of the town, at the extremity of the present street. A licence to crenellate his manor-house here was granted to Rich. de Champernowne, 8th Edw. III. One wing of the house is standing, with a vaulted substructure of granite, and a dining-room over. The *ch.* is mainly Perp., and remarkable for a true spire, that is, a spire tapering from the ground. It is 134 ft. in height, and was rebuilt about the year 1621. The interior of the ch. has been lately repaired. Observe the granite pillars in the interior, and on the N. wall, on the outside, a curiously sculptured doorway. There are some monuments with effigies of the Champernownes. Two

Route 15.—*Mothecomb.*—*Revelstoke.* Sect. I.

old conduits should be noticed in the streets leading E. and N. In Feb. 1643, Sir Nicholas Slanning, having entrenched himself near this town, with 2000 men, was defeated by the Devonshire club-men.

Ermington (Fawn Hotel), with its leaning spire (see Rte. 16), is 2 m. from Modbury, and on the road from this place to Ivy Bridge (Rte. 7), from which it is distant 3 m.

Proceeding from Modbury on foot by the coast of Bigbury Bay (which the pedestrian will find a pleasant circuit)—

2 l. *Fleet House* (— Splatt, Esq.). Here the pedestrian will leave the road, and walk through the park, and along the shore of the Erme to the sea, about 3 m. If, however, there should be a chance of his meeting the flood tide, he must take the road to the rt., near the head of the estuary, through the woods of Fleet House to Holbeton. Fleet House was for many years the seat of the Heles. It dates from the reign of Eliz., but the principal fronts are modern. The Bulteels, who, until very recently, were the owners of Fleet, trace their descent from the Crockers, one of the oldest of Devonshire families.

"Crocker, Cruwys, and Coplestone,
When the Conqueror came, were at home."

At the head of the Erme estuary, on the l. bank, on a farm called *Oldaport*, are the remains of a large walled camp or fortification, enclosing nearly 30 acres. They consist of the foundations of 2 round towers, and of walls 5 ft. thick, with 2 entrances 9 ft. wide. The farmhouse was formerly the residence of the family of De la Port. These remains will perhaps repay the attention of the antiquary. They may possibly be of Roman origin. The "Ardua" of the geographer of Ravenna has been fixed at Ermington by some authorities.

2 *Holbeton*, deserving notice only for its retirement in an uninteresting but highly productive district.

1½ *Mothecomb*, a little hamlet at the mouth of the Erme. We now pursue our way along the solitary cliffs towards the western horn of Bigbury Bay, among rocks of the grauwacke formation, beautifully coloured, hung with ivy and samphire, and everywhere broken into the most wild and romantic recesses, in which clusters of fragments are buffeted by the sea. Near the end of the bay, where the shore makes a decided turn to the southward, stands the

4 *Ch. of Revelstoke*, a lonely old building, rough with lichens, weathered by storms, and perched on the verge of a low craggy cliff, up which comes the salt foam to the churchyard. Not a house is in sight; the solitary hills and waves encompass the building, which with its mouldering tombstones might well represent the imaginary scene of the poet—

"Where lay the mighty bones of ancient men,
Old knights, and over them the sea-wind sang
Shrill, chill, with flakes of foam."

Near at hand the visitor should notice a cliff of beautiful outline and varied colouring, rising abruptly from the waves, and diversified at the top by verdant hollows, in which wild fennel grows luxuriantly. Close to it there is a path down to the sea.

From Revelstoke Ch. the pedestrian can cross the hills direct to Newton Ferrers, about 2 m., or add ½ m. to his walk by proceeding round

Stoke Point, where the slabs of slate by the sea are on a grand scale. Their size can be appreciated when a fisherman is seen upon them angling for rock-fish. Having crossed the hill from this point, we shall find that the land breaks suddenly into a dell, through which runs a lane to the wild village of

Noss, a straggling group of cottages, "set in masses of green, and among narrow lanes and paths running hither and thither." It is situated on the southern side of an inlet from the Yealm Estuary, and opposite the old town of *Newton Ferrers* and a hamlet called *Bridgend*, the 3 being collectively known as *Yealm*. The scene is novel and striking, and the little road winding along the wooded hills of the shore may remind the traveller of those skirting the Swiss lakes. In 1 m. it will lead him to a ferry near the mouth of the estuary. In 1849 Noss was ravaged by the cholera, attracted no doubt by the mud banks and want of drainage; and there is a tradition that about 160 yrs. ago all its inhabitants, excepting 7, were swept away by a pestilence. A public-house in Newton Ferrers is said to be the only one in the parish.

The *Yealm Estuary*, although seldom visited, is rich in the picturesque. The water is transparent, the course of the inlet tortuous, and the hills which enclose it heathery or wooded, and fringed at their bases by a margin of rocks. There is a wildness in this remote inlet which is very pleasing. Having crossed the ferry, the pedestrian may proceed by *Wembury* and its weather-beaten ch. on the margin of the sea; or, along by-roads and paths, either by *Plymstock* (a fine screen) and the Laira Bridge, about 7 m., or by Hooe Lake, and ferry over the Catwater, about 5 m., to

Plymouth (Rte. 7).

In the ch. of *Wembury* hangs the iron helmet of Sir Warwick Hele, and there are several monuments to this family, who had here a stately mansion, built by Sir John Hele, serjeant at law, some time in the 16th cent. It was seated on a tidal lake, and for the beauty of its prospects was declared by old Fuller to be "almost corrival with Greenwich itself." The house was pulled down 1803 by the Lockyers, who had purchased the property.

ROUTE 16.

TOTNES TO PLYMOUTH (TURNPIKE ROAD). ERMINGTON; YEALMPTON.

By this route there is little to call for notice till the tourist reaches

9 *Ugborough* (1½ m. from Kingsbridge Road Station.) *Ugborough Castle* on the l., and the eminence of *Ugborough Beacon* on the rt. The ch. commands a fine view. About 1 m. from the village is *Fowellscombe*, a Tudor mansion dating from 1537.

3 *Ermington* (Fawn Hotel), known for the leaning spire of its ch. The tower and spire (said to have been bent by lightning) are E. Eng.; the body of the ch. (in a sad state of neglect) Perp., with Dec. portions in the chancel. The altar (here strictly a communion *table*) is detached about 6 ft. from the E. end, and sur-

rounded by a massive Jacobean balustrade of oak; probably a unique example of this Puritan arrangement, which Laud insisted on altering. The Elizabethan monument in the N. chancel aisle is that of Christopher Chudleigh. A delightful lane runs from this village to *Ivy Bridge* (Rte. 7).

3½ *Yealm Bridge*. Here, some height above the level of the river, is the celebrated *Yealm-bridge Cavern*, stored with the fossil remains of animals. These consist of the bones and teeth of the elephant, rhinoceros, horse, ox, sheep, hyæna, dog, wolf, fox, bear, hare, water-rat, and a bird of considerable size, and are all contained in a layer of loam, forming the upper bed of a series of sedimentary deposits of from 18 to upwards of 30 ft. in thickness. Many are gnawed, and associated with the fœcal remains of the hyæna, and the limestone roof is beautifully polished, as if by the passing to and fro of animals which inhabited the cave. Farther down the river, at Kitley, is another cavern of larger dimensions, but containing no bones; while the floor is little raised above the level of high water. It is therefore supposed that the *Kitley cavern* remained below the surface of the river when that of Yealm-bridge was raised high and dry by an elevatory movement of the land, and so became fitted for the reception of hyænas.

¼ *Yealmpton*. The *ch.* is well worth a visit. It was partly rebuilt (Butterfield, architect) and otherwise restored at a cost of many thousands by the late Mr. Bastard, to whom there is a memorial window, erected by his tenants and friends in testimony of their regard for him. The walls of the ch. are inlaid with various marbles. In the N. aisle is the interesting *brass* of Sir John Crocker, "Cippornrius" (cupbearer), "acsignifer" to Edw. IV., d. 1508. Sir John distinguished himself in suppressing Perkin Warbeck's rebellion in 1497. Beyond this town the traveller will observe to the l. *Kitley*, seat of the Bastards, and, on the opposite side of the river, *Puslinch* (Rev. J. Yonge), where there is a fine portrait of Dr. Mudge, painted by *Northcote* in his happiest style.

7 *Plymouth* (Rte. 7).

ROUTE 17.

EXETER TO BARNSTAPLE AND BIDEFORD, BY CREDITON. — NORTH DEVON RAILWAY. (SOUTH MOLTON; TORRINGTON.)

(The traveller will approach the magnificent coast scenery of North Devon most easily by this route. From Barnstaple, a coach, meeting certain of the trains, runs to Ilfracombe, and another, by Paracombe, to Lynton and Lynmouth. Clovelly and Hartland are best reached from Bideford. During the summer months a coach runs from the Coplestone Stat. on the N. Devon Rly. to Bude, by North Tawton, Hatherleigh, and Holsworthy. This is a long and a very uninteresting day's drive. (The rly. in progress to Okehampton will have extension lines to Bude and to Torrington, but these are not yet (1865) begun.) Bude (see CORNWALL, Rte. 25) is better reached from Launceston, or (by the pedestrian) by walking along

DEVONSHIRE. *Route 17.—Brampford Speke.—Crediton.* 161

the coast from Hartland, through Morwenstow.)

The tourist may leave Exeter from either the *Queen Street* or the *St. David's Stat.* Both stations serve for the N. Devon Rly.

The line runs northward by the vale of the Creedy, passing on rt. *Pynes House*, seat of Sir Stafford Northcote, Bart., M.P. On rt. lies the village of

Brampford Speke. The family of Speke was once very powerful in Devon. "There are yet in remembrance," says Westcote, in his *Survey* (1630), "certain by-paths over enclosed lands, which they call *Speke's Paths*, as lawful for him and his people to ride, go, and drive that way, but for no other; but they are all wellnigh forgotten and shut up now." The *church* of Brampford Speke, which was well and carefully restored while the Rev. G. C. Gorham held the living (Bp. Philpotts contributing), contains an ancient *chantry* of the Speke family, who also founded the chapel of St. George in Exeter Cathedral. The tower is very good.

4½ *Newton St. Cyres Stat.* l. *Newton House*, J. Quicke, Esq., whose family has possessed it since the reign of Elizabeth. 2 m. beyond Newton the line passes *Downes*, James Buller, Esq. (rt.), and leaves the river Creedy.

7 m. *Crediton* (*Inn:* the Ship), situated in a valley opening to the small river Creedy. It owes its modern appearance, like Tiverton, to the ravages of fire, but is a very ancient town, the birthplace of the Anglo-Saxon Winfred, better known as *St. Boniface* (the first preacher of Christianity in Central Germany, and the founder of the famous monastery of Fulda—he was the patron of innkeepers, hence called "Bonifaces"), and the seat of the Devonshire bishopric from A.D. 909 to 1050, when the sees of Devon and Cornwall were united and established at Exeter. Thus the inhabitants say—

"Kirton was a market town
When Exter was a vuzzy down."

It was once famous for the manufacture of woollen goods; but the clothier is now superseded by the shoemaker, who drives the busiest trade in the place. The old saying is however extant—"as fine as Kirton," *i.e.* Crediton, "spinning." The first skirmish with the Devonshire rebels, in 1549, took place here. The "rebels" had assembled at Crediton, and made a "mighty rampiere" at the town's end, which they fortified, together with some barns adjoining. Sir Peter and Sir Gawain Carew, who had ridden from Exeter "to have speech of the rebels," were denied access to the town. There was a skirmish, and the barns were set on fire. "The barns of Crediton" was henceforth the rallying word of the insurgents. (See Froude, *H. E.*, vol. vi.) Near the town are *Shobrook Park*, J. H. Hippisley, Esq. (where are some good modern pictures by *Wilkie, Eastlake, Webster, Lee*, &c.),—the park, through which there is a footpath, deserves a visit; *Downes*, James Buller, Esq.; and *Creedy Park*, Major-Gen. Sir H. R. F. Davie, Bart., M.P.

The *Ch.*, dedicated to the Holy Cross (and restored 1855—Hayward architect—but much remains to be done), is a large and handsome building, chiefly Perp., with a central tower, of which the lower part is Trans. Norm. In the S. chancel porch is an E. E. piscina. The windows are excellent, particularly the E. and W. There is a lofty and light clerestory, extending through nave and chancel. E. of the latter is the *Lady Chapel*, of early Dec. character (the tracery of the windows is

Perp. insertion), and well deserving restoration. It served as the Grammar School from Edward VI.'s reign until 1859, when the present schools were completed. This ch. before the Reformation was collegiate—the first in rank among the col. churches of the diocese — and the long and stately chancel was occupied by the stalls of its 18 canons and 18 vicars. The manor belonged to the bishops of Exeter, who made it one of their favourite residences. (Whilst Bp. Walter Stapeldon was celebrating mass in the church on the feast of St. Peter ad Vincula, August 1, 1315, a blind man who had been praying before the altar of St. Nicholas suddenly recovered his sight. The bishop investigated the matter in the adjoining Lady Chapel, and "ordered the bells to be rung in thanksgiving." The man was a fuller of Keynsham, who had lost his sight as suddenly as he regained it during the previous Easter week. He had dreamt that he would be cured if he should visit the ch. of the Holy Cross at Crediton.) At the E. end of the S. chancel aisle is an altar-tomb of the 14th centy., with male and female figures, said to be those of Sir John Sully and his wife. The knight had fought in most of the Black Prince's battles, and died when upwards of 105. On the N. side of the chancel is the effigy of Sir Wm. Peryam, chief baron of the Exchequer, 1592. "True honour," says Westcote, "kept him company to the grave, and returned not with the heralds, by whom he was, according to his degree, laudably interred." The altarpiece represents Moses and Aaron supporting the Decalogue—a surprising performance, reported to be a copy of one formerly existing in Exeter cathedral. In the parvise chamber is a library (the collection of a former vicar) of nearly 1000 vols. There is a fine copy of Walton's polyglott. To the late vicar of Crediton, the Rev. Samuel Rowe, we are indebted for 'A Perambulation of Dartmoor,' an entertaining account of the most curious and delightful district in this county (although the reader should be warned against the wild "helio-arkite" theories adopted by the author, and quite unsupported by facts).

Opposite the Ch. are some excellent parochial schools (Hayward, architect), and at the head of the town the *Grammar School*, completed 1859 from Hayward's designs. It is a large and fine Elizabethan building, with residences for 2 masters. The foundation is a good one, with scholarships for either university attached. In an orchard l. of the road, a short distance beyond the Grammar-School, is a desecrated chapel (one of 7 which formerly existed in different parts of the parish), of E. Eng. date, and remarkable for the design of its E. and W. ends, which have 3 lancets of equal height in each. There was no W. door.

A beautiful and curious view of Crediton is gained from *Down Head*, a few minutes' walk from the town. The view from *Posbury Hill* (S.W.) is also extensive. The summit has been fortified, and on *Blackadown*, opposite (whence the view is still finer), are remains of another camp, with triple foss. These heights both commanded an ancient road from Crediton to the N. coast of Devon. They look on one side toward the northern range of Dartmoor, and on the other across a wide stretch of rich country, toward the Blackdown hills, which divide Devon from Somerset. (See Rte. 1.)

The geologist may find on *Posbury Hill* a large patch of igneous rocks in the new red sandstone.

On the road between Crediton and Okehampton is

Sandford, E. of Crediton, considered the most fertile parish in Devonshire. The soil rests on the red sandstone. But the whole of this neighbourhood is unusually rich and productive. The *Lord's Meadow*, a broad open field extending from the Crediton valley to the Creedy river, retains the celebrity it enjoyed in Westcote's days. "The soil," he says, "is very fertile both for corn and pasture, insomuch as it is grown to a general proverb throughout the whole kingdom,—'as good hay as any in Denshire;'—and here in the country—'as good hay as any in Kirton;'—and there—'as good as any in my lord's meadow'—than which there can be no better." Westcote himself was born (1567) in the parish of

Shobrook, adjoining Crediton, where the *Ch.* has some Norman portions, Shobrook was also the native parish of the Bodleys, one of whom, Sir Thomas, founded the Bodleian Library at Oxford. They removed first to Crediton, and then to Exeter.

[3¼ m. N., on the banks of the Creedy, stands *Dowrish House*, Mrs. Clayfield, formerly mansion of the Dowrishes, and built in the reign of King John. The gatehouse and centre of the old structure still remain. Here are preserved some portraits of the Dowrish family; and " a marble table inlaid with cards and counters, showing the 2 hands of piquet held by a Mr. Dowrish and an ancestor of the present Sir Stafford Northcote, who were playing together, when Mr. Dowrish, thinking he had won the game, betted the manor of Kennerleigh, and lost it. The Northcotes hold it at the present time. The marble table was made to commemorate the event."

7 *Bow*, or *Nymet Tracy*, an improving village, cheerfully situated on the slope of a hill. The church is of no great interest: it has a carved screen; the tower and chancel were originally E. Eng. Beyond the road becomes interesting on its approach to Dartmoor. *Cawsand Beacon*, 1792 ft., and *Yes Tor*, 2050 ft., the highest point in the South of England, are the most conspicuous summits. The chapel of *Broad Nymet*, 1 m. from Bow, is E. E. in character and worth notice.

Nearer Okehampton, about 1½ m. off the road to the rt., is the village of *Sampford Courtenay*, in which the formidable insurrection in the reign of Edw. VI. first broke out. (See Froude, 'Hist. Eng.,' vol. vi.) The rebels, having unsuccessfully besieged Exeter, were defeated by Lord Russell at Clist St. Mary. Sampford C. *Ch.* (Perp.) is a fine building with a lofty tower.]

11 m. *Yeoford Stat.* (From this stat. a branch line of rly. is in progress (1865) to Okehampton. A portion, as far as North Tawton, will probably be shortly opened. The line will be continued by Lidford to Tavistock.)

13½ m. *Coplestone Stat.* In the middle of the village here is *Coplestone Cross*, a very ancient monument, in all probability of Saxon date. It is about 12 ft. high, and rudely ornamented with scroll-work. The family of Coplestone, "Esquires of the White Spur," as they were called, took their name from this cross, a fac-simile of which was erected by the late Bishop of Llandaff in his village of Offwell, near Honiton.

15½ m. *Morchard Road Stat.* rt. *Morchard Bishops*, 2 m. The line, having crossed the summit-level in a deep cutting, has here entered the vale of the Taw, which it is to follow to its destination.

18¼ m. *Lapford Stat.*, from which *Denridge* and *Pidley*, once the seats of the Radford and St. Leger families, but now farmhouses, are respectively 3 and 4 m. E. *Bury*, ¼ m. S. on the l. bank of the river, and *Kelland*, 1 m.

S. on the road to Zeal Monachorum, are also old manor-houses. In Lapford *Ch.* is a very good screen, without paint. The tower is Perp. and fine.

[*Coleridge*, some 4 m. W., has a Perp. ch. with a beautiful screen of the same date, the doors of which are perfect. This is one of the best and most characteristic examples of the roodscreens so common in Devonshire. There is a figure of Edw. V. in coloured glass; and an effigy in armour of John Evans, 1514, probably the donor of the screen. Two bench ends have inscriptions demanding prayers for him.]

21½ m. *Eggesford Stat.*, 1 m. N. of *Eggesford*, property of the Earl of Portsmouth, who resides at *Howard House*, in the adjoining parish of Wemworthy. [At Brushford, near W., the Eggesford fox-hounds are kennelled. rt. 1½ m.—

Chulmleigh (*Inn:* King's Arms), a small market-town, near the junction of the Little Dart with the Taw, and on the Roman road from Exeter into Cornwall by Stratton. A good roodscreen and a very fine Perp. tower, one of the best in the district, are the chief things to be noticed in the ch., which is itself Perp. In the neighbourhood are some curious houses. W., between the rail and the road to Barnstaple, you may find *Colleton Barton* (— Williams, Esq.), built 1612, and rich in antique carving; N. 1½ m. *Leigh House* (R. Preston, Esq.), of Eliz. date; and 5½ m. E., near the farmhouse of *Affeton Barton*, the ruins of the splendid *seat of the Affeton family* in the 13th and 14th cents., consisting of a gate-tower with spiral staircase. Affeton was subsequently occupied by the Stucleys; and the neighbouring ch. of *W. Worlington* (a strange old building with a wooden spire) contains a sumptuous monument to Sir Thomas Stucley (d. 1663), whose brother was Cromwell's chaplain. To this family belonged, temp. Eliz., the hero called "the lusty Stuckeley," who, says Westcote, "projected to people Florida, and there, in those remote countries, to play Rex." He afterwards became the Pope's pensioner, and was sent by him to Ireland to assist the papal cause; but, putting in to Lisbon on his way, was persuaded by King Sebastian to join his expedition to Barbary, where he fell in the battle of Alcazar. His career is as characteristic of the times as those of the famous Shirley brothers of Weston in Sussex. The little church of *Creacombe* (rebuilt 1857), about 4 m. N. of W. Worlington, in a wild and uninteresting district, contains a triangular-headed S. door, undoubtedly Saxon. The font is a plain circular bowl, probably of the same date.]

25 m. *South Molton Road Stat.* rt. 8 m. is the town of S. Molton. (*Inns:* George; White Hart.) This is an old town situated at the N. edge of the carboniferous rocks, and on the river Mole, from which it derives its name. (The Mole descends from Exmoor, the springs of one of its branches rising near "Mole's Chamber.") Before the Conquest the manor was included in the demesne of the crown; but in the reign of Edw. I. was held by Lord Martyn of the Earl of Gloucester, by the service of providing a man, with a bow and 3 arrows, to attend the earl when hunting in "Gower," in Wales. A butcher of this place, named *Samuel Badcock*, distinguished himself by his learning. He was a dissenting minister, and born in 1747.

The *Church* is Perp., and the shell of a very fine building, but choked and spoilt by ill-arranged sittings. The tower (140 ft. high, including vane) is one of 3 ascribed to the same architect; the other two are Bishop's Nympton and Chittlehampton. These are locally known as "Length," "Strength," and "Beauty." S. Molton is "Strength," a title which the thick walls and massive buttresses at once approve. Within the ch. is a very fine stone pulpit (Perp.), much resembling one at Chittlehampton. The figures are modern. The tower of *Bishop's Nympton* (4 m. E.), although only 100 ft. high, is "Length;" but it really is the highest in proportion to the square of its base. There is a Norman font in this ch.

Castle Hill, the seat of Earl Fortescue, is about 3 m. distant on the Barnstaple road. A triumphal arch, and the artificial ruin of a castle, crown the hills near the house. The park is above 800 acres, finely wooded. The hall of the castle is decorated with stag-heads from Exmoor, the date and particulars of the chace being inscribed under each pair of antlers. The church of *West Buckland*, 2 m. N., has an ancient screen. Middle-class schools have recently been established at West Buckland, with considerable success. *King's Nympton Park* (J. Tanner, Esq.) is about 6 m. S. The park dates from the reign of Henry VIII., when it was enclosed by *Sir Lewis Pollard*, a Justice of the King's Bench, and native of this parish. 1 m. S.W. are extensive quarries of black limestone.

Antiquaries suppose that the Roman station *Termolum* was situated between South Molton and Chulmleigh; and that a Roman road traversed the county from the neighbourhood of Honiton to Stratton, by Cadbury, Chulmleigh, Clovelly Dikes, and Hartland.

[*North Molton* is 3½ m. N. by E. of its sister town, and contains a fine Perp. *Church*, restored in 1849. The screen is good, and richly decorated; the oak pulpit has niches with the original figures painted and gilt. The Perp. font is unusually fine; the octagonal basin is richly arcaded, moulded, and foiled, and the stem has figures under canopies. The tower, not so fine as that of S. Molton, is 100 ft. high. Near the town are *Court Hall* and *Court House*, old ivied mansions, the property of Lord Poltimore, but the latter belonged formerly to the Earl of Morley; in the hilly country, away to the E.N.E. some 7 m., two ancient manor-houses, now occupied by farmers, but once the seats of the families of Bottreaux and Columb. Another curiosity is the *Flitton Oak*, a giant of its kind, standing on a spot where 3 roads meet, 2 m. N.W., towards High Bray, on the property of Lord Poltimore. At 1 foot from the ground it measures 33 ft. in circumf., and at 7 ft. it branches into 8 enormous limbs. It is supposed to be little less than 1000 years old. The species, says Loudon, is Q. sessiliflora. Along the upward course of the Mole the mining of copper has been pursued from a very early time. On the ascent of the beautiful wooded valley we soon reach the openings made by the "old men," and then the works of the *Poltimore*, where both old and modern men have been busy. The ores of the copper here are the red and grey, and the green carb., but what renders the lode of particular interest is that the gossan yields gold, at the rate, it is said, of 8 dwts. to the ton. Higher up the stream is the *Britannia*, where the precious metal has been found in grain; and still further to the N. the *Prince Albert* copper-mine.]

28 m. *Portsmouth Arms Stat.*, where the inn is on the banks of the Taw and the high road to Barnstaple

32½ m. *Umberleigh Stat.*, on the road from S. Molton to Torrington. There is some picturesque scenery about Umberleigh bridge, which here crosses the Taw.

[rt. 3 m. is *Chittlehampton*, where is a ch. of Perp. date, with a magnificent tower, "the nearest approximation to the highly ornamental structures of

Somersetshire in this county. There is nothing in its detail which is not of the most pure and faultless description; and the admirable grouping of the pinnacles, with its general arrangement and proportion, leave it without a rival in Devon." It is "Beauty," whilst Bishop's Nympton and S. Molton are "Length" and "Strength." In the ch. is a stone pulpit, with figures and canopies of excellent design. It is of the same date as the tower. The panelled roof of the N. chancel aisle should be noticed. The ch. is dedicated to St. Hieritha (called St. Wuth), said to have been born at Stowford, an adjoining hamlet, and who, says Leland (Itin.), "suffered the next year after Thomas Becket." Nothing is really known of her. Here are *brasses* for John Cobleigh and 2 wives, c. 1480.

1 m. l. of Umberleigh Stat. is *Atherington*, where the ch., originally E. Eng., was greatly altered and added to in the Perp. period. The tower deserves notice; but the great feature is the magnificent roodscreen, one of the finest examples in Devonshire. The most perfect part is that which separates the N. nave aisle from that of the chancel. It is of oak unpainted, rising nearly to the roof; and displays a wonderful variety of details, some of which (especially the ornaments in the groining) indicate the late period of the work. Above the canopies are pedestals for 5 figures. There is some fine stained glass (fragments) at E. end of chancel aisle; and an altar-tomb with *brasses* for Sir Arthur Basset and 2 wives, circ. 1540.]

[6 m. beyond Atherington is *Torrington* (*Inn:* Globe), situated very pleasantly on an eminence sloping to the Torridge. It is an ancient place, containing fragments of a castle founded by Richard de Merton in the reign of Edw. III. The site is now a bowling-green, and commands an extensive view.

Torrington and its neighbourhood have some historic associations. Githa, the mother of Harold, was endowed with lands of this tything; and during the Rebellion stirring incidents occurred in the town and on the adjacent hills. In 1643 a body of rebels advanced from Bideford to attack Colonel Digby, who had marched upon Torrington to cut off the communication between the N. of Devon and Plymouth. No sooner, however, were they met by a few of the Royalist troopers than they "routed themselves," to quote Clarendon's words, and were pursued with much slaughter. The consequences of this action were the immediate surrender of the fort of Appledore, and subsequently of the towns of Barnstaple and Bideford. "The fugitives," says Clarendon, "spread themselves over the country, bearing frightful marks of the fray, and telling strange stories of the horror and fear which had seized them, although nobody had seen above six of the enemy that charged them." In 1646 the townspeople were witness to a far more fatal engagement, when Fairfax came by night upon the quarters of Lord Hopton. The action which ensued was furious but decisive, and the Royalists were totally defeated. Upon this occasion the ch., together with 200 prisoners and those who guarded them, were blown into the air by the explosion of about 80 barrels of gunpowder. The capture of Torrington was the death-blow of the King's cause in the west. In 1660 the celebrated General Monk was created Earl of Torrington. In 1669 the town gave the title of Earl to Admiral Herbert; and, in 1720, of Viscount to Sir George Byng. The Monks—now represented by the physician Dr. Munk—were seated for many generations at the manor-house of *Potheridge*, near *Merton*, a village 7 m. distant, between Torrington and Hatherleigh; but their mansion, sumptuously rebuilt about 1670 by the General, when Duke of Albemarle (he was born at Potheridge), was pulled down in the last centy. The stables, however, remain to this day, and will give the visitor some idea of the magnificence of the ancient building.

Annery, N.W., in the valley of the Torridge (W. Tardrew, Esq.), was for a long period the seat of the Hankfords. Here was born and died Sir William H., Chief Justice in the reigns of Hen. V. and VI.; the judge who, according to the Devonshire tradition, committed P. Henry. His monument may be seen in *Monkleigh* Ch. A local tradition asserts that he was shot in his own park at Apnery, by his keeper, whom he had reprimanded for negligence. He had " plotted for himself a violent death," says Westcote. An oak in the park, under which he is said to have fallen, is still called the " Hankford oak."

John Howe, a dissenting minister of some celebrity, b. 1630, lived for several years at Torrington.

Captain Palmer, R. A., has here a beautiful early portrait, by *Sir Joshua Reynolds*, of Mrs. Field, sister-in-law of the Rev. Joshua R., as well as family portraits by *William Doughty*. Sir Joshua's eldest sister, Mary, married John Palmer, Esq., of Torrington. The house is near the ch., and in its arrangements little altered since Dr. Johnson dined in it, 1762.

Torrington *Ch.*, originally Dec., suffered in the Civil War (see *ante*). In the ch. of *St. Giles-in-the-Wood* are *brasses* for Eleanor Pollard, 1430; Margaret Rolle and children, 1592; and John Risdon, 1610. There is a small ch. at *Little Torrington*, which has been excellently restored with stained glass, &c.

The scenery between Torrington and Bideford well merits notice, the oak being abundant. The road skirts the river, and commands a good view of the *Aqueduct of the Torridge Canal*, which crosses the valley on 5 arches. This canal, completed in 1824, was one of the patriotic works of the late Lord Rolle. It enters the river near Wear Gifford about 3 m. from Torrington.

In the town you may visit a manufactory of gloves; at *Wear Gifford*, 2 m. N., a very curious manor-house, described Rte. 18; and at *Frithelstock*, 2½ m. W., the remains of an old priory, founded by Robert de Bello Campo in the reign of Hen. III. In the neighbourhood are *Cross House* (Mrs. Stevens), at present occupied by Sir Trevor Wheler, Bart.; *Stevenstone House*, a seat of the late Lord Rolle; and about 6 m. towards Hatherleigh, *Heanton House* (Lord Clinton).]

4½ m. from Umberleigh Stat. the Rly. passes through some of the prettiest scenery in the Taw valley, where the ch. of *Bishop's Tawton* rises on the rt., and l. the woods of *Tawstock Court*, seat of the Wreys. The view here is said to include the most valuable manor, the best mansion, the finest ch., and the richest rectory in the county. Tawstock Court was built in 1787. A gateway (1574) is the only remnant of the mansion of the Bouchiers, occupied by Fairfax in 1646; but the park abounds in oaks which have flourished in times long past. Tawstock *Ch.*, very good Dec., with Perp. windows inserted in the nave, contains monuments of the Bouchiers Earls of Bath, the ancestors of the proprietor of Tawstock Court; and an early effigy in wood. In a room over the vestry are fragments of old armour and banners. *Bishop's Tawton*, on the opposite side of the valley, is said (but solely on Hoker's authority—there is no ancient evidence) to have been the seat of the Devonshire bishopric before the see was fixed at Crediton. The ch. has some Dec. portions, including a spire, an unusual feature in Devonshire.

39½ m. *Barnstaple Stat.* [Here coaches meet certain of the trains for *Ilfracombe*, and for *Lynton*. A rly. has been authorised from Barnstaple to Ilfracombe, but is not yet (1865) commenced. The direct turnpike-road to Ilfracombe, 11 m., is pleasant, but of no special interest. The pedestrian, and those who do not travel by the coach, will do better to take the longer road (12½ m.) by *Braunton*, which is described in the following route. The coach-drive to Lynton by Paracombe is a very beautiful one, but calls for no special notice.] Pop. in 1861, 8127.

Barnstaple, for brevity called *Barum* (*Inns*: Golden Lion; Fortescue Arms), the capital of N. Devon, is much admired for its position on a broad river and in a verdant vale. It boasts a considerable antiquity, having formed a part of the demesne of the Saxon kings. Athelstan is said to have chartered it, and to have repaired the town walls; and after the Conquest it was dignified with a castle and a priory, founded by Judhael de Totnais, the latter dedicated to St. Mary Magdalen. No remains of these buildings are now to be seen. The mound is the only vestige of the castle; and the name of *Close*, or *Maudlyn Rack Close*, of the priory. Athelstan's charter is at least doubtful; but the town was certainly incorporated by Henry I., and has sent members to Parliament since the reign of Edward I. The port furnished 3 ships for the fleet which defeated the Armada. During the Civil War there was much fighting in and about Barnstaple, which Clarendon (who was for some time Governor of the town) pronounced "the most miraculously fortified place that I know." Prince Charles was sent here for some time for security. The remains of the ancient fortifications are interesting. In the Grammar School here were educated Bishop Jewell, his antagonist Harding, and Gay the poet, who was born either in the town, or in a house under Coddon Hill, close without it.

There is not much in Barnstaple to interest the stranger, but the "lions," such as they are, he will probably like to visit. They may be enumerated as follows:—

The *Ch.*, dedicated to SS. Peter and Paul, is not remarkable. Its spire was shattered by a violent thunder-storm in 1816. The building, which has been modernized, contains a powerful organ. Two new churches, that of the *Holy Trinity* (Macintosh, architect), and that of *St. Mary Magdalen* (Ferrey, architect), have been built since 1845.

The *Bridge*, supposed to have been built in the 13th cent. It was widened in 1834, and consists of 16 arches, 8 less than the bridge at Bideford. The view from it is very pleasant; the river Taw and its vale having a fine background on the E., called *Coddon Hill*.

Queen Anne's Walk, on the quay, W. of the bridge, a colonnade intended originally for an Exchange and erected in the reign of Queen Anne. It was rebuilt by the corporation in 1798.

The *North Walk*, further W., a promenade by the side of the river, and planted with trees, after the fashion of the French.

Barnstaple is distinguished as the birthplace of *Lord Chancellor Fortescue*, 1422. It is noted in the county for a large fair, called pre-eminently *the Barnstaple Fair*, which begins on the 19th of September, and is attended by some ancient customs. On the morning of its proclamation the mayor and corporation meet their friends in the council-chamber, and partake of spiced toast and ale; and during its continuance a glove decked with dahlias is protruded on a pole from a window. Upon the second day a stag is hunted on Exmoor, and the incidents of the sport are sometimes as amusing as those of the far-famed field-days at Epping. The town has a manufacture of lace, and several potteries are at work in the neighbourhood. The clay is found in the adjoining parish of Fremington. Clarendon informs us that in the Rebellion, when Sir Richard Greuville was stationed at Okehampton, he formed the strange design of cutting a deep trench from Barnstaple to the English Channel, a distance of about 40 m., by which, he said, he would defend all Cornwall, and so much of Devon, against the world. Lady Fanshawe, in her curious Memoirs, speaks of Barnstaple as "one of the finest towns in England." "They have," she says, "near this town, a fruit called a massard, like a cherry, but different in taste, which makes the best pies with their sort of cream I ever eat." The visitor should decide this question of taste for himself; but let him on no account omit "their sort of cream."

Good *views of the town* are to be obtained from *Coldon Hill* (E. alt. 623 ft.) and from the Bideford road. Pleasant walks are to be found on the l. bank of the Taw, E. and W. from the end of the bridge. On that side of the river is the rail of the N. Devon Extension, completed 1855 to Bideford. Fremington, the first station, is the boundary of the deep water, the channel near Barnstaple being choked by sand. It is 6 m. from Barnstaple to the mouth of the river.

In the neighbourhood are *Upcott*, *Pilton House* (J. Whyte, Esq.), *Brynsworthy*, (S. T. M. May, Esq.), *Bickington House* (C. Roberts, Esq.), and *Fremington House* (W. A. Yeo, Esq.). Fremington has a fine collection of exotics. *Raleigh House*, anciently a seat of the Raleighs, was long since converted into a woollen factory, and subsequently into a lace-mill. About 4 m. N.E. is *Youlston Park* (Sir A. Chichester, Bart.), and 6 m. in the same direction *Arlington Court* (Sir A. P. B. Chichester, Bart.).

[In *Pilton* ch., ½ m. N., a stand fo*.* the hour-glass, in the shape of a man's arm, is still affixed to the pulpit. One of the bells of the ch. bears this ringing inscription:—

" Recast by John Taylor and Son,
Who the best prize for church bells won
At the Great Ex-hi-bi-ti-on
In London, 1—8—5 and 1. "

At *Marwood*, 3 m. N. of Barnstaple, there is a fine Perp. ch., with much excellent carved work. The tower is handsome, and there is a good E. Eng. piscina.

The ch. of *Swimbridge*, 5 m. on the road to S. Molton (late Perp. with Dec. tower), contains a beautiful screen (Perp.), a stone pulpit, and a specimen of that anomaly the humorous epitaph. It is to the memory of John Rosier, attorney and "Auncient of Lyon's Inn," and begins—

" Loe with a warrant seal'd by God's decree,
Death, his grim sergeant, hath arrested me."

It runs through a dozen lines in a similar strain.]

42½ m. *Fremington Stat.*

46 m. *Instow Quay*, a small but rising watering-place, situated at the junction of the Taw and the Torridge. It has a view of the sea, of Lundy Island, the Barnstaple Bar, the sands of Braunton Burrows, Northam Tower, commonly called Chanter's Folly, as built by a person of that name, and the busy village of Appledore. A pleasant road leads from Instow Quay along the shore of the river, passing *Tapley Park* (Mrs. Cleveland) to

3 m. by this road, 48½ from Exeter by rail, *Bideford* i.e. By-the-Ford. Pop. in 1861, 5742. (*Inns:* New Inn; Commercial Inn.) This town, considering the unpretending character of the surrounding scenery, is as prettily placed as any in

Devonshire. It is built in wide, airy streets, on a hillside shelving to the water, and commands delightful views of the broad meandering Torridge and its vale. These are seen to advantage from the bridge and the windows of the New Inn. Towards the sea the river is adorned by the woods of Tapley, the Tower of Northam, and the villas of Instow. In the other direction it winds glistening a little distance, and then loses itself among the folds of the hills, the sweeps of which are particularly graceful. It is navigable to Wear Gifford, from which place there is a canal to Great Torrington.

The *Bridge* is a favourite promenade of the inhabitants. It is 677 ft. in length, and spans the river on 24 pointed arches. It was erected about the beginning of the 14th cent. by Sir Theobald Grenville, who, according to a legend, was encouraged in the work by a vision which appeared to one Gornard, a priest. Attempts having often been fruitlessly made to discover a foundation, Father Gornard was admonished in a dream to search for a rock which had been rolled from the hill into the river. This was told to Sir Theobald, who set workmen to look for the stone. It was soon discovered, and on this solid basis the bridge was thrown across. Adjoining it is a broad quay 1200 ft. long, which also forms a very agreeable walk.

The *Church*, dedicated to St. Mary, dated from the 14th cent., and in 1738-9 was the curacy of *Hervey*, author of 'Meditations among the Tombs.' The old ch. was entirely spoilt by churchwardenisms of various dates and eccentricities; and a new one is (1862) in course of erection on its site. In the churchyard is the following epitaph:—

"Here lies the body of Mary Sexton,
Who pleased many a man, but never vex'd one:
Not like the woman who lies under the next stone."

On the hill opposite Bideford the stranger will notice a small battlemented structure, called *Chudleigh Fort*, which was built by Major-Gen. Chudleigh at the breaking out of the Rebellion. It shortly afterwards surrendered to the king's troops, under Colonel Digby. The hill commands an excellent view of Bideford and the surrounding country.

There are many pleasant walks in the neighbourhood, viz. down the l. bank of the river; along the new Torrington road to *Yeo Vale* (Mrs. Morison) and *Orleigh Court* (— Lee, Esq.), about 5 m. distant, the latter estate containing a remarkable outlying patch of greensand, 36 m. from the greensand of Great Haldon; and along the rt. bank of the river to the village of *Wear Gifford*, 4 m., where there is an oak mentioned by Loudon as 28 ft. in circumference, and as covering with its head a space 92 ft. in diameter. Other seats near the town are, *Moreton House* (Sir G. S. Stucley, Bart.), and *Abbotsham Court* (R. Best, Esq.). *Portledge* (Rev. J. T. P. Coffin) has belonged to the family of Coffin for many centuries.

At *Wear Gifford* is an ancient house (property of Earl Fortescue), one of the most interesting in Devonshire. It is of the 15th cent., with embattled tower gateway, and was for many years used as a farmhouse, but has been recently restored as an occasional residence by its proprietor. The wall which surrounded the outer courts, was so injured in the Rebellion, that only the gatehouse and doorways remain. The hall occupies the centre, between gabled wings, and has a handsome roof, with hammer-beams, tracery, cusping, and pendants, of superior detail. The house itself contains panelling exquisitely worked, antique pictures and tapestry. The Giffords were lords of the manor of Weare Gifford from a period soon after the Conquest. It passed through heiresses to the Trewin and Densil families, and again through an heiress (temp. Hen. VI.) to the Fortescues. It was perhaps the first Fortescue of Weare (a son of Henry VI.'s Chief Justice) who built the existing house. The *Ch.* has Dec. nave and chancel, with very fine Perp. roof in the latter. There is an altar-tomb with Gifford effigies; and some 17th centy. Fortescue monuments. Read the inscription on that of Hugh Fortescue, d. 1648. Here is also a modern *brass* by Hayward, of Exeter.

The greatest natural curiosity near Bideford is the *Pebble* or *Boulder Ridge* on Northam Burrows, at the mouth of the Taw and Torridge, about 4 m. distant. The most agreeable route to it is by the l. bank of the river for 2 m., and then by a lane (¼ m.) to the village of *Northam*. From that place a steep hill descends to *Northam Burrows*, a level plain of turf of 1000 acres, formed by the sandy deposit from the sea and rivers, and now protected from the waves by the Pebble Ridge. This remarkable barrier extends about 2 m. in a straight line, like an artificial embankment, and is also curious as showing that large stones as well as shingle travel along the shore from their native rocks. It is about 50 ft. wide and 20 ft. high, and consists of rolled slate-stones, or pebbles, which vary in size from ½ a foot to 2 ft. in diam. It is singularly uniform and compact; on the one side sloping steeply to the turf of the Burrows, on the other, at a less inclination, to a broad area of sand; but scarcely a pebble is to be found on the turf or the shore beyond the base of the ridge. In this form it stretches from the distant cliffs to a point opposite the bar of the rivers; but once within the influence of this obstruction, it loses its character of a ridge, and lies heaped upon sloping sandhills. The shore scene is exceedingly wild, and the view of the coast, of Lundy Island, and the estuary of the Taw and the Torridge, most interesting. At low water the dangerous bar is seen stretching athwart the entrance of the rivers; and on the Braunton Burrows opposite are the two lighthouses, which are to be brought into one by a vessel standing for the harbour. A large new hotel is at present (1865) building on the Northam Burrows.

It is a short walk from the Burrows to the village of *Appledore*, on the shore of the Torridge, where you can take a boat to Bideford, and so vary the route homewards. Appledore is interesting for its antiquity, and for a legend of the Danish warrior Hubba, who is said to have landed near this village, in the reign of Alfred, from a fleet of 33 ships, and to have laid siege to a neighbouring castle, called Kenwith, the site of which is now only surmised to be a hill called *Henny Castle* (near *Kenwith Lodge*, Dr. Heywood's), N.W. of Bideford. The strength of this place, however, proved too great for its assailants. Hubba was slain under its walls, and his followers driven with slaughter to the shore. At one spot, it is said, they rallied, and so checked their pursuers as to be enabled to regain their ships; and a field by the roadside, near the village of Northam, is to this day pointed out as the place where they turned, and has been known from time immemorial as the *Bloody Corner*. Biorn Ironside, the companion of Hubba, was slain in this headlong retreat, and the magical Raven banner was taken by the Saxons. It was a black bird, probably a stuffed specimen of the raven, which hung quiet when defeat was at hand, but clapped its wings before victory. Hubba, we are told, was buried beneath a cairn on the shore, and the name of *Hubblestone* would seem to mark the locality. This defeat took place in Devonshire (Sax. Chron. ad ann. 877-78); but the identification of the site with Henny Castle is quite uncertain.

In the year 1646 Bideford was

ravaged by the plague, but in 1832 and '49 it escaped the cholera. There is a monument in the ch. to a Mr. Strange, who made himself remarkable for his charity during the plague of 1646. The town is considered one of the healthiest in the county. Among its natives was *John Shebbeare*, the political writer, who paid the penalty of a libel in the pillory at Charing Cross. He was born in 1709, and is best known by his 'Letters to the People of England.'

The neighbourhood possesses some interest for the geologist. Beds of *anthracite* stretch across the hills from Bideford to Chittlehampton, the principal seam having an average thickness of 7 ft. The mineral has been extracted, like the metallic ores, by mining; but the beds are of such irregular thickness that a heavy expense attends their working; 58 tons in the week have, however, been produced by one of the pits. Anthracite is used chiefly for drying malt and lime-burning. In a decomposed state it makes a black paint. Between Peppercombe and Portledge Mouth in Bideford Bay is an outlying patch of *new red sandstone*, 17 or 18 m. from the nearest points of that formation at Hatherleigh and Jacobstow; and at Orleigh Court, as before mentioned, a few isolated acres of *greensand*, yet further removed from its kindred hills. Good examples of *raised beaches* may be observed N. and S. of the united embouchure of the Taw and the Torridge. The gravel or sand of the latter river is converted into hollow bricks, tiles, &c., in the *North Devon Pottery*, near the town.

The visitor of Bideford will make a point of visiting the romantic village of *Clovelly* (11 m.) and the park of *Clovelly Court*. If he travels by carriage or on horseback, he must procure at the New Inn a key of the drive called the *Hobby*. If on foot he can step over the gate. For Clovelly, see the following route.

ROUTE 18.

LYNMOUTH AND LYNTON TO HARTLAND, BY COMBE MARTIN, ILFRACOMBE (BARNSTAPLE), AND CLOVELLY.

This route embraces the whole of the grand coast scenery of N. Devon. Lynton may be reached from Barnstaple (see the preceding route) or from Taunton, by Watchet and Porlock (a very fine and striking approach). This latter line is described in Rte. 19.

Lynmouth. (*Inn*: Lyndale Hotel.) *Lynton*. (*Inns*: Castle Hotel; Valley of Rocks; Crown; Globe.) At Lynton telescopes are employed at the rival houses for the prompt discovery of the approaching traveller. He had better, therefore, determine beforehand on his inn, or he may become a bone of contention to a triad of postboys, who wait with additional horses at the bottom of the hill to drag the carriage to its destination.

Lynton and Lynmouth are situated on the outskirts of Exmoor, amid scenes far finer than any other of the southern counties can boast; characterised by subalpine valleys, impetuous streams, wild gloomy ridges, and precipices and crags which would elicit admiration even in mountainous Wales. Two noisy torrents here effect a junction close upon the sea, the E. Lyn flowing with hoarse murmurs down a magnificent ravine, the W. Lyn winding a less imposing but lonely and richly wooded valley. So sharp is the descent of these rivers from the moor, that they suddenly swell after rain of any continuance, and at these times present a spectacle of grandeur which the beholder will not easily forget. The waters then rush down with a mighty noise, and a speed the eye cannot follow.

Lynmouth is seated at the mouth of these formidable streams, and is shut in by a precipice called *Lyn Cliff* and fir-clad heights. A steep winding road leads from Lynmouth to Lynton, which is not placed in quite so interesting a position as its neighbour, but is raised above the noise of the torrent, and commands a view of the dark ridges of Exmoor, and of that which separates Lyndale from the sea.

Lynmouth is thus described by the late Robert Southey:—" My walk to Ilfracombe led me through Lynmouth, the finest spot, except Cintra and the Arrabida, that I ever saw. Two rivers join at Lynmouth. You probably know the hill-streams of Devonshire; each of these flows down a combe, rolling down over huge stones like a long waterfall; immediately at their junction they enter the sea, and the rivers and the sea make but one sound of uproar. Of these combes, the one is richly wooded —the other runs between 2 high, bare stoney hills. From the hill betwe, n the two is a prospect most magnificent; on either hand combes, and the river before the little village—the beautiful little village, which, I am assured by one who is familiar with Switzerland, resembles a Swiss village. This alone would constitute a view beautiful enough to repay the weariness of a long journey; but, to complete it, there is the blue and boundless sea, for the faint and feeble line of the Welsh coast is only to be seen on the rt. hand if the day be perfectly clear."

A week or a fortnight may well be passed at either of these places. Lynton is generally preferred by visitors who spend their time in exploring the neighbourhood, but Lynmouth has greater charms as a residence, and will be chosen by those who like to have a mountain scene always in view, and to watch the clouds curling about the heights. The neighbourhood is a paradise for anglers; the Lyns, and the other streams of Exmoor, swarm with trout, and their pursuit necessarily leads the fisherman through wild and romantic scenes. The mode of lionising the neighbourhood is on pony or donkeyback, or, far better, on foot. The roads are ill adapted for carriages, being steep and circuitous. Posting is therefore both tedious and expensive. The stranger should be informed that the hotels will board him by the week at a cheaper rate than they will furnish bed and meals separately, and that the charge for ponies is less when they are taken by the day.

The chief points of interest in the neighbourhood are—

1. *Lyndale, Valley of Rocks, Lee Bay.*
2. *Valley of the W. Lyn.*
3. *Heddon's Mouth.*
4. *Brendon valley.*
5. *Glenthorne; path along the Exmoor coast.*
6. *Porlock, Bossington Hill, Dunkery Beacon, Culbone.*
7. *Exmoor.*

No. 1 may be seen in one day; 2 and 3 may be comprised in the route to Combe Martin and Ilfracombe; 4 and 5 should each be made the object of a separate day's excursion, although it is quite possible to include them in one ramble; 6 may have been already seen by the traveller on his road to Lynton.

(1) *a.* First then for *Lyndale* and *Waters' Meet.* Starting from Lynton, the stranger should descend to Lyn-

Route 18.—*Waters' Meet.—Valley of Rocks.* Sect. I.

mouth through the beautiful wooded grounds of *Lynton Cottage* (Mr. Sanford), having given orders that his pony should be taken round to await him below. He will next visit the *grounds of Sir W. Herries*, which occupy the ravine through which the W. Lyn comes hurrying under *Lyn Cliff*, where it falls in a cascade; and if inclined to extend the ramble, a path will lead him up the stream nearly ½ m.; and "perhaps nowhere," says 'the Sketcher' (Blackwood), "is to be found so much beauty of painter's detail, of water, foliage, stones, and banks, within so small a space." The *Filmy fern* grows here abundantly, and the turf is chequered by the ivy-leaved *Campanula*, while the sweet-scented *Lastræa oreopteris* and *L. Filix mas paleacea* attain an unrivalled luxuriance ('Ferny Combes,' 1856). Having fully explored this romantic retreat, he is advised to mount his pony and proceed up the gorge of the E. Lyn, or *Lyndale*, as far as the junction of 2 branches of the river, at a spot prettily named

Waters' Meet (about 2 m., to which there is also a path along the rt. bank through the woods, but it is longer and more fatiguing). Here the scenery is most beautiful. The sides of the ravine are covered with woods, the haunt of the wild deer of Exmoor, and rocks in various places protrude as cliffs, or lie coated with moss under the oaks on the hillside. Far below, where the foamy torrents unite, stands a rural little cottage, the property of the Rev. W. S. Halliday of Glenthorne. From this spot you can proceed ½ m. further to *Ilford Bridges*, and thence cross the hills to

Lyn Cliff, or, if on foot, you can climb from Waters' Meet at once in the same direction. The view of Lyndale from these heights, and the grandeur of the surrounding country, will be ample recompense for the fatigue of the ascent. After contemplating the depths of the valley, raise your eyes to the dark ridges of Exmoor stretching in deep purple E. and W. and N. to the sea. At the close of the autumn these desolate hills have donned their most gloomy garb and are in character with wintry skies. Arrived at *Lyn Cliff*, you must gain a point a little E. of the summer-house, so as to command the length of the gorge. *Countesbury* and its ch. will be seen aloft in the distance, on so dreary a hill that you will shiver to think of a winter's night in that forlorn and exposed village. Lyn Cliff is a good point for a view of the ledge on which Lynton, it is said, looks dropped by chance, and of the hollow in which Lynmouth lies embedded. Hence also you may travel in imagination some distance towards Porlock, for the upland of Countesbury is open before you, and the brown moor stretching beyond it for miles; whilst an idea may be gained of the size of the hills by carrying your eye from the depths of the valley to the distant summits. From Lyn Cliff the wanderer can descend to *Lynbridge, Cherry Bridge*, or *Barbrick Mill*, and at any of these places cross the W. Lyn and return to Lynton by a horse-road opposite Lynbridge. He will probably have returned to his hotel about the time for a luncheon. He can next proceed to the

b. Valley of Rocks. This wild and interesting scene is about 1 m. W. of Lynton, and approached either by the *North Walk* above the cliff, or by a carriage-road. The former should be selected. It is a path cut midway along a rapid slope of about 700 ft., and forms a narrow terrace commanding a fine sea view, the cloud-like mountains of Wales in the distance, the gorge of the E. Lyn (in perspective), and a sweep of dreary coast terminated by the *Lynmouth Foreland*.

After skirting the sea for about a mile you come to a gap in the hillside, and through this colossal portal, between 2 masses of bare pyramidal limestone, you enter the *Valley of Rocks*, which may well astonish the traveller when they first break upon his view, rising abruptly from the face of the slope in crags and pinnacles. In a few minutes he will be passing below them. Southey describes it as "a spot which is one of the greatest wonders indeed in the West of England. Imagine a narrow vale between 2 ridges of hills somewhat steep: the southern hill turfed: the vale, which runs from east to west, covered with huge stones and fragments of stone among the fern that fills it; the northern ridge completely bare, excoriated of all turf and all soil, the very bones and skeleton of the earth; rock reclining upon rock, stone piled upon stone, a huge terrific mass. A palace of the pre-Adamite kings, a city of the Anakim must have appeared so shapeless, and yet so like the ruins of what had been shaped after the waters of the flood subsided. I ascended with some toil the highest point; 2 large stones inclining on each other formed a rude portal on the summit. Here I sat down. A little level platform, abou-2 yds. long, lay before me, and then the eye immediately fell upon the sea, far, very far, below. I never felt the sublimity of solitude before."

One of these rocks is known as the *Chimney Rock*, and another, which throws its shadow on you as you turn into the valley, by the whimsical name of *Rugged Jack*. Having threaded this pass, the traveller will find himself upon the greensward of the valley itself; the *Castle Rock* rising like some Norman ruin on the rt., and the crag called the *Devil's Cheesewring*, or *Cheese-press*, from the hillside opposite. He is now in the heart of the stony vale, which descends obliquely towards the sea, but at a great elevation, and will probably rest to contemplate the wild and singular scene. He may ponder meanwhile on the probability of a mighty torrent having once rolled through this trough-way to the sea, and of the land having been afterwards upraised to its present position. A human interest also attaches to this lonely glen. From time immemorial it has been known as the *Danes*; and tradition acquaints us that a party of those marauders, when pursued from a neighbouring village, were here overtaken and slaughtered; and in connection with the legend it is a curious circumstance that a number of bones have been discovered in cutting a path up the Castle Rock.

You will ascend the Castle Rock. This, at one time, was a feat requiring some agility; but a few years ago one John Norman received permission from the lord of the manor to make paths and destroy rocks that he might levy toll on the stranger. It must be allowed that he has executed his work in a masterly manner. The walk along the cliff is worthy of a Telford, and the path up the Castle enables the veriest coward to ascend to the summit; but the native wildness of this huge ruinous crag is gone for ever. On all sides it is covered with rubbish; a terrace has been levelled near the top, and, sad to relate, the weather-beaten rocks have been actually hewn into seats and tables. Here may be seen a block of several tons weight, so nicely balanced, that a heave of a crowbar would send it thundering to the sea; and at the base of the cliffs the mouths of several caverns which are said to extend a long way underground, and can be visited by one of Norman's paths. The view is, of course, very extensive, and in a westerly direction the eye ranges from *Duty Point* and *Lee Bay* to the great promontory of *High Veer*.

Route 18.—*Lee Abbey.*—*Glenthorne.* Sect. I.

From the terrace a stair-way has been cut to the summit, and the steps afford several good sections of fossil shells. After his visit to the Castle Rock the traveller can descend to the beach at the end of the valley, and examine the cliff, which, in appearance, is identical with the vesicular *volcanic ash* of Brent Tor. He should also direct his attention to the pile of rocks called the *Cheese-press*, and explore the wilderness of pinnacles and crags around the *Chimney Rock* and *Rugged Jack*. The walk may be extended to *Duty Point*, just W. of the valley, and a little further to

Lee Bay (1½ m. from Lynton), a magnificent crescent of foliage and heights. At one part of it, called *Crock Meadows*, a small landslip has occurred. Behind the shelter of Duty Point stands

Lee Abbey, the modern mansion of C. Bailey, Esq., shown on Wednesdays. Adjoining the house are artificial ruins. Here, in former times, stood the splendid abode of the De Wchehalse, a noble family of Holland, who, about 1570, during the persecution of the Protestants by Alva, escaped with their property to England. In the reign of Charles II. Sir Edward de Wchehalse was the head of this house, and one of the most powerful barons in the W. of England, but his daughter, his only child, proved the unfortunate cause of destruction to the family. She was wooed and won by a nobleman in high favour with James II.; but the lover proved faithless, and the deserted maiden was one day found lifeless under the rocks of Duty Point. The father in vain sought redress by petitioning the king, and, when Monmouth landed at Lyme, De Wchehalse and his adherents hastened to support him. After the battle of Sedgemoor the unhappy parent returned to Lynton, but the emissaries of the king were soon despatched to apprehend him, and, on their approach by the neighbouring valley, De Wchehalse and the remainder of his family embarked in a boat to escape. The night was, however, stormy, and they are supposed to have all perished, as they were never heard of again. The monument and shield of De Wchehalse may be seen in Lynton church.

(2 and 3) The *Valley of the W. Lyn*, and *Heddon's Mouth*, may both be seen on the way to Combe Martin and Ilfracombe. (See *post*.)

(4) Another beautiful and favourite ride from Lynton is by the following course. Ascend Lyndale to Ilford Bridges. Take the road on the l. to *Brendon* Church. Descend into the *valley of Brendon* (a splendid ravine much resembling Lyndale), and proceed to the Lynton and Porlock road; returning by Countesbury Hill.

Oare Water and *Budgery Water* may be made the objects of a separate excursion by those fond of fishing or scenery. On the heights above Oare Valley the botanist should look for *Lycopodium alpinum*. The *Oak-fern*, or *Polypodium dryopteris*, grows abundantly on Exmoor.

(5) *Glenthorne*, the seat of the Rev. W. S. Halliday, is situated in a singularly romantic dell on the coast, about 5 m. from Lynton for a person on foot by Mr. Halliday's coast-path, and 8 m. for carriages, as the road on its descent to Glenthorne is drawn out by many twists and turns. The coast-path deserves to be particularly described. Commencing a little beyond Countesbury, and running through Glenthorne to Porlock, it is cut on the side of the huge sea-slopes, and commands at all points views of the Welsh mountains and Bristol Channel. It is called a

horse-path, but few would venture along it otherwise than on foot. It passes round several deep recesses, each with its stream and wood of oaks, and, approaching Glenthorne, is girt by rocks, superb in colour, and here and there by old trees most wonderful in form, flattened, as it were, by the wind against the hillside, to which they seem to cling with fantastic arms. At several points are seats of rosy stone, and these like the rock are festooned with creepers, ferns, and mosses. Beyond the grounds of Glenthorne the path proceeds to Culbone and Porlock through oak coppice; but at intervals are deep hollows, worn by the streams, and these are invariably filled with trees of considerable size. Below, on the cliffs, the traveller will remark the contortions of the strata. In the woods may be found *Asplenium septentrionale*.

The road from Lynmouth ascends at once to a height of about 1100 ft., and proceeds on that level to the descent to Glenthorne. ¼ m. short of *Countesbury*, 1½ m., is an old camp (rt. of the road) commanding an excellent view of the ravine at Waters' Meet; and, 3½ m. beyond this village, the boundary of Mr. Halliday's property, called *Cosgates Feet Gate*, from which a track on rt. leads by the valley of Oare to Brendon and Watersmeet. Here the traveller will see, on the l., the camp of *Oldbarrow*, known as one of the most perfect in Devonshire; and he will look down upon the woods of *Glenthorne*, to which he will now descend by a series of zigzags. The house is situated about 1000 ft. below the Porlock road, and 50 above the shore, at the base of mountainous slopes, thickly wooded and mantled with heather and fern. It stands on a small grassy platform abutting on the cliff, and a little to the W. of a beautiful dingle by which a stream and a path descend to the beach. Within the mansion, which is occasionally shown, are many curiosities—antiquities from Greece and Italy, a collection of armour, rare cabinets, and among some pictures the Spectre Ship, by *Severn*, in illustration of Coleridge's 'Ancient Mariner.' In the servants' hall there is a fireplace which belonged to Card. Wolsey, and on Palermo Point, above the house, a group of marbles from Athens and Corinth. The scenery, however, is the chief attraction of Glenthorne, and let no visitor neglect to explore the paths on the sea-slopes E. of the house. They run through a wood of most venerable oaks, many twisted in fanciful shapes, and one, in particular, forming an arch over the path.

(6) To *Porlock* (including *Culbone*), 13 m. post. The road is that to Glenthorne as far as the boundary of Somerset.

From the border the road traverses the long ridge of *Oare Hill*, black moors stretching in advance for miles, and occasionally perhaps varied by one of those grand cloud effects, when mists come whirling over the hills in wreaths, and here and there open to show patches of green as brilliant as chrysophrase. The *descent to *Porlock* is finer of its kind than anything in Devonshire—on the rt. the wild mountain of Dunkery, and a middle ground of woods and hollow glens; in front the rugged ridge of *Bossington* and the broad vale of Porlock (bearing some resemblance to that famed Welsh scene on the Clwyd); on the l. a crescent-shaped bay, the Bristol Channel, and the many-coloured mountains of Wales. At Porlock (see Rte. 19, and the *Handbook for Somerset*) there is a humble but hospitable little *inn* (the Ship), garnished with antlers of the red deer; and the traveller may here well spend a day or two in making the ascent of *Dunkery Beacon*, which has a base 12 m. in circumference, and commands perhaps the noblest prospect in the W. of England, the summit, crowned with the remains of old fire-beacons, being about 4 m. distant; and in excursing along the coast by *Ashley Combe* (Earl of Lovelace) to the remarkable hamlet of *Culbone* (3 m.), consisting of some cottages and a miniature ch., "situated in as extraordinary a spot as man in his whimsicality ever fixed on for a place of worship," so shut in by woods and hills 1200 ft. high as to be excluded from the sun for 3 months in the year. From Ashley Combe he should also walk or ride up a wooded glen to a farm of Lord Lovelace's called the *Pet*, situated in a gloomy but most imposing amphitheatre, chiselled by some streams from the black hills of the moor. One on foot can scramble to the summit, and return by high road to Porlock, but the path for horses has been lately overwhelmed by a landslip. You should also not forget to walk about 2 m. on the Minehead road for a view of *Holnicote* (Sir T. D. Acland, Bart.). You will there behold a background of the dark mountainous Dunkery, a mid distance of ferny glens and heights most beautifully wooded, and a foreground of slopes rising in graceful undulations from a vale. It is to be sincerely hoped that cultivation will never ascend Dunkery, which now, in its sombre garniture of heather, may well be the delight of the proprietor of Holnicote. This neighbourhood more properly belongs to the *Handbook of Somerset* (in which it is fully described), but it may be added that *Bossington Hill* is traversed by paths which command certainly a far more beautiful though not so extensive a view as Dunkery; and that there is a curious cavern at the sea-point of the hill.

(7) *Exmoor* occupies an area of about 14 sq. m., and is still to a great extent uncultivated—a waste of dark hills and valleys tracked by lonely streams. It attains its greatest elevation on the E., where *Dunkery Beacon* rises 1668 ft. above the sea; but on the W. its hills are of little inferior height, *Chapman Barrows* being 1540 ft., and *Spm Head* 1610 ft. On its borders it is pierced by deep wooded ravines, of which the traveller has a magnificent example in Lyndale. The central part of this region, about 20,000 acres, formed the ancient *Forest of Exmoor*, for which an Act of enclosure was obtained in 1815, when it was purchased by the late John Knight, Esq., of Wolverley Hall, Worcestershire, who proposed converting it to a less interesting but more profitable land of meadows. With this object he encircled the whole forest with a ring fence, and commenced building a castellated mansion at Simonsbath, but this he soon found occasion to abandon, together with many of his projected improvements, for the speculation proved anything but a golden adventure. A considerable acreage has, however, been brought under cultivation, and this is now leased in separate farms by the proprietor of the forest, Mr. Frederick Knight; the principal drawback to success being the strong winds and chilly mists which prevail in so elevated a district. The soil is in general of a fair quality, although the hard sandstones below the soil, being little liable to decompose, are somewhat unfavourable to fertility. Extensive tracts, however, still remain, both in the forest and surrounding highlands, in a state of nature, delighting the eye by the grandeur of their unbroken outline and the rich beauty of their colour; and here, over slopes of heather, interspersed with the dwarf juniper, cranberry, and whortleberry, roams the "Exmoor pony," a breed of the native English horse, carefully preserved by Sir Thomas Acland, and the red forest deer, which still makes its lair in the extensive covers on the

moor-side. This is the only corner of England in which the red deer is still to be found in a thoroughly wild state. A stag is now and then roused on the Quantock Hills, but Exmoor itself is their head-quarters. A very pleasant book on the 'Chase of the Wild Red Deer in the Counties of Devon and Somerset' has been written by C. P. Collyns, Esq. (Longman, 1862), himself a veteran sportsman, resident at Dulverton.

Since the year 1841 the farms on Exmoor have been chiefly under the management of Mr. Robert Smith, the resident agent of Mr. Knight, and under his superintendence upwards of 4000 acres have been let on lease, in addition to the land previously occupied. The water-meadows made by this gentleman are well worth the attention of those interested in agriculture.

But the farmer is now likely to be driven by the miner from his settlement on Exmoor. In 1851 a specimen of the white carbonate of iron was sent by Mr. R. Smith to the Great Exhibition. Its value suggested the expediency of a further search, and this led to the discovery of abundant iron-lodes, including the hæmatites and other ores hitherto supposed peculiar to Staffordshire and S. Wales. Large districts of the moor are now in the hands of three of the principal iron companies in the kingdom, viz. the Ulverstone of Lancashire, and the Dowlais and Plymouth of S. Wales. Their steam machinery is expected to raise about 300,000 tons of iron-ore annually. Two lines for a mineral railway have been surveyed, the one to Porlock, the other to Lynton; but it is not yet determined which will be adopted. A new district ch., erected principally through the exertions of Mr. Knight, was consecrated 1856.

The road from Lynton to Simonsbath ascends Lyndale to Ilford Bridges, and there divides into 4 branches. On rt. one climbs the hill towards Barbrick Mill, and another passes up the valley to *Combe Park*, seat of W. Collard, Esq. Forward, a third runs direct for the heights of the moor, where it joins the fourth, which turns l. from Ilford Bridges, up a ladder-like hill towards Brendon ch. Having ascended to the upper regions (by either of the two roads last-mentioned), the traveller will have *Scob Hill* on his l., a heathery eminence, on which the deer are frequently to be seen in the early morning and evening, and which is said to be a favourite resort of vipers. He will then proceed by a good and easy road along the moor, with a wide extent of wild country opening around him. To the rt. he may observe the hills in which the Barle and the Exe have their fountains; and in whose vicinity are the bogs called the *Black Pits* and *Mole's Chamber* (now cultivated; 4 m. from Simonsbath, and 1 m. from the Black Pits), the last so named from an unfortunate farmer, who was lost in it with his horse when hunting. He will enter the ancient forest, now the property of Mr. Frederick Knight, at *the double gates* across the road. He will there notice the views rt. and l., and also the ring fence, as yet the only intruder (save the road) on the solitary scene. 1 m. l. of the double gates, in a bottom called the Warren, are some remains of a building which was once the stronghold of the *Doones of Badgeworthy*, a daring gang of robbers who infested the borders of the moor at the time of the Commonwealth, and of whom the tradition is still extant. They are said to have been natives of another part of England, and to have entered Devonshire about the time of Cromwell's usurpation. It is certain that for many years they were a terror to the neighbourhood of Lynton, and long succeeded in levying black mail on the farmers,

Route 18.—*Simonsbath*.   Sect. I.

and in escaping with their booty to this lonely retreat, where none dared to follow. At length, however, they committed so savage a murder that the whole country was aroused, and a large party of the peasantry, having armed themselves, proceeded at once to Badgeworthy, and captured the entire gang. This exploit ended the career of the Doones, for they were shortly afterwards tried for their numerous crimes, and deservedly executed. 1½ m. beyond the double gates the traveller will pass the Exe, here a rivulet, draining from a bog called *the Chains*, where the moor is impressively desolate. In another ½ m. he will open to view the valley of the Barle, and begin the long descent upon Simonsbath, the ruinous wall and flanking towers commenced by Mr. Knight skirting the road on the l.

Simonsbath is a solitary settlement in a moorland valley, encircled by some fine old trees, originally planted as shelter to a rough house of entertainment which formerly stood here. The place consists of Mr. Knight's unfinished mansion, now a picturesque ruin, a small house adjoining it, occupied occasionally as a residence by the present lord of Exmoor, a small public-house, and various outbuildings, including the shop of a blacksmith, the yard of a carpenter, and the store of a general dealer. The view is wild. The Barle courses along a valley between swelling moorland hills, and the eye ranges down a vista formed by promontories which successively bend the river from side to side. (*Ring Castle*, an old entrenchment on the river, is traditionally said to have been built by the pixies as a defence against the mine spirits.) *Simon's Bath* itself is a crystal pool on the river, above the house, so called, it is said, from one Simon, a king, who is said to be interred under a large barrow called "Symonsborough," on the Blackdown Hills. (See Rte. 1.) And here the dreamer should be informed that this Simon, in all probability, is no other than King Sigmund of the 'Niebelungen,' well known to the Anglo-Saxons,—for this pool on the Barle is a very suitable place for recalling a "vision of old romance."

The Barle is an excellent trout-stream; although the fish, "though numerous, are not large, and are not yellow-bellied and pink-fleshed as they ought to be, and as the fish are in the neighbouring Badgeworthy and Oare waters."—*G.T.* Tickets are necessary for fishing all these waters; and the angler should inquire at Lynton about them. 2 beds and 2 tickets for the three waters are to be had at Simonsbath; and tickets for the Barle may be had at the Red Deer inn, 2 m. S.E. of that place.

Exmoor is rich in stories of a certain "Faggus" (Fergus?), a robber, who had an "enchanted strawberry horse," which fought for its master with hoof and teeth. Once on Barnstaple Bridge, when they were on the point of taking "Faggus," the horse leaped the parapet, plunged 40 feet down into the water, and swam away. Faggus was at last taken by a "policeman" disguised as a beggarman, who passed a rope through the bacon-rack in a cottage where the robber happened to be resting, and swung him up feet foremost. In the mean time another "policeman" shot the horse in the stable.

The pedestrian—who will find his reward in longer excursions over the wild country of Exmoor—may be told of the following walk, which is recommended in a charming little volume prettily named 'Ferny Combes' (1856). To *Simonsbath*, and thence down the Barle to Landacre Bridge and *Withypool* (*Inn:* Royal Oak); and further down the stream, (about 5 m.), between hills, wild and bare on the one side, beautifully wooded on the other, by *Tor's Steps* (perhaps Thor's Steps), an ancient British bridge formed of huge blocks of stone, fixed as piers and pathway. Then across the hill to *Winsford* (a very good *inn*); and, by a lane just wide enough for a small carriage, to *Exford;* from which a road leads to the top of Porlock Hill. Descend to *Porlock*, and return home by *Culbone* and *Glenthorne.*

The stranger, before he leaves Lynton, should explore the course of the *W. Lyn*, and that remarkable valley opening to the sea at *Heddon's Mouth*, about 6 m. W.; but both may be seen in his route to Combe Martin and Ilfracombe. (A coach runs to Barnstaple, a beautiful drive, daily in summer. According to the charges of postboys, Lynton is 47 m. from Bridgewater, 13 from Porlock, and 20 from Ilfracombe.)

There are three roads by which he can proceed to Ilfracombe from Lynton. Should he select the circuitous and comparatively uninteresting carriage-road, he can visit Combe Martin (about 15 m.), but will travel by *Paracombe* (6 m.), and leave Heddon's Mouth a long way to the N.; and Combe Martin also will escape him, unless he keeps a wary eye on his driver, as it is a common trick with these worthies to forget their orders, and hurry direct from Lynton to Ilfracombe. The other roads are adapted only for horsemen or pedestrians, but are far to be preferred in point of scenery. The first passes through the Valley of Rocks, and by Lee Bay and Woodabay near Martinhoe to Heddon's Mouth and Trentishoe; the second, along the carriage-way by the valley of the W. Lyn, and over a moor, to the same destination, being about ½ m. longer than that by Lee Bay, which is decidedly the most interesting. By either of the latter routes we can reach the superb valley which opens to the sea at

6 *Heddon's Mouth* (the Hunter's *Inn*, a small house at which pedestrians may very well pass a night), enclosed by huge boundaries hung with wood, fern, furze, and heather, and considered by many persons the finest valley in the county. The stranger with time at his command should walk by the side of the stream to the shore at Heddon's Mouth (i. e. the *Giant's* Mouth,—*etin*, A.-S. a giant—the rocks open at the shore like a gigantic mouth), and also ascend to the Parsonage, from which a most charming path will lead him along the hillside to the cliffs, and round the point. Through openings in the wood he will obtain glorious peeps of the deep valley, of the blue sea, and mountain coast of Wales; and, if a botanist, may find among the mosses the *Orpine* or *Livelong*, a large red *Sedum*, rare in England. (The coast at Martinhoe, which the pedestrian will have passed in reaching Heddon's Mouth from Lynton, is the scene of a curious version of a widely-spread legend. Sir Robert Chichester, anciently of Croscombe, in Martinhoe, is said to be compelled, for his sins, to haunt the base of a cliff on the sea-shore. He is condemned to weave traces from the sand, which he is to fasten to his carriage, and then drive up the face of the crag, and through a narrow fissure at the summit, which is known as "Sir Robert's Road.") From the valley of Heddon's Mouth a steep zigzag road rises through pine woods to the hamlet of

Trentishoe, where the diminutive ch., of no great architectural interest, should be noticed. From this place the pedestrian is advised to strike across the hills (on which grows the large trailing *Lycopodium claratum*) direct to Combe Martin, by the

Route 18.—*Combe Martin.* Sect. I.

summits of *Trentishoe Barrow, Holstone Barrow* (alt. 1187 ft.), *Great Hangman* (alt. 1083 ft.), and *Little Hangman*. The most remarkable scene which he will observe by the way is the wild deep glen of *Shercombe*, with loose stones on its precipitous sides, situated between Holstone Barrow and Great Hangman Hill. It is particularly striking when viewed from the sea, and is watered by a small stream which affords nourishment to the *bog pimpernel* and other marsh flowers, and falls over the cliff in a picturesque cascade. The Hangman Hills form a point from which the high land of Exmoor sweeps to the S.E. by a curved line passing by Paracombe, Chapman Barrows (1540 ft.), Span Head (1610 ft.), and North Molton Ridge (1413 ft.). On the descent from Little Hangman, the traveller should observe the variety and beauty of the colours on the cliff. The hill derives its name from the

Hanging Stone, a boundary-mark of Combe Martin parish, and so called, it is commonly said, "from a thief, who, having stolen a sheep and tied it about his neck to carry it on his back, rested himself for a time upon this rock, until the sheep struggling slid over the side and strangled the man." A Hangman's Stone is found in several parts of England—for instance, near Sidmouth, and in Charnwood Forest, Leicestershire—and of all the same wild tale is told; but a connection may be seen between these names and that of Stonehenge, which signifies the Hanging (or uplifted) Stones—*Stane-hengen*, Saxon—and is supposed to have been derived from the imposts, which formed a corona on the outer circle.

6 *Combe Martin.* (*Inn:* King's Arms, commonly known as the Pack of Cards, and bearing no fanciful resemblance to one of those unstable pagodas built by children. It was erected as a marine residence by an eccentric individual who lived some years ago near Barnstaple.) This long irregular village lies in a valley opening to a rocky picturesque bay, and in the reign of Hen. II. belonged to the Norman baron Martyn de Tours, after whom it was called. It is well known for its *silver-lead mines*, which have been worked at intervals from the time of Edw. I. Camden informs us that they partly defrayed the expenses of the French wars of Edw. III., and that Hen. V. also made good use of them in his invasion of France. From that period they seem to have been neglected until the reign of Eliz., when a new lode was discovered and worked with great profit by Sir Beavis Bulmer, Knt., as appears by the following quaint inscription on a silver cup presented by the Queen to William Bourchier, Earl of Bath, when lord of th manor :—

" When water workes in broken wharfes
   At first erected were,
And Beavis Bulmer with his arte
   The waters 'gan to reare,
Disperced I in the earth did lye,
   Since all beginninge olde,
In place called Coombe, where Martyn longe
   Had hydd me in his molde.
I dydd no service on the earth,
   And no man set mee free,
Till Bulmer, by his skille and change,
   Did frame mee this to bee."

Another cup, weighing 137 oz., and, like the former, made of Combe Martin silver, was presented by Elizabeth to Sir R. Martin, Lord Mayor of London. It bore an appropriate inscription, beginning thus :—

" In Martyn's Coombe long lay I hydd,
   Obscured, deprest with grossest soyle,
Debased much with mixed lead,
   Till Bulmer came, whose skille and toyle
Refined me so pure and cleane,
   As rycher no where els is seene."

Mr. Webber, of Buckland House, near Braunton, is in possession of a letter from Charles I. to one of his ancestors, showing that these mines were then considered of importance; but there is no proof of their having been worked in that reign. In more recent times they have been open, as formerly, only at intervals. Some adventurers embarked in them in 1813, and again in 1835, when, after an expenditure of 15,000*l*., a lode was found which promised to be remunerative. The speculation, however, was ultimately abandoned. The lodes occur in beds containing limestone, and immediately under the slates. The mines are 2 in number, the shafts being sunk to the depths of 40 and 102 fath.; the *levels* are driven under the village, and an *adit*, or subterranean passage for drainage, passes under the hotel towards the sea. A *smelting-house* was erected in 1845 at the mouth of the valley, where it forms a picturesque object among the trees. The produce of the Combe Martin mines has been here reduced to plates weighing 1200 and 1800 oz., and the company also smelt a large proportion of the Cornish lead-ores.

The *Ch.* is a most interesting old battlemented building constructed of a rose-coloured stone, the angles of which are as sharp as if recently cut. It is Perp. (nave and aisles) and E. Eng. (chancel), with a very fine Perp. Tower, of the character usual in the best churches of N. Devon (see Intro. *Devon*). Its height is 99 ft. There is a small niche containing a figure on the face of each buttress in the 3rd stage; and a large canopied niche with the patron, St. Peter, above the W. window. Within the ch. remark the screen; an excellent example, though not one of the richest. There are some good paintings of the Apostles on panels at the base. Remark the narrow E. Eng. door on the S. side of the chancel, and the painted tombstones in the churchyard. A hand holding a knife and cutting the stalk of a flower would appear to be a favourite device. In the S. aisle is a mural monument to the memory of — Hancock, wife of Thomas Hancock, " sometime His Majesty's principal sercher (*sic*) in the port of London," with an effigy the size of life exquisitely and elaborately sculptured in white marble. It bears the date 1637. Dame Hancock is represented in the dress of that time, covered with point lace, and looped with knots of riband: she has a pearl necklace round her throat and her hair in curls, and bears some resemblance to the portraits of Henrietta Maria, queen of Charles I. This monument has been restored through the taste and spirit of the present vicar, who has done much for his ch., which is in excellent order.

A curious ceremony, called "Hunting the Earl of Rone," was kept up in Combe Martin till 1837. There were mummers representing — the Earl of Rone, wearing a grotesque mask, a smock-frock, and a string of 12 sea-biscuits round his neck; a hobby-horse, masked, and armed with a "mapper," an instrument shaped like a horse's mouth, with teeth, and able to be opened and shut quickly; a fool, masked; a donkey with a necklace of 12 biscuits; and a troop of grenadiers armed with guns. On Ascension-day the grenadiers marched to Lady's Wood, near the village, and found the "Earl of Rone" hidden in the brushwood. They fired a volley, set him on the donkey with his face to the tail, and thus took him through the village to the sea, joined by the hobby-horse and the fool. At certain stations the grenadiers fired, and the Earl fell from his donkey mortally wounded. The spectators had to contribute blackmail, and if they refused the hobby laid hold of them with his "mapper." An Earl of Tyrone is said (?) to have been taken by soldiers in the Lady's Wood during the Irish rebellion, and to have lived for some time on a string of sea-biscuits which he had taken from the little vessel that landed him on the coast.

Combe Martin Bay is so shut in

by rocks that it might easily be made a harbour, and the idea of converting it to such a purpose has been entertained by the railway company called the North Devon Extension. The pebbles of the beach are burnt into lime; and *laver* is gathered at low tide and eaten in some quantity by the poor of the village. Should the visitor be partial to it and like to seek it for himself, he should know that the *porphyra laciniata* has the finest flavour and is equally common with the green laver. "It is elegantly dotted with closely-set grains of a dark violet-purple in winter and early spring, when the plant is collected for table."—*The Seaside Book.*

In the neighbouring parish of *Berrynarbor* is a farmhouse called *Bowden*, celebrated as the birthplace of *John Jewel*, Bishop of Salisbury' 1522, author of the 'Apology of the Church of England,' which so delighted Queen Elizabeth that she commanded it to be read in every ch. within her kingdom. "So devout in the pew where he prayed," says Fuller, " diligent in the pulpit where he preached, grave on the bench where he assisted, mild in the consistory where he judged, pleasant at the table where he fed, patient in the bed where he died, that well it were if, in relation to him, ' secundum usum Sarum' were made precedential to all posterity." The opponent of Jewel, Thomas Hardyng of Louvain, was born in the neighbouring parish of Combe Martin. Jewel's family had dwelt at Bowden for many generations. The *Ch.* of Berrynarbor contains Norman and E. Eng. portions (nave and chancel), with a Perp. S. aisle, and a very fine Perp. tower 80 ft. high, which perhaps exceeds that of Combe Martin in beauty. Observe the W. window, excellent in its details; the niches and canopies on each side of the 3rd stage; and the pierced battlements with pinnacles. These last are corbelled out over the face of the wall—a peculiar arrangement which, however picturesque, has resulted in reducing the part above the stringcourse to a ruinous state. It is held together by spans of iron. The font is Norm.

Towers of similar character (but not equal) to those of C. Martin and Berrynarbor exist at *Arlington* and *Kentisbury*. These 4 are the finest in the district. Arlington Ch. itself is modern (Gould, architect), the old tower being retained.

In the village of *Berrynarbor*, adjoining the churchyard, the traveller will find the remains of a house orinally built in the reign of Edw. IV., and once decorated externally with elaborate carvings in stone, with friezes and mouldings, and the arms of Plantagenet and Bonville. Nearly all these decorations were removed a few years ago by the proprietor, the late Mr. Basset, to ornament a building in his garden at Watermouth.

The carriage-road from Combe Martin to Ilfracombe (3 m.) passes through Berrynarbor; but one on foot is advised to walk to Ilfracombe along the coast by Watermouth, the distance being nearly the same. Close to Watermouth, on the shore, is

Smallmouth, remarkable for its 2 caverns. The one gives you a peep of the pretty bay of Combe Martin, as "a sun-gilt vignette, framed in jet." The other is entered through a narrow chink, but expanding leads into a pit open to the sky, which is seen through a network of brambles. Hence this cavern has been called *Brier Cave*.

1 *Watermouth* (A. D. Basset, Esq.), a Gothic building commenced about 40 years ago by the father of the present proprietor. The situation is romantic, and the grouping of the neighbouring knolls and ridges strikingly beautiful. The castle stands at the edge of a green basin, little raised above the sea, but screened from it by a natural embankment of rocks.

DEVONSHIRE.   *Route 18.—Ilfracombe.*   185

The richest woods enclose this vale, and a stream runs sparkling through the grass. This beautiful spot is viewed to most advantage from the sea, as the feudal-looking mansion and its verdant pastures are thence seen in connection with the bleak coast of Exmoor and rocks of Ilfracombe. The cove should be visited, for it is a wild and cavernous recess. It is the mouth of the little stream, and one side of it is formed by a hillock popularly known as *Saxon's Burrow*. Between it and Ilfracombe is the ferny dell of *Chamber Combe*.

2½ *Ilfracombe*. (*Inns*: Britannia Hotel; Clarence Hotel; Packet Hotel.) This little watering-place is well known for the picturesque forms of the surrounding hills. But its principal attraction is the coast, which, stamped with a peculiar character by the irregularity of its outline, presents a front of huge dark rocks and chasms. Here there are no ranges of lofty cliffs descending to the sea in mural precipices; but a chain of unequal heights and depressions. At one spot a headland, some 500 ft. high, rough with furze-clad projections at the top, and falling abruptly to a bay; then, perhaps, masses of a low dark rock, girding a basin of turf, as at Watermouth; again, a recess and beach, with the mouth of a stream; a headland next in order: and so the dark coast runs whimsically eastward, passing from one shape to another like a Proteus, until it unites with the massive seafront of Exmoor.

This rocky shore has also interest in another respect. It is a favourite haunt of those wonderful and beautiful forms of life so recently brought to our notice by such men as Gosse, who at Ilfracombe found his *acornshell*, with "its delicate grasping hand of feathery fingers"—his *madrepore*, "translucent, looking like the ghost of a zoophyte"—his *polype*, with "its mimic bird's head" —and his *anemone*, which, cut across transversely, "feeds at both ends at the same time." 'A Naturalist's Rambles on the Devonshire Coast' (Van Voorst) may well be recommended to those who are fond of such pursuits, and who will here find that the tides are very favourable for their purpose, the lowest water of the spring-tides occurring near the middle of the day.

The manor of Ilfracombe has belonged to many noble families and distinguished individuals—the Champernownes, Sir Philip Sidney, the Martyns, Audleys, and Bourchiers, Earls of Bath. The pier was originally built by the Bourchiers, and enlarged in 1829 by Sir Bouchier P. Wrey, Bart., the present lord of the manor.

As a seaport the town was once of some consequence, having contributed 6 ships to the fleet of Edward III., while one only was sent from the Mersey; a fact which is curious as showing the change which time has effected in the relative importance of these harbours. Ilfracombe has been the scene of some historic incidents. In 1644, during the Rebellion, it was taken by a body of horse under Sir Francis Doddington: and in 1685, after the defeat of the Duke of Monmouth at Sedgemoor, Colonel Wade and a number of fugitives here seized a vessel, which they victualled and carried to sea. They were, however, intercepted by a frigate and forced to return. The colonel was afterwards captured near Lynton, but ultimately pardoned.

The *Harbour* is a romantic recess, protected very completely by ramparts of rock. It runs parallel with the shore, from which it is separated by *Lantern Hill* and a stout ridge of slate; whilst *Helesborough*, a headland 447 ft. in height, juts out at the entrance.

On Lantern Hill stands the *lighthouse*, about 100 ft. above the sea, a quaint-looking building for the purpose, and, in fact, an ancient chapel formerly dedicated to St. Nicholas, and the resort of pilgrims, but which probably at all times displayed a light for the guidance of fishermen. A part of it is now fitted as a news-room for the inhabitants and visitors.

The *Ch.*, a venerable structure, in a delightful situation, is of various periods—Norm., Trans., and Dec. The tower, which rises in the centre of the N. aisle, and projects into the ch., is Norm., with Perp. battlements and pinnacles. The corbels in the nave are curious, and the Dec. piscina very good. Here are monuments to the memory of the mother of John Prince, author of the ' Worthies of Devon,' and Capt. Bowen, R.N., who fell in the disastrous attack upon Teneriffe by Nelson. The historian Camden was prebendary of this ch.

The *Baths*, a Doric building erected in 1836, communicate by a tunnel with a part of the shore which was formerly inaccessible from the land except at low water. The cliffs present a picturesque scene, and are pierced with a large cavern called *Crewkhorne*.

In the immediate vicinity of the town you should visit *Lantern Hill; Capstone Hill*, just W. of the harbour, and marked by a flag-staff; the *Sea-walk* round Capstone Hill to a cove called Wildersmouth; the summit of *Helesborough*, alt. 447 ft., crowned with one of those old earthworks called "Cliff-castles," containing nearly 20 acres, and protected on the land side by a double entrenchment. You may ramble from this headland through the village of *Hele* to *Watermouth, Smallmouth,* and *Combe Martin*; and E. of the town, along those irregular furzy hills called the *Seven Tors*. The coast in that direction is very lonely and rugged, and well seen from a sloping tongue of land named *Greenaway's Foot* (½ m. E.),

adjoining which there is a recess with a vertical cliff called the *Lover's Leap*. Here an artist should notice the pink hue and satin lustre of the rocks where faced by the surface of the laminæ, and their inky blackness where broken against the grain. The sea is deep and rolls with grandeur to the shore, while the distant mountains of Wales, the island of *Lundy*, and *Bull Point* on the W., are features in the prospect. Below the Tors is a little cove in which True Maiden-hair grows. It is called *White Pebble Bay*. The Tors are closed, but by payment of a small toll you may obtain admission to the paths.

A botanist may here revel in his delightful pursuit. Hear the authoress of ' *Ferny Combes*' —

"The most striking flowers of N. Devon belong to the coast. The *vernal squill*, the sweet-scented *ladies'-tresses*, and the golden blossoms of the *yellow-wort*, opening only in the sunlight, are to be found near Ilfracombe, as well as the *samphire*, the *sea-lavender*, and the beautiful *wild balm*, a rare plant."

The visitor to Ilfracombe has an opportunity of exploring the finest scenery in the county by a ride to Lynton. He can also make an excursion in a westerly direction to the *Valley of Lee, Rockham, Morthoe*, and the *Woolacombe Sands* (about 6 m. distant). The ch. of Morthoe (4¼ m.), restored 1858, has an E. Eng. chancel, a Perp. nave, and in the S. transept a chapel dedicated to SS. Catherine and Mary Magdalene, founded by Wm. de Tracey, vicar of Morthoe, 1322. His monument is here, with rudely traced effigy, fully vested, and holding a chalice. It was assigned by Camden (but without reason) to the murderer of Becket, and the female figures (SS. Catherine and Mary Magdalene), who also appear on it, were locally said to be his " wife and daughter." The tomb is certainly not his; but there is reason to believe that he lived in this neighbourhood for some time after the murder, and before he made his confession to Bishop Bartholomew of Exeter. His name figures in the local tradition of this district. In the "Crookhorn" cavern, W. of Ilfracombe, he, say the boatmen, "hid himself for a fortnight after the murder, and was fed by his daughter;" and to the Woollacombe sands he was banished "to make bundles of the sand, and wisps of the same." He may be heard howling there on stormy nights. The Truceys were barons of Barnstaple, but according to tradition never prospered after the commission of this crime. Their descendants are supposed to languish under the curse of Heaven, and hence

"All the Traceys
Have the wind in their faces."

You should walk to the end of the Warren, forming the N. point of Morte Bay. There is a magnificent sea-view, with Lundy Island in the distance. Off the point is the *Morte Stone*, the *Rock of Death* (?), on which no less than 5 vessels were lost in the winter of 1852. There is a whimsical saying, that no power on earth can remove it but that of a number of wives who have dominion over their husbands. "A woman's hair," runs the proverb, " can draw more than a yoke of oxen." It is, according to another local saying, "the place which heaven made last, and the devil will take first." *Actinia Aurora* abounds on the Morte Stone in many varieties. On this coast it is only found here, and at Lundy Island. S. of Morthoe are the sands, and

Barricane, a delightful spot, where the beach almost entirely consists of shells, many beautiful and curious. Among the rarer species Mr. Gosse mentions the *wentle-trap*, *elephant's tusk*, *cylindrical dipper*, and *bearded nerite*. The beautiful oceanic "blue snail," *Ianthina communis*, is sometimes washed up alive, and in large quantities. *Villula limbosa*, on which the Ianthina is said to feed during its voyage, is also not uncommon during the summer months.

Steam-packets ply between Ilfracombe and Swansea from May to October, and to Bristol throughout the year. The Cornish boats also call off the harbour on their passage between Hayle, Padstow, and Bristol.

Proceeding to Barnstaple, 2 roads are open to our choice; one direct, 11 m., and another by Braunton, 12½ m. The latter is by far the most picturesque. It climbs in about 2 m. to the high land above Ilfracombe, and descends a long lonely valley, hedged in by wooded hills, which sweep round in crescents, the haunt of owls and echoes. On the rt. is *Curn Top*, where many years ago a Jew pedler was murdered, and where, according to the wild tale, his ghastly head may occasionally be seen moving among the bushes.

8 *Braunton*, situated in a country remarkable for its fertility, and deriving its name from St. Branock, "the King's son of Calabria," who is said to have arrived in England from Italy in the year 300. On the summit of the neighbouring hill are the remains of his chapel, which, the inhabitants aver, is as firm as a rock, and has resisted the efforts of all who have attempted to remove it. The *Ch.* will repay a visit. The width of the roof is imposing, covering the nave, which is without aisles, and the carving is in good preservation. The emblems of the Crucifixion, Apostles, &c., are worked on the seats and the panels of the roof; and on one of the latter a sow with a litter of pigs. These are in allusion to a legend that St. Branock was directed in a dream to build a ch. wherever he should first meet a sow and her family. This interesting party he is said to have

encountered on this very spot, and here, accordingly, he founded the church. The ch. has an E. Eng. chancel, with a Perp. tower in the place of the S. transept. The font is Norm. There are S., W., and N. porches. The original form of this very curious ch. is a problem for the archæologist. "I forbear," says Leland (Itin.) "to speak of S. Branock's cow, his staff, his oak, his well, and his servant Abel, all of which are lively represented in a glass window of that ch." This has long perished.

On the coast, a short way from the village, is the district of blown sand called the *Braunton Burrows*, where there is a *lighthouse* for directing vessels to the entrance of the Taw and Torridge, and the ruins of an old building called *St. Ann's Chapel*. Many curious plants find a congenial soil among these sandhills, particularly the *round-headed club-rush*, one of the rarest in Britain (Gosse). Mr. Gosse also mentions the *small buglos*, the rare *musky stork's-bill*, the *viper's buglos*, the *prickly saltwort*, the *fuller's teazel*, 2 species of *spurge, euphorbia peplus,* and the more uncommon *euphorbia Portlandica*. There is a good example of a *raised beach* between the burrows and Baggy Point, the S. horn of Morte Bay, where the great sea stock is to be found upon the cliffs.

Beyond Braunton the road reaches the river Taw at the farmhouse of *Heanton Court*, once a seat of the Basset family, and in 1¼ m. commands a very pretty view of

4¼ m. *Barnstaple* (see Rte. 17).

From Barnstaple proceed by rail to Bideford, 9 m. (see Rte. 17); thence the distance to Clovelly is 11 m. (If the tourist travels by carriage or on horseback, he must procure at the New Inn a key of the drive, at Clovelly, called the *Hobby*; if on foot, he can step over the gate.)

Proceeding to Clovelly—

4 m. from Bideford, about 1 m. off the road rt., is *Alwington* ch., with a fine Perp. tower of unusual character. It diminishes rapidly from the ground, and is very picturesque. *Parkham* ch., 1 m. farther W., has Norm. font and S. door, and a good Perp. tower.

7 Here, on the rt., one of those wild hollows, so numerous on this coast, descends to *Buckish Mill*, a fishing village, and a pretty object in the view from Clovelly. From the upper end of the village a path leads eastward through a glen, commanding from one point a little patch of sea, which appears as if it had been caught up and imprisoned by the hills.

¼ Turn into the *Hobby* by the gate on the rt. The coast from Buckish Mill to a point not far from the promontory of Hartland is covered by a dense mass of foliage sloping to precipitous cliffs. The *Hobby*, which was a special pet with its late projector and proprietor, Sir J. H. Williams, is an excellent road passing for 3½ m. along this magnificent sea-boundary, winding the whole distance through woods; sweeping inland occasionally to pass shadowy dells, where streams fall to the shore; and commanding at all points extensive views over the Bristol Channel to the Welsh coast. After pursuing it about 2 m. the stranger should look out for Clovelly, which is seen from the Hobby to great advantage.

3¼ *Clovelly.* (*Inn:* New Inn.) It is difficult to describe this remarkable village further than by saying that it is the most romantic in Devonshire, and probably in the kingdom. It is hung, as it were, in a woody nook, to which a paved path slants in zigzags from the gate of the Hobby. But soon this little road has to break into steps, and in this form it descends through the village to the pier, some 500 ft. below. A brawling stream accompanies the stair-flight, and is crossed at one or two places by foot-bridges. The view is superb

Route 18.—*Bideford Bay.*

—the Welsh coast about Milford Haven; Lundy Island, generally more distinct, but sometimes entangled with clouds; and the vast plain of the sea, streaked if it be calm with white watery lanes. Midway in the village is a terrace of about a dozen square yards, commanding the coast E. and W. In the former direction the glen of *Buckish Mill* forms a pretty break in the range of woods and cliffs, while near at hand a small waterfall (called *Freshwater*) tumbles to the shore.

Here the traveller should rest a day at the little inn, which will entertain him with great hospitality. If it happens to be the autumn, he may regale at breakfast upon herrings which have been captured over night; for Clovelly is famed for its fishery, and every evening about sunset the boats may be observed leaving the shore, to *drive* for herrings or mackerel. The night is selected for this kind of fishing, as success mainly depends upon the shoals coming blindly upon the net, when they get entangled by the gills. Moonlight and a phosphorescent sea are therefore unfavourable. In thick weather a Clovelly boat has captured as many as 9000 herrings at a haul; and they are commonly taken here in such numbers as to be sold by the *maise*, which consists of 612 fish, and is valued from 18s. to 25s. Clovelly *Church* has some early portions; and contains a good *brass* to Robt. Cary, 1540.

Bideford Bay, which is well seen from Clovelly, is included between the points of Morte and Hartland, and may remind the traveller of Torbay. It is gracefully girded by cliffs, and a chosen haunt of fish; but it differs from Torbay in being exposed to westerly winds. Clovelly answers to Brixham as the station of the trawlers, and supplies the markets of Bideford and Barnstaple, and even of Bristol and Wales. Pilchards are occasionally taken by the drift-net, but the shore is too rough for their wholesale capture by the seine. They rarely, however, come in shoals so far up the Channel. In the reign of Queen Anne French privateers made so many prizes on this part of the coast, that they are said to have called it the *Golden Bay*.

Travellers who like to build castles by moonlight may frame the most beautiful and airy erections at Clovelly. For this purpose they should seat themselves on the little terrace of the inn, when the village is hushed in repose, the owl hooting in the wood, "the single broad path of glory" on the sea, and the restless tide just heard among the rocks.

The *pier* should be visited by daylight, as it commands a fine view of the coast. It was erected by George Cary, Esq., whose family had possession of the manor as early as the reign of Richard II. The traveller, having gleaned a treasury of recollections at the village, should next proceed to

Clovelly Court, of which an entrance called the Yellaries Gate is at the top of the hill. If unequal to a walk, he will be allowed, under the escort of a guide, to drive round the park; but it is, perhaps, needless to admonish him that by such a lazy course half its beauties will escape him. The richest scenery of this enviable retreat is to be found on the coast, which may be easily explored by excellent paths of gravel and turf. In every part it presents a wilderness of grotesque old oaks and cliffs, and seats are placed in rare nooks and seclusions, where the weather-worn rocks protrude themselves for admiration. All the beauties of this rugged woodland are summed up in the *Deer Park*; and there the mural precipice, whimsically known as *Gallantry Bower*, falls from a height of 387 ft. to the sea. The finest view in the neighbourhood is commanded by the summit. The hills immediately W. are so beautifully grouped that one might suspect nature had been studying the picturesque when she arranged them. Rooted together in the valleys, but rising at various distances in ridges and knolls, they seem to mock the ocean with their waves of foliage. From this, the highest point of the park, the visitor should descend to *Mill Mouth* and the beach, where, at the base of Gallantry Bower, are some fragments of the cliff most curiously curved, the bands of slate resembling the ribs of a ship. They are dark in colour, and one is called the *Black Church Rock*. The coast, from the mouth of the Taw and Torridge to Boscastle, in Cornwall, belongs to the carboniferous formation, which is everywhere remarkable for the contortion of the strata. The view westward from these ruinous old crags shows the sea-front of those hills which appear so charming from the high ground, and you may search far to find cliffs with a more varied outline. At one spot a cascade of some pretension tumbles to the shore, and is no mean addition to the scene.

The mansion of Clovelly Court is a handsome structure erected in 1780: the old house and its gallery of pictures were destroyed by fire. Clovelly is the nearest port to

Lundy Island (*lundi*, Icelandic— a *puffin*), distant about 18 m., so those who have a relish for exploring places seldom visited can here best embark on a trip to Lundy. The island is a wild seclusion, about 3 m. in length by 1 in breadth (1800 acres), " so immured with rocks and empaled with beetle-browed cliffs, that there is no entrance but for friends." In times long past it belonged to a noble family named Morisco, one of whom, says Matthew Paris, having conspired against the life of Hen. III., fled to Lundy and turned pirate, and grievously annoyed the neighbouring coast, until surprised with his accomplices and put to death. Here also, it is said, King Edw. II. endeavoured to shelter himself from his troublesome wife and rebellious barons. But the principal event in the history of Lundy is its capture by a party of Frenchmen in the reign of William and Mary. A ship of war, under Dutch colours, anchored in the roadstead, and sent ashore for some milk, pretending that the captain was sick. The islanders supplied the milk for several days, when at length the crew informed them that their captain was dead, and asked permission to bury him in consecrated ground. This was immediately granted, and the inhabitants assisted in carrying the coffin to the grave. It appeared to them rather heavy, but they never for a moment suspected the nature of its contents. The Frenchmen then requested the islanders to leave the ch., as it was the custom of their country that foreigners should absent themselves during a part of the ceremony, but informed them that they should be admitted to see the body interred. They were not, however, detained long in suspense; the doors were suddenly flung open, and the Frenchmen, armed from the pretended receptacle of the dead, rushed with triumphant shouts upon the astonished inhabitants and made them prisoners. They then quickly proceeded to desolate the island. They hamstrung the horses and bullocks, threw the sheep and goats into the sea, tossed the guns over the cliffs, and stripped the inhabitants even of their clothes. When satisfied with plunder and mischief they left the poor islanders in a condition most truly disconsolate. During the Rebellion Lundy Island was held by Lord Saye and Sele for the king. From the middle of the last centy. it has belonged to different families in succession, and in 1840 was sold for 9400 guineas. It is now the property of Wm. Heaven, Esq. On the highest point of the island is a Trinity Board lighthouse, with a revolving higher light, and a fixed lower one. To the geologist Lundy possesses considerable interest as affording sections at the junction of the granite and slate; the former rock predominating in the island, the latter appearing at the southern end. The cliff scenery is wild and sombre, and the shore girdled by a number of insular rocks. On the S. side, adjoining the landing-place, are *Lamatry* and *Rat Island* (the latter is one of the few remaining citadels of the *Mus rattus*, or aboriginal black rat, once lord and master of its race throughout Europe. The *mus decumanus* crossed the Volga in 1727, and in 1730 crossed the Channel. They have nearly exterminated their predecessors). On the E. the *Knoll Pins, Gannets, Seals,* and *Gull rocks;* on the N. the dangerous reef of the *Hen and Chickens,* a submarine prolongation of the island; and a pyramidal fragment called the *Constable,* because, overlooking the shore, it seems to keep watch like a sentinel. On the S.W. point is a singular chasm, called the *Devil's Limekiln,* having an outlet to the sea, like the Frying-pan in Cornwall; and a rock opposite the opening, which, it is said, would exactly fit it, and is for that reason named the *Shutter.* The antiquities consist of the ruins of *Morisco's Castle* and a *chapel* dedicated to St. Ann. Other curiosities are a building at the northern extremity of the island called *Johnny Groat's House,* and near the southern end the *lighthouse,* elevated 567 ft. above the sea, and erected in 1819. Lundy is a favourite resort of the Gannet or Channel Goose, and during the breeding season the cliffs are alive with various species of sea-birds. The island is quite treeless. The great and especial charm of Lundy is "the perfect purity and freshness of colour which surrounds one on every side. In few other places does one see such delicate purples and creamy whites as the fragrant Lundy heather exhibits; such pure greens, and yellows, and orange tints as those of the Lundy furze-brakes; and such vivid, sparkling whiteness as that of the granite peaks which crop out continually among the varying undulations of richest verdure."—*G. T.* The *Actinia Aurora* has one of its N. Devon *habitats* here, the other being on the Morte Stone (see the present Route, *ante*). It flourishes here in vast colonies among the slates of the southern coast, double and treble the size of the Morte specimens, and of every colour and variety. Other anemones also are frequent.

Proceeding on our route from Clovelly—

At *Clovelly Cross,* where we rejoin the high road, are the remains of an ancient camp, now known as *Clovelly Dikes,* or *Ditchen Hills.* It is an earthwork of considerable size, circular in form, and encompassed by 3 great trenches about 18 ft. deep. This very remarkable camp commands the only ancient practicable post-road in the N.W. of Devon. With this exception the road to Hartland has little interest. The pedestrian can pursue a more agreeable but longer route through the park of Clovelly Court, and by the coast and Hartland Point to the mouth of Hartland valley, whence he can walk inland to the town of that name.

Hartland Point (alt. 350 ft.), called the Promontory of Hercules by Ptolemy, and Harty by Camden, occupies the angle at which the Devonshire coast strikes to the S.W., and is opposite to a distant Welsh headland, from which the cliffs of Wales trend to the N. It forms, therefore, the boundary of the old "Severn Sea," the Channel here expanding its jaws as if to receive the rolling waves and clearer water of the Atlantic. It is singular in its shape, projecting in a ridge about 370 ft. from the neighbouring cliff; the summit being craggy where it abuts upon the mainland, but for a distance of 250 ft. a flat and grassy platform, of an average width of 30 ft., and bounded by sheer precipices of 300 ft. The view of the coast-line on either side of Hartland Point is magnificent. Inland, Hartland Abbey is seen stretching across the vale, with the lofty ch.-tower on the hill above it.

In a recess a little W. of this promontory you may find a concave rock, so curved and smooth as to bear no fanciful resemblance to the interior of a vessel stranded on the shore. You may squeeze yourself at low water through an adjoining headland by means of a chink in which the sea "blows" at a certain state of the tide, and in another chasm look through a natural chimney at the sky; and this headland itself is well worth examining by those who visit Hartland, and may be recognised as separated by a valley from the high land, and as forming a point at which the coast makes a sharp turn to the southward. The shore towards Hartland Quay presents a scene most wild and dismal, and affords striking examples of arched and otherwise contorted strata. It is everywhere cumbered by ruinous walls of rock at right angles to the sea; the cliffs are ribbed with bars of red schist, but the dreary chaos is in a measure enlivened by cascades which leap from above.

5 (from Clovelly) *Hartland Town* — so called to distinguish it from *Hartland Quay*—(*Inn*: King's Arms, countryfied and good), a retired place situated 2 m. from the sea, at the head of the wooded vale of Hartland Abbey, which, with the old Abbey-ch., the promontory of Hartland, and the neighbouring coast, are the objects of interest. The parish is said by Leland to have derived its name "from the multitude of stags."

Hartland Abbey (Sir G. S. Stucley, Bart.), one of the best-endowed and most considerable in Devonshire, is said by Risdon to have been founded by Githa, the wife of Earl Godwin and mother of Harold, in honour of St. Nectan, who, she believed, had preserved her husband from shipwreck in a dangerous storm. Githa's foundation was for secular canons, who were replaced by Augustinians, temp. Hen. II., under the auspices of Wilfrid de Dinham. At the Dissolution, the Abbey, valued at 306*l.* a year, was granted to Wm. Abbot; and passed through various hands into those of the Buck family about 1824. St. Nectan, to whom the abbey was dedicated, is said to have been the son of a Welsh "kinglet." His relics were preserved here. The present mansion was built about 70 yrs. ago, after the plan of the ancient abbey, of which the (E. Eng.) cloisters were preserved in part as an ornament for the basement story. The house contains old carving and pictures, and is situated in a delightful seclusion. It is begirt by woods, in which the fern tribe grow luxuriantly, particularly *L. dilatata*.

The parish *Church* of Hartland (1¼ m. W.), dedicated to St. Nectan, is an exceedingly interesting building, and has recently undergone a careful restoration by Sir Geo. and Lady Elizabeth Stuckley. Nave, aisle, and chancel are late Dec. The tower is Perp., with a very fine arch opening to the ch. The tower is 111 ft. high, plain, with the exception of a niche on the E. side, in which is a figure of St. Nectan. The *screen*, extending across the whole ch., is nearly perfect; it is early Perp., and one of the best examples in the N .of Devon. The cradle roofs are good, and that in the N. chancel aisle has the bosses gilt and panels painted. The carved oak pulpit, with its canopy, should be noticed; and upon it the figure of a tusked goat, and the inscription

"God save King James Fines"—the word fines and the goat have puzzled the brain of the antiquary. The Norman font is sculptured with quaint faces looking down upon other quaint faces on the pedestal; the group (according to the Rev. Mr. Hawker of Morwenstow) being emblematical of the righteous looking down upon the wicked. There is a Norm. door on N. side of the ch. The oldest monument in the ch. bears date 1610, and is on the rt. of the E. window; a brass to Anne Abbott is of 1611. The visitor will also notice on the wall l. of the altar an inscription to the memory of a Cavalier. In the ch.-yard the visitor will remark the singularly broad slabs of stone which are used as stiles; and by the chancel door the tomb of one Docton, bearing a quaint inscription, beginning, "Rejoice not over me, oh my enemie." The sexton will tell you that the stone was once surrounded by a brass rim inscribed with the following verse:—

"STOKE ST. NECTAN, HARTLAND.

Here lies I at the chancel door;
Here lies I because I'se poor.
The further in, the more 's to pay;
But here lies I as warm as they."

The tomb, however, gives the lie to the assertion of poverty, and the lines may in fact be seen elsewhere (as at Kingsbridge). The view over the valley and sea from the church-tower is very striking. From the ch. the stranger is recommended to pay *Hartland Quay* a visit, and to walk to the end of the valley, where he may gain some idea of the dreariness which characterises the coast of the carboniferous formation. He should descend upon the rocks for a view of the cliffs, with their black and rusty bands of slate, and remarkable contortions. On the W. rises *St. Catherine's Tor*, a conical hill connected with its neighbours by a massive ancient wall; and on its summit have been discovered the foundations of a Roman building.

There are many beautiful scenes here on the coast, in a district little visited and thinly inhabited. In *Milford Valley*, to the W., a lively rivulet seeks the beach in a series of falls. It first leaps 100 ft., then falls again and again, and at last joins the sea. " Neither will the lover of the beautiful think lightly of the valley and mouth of *Welcombe*, or the glen of *Marsland*, whose winding stream, filled with excellent but small trout, separates Devon and Cornwall."— *Ferny Combes.*

ROUTE 19.

TAUNTON TO LYNMOUTH AND LYNTON, BY WATCHET, DUNSTER, AND PORLOCK.

This is by far the most striking approach (though not the easiest, which is by the N. Devon Rly. to Barnstaple, and thence by coach) to Lynmouth. The tourist will proceed from Taunton to Watchet by rly. (14¼ m.), and may post thence to Lynmouth through Porlock. (The distance from Watchet to Lynmouth is 24 m.) The pedestrian will find resting-places at Dunster, at Minehead, and at Porlock. The whole of the road from Dunster to Lyn-

[*Dev. & Corn.*]

mouth is full of beauty and interest; and the prospects are among the grandest in the W. of England.

The rly. from Taunton to Watchet (14½ m.) passes under the Quantock Hills, and has stats. at Bishop's Lydeard, Crowcombe, Heathfield, Stogumber, and Williton.

Watchet (*Inn:* the New London) is a place of no great interest, its principal business being the transportation of iron-ore to Wales. The shore is flat, but rocky. The remains of the Cistercian Abbey of Cleeve (about 2 m. from Watchet), founded by Wm. de Romana, Earl of Lincoln, in the reign of Hen. II., are worth a visit.

The tourist should proceed to Dunster by *Blue Anchor* (2 m.), a small watering-place commanding a beautiful view. Around the alluvial plain to the W. of it, the hilly ranges circle in amphitheatrical order, wild and heather covered, sweeping in undulating outline from Minehead to the Quantocks. In advance of them rises the tower-crowned cone of Dunster, and through the vista of the valley of Avill looms the giant Dunkery. Alabaster occurs here on the shore, in irregular veins, and is collected and ground for cement.

A road runs direct from Blue Anchor to

3½ m. *Dunster* (*Inn:* Luttrell Arms). Dunster is a good centre for a few days' stay, the places of interest accessible from here being— the Castle, Grabhurst Hill, Cleeve Abbey, Blue Anchor, Minehead, Porlock, Culbone, and Dunkery Beacon. (The greater part of these places will be found fully described in the *Handbook for Somerset*.) The inn is a 16th centy. house. The ch., Perp., with some monuments of Mohuns and Luttrells, worth notice, in its chancel. Dunster Castle, the ancient seat of the Mohuns, and of the Luttrells from the reign of Hen.

VII., is shown during the absence of the family (the grounds are always to be seen). It dates almost entirely from the year 1580, the great gateway alone being as old as Edw. III. The castle was taken by the Marquis of Hertford in 1643, and afterwards by Admiral Blake. The view from the site of the ancient keep is fine; but not so fine as that from Grabhurst Hill, or Conygar, the flank of which we descend, toward

2½ m. *Minehead* (*Inns:* Duke of Wellington; Feathers), a pleasant little watering-place, with a lovely neighbourhood. In the ch. is the supposed monument of Bracton (Judge temp. Hen. III., and famous for his treatise on the Common Law of England), born at Bratton Court, about 1 m. W. of Minehead. There is a fine view from the hill above the upper town.

The drive from Minehead to Porlock is one of the most beautiful in Somersetshire. On each side of the road rise hills of varied outline, covered with fern and heather; whilst the rugged valley charms by its abundant woods, grouped over broken ground, and mingled with corn-fields. Cottages and homesteads here and there peep through the trees with a gabled roof or latticed window, and the hedgerows glitter with the bright leaves of the holly, which abounds throughout the district. At

2½ m. we pass the hamlet of *Holnicote* (Holne, hollyne = holly); and l. the park of Holnicote (Sir T. D. Acland, Bart.), of which the mansion was burnt in 1799. Its timbered slopes are seen in connection with the huge side of Dunkery, and a middle distance of hollow wooded glens. Let no artist sleep over this part of the road. From Holnicote the traveller descends into the vale of Porlock, and soon crosses a mountain-stream, the *Horner*, which flows from Dunkery by a romantic valley. It is a wild, noisy spirit, so named from the British *hwrnwr*, the Snorer.

2 m. *Porlock* (*Inn:* the Ship, a humble but most hospitable house, its entrance garnished with the antlers of the red deer). The village is picturesque, standing in a fertile vale about 1 m. from the sea, in an amphitheatre of hills formed by the dark masses of Exmoor. The ch. contains some monuments of interest. Dunkery and Bossington Beacons, and the hamlet of Culbone, are the chief places to be visited from Porlock. Dunkery (1668 ft. above the sea) is the highest point of Exmoor and of Somersetshire. (The walk to its summit is about 4 m. from Porlock.) The Malvern Hills, and the crests of Dartmoor toward Plymouth are both said to be visible from Dunkery on a clear day. The view from *Bossington* (801 ft.) is more beautiful though not so extensive. *Culbone*, 3 m. from Porlock, is a most romantic hamlet, with the tiniest of churches, on a plain of about ¼ of an acre in extent, 400 ft. above the beach, and hemmed in by wooded hills rising to a height of 1200 ft. (See these places further noticed in Rte. 18—Excursion from Lynmouth.)

A rough but very romantic road runs from Porlock to Countesbury (2 m. from Lynton), by Culbone and Glenthorne; it will be the best for the pedestrian.

The carriage-road ascends Porlock Hill into the moor, winding upwards and commanding magnificent views (the finest perhaps in the district) in its ascent. (The tourist should look out for this great view, which is thoroughly Alpine.) 7 m. from Porlock we reach the boundary of Devon and Somerset—a fence and gate intended to keep the half-wild sheep and ponies in their respective counties; rt. is the camp of *Oldbarrow*; and far below, in a deep dell by the sea, *Glenthorne* (see Rte. 18). 3 m. farther we reach *Countesbury*; and then descend rapidly toward the gorge of

1½ m. Lynmouth (see Rte. 18).

ROUTE 20.

BAMPTON TO HOLSWORTHY, BY SOUTH MOLTON AND TORRINGTON.

(Bampton and Dulverton will be most easily approached by the rly. now (1865) in progress from Taunton to Barnstaple. At present Tiverton is the nearest accessible point by rly.)

BAMPTON (*Inn:* White Horse) is a small secluded town embedded among hills in a singularly beautiful country. It is 7 m. from Tiverton Stat., by 2 roads, the new and the old, but on these the only public conveyance is a van 3 times a week. The objects of interest in the immediate neighbourhood are the *limestone quarries*, the view of the town and valley from *Bampton Wood* (W. side of the old Tiverton road), and the scenery of the first mile of the *Wiveliscombe road:* at a little distance, *Pixton Park*, the mountain town of *Dulverton*, the border of *Exmoor*, and, on this, the hill of *Haddon Down* (5 m. N.E., and 1140 ft. high), which people often visit for the sake of the view. For

K 2

the sportsman there is trout-fishing on the Exe and Barle, and stag and fox hunting, in the proper season, round Dulverton.

Bampton is principally known for its 4 great fairs, which are held in the months of March, June, October, and November. At these times it presents an interesting scene, and is a busy market for cattle, sheep, and Exmoor ponies. With respect to the ponies, the stranger should look well to his purchase. It is a common trick to offer, as a colt, a wild animal which has never been troubled with saddle or bridle, but which is, nevertheless, the mother of a numerous offspring. 14,000 sheep have been brought to the Oct. fair, which is the largest, and held on the last Thursday of that month.

Bampton had formerly a *castle*, (which Richard Cogan had a licence to castellate in 1336) which stood on a fir-crowned knoll on the Wiveliscombe road, at the E. end of Castle Street. This knoll is now called *the Mount*. It belongs to Mr. Badcock, and near it are some very fine beeches, particularly one called *the Beechentree*. At the W. end of Castle Street is the *Ch.*, a Dec. (chancel) and Perp. (nave) building, with carved roof and screen (neither very fine), and fragments of stained glass. You should see the view from the churchyard, where you may seat yourself on stone benches, built around 2 aged yews, whose chinks are filled in with masonry. At *Petton*, in this parish, is a small chapel (a simple parallelogram) of E. Eng. date, with a rude Dec. roof S. of the town is a picturesque hillside, the leading feature of the valley. It is a rugged escarpment, formed by the refuse of *limestone-quarries*, which have been worked for many years, and supply the neighbouring country as far as S. Molton. There are in all about 15 quarries, each with a name, and each with a kiln ; but some have 2 kilns. One of the most worth seeing and easiest of access is *Karsdon*,

on the E. side of the old Tiverton road. In this is a wall of solid rock, dipping N. and E., but nearly vertical. In other quarries the strata may be observed in a different position, and in some curved and contorted. The limestone is in colour a delicate blue and pink, and appears to be identical with those of Plymouth and Torquay. The quarries command an excellent view of the town.

Bampton is noticed by early historians. The Saxon Chronicle informs us that in the year 614 Cynegils, King of the West Saxons, here (if the Beamdune of the Chronicle represents this place) fought a furious battle with the "Wealas" or Britons, when the latter were defeated with a heavy loss. The principal seats in the neighbourhood are *Combehead*, H. Badcock, Esq.; *Pixton Park*, Earl of Carnarvon, but rented by Fenwick Bissett, Esq.; *Wonham*, J. Collins, Esq.; *Timewell House*, John Bere, Esq.; *Lower Timewell House*, Rev. R. Bere; *Stoodleigh Court*, T. Daniel, Esq.; *Stockeridge*, also the property of Mr. Daniel; and, in the parish of Hockworthy, the old mansion of *Hockworthy Court Hall*, Godfrey Webster, Esq. The ch. of *Clayhanger*, 4½ m. E., has an ancient screen.

Every visitor to Bampton should extend his ramble to *Dulverton*, a romantic little town, 5 m. distant, under the heights of Exmoor, and in the county of Somerset. If bound to Lynton, he can post to his destination from Tiverton or Exeter, by way of Bampton and Dulverton, and through Exmoor Forest, passing for a short distance over the turf of the moor. This route is frequently selected by travellers ; and for those fond of scenery a more delightful one cannot be chosen. The road to Dulverton passes by one long ascent and descent to Exbridge. At the top of the ascent is *Combehead*, H. Badcock, Esq., a charming seat, embosomed in woods, and overlooking many huge hills and deep valleys. The house is partly seen on the l. The descent to Exbridge affords a view of the country rising to Exmoor, and immediately in front of a remarkable hill dividing the valleys of the Barle and the Exe, which flow united under Exe bridge in a turbulent river 40 or 50 ft. broad.

Exbridge (*Inn*: Blue Anchor), 2½ m. from Bampton, is a small hamlet in a broad vale or basin, and favourite head-quarters with the angler. Both the Exe and the Barle abound with trout. The traveller should notice the view from the bridge. About 1 m. beyond it the road enters a valley covered with trees as far as the eye can reach. This is *Pixton Park*, property of Herbert Earl of Carnarvon. Here the traveller is shaded by oak and beech, and in close proximity to the Barle, which will be seen between the trunks of the trees. Towards the close of day he may expect a salute from one of the largest rookeries in the kingdom, and on the opposite hill, in the park, is one of the largest heronries.

Dulverton (*Inns*: Red Lion; Lamb; White Hart), 5 m. from Bampton, in an amphitheatre of hills, which are wooded in large covers for the red deer. An impetuous torrent, the Barle, dashes past the town under a bridge of 5 arches, and running noisily over ledges of rock escapes from the basin by the narrow entrance, where the woods of Pixton Park climb the slopes, and the house frowns from a height, like a castle defending the pass. Dulverton is a one-sided place. It is situated in a cul-de-sac of hills bounded N. by the great waste of Exmoor. It is therefore of no commercial importance. There is a *silk factory* on the river, but it is worked but leisurely. The land in the neighbourhood is poor, and oats, sheep, and cattle its principal produce. To an artist or sportsman Dulverton has many attractions. The scenery is beautiful; the trout-fishing free to the public as far as the border of the forest; the stag and fox hunting on Exmoor of a very peculiar and exciting description. The wild deer are hunted every season, the hounds being kept either at Dulverton or Lynton; but they are by no means so numerous as they were some years ago, when they abounded in the covers near the town, and were frequently to be seen from the churchyard. Their antlers and skins will be observed in the inn.

At Dulverton you should notice the views from the churchyard and bridge. You should walk down the path below the bridge, and explore the upward course of the river; and, above all, you should ascend to an open spot called *Mount Sydenham*, in a wood above the church. The prospect it commands is truly most magnificent. Towards the N. you will look up the valley of the Barle—a wild and solitary valley, where no road has yet penetrated beyond a certain point. Its sides are the wooded covers of the red deer; the heights above them naked heaths. You will command the windings of the river in long perspective for many miles. A short but delightful excursion is to ascend *Catford's Lane* to Mount Sydenham (a rocky platform at the top of the hill, l. of the path), and to *Higher Combe*, a hunting-box of Sir Thomas Acland's, and return by the Barle. This will give you some idea of the indescribable beauty of the moorland glens. You will gain views over the greater part of Devon and Somerset, and behold the mountainous chain of Dartmoor on the distant horizon.

Those who are bound to Lynton may post to it from Dulverton, over the forest, but they will find the road hilly, and in some parts bad. For an equestrian or pedestrian it is an interesting route; for a carriage preferable one would be by the Dunster road, as far as *Timberscombe*, a drive of great beauty. From Timherscombe a cross road leads to Porlock. The distance by the forest from Dulverton to Lynton is 23 m. (charged 26 post), an easy walk in a summer's day. *Red Deer* is the halfway house, and a good road runs from Red Deer by *Simonsbath* to Lynton. Simonsbath is a wild spot, 2 m. from Red Deer, and 9 m. from Lynton (see Index).

From the centre of Dulverton the huge fir-clad hill on the W. is a prominent object, rising high above the roofs. It is called *Part of Ibbb's*, in accordance with a whimsical nomenclature common in the town. Thus one house is called Part of Kennaway's, another the Huntsman's House.

Near Dulverton are *Combe*, an old mansion 1 m. S. (John Sydenham, Esq.); *Hollam House* (Miss Brague), just above the town; and *Barons Down* (Stuckley Lucas, Esq.). Dulverton is 17 m. from Dunster, a beautiful drive; 15 m. from S. Molton, post, and rather more by an ancient trackway, which passes, 5 m. N.W., *Tor's Steps*, a very wild but most charming spot, where a series of rude stones cross the Barle. There are ironmines on Exmoor, and lead-mines near *Molland*, in the adjoining county. The principal landowners are the Earl of Carnarvon and Sir Thomas D. Acland, Bart., whose seat in Somerset is Holnicote, near Minehead; in Devon, Killerton, near Exeter. The hill above Hollam commands one of the finest views in the neighbourhood.

The *church* of Dulverton has been recently restored. The town, says Fuller, was the birthplace of *Humphrey Sidenham*—"Silver-tongued Sidenham"—an eloquent preacher, who died 1650.

Proceeding on our route from Bampton, we pass W. through a country of little interest to

18 *South Molton* (see Rte. 17, where *North Molton* is also described). Proceeding on this route, we reach

5 m. rt. *Chittlehampton* (see Rte. 17); and then, after crossing
2 m. *Umberleigh Bridge*,
1 m. *Atherington* (Rte. 17),
6 m. beyond is
Torrington (Rte. 17).

[The market town of *Hatherleigh* (*Inns*: George; London Inn) is 11 m. S. of Torrington, on the high road to Plymouth. It is situated on an outlying patch of new red sandstone, but in a barren country, where the cold and unfruitful soil has retarded changes which have elsewhere occurred for the benefit of the community, and—

" The people are poor as Hatherleigh Moor,
And so they have been for ever and ever.'

Beside these, which are said to be local rhymes, others are frequently repeated:—

"I, John of Gaunt,
Do give and do grant
Hatherleigh Moor
To Hatherleigh poor
For evermore."

The *church* is Perp., and has remains of a fine screen, and of an oak ribbed roof, of which the wall plate is richly carved. *Nath. Carpenter*, the mathematician, was born near Hatherleigh, in the parsonage-house of *North Lew*, 1588. His ' Opticks,' says Fuller, would have been a masterpiece if perfectly printed. But to his grief he found the preface casing Christmas pies in his printer's house, and could never afterwards recover it from his scattered notes. All the seats in N. Lew Ch. are good and open, with carved work (emblems of the Passion, &c.) on the panels. On one is the date 1537.]

Proceeding again from Torrington:—

5 rt. 1 m. is a large square entrenchment, called " Henbury Fort," and probably Roman; it is made by 2 banks, with a ditch between them;

and 1 m. further N. (E. of *Buckland Brewer*) a smaller work of a similar shape in a wood.

3½ *Woodford Bridge*, where the road crosses the Torridge, here flowing towards the S.E.

7½ *Holsworthy* (*Inns*: White Hart; Stanhope Arms), a town about 9 m. from Bude Haven, and 3 m. from the Tamar, the boundary of the county. The *Labyrinth*, formed of beech-trees, planned and laid out by Lord Mahon in 1821, is the only thing to be seen in it. Earl Stanhope is the lord of the manor. In the neighbourhood are many interesting churches, such as those of *Bridgerule*, *Launcells*, and *Kilkhampton* (see *Cornwall*, Rte. 25). These, for the most part, are of Early Perp. date, and contain some old and curious woodcarving. The emblems of the Passion are generally represented on the bench-ends. The 30 pieces of silver appear as 3 lines of circular dots, 10 in each. In the direction of Hatherleigh are the ancient seats of *Dunsland*, W. B. Coham, Esq.; *Coham*, W. B. Coham, Esq.; and *Burdon*, near High Hampton, C. Burdon, Esq., in whose family it has remained since the reign of Richard I.

[Hatherleigh and Holsworthy will be accessible by the rly. to Bude Haven, in connection with the Okehampton line. There will also be a branch to Torrington, and thence to Barnstaple. (See the course of these rlys., now, 1865, about to be commenced, on the map.)]

SECTION II.
CORNWALL.

ROUTES.

ROUTE	PAGE	ROUTE	PAGE
21. *Launceston* to Truro, by Bodmin. (Road: over the Bodmin and Goss Moors, Brown Willy and Roughtor; Hantergantick, Dozmare.)	201	25. Plymouth to *Bude Haven*, by Saltash, *Callington*, Launceston, and *Stratton*. (The Coast from Bude to Morwenstow.)	270
22. Launceston to Truro, by *Camelford*, *Wadebridge*, and *St. Columb*. (The North Coast. *Boscastle*; *Tintagel*; *Delabole Quarries*; *Padstow*; the Vale of *Mawgan*; *Newquay*.)	212	26. Truro to *Falmouth*, by *Penryn*. (Falmouth *Harbour* and *Inlets*).	280
23. Plymouth to *Truro*, by *Saltash*, *St. Germans*, *Liskeard* (the *Cheesewring*, *St. Neot's*), *Bodmin*, *Lostwithiel* (*Restormel*), *St. Blazey*, and *St. Austell*. [Cornwall Railway.] (*Perranzabuloe*; *Perran Round*; *the Coast*)	230	27. Truro to *Penzance*, by *Redruth* (*Portreath*, *Carnbrea*), *Camborne*, and *Hayle* (*Lelant*, *Ludgvan*). *Mount's Bay*, *Madron*.	285
24. Plymouth (*Rame Head*) to Falmouth, by *Looe*, *Fowey*, and St. Austell. (The South Coast.)	261	28. Truro to Penzance, by *Helston* and *Marazion*. The *Lizard*. (The Coast from Helston to Penzance.)	300
		29. Excursions from Penzance. (*St. Michael's Mount*, *St. Ives*, *Gurnard's Head*, *Cape Cornwall*, *Land's End*, *Lamorna Cove*, *Scilly Islands*.)	315

ROUTE 21.

LAUNCESTON TO TRURO, BY BODMIN. (ROAD: OVER THE BODMIN AND GOSS MOORS. BROWN WILLY AND ROUGHTOR; HANTERGANTICK, DOZMARE.)

Launceston is generally reached from Plymouth by rly. as far as Tavistock (DEVONSHIRE, Rte. 13), and thence by road (12 m.) through Milton Abbot. This is a pleasant road, commanding some picturesque scenery. An omnibus (meeting certain of the trains) now runs from Tavistock to Launceston; but the rly. is nearly completed to the latter place, following the valleys of the Tavy, the Lyd, and smaller rivers. When the rly. from Crediton (Yeoford, see Rte. 17) to Okehampton (and Lidford, where it will join the line from Tavistock) is completed, Launceston will be easily reached from Exeter by that route. The distance from Okehampton is 18 m.

Launceston (*Inns*: White Hart; King's Arms. Pop. in 1861, including St. Thomas's and St. Stephen's,

K 3

4489) is situated in a fertile district, and about 2 m. from the rt. bank of the Tamar. It was anciently called *Dunheved—Sax.* " Hill-head," or, the " top of the hill." (The word occurs elsewhere. Bishop Stapledon dates a letter from " Dounheved juxta Shaftesburi "—now Donhead.) Its modern name, a corruption of *Lan-cester-ton,* signifies the *Church-Castle-town,* or *enclosure* of the castle town; *Lan* being an enclosure —*i. e.* set apart or sacred to some particular purpose; and as the churches were probably the first enclosures thus set apart, the word became identified with them.

The objects of curiosity are the castle, the ch., and some trifling remains of an old priory; in the neighbourhood — Werrington Park, Endsleigh, and Trecarrel, once the seat of an ancient and now extinct Cornish family of the same name.

The *Castle* is one of three at present standing in this part of the country; the others being Trematon, near St. Germans, and Restormel, near Lostwithiel. These castles have many features in common, especially the high circular keep. They differ at once from the existing remains of earlier Norm. fortresses, and from those of the Edwardian period; and date, in all probability, from the long reign of Henry III. The circular keeps of Totnes and Plympton, in Devonshire, may be compared.

The height of Dunheved gradually declines and narrows towards the N.; and near its point, but still high above the river Kensey, a natural knoll of trap rock has been scarped down, and terraced. Upon the summit, 100 ft. above the river, is a circular keep tower, 18 ft. diameter inside, and the walls of which are about 12 ft. thick. Around this, leaving a passage perhaps 10 ft. broad, forming the "chemin de ronde," is a concentric wall, placed like a coronal upon the cap of the hill. Around and outside it is a narrow walk, possibly once defended by a parapet. All this part of the castle is very late Norman.

The inner tower had a ground-floor and two stories. The door is on the N. side, and is the only opening of any kind into the lower chamber, which probably was for stores. This chamber was lofty, and had a boarded roof, which formed the floor of the 1st story.

On the l. of the entrance passage a stair formed in the thickness of the wall led to the first floor, and in its way winds half round the circle. It is dark, having no windows. The first floor was just clear of the outer wall, and had 2 windows, on opposite sides. The stair enters at the side of one of these, and passing through the opposite side ascends, also in the wall, to the second floor. The first floor, on which was the principal apartment, has a chimney-piece and hearth on the N. side. The roof of this, and the floor of the upper story, were of wood. Much of the wall at this elevation is destroyed, but it is evident that the stair ran on to the upper story, and thence to the battlements, now wanting. The walls gather in, dome-like, with the 2nd floor roof. This tower is very plain, but its entrance arch (the present one is on the ancient pattern), and passage, and stair have all pointed (Trans. Norm.) arches. The fireplace is mutilated, but its side joints and corbels are decidedly Norman.

The annular wall has a southern entrance, therefore not opposite to that within. On the l. from the entrance a passage in the wall leads to the battlements. Towards the N.E. there has been a "Garderobe" in the wall, with a sewer and loophole; above also there appears to have been a sewer. The top of this annular wall is on a level with the first floor of the tower, and the joist-holes round the exterior of the latter show the space between to have been roofed with timber. The base of this wall, out—

side, batters, and at the top of the slope is a bold well-cut cordon of stone. The tower is rent by a slight fissure, and tilted up towards the W. side. The annular wall is rent, but not tilted. It seems, therefore, probable that the tower held together, and so was lifted bodily by the power which has evidently been used, whereas the wall gave way. All the work is rudely built of slate, with very little ashlar remaining.

These 2 buildings crown the knoll, and, from the outer entrance, stairs descend the steep to a gate-tower at the base of the mound. These stairs and a part of the wall are modern, but it is evident that there was always a stair here covered by a wall on each side, roofed with timber, and on the E. side no doubt battlemented. Probably the base of the mound was also girt by a low wall of which the gate-tower formed a part of the circuit. Traces of the walls are seen on its W. side, and there is a small platform also included. The gate tower is Trans.-Norm.

The rest of the space is occupied by the courts (ballia) of the castle, the area of which is considerable, and until recently held the County Courts. The mound occupies the N.E. corner. A wall skirting the mound, a little above its base, appears to have encircled the whole. It may be seen extending along the S.E. face. Thence it swept to the W., and included the S. gatehouse, temp. Hen. VIII, still standing, with pointed drop arch, large opening, portcullis grooves, and traces of the ribs of the vault. Outside is the same cordon seen in the keep; a drawbridge led across the ditch from this gate. The arches in a part of the bridge, lately walled up, may still be seen. The wall W. of the gate remains in parts. The N. gate has a drop arch, but, within, its lodge arch is sharply pointed.

On the N. and W. sides the castle defence is a deep natural valley; on the S. and E. the valley has been deepened, and still, though built upon, bears the name of Castle-Ditch. The Deer Park, still so called, extended S.W. from the Castle gate. This gate is late Perp., but it is evident that the whole of the rest of the building—gate, tower, annular wall, and circular keep, are by one hand, and of one time. It is very possible, from the aspect of the place, that even in its unscarped state it was naturally strong, and may have been employed by the Celts or Saxons for defence. At present nothing is visible that can be regarded even as Early Norman.

Launceston Castle was held of the Conqueror by the Earls of Moreton. From Earl William it reverted to the crown, and in the 11th year of Edw. III. was merged in the Duchy of Cornwall. It appears to have been a ruin as early as the reign of Edw. III., and Carew speaks of its crumbling condition in 1602. In 1645 it was fortified for Charles I. by Sir Richard Grenville, and in March of the following year the garrison surrendered to the parliamentary troops under Fairfax. This was the closing scene in the military annals of the castle. The Dukes of Northumberland, High Constables of Launceston under the Duchy, have expended a considerable sum in most judicious repairs, which are calculated to prevent for some time any further decay. The precinct has been tastefully laid out as a public pleasure-ground.

The *Ch. of St. Mary Magdalen* is a late Perp. building, which has been recently restored. It is entirely constructed of granite, and was erected in 1524 by Sir Henry Trecarrel, of Trecarrel; the story being that Sir Henry, instead of finishing his house, used the stone which had been cut for that purpose in building this church. The whole structure is panelled, and the panels are filled with armorial bearings, flowers, and other emblems. Amongst other carvings occur St. Martin parting his cloak, and shields with the Trecarrel arms. A number of shields encircle the edifice, embossed with letters, which together form an invocation to the saint, and an apostrophe on the sacredness of the locality. The tower, which stands apart, but is connected with the ch. by a large vestry-room, is of earlier date, and built of a different material. The S. porch is remarkable for its beauty. The chancel contains the monumental tomb of Sir Hugh Piper, "the famous loyalist of the West," and his Dame Sibylla, "very livelily represented in marble," the one in armour, and the other in brocade. The wooden pulpit is polygonal and curious.

A Norman arch with 8 jamb shafts and chevron mouldings, forming the entrance of the White Hart Inn, was removed from the ruins of the *Priory*, founded for Augustinian monks in the reign of Hen. I. by Warlewast, bishop of Exeter. Several fragments of the Priory are incorporated with the houses now occupying its site, which was described by Leland as "in the far west part of the suburb of the town, under the root of a hill by a fair wood-side."

In addition to these ruins of castle and priory, some remains of the town walls may be seen in Launceston. The only gateway now standing is that on the S.E., which is of Decorated date, and forms the entrance from Devonshire. *St. Stephen's*, 1 m. N., is a fine granite ch., with a Perpendicular tower and in part Early Eng. nave.

In the ch. of St. Thomas, close to Launceston, there are a very ornamental pair of doorhinges of the 15th cent., and a good font.

Werrington, belonging to the Duke of Northumberland, and *Endsleigh*, the cottage of the Duke of Bedford, are both situated on the Tamar, the one 2 m. N., and the other 9 m. S. The large park of Werrington, overgrown with fern and well stocked with deer, is picturesque. Tickets of admission to Endsleigh (*Devon*, Rte. 13) may be obtained at the White Hart. *Trebartha Hall*, the seat of Francis Rodd, Esq., and *Trecarrel*, are also worth seeing. Trebartha is in the parish of Northill, about 7 m. towards Liskeard, under the rocky escarpment of the moors. S.W. of the house a tributary of the river Lynher falls in a cascade, where the botanist may find *Hymenophyllum Tunbridgense*, or filmy-leaved fern, a rare plant. (*Hymen. Wilsonii*, nearly related to H. Tunb., grows abundantly on Zennor Down, near the Gurnard's Head). *Trecarrel* stands on the banks of the Inny, ½ m. W. of the church-town of Lezant, which is about 4 m. on the road to Callington. The old mansion was built about 1540, by Sir Henry, the last of the Trecarrels, and in the Rebellion was honoured by a visit from Charles I., who slept in it on his road into Cornwall. The hall and a small chapel of granite are in excellent preservation. The hall has a fine cradle roof; and in the wall over the dais a square opening from the lord's chamber. The Chapel, detached from the house, standing in the centre of the quadrangle, has the walls and roof perfect. At the E. end the altar platform remains; with piscina and pillar bracket for an image. This part of the building is the whole height; the W. part is in two stories, with fireplace and garderobe in the upper room. All is late Perp., though some portions appear earlier than Sir Henry's time, to whom the building of the house is usually assigned. He may have completed it, and have left unfinished the rooms beyond the daised end of the hall, using the stone for St. Mary's Ch. The hall is now used as a cider-cellar; the house is a farmhouse; and, alas! the little chapel a hen-roost. From Lezant you should proceed 1 m. further along the highroad to the *Sportsman's Arms*, a convenient house of entertainment. A lane leads direct from it to the *Carth-*

amatha Rocks, on the Tamar (1 m.), one of the finest points of view in the county. Another excursion may be made to *Lidford* and *Brent Tor*. (Rte. 6.)

At Launceston, in 1643, when the fortunes of Charles were at a very low ebb, the tide of a sudden turned and drove the Roundheads out of Cornwall. Sir Ralph Hopton and Sir Beville Grenville were shut into the county by Sir Alexander Carew and Sir R. Buller, who lay at this town to prevent their escape. The Parliamentary commanders, to beguile their inactivity, instituted legal proceedings against "divers persons unknown, who had lately come into Cornwall, armed *contra pacem*." Upon this Hopton appeared, and, producing the commission of the king to the Marquis of Hertford, appointing him general of the West, and his own commission from the marquis, obtained a verdict of acquittal, and was thanked by the jury. Hopton then, in turn, preferred an indictment against Buller and Carew. The jury found them guilty, and an order was granted to raise the *posse comitatus*, "for the dispersing that unlawful assembly, and for the apprehension of the rioters." A force of 3000 well-armed foot was speedily in motion; Buller and Carew were driven from Launceston, and the Royalists found themselves masters of Cornwall.— "The gentlemen of this county," says lady Fanshawe, in her *Memoirs*, "are generally loyal to the crown and hospitable to their neighbours, but they are of a crafty and censorious nature, *as most are so far from London*."

A rly. is authorised from Launceston by Camelford to Bodmin.

Proceeding on our route, we leave Launceston by the *Old Falmouth road*, which, passing for a long distance over elevated moors, the "backbone" and watershed of Cornwall, is one of the most bleak and lonely in the kingdom. It is, however, improving, and much changed since the days when a traveller could find on it "neither horse-meat nor man's meat, nor a chair to sit down."

3 m. rt. to Penzance by Camelford. (Rte. 22.)

1 m. *Holloway* (Holy-way) *Cross*, where one of the ancient crosses stands near the turnpike. It is the usual type of Cornish cross—a circular disk of granite, with a cross on it in low relief, standing on a short flattened shaft.

½ m. The road passes the *Inny*, a tributary to the Tamar. On its wild, granite-strewn banks in the parish of *St. Clether*, are remains of a little chapel over *Basil's Well*, a spring which rises under the altar.

3 m. *Fivelanes*. rt. *Alternun*, one of the most extensive but barren parishes in Cornwall. Its chief produce is said to be water. It derives its name from St. Nunn, to whom its well is considered sacred. The *Ch.* is a fine building, with the altar-rails extending across the aisles as well as between nave and chancel.

½ m. *Trewint* (Corn. "white place"). 1 m. beyond this village the traveller rises into the *Bodmin Moors*—highlands of granite, which extend to within 4 m. of the county town. Considerable portions of this district, and especially the valleys, have of late years been enclosed and brought under the plough; yet much remains to interest those who are fond of wild scenery. For many miles the waste stretches forth its tinted hills in one expanded scene of sterility, whilst in various directions rise solitary *carns*, which, heaped with granite, show apparently all that the moor possesses of value. A mineral treasure is, however, extracted from the valleys, which, during the course of ages, have been silted up by disintegrated granite, throughout which is disseminated a considerable quantity of tin. The traveller will find every *bottom*, as the Cornish term their valleys, furrowed by stream-works, most of which have long since been abandoned: few are now in activity. The road crosses the Fowey river (here a mere streamlet), descending from its source on Brown Willy, about 1 m. before reaching

3 m. The *Jamaica Inn*, hitherto a solitary half-way house, but now likely to be centred in a village, as a ch., parsonage, and school, have been erected here by Mr. Rodd, of Trebartha Hall, the proprietor of the land; — establishments hailed with much satisfaction by the moor-men, who declare that their children "are quite mountainerers, wildings, wild asses, and transgress." This inn is frequented by sportsmen in the winter, and affords somewhat rude accommodation. On a small farm in its vicinity, in the occupation of his father, was born the astronomer *Adams*, so justly celebrated for the discovery of the planet Neptune. It is in the parish of *Laneast*.

[From the Jamaica Inn the tourist may conveniently visit the hills of Brown Willy and Roughtor; the romantic valleys of Hanter-Gantick and Hannon; and Dozmare Pool, among the wild hills to the S.

(a) The 2 Cornish mountains, *Brown Willy*—a corruption of *Bron*, a breast; *Wella*, a beacon (Cornish: Bron, though literally a breast, is used to signify a hill so shaped; Bronwelli, a look-out hill)—and *Roughtor*, of the respective heights of 1368 and 1296 ft., are situated about 3 m. N. of the inn. An excursion to their summits offers a rich treat to those fond of such adventures; but a pocket compass should be taken, as these elevated moors are frequently enveloped in mists, which give no warning of their approach, and limit the view to a circle of a few yards. Deep bogs—of which there is a formidable specimen N.W. of Roughtor—may be entered under such circumstances, from which the traveller without this guide will find a difficulty in extricating himself. Brown Willy, separated from the Jamaica Inn by a hill called *Tober* or *Two Burrows* (alt. 1122 ft.), is a ridge lying a few points E. of N. and W. of S., parallel with Roughtor, and marked by 4 distinct hummocks. In a comparison of the 2 mountains, Brown Willy may be designated as the more beautiful, Roughtor the more imposing, the latter being literally covered by a monster meeting of rocks. Immediately under Brown Willy, to the S.W., a bottom is occupied by a large stream-work, called Brown Willy, in which the traveller may witness the operation of streaming for tin. The crest of the ridge is roughened by masses of granite, which, fashioned in squarer forms than those on Roughtor, give an appearance of a less irregularity to the outline. The summit, crowned by a pile of stones, commands a view extending into Somerset and to the remotest parts of Devon and Cornwall. The superb height of Roughtor rises close at hand, and on the solitary waste which stretches northwards from Roughtor and Brown Willy, in the direction of Davidstow Moor, are the works of the *Roughtor Copper Mine*, an adventurous but unprofitable concern belonging to the shareholders of that great Devonshire mine, the Devon Consols. Under the E. side of the hill lies a small pool of water, called *Fowey Well*, as the source of the river Fowey, and S.W. the rocky eminence of *Garrah*, 1060 ft. above the level of the sea. Below Garrah (¼ m. S.W. of it) is the lonely little entrenchment known as *Arthur's Hall*. The granite of the Bodmin range is well characterised by that of Brown Willy, which is composed of white crystalline felspar, grey quartz, and two kinds of mica, one of which is white and transparent, the other opaque, and of a dark garnet colour. The black mineral schorl is occasionally disseminated through the mass in minute crystalline grains. A valley, now partly cultivated, separates this mountain from *Roughtor*, which should certainly be ascended for a nearer view of the enormous carns of granite, which, covering it on all sides, give a ruggedness to its outline even when viewed at a distance of 30 m. They consist of some of the largest blocks in Cornwall, lodged one upon the other in very curious and critical positions, and at the summit weathered into spheroidal masses, which strikingly illustrate the decomposition of granite, and exhibit on their upper surfaces a network of those irregular cavities called *rock basins*. On the summit of the hill (which is in the parish of Simonward) are traces of a chapel dedicated to St. Michael (licensed Nov. 1535). No hill in Devon or Cornwall can be matched for magnificence with Roughtor, which ought surely to be preserved from the quarryman, as the grand feature of the county. The red lichen *Lecanora perella* is found in the caverns and crevices, and collected for the purposes of a dye. In the barren valley, under the N.W. side of the hill, are a number of those circular enclosures, or *hut-circles*, so common on Dartmoor; and near the bank of the stream a monument of unhewn granite, which strikes the attention from the loneliness of the surrounding hills. It bears an inscription and marks the scene of a sanguinary murder. Upon a low eminence, immediately W. of Roughtor, lies a *logan stone*, about 4 ft. in thickness, 15 in length, and 12 in breadth. The upper surface is flat, and the ponderous mass is moved easily by a push, or by the weight of a person stepping upon it. So perfect is the balance, that the oscillation continues for some seconds after the stone has been set in motion. Accident appears to have had the greatest share in producing these effects, as the block has been evidently curtailed at its eastern extremity by the operation of *pooling*.

(*b*) The traveller may hence extend his excursion to *Hanter-Gantick* (i. e. "*Hender*," aged; "Gantic," opening),

sometimes designated the Cornish Valley of Rocks, — or to *Hannon Valley*, from the sides of which rise 2 isolated crags, known as *the Devil's Jump*. The former is situated some 5 m. down the Lank (Du — or Black Lank), a stream which flows S.W. and between Rowtor and Brown Willy ; the latter about 2½ m. down a tributary of the Camel, which, running in a similar direction, is to be found on the N.W. side of Roughtor. Between "Devil's Jump" and Roughtor there is a very good *stone circle* on Stannon Down.

Hanter-Gantick is also 1 m. S. of the church-town of *St. Breward*, or Simon Ward, as it is commonly called. It is a deep romantic valley, desolated by rocks of granite, which, shaped by the elements into cubes, cover the slopes and lie heaped together by hundreds on the adjacent heights. It is a scene befitting the genius of a Salvator, and one of the most extraordinary of its kind in the country. The declivity of the higher part of the valley is abrupt, and here the stream thunders through the obstruction in a series of cascades. A descent to its banks will repay the labour, although a ladder is almost required in the passage from stone to stone, and a thick growth of brake offers additional impediments. The finest *coup d'œil* is obtained from the hillside which fronts this portion of the valley. Hence the entire scene is displayed, and its rugged effect well contrasted by the azure tints of Brown Willy, which rises in the distance. A few years ago Hanter-Gantick was as solitary as it is wild, but it is now the site of granite-works. Between it and Wenford Bridge is the hamlet of *Lank* ("*Lank*," a young place ; the adjoining river is "*Du* Lank," *Black* Lank, probably in reference to the colour of the water in such a deep wild ravine); and on *Lank Down* the *Lank Rocks*, 2 carns of granite, which

Route 21.—*Hannon Valley.—Dozmare Pool.* Sect. II.

are called by the country people *the King's and Queen's Houses*. The *Ch. of St. Breward* has Norm. portions (N. aisle, font, and perhaps part of nave and tower?). There are some carved bench-ends. The ch. was originally built by the Peverells, soon after the Conquest. Of St. Breward nothing is known. The name Simonsward is perhaps a relic of the Saxon *Sigmund* (see *Devon*, Rte. 1), whose name is found in similar wild districts. Simonsward may have been the "mark" or boundary of some early Saxon settlement.

(c.) *Hannon* (i.e. "Half-way") *Valley* is situated about 1 m. W. of *Advent* (S. Tanc locally), and through this the streams rising N. of Roughtor discharge their waters into the Camel. It has been invested with features of particular interest by a thunder-storm, which, falling with unusual violence in the summer of 1847, principally upon the high land W. of Roughtor, occasioned a flood in the Camel, which swept away many of the bridges, and destroyed a large amount of property on its banks. The bed of this valley was ripped open by the accumulated waters, and the stream now flows between white banks of granite and quartz, varied by the intrusion of rocks of a different character. From the sides of the lower part of the valley rise the crags which are known as the *Devil's Jump*. That on the l. bank, when seen from beneath, resembles a tower about 50 ft. in height. In the bed of the stream, immediately below this rock, lies a block of a white crystalline stone, about 24 ft. in length, by 8 in breadth, which, abutting upon a deep and clear pool, would seem to have been expressly placed there to serve the purposes of the bather. At the extremity of this valley a solitary tree will be seen standing amid ruins occasioned by the flood. It is connected with an alarming adventure which befel a farmer residing in the neighbourhood. On the day of the storm he was making his way to Camelford, and about to cross the stream by a foot-bridge, when a sudden increase in the volume of the torrent rendered the passage impracticable, and at the same time, by occasioning an overflow of some low ground in his rear, cut off his retreat. Two trees presented the only means of escape. He hastily climbed upon one, but, thinking this the weaker of the two—and it was afterwards carried away—he removed into the other, which fortunately resisted the fury of the inundation.

Nothing in Cornwall exceeds in beauty the walk (though rather a rough one) between the Devil's Jump and Wenford Bridge. It is a great treat for a botanist, a fisherman, or an artist, who will meet with asphodels, bog pimpernels, sundew, sphagnums, ferns of many sorts, with trout and *peal*, and some very pretty scenery.

From Wenford Bridge there is a rly. passing by Bodmin to Wadebridge; but passengers are only conveyed between the two last-named places.

(d) 1¼ m. S. of the Jamaica Inn lies *Dozmare Pool* (pronounced *Dosmery*)— i.e. "*Dos*," *a drop;* Mor and Mari, *the sea;* from the old tradition that it was tidal—890 ft. above the sea, a melancholy sheet of water, about 1 m. in circumf., and from 4 to 5 ft. in depth. A lofty hill, called *Brown* or *Bron Gilly — Bron Gilla*, a secluded hill or breast—alt. 1100 ft., is the mark by which the traveller can direct his course. On the N. side of Bron Gilly are the remains of an ancient village, probably of tinners or *streamers*, as they are locally called. Below this the pool is situated, on a table-land which borders the deep vale of the Fowey. The traveller will pass in a bottom on his rt. hand a stream-work called the *Poor Man's Endeavour*, in which may be seen an interesting section displaying the following series of deposits. Disintegrated granite, 1 ft.; black bog, the lower part filled with hazel-branches, 6 ft.; disintegrated granite, 2 ft.; bog of a lighter colour than that above, and containing decayed fragments of wood, 4 ft.; and below this again another bed of granitic soil, which is streamed. The pool is the theme of many a marvellous tale, in which the peasants most implicitly believe. It is said to be unfathomable, and the resort of evil spirits. Begirt by dreary hills, it presents an aspect of utter gloom and desolation. The country people represent it as haunted by an unearthly visitant, a grim giant of the name of Tregeagle, who, it is said, may be heard howling here when wintry storms sweep the moors. He is condemned to the melancholy task of emptying the pool with a limpet-shell, and is continually howling in despair at the hopelessness of his labour. Occasionally, too, it is said this miserable monster is hunted by the devil round and about the tarn, when he flies to the Roche Rocks, some 15 m. distant, and, by thrusting his head in at the chapel window, finds a respite from his tormentor. Such is the legend of *Giant Tregeagle*, of whom some have told that he was a wicked seigneur, once residing on the site of this dismal lake, by which his mansion was of a sudden engulfed, while his park was at the same time transformed into the barren waste which is now known as the Bodmin Moors.

"In Cornwall's famed land, by the Pool and the Moor,
Tregeagle the wicked did dwell;
He once was a shepherd neglected and poor,
But, growing ambitious, and looking for more,
Sad fate this poor shepherd befell."

Tregeagle, however, was a veritable person, the dishonest steward of Lord Robartes at Lanhydrock (where a room in the house is still called Tregeagle's), who maltreated the tenants under his charge, and amassed money sufficient to purchase the estate of *Trevorder*, in St. Breock, where he distinguished himself as a harsh and arbitrary magistrate. Hence the evil reports which one hears of him. The traveller may glean amusement at the Jamaica Inn, by broaching the subject among the moor-men. One will then narrate how he was startled by the noise of a coach and the cracking of whips, when cutting turf near the pool after dark, and declare that he distinctly heard the coach plunge under water. Another will tell how he has seen upon the solitary shore a strange light, "like fire in a furze-bush." And all will most emphatically declare that there is "certainly somebody there, let people say what they *wool!*" Until very recently there was no visible outlet to this mysterious tarn, since the water imperceptibly oozed through a bog on its western side. Hence another story of a whirlpool and subterranean channel communicating with the subjacent valley. A trench cut through this morass has now partially drained the lake, and gives the water a free passage to more inclined ground, where it soon joins a branch of the Fowey rising near the high road, ½ m. W. of the Jamaica Inn. Another tributary to this river has its source under *Hawk's Tor* (alt. 900 ft.), 1 m. W. of the Four-hole Cross.

From Dozmare Pool the pedestrian can cross the moor direct to *St. Neot*, about 5 m. (Rte. 23); or by a circuitous route include *Treveddoe*, in the parish of Warleggan, a most ancient tin stream-work still in activity, and having, in addition to the excavations of the streamers, shafts 60 fath. deep, which are said to have been sunk by the "old men" (Treveddoe has also a curious old manor-house, now a farm); or he can travel to *Liskeard* by a road from the Jamaica Inn, 9 m.; or, by a longer route on foot over the moor, visit on his way *Kilmarth Tor*, the *Cheesewring*, the *Hurlers*, the *Trevethy Stone*, the

Well of St. Cleer, and the interesting memorial known as the *Half Stone* (all described in Rte. 23); and in the latter route, as the tors of Kilmarth and the Cheesewring are plainly seen from the vicinity of Dozmare Pool, the stranger will have no difficulty in directing his course.]

Proceeding from the Jamaica Inn towards Bodmin:—

1½ m. Here, leaning towards the road, is the *Four-hole Cross*, a lonely impressive monument, bearing every mark of extreme antiquity, and situated in a wild and elevated part of the moor. The top is mutilated, and of the 4 holes which once stamped the figure of the cross, 2 only are now remaining. The pillar was evidently once ornamented with scrollwork, which, with the exception of a few lines, has been so greatly effaced that it can only be made out by certain lights. It is of the Celtic *knotwork* character.

3½ m. *Temple*, a miserable hamlet on a manor which belonged to the Knights Templars. They had a ch. here which long since fell into decay, but still remains as a ruin. It is of late Norm. period. The font lies in the midst, with a young tree growing out of it. Adjoining the village are the rugged rocks of *Temple Tor*. The parish of Temple is the centre round which 12 parishes, collectively known as " the Moors," are ranged.

1½ m. rt. *Pererell's Cross*, close to the roadside; 1. *St. Bellarmine's Tor*, and adjoining is another small tor called " Colvannic," near the hamlet of " Pound Scawens " (i.e. the pound by the elder-trees), on the Bodmin and Launceston turnpike road; and at a distance of about 2 m. *Cardinham Bury*, an entrenchment of a circular form, Barrow of *Caer dinas*, or Cardinham, *i.e.* the fortress of rocks, giving its name to the parish, and also formerly to the resident family. Walter de Cardinham was the Norm. settler here.

1 m. rt. a road branches to *Blisland* (said to signify "happy church," but, query?), 2 m., where is a ch. of some interest. The chancel is E. E., the aisles Perp., the S. door and font Norm. There is a *brass* for John Balsam, rector, 1410, in chasuble. During repairs in the rectory 2 ancient silver crucifixes were found. The parish was known as " Blisland juxta Montem," from the neighbourhood of Roughtor.

2 m. *Council Barrow*, rt. of the road.

2 m. l. an old *cross* in a field near the turnpike.

1 m. *Bodmin* (*Inns:* Oliver's Royal Hotel; Gatty's Town Arms), situated nearly in the centre of the county, about 12 m. from the Bristol and English Channels. Here are held the sessions and assizes.

(For Bodmin and its neighbourhood see Rte. 23. The *Bodmin Road Stat.*, on the West-Cornwall Railway, is at Glynn Bridge, 3 m. from the town. An omnibus meets every train.)

Proceeding again on our route—

2¾ m. l. *Lanivet*. The Perp. ch., much dilapidated, is of little interest. The churchyard contains 2 ancient stone crosses, one 10, the other about 11 ft. high. To the l., ½ m. distant, are the remains of what is known as *St. Bennet's Monastery*, a small religious foundation, of which the history is very uncertain. The domestic portion of the building (15th cent.), with its shafted windows and ivied tower, was very interesting until mutilated and cockneyfied in 1859. The mine-works have also contributed to spoil the scene.

A road here branches S. to *St. Austell*, 8 m. (Rte. 23).

Beyond Lanivet the traveller enters a barren country, which, rising to the *Tregoss Moors* (celebrated until lately for the ponies bred on them), extends many miles.

3 m. a railway for the conveyance of ore, &c., passes from the highroad here to St. Blazey.

3½ A road on the l. leads to the village of *Roche* (1 m.), which is distant about 2 m. from the bleak hill of *Hensbarrow* (*Hên-barrow*, i. e. old tumulus) (alt. 1034 ft.). Roche *Ch.* is modern, of the meeting-house type, but contains an old font of the Norm. character, but doubtful date, so common in Cornwall; it is ornamented with two purses (?) interlaced. In the churchyard is a rude cross. The *Roche Rocks*, ½ m. S. of the ch., and 680 ft. above the sea, consist of several great masses piled together in rude confusion to a height of 100 ft.; and in the heart of the group are the remains of a little chapel in the Dec. style, dedicated to St. Michael, and said to have been once tenanted by a hermit, and more recently by a solitary leper. The spot is lonely, and well suited to the wild tales attached to it, such as that of Giant Tregeagle, who is said to fly over the moors, on stormy nights, to seek a shelter here from his unearthly pursuer. Close at hand rises a spring which is said to ebb and flow, and at some little distance is the "wishing-well" of St. Roche, to which village maidens still repair on Holy Thursday, to throw in pins and pebbles, and predict coming events by the sparkling of the bubbles. The Roche Rocks consist of quartz and schorl, constituting schorl rock, which is in a friable state.

1½ m. The traveller is now passing over the *Tregoss Moors*, the fabled hunting-ground of King Arthur, and may see to the rt. the granite eminences of *Belovely* or *Belouda Beacon* (alt. 765 ft.), and *Castle an Dinas* (alt. 729 ft.), the latter crowned with an encampment, and interesting to the geologist for a variety of altered slate. "Castle an Dinas," i.e. masonry castle in the *earth*-work, not, as is sometimes said, Castle of the Danes: it is a very common name in Wales.

3¼ m. The *Indian Queens*, a lonely inn in a wild unsheltered situation on the moor.

¼ m. *Fraddon*.—To the l. of this hamlet, ½ m., lies *Calliquoiter Rock*, containing variable mixtures of schorl with granite. The summit of the hill is 690 ft. above the level of the sea. Beyond Blue Anchor the new road to Truro branches off on the l. It runs by the church-town of *Ladock*, and through one of the prettiest valleys in the county. The parish of Ladock is well known for its *streamworks*. They have produced a quantity of tin, and some of the largest pieces of gold which have been found in Cornwall.

1 m. The church-town of *St. Enoder*. The small ch. has an early Dec. nave. St. Enoder is said to have died in Cornwall early in the 5th cent. l. the village of *Summercourt*, noted for its annual cattle and sheep fair, on Sept. 25, in which 3000 head of stock commonly change hands.

3 m. *Mitchell*, or *St. Michael*, before the Reform Act a borough town returning 2 M.P.'s.—A cross road leads to *Newlyn*, 2 m.: and 1½ m. N. of Newlyn is the manor-house of *Trerice*, the old seat of the Arundels, now belonging to Sir T. D. Acland, Bt., by whom it has been restored. It has carvings in panel representing many of the old houses in the county, and is well worth seeing.

6½ m. *Truro* (*Inns*: Tedder's Royal Hotel; Lenderyou's Red Lion Hotel). (See Rte. 23.)

ROUTE 22.

LAUNCESTON TO TRURO, BY CAMELFORD, WADEBRIDGE, AND ST. COLUMB. (THE NORTH COAST.—BOSCASTLE; TINTAGEL; DELABOLE QUARRIES; PADSTOW; THE VALE OF MAWGAN; NEWQUAY.)

(The rly. from Launceston by Camelford to Bodmin will run somewhat S. of the road followed in the present route.)

Launceston (Rte. 21).

A wild and dreary road, skirting *Laneast* and *Wilsey Downs*, hills traversed by the junction-line of the carbonaceous and grauwacke formations, leads to

12 m. *Davidstow* (pronounced Dewstow), a poor village, in one of the bleakest districts of Cornwall, but with an interesting *church*. The sterile expanse of Davidstow Moor stretches S. to Roughtor and Brown Willy, the 2 Cornish *mountains*. About 3 m. N., on Wilsey Down, is *Warbstow Barrow*, an ancient fortification of considerable size. A long mound in the centre of it is called by the country people *King Arthur's Grave*.

3½ m. *Camelford* (*Inns:* King's Arms; Darlington Arms), situated in an elevated and hilly part of the county, on the skirt of the moors, and on the *Camel*, or *Alan*, here but a rustic stream, which, rising in the parish of Davidstow, flows by Wadebridge and Padstow to the sea. The figure of a camel crowns the town-hall, as a weathercock, placed there by the corporation, in happy ignorance, it is to be presumed, that their town has derived its name from " *Crum heyle*," the *crooked river*. The Camel abounds in peal and trout.

The parish ch., called *Lanteglos*— *i. e.* the " Church enclosure,"— is 1½ m. W. It is ded. to St. Julitta, and contains E. E. (chancel), Dec., and Perp. (nave) portions. The Perp. E. windows of chancel and S. aisle are good. The heraldic bosses on the roofs of both should be noticed. The arms of Coryton, Trelawny, and Trecarrel are conspicuous on that of the S. aisle. The fine octangular font is E. E. (A Norm. font is preserved at the Vicarage.) The W. tower is E. E.

[The Ch. of *Advent*, 2 m. E. (ded. to St. Adwen, locally *St. Tane*), contains E. E. portions, and is interesting. The N. transept and W. tower (both E. E.) deserve notice. In the latter the wall of the newel projects into the N. aisle, and is pierced for a lancet light. There are remains of gilding and colour on the roof (Perp.) of the nave.]

Camelford was made a free borough by Richard king of the Romans, and incorporated temp. Chas. II. It had for years returned a member to Parl., when it was disfranchised by the Reform Bill. In 1791 it was represented by *Macpherson*, the author of Ossian. *Captain Wallis*, who discovered Otaheite, was born at *Fentonwoon* (Fenton-woon, i. e. spring or well on the downs), now a farmhouse, ½ m. S., near the river-side.

The neighbourhood of Camelford, according to tradition, has been the scene of 2 sanguinary battles—one between King Arthur and his rebellious nephew Mordred (date 542), in which, it is said, Mordred was slain, and King

CORNWALL. *Route 22.—Boscastle.* 213

Arthur wounded mortally; the other between the Britons and the Saxons under Egbert (date 823).

Several excursions of high interest can here be made. Camelford is the nearest town to *Roughtor* and *Brown Willy* (Rte. 21), the former of which has a magnificent appearance, as it rises in a craggy ridge over intervening hills. In his route to this mountain the traveller will cross a cart-track on the moor, bordered by upright stones, which are ranged along it at regular distances. It will give him an idea of the dreary character of this district. It extends from a place called Watergate to Fivelanes, near Launceston, and the stones were erected by the minister, who had to traverse the waste on Sundays. They are intended to serve as guides in misty weather; a long post occurs at intervals of ½ m., and is marked on the Watergate side with the letter W., and on that towards Fivelanes with the letter F. The visitor to Camelford can also make an excursion to the wild valley of *Hanter Gantick*, by the *Devil's Jump* (both described in Rte. 21). His shortest route is by the ch. of *Advent* (see *ante*). In the third field beyond this ch., by the side of the path, stands a venerable, time-worn granite *cross*, about 9ft. in height. In this excursion he will notice the effects of a flood which occurred on the Camel in the summer of 1847. It was occasioned by a singularly heavy rain, which, accompanied by thunder and lightning, fell without intermission from 10 A.M. to 4 P.M. It swept away a number of bridges and destroyed much valuable property. Fortunately an engine happened to be at Wenford Bridge, near St. Mabyn, the terminus of the Wadebridge railway, when the head of water was seen rushing down the valley; and the engineer, starting off, gave the alarm to the farmers living along the banks, so that many had time to drive away their cattle, and remove their most valuable effects.

To the N. of Camelford lies one of the most interesting districts in Cornwall, since it comprehends *Boscastle*, the ruins of *King Arthur's Castle of Tintagel*, the magnificent line of coast between these points, and the celebrated slate-quarries of *Delabole*. In a visit to the sheep-market of Camelford the stranger will be reminded of his vicinity to slate-quarries, since the partitions are each formed of a single slab of that material.

The traveller can proceed to Boscastle or Tintagel by *Slaughter Bridge* (1 m. N., and now corrupted into *Sloven's Bridge*), which lies on the road from Delabole to Launceston, and is said to have been named as the spot where King Arthur received his death-wound. *Worthyvale*, at a short distance from the bridge, was a manor-house of the ancient lords of Boscastle.

4½ m. *Boscastle* (*Inn:* Wellington Hotel). This little town is situated upon a steep hill, sloping to a valley, which at a short distance is joined by another, each coursed by a rapid stream, when they are together deflected towards the harbour and inlet of Boscastle. The "port" is in a kind of ravine, and is somewhat like Balaclava on a small scale. The scenery in the neighbourhood is most romantic, and the country broken by deep furzy *bottoms*. Of the grandeur of the coast it is impossible to speak too highly. Boscastle has been so called from a baronial mansion, a residence of the Norman family of De Bottreaux, by which it was once dignified; and it still retains such names as Moise, Amy, Benoke, Gard, and Avery (? Yvery). It has a Valency brook, and a Palais and a Jardin. A green mound is the only mark of the castle of the De Bottreaux. In the reign of Henry VI. the heiress of the family was married to Robert

Lord Hungerford; and as the possessions of that nobleman were situated at a distance of 100 miles in an easterly direction, it is probable that at this period the castle fell into decay. From the Hungerfords it descended to the Earls of Huntingdon, who retained it till the reign of Elizabeth, and whose heir in the female line, the Marquis of Hastings, is still Baron Bottreaux. The herald will remember the "3 toads" and the "griffin segreant," the arms of the Lords Bottreaux, in the ample quartering of the house of Hastings. The manor some years since came into the possession of the late T. R. Avery, Esq., who greatly improved the place and developed its trade, and it still belongs to his family.

The parish ch. of *Bottreaux*, or *Forrabury*, with its "silent tower," from which it is said the merry peal has never sounded, is situated above Boscastle, and close to the soaring headland of Willapark Point. It is dedicated to St. Symforian, who, according to the tradition, was buried in it, and hence, perhaps, the name Forrabury. St. Symphorian, however — martyred A.D. 180 — was really interred at Autun, of which place he was a native. An ancient granite cross, resting upon a pedestal of limestone, stands outside the churchyard. *Within*, the ch. displays E. E. portions in the chancel and very early (Sax.?) arches in the transepts. There are some good bench-ends, and the circular font is of Norm. character. The following legend is connected with the church. Upon its erection, the inhabitants, long envious of the musical bells of Tintagel, determined to have a peal of their own. Lord de Bottreaux, then residing at his castle, aided the project, and a celebrated founder in London was directed to cast the bells. They were despatched by sea. The vessel freighted with them arrived safely off Boscastle, when the bells of Tintagel were swinging with sullen roar. The sound boomed over the waves to the ear of the pilot, who, elated by the welcome of his native village, piously thanked God that he should be ashore that evening. "Thank the ship and the canvas," exclaimed the captain; "thank God ashore." "Nay," said the pilot, "we should thank God at sea as well as on land." "Not so," quoth the captain; "thank yourself and a fair wind." The pilot rejoined; the captain, after the manner of captains, grew choleric, swore, and blasphemed. The ship meanwhile had closed the land, and the dark headland of Willapark and the precipices of the Black Pit were seen crowded by the inhabitants, eagerly expecting the precious freight. Suddenly a heavy bank of clouds, having gathered in the west, darkened the entire sky; a furious wind arose, and lashed the sea into mountainous billows. The vessel became unmanageable, and, driving towards the coast, capsized, and foundered, when all on board perished except the pilot, who alone, supported by a part of the wreck, was washed ashore, unhurt. The storm continued with extreme violence, and it is said that during the pauses of the gale the clang of the bells was distinctly heard, tolling from the ocean depths, and to this day the inhabitants recognise these solemn sounds during the storms which so frequently assail this part of the coast. See the very striking lines by the Rev. R. Hawker of Morwenstow, entitled 'The Silent Tower of Bottreaux.'

The harbour of Boscastle is ½ m. from the upper town. It has been excavated by the waves, and is truly romantic — a little winding inlet, not a stone's throw in breadth, and opening under the headland of *Willapark*. The name occurs elsewhere on this coast — near Combe Martin for example — and signifies "look-out field;" *Welli*, a look-out; *parc*, a field. The sea is here in constant agitation, and the cove itself affords no security to shipping; but a small space at its extremity, of size sufficient to admit two or three vessels at a time, is enclosed by a diminutive pier, and this, properly speaking, is the harbour of Boscastle. Everything about this place denotes the boisterous seas to which it is exposed; boats are made fast by cables which would ordinarily hold a ship, and, stretched along the pier, lie enormous hawsers, thicker than a man's thigh, which are employed in checking the impetus of vessels when they enter the harbour. Immediately beyond the pier is a seat, from which the stranger can view at his leisure an interesting phenomenon. A fissure in the opposite rocks, passing underground about 50 ft., communicates with the open sea, and from this, at intervals, a column of water is violently projected across the harbour, accompanied by a loud report. But the effect is produced only within an hour of low-water, and when the sea is agitated. From the same spot may be observed another, but more distant phenomenon of a similar kind. A hole pierces an island-rock called *Meachard*, lying outside the harbour, and, as the waves roll by, the spray is occasionally *blown* from it like a jet of steam. During the summer a number of seals are taken by the Boscastle fishermen. The coast is everywhere undermined by deep caverns, which, when the sea is smooth, the fishermen enter in their boats and explore with torches. The seals, which are fond of lying on ledges in these gloomy retreats, are confounded by the light, and fall an easy prey. They are killed for their oil and skins, which are considered of sufficient value to repay the risk of the adventure.

Immediately W. of the harbour rises *Willapark Point*, a magnificent headland, crowned with a low tower, erected as a prospect-house. On its W. side the cliffs recede and form a gloomy chasm, appropriately called the *Black Pit*, since the rock is here so singularly dark that it may be easily mistaken for coal. This headland, when viewed from the point to the W. of it, forms one of the finest cliff-scenes on the coast; its huge and sombre flanks of slate being contrasted by the light-tinted slope of *Resparvell Down*, a barren ridge which fills in the background, and is in keeping with the desolate cliffs and boisterous ocean. Standing upon this point W. of Willapark, the stranger is upon the boundary of two great formations,—the carbonaceous and grauwacke groups, which respectively prevail in Devonshire and Cornwall. The boundary-line passes from Boscastle across the county in the direction of Launceston, and is tolerably well marked as far as S. Petherwin. Northwards, to the extremity of the county, the coast in every part exhibits the singular contortions of the carboniferous strata. From this point the traveller will observe immediately W. of him a slate-quarry, called *Grower*, worked in the face of the grauwacke cliff. The *guide-chains*, by which the stone is raised, are actually fastened to the bottom of the sea, and on as wild a shore as can well be imagined. From the character of the rocks in this neighbourhood the soil is perfectly black.

A delightful excursion can be made from Boscastle to *Crackington Cove*, a romantic spot 4½ m. E. The road passes over *Resparvell Down* (alt. 850 ft.), which is terminated towards the sea by *High Cliff* (alt. 735 ft.). This down commands a fine view over the Bristol Channel, and along the coast, embracing headland after headland, in magnificent perspective. A quarry for slate is situated on the cliff ¾ m. W. of the cove. *Crackington Cove* is a recess on the E. side of a small bay, which is bounded on the W. by the picturesque promontory of *Cumbeak* (alt. 333 ft.), and on the E. by *Penkinna Head*, which rises above the sea-level about 400 ft. The latter is an imposing mass of dark slate, varied by white lines of the rock the quarrymen call *harder*, which show, even at a distance, the contortions of the strata. The general direction of the beds may be observed at low water, when parallel ridges, among many which are contorted, stretch along the beach towards the W.N.W. At the head of the bay the cliffs slope to the shore in imposing curves, forming inclined planes from 100 to 150 ft. in length; and the retreat of the tide leaves dry under Penkinna Head a rugged bed of rocks, among which are several beautiful stones variously coloured green, white, and brown, and marked by a network of white or yellow quartz veins, which the wear of the sea has brought into prominent relief. This bay appears intended by nature for a harbour, and a company who are working a slate-quarry about a mile up the valley have contemplated throwing out a pier from Carnbeak. The slate of the cove was some years ago quarried on the face of the cliff; but the stone proving of an inferior quality, the works were abandoned.

Minster Ch., a small antique building 1 m. N. of Boscastle, deserves notice as situated in a striking and picturesque nook among the hills. Close at hand is a waterfall of about 150 ft. The chancel has E.E. portions, and the tower—of which only one stage (not above the roof) exists—has a very early western arch. At *Lesnewth* (i. e. New Court), 1½ m. W. of Minster, is a ch. with Norm. and E.E. portions, and a good Perp. tower.

The distance from Boscastle to *Tintagel* is about 3 m., the intermediate country, though hilly, bearing some resemblance to a natural terrace, bounded on the seaboard by precipices, and on the land-side by a range of elevated hills, the reputed border of the old Saxons and Britons. Proceeding from Boscastle towards Tintagel (you should walk by the coast)—

2 m. *Longbridge.*—At this spot the road crosses a deep *bottom*, through which a brawling stream flows to the sea, and a mile up the valley falls nearly 40 ft. in a cascade called *St. Nighton's Keive*. St. Nighton is probably the same as *St. Nectan*, to whom Hartland ch. is dedicated (*Devon*, Rte. 18). Owing to a thick growth of brake it is a difficult task to walk through the valley to this waterfall. The better plan is to turn off the road at a farmhouse named Trethevey, standing at the top of the descent into the bottom. From this place, by pursuing a lane for about a mile, and then crossing 3 or 4 fields, the cascade may be reached without trouble. The valley is abruptly terminated by a barrier of rock, through a chasm of which the stream is hurried to a fall, and tumbles about 30 ft. into a circular basin, or *keive*. From this it passes through a natural arch, and, gushing under and over a large slab of stone, which is curiously fixed in the opening, is precipitated again 10 ft. into a dell dark with foliage. Altogether the scene is romantic and interesting, and will well repay a scramble even through the briers of the valley. A few yards below the fall the water is confined by a dam, and here there is a large rectangular mass of schist, about 20 ft. long by 6 ft. broad, of so uniform a shape that it might be imagined to be a monumental stone raised over the remains of some solitary giant who had haunted the spot. The genii loci were, however, of less ponderous bone, for a story is told of two mysterious old ladies, who here lived in such secret retirement, that they actually died with their names unknown by the gossips of the neighbourhood. Many a tale now circles at their expense, and, among others, that they lived upon snails, which are particularly numerous in this part of the country. One on foot

should walk down the valley—which is known as "the Valley of Rocks"—from the bridge to the sea. This is the prettiest part of it; it is roughened by schistose rocks, and contains Trevillet watermills, which are proper subjects for the pencil, and have been painted by Creswick under the title of " The Valley Mill." You should proceed by the cliffs to Tintagel. On the W. side of the bay into which the valley opens is a dark little recess, called *Bossiney Hole*, shut in by lofty precipices. During the summer and autumn this spot, at low water, is a scene of singular bustle, as a number of donkeys are then employed in scrambling up and down the rocks, carrying bags of sand, which are sold to the farmer as a top-dressing for the land. A headland called *Willapark*, resembling the point at Boscastle, juts out to the W. of it, and opposite to the village of *Bossiney*. As seen from the W. it presents a sheer precipice of a very striking and beautiful appearance, a perfect wall, tinted with yellow lichens. Bossiney is a mere hamlet of beggarly cottages, but it has been represented in Parl. by Sir Francis Drake, Sir Francis Cottington, and other distinguished persons. In 1695 its member was John Tregeagle, son of " Giant Tregeagle," and sheriff of the county. The village is remarkable for being built round a large barrow, on which it was the custom to read the writ for the election of M.P.s before the borough was disfranchised.

1 *Trevena* (*Inn:* the Stuart Wortley Arms). This village is in the immediate vicinity of the headland of *Tintagel* (locally pronounced *Doundudgel;* the name is said to signify the "impregnable fortress,"), which, celebrated as the most romantic scene in Cornwall, derives additional interest from being crowned with a ruinous castle of high antiquity, the reputed birthplace and residence of King Arthur. The promontory strikingly illustrates an action of the sea which tends to separate headlands from the mainland and convert them into islands; and consists of a peninsula, united to the coast by a neck of broken rocks, pierced by a long dark cavern, or rather tunnel, which may be visited at low water. A wild hollow, commencing at Trevena, opens to the sea in the rocky recess under Tintagel, and the stream which flows through it falls over the precipice in a cascade. So abrupt is the cliff at this spot, that vessels were formerly brought alongside for the purpose of shipping slate. This hazardous practice is now discontinued, but a wooden stage, projecting over the cliff, and other machinery employed in loading the vessels, still remain, and are a happy addition to the picturesque. The ruins of the *castle* are situated partly on the mainland and partly on the peninsula, being separated by the deep chasm or gap occasioned by the partial destruction of the isthmus. Considering the exposure of the locality, and the number of years which must have elapsed since the erection of the building, it is surprising that any portion should exist. The ruins, however, occupy an area of some extent, and consist of dark disintegrated walls, which are pierced by small square apertures and arched entrances. The different parts of the castle are said to have been once connected by a drawbridge, and this is not improbable, as the neck of land is continually diminishing under the repeated assaults of the sea, so that the chasm, if indeed it existed, must have been inconsiderable when the castle was built. In addition to the ruins which stand on its heights, the remains of an ancient landing-place, called *Porth Hern* (the Iron Gate), may be seen at the base of the promontory. These consist of a massive bastion and gateway, which, like the outer walls of the castle, have been sometimes considered to date from the time of the early Britons. The walls are built of the slate of the country, with

[*Dev. & Corn.*]   L

coarse mortar full of small gritstones. "The lower part of the chapel, with a W. porch and a solid altar, may be traced, with a burial-ground close to it. Another part is erroneously called the church, but was clearly a domestic building with a round staircase and a garderobe; the pit of another garderobe turret also remains, with part of one of the closets over it. This work appears to be of the 13th cent. There is a pointed arch to the doorway, and the walls are at present not more that 2 ft. 6 in. thick. . . . The work on the main land and on the island appears to be all of the same character, and had doubtless been connected by a drawbridge. The whole appears to be of the beginning of the 13th cent. with some later alterations."— *J. H. P.* There is, however, very little from which to form an accurate judgment as to the date of these remains, since there are no mouldings or cut stone fragments. The walls are falling away year by year with the cliff. The island will be visited by every intelligent traveller, the ascent now presenting little difficulty, as a winding path has been cut in the face of the cliff, although it must be admitted that the remark of Norden still applies—" he must have eyes that will scale Tintagel."

The early history of Tintagel Castle is to be gleaned only from tradition. There is no authentic record of its origin; but the tradition which has connected Tintagel with Arthur, the "flower of kings," is of unknown antiquity, and—although the existing remains are no doubt of far later date—a principal stronghold of the old "princes" of "West Wales"—by which name Cornwall and part of Devonshire were frequently called—may very probably have existed on this site. In the mediæval romances belonging to the cycle of Arthur the name of Tintagel frequently occurs—most frequently in the romances of Tristrem, where Tintagel is made the castle of king Mark of Cornwall. "Tintagel," it is said in one of them—

"estoit un chastel
Qui moult par art e fort e bel,
Ne cremoist asalt ne engin qui vaille
Sur la mer en Cornouaille."

The walls, continues the description, were painted with various colours, and had been laid under a powerful spell, by means of which the castle became invisible twice in the year (see the Romans de Tristan, ed. Michel). In Domesday Tintagel is mentioned by the name of *Dunchine* ("the castle of the cleft," from the *chine* separating it from the mainland). Soon after the Conquest it was a residence of the Earls of Cornwall, and in 1245 Earl Richard, the son of King John, entertained in it his nephew David Prince of Wales. Subsequently it became the property of the crown, and was occasionally used as a prison—the Lord Mayor of London having been sent here in 1385, according to Carew, "for his unruly mayoralty condemned hither as a perpetual penitentiary"—until the reign of Elizabeth, when Burleigh, considering the cost of keeping it in repair too onerous, allowed it to fall into ruins. It now belongs to the Duchy. Such in a few words is all that we know of Tintagel, but the stranger, as he contemplates its mouldering time-worn stones, will probably recall the romantic stories of King Arthur and his stalwart knights, and re-erect the castle "in the air," gay with a pageant of ancient days, and echoing the wild music and clanking harness of warriors; for, in truth, the solitude and magnificence which now characterise the spot are well calculated to encourage a truant fancy. The ruinous walls are remarkable for their dark and sombre hue, unrelieved by the usual patchwork of lichens; and the stones, worn to sharp edges by the weather, being laid on the bare rock, the direction of their laminæ coinciding with those of the

CORNWALL.   *Route 22.—Tintagel—King Arthur.*   219

cliffs, can be scarcely distinguished from the ground at a little distance. The slate of the promontory well merits notice. Where removed from the more destructive influence of the waves, it has been singularly weathered by wind and rain into a multitude of little basins and ridges, presenting an appearance similar to that of a body of snow or ice which has been for some time exposed to the sun's rays. Some of these slate "rock basins" are whimsically called *King Arthur's Cups and Saucers.* On the W. side a grotesque mass of slate rises in a jagged pillar, about 40 ft. high, and appears as if it had been acted upon by a corrosive acid. A spring of fresh water rises on the summit of the promontory, and a few sheep pasture on the turf, and occasionally fall into the sea. The flavour of the *island* mutton is considered particularly fine. The botanist will observe that the cliffs are hung with *samphire,* and may procure specimens of *Trifolium stellatum* from their rocky crevices. The character of this iron-bound coast is well seen at Tintagel. The sea front, mostly composed of slate, presents a series of inaccessible headlands and gloomy recesses, illustrating the influence of the "Atlantic drift," which is especially directed into the Bristol Channel. The sea is here ever heaving in long undulations, and, the water being deep to the land, the base of the cliffs is worn by the roll of the waves into a concave surface, which presents an effectual barrier to escape in shipwreck.

This is not the place to discuss the question of the historic existence of Arthur—whom, however, Mr. Rees and Dr. Guest, the two best authorities on the subject, consider to have been a true prince of Cornwall, who long withstood the westward advance of the Saxons. Of his origin as the great hero of romance there are many versions,

but on this spot we shall of course prefer that given by the Laureate—

" And that night the bard
Sang Arthur's glorious wars, and sang the king
As well nigh more than man, and railed at those
Who called him the false son of Gorlois :
For there was no man knew from whence he came;
But after tempest, when the long wave broke
All down the thundering shores of Bude and Boss,
There came a day as still as heaven, and then
They found a naked child upon the sands
Of wild Dundagil by the Cornish sea;
And that was Arthur; and they fostered him
Till he by miracle was approven king :
And that his grave should be a mystery
From all men, like his birth . . . ."

The local pronunciation of the castle —"Dundagil"— is here adopted. The scene of Arthur's disappearance in the fatal battle of Camlan, fought against the traitor Modred—

" That great battle in the west
Where I must strike against my sister's son,
Leagued with the lords of the White Horse, and knights
Once mine, and strike him dead, and meet myself
Death, or I know not what mysterious doom"—

is fixed by local tradition at Camelford (see *ante*), and by certain of the romancers, followed by Tennyson ('Morte d'Arthur'), in Lyonnesse — the mysterious submerged district between the Land's End and the Scilly Isles. The grave of the "clear-faced king" remains a mystery. A stone with his name on it is pointed out at Slaughter Bridge, near Camelford. A well-known mediæval story asserted that his tomb was opened at Glastonbury—where the historic Arthur may very possibly have been interred—in the reign of Hen. II., the tomb having been marked by the line—

" Hic jacet Arturus, rex quondam rexque futurus."

At Tintagel it is still believed that he haunts the battlements of his castle in the shape either of a gull or a raven, it is not certain which, but neither of these birds is willingly shot by the natives. This belief is

L 2

referred to by Don Quixote—"Have you not read, sir, ... the famous exploits of King Arthur? .. of whom there goes an old tradition that this king did not die, but that by magic art he was turned into a raven; and that in process of time he shall reign again, and recover his kingdom and sceptre; for which reason it cannot be proved that, from that time to this, any Englishman has killed a raven."—Bk. ii. ch. 5. "Guenivere," the name of Arthur's faithless queen, is still common in Cornwall under the form of "Jenuifer."

Tintagel, in early days, was the gateway into the Celtic peninsula, the only military road passing it on its course along the N. coast of Devon and Cornwall. Hence its ancient importance, and the battles which occurred in its immediate vicinity. The boundary of the Celt and Saxon may still be traced from the Tamar to Tintagel by the names of the villages—Michaelstowe, Jacobstowe, Davidstowe, Morwenstowe, &c.—but the real history of the gradual advance of the Saxons into Cornwall, and of the boundaries of the two races at different periods, has still to be accurately traced.

The *Ch. of Tintagel* (dedicated to St. Marcelliana), which stands on an exposed spot above the lofty cliffs W. of the castle, and has been subjected to restoration, will repay a visit. It contains Saxon portions (transept arches?); Norm. (chancel arch and font, remarkable, on 4 spreading legs); E. E. (western tower arch); and Dec. and Perp. elsewhere. The N. chancel arch, or Lady-chapel, has the original stone altar. The roof of the porch is formed of 4 large slabs. In the nave is a good *brass* for Johanna Boon, circ. 1430, and in the S. transept an incised slab with countersunk head of the effigy, temp. Edw. I. The ch. once belonged to the Abbey of Fontevrault in Normandy. Edward IV. bestowed it upon the collegiate ch. at Windsor, and at present the dean and chapter of that establishment attach the great tithes, and are the patrons of the living. The chief furniture of the ch. is decorated with the cross of St. George accordingly. The vicar of Tintagel is constable of the castle. The stranger will notice in the churchyard the green mounds—almost barrows—of some old graves, and some ancient tombstones commemorating a family of the name of Arthur. It is a curious circumstance that this name is common in the country round King Arthur's Castle.

1 m. S. of Trevena is *Trebarwith* (pronounced Trebarreth) *Strand*, the sandy shore of a bay about a mile in width, and deservedly a favourite spot with artists; not only is it intrinsically beautiful as a coast-scene, but it offers facilities for the study of the sea in its greatest purity, the billows being unsullied by earthy particles held in suspension. The rocky cliffs of this part of Cornwall have, in particular, been painted by Creswick, and in many points resemble Italian coast-scenery. It is worthy of notice that the "pietra forte" of Florence—although little older than the London clay—has been so modified by subterraneous heat that it was once considered a very ancient formation, and was classed with the Cornish killas under the name of *grauwacke*.

From Tintagel the traveller should return to Camelford by the *Delabole Quarries*, which are 4 m. from Trevena and 2 m. from Camelford. They are celebrated for producing the best slate in the kingdom, and have been worked many years, being mentioned by Carew, who wrote in the reign of Eliz. On the road he will pass another large quarry called *Bowethick*, or *North Delabole*, situated in a valley rendered picturesque by protruding rocks, and opening to the sea at the little cove of *Port William*. 2 villages owe their origin to the Delabole quarries, *Pengelley* and *Medrose;* the best accommodation is to be found at

4 m. *Penjelley*, i. e. head of the grove (*Inn:* the Old Delabole Inn). The quarries present one of the most astonishing and animated scenes imaginable. The traveller suddenly beholds 3 enormous pits, which, excavated by the uninterrupted labour of centuries, are encompassed by dark blue hills of rubbish, continually on the increase, and slowly encroaching upon the domain of the farmer. The scene is enlivened by a throng of men busily engaged in various noisy employments, while waggons and horses are everywhere in rapid motion, and steam-engines are lifting with a harsh sound their ponderous arms, and raising loaded trucks from the depths of the pit, or masses of slate of several tons' weight, which are seen slowly ascending *guide-chains* to stages which overhang the quarries. The stranger should obtain the services of one of the "captains"—superintendents—who are always willing to act as guides, and to explain the different operations to which the slate is subjected. The quarry nearest Pengelley is perhaps the most interesting of the 3. This is about 260 ft. in depth, and divided by a ridge no broader than a cartway from the middle pit, which is now considered the most valuable, as it has not yet been excavated to any considerable depth, and the slate is of a prime quality. The third or upper pit is the largest. It has been worked for a long period, and is now nearly exhausted, and the machinery being old, and the sides of the quarry loose and unstable, this pit is often the scene of melancholy accidents. Upon the edge of each quarry is the *Papote Head*, a projecting platform, from which a number of *guide-chains* are stretched like the shrouds of a ship to the base of the pit. The slate is first loosened by small charges of gunpowder; it is then torn up by wedges and crowbars, and placed in trucks, which, being attached to a wheel which traverses a guide-chain, are drawn up by the steam-engine some feet above the *Papote Head*. Moveable stages, called *hatches* or *tables*, are then run out under the trucks, which, being lowered upon a framework on wheels, are drawn away by horses to the different workshops, where the slate is split into various sizes, according to the purpose it is intended to serve. The water is pumped from the quarries by water-wheels into an adit, and the slate is shipped at the little harbours of *Port Gavorne* and Boscastle, the former being the principal port in the summer, the latter in the winter, as affording the best shelter to the vessels. About 1000 men are employed in these works, who raise on an average 120 tons of slate per day, which, manufactured on the spot into roofing slates, cisterns, and other articles, are exported to various parts of the United Kingdom, and to France, Belgium, the West Indies, and America. The roofing slates of Delabole are particularly famous, and are divided into nine sizes, called respectively Ladies, Countesses, Duchesses, Queens, Rags, and Imperials. If the stranger should be desirous of comparing the produce from the different quarries, he can ascertain the quality by the *sound* when the stone is struck, which should be clear and sonorous; by the *colour*, since the light blue is firm and close, the blackish blue of a loose texture and apt to imbibe water; and lastly by the *feel*, a good stone being hard and rough to the touch, and a bad one smooth and oily. The best slate from any quarry is called the *bottom-stone*, and at Delabole is found at and below a depth of 24 fath. from the surface. The name *Delabole*, or *Dennabowl* (sometimes corrupted into Dilly-bolly), is in Cornwall often associated with patches of barren soil, and there are furze-crofts on many estates which are thus denominated. On the eastern edge of the Bodmin Moors we find a Dennabowl

in close proximity to *Stonyford*, a name which sufficiently denotes the character of the district. The country in the vicinity of Pengelley bristles with hedges of slate, and the sides and roofs of out-houses are here frequently formed of single slabs of that material. The neighbourhood is a convenient one for the builder, as the proprietors of the quarries are too happy to have the *deads* removed, since their accumulation involves the sacrifice of much valuable land. Fine specimens of the "Cornish diamond," or rock crystal, have been found in these quarries.

Proceeding from Camelford towards Wadebridge—

3 m. *St. Teath*. In the ch. see a curious pulpit, carved and coloured. It was presented to the parish in 1630 by the family of Carminowe, who claimed descent from King Arthur, and in the celebrated Scrope and Grosvenor quarrel proved that they had borne the disputed arms (azure, a band or) from time immemorial. In the E. window of the S. transept is the shield of Hen. VII., with other heraldic bearings. There are some good seat-ends, and an effigy in the N. transept (of the 13th cent. ?). Near St. Teath (pronounced St. *Teth*) is a wayside cross, with 3 holes only, standing in the hedge. Of St. Tethe, or St. Etha, nothing is known. 1. about 2 m. lies the remote church-town of *Michaelstow*. The ch. has Dec. portions (nave; where the piers on the S. side are of granite, with foliated capitals of Caen stone), and Perp. (S. aisle and tower). There is a good open roof to the S. aisle, and the N. aisle has a chantry (divided off by screen) at its E. end. The font is Norm. There are some fragments of stained glass. In this parish is *St. Syth's* (Osyth's?) beacon — an earthwork rising to a great height.

3 m. rt. *St. Kew*. The *Ch.* here should be seen. It is of the early part of the 15th cent., somewhat resembling Bodmin. The tower is fine. The cradle roofs deserve notice. There are incised slabs (17th cent.) in the chancel and N. aisle. Almost every window has remains of stained glass, and in the E. window is a Root of Jesse (15th cent.), said to have come from Bodmin. The wild boar which figures in one of the windows is said to have been killed in Lemon woods by a man named Lanow; the name also of the parish before the dedication of the ch. to St. Kew, of whom nothing is known. On the same side of the road, at a distance of about 5 m., is *Endellion*. The ch. is of no great interest. In the parish is Port Issyk (issic, i. e. *lower* port)—corrupted into P. Isaac—whence the Delabole slate is exported. 1. *St. Tudy. Hengar House*, a seat of Sir Henry Onslow, Bart., is enriched by some tapestry and paintings. In the ch. are monuments of the Nicols family, one dated 1597.

2 m. l. *St. Mabyn*, and near it an earthwork called *Killbury* or *Kelly Rounds*. The church-tower of St. Mabyn (75 ft.) is one of the loftiest in the county. There are grotesque corbels at the angles of the upper stages, and 4 statues in niches at the top. The tower stands on an eminence. The ch. is for the most part Perp. The E. window is a memorial for Francis Hext and wife.

2 m. *Wadebridge* (*Inns:* the Molesworth Arms; Commercial Hotel), a town remarkable for its bridge, the longest and one of the oldest in the county, but partly reconstructed a few years since. It is a picturesque structure of 17 arches, built in 1485, and is said to have originated in the exertions of a Mr. Lovebond, vicar of Egloshayle, who, affected by the continual loss of life at the ferry, raised by subscription a fund sufficient to pay the cost of its erection, and at his death bequeathed an annual sum of 20*l.* to be applied towards its maintenance. A railroad runs from this town to Bod-

min, and a branch extends in the direction of Camelford to Wenford Bridge, near the rocky valley of *Hunter-Gantick*. (Rte. 21.) The trains carry passengers as far as Bodmin, but are principally employed in bringing copper and iron-ore from the Lanescot and other mines, and conveying imports and sea-sand for manure up the country. The valley of the Camel, through which it passes, contains the prettiest scenery in the neighbourhood. The situation of *St. Breock Ch.* is especially pleasing. The parish ch. of *Egloshayle (the ch. by the river)* stands on the rt. bank of the Camel, and may be seen from the bridge. It is Perp. throughout; and the tower, which is a fine specimen, was probably, as well as the S. aisle, the work of Lovebond (d. 1490), the vicar who built the bridge. In the moulding of the W. door is a serpent, triumphant on one side, depressed on the other. In the chancel is an incised slab to the Kestells, 1522. The pulpit (late Perp.) is no doubt Lovebond's work. His shield or device is the 3 hearts with fillet. *St. Breock Ch.*, which has been restored, is mostly Perp., except the tower, which is Dec., and the very fine font, also of Dec. form. In the chancel is a *brass* for a civilian and 2 wives, circ. 1578 (Tredinicks?). About 5 m. on the road to Bodmin is *Pencarrow* (Lady Molesworth); and 5 m. N. by E., in an elevated, unfrequented part of the country, *St. Endellion*, with a weather-stained *ch.*, dating from the reign of Hen. VI. (see *ante*); and on an opposite hill some remains of *Roscarrock House*, formerly residence of the ancient family of Roscarrock, a ponderous building, castellated and loop-holed, and entered through a heavy arch of granite.

An excursion can be made from Wadebridge by a wild bleak road, or by the river, to

Padstow (by road 8 m.). (*Inns:* Commercial Hotel; Golden Lion. Steamers ply between Padstow and Bristol, calling at Swansea and Ilfracombe.) This is one of those antiquated unsavoury fishing-towns which are viewed most agreeably from a distance. It is situated about 1 m. from the sea, near the mouth of the Camel estuary, and derives its name from St. Petrock, to whom the ch. is dedicated. Athelstane, on his conquest of Cornwall, is said to have given this place the name of "Athelstow," but it soon took that of Petrockstowe, contracted at last to "Padstow." It appears to have been a seaport of some consequence in early days, and is mentioned as having contributed two war-ships fully equipped for the siege of Calais (Edw. III.). Its prosperity, according to a tradition, declined in the reign of Hen. VIII., in consequence of an accumulation of sand at the mouth of the harbour.

The *Ch.*, which is late Dec., has been restored throughout by Miss Prideaux Brune, of Place. The slender pillars, with banded capitals and lofty arches, deserve notice. The windows have all been filled with stained glass, and the timber roofs are new. The font, with an arcade and figures of the 12 apostles, is ancient, with the exception of the 4 side shafts. It is of "Caraclew" stone (*i. e. Car-a-clew* = grey rock). Most of the ornamental work, door-jambs, mullions, window-dressings, and fonts, of this district are made of Caraclew, a good stone, but of an ugly cold slaty grey colour. This font was once regarded by the inhabitants as endued with a marvellous property, which was held in high esteem by the *mauvais sujets* of the town. This was nothing less than the virtue of preserving those who had been baptized in it from the gallows. About 50 years ago, however, much to their discomfiture, a man named Elliot, who had been duly christened in it, was convicted of robbing the mail and hanged. In the ch. is a monument (1627) to Sir Nicholas Prideaux.

Place House (Charles Prideaux Brune, Esq.), the ancient seat of the family of Prideaux, stands, encircled by trees, upon the high ground above Padstow. It was erected in 1600 upon the site of a monastery said to have been founded by St. Petroc, and destroyed by the Danes in 981. It contains numerous pictures, including several of the youthful productions of the Cornish artist *Opie*, who, before leaving the county, made an expedition to Padstow, and painted all the Prideauxs and their servants, and even the family cats. Among the portraits are those of *Humphrey Prideaux*, the learned Dean of Norwich, who was born here, and Harriet Villiers, Duchess of Cleveland. There is a large painting of Jupiter and Europa, some good landscapes, cattle-pieces, and a Madonna and Child. In the neighbouring parish of St. Merryn is *Harlyn*, the seat of the Peter family; and in that of St. Issey some slight traces of *Halwyn*, where, according to the tradition, a Champernowne and his lady lived in separate establishments on opposite sides of the estuary, but contentedly singing

„That verdant bill and silver stream
Divide my love and me."

The ch. of *Little Petherick*, 3 m. on the Wadebridge road, has been admirably rebuilt, on the plans of Mr. W. White, by the late vicar, Sir Hugh Molesworth, Bart. It contains a valuable copy of Fox's Book of Martyrs, 3 vols. folio, published 1684.

Padstow Harbour, though much obstructed by sand, with an entrance narrow and dangerous, and a bar called the *Dunbar* (*Dune bar*) within its mouth, is the only place of shelter on the N. coast of Cornwall; and during gales from the N.W., when a refuge on this iron-bound shore is particularly required, its entrance is attended with considerable risk, as at these times there is an eddy of wind within the point by which vessels are likely to be taken aback and driven upon the sands. A capstan has, however, been placed on *Stepper Point* (227 ft. above the sea), and when a vessel is expected a pilot-boat waits within the headland, so as to carry a hawser on board in time to prevent these fatal effects. But it is intended to construct a harbour of refuge here. The sands are thought to be now on the decrease, owing to the amazing quantity which is annually taken from the Dunbar, and despatched for manure up the country. They are said to be the richest in the county in carb. of lime, of which they contain 80 per cent., and are in such demand that the amount thus carried away in the year has been estimated at no less than 100,000 tons. A *raised beach* may be seen at the mouth of the harbour. The E. shore of the estuary is desolated with sand, which, piled in a series of naked hills, gives great wildness to the view from Padstow, but has rather a cheerful appearance on an overclouded day, when it delusively appears brightened by sunshine.

This sand has partly buried an ancient chapel, dedicated to *St. Enodoc* (locally " Sinkineddy "), and situated under the E. side of *Bray Hill*, a barren eminence 209 ft. above the sea, lying a short distance N. of Padstow, but on the opposite side of the harbour. The sand is piled around this building to the level of the roof, and has been excavated to allow a passage to the door, but is now fixed by turf. Its accumulation appears to have been arrested at a distant period, as there are several ancient tombstones upon the surface. Observe one on the N.E. side of the churchyard with a quaint inscription and date 1687. This little ch. was built about the year 1430, to supply the place, it is thought, of an ancient *oratory*, traces of which were revealed about 50 years ago, but only for a short time, by the shifting of the sand on Bray Hill. On approaching the existing ch. little else is seen than its crooked spire of slate-stone, blackened by the salt breezes and encrusted with yellow lichens. The seats in the interior are wormeaten, and ornamented with carving so rude that it might be imagined coeval with the ark. Some scarlet and gold remains on the roof panels. The antiquary, however, will regret the necessity for the late repairs, which have obliterated some of the most interesting features of this little fanc. Its Norman font, a plain circular bowl with cable moulding at the base, is an indication of the existence of a ch. prior to the present structure. Connected with this building, a story is told, that some years ago the clergyman, in order to preserve his emoluments and fees, was in the habit of descending into the pulpit by a skylight. Service is now performed in it once a fortnight. St. Enodoc is in the parish of *St. Minver*, where is a very interesting E. E. church with Perp. additions. The W. tower is E. E. The nave is nearly filled with seats having well-carved ends. There is a *brass* to Roger Opy and wife, 1517. Some incised slate slabs have been arranged behind the altar. Between Wadebridge and St. Enodoc is a small chapel on the sandy shore of Padstow harbour called *St. Michael*, or the Rock Church; it is in most features like St. Enodoc Ch., but without tower and spire. The font is almost exactly the same. Against its eastern wall, on the outside, is a good head of a large cross without a staff.

On the opposite side of the estuary, and near Trevose Head (4 m. W.), the stranger may find the tower of another old ch., dedicated to *St. Constantine*, which the sand invaded with more fatal effect. In its vicinity the *Feast of St. Constantine* used to be annually celebrated, and has been discontinued only a few years. Its celebration consisted in the consumption of limpet-pies, and service in the ch., followed by a hurling match.

Near the mouth of the harbour are 3 *island rocks*, which are visited in the summer by parties of pleasure, or persons in search of gulls' eggs. There is risk, however, in the adventure, as a ground-sea sometimes rises without warning, and cuts off the retreat.

At *Porthqueen* (*i. e.* Porthgwin = White Porth) and *Kellan Head* (alt. 209 ft.), situated on the coast between Padstow and *Port Isaac*, are fine specimens of trap-dykes. At Kellan Head the intrusive rock has caught up fragments of slate, which appear to have been much altered by the heat of the igneous mass.

Trevose Head (4 m. W.) is a good point for a view of the coast, since it is situated about midway between Hartland and St. Ives, and projects boldly into the Channel. The lighthouse was erected 1847. It exhibits two fixed lights, one upon the summit of the tower (alt. 204 ft.), the other at the base, and 129 ft. above high-water mark. Between *Pentire Point* and Trevose Head the cliffs show the effects of considerable disturbance. On the W. side of the latter headland trappean rocks are singularly mixed with arenaceous beds and argillaceous slates. Organic remains occur abundantly in the slates and calcareous beds near *Dinas Cove*, S.W. of Padstow.

Proceeding from Wadebridge towards St. Columb:—

2 m. Before reaching this milestone a small stone *cross* l. on the roadside. rt. to Padstow, 6 m. (It was here that Mr. Norway was murdered by two brothers named Lightfoot, Feb. 8, 1840. The murderers were hung at Bodmin, and confessed all the circumstances of their crime. On the evening of the murder, Norway's brother, chief officer of the

ship 'Orient,' then about 7 m. N.N.W. of the island of St. Helena, dreamt that he saw the murder perpetrated, with all the facts as they occurred,—excepting only that a house which he well knew, seemed in his dream to be l. instead of rt. of the road. See the whole remarkable story in Carlyon's 'Early Years and Late Reflections,' vol. i. p. 219.)

1 m. *No Man's Land.* Here the traveller ascends the wild highland of St. *Breock Downs* (alt. 739 ft.), which has a particularly black and gloomy aspect, even at a distance. l. 1 m. is a rock called the *Druids' Altar*; and 1½ m. the *Great Stone*, at the intersection of 4 cross-roads.

1½ m. rt. *St. Issey Beacon*, a conspicuous landmark. l. *St. Breock Down*. ½ m. Here, l. of the road, may be seen 6 upright stones, the remnant of 9, which once stood in a row, and were known as the *Nine Maidens* (in Corn. " Naw Wawrs," the "nine sisters"). They are generally considered sepulchral monuments.

3 m. *St. Columb Major* (*Inn:* Red Lion, kept by Polkinhorne, an excellent guide to the district, and most civil and obliging landlord). This town is situated about 5 m. from the sea, and derives its name from St. Columb—not the famous St. Columb-kille, but a sainted Irish virgin, who in the 5th cent. preached in Cornwall. Her remains rested in the same tomb with SS. Patrick and Bridget in Down Cathedral. The town is seated upon an eminence, the reputed site of a Danish fortification. The *Church*, which is of great size and beauty, is Early Dec. (piers and arches of nave, S. porch door, S. transept window, and font), and Perp. (all the remaining portions). In the chancel observe the stone altar, found in 1846 under the floor, and now placed on 4 granite shafts—in all probability its original supporters. The chancel was once 10 ft. longer, but was injured by an explosion of gunpowder in 1676. The window of the S. transept is a fine example. The font has grotesque faces, protruding tongues at each other, on the sides. There are S. and N. porches; and the W. tower (Perp.) stands on open arches W., S., and N. Much has been done for this ch., which has some good open seats. Mr. Butterfield has given plans for its adaptation as the cathedral of Cornwall. In the ch. are 3 *brasses*—Sir John Arundell, Kt. of the Bath (1545), and 2 wives; Sir John Arundell (d. 1590) and wife (engraved circ. 1630); and John Arundell (1633) and wife. In the churchyard is a small and curious cross. The manor of St. Columb belonged to the priory of Bodmin, whence it passed to the Arundells, and early in the present cent. to T. Rawlings, Esq., of Padstow. The *Rectory*, which has been lately restored, is quadrangular and moated; and is said to have been intended for a college of 6 priests. The timber used in the construction of the church is said to have been grown upon Tregoss Moors, the fabled hunting-ground of King Arthur (the Cornish word *goss* is a corruption of *coes* or *coed*, a wood); but the traveller will admit that there is nothing to countenance the tradition in the present appearance of this district, which is as bald as a desert, and even in Leland's time (Hen. VIII.) was described as " a morish ground al barren of woodde." Some good Gothic houses have been lately erected in the town.

Trewan (R. H. S. Vyvyan, Esq.) stands on an eminence above St. Columb, of which it commands a fine view in connection with a long distance of hill and valley. It is a battlemented building of the 15th cent., which for a long period had fallen into decay, but it has recently been restored by R. H. S. Vyvyan, Esq. The ancient granite entrance hall has been preserved, and is a fine specimen of the architecture of the Elizabethan period. *Carnanton*, seat of H. Willyams, Esq., inherited from Noy, the attorney-general of Charles I., who, says Fuller, "was wont pleasantly to say that his house had no fault in it save only that it was too near unto London," and *Nanswhyden*, Miss Brune, are near this town. The latter formerly belonged to Mr. Hoblyn, who published an edition of the Stannary laws. He was speaker of the Stannary parliament, and died in 1756. His monument may be seen in the ch.

St. Columb is an excellent centre from which to visit many of the places described in the present route and in Rte. 21. It is the only spot, however, from which the very interesting range of coast between the Towan and Trevose Heads—forming Watergate Bay—is conveniently accessible. This line of coast of about 20 m. is at no point farther distant than 8 m. from St. Columb. The spots specially to be visited are the vale and village of Mawgan, the watering-place of Newquay, and the coast between Piran Sands and Trevose Head, including the little bay known as Bodruthan Steps. (Walk to Mawgan through the Carnanton woods—in which the ferns are magnificent—or drive by the lodge through the grounds, permission being given.)

The Vale of *Mawgan* or *Lanherne*, which stretches in a direct line from the town of St. Columb to the lonely little "Porth" or cove in which it terminates, is perhaps the most beautiful "combe" on the N. coast of Cornwall. Throughout, it "presents a succession of lovely scenery: the groves of Carnanton, once the seat of Noy, Charles I.'s able, though miserly and crabbed, attorney-general (his heart at his death was found shrivelled up, say his biographers, into the substance of a leathern penny purse); the grey convent at Lanherne, formerly the manor-house of the Arundels, devoted by one of the family to the reception of nuns driven here by the first French revolution; the old church tower of Mawgan, embowered in its grove of lofty Cornish elms (the small-leaved variety, strangely neglected in other parts of England)."

The *Church* of St. Mawgan (3 m. from St. Columb) is throughout Perp., with a fine tower, 70 ft. high, from the top of which the view down the valley is striking. The ch., which contains many of the old carved bench-ends, has been restored by Butterfield, who also designed the new parsonage. There are *brasses* for—a priest, circ. 1420; Cecily, dau. of Sir John Arundel, 1578; a civilian, circ. 1580; and Jane, dau. of Sir John Arundel, c. 1580. "She served 5 queens," runs the inscription. This brass is a palimpsest, and has on the reverse portions of 2 Flemish brasses, circ. 1375. The nuns of Lanherne buried in the transept until lately. In the churchyard is a very interesting *cross* of the 14th cent. Under 4 niches at the summit of an octagonal shaft are—the Almighty Father with the dove holding a crucifix, the usual representation of the Holy Trinity; an Abbot; an Abbess; and a King and Queen, the latter kneeling at a lectern; below, an angel holds a scroll, which rises to the queen's crown. The work is well executed and well preserved. Here is also the stern of a boat, painted white, and erected in the place of a tombstone over the grave of 10 unfortunate fishermen who, on a winter's night of 1846, were drifted ashore in their boat, a ghastly crew, frozen to death. Adjoining the ch. is the old manor-house of the Arundells, *Lanherne*, for the last 50 years a Carmelite nunnery. It became the property of the Cornish Arundells in 1231. On their extinction in 1700 it passed to Lord Arundell of Wardour, and in the beginning of the present cent. was assigned by its proprietor to a sisterhood of nuns, who, driven from France to Antwerp by the Revolution, had emigrated to England when the French entered Belgium. It has always belonged to a Roman Catholic; and in one of the walls is a secret chamber in which, it is said, a priest was concealed for 18 months in the reign of Elizabeth. One side of the house is ancient (circ. 1580?); the other 150 years old. The inmates are an abbess and 20 nuns, 18 English and 2 French women, who inhabit the modern portion of the building. The chapel, fitted up in the style of Louis XIV., is the only room to which strangers can gain access, but it is hardly worth seeing. It is situated in the ancient part of the house, and contains some copies from the old masters, and a silver lamp burning perpetually before the high altar. The nuns occupy a gallery closely boarded and curtained, for even the officiating priest is denied a view of them. Strangers may here attend mass, but they are not allowed to advance from beneath the gallery whilst the nuns are in the chapel. The convent gardens, surrounded by high walls, are used for exercise and burial, the cemetery containing an ancient *sculptured cross*, the shaft covered with knot-work, which originally stood in the parish of Gwinear.

From Mawgan you should walk down the valley to the coast, and visit *Mawgan Porth*, and the romantic little bay called *Bodruthan Steps*, about 1 m. to the N. of it. The sea view from the top of the cliffs, looking out over the bay, is almost unrivalled. "Across the beds of seapink, our feet sinking deeper in its soft cushions at every step we take . . . we stand at the cliff-edge. . . . I grant the most patriotic Cornubian at once, that nowhere, at no time, had we looked on a scene like this. Twenty miles of cliff, a hundred of rolling water outspread before us—a score or more of lesser bays, each with their own golden sands and gleaming promontory indented within the embrace of the one noble bay."— *G. F. J.* These are the seas which Hook delights to paint. Before him

"no artist seems to have truly felt the gladness and glory of our blue waters."—*F. T. P.* There is excellent fishing (trout and peal) in the stream which runs through the Mawgan valley. The coast at Mawgan Porth is pierced with caverns in all directions, said to be of unknown extent. The largest has an entrance about 300 ft. high, and extends inward for about 800 ft. *Bodruthan Steps* (formerly reached by numerous *steps* down the cliffs) is a bay N. of Mawgan Porth, with a beach of fine sand—slate cliffs of 400 ft. high, pierced by numberless caverns—and some weatherworn and fantastic masses of rock studding the sands themselves. One of them is known as "Queen Elizabeth's Rock," and really resembles the well-known small crowned head and spreading ruff. The view extends from Trevose to the Towan.

St. Columb Minor is 5 m. from St. Columb, near the sea, in a valley W. of Mawgan. The ch. is late Dec., with a fine W. tower. In its vicinity are *Rialton*, which gave title to the statesman Sidney Godolphin, and the ruins of

Rialton Priory (so called), which are now, however, rather a subject for regret than admiration, as they have been much mutilated within the last few years. Rialton belonged to the priory of Bodmin; and this house was built about the end of the 15th cent., by Thomas Vivian, then prior of Bodmin, whose tomb remains in Bodmin church. On the coast is the little harbour of

Lower St. Columb Porth, where the traveller may witness the phenomenon of a *blow-hole*, through which, at intervals, the sea is forcibly driven, when the tide is at a certain height.

Newquay (*Inns:* Old Inn; Red Lion; lodgings are scarce and very indifferent), 7 m. from St. Columb, and 2 m. W. of St. Columb Minor, is a small but rising watering-place where the pilchard fishery is pursued on a considerable scale. It is situated at the W. end of *Watergate Bay*, under the shelter of *Towan Head*, and its sandy beach runs 3 m. E. beneath a range of romantic cliffs, which are particularly fine at a place called *Filorey* between Newquay and Mawgan. The eastern side of Newquay Bay is closed by an island, which forms the Trevalgey Head. It is approached by a wooden bridge across the ravine 20 ft. wide, which separates it from the mainland. In a W. direction, between Towan Head and Piran Bay, the coast presents the following series of sandy coves which are girded by cavernous cliffs:— *Fistral Bay*, bounded on the W. by *Pentire Point* and the *Goose Rock*; *Crantock Bay*, with the estuary of *the Gannel*, which is little else than sand— the islet called the *Chick* is off the W. point; *Holywell Bay*, so named from a spring of fresh water in a cavern accessible only at low tide; the bay terminates on the W. with *Penhale Point* and the outlying rock termed the *Carters*.

Newquay is the northern terminus of a *railroad* commenced by the late Mr. Treffry, of Place House, Fowey, which runs from one coast of the county to the other in a line from Par to Newquay, a distance of about 20 m. Passengers are not conveyed by it.

The neighbourhood of Newquay has much interest for the geologist. He may find a bed of fossiliferous limestone, resting on variegated slates, in the small island lying off Lower St. Columb Porth; and in the cliffs of Watergate Bay a very excellent section of these slate-beds, and a fine example of an elvan (about 2 m. W. of Mawgan), which cuts the grauwacke cliff nearly at right angles to the strike of the beds. At Newquay the blown sand is consolidated into a very interesting rock—a recent sandstone, which is still in the course of formation, owing to the infiltration of water holding iron in solution.

It is sufficiently compact to be quarried for building purposes, and when ground and burnt forms an excellent cement, and has been used as such in Newquay pier. As a building stone it has been employed in the construction of the neighbouring ch. of *Crantock*. When first raised it is somewhat soft, but becomes hard by exposure, in consequence of the evaporation of the water contained in it. The cliffs between Newquay and Trevose Head illustrate, in a striking manner, the destruction of a coast by heavy breakers. In *Crantock Ch.*, which has Dec. and E. E. portions, is a curious circular *Font*, date 1473. The ch. was collegiate.

Trerice, the ancient mansion of the Arundells of Lanherne, is situated about 3½ m. from Newquay. (See Rte. 21.)

2 m. S.E. of St. Columb is the eminence of *Castle an Dinas—Brit.* " the earth fort," in contradistinction to a castle of " stane and lime" —(alt. 729 ft.), crowned with an elliptical doubly entrenched camp of 6 acres, which tradition proclaims *the hunting-seat of King Arthur*, who, according to the legend, chased the wild deer on the Tregoss Moors. The geologist as well as the antiquary may find amusement in this old castle, for the alteration of slate by the proximity of granite is well seen on the hill. Observe the schorl which has been introduced among the laminæ.

The *Roche Rocks* (Rte. 21) are about 5 m. distant in the same direction. 4 m. S.W. is the village of *Colan*, of interest for its ch., which was founded 1250 by Bishop Branscombe, but much altered in the Perp. period.

For the remainder of this route see Rte. 21.

ROUTE 23.

PLYMOUTH TO TRURO, BY SALTASH, ST. GERMANS, LISKEARD (THE CHEESEWRING, ST. NEOT'S), BODMIN, LOSTWITHIEL (RESTORMEL), ST. BLAZEY, AND ST. AUSTELL [CORNWALL RLY.]. (PERRANZABULOE; PERRAN ROUND; THE COAST.)

The *Cornwall Rly.* from Plymouth to Truro, and the *West Cornwall Rly.* from Truro to Penzance, now carry the iron road to within 10 m. of the Land's End; but the construction of the Cornwall Rly. has been attended by difficulties of no ordinary kind. An estuary had to be spanned, and the line conducted over the rocky hills of a semi-mountainous country, and across numerous deep valleys. It was a labour for a Hercules, but Mr. Brunel accomplished the feat. In May 1859 the rly. was opened to public traffic. Its completion, however, had occupied 12 years, and in the short space of 60 m. there are no less than 7 tunnels, and 43 viaducts, of which some are 150 ft. in height. The greatest of the many difficulties was to cross the Tamar, the boundary of the county, where the estuary was ¼ m. wide, and impassable at one bound, and where the water in mid stream was 70 ft. deep. This was accomplished by the late Mr. Brunel, below the level of the Tamar and its bed, in the very remarkable structure the

Royal Albert Bridge. This extraordinary viaduct—which for novelty and ingenuity of construction stands unrivalled in the world—carries the rly. at a height of 100 ft. above the water from the hills of Devon to those of Cornwall, on 19 spans or arches, of which 2 alone bridge the estuary in gigantic leaps of 455 ft. Its total length is 2240 ft., or nearly ½ m., its greatest width only 30 ft., but its height, from the foundation to the top of the tubes, 260 ft., or 50 ft. greater than that of the Monument. The estuary is here at its narrowest point, but broader than the Thames at Westminster, and not to be spanned without the aid of a central pier. To found and build such a structure was the first great difficulty. The second was to hang the roadway; for as a central pier afforded no point to which chains could be secured, it was impossible to erect a suspension bridge similar to the Britannia. The supports of the roadway must be made in a manner self-supporting, and this Mr. Brunel effected, by an ingenious combination of the arch, the tubular girder, and suspension chain. The main chains which stretch from the shore to the central pier, and from which the roadway hangs, are attached at the ends to enormous iron tubes, which in two magnificent curves bridge the estuary. Thus each tube gives support to the chain, and forms with it a double bow, or ellipsis. The chief labours of construction were to build the central pier, and to raise the tubes. Each weighs about 1200 tons, and to uphold such a mass of iron it was necessary that the foundation should rest on the solid rock. But to reach this was no easy matter. The depth of water was 70 ft., and the river bed, of mud and gravel, 20 ft. It was accomplished by means of a novel application of the cofferdam principle. A cylinder of wrought iron, 100 ft. in height, 37 ft. in diam., and weighing 300 tons, was sunk on the spot selected. The water was pumped out and air forced in, and the men set to work as in a diving bell. But the labour was most severe. The excavation was carried on under a pressure of 38 lbs. to the inch, which produced distressing symptoms, and in one instance a fatal effect; and although less felt after a time, when 40 men could work together with little inconvenience, it was gratifying to all parties to see the granite pile emerge above the surface of the river. Then commenced a series of very interesting operations. One of the tubes was put together on the shore, floated out on pontoons—each 50 ft. in length—and lodged at high water upon the bases of the piers, which were to rise simultaneously with the arch as it was lifted by hydraulic pressure. Each tube is elliptical in form, and constructed throughout of inch boiler-plate, strengthened inside by ties and diaphragms. It is 12 ft. in height, and 17 ft. in width. The process of placing the two tubes in position occupied from 5 to 6 months. The western tube was first raised. Twice a week it was lifted by the presses 3 ft., and in the following 3 days the masonry was built up another 3 ft. Thus the progress was 6 ft. per week, and at the end of each week the 6 ft. joints of the iron columns of the central pier were added. These pillars are of colossal dimensions. They are 4 in number, octagon in their shape, 10 ft. in diam., and 100 ft. in height. They stand 10 ft. apart in the centre of the granite pile, and are bound together by a lattice-work of wrought iron. Each weighs about 150 tons. On the top, like a capital, rests the standard, a mass of 200 tons, to which the tubes are bolted. The piers which carry the roadway to the hills are of more moderate proportions. They are each formed of double columns of stone, braced together by a girder of boiler-plate, but the main piers on the shore are of more massive construction. They have to share with the central pier the weight and thrust of the bridge. They are 190 ft. in height from the foundation, and of solid masonry 29 ft. by 17. Such, in brief, is an outline of the Saltash viaduct, which will probably remain unsurpassed for many years to come. It is longer by 300 ft. than the far-famed bridge of Anglesea, but it has been erected at a much less cost. Its strength, too, has been severely tested. Each span was subjected to a dead-weight strain, uniformly distributed, of 2300 tons. This amounted to about 5½ tons per inch of the section of the tube, but the weight of the heaviest train will be less than ½ ton per inch. The pressure of the structure on the base of its central pier is calculated at 8 tons per foot, or double the pressure of the Victoria Tower on its foundation.

[The old road from Plymouth into Cornwall passes through Devonport and its fortifications to the ferry across *Hamoaze*, where the carriage and horses are placed upon the *steam-bridge*, established 1831, by the late J. M. Rendel, the engineer, then residing in Plymouth. It was a novel invention for crossing rivers, and was first applied by Mr. Rendel to the Dart, then at Torpoint and Saltash, and afterwards at Southampton and Portsmouth. Its value was recognised by the Royal Soc., who awarded for it the Telford medal. The passage occupies about 8 minutes. The floating bridge passes among numerous ships laid up in ordinary.]

The Rly. from Plymouth and Devonport to the steam ferry at Saltash commands a fine view of the *Hamoaze*; and, on its opposite shore, of the woods of *Thankes* (Lord Graves) and of *Antony* (seat of the Carews), the town of *Torpoint*, the *St. Germans river*, and the old keep of *Trematon* rising from a bank of foliage. At Saltash the estuary is considerably contracted, and here the Cornwall Railway spans it by the *Royal Albert Bridge*.

4¼ m. *Saltash Stat.* (*Inn*: Green Dragon Hotel.) This town, inhabited principally by fishermen, climbs the steep shore of the Tamar, and from the river presents a very striking appearance, the acclivity being abrupt, and the old houses hanging in tiers one above the other. The picturesque effect of this grouping is considerably heightened by a variety of colours, arising from a strange jumble of materials. One house is constructed of stone, another of brick, a third fronted with plaster, and a fourth with slate. The principal "sight" at Saltash is the view from the high ground above the town, where the roads branch towards Trematon and Callington. It is of great extent and beauty, comprising Hamoaze and its wooded shores, the wonderful viaduct, the arsenal, steam-yard, and dockyard of Devonport, Mount Edgcumbe, the winding river and distant ocean. To this may be added, for those who find pleasure in the monuments of the dead, a sumptuous tomb to 3 brothers Drew in the old *Chapel of St. Nicholas*. This chapel contains Dec. and Perp. portions, and has a tower which may be very early Norm. The roof-bosses are curious. Among their ornaments occur the arms of Richard King of the Romans (son of King John and Earl of Cornwall), and of his son Edward, also Earl of Cornwall. A tablet inserted in the wall of this building is inscribed,—"This chapple was repaired in the Mayoralty of Matthew Veale, Gent., anno 1689." The Mayor of Saltash is an important personage: he takes precedence of the Mayor of Plymouth, and by virtue of his office is also coroner for the borough of Plymouth.

The Roman road, proceeding west from Exeter (a branch of the Ikenild Way), crossed the Tamar at this point; and the "Statio Tamara" of the Itineraries was no doubt at King's Tamerton, immediately above the river, on the Devonshire side. The right of ferry at Saltash, temp. Edw. III., was granted to a soldier who had been wounded at Poictiers. (See *Sir H. Nicolas's Hist. of Navy*).

(An excursion up the Tamar, as far as the Weir-head and Morwell Rocks, is one of the most interesting in the county. See DEVON, Rte. 7; and CORNWALL, Rte. 25.)

Saltash is known for its fishermen, but more so for its fishwomen, who are celebrated for their prowess at the oar, and not unfrequently bear away the prizes at the different regattas. It was an ancient borough previous to the Reform Bill, by which it was disfranchised, and has been represented in Parliament by Waller the poet and Clarendon the historian, who was its member in the Long Parliament. In 1643 it was the scene of a furious engagement, when Lord Mohun and Sir Ralph Hopton drove Ruthen, the governor of Plymouth, across the Tamar, in spite of the cannon which he had planted in the narrow avenues, and of the fire of a ship of 16 guns. Ruthen had been previously beaten on Broadoak Down near Liskeard.

St. Stephen's is the parish ch., and about 1 m. from the town. It has a lofty tower; and a fine Norm. font, in all respects resembling that at Bodmin (see the present Route, *post*). An old *lich-stone* lies just within the porch of the churchyard. Having walked to St. Stephen's, the stranger will probably extend his ramble, as at this place he comes in view of the ancient

Castle of Trematon rising from a wood. (It is seen rt. of the rly. after passing Saltash.) It is separated from the church by a deep valley pierced by an inlet from the Lynher Creek, at the head of which a small hamlet nestles under the shelter of the hill. The remains of this castle are considerable, but not so picturesque as many other ruins, on account of the red colour of the stone. They are, however, beautifully decked with ivy and encircled by lawns and shrubberies. The mansion, which contains some fine paintings, was erected about 30 years ago by the late B. Tucker, Esq., partly at the expense of the castle walls. Trematon is supposed to have been built about the time of the Conquest, and to have been given by Wm. I. to the Earl of Cornwall. At a later period it was annexed to the Duchy. A Stannary Court was anciently held in it, and Gilpin remarks that " *Trematon law* is almost to this day an object of reverence among the common people of Cornwall." During the riots in 1549 the castle was plundered by the rebels, who, enticing out the governor by the pretence of a parley, intercepted his return. The ruins are encircled by a moat, and consist of the walls of the keep (13th centy.) and base court, and of a square massive tower at the entrance, pierced with an archway, which is furnished with grooves for a portcullis. The keep is of an oval form, and commands a very beautiful prospect. Strangers are admitted on week-days. Between the castle and the village of Trematon is a wayside octagonal *cross* about 4 ft. high.

The *Lynher* or *St. Germans River* (which the rly. crosses by a viaduct) and its numerous branches afford the means of pleasant water excursions: their shores being hilly and covered with wood. [*Antony*, the seat of the family of Carew (pron. *Carey*), is bounded partly by this creek and partly by the Tamar. The house was built by Gibbs in 1721, and contains a collection of pictures by *Holbein*, *Vandyke*, *Sir Joshua Reynolds*, *Kneller*, *Lely*, &c. Among them is a portrait, of Richard Carew, the author of the 'Survey of Cornwall,' and a head of Sir Kenelm Digby, by *Vandyke*. A monument to the same Richard Carew will be found in the neighbouring ch. of *Antony*. A group of ilex oaks in the grounds of Antony, planted about 1725, contains perhaps the largest and oldest trees in England of this species. A ferry crosses *Antony Pas-*

sage to Trematon, and below it is *Beggar's Island*. (The story, given in Carew's 'Survey,' runs that a Carew found two beggars fighting in his grounds at Antony, landed them on this island, told them to fight it out, and left them.) Above Antony House the voyager to St. Germans passes below the woods of *Shillingham*, the original seat of the Buller family (there are small remains of the chapel of the house); and then *Ince Castle*, now a farm-house, but once a mansion of the Earls of Devon, and in the civil war garrisoned by the Royalists. Ince is a 16th centy. house, and a solitary example of a brick building in a stone country. It was for some time a seat of the Killigrews, one of whom was painted with his neighbour Carew by Vandyke (the picture is in the Vandyke Gallery at Windsor). The house is a square with 4 corner towers; and, says tradition, *one* Killigrew kept a wife in each tower, neither of whom knew of the existence of the others.]

9½ m. *St. Germans Stat.* (7 m. by road, 10 m. by water, from Saltash, and a favourite boat-excursion of about 14 m. from Plymouth). (*Inn:* Eliot Arms.) This was once a borough town, but is now little more than a village, and important only for its *Church*, which is of great interest in itself, and to be regarded with reverence as having been the cathedral of the Cornish bishopric from its first establishment, temp. Athelstan, to its final union with the see of Exeter under the Confessor. After the grant of Petrockstowe or Bodmin to the see, the cathedral was there and at St. Germans indifferently (see Bodmin, *post*). In its present state the ch. consists of a nave, flanked by 2 western towers, and S. aisle. The chancel and a part of the nave "fell suddenly down on a Friday in 1792." The N. aisle was taken down about the end of the last centy., and a part of its site is now

Route 23.—*Port Eliot.* Sect. II.

occupied by the Port Eliot pew. The W. front, with its towers hung with ivy and fern, is striking and venerable. The central doorway, much enriched, is Norm., but of late character. The N. tower is Norm. in the 2 lower stages, with an additional E. E. story, which is octagonal. The S. tower is Norm. in its lower stage, and Perp. above. The position of these towers may be compared with that of the transeptal towers at Exeter and Ottery St. Mary (see DEVON, Rtes. 1 and 3). The interior of both towers should be seen. In the E. arch of the S. tower stands the Norm. font (fig. by Van Voorst). 2 Norm. piers remain on the S. side of the nave. The *S. aisle* has good windows at its eastern end, which is Dec. Between the 2 eastern windows is a beautiful saint's niche, called the "Bishop's Throne." Here are also sedilia and a piscina. The western part of this aisle and its porch are Perp. At the E. end of the nave is a very fine early Perp. window of 5 lights, cusped, 3 stories high. Observe a very ancient "miserere" stall, representing a man carrying a hare across his shoulder on a stick, with dogs in couples (it has been claimed as the earliest woodwork in the diocese); and a pleasing memorial (designed by a brother officer, and erected by the tenants on the estate) to Capt. Granville Eliot, (Coldstream Guards), killed at Inkermann. The ch. is in a state which imperiously calls for restoration. The religious house here was first founded by Athelstan (?) for secular canons, who were changed for regulars (Augustinians) by Leofric, first Bishop of Exeter. The churchyard has been lately incorporated with the lawn of

Port Eliot (Earl of St. Germans). Port Eliot is on the site of the Priory, and one or two rooms of the old building exist. The house is well stored with paintings by *Rembrandt, Opie, Reynolds,* and other masters.

The following are by *Reynolds:*—
Harriet Eliot (mother of 1st Lord E.), daughter of James Craggs, Esq., Secr. of State.
Edward 1st, Lord E.
Ann E., his sister, married Capt. Bonfoy, R.N.
Edward E., when young, ⅜ length.
Ditto, ⅜ length.
Ditto, at a later period, ⅜ length.
Richard E., brother of 1st Lord.
John E., another brother, Captain R.N.
Edward James E., eldest son of 1st Lord.
Hon. Capt. John Hamilton, R.N.
Sir Josh. Reynolds.
Large picture of *Richard E. and family,* 1746, the first painting by the artist in which several figures are grouped together.
View of Plymouth, from Catdown, a long narrow landscape, painted 1748, the year before Reynolds went to Italy.

Here are also portraits of John Hampden (the only one known), and of Sir John Eliot, ancestor of Lord St. Germans, and Hampden's associate and friend. He died a prisoner in the Tower, where he was buried, as the king would not allow his remains to be removed to St. Germans. An admirable Life of Sir John Eliot by Mr. Forster (London, 1864) has given increased interest to this portrait, and to his ancestral home.

At *Erth* are remains of a domestic chapel of the 13th centy.

Cuddenbeak (the wooded promontory), a farmhouse situated on the river in the position indicated by the name, occupies the site of the ancient palace of the bishops. The traveller will notice the Cornish elms, straight as arrows, which are ranged along the road-side near the ch.; and at the extremity of St. Germans an old village tree (a walnut), so common in Devon and Cornwall, with the earth heaped round it as a seat for gossips. In the parish are *Bake,* a property of Sir Joseph Copley, Bart.; *Catchfrench,* F. Glanville, Esq.; and *Coldrinick,* C. Trelawny, Esq. The road from Saltash is very pretty at *Nottor Bridge,* and at *Tideford,* 1 m. from St. Germans.

[From St. Germans the ecclesiologist may visit the churches of Sheviock and Antony, both well worth seeing, and return to Plymouth by the flying bridge across the Hamoaze. The distance to Tor Point, where the ferry crosses to Devonport, is about 10 m.

Sheviock Church, dedicated to SS. Peter and Paul, is one of the best examples of a 14th centy. ch. in Cornwall. Tywardreth, near Fowey, resembles it. Carew gives us the legendary history of its foundation, recounting how it was built by one of the Dawneys, lords of the manor of Sheviock, whilst the dame of this Dawney was at the same time erecting a barn; and how the cost of the barn exceeded that of the ch. by 3 halfpence; "and so," says our author, "it might well fall out, for it is a great barn, and a very little ch." Since Carew's time, however, the odd halfpence, and a trifle more, have been expended on the ch., particularly in 1851, when the chancel was restored in memory of the Rev. Gerald Pole Carew, by his widow, during the incumbency of the Rev. J. Somers Cocks. It now contains noble painted windows, designed by Street and executed by Wailes, on which are represented our Saviour, and SS. Peter, Paul, Stephen, and Alban; and, in the chancel, several paintings after Overbeck, within circular medallions. Among the subjects are the Annunciation; Our Lord in Majesty, seated on a rainbow; Our Lord with Martha, Mary, and Lazarus; and the first miracle in Cana of Galilee. In the N. aisle is the effigy of a knight (Dawney?) of the 15th centy.; and in the transept a fine monument, with effigies, to Edward Courtenay and his wife, heiress of Sir Nicholas Dawney. The body of the ch., excepting the N. aisle, dates from the 14th centy.; the N. aisle was added in the 15th. The churchyard cross, of carved granite, is a memorial to Lieut. Glanville, 2nd Bengal Europeans, killed at Cawnpore, 1857.

Trethill, ½ m. S.E. of Sheviock, belonged to the family of Wallis, one of whom discovered Otaheite.

2½ m. beyond Sheviock is *Antony* (*in East*), situated on the shore of the *Lynher Creek*, which has here the appearance of an extensive lake. The church stands high, and was struck by lightning on Whitsunday, 1640. The view from the churchyard is magnificent, and was greatly admired by J. M. W. Turner. To the E. the woods of Antony form a promontory, and in the distance rise the Dartmoor tors. The *church*, dedicated to St. James the Less, is said to have been built in 1420. It has been (1862) well restored (W. White, arch.). Most of the windows are filled with memorial stained glass by Willement and others. The carved oaken seats are exact copies of those found in the ch. An old silver-gilt chalice (16th cent.) is among the plate. There are monuments to Richard Carew, author of the 'Survey of Cornwall,' 1620; a *brass* for Margery Arundell, 1424, said to be the foundress of the ch.; and a tablet to Captain Graves, R.N., who played a gallant part in the attack on St. Jago in the reign of George II.]

From St. Germans the rly. curves inland, passing J. *Catchfrench* (F. Glanville, Esq.), (Catchfrench, "Chasse franche," an old Norm. "freewarren"), and an ancient entrenchment called Blackadon Rings; and rt. an entrenchment on Padderbury top. The woods of *Coldrinick* (C. Trelawny, Esq.) are then passed rt.

14¾ m. *Menheniot Stat.* Here is Poole Court, a long-deserted mansion of the Trelawnys, which served for many years as the poorhouse. The *ch.* possesses an ancient spire, of which there are few in the county. Bishop Trelawny, the hero of the ballad "And shall Trelawny die?" was christened here.

rt. of the station is the eminence of *Clicker Tor*, and its jagged rocks protruding from the fern and turf.

It is geologically remarkable for being of serpentine. On each side of the tor for the rly. crosses a valley by a lofty viaduct, and on the Plymouth side by the most ornamental on the whole line. It is a beautiful piece of woodwork, and a most picturesque object in connection with the richly wooded valley it spans. 3 m. beyond we reach

18 m. *Liskeard*, anciently *Liskerret*, i.e. court on an eminence (the prefix *Les* or *Lis*—Welsh *Lhys*—indicated that the place was the abode of a prince or chieftain, as Lestormel, Lespryn, Lestwithiel, vulgo *Restormel*, Respryn, and Lostwithiel) (*Inns:* Webb's Hotel; Bell Hotel; Commercial Hotel), situated in an elevated but rich and well-cultivated country. The monuments of antiquity in the neighbourhood are the objects of interest; the town itself contains nothing worth notice. At its eastern end is the site of a castle which gave Liskeard its ancient name. It is now laid out as a public walk, and has, in the centre, a small mean building, called a grammar-school, in which the learned Dean Prideaux and Dr. Wolcott, better known as Peter Pindar, received the rudiments of their education. A walk leads from this spot over fields which were once the castle park, and where a good view is obtained of the surrounding country, particularly of *Caradon* (i.e. rocky down) *Hill* (alt. 1208 ft.), cavernous with mines, and bounding the wild district of the Bodmin Moors. In 1643 a battle was fought on Braddoc Down, between Liskeard and Lostwithiel, in which Ruthen, the governor of Plymouth, was defeated by the royalists under Sir Ralph Hopton, who, without the loss of an officer, took the enemy's cannon and colours and 1250 prisoners. Hopton then established his quarters in Liskeard, which in 1644 and 45 was honoured by the presence of Charles I. In 1620 the town was represented by Sir

Edward Coke, the great lawyer, and in 1775 by Gibbon the historian.

The stranger will find the following objects and excursions in this neighbourhood very interesting; and if a botanist, may look for *Anchusa sempervirens*, or *evergreen alkanet*, a rare plant, on heaps of rubbish in the lanes.

(*a*) A *walk to Looe*, along the towing-path of the canal, 9 m., which passes down a valley very prettily wooded. The canal begins at *Moorswater*, 1½ m. W., and there communicates with a railway, which runs a circuitous and inclined course of 6½ m. to the *Caradon Copper Mines*, and of 8¼ to the granite-quarries of the *Cheesewring*. Persons are allowed to walk along the rail, but it is a roundabout way of reaching the moor. Towards evening the produce of the mines and quarries is brought down to Moorswater in detached trucks, which follow one another in succession, under the control of breaksmen, and are drawn back the next day by horses. Moorswater valley is spanned by one of the longest and loftiest of the rly. viaducts, 146 ft. in height, and passing from hill to hill on tapering piers of stone and timber one-third of the height. At Moorswater there is a granite-cutting establishment belonging to the Cheesewring Company, where the stone is carved by hand and polished by steam-power.

St. *Keyne's Well* (½ m. E. of the interesting ch. of the same name, which is 2½ m. on the road to W. Looe), a spring of rare virtues in the belief of the country people, and covered in by old masonry, upon the top of which grow five large trees, a Cornish elm, an oak, and three antique ash-trees, on so narrow a space that it is difficult to imagine how the roots can be accommodated. According to the legend, St. Keyne presented this well to the inhab. in return for the ch. which they had dedicated to her; and it is said to share with *St. Michael's Chair* at the Mount a marvellous property by which the husband or wife who can first obtain a draught of water from the spring will acquire the ascendency. This mystical well is the subject of a ballad by Southey, which concludes with the following lines :—

" I hasten'd as soon as the wedding was o'er,
And left my good wife in the porch,
But I' faith she had been wiser than I,
For she took a bottle to church."

At *Duloe*, 2 m. beyond the village of St. Keyne, on a farm opposite the ch., and in a field, a gun-shot 1. of the road, are the remains of an ancient *circle* of large upright stones, about 30 ft. in diameter. The old monument, however, is in a very mutilated condition. A hedge bisects it, one stone lies prostrate in the ditch, five only stand upright, and there appear to be wanting to complete the circle. The stones, which are rough and unhewn, are principally composed of white quartz, and one is about 9 ft. in height. Duloe *church* has (1862) been almost rebuilt by the rector, assisted by the Rev. Thomas Bewes, who is owner of much land in the parish. Melittis melisophyllum (Cornish balm) is found in this and the neighbouring parishes. Between Duloe and the village of Sandplace (on the canal) is a celebrated spring, sacred to *St. Cuby* (St. Cuby is believed to be *St. Cuthbert*), and commonly called *St. Kiby's Well*. Dr. Scott, the present master of Balliol College, was for some years rector of Duloe, and there, we understand, the sheets of the Greek Lexicon, so well known as "Liddell and Scott" were revised. (For the excursion below this point, and for Looe itself, see Rte. 24.)

(*b*) *Clicker Tor*, 3 m. on the high road to St. Germans, a rugged and picturesque eminence known to the geologist as consisting of dark green *serpentine*, which is traversed by veins of amianthoid asbestus. The white Cornish heath, *Erica vagans*, which appears confined to a soil of serpentine, is said to have been found on the hill, but is not here now.

(*c*) N. of Liskeard are many objects of curiosity which a person intending to return to Liskeard may most conveniently visit in the following order :—The Caradon Mines, Trevethy Stone, Cheesewring, Sharpitor, Kilmarth Tor, Cheesewring again, Hurlers, Half Stone, St. Cleer.

The *Caradon Copper Mines*, at present yielding a considerable return, are excavated in solid granite, and situated at the foot of *Caradon Hill* (alt. 1208 ft.), which should be ascended for the view.

Trevethy Stone, or the *Grave-house* (called Trethevy Stone by the natives), about 1 m. E.N.E. of St. Cleer ch., is a cromlech consisting of a slab about 16 ft. in length by 10 ft. in breadth, supported in a slanting position by 6 upright stones, forming a kistvaen, or stone chest, and raised upon a tumulus. Another block has fallen within, so that a person can enter the enclosure, which is now used as a tool-house by the neighbouring cottagers. The height from the ground to the upper point of the table-stone, near which is a small circular hole, is about 16 ft. At the base of one of the upright stones is a square aperture, from which the stone appears to have been cut to form an entrance. The Trevethy Stone is one of the largest cromlechs existing in Cornwall, and derives additional interest from its elevated position, which commands the country for many miles. A short distance W. of it the railway crosses the foot of a down, which was formerly covered with blocks of snow-white quartz, of which many still remain.

Cheesewring. This remarkable object consists of tabular blocks of granite heaped one upon the other after the manner of cheeses to the height of 24 ft., but has probably acquired its name from its supposed resemblance to the press employed in the preparation of cider, in squeezing out the liquor from the *cheese* or pounded apples. It derives its extraordinary appearance from the circumstance of the stones at the base being less than half the size of those they support, which are 10 and 12 ft. in diameter. Hence the shape of the pile is that of a huge fungus, with a stalk so slenderly proportioned for the weight of the head, that the spectator will find it hard to divest himself of the idea of its instability. (There is not the slightest foundation for the assumption that the Cheesewring, or similar piles of rock, such as Bowerman's Nose on Dartmoor, or those on Ripon moor in Yorkshire, ever served as "rock idols." The suggestion seems to be due originally to Borlase.) A few years ago it was unfortunately discovered that the granite which formed the substance of this hill was of a superior quality; a railway was conducted to the spot, buildings were erected, and the destructive quarryman is now at work within a few feet of the Cheesewring itself. By a lease recently granted by the Duchy, bounds have been set to the quarry, in order that this far-famed curiosity should escape the general havoc; but the ground about it is covered with rubbish, and the neighbouring rocks, which add so much to the effect of the scene, are daily diminishing in their numbers. The eminence commands an imposing prospect. N. and S. two seas form the horizon, and N.W. Brown Willy lifts his head, and offers a landmark to those wishing to proceed to the Jamaica Inn. On a clear day you may see across Devonshire from Hartland to Plymouth, and both Dartmoor and Exmoor enter into the view. About the middle of the last century a rock near the Cheesewring was the retreat of a very singular character — one *Daniel Gumb* — who, locally known as the Mountain Philosopher, was born of poor parents in the parish of Lezant, and brought up as a stone-cutter. As a mere boy he showed a fondness for books, and at a more advanced age directed his studies to mathematics and astronomy, and was oftener seen mapping the stars upon the granite than labouring at his vocation. He abandoned all idea of making a fortune by stone-cutting, and taxed his ingenuity for the reduction of his expenses, which pressed sorely on his time to the exclusion of his favourite pursuit. With this object he searched upon the moor for a rock which might be converted into a house, and, finding a mass of granite in the vicinity of the Cheesewring well adapted to his purpose, he excavated the ground beneath it, and formed a rude dwelling, in which, with his wife and family, he lived rent and tax-free for many years. As a result of his studies, he left the slab, which had served him for a roof, scored with diagrams illustrative of some of the most difficult problems of Euclid. His cavern, situated near the foot of the hill, was long preserved from destruction as *Gumb's Rocks*. The roof had fallen, but the "bedroom," bearing the date 1735, and the stone from which the philosopher was accustomed to star-gaze, were pointed out. Unfortunately they have now altogether disappeared before the march of those barbarians known as quarrymen.

Several rocky tors are situated in this neighbourhood. *Sharpitor*, or *Sharp Point Tor* (1200 ft.), rises in a beautiful cone immediately N. of the Cheesewring, and bears upon its western slope the remains of those ancient enclosures called *hut circles*, and lines of stones.

Kilmarth (1277 ft.), directly N.

by W. of Sharpitor, and the grandest of the group, stretches E. and W. in a ridge which is nearly precipitous on its N. flank. The granite heaped upon this hill presents the most fantastic forms, and the solitude of the spot is as yet undisturbed. A pile of rocks, starting upward from the crest and W. of the summit, presents the appearance of a leaning tower, the upper surface outlying the base. 2 other hills, rising N. of Kilmarth, will strike the attention by the grandeur of their irregular outline. These are *Hawk's Tor* (the easternmost) and *Trewartha Tor* (1050 ft.). Another of this group of tors is called King Arthur's Bed (*beth*, i.e. *grave?*). Some *hut circles*, remains of *avenues*, lines of stones, and vestiges of ancient stream-works, may be found between Kilmarth and the Jamaica inn.

About 1 m. S. of the Cheesewring are *The Hurlers*, formerly three large intersecting circles, with their centres in a line, and named in accordance with a tradition that they were once men who, amusing themselves by hurling on the sabbath, were transformed into stone. Hals, a writer on Cornish antiquities, adverting to this legend, quaintly remarks, "Did but the ball which these hurlers used when flesh and blood appear directly over them immoveably pendent in the air, one might be apt to credit some little of the tale; but as the case is, I can scarcely help thinking but the present stones were always stones, and will to the world's end continue so, unless they will be at the pains to pulverize them." It is to be regretted that the possibility of their conversion has been fully demonstrated, and that many of these unfortunate hurlers have been long since reduced to their original dust, or been cut in twain or embowelled to serve the purposes of the farmer. One circle is destroyed with the exception of two of the stones, and the others are very imperfect.

The stone commonly called the *Other Half Stone*, in a field about ¾ of a m. S.S.W. of St. Cleer Church, is a granite shaft of a cross with a broken mortice on the top, in which the cross was inserted: it is covered with the interlacing knot-work common in Cornwall and Ireland. The Half Stone is the base of this or some other cross; it consists of a square stone with a very large mortice in the top with *Doniert* plainly written. What follows is rather conjectural, but it has been read *Doniert rogavit pro anima*. Doniert, according to Carew, is Dungarth, son of Caradoc king of Cornwall; drowned A.D. 872. This occupies the whole of one side; on the other are 4 panels, each containing an excellent specimen of the interchanged knot. More recently, in consequence of the fact that tradition makes mention of a sepulchral chamber beneath these stones, a deputation from the Plymouth branch of the Exeter Dioces. Archit. Soc. visited the spot, and, on making extensive excavations, discovered a cruciform chamber, in a good state of preservation, but containing no relics.

The *Well of St. Cleer*, the ivy-mantled ruin of the *baptistery*, or chapel, by which it was enclosed, and an ancient *cross*, about 9 ft. high, form a group by the road-side, 100 yards below the church; — "memorials," says the author of 'Notes in Cornwall,' "of the innocent and reverend custom of the ancient church to connect close together the beauty of Nature and the beauty of Religion by such means as the consecration of a spring or the erection of a road-side cross." The chapel was destroyed by fanatics in the civil war, but appears to have been similar in size and construction to that which now stands by Dupath Well near Callington (Rte. 25). The great slabs of granite, which once formed the roof, and now lie heaped in a confused ruin, are very striking. (It is said that the chapel is about to be rebuilt by a neighbouring proprietor.) The well is said to have been once used as a *bowssening*, or *ducking pool*, for the cure of mad people.

St. Cleer, 2 m. N. of Liskeard, is situated in a wild mining district at the foot of the moors. The road from Liskeard crosses *St. Cleer Down* (alt. 753 ft.), a stony height commanding a fine view, and then enters the church-town of St. Cleer, so called after the founder of the order of Poor Clares, out of Cornwall known as St. Clare. The stranger will notice the tower of the ch. 97 ft. high, and, on the N. side of the building, a Norman doorway with zigzag moulding, now walled up.

(*d*) Those who are fond of wild scenery will derive much pleasure from a walk from Liskeard, by the Jamaica inn and Brown Willy, to Camelford, from which they can visit Tintagel, on the N. coast (Rte. 22).

Golytha Rock, in the bed of a stream, ½ m. below Dreynes Bridge (on the road to the Jamaica Inn), originating 3 small but pleasing falls, is well worthy of a visit. The river Dreynes pursues its course from the moors through this beautiful wild valley till it unites below the rly. at " Two Waters foot" with the S. Neot river. The two united form the *Fowey* river. It is to be hoped that collectors (misnamed botanists) will not wantonly destroy the ferns and other wild plants they may find, as they are too much in the habit of doing. The name Golytha, "obstruction," is the same as the Welsh "golydda," and applied to these rocks it is perfectly significant.

(*e*) The Perp. *Ch. of St. Neot*, about 4 m. N.W. of Liskeard, has been long celebrated for its stained glass windows. They were constructed at different periods between 1400 and 1532, and restored in 1829 by the Rev. R. G. Grylls, the patron of the living, after exposure to neglect and spoliation for 300 years. The work is creditable, although completed before the days of true restoration : it has been executed with great care and expense. The windows are known as St. George's, St. Neot's, the Young Woman's, the Wives', the Harris, the Callawaye, the Tubbe, the Chancel, the Creation, the Noah, the Borlase, the Motton, the Redemption, the Acts, and the Armorial. In St. George's are depicted the surprising adventures of our patron saint, viz. :— fighting the Gauls—killing the dragon — receiving his arms from the Virgin—taken prisoner by the Gauls —restored to life by the Virgin— ridden over by the king's son—torn to pieces with iron rakes—boiled in lead—dragged by wild horses—and, finally, beheaded. In St. Neot's window we find incidents of a less stirring but as marvellous a description, for the legend of St. Neot is one of the most fanciful in the whole calendar of saints. He is said by some to have been the uncle of King Alfred, and by others a poor shepherd, who first distinguished himself by impounding in a ring of moor-stone some obstinate crows which he had been set to scare from a corn-field. This "pound" is still shown on Gonzion Down, near the ch. ; it is a square earthen fort. This remarkable feat at once brought him into notice, and to establish his fame he retired from the world and became a hermit. A belief soon spread that he was specially favoured by Heaven and invested with a strange power over man and beast. Many are the wild tales of his miraculous performances — one is of his " holy well," which an angel stocked with fish as food for St. Neot, but on condition that he took but one for his daily meal. The stock consisted but of two, but of two for ever, like a guinea in a fairy purse. It happened, however, that the saint fell sick and became dainty in his appetite ; and his servant, Barius by name, in his eagerness to please his master, cooked the two, boiling the one and broiling the other. Great was the consternation of St. Neot, whom for a moment the sight had completely overwhelmed; but, recovering his presence of mind, he ordered the fish to be thrown back into the spring, and falling on his knees most humbly sought forgiveness. The servant returned, declaring that the fish were alive and sporting in the water, and when the proper meal had been prepared, the saint on tasting it was instantly restored to health. (St. Corentin in Brittany had but one fish, from which he took a small slice daily, and then replaced it in the well.) At another time St. Neot was praying at this well, when a hunted deer sought protection by his side. On the arrival of the dogs the saint reproved them, and, behold! they crouched at his feet, whilst the huntsman, affected by the miracle, renounced the world and hung up his bugle-horn in the cloister. Again, the oxen belonging to the saint had been stolen, and wild deer had come of their own accord to replace them. When the thieves beheld St. Neot ploughing with his stags they were conscience-stricken and returned what they had stolen. Such stories as these are represented on the window, and many more may be gathered from the country-people, who affirm that the ch. was built by night, and the materials brought together by teams of 2 deer and 1 hare. They also show in the churchyard the stone on which the saint used to stand to throw the key into the keyhole, which had been accidentally placed too high. (St. Neot was of small stature, and either this lock or another was in the habit of descending, so that his hand could reach it.) The Young Woman's window dates from 1529, and was the gift of the village maidens. It contains the figures of St. Patrick, St. Clara, St. Mancus, and St. Brechan—the last a Welsh

king, whose 24 sons were all missionaries in Cornwall. In other windows are represented various subjects from the Old Testament, and in one the 9 grades of the angelic hierarchy. (The work and drawing in all these windows is very rough, but a rich general effect is produced. They have all been fully described by the vicar, the Rev. H. Grylls, in his 'Descriptive Sketch of the Windows of St. Neot's,' published by Parker in 1854.) The present ch. is of Perp. architecture, dating from the reign of Edw. IV., 1480. In a former building had been deposited the remains of St. Neot, which in 974 were carried away by the founders of Eynesbury Abbey, in Huntingdonshire. An arm, however, was left behind, and this was long preserved in a stone casket, which may still be seen in the N. aisle. Above it is an inscription supposed to have been written about the time of the Reformation. The ch., like many others in Cornwall, has a K. Charles letter. (See *Introd.*) The tower of this ch., erected in the beginning of the 14th centy., is exceedingly beautiful, and well worthy of a careful examination, as good *towers* of that date are uncommon. The granite groining of the porch-roof is worth notice, and there is some stained glass in the window of the parvise above. Against the S. wall of the ch. is a fine shaft of a cross, covered with interlacing knotwork; it should be restored to its old situation by the churchyard gate. St. Neot's Well, in a meadow near, was arched over in granite by the late General Carlyon. It was in this well that he stood up to his chin daily, and chanted through the Psalter. The old name of the parish was Neotstow, and it is said to have been in a ch. on this site that King Alfred was praying (during a hunting expedition into Cornwall) when a change took place in his life. (See Asser.) The burial-ground contains the tomb of one Robins, who be-

[*Dev. & Corn.*] M

queathed a sum of money to the poor of this parish on a condition recorded on the stone:—

"If this stone be not kept in repair, The legacy devolves unto the heir."

About 2 m. W. of St. Neot, in the parish of Warleggan, is *Treveddoe tin stream-work*, which is worth seeing, and noticed in Rte. 21. Warleggan Church is poor, but the parsonage garden is indeed beautiful. Trengoffe (*i. e.* strong stream) in this parish well shows the favourite situation for an old manorhouse of 16th cent. There is a curious avenue of sycamores. Between Liskeard and Lostwithiel the botanist may observe, on heathery ground, *Viola lactea*, the *cream-coloured violet*, a rare plant, also found in the neighbourhood of Tunbridge Wells, and fond of the pure air of the hills.

———

The old turnpike-road from Liskeard to Lostwithiel (11½ m.) runs over a bleak and elevated country, commanding extensive views. Numbers of Celtic barrows meet the eye; and above Largin wood a square redoubt, a relic of the fight of Braddoc Down (see *post*).

The *Rly.*, leaving Liskeard, crosses the valley of the Looe river at Moorswater by a lofty viaduct (see *ante*). 3 m. it reaches the little stat. of

21 m. *Doublebois*, where it runs parallel to the old turnpike, but on the side of the hill above, and crossing the spurs of the hill by viaducts, the highest of which is 151 ft. The scenery all along this valley is very pretty. The junction of the Dreynes river with that of St. Neot is seen rt.; and soon after passing Doublebois station the little manor-house of Pengelley (head of the grove), called *Treverbyn Vean* (Col. C. Somers Cocks), to which is attached a curious manorial service. The lord of the manor has to present a grey cloak (*cappa grisea*) to the Duke of Cornwall on his crossing the border of the county from Devonshire. This holding was granted to the Lord de Moleyn in 1543. The house of Treverbyn is the creation of its present owner. The dining-room is panelled with cedar brought from Bermuda by Admiral Boscawen; and the timber roofs of the entrance hall (with Minstrels' Gallery), dining and drawing-rooms, were made from the teak of the 'Orinoco,' which took Col. Cocks' battalion of the Coldstreams to the East in 1854. There is some very good tapestry in the drawing-room, which also contains a chimney-piece with the legend of St. Neot, designed by W. Burges, and displayed in the Exhibition of 1862. The collection of rhododendrons in the grounds is unusually large.

27 m. *Bodmin Road* stat. at Glynn Bridge (the town is 4 m. distant; an omnibus meets every train). 1. is *Braddoc Down*, where the Parliamentarians were defeated by Hopton in 1643. (*Braddoc*, Brit. "treachery," has been corrupted into Broadoak.) Probably the name of *Treachery* was given for some deed of which the numerous barrows or tumuli are the existing records. rt. is Largin Castle (see *ante*). 2 m. S. is *Bury Down*, crowned by a circular entrenchment (possibly connected with the rampart called the Giant's Hedge—see Rte. 24).

Bodmin (*Inns*: Oliver's Royal Hotel; Gatty's Town Arms;—Pop. in 1861, 4466) is situated nearly in the centre of the county, about 12 m. from the Bristol and English Channels. Here are held the sessions and assizes.

Bodmin, in early times, was the largest town in Cornwall, and to the period of the Dissolution particularly favoured by the religious orders, who possessed several establishments in the neighbourhood, and one important convent in the town itself. This is said to have been originally founded by Athelstane in 936 for

Benedictines; but it was refounded for Augustinian canons by Wm. Warelwast, Bishop of Exeter (1107-1136). The ch. possessed the body of its patron, St. Petrock, who is said to have been a native of Wales educated in Ireland, to have crossed to Padstow in 518, and to have settled in Bodmin, where he died in 564. 4 churches in Devonshire and 9 in Cornwall are dedicated in his honour. It was usual to make manumissions of serfs before the altar of St. Petrock; and the priory possessed a copy of the Gospels written in the 9th cent., at the end of which are 46 entries of such manumissions,—all before or immediately after the Conquest. (This MS. is now in the Brit. Mus.) In 994 Æthelred granted the monastery of St. Petrock's to the Bishops of Cornwall, whose original seat seems to have been St. Germans; but from this time until the establishment of the united sees of Devon and Cornwall at Exeter the place of the Cornish see was indifferently St. Germans and Bodmin. (See Pedlar's 'A.-S. Episcopate of Cornwall.') Great efforts—the success of which is earnestly to be desired—have recently been made to re-establish the Cornish see, and to fix it once more at Bodmin. The income of the priory at the Dissolution was 289*l*. The site of the domestic buildings (S. of the ch.) is marked by the present priory-house, in the garden of which are many fragments of capitals and columns dating from the 13th cent., and a few of early Trans. character.

The existing parish *church* was (according to Dr. Oliver) also that of the priory, the choir serving for the convent, the nave for the parishioners. It is the largest ch. in Cornwall, dating, for the most part, from 1470, when it seems to have been rebuilt, with the exception of the tower and some part of the choir. The tower was capped by a spire 150 ft. high, destroyed by lightning in 1699.

There is a S. porch and parvise. The Norm. font (fine) should be noticed, and the tomb of Prior Vivian (1533) at the end of the N. aisle, where it was placed in 1819. This prior was titular Bishop of Megara, and acted as suffragan to the see of Exeter from 1517 until his death. An ugly transparency (resembling that by West, about to be removed from St. George's Chapel at Windsor) serves for an east window. The chapel at the back of the high altar, in which was the shrine of St. Petrock, was destroyed in 1776. The ch. has an excellent peal of bells and chimes, which play an old Flemish air at the hours of 4, 8, and 12.

In the yard, E. of the chancel, stands the ivy-clad chapel of St. Thomas, Dec., with good 3-light window, sedilia, piscina, &c.

Bodmin had formerly several other chapels, long since destroyed. *Berry Tower*, however, on the hill to the N., is a relic of the Chapel of the Holy Rood.

The Town-hall is old, and has a curious carved wooden doorway in the street, 16th cent. There is a wooden doorway in the High Street, going towards the Asylum, a flat-headed trefoil, probably early 14th cent., in a small hostelry of humble character.

Bodmin has a *Literary Institution*, and on its outskirts the *County Gaol* and *County Lunatic Asylum*, which may be visited by strangers, subject to certain regulations.

In 1549 Bodmin was the scene of a singular execution. The Cornish rebels having encamped in the neighbourhood, the inhab. of this town obliged Boyer, their mayor, to allow them the necessary supplies. Shortly afterwards the insurgents were defeated near Exeter by Lord Russell, and the provost marshal, Sir Anthony Kingston, was despatched into Cornwall to bring the fugitives to justice. Upon entering the county, Kingston informed Boyer by letter that he would dine with him on a certain day, and at the appointed time arrived accompanied by a train of followers. The mayor received him with hospitality, but a little before dinner Kingston took his host aside and whispered in his ear that one of the townspeople was to be executed, and requested that a gallows might be erected. The mayor ordered it to be prepared, and as soon as dinner was ended Sir Anthony demanded whether the work was finished. The mayor answered that all was ready. "I pray you," said the provost, "bring me to the place;" and he took the mayor by the arm, and, beholding the gallows, asked whether he thought that it was strong enough. "Yes," said the mayor, "doubtless it is." "Well, then," said the provost, "get thee up speedily, for it is prepared for you!" "I hope," answered the poor mayor, "you mean not as you speak." "In faith!" said the provost, "there is no remedy, for thou hast been a busy rebel." Accordingly the mayor was strung up without further ceremony.

On *Halgaver*, or the *Goat's Moor*, 1 m. S., there was anciently held, in the month of July, a carnival, which antiquaries consider originated with the Saxons. A Lord of Misrule was appointed, before whom any unpopular person, so unlucky as to be captured, was dragged to answer a charge of felony; the imputed crime being such as his appearance might suggest—a negligence in his attire, or a breach of manners. With ludicrous gravity a mock trial was then commenced, and judgment as gravely pronounced, when the culprit was hurried off to receive his punishment. In this his apparel was generally a greater sufferer than his person, as it commonly terminated in his being thrown into the water or the mire. There is no doubt as to the antiquity of this curious jubilee:—
"Take him before the mayor of Hal-gaver"— "Present him in Halgaver Court"—are old Cornish proverbs.

At *St. Lawrence*, 1 m. N.W., are remains of a *hospital for lepers*, consisting of some pointed arches and dilapidated walls. This hospital was incorporated by Queen Eliz., 1582. St. Lawrence is now only celebrated for an annual horse-fair (Aug. 10).

A good view of Bodmin may be obtained from the *Beacon Hill*, S of the town. The pillar on the hill is a monument to the late Major-Gen. Sir Walter Raleigh Gilbert. About 2 m. from Bodmin Ch. a Roman camp was traced early in the present cent., from which coins of Vespasian, Samian ware, &c., were dug.

The chief *excursions* are to the *Glynn Valley* and the *Pencarrow Woods*. The Bodmin Road Stat. (on the W. Cornwall Rly.) is at

Glynn Bridge, 3 m. on the road to Liskeard. Above it is *Glynn* (Lord Vivian), below it *Lanhydrock* (T. J. Agar Robartes, Esq; see *post*, Exc. from Lostwithiel), both beautiful seats on the banks of the Fowey. Glynn was the old family seat of the Glynn family until bought by the late Lord Vivian. The house had been nearly destroyed by fire, and was renovated and much improved by its new proprietor. Among the pictures at Glynn is a portrait by *Reynolds* of Mr. Craunch of Plympton, by whose advice the young artist was sent to London to be placed under Hudson. On the road to Glynn Bridge the old entrenchment of *Castle Kenyoe* (or Canyke) is passed on the rt.

Pencarrow, the seat of the late Colon. Secretary, Sir Wm. Molesworth, Bart. (and now of Lady Molesworth), lies to the N. of Bodmin. S. of the park are *Dunmeer Wood* and *Dunmeer Castle*, the objects of the excursion. A walk of 1½ m. by the side of the Wadebridge railway will bring you to *Dunmeer Bridge*. Dunmeer Castle is ½ m. to the N. of it. Further N. 1 m. is a smaller entrenchment called *Penhar-*

g tic Castle, overhanging the railway and the l. bank of the river. *Boscarne*, a farmhouse 1 m. W. of Dunmeer Bridge, was formerly a seat of the Flamanks ; and *Park*, ½ m. W. of the N. entrance to Pencarrow, of the Peverells and Bottreaux. The skirts of Dunmeer Wood are the habitat of *Ligusticum Cornubiense*, one of our rarest plants.

Several longer excursions can be made from this town, viz.—to *Wadebridge* (Rte. 22), by rly.—to *Lostwithiel* (*post*), say by a circuitous ramble over Halgaver to *Helmên Tor* (Rte. 23) and *Lanlivery*, returning by road—to the *ruins of St. Bennet's Monastery* near Lanivet, 3 m., and the *Roche Rocks*, 8 m. (see Rte. 21)—to *Blisland* (where is a Church worth visiting, see Rte. 21), on the border of the moors, and the rocky valley of *Hanter-Gantick*, 2½ miles from Wenford Bridge—to the *Four-hole Cross*, *Brown Willy*, and *Roughtor*, sleeping a night at the Jamaica Inn (Rte. 21)—and, lastly, to *St. Neot* (present route, *ante*), by *Cardinham Bury*, and the old tin stream-work of *Treveddoe* (see Rte. 21).

Brynn (a small hill, *i. e.* hillock), W. of Bodmin, in the parish of Withiel, was the birthplace of *Sir Beville Grenville*, the royalist leader, victorious in the fight of Stamford Hill, and killed in the battle of Lansdown. *Withiel* (Corn. *elevated*) Ch. has a good Perp. tower, which, together with the old parsonage, are said to have been built by Prior Vivian of Bodmin. The tower of *St. Wenn* Ch. (2 m. W.) is very fine Perp.

It is 7 m. from Bodmin to Wadebridge by rly. This line extends to *Wenford Bridge*, 7 m. up the course of the Camel. It was opened in 1834 for the transport of ore and sea-sand, and in 1846 was purchased by the S. Western Company. Passengers are carried only between Bodmin and Wadebridge.

Leaving the Bodmin Road Stat., the railway passes on a viaduct the deep *Treycur Bottom*, which leads to the Glynn valley. The dell is a mass of foliage, and a very favourite haunt of the woodcock. To the N. are the Bodmin moors, and westward Hensbarrow, the Roche Rocks, and crested Helmên Tor.

[From the high ground beyond *West Taphouse*, a lonely public-house under the bleak height of *Fire Barrow Down*, are seen l. the wooded hills and valleys of Boconnoc, one of the most beautiful prospects in the county. Nearer the road rises *Boconnoc Cross*, erected 1848 by the Hon. George Fortescue.] The railway descends through the valley of the Fowey river, with Restormel Castle rt., to

30½ m. *Lostwithiel* (*Inn:* the Royal Talbot ;—Pop. of parish in 1861, 1017), seated in the deep valley of the Fowey. It is fancifully said to be *lost within the hill*; but the name is a corruption of *Lestwithiel*, *the Supreme Court*. This town is one of the most interesting in Cornwall. It was that in which the elections for the county took place until the Reform Bill. The *Ch. of St. Bartholomew* is almost entirely of the 15th and 17th cents., with the exception of the tower and spire, which are of the 13th, and form "a composition as beautiful as it is unique. The gablets surmounting each side of the octagonal belfry, though of a plain character, produce an effect of richness unsurpassed by any parapet."—*E. W. Godwin*, who suggests that the design (unique only in England) may have come from Normandy. The E. window is of the 14th cent. The ch. was materially injured by an explosion of gunpowder during its occupation by the Roundheads under Essex in 1644. On the font is the figure of a man on horseback holding a hawk. Near the ch. are remains of the so-called *Stannary Court* and *Prison*, which are in all probability those of a Hall of Exchequer and other buildings erected by Edmund Earl of Cornwall (son of Richard King of the Romans), temp. Edw. I. The windows of the hall are modern and doubtful restorations. Earl Edmund probably built the first ch., of which the spire and tower are relics. The curious and picturesque bridge (soon, it is said, to be replaced by a modern monstrosity) dates from the 14th cent. The trout of Lostwithiel are considered very excellent. The excursions from this place are to Restormel, Lauhydrock, Bocounoc, and to Fowey by the river.

The ivy-mantled ruin of *Restormel Castle* (Res or *Les*-tormel, *i.e.* the Court of Assembly or gathering—*i. e.* for battle: it is still often called *Lestormel*) crowns a hill on the valley side, 1 m. N. This building was originally one of the palaces of the Norman Earls of Cornwall, and was the fortress of the neighbouring town. It is described by Leland as " unroofed and sore defaced" in the time of Henry VIII., and appears to have been a ruin in the days of Eliz. " The whole castle," says Norden, writing in that reign, "beginneth to mourne, and to wringe out hard stones for teares; that she that was embraced, visited, and delighted with great princes, is now desolate, forsaken, and forlorne." Restormel was, however, garrisoned in the civil war by the Parliament, and taken by Sir Richard Grenville, Aug. 21st, 1644. It is a circular structure, with gate-house on the W., and a projecting tower E.N.E., the whole surrounded by a deep moat. This is said (and probably with truth—since the castle resembles in plan those of Launceston and Trematon—see *Launceston*, Rte. 21) to be the work of Richard King of the Romans, temp. Hen. III. It is beautifully situated, overlooking the wooded valley of the Fowey. At the foot of the hill stands *Restormel House*, residence of C. B. Sawle, Esq., but property of the Duchy. The road to this mansion is the road to the castle. At the farmyard behind the house turn l. up the hill, and rt. in the field above, where a stile shows the way into the wood. In the drive through the park you pass *Restormel Mine*, which the Queen entered when she visited Cornwall. It is worked for iron, which is contained in a crosscourse.

Lanhydrock House (T. J. Agar Robartes, Esq., M.P. for E. Cornwall), 2¼ m. N.W., is a granite edifice, mainly in its ancient condition, and was formerly the seat of the Robartes, Barons Truro and Earls of Radnor. The N. and S. wings bear date, respectively, 1636, 1642; the gateway 1651. The house is approached by an avenue planted in 1648, and contains a gallery 116 ft. in length, the ceiling of which is adorned by a rude stucco relief of the Creation. Lanhydrock was garrisoned for the Parliament in the civil war—(the head-quarters of Essex's army were at Lespryn, at the foot of the avenue of sycamores; those of the Royalists, under Sir Beville Grenville were at Boconnoc) —and surrendered in 1644 to the king, who bestowed it on his general Sir Richard Grenville, but the Parliament restored it to its original owner. " Lanhydrock stands almost untouched, as if it had been buried alive since the days of the Puritans. ... Lord Robartes, its builder, was a stanch Presbyterian; and the library collected by himself and his chaplain—one Hannibal Gammon— stands on the old shelves of the long gallery as if its Roundhead purchasers had been using it only yesterday ... rare old tomes ... a large part seasoned with many a bitter MS. marginal note against prelacy and popery. ... The avenue was planted under orders sent by Lord Robartes from London, when he had become Conservative, and had been clapped by Oliver Cromwell into the Gatehouse."— *Quart. Rev.* vol. 102. The carved oak panelling in this gallery, its ceiling, and the Flemish tapestry and cedar panels in the drawing-room, should be noticed. Out of one of the bed-rooms there is a hiding-room behind the panels. The Tregeagle of the old legends was steward to Lord Robartes, and a room is still called "Tregeagle's room." There are some family portraits worth notice. The private gardens are very pretty. The *Ch.* at the back of the house is without interest, except for a cross which stands by the porch.

Boconnoc (the residence of the Hon. G. M. Fortescue), 4 m. E., was purchased in 1709 by Governor Pitt, the grandfather of the great *Earl of Chatham*. It is now the property of Lady Grenville, whose seat is the beautiful Dropmore, near Maidenhead. In the mansion are some good paintings by *Kneller, Lely,* and *Reynolds,* and a bust of Lord Chatham. Lady Grenville became possessed of this property on the death of her brother Lord Camelford, who erected the obelisk in the park to the memory of his friend Sir Philip Lyttelton. This obelisk stands in a redoubt made at the time Charles I. had his head-quarters at Boconnoc, and was the rear of the position of his line when the battle of Braddoc Down was fought. The Roundheads were posted opposite, with the valley between. After firing at each other for some time with no result, Sir Ralph Hopton went down the valley, charged up the hill of Braddoc, utterly routed the Roundheads, pursued them through Liskeard, and took possession of that town. The grounds of Boconnoc are generally considered the finest in the county. The lawn consists of 100 acres, and the woods stretch far over hill and valley, watered by tributaries to the little river *Lerrin*. A carriage-road, 6 m. long, runs through them.

In Braddoc ch. there are remains of old glass; emblems of the Passion, alternating with modern arms, &c., and a chalice of the 15th century.

The valley of the Fowey between Lostwithiel and the coast is remarkable for some of the most delightful scenery in Cornwall. To view it to advantage the traveller should take a boat and descend the stream. In 2½ m. the banks suddenly open out, and the glassy reaches of an estuary are beheld winding towards the sea. The most notable points are the Ch. of St. Winnow, and the romantic inlets flowing to Lerrin and St. Cadoc. The distance to Fowey (Rte. 24) is about 7 m.

Pelyn House, seat of Nicholas Kendall, Esq., M.P. for E. Cornwall, 1½ m. from Lostwithiel, was burnt down in April, 1862.

[From Lostwithiel you may visit St. Blazey and its neighbourhood, proceeding either by road, 4 m., or by rail to Par, whence St. Blazey is 1½ m. distant. By road, ½ m. rt., is seen the fine tower of *Lanlivery Ch.* N. of it are the rugged hills of *Red Moor* and (3½ m.) *Helman Tor* (see *post*). At Red Moor is an old tinwork, with remains of Jews' houses and smelting-places. Several ingots of tin have been found here, and a figure in tin (now at Lanhydrock), 12 or 14 in. high, a rude representation of either Moses or the First Person of the Trinity. It has Hebrew characters on the back and front, and 2 horns or rays projecting from the sides of the head. A lane and a church-path lead from Lanlivery Ch. to Luxulian, the Treffry Viaduct, and Valley of Carmears, and afford a delightful, but circuitous, walk to St. Blazey. The direct road passes the Fowey Consols, and then descends to

2 m. *St. Blazey (Inn:* the Packhorse), a town seated under an amphitheatre of wooded heights, 1½ m. from the harbour of Par. It is named after St. Blaise, the patron of woolcombers, who was bishop of Sebaste in Armenia, but has the honour of a place in the Church of England calendar. He is said to have landed at Par (3rd centy.)

on a visit to England, and to have been subsequently tortured with iron combs, and martyred, during the persecution of the Christians by the Roman emperor Licinius, A.D. 316. His memory is to this day perpetuated at St. Blazey, and in the manufacturing districts in the N. of England, by a festival on the 3rd of Feb. There is a figure of St. Blaize in the ch. On the hills above the town is *Prideaux*, the seat of Sir Colman Rashleigh, Bart., an ancient quadrangular mansion with stairs of granite; and, on a height adjoining it, the remains of an earthwork known as *Prideaux Warren*. On the road to Par is a large iron-foundry.

There is much that is interesting within reach of St. Blazey and its neighbour St. Austell. There are the important copper-mines of *Fowey Consols* and *Par Consols*, the great tin-mine of *Charles Town*, the open mine of *Carclaze*, the *china-clay works*, and *tin stream-works*, the romantic *Valley of Carmears*, the *Treffry Viaduct*, and the busy ports of *Par* and *Charles Town*; and at greater distances, *Fowey, Restormel Castle, Hensbarrow Roche Rocks*, and the picturesque fishing-towns of *Mevagissey* and *Gorran Haven* (see Rte. 24).

The valley of *Carmears* (or *Cairnmens*) is more especially the "sight" of St. Blazey, from which it is a walk of about a mile. It is a beautiful romantic scene of wood and rock, —one of the finest, if not the very finest, of the Cornish valleys. It leads towards Luxulian, and the highlands of Hensbarrow, and derives its name from the granite tors which rise from its sides. The railway from Par to the china-clay works of Hensbarrow and the quarries of Luxulian offers a road to the valley. You will find it at the entrance of St. Blazey from Lostwithiel. This rail and a stream—each of which is walled magnificently with granite—run side by side to the Carmears, which open

beautifully to view on a turn to the l. From the gorge which forms the portal the rail ascends a long and steep incline, to the rt. of which a cascade thunders through a wood. But you should here leave the rail, for you can return by it from the viaduct, if desirous of viewing the scenery from the high ground. A walk of about 2 m. up the valley will bring you to the

Treffry Viaduct, a magnificent granite structure, erected at the sole cost of the late Mr. Treffry, of Place House, Fowey. It is elevated more than 100 ft., and carries the Hensbarrow railway—also the work of Mr. Treffry, and which he had contemplated extending to the N. coast— and a stream for working the incline, across the valley, the latter flowing in a passage below the roadway. Beyond the viaduct the valley grows bare and stony, its sides bristle with granite rocks, and at the distance of a mile rises the ch. tower of

Luxulian.—This parish is known chiefly for its granite, a very beautiful material, of which the lighthouse and beacon on Plymouth breakwater were built. Boulders of porphyry are also found lying about the moors of Luxulian, St. Wenn, and Withiel; and it was from one of these (of a deep pink colour, blotched with black hornblende) that the sarcophagus of the Duke of Wellington was made. The block (which was on the property of William Rashleigh, Esq., of Menabilly) weighed 70 tons, was wrought and polished by steam power, and converted into a sarcophagus at a cost of 1100*l*. The *granite quarries* are at present directly opposite Luxulian, but they are continually advancing along the valley side. The rail joins the branch from Hensbarrow at the viaduct. The *church* of Luxulian is an ancient structure, and its tower was the depository of the Stannary records during the civil war. The ceiling is handsome.

In the village is a little *baptistery*, so common in Cornwall, projecting from the bank, with granite roof and sides. The moors in the neighbourhood are wild and rocky, and contain some of the most important of the tin stream-works. A walk over these hills will introduce the stranger to scenery characteristic of the Cornish highlands. He may visit the *Whispering Stone*, 1 m. N., on the estate of Tregarden, and there hear, as by magic, a gentle whisper breathed on the opposite side of the valley; and he may extend the excursion to the granite rocks of *Helmén*, a bold carn, rising from Red Moor, about 2 m. further N., and there search out the logan-stone on its southern slope, and enjoy on its crest a view stretching from sea to sea. In wandering about the moors by Helmén Tor you may on Creggan (heathy) Moor find an old and curious little conventicle, very picturesque, with its old burial-place and well. It is in Lanivet parish.

The *Fowey Consolidated Mines* are situated on a hill, 1 m. from St. Blazey towards Lostwithiel, and command a panoramic view. They form one of the most important groups of the Cornish copper-mines, and are worked with all the latest improvements. Here is the celebrated *Austen's engine*, a veritable Cornish giant, raising from a depth equal to " the Monument 8 times piled on itself," in every minute that flies, more than 38,000 gallons of water; and here, also, is a *man-engine*, by which the miner is carried up and down the shaft with ease and rapidity. The works of this mine—as well as those of the Par Consols—are conducted on the largest scale, and may well be selected for examination.]

The station beyond Lostwithiel is 34¾ m. *Par*, 1½ m. S. of St. Blazey, where an active pilchard-fishery is pursued, and a great quantity of ore, china-stone, and china-clay is shipped to Swansea and the potteries. This was Mr. Treffry's harbour, and it is mainly formed by one of those great works which will immortalise his name—a *breakwater*, 450 ft. in length, constructed entirely at his expense. Par is known for its group of copper-mines, now worked as one under the title of *Par Consols*, a most busy scene on the sloping hill above the shore. The condition of this concern is at present very flourishing, and mainly to be attributed to the enterprise of the late Mr. Treffry, who was one of the principal proprietors. The *country* in which the mine is excavated is slate, and the engine a very colossus in size and power. By means of the muddy water it continually discharges a considerable tract of ground has been formed around the harbour, and on this are erected smelting and other works. The rly. crosses the canal and tramroad by a granite skew bridge. It skirts the shore and commands a pretty view of the bay. The distant cliffs are of many colours, pierced by green rifts and chasms, and curtained by shrubs.

From Par a long hill leads to the village of *St. Blazey Gate*, on a lofty height from which the works of *Par Mount* and other mines are seen S. At Biscŏvéy the road passes rt. a very good *ch.*, mainly built by the late General Carlyon, from the designs of Street, and descends to a woody region.

rt. of the railway is *Tregrehan* (*i. e.* " the granite-place "), the beautiful seat of Major Carlyon, but where the park, covered with noble trees, is undermined in every direction by the works of *Old Crinnis*. A stranger, however, would never suspect it. On the rt., 2½ m. from St. Austell, a lane leads to a very pretty valley, where there are quarries in the limestone, tin stream-works, and china-clay works. One on foot might walk this way to Carcluze, and then descend upon St. Austell. The railway curves N. and reaches

39¾ m. *St. Austell* (*Inns:* White Hart; Globe. Pop. of parish in 1861, 11,893). This ancient town has a place in history as captured by Charles I. in 1644. It is seated on a southern slope of one of the great hills, and is a place of some bustle from the continual transit through its streets of heavy waggonloads of china-clay for the harbours of Par and Charlestown. It is an old-fashioned and somewhat gloomy town, but can yet boast its cheerful villas on the outskirts. The rly. station is on the N., and beyond it one of the viaducts, for which the line is remarkable, spans the adjacent valley.

The *Ch.* (ded. to St. Austell, of whom nothing is known) is one of the best in the county, and ranks among the few Cornish churches which are richly ornamented (St. Mary at Truro, Probus, and Launceston, are the 3 which in this respect most resemble it). The chancel is Early Dec. (circ. 1290); the nave and tower Perp. The chancel is not parallel with the nave. The font is of the Norm. type common in Cornwall, with 4 shafts at the angles, having masks for caps. On the buttresses of the S. side of the ch. are represented the ladder, spear, nails, and hammer, implements and emblems of the crucifixion, but which pass with the vulgar for miners' tools; and over the porch appears an inscription which has proved a sore puzzle to antiquaries, but is generally deciphered as the Cornish words *Ry-du, Give to God.* The tower is richly ornamented with figures in niches, representing the Almighty Father supporting the crucified Saviour, Joseph and Mary, 3 saints or bishops, and the 12 apostles. With Probus, says 'The Civil Engineer,' this tower divides the honours of the extreme west, and it is particularly noted for its groups of niches, and the small elaborate decorations of its belfry-story and parapet. The ch. sadly requires restoration and reseating. Harte (author of the 'Life of Gustavus Adolphus') died Vicar of St. Austell in 1774. The *Market-house* and *Town-hall*, adjoining the ch., are of granite, and spacious. By the entrance to the town-hall is a paving-stone on which proclamations are read, and (the story runs) a witch was burnt. But the handsomest modern building is the *Devon and Cornwall Bank*, opposite the White Hart. It is of granite and marble. Another structure of some interest, but of a very different date, may be found in the valley, to the l. of the Truro road. This is *Menacuddle Well*—i.e. *maen-a-coedl*, the hawk's stone—and the remains of its little chapel or baptistery. It is situated in the grounds of Mr. Martin, who allows the pilgrim to visit it. It is in a pretty spot, where the river tumbles in a fall (the wood which surrounded it has (1862) been cut down). 1¼ m. S. on the road to Pentewan is *Penrice*, Sir J. Sawle Graves Sawle, Bart., and near Mevagissey, at a distance of 5 m., *Heligan*, the seat of John Tremayne, Esq. Heligan —i.e. "the willow-trees"—is one of the finest seats in the west country. The house, though extremely ugly, is commodious. In the gardens are some of the largest Himalayan Rhododendrons in the kingdom. Adjoining Charlestown is *Duporth*, the charming residence of G. G. R. Freeth, Esq. The garden is "a little paradise." St. Austell has a *Literary Institution*, in union with the Society of Arts in London. (Mevagissey and Veryan Bay are best reached from St. Austell. See this part of the coast described in Rte. 24.)

[There are many interesting points in the neighbourhood, some of which have been already enumerated at St. Blazey (*ante*). To continue their description, there is—

Charlestown, one of the largest tin-mines in the county. The name also attaches to *Polmear*, the port of St. Austell, 2 m. distant.

Pentowan, i.e. head of the sand-hills or "towans," 4 m. S., has a small harbour for ore and china-clay. The stream-works (formerly worked up the valley) have in some places been carried on at a depth of 50 ft. below the level of the sea. In the tin-bed were found the roots and stumps of oak-trees in their natural position, showing clearly that a considerable change in the relative level of land and water must have here occurred. Here also the horns of the so-called Irish elk have been found, rendered entirely metallic by tin ore, which had taken the place of the lime. Some canoes of oak, chained together, have also been found here, but were destroyed for firewood by the streamers. Pentowan gives its name to an excellent building-stone quarried in a fine-grained elvan, composed of felspar, quartz, and crystals of mica, and remarkable for containing fragments of the slate-rock which it traverses. The harbour here is connected with St. Austell by a railway.

Carclaze, however, is the greatest curiosity — an immense tin-quarry, which, from time immemorial, has been worked open to the day (ancient implements — of course *said* to be Phœnician — have been found here). The stranger will find Carclaze by proceeding along the road to Lostwithiel as far as the Mount Charles public-house, about 1 m., and by then taking a road on the l. to the china-clay works. From these works a cottage will be seen at the top of the hill. This is the blacksmith's shop of Carclaze, which is at the summit of a solitary moor (alt. 665 ft.) commanding a fine prospect along the coast.

The view of the mine (now worked for china-clay — *kaolin* — as well as tin) is truly astonishing. The traveller suddenly discovers an enormous excavation, about 1 m. in circumference, and more than 130 ft. in depth, containing streams and stamping-mills, and a number of miners and labourers employed in extracting and dressing the ore. But the circumstance which renders Carclaze (the *grey rock*) so eminently imposing is the whiteness of the cliffs, as contrasting with the brown surface of the moor and the black coast in its vicinity. It requires, indeed, no great stretch of the imagination to fancy Carclaze a work of enchantment, and a chasm which has been opened by some potent magician in a mountain of silver. The country here consisting of a disintegrated schorlaceous granite, of the consistence of mortar, the mine has been necessarily worked open to the day, but at a certain depth the granite becomes more compact, and allows of *mining*. The white sides of the quarry are marked by black strings of schorl, oxide of tin, and quartz, which, unconnected with any lode, but filling the joints of the granite, appear to separate the cliffs into rectangular divisions. The ancient and present condition of the granite is a curious consideration. The material was once a solid rock, traversed by cracks, in which hard crystalline substances were gradually deposited. By the decomposition of the felspar the ancient rock has been reduced to a pasty consistence, and has crumbled to pieces, while the original fissures have been filled with mineral matter, which stands out in prominent relief. The view from Carclaze of the distant bay and intervening wooded hills is exceedingly beautiful, and would alone repay a walk from St. Austell, but to enjoy it to perfection you should go to the remains of a tor at the eastern end of the height. From that point you will see Dartmoor in the far E., to the N.E. the Bodmin moors, with Roughtor and Brown Willy, and N.W. Hensbarrow crowned by its tumulus.

2 m. N. of Carclaze, on the E. flank of Hensbarrow, is *Beam Mine*, which, like Carclaze, was originally quarried, but is now mined.

Before the stranger leaves this neighbourhood he should visit the *China-clay works*. The granite which he has seen in Carclaze is locally known as *soft growan*, and abounds in the parishes of St. Stephen in Brannel, St. Dennis, and St. Austell. It often contains talc in the place of mica, and is characterised by the partial decomposition of the felspar. In some localities this *growan* is tolerably firm, when it resembles the Chinese *petuntze*, and, quarried under the name of *china-stone*, is extensively employed in the potteries. This is ready for the market when cut into blocks of a size convenient for transport; but the softer material, which is dug out of *pits* and called *china-clay*, *porcelain-earth*, or *kaolin*, requires a more elaborate preparation, for the purpose of separating the quartz, schorl, or mica from the finer particles of the decomposed felspar. This clay is dug up in *stopes*, or layers, which resemble a flight of irregular stairs. A heap of it is then placed upon an inclined platform, under a small fall of water, and repeatedly stirred with a *piggle* and shovel, by which means the whole is gradually carried down by the water in a state of suspension. The heavy and useless parts collect in a trench below the platform, while the china-clay, carried forward through a series of *catchpits*, or tanks, in which the grosser particles are deposited, is ultimately accumulated in larger pits, called *ponds*, from which the clear supernatant water is from time to time withdrawn. As soon as these ponds are filled with clay, they are drained, and the porcelain earth is removed to the *pans*, in which it remains undisturbed until sufficiently consolidated to be cut into oblong masses. These are carried to a roofed building, through which the air can freely pass, and dried completely for the market. When dry they are scraped perfectly clean, packed in casks, and carried to one of the adjacent ports to be shipped for the potteries. Such, until recently, was the universal mode of preparing the clay; but the process is now accelerated by 2 important improvements. These are—the construction of the cisterns as filters, and the introduction of a machine by which 2 tons of the earth can be dried in 5 minutes. By these means a saving of time, estimated at 4 months, is effected. China-clay is used in bleaching paper and calico, and to give them weight and body, as well as in the manufacture of china and the finer kinds of earthenware. It was first found in Cornwall (at Tregonan, near Helston) in 1768, by W. Cookworthy, a quaker of Plymouth, and at the present day is exported to an annual amount of about 80,000 tons, valued at 240,000*l*.

To the l. of the road from Mount Charles to Pentowan, in a field directly N. of the woods of Duporth, is an upright block of granite called the *Giant's Staff*, or *Longstone*, to which the following legend attaches. A giant, travelling one night over these hills, was overtaken by a storm which blew off his hat. He immediately pursued it, but, being impeded by a staff which he carried in his hand, he thrust this into the ground until his hat could be secured. After wandering, however, for some time in the dark without being able to find his hat, he gave over the pursuit and returned for his staff; but this also he was unable to discover, and both were irrecoverably lost. In the morning, when the giant was gone, his hat and staff were both found by the country-people about a mile asunder. The hat was found on Whitehouse Down, and bore some resemblance to a mill-stone, and continued in its place till the autumn of 1798, when, some soldiers having encamped around it, they fancied, it is said, as it was a wet season, that this giant's hat was the cause of the rain, and therefore rolled it over the cliff. The staff, or *Longstone*, was discovered in the position in which it remains; it is about 12 feet high, and, tapering towards the top, is said to have been so fashioned by the giant that he might grasp it with ease.

The *Roche Rocks* (Rte. 21) are 4½ m., and *Hensbarrow* about 4 m., N. of St. Austell. The summit of Hensbarrow is 1034 ft. above the level of the sea, and therefore commands a view which will well reward you for its ascent. For Mevagissey and the coast W. see Rte. 24.]

[Proceeding from St. Austell towards Truro, by the old turnpike-road, 14 m., we pass on the l. the ancient tin-mine of *Polgooth* (the *pool* which *twists* or turns), a most extensive excavation. It contains no less than 50 shafts, and a single lode has been worked the full length of a mile. 17,000*l*., however, were expended before the speculation yielded any return, when the profits are said to have averaged 1500*l*. a month. The lodes of *Polgooth* are remarkable for intersecting each other in a very uncommon manner.

3½ m. The road crosses a hill with fine view of the sea and coast. rt., at the summit, is the tin-mine of *Hewas*, in which specimens of gold, and some remains of the furnaces of the Jews, who formerly worked the mine, have been discovered.

¼ m. *Hewas Water*, a village in the valley. From the turnpike on the hill a road on the l. leads to Tregony. 2 m. along this road the traveller will have on his l. *Pencoose Castle*, a circular entrenchment near *St. Ewe*, the church of which place has a spire, a thing of note in Cornwall.

1¼ m. The old seat of *Pennance*, "head of the brook," with its avenue. Beyond it on rt., near the roadside, is another ancient camp in the shape of a ring.

We now begin a series of formidable hills extending to Truro. In the next valley lies Grampound.]

The railway from St. Austell passes farther inland than the turnpike-road, and reaches 46¼ m. *Grampound Road Stat*. (This is the nearest station to St. Columb (Rte. 22), 9 m. across the country. Polkinhorne, the landlord of the Red Lion at St. Columb, will send a carriage to this station if written to in due time.)

Grampound (Grand Pont (?): the name suggests the pounds of Dartmoor, A. S. *pindian*, to enclose), a village of great antiquity, supposed to have been the *Voliba* of Ptolemy, is situated upon the river Fal, here only a small stream. It has been chiefly known in our times as a " rotten borough," so notorious for venality that it lost its right of returning 2 M. P.'s before the Reform Bill. In 1620 *John Hampden* was first returned to Parl. as its member. An old chapel, now a market-house, and granite cross, are the only curiosities; but in the neighbourhood of the village there are no less than 6 camps on the Fal. One, of an irregular shape, is on *Golden* farm, 1 m. S., on the rt. bank; a second on the St. Austell road, ½ m. N.E.; a third on the Truro road, 1 m. W.; a fourth, of a quadrangular form, 1 m. N. and close to the l. bank; a fifth, called *Resugga Castle*, on the same side of the river, a little further N.; and a sixth, which is circular, on *Barrow Down*, 1 m. W. of Resugga. Grampound is the nearest point on the high road to *Giant Tregeagle's Quoits*, on the shore, about 9 m. distant. (For them and for Veryan Beacon see Rte. 24.)

In *Cuby Ch.* at *Tregony*, 2½ m. from Grampound, is an interesting old font. In this village also are some trifling remains of a *castle* which is said to have been built by Henry de Pomeroy when Richard I. was in the Holy Land. *Trewarthenick*, belonging to the Cornish family of Gregor, is a handsome seat on the neighbouring hills.

3 m. W. of Tregony is *Ruan Lanihorne*, of which *Whitaker the antiquary* was for 30 years rector, his remains being interred in it; and 5 m. S.W. *Lamorran*, with a ch. and ivied tower of a priory, washed by the waters of *Lamorran Creek*, and opposite the ch. an ancient granite cross. A painted window inserted in Lamorran ch. 1858 represents the leading events in the life of our Saviour. In the parish of Ruan Lanihorn there were till quite lately the remains of two castle towers on the shore of the creek below the church. The history of the castle is unknown—the yard wall yet exists.

Beyond Grampound road the railway passes l.

Trewithen (the place of trees), the seat of C. H. T. Hawkins, Esq., nephew of its former proprietor, Sir Christopher Hawkins, Bart. This old house stands on high ground, and commands an extensive panorama of wild hills. It contains among other pictures a genuine sketch of Charles I. on horseback by Vandyke, of which there is a duplicate in Buckingham Palace. Part of this estate has the poetical name of *Golden Farm*, which, however, is not derived from the autumnal tints of the woods, or the treasures of a streamwork, but from an old Roman Catholic family. There is a tradition of a Roman Catholic priest having been hidden in the house at Golden, caught at last, and executed. As before stated, there are remains of an *encampment* at Golden.

½ m. beyond Trewithen is

Probus (Inn: Hawkins Arms), a village situated on high ground, 305 ft. above the level of the sea. It is well known for its *Ch.* (date about 1470, but rebuilt lately). The tower is the loftiest and the most beautiful in the county, and bears a close resemblance to that of Magdalen College, Oxford. It is a very perfect specimen of Late Perp., and, strange to say, was built in the reign of Elizabeth, when Gothic architecture had perished out of the land. Did we not know the contrary, its date would be fixed but little later than that of the ch. It is entirely of wrought granite, and in every part covered with sculptured devices. The height is 125 ft., and the angles are supported by buttresses which, as they ascend, diminish in size, and terminate in clusters of foliated pinnacles. There are also intermediate pinnacles, which give extreme lightness and elegance to the structure. The ch., which has been thoroughly restored, is dedicated to SS. Probus and Grace, a married pair, and the front of the gallery, constructed of panels taken in 1723 from the old rood-screen, bears the following legend, which has, no doubt, a reference to the names of these founders of the building:—" Jesus hear us, thy people, and send us *Grace* and *Good* for ever." The 5th of July was probably dedicated to these saints, as from time immemorial a fair called *Probus and Grace* has been annually held here on the first Monday after this day, and the following Sunday has been celebrated as a feast Sunday. Nothing is known of SS. Probus and Grace, but during the rebuilding of the body of this church, 1850, two skulls were found together, built up in the wall, corroborative of the tradition of the parish that the skulls of the two saints were so disposed of. They were carefully reburied in the church, beneath the altar. The antiquary will find the brasses of John Wulvedon (1514) and wife, with an inscription, in good preservation in the Golden Aisle. A font and pulpit in the Perp. style, and a small window near the S.W. door, have been lately added to the ch. as memorials. The family vault of the Hawkinses is in this ch.

[Proceeding from Probus by road —to the rt. is *Trehane*, seat of the Rev. William Stackhouse. The road descends a long hill, and then traverses a picturesque valley, resembling those of Devonshire, to

2 *Tresilian Bridge*, where the gatehouse of *Tregothnan* (Viscount Falmouth) is passed on the l. Tresilian was the property of Justice Tresilian, and is historically interesting as the place where the struggle between Charles and his Parl. was brought to a close in Cornwall by the surrender of the royal army to Fairfax, 1646. We here enter the long straggling village of *West Taphouse*, and for a mile skirt the shore of an estuary. At one point we obtain an extremely pretty view down the vista of the creek, and of the woods of Tregothnan rising from the margin. We then leave the valley, and climb the last hill towards Truro, shaded by the venerable trees of *Pencalenick*, the seat of Mrs. Vivian; *Penair*, seat of the late Admiral Barrington Reynolds, is also l. of the road; and *Polvhele*, the seat of the old family of that name. *Tresawsen*, a farmhouse in the parish of *Merther*, was formerly in the possession of the Hals family, and for some time the abode of *William Hals*, author of the 'Parochial History of Cornwall.'

3¾ *Truro*. Upon entering it, *Tregolls*, the residence of Sir S. T. Spry, will be observed on the l.]

The railway, crossing several feeders of the Falmouth river, reaches 53¾ m. *Truro*.

(The line is continued to Falmouth by Penryn; see Rte. 26.)

Truro (*Inns:* Tedder's Royal Hotel; Lenderyou's Red Lion Hotel: Pop. in 1861, 3117) is pleasantly situated, and is considered the metropolis of Cornwall, though Bodmin is the county town. It is seated in a valley at the junction of 2 streams with an inlet of the sea, called the *Truro River*, which joins the Fal near Tolverne Ferry. The name Truro is probably Tre-riu or Tref-riu, i.e. town-place on a *declivity*. (A village in Carnarvonsh. is the same.) The Earls of Cornwall had a castle here. This building is mentioned by Leland (temp. Hen. VIII.) as "now clere down," but the scarped mound where it stood may be seen to this day (on the high ground at the top of Pydar-street, to the l.). It is crowned by a modern circular wall, surrounded by a circular terrace, arrangements which render it probable that this castle resembled Launceston in plan. Others derive the name of the town from *Tru-ru*, the *Three Streets*, while Borlase explains it as *Tre-cur, the town on the* (Roman) *road.* Truro stands in the centre of a mining district, and largely exports the ore. It was formerly dignified as one of the coinage towns for tin, and the old *Coinage Hall* of the 15th cent., which has been lately pulled down, served for some years as the court of the vice-warden of the Stannaries, who now adjudicates on mining matters in the Town Hall, a handsome modern Italian building. The *Cornish Bank* adjoining it, an edifice in the Pointed English style, has been erected on the site of the Coinage Hall.

East Huel Rose, i.e. east works on the *rhos* or *moor*, near Truro, was one of the largest lead-mines in the county. *Huel Garras* is celebrated for having at one time produced 100 oz. of silver for every ton of lead.

The *Ch. of St. Mary* is a handsome specimen of the Perp. of Hen. VII.'s time, the old part built chiefly of Roborough stone. The tower and spire are modern. There are 9 windows of stained glass, and the whole building has been improved and restored of late years. (A part of one of the aisles has been pulled down and rebuilt, so as to enlarge the street, in a sloping direction, which has a singular effect.) See a monument dated 1636 in the chancel, with an inscription recording the singular adventures of one Phippen, a native of Dorsetshire. At the E. end of the town is the *Ch. of St. Paul*, and at the W. end *St. George's Ch.*, schools, and parsonage, a group of buildings completed 1858.

The *Royal Institution of Cornwall* (establ. 1818), a society which has published in its Reports many valuable papers relating to the curiosities of the county, meets at Truro in the autumn. The Lecture-room and Museum are in Pydar-street, and the latter is well worth seeing. Among other things it contains a *collection of Cornish birds*, including some rare specimens. One of the most curious is a cormorant strangled by a conger eel, taken in Looe Harbour. In seizing the fish the bird struck its lower mandible through the upper lip of the conger, and, being unable to swallow it or to disentangle itself, was, after a struggle, strangled by the coils of the eel round its neck. Cabinets of Cornish minerals and fossils; numerous antiquities which have been found in the neighbourhood, particularly some portions of the old ch. of St. Piran (see *post*); a number of foreign birds, mostly East Indian; skulls of the Ceylonese, believed to be the only curiosities of the kind in England; and specimens of 2 varieties of the elephant of Assam.

The *County Library*, established in 1792, occupies a portion of the house. A reading-room is attached.

The *Royal Cornwall Horticultural Society* is also established in Truro. The botanist will find in its hortus siccus most of the plants indigenous to the county.

Foote, the comedian; *Polwhele*, author of a history of Cornwall and Devon; and *Richard* and *John Lander*, the explorers of the Niger, were natives of this town. To commemorate the exploits of the Landers, a Doric column has been erected in Lemon-street. The house in which Foote was born, on the N. side of Boscawen-street, is now the Red Lion Hotel. The late *Lord Vivian* was also a native of Truro, as well as *Henry Martyn*, the missionary, b. 1781; *Thomas Harreis*, M.D., founder of the London Missionary Soc., b. 1734; and *Henry Bone*, R.A., the celebrated miniature-painter, who was born here in 1755: Martyn, who died of fever or plague in Persia 1812, and translated the N. T. into Persian, was the son of a miner. A very clear rivulet flows through the town, and is led in streamlets through almost every street and alley. In the neighbourhood are several seats. On the London road, *Tregolls*, Sir Samuel Spry; *Penair*, Lady Reynolds; *Pencalenick*, Mrs. Vivian; and *Tregothnan*, Viscount Falmouth. On the road to Helston, *Killiow*, Rev. John Daubuz; *Killiganoon*, late Admiral Spry; and *Carclew*, Sir Charles Lemon, Bart. *Polwhele*, where Col. Polwhele, son of the county historian, resides, is situated 1½ m. N., on the road to St. Erme and Mitchell.

In the town or its immediate vicinity you will find *paper-mills* and *iron-foundries*; and at Garras Wharf, at *Carvedras*, on the Redruth road, and at *Calenick*, on the old Falmouth road, *tin smelting-houses*. The churchyard of *Kenwyn*, 1 m. N.W. on the road to Perranzabuloe, commands a very interesting view of the surrounding country.

St. Clement's Ch., 2 m. E. of Truro, is beautifully situated on the shore of the Tresilian Creek. The Polwhele aisle (or transept rather) is of the 13th cent. At the Vicarage the antiquary will find one of the oldest of the Cornish crosses. It is called the *Isnioc Cross*, and the following inscription is engraved upon it in an abbreviated form: "*Isniocus Vitalis Filius Torrici.*" St. Clement was martyred by Trajan, and, according to the legend, was thrown into the sea with an anchor and cable fastened to his neck. It is a pleasant walk to this ch. by Malpas and the shore of St. Clement's Creek.

The *Truro River* presents some beautiful scenery. One of the prettiest parts is at King Harry's Passage, across to the district of Roseland, i.e. Rhosland—moorland—consisting of the parishes of Veryan, Gerrans, Philleigh, St. Just, and St. Anthony. (See Rte. 25.) Below *Malpas*— "smooth passage"—a very common name in Wales, pronounced *Mopus* (2 m.), the l. bank is enriched with the woods of *Tregothnan*, Viscount Falmouth. The house, built by Wilkins in, the Tudor style, contains among other pictures some works by *Opie*, and portraits of the great Duke of Marlborough, George Prince of Denmark, Queen Anne, and their son the young Duke of Gloucester. The road from the lodge-gate runs a long distance through the park, which is enlivened by herds of deer, and occupies a range of hills bounded by the rivers Truro and Fal. Below Tregothnan the latter river joins the stream, and both shores are clothed with wood, that on the rt. forming the grounds of *Trelissic*, residence of the Hon. Mrs. Gilbert. Below Trelissic the river expands and loses its name in the *Roadstead of Carrick*, the main branch of Falmouth Harbour. The *Ch. of St. Michael Penkivel* (Pen-kivel, Headland of the *Horse*, to distinguish from many other St. Michael's in the county), near the l. bank of the Truro river, was a fine structure of the 14th cent., but has been entirely rebuilt by Lord Falmouth, under the direction of Mr. Street. It contained in the tower a curious oratory with stone altar, which has been replaced. 2 other chantry altars, with tombs and sedilia of the 14th cent., have been preserved, one at the end of each transept. In the body of the building is a monument to the memory of Admiral Boscawen, by Rysbrach, and a metal tablet, date 1515, which teaches you to

"Pray for the soule of Master John Trembrass,
Master of Artes, and late parson of this church."

Truro is generally the starting-point for an excursion to the ruins of the *Ch. of St. Piran*— most interesting memorials, which, lost for 10 centuries, were exposed to view in 1835 by the shifting of the sand which had been blown over them. They are situated in the parish of Perranzabuloe, on the N. coast, and distant from Truro about 8 m. A wild, dreary road leads over the hills to *Perran Porth* (an *Inn*, Tywarnhayle Arms), a small bathing-place in a sandy cove, bounded on the E. by the solitary district in which St. Piran's ch. was buried. For many miles in that direction the coast has been desolated by sand, which, from time to time blown inland from the shore, has been slowly accumulated. Camden, Norden, Carew, and Borlase bear witness to its encroachment in different years, and the name of the parish—*Perranzabuloe*, or *Perran in sabulo*—is presumptive evidence as to the character of the district at a remote period. (All this sand is blown in through a narrow crevice in the rocky cliff; and it would appear that a few yds. of strong stone wall filling up this crevice would have saved hundreds of acres from destruction.) The *arundo arenaria*, planted to bind and fix the mass, occasionally a specimen of *convolvulus soldanella*, a thin, mossy vegetation in the hollows, and rabbits countless as the sands themselves, are the only living objects that enliven it. The ruins of St. Piran's ch. are about 2 m. from the Porth, in the heart of these sandy dunes, and the remains of another ch. of less ancient date, and a 4-hole cross, are in their immediate vicinity. A direct scramble across the sands will be found laborious; the better plan is to skirt them; but the stranger will experience difficulty in finding the ruins without a guide. (The visitor should ask for the *hamlet of Rose*—the nearest to the churches—where he will obtain a guide. An old man named Kitto, who lives there, was present at the disinterment of the oldest ch., and his services will be found useful. The district is a very puzzling one; and the stranger who depends on his unassisted powers of discovery runs a great risk of leaving without having seen the first ch. at all). The following legend is supposed to explain the origin of this curious little shrine. At the end of the 4th centy. St. Patrick visited Cornwall on a crusade against Druidism, and, finding his efforts successful, returned to Ireland, and, consecrating 12 bishops, sent them over to complete the good work. St. Piran was one of these. He is said to have crossed the sea on a mill-stone, and, landing at St. Ives, proceeded E. 18 m., when he pitched his cell and began his ministry. Such is the legendary account of St. Piran's settlement in Cornwall. The distance he is said to have travelled from St. Ives would have carried him among the miners of St. Agnes, and he is now considered the especial guardian of tinners, and has from time immemorial been annually fêted by these people on the 5th of March. The saint is said to have died some time in the 5th centy., and then, it is concluded, a ch., according to the custom of the Celtic Christians, was built over his remains. For about 2 centuries this building was probably used for the rites of religion, and antiquaries conjecture that it was submerged by sand either in the 8th or 9th centy., but many years before the subjection of Cornwall by the Saxons. At this catastrophe the 2nd ch. was in all probability erected, as near as possible to the spot consecrated as the burial-place of the saint, but protected from the sand by a stream of water, which experience had shown would arrest its progress. This edifice remained safe for ages, and was considered in such security in 1420 that it was rebuilt on a larger scale. For another centy. the sands were held in subjection, but, the stream having been diverted by some mining operations, they once more pursued their desolating career, and soon menaced the building with destruction. Borlase, in the middle of the last centy., briefly remarks, "The 2nd ch. is in no small danger;" and so rapid was the accumulation of the sand that parishioners now alive remember the porch having been buried in a single night. The danger at length appeared so imminent that the inhabitants were obliged to remove the building. In 1803 the tower, windows, and porch were taken down, and the ch. erected again at a distance of 2 m. The tradition of the old ch. had been still preserved, when in 1835 the shifting sand disclosed the long-lost relic; human efforts aided the exhumation, and at length the little edifice, with its adjoining baptistery, stood forth perfect as on the day on which they were overwhelmed. In the winter the spring of St. Piran, its course being choked with sand, forms a small lake, and overflows the building to the height of 6 ft. The ch. lies nearly E. and W., its extreme length being 29 ft. and breadth 16½ ft. The principal entrance was on the S. side, a small arched doorway of primitive construction, surrounded by a curious cable moulding, and ornamented with 3 heads rudely chiselled in a soft stone. It was unfortunately destroyed within a fortnight after the discovery of the building. The heads and a few stones of the moulding are now in the museum at Truro. (It has been questioned by competent authority whether these heads, 2 of which terminated a dripstone over the door, are earlier than the 12th cent.

The 3rd head seems to have been in the centre, over the door, as is common in Norm. dripstones.) The steps by which the doorway was entered remain, and are much worn. On the same side of the ch. was a rude window, within the head of which a stone was laid across to support the weight of the wall, although the radiating stones, which formed the arch, appeared to uphold the ponderous mass. The N. and W. side of the ch. are dead walls; that on the E. was pierced with an altar window and priest's door, which fell during the removal of the sand. The masonry is of the rudest description, and affords a striking proof of the antiquity of the ch. No lime has been used by the builder, but china-clay and sand employed in its stead, and in this the stones are embedded without much regard to arrangement, consisting of blocks of granite, elvan, and slate, many smooth and rounded as if taken from the beach or the channel of a stream. "On the whole," says Mr. Haslam, "the masonry looks like that of persons who had seen Roman work, and perhaps assisted in it, without learning the art; and who had seen lime and used it, but without learning how it was prepared for use, and who pitched upon this white substance, china-clay, as resembling lime." The floor of the ch. consists of a hard and level concrete. The altar was removed in 1835, and St. Piran's remains, but headless, were discovered beneath it. This altar has been since rebuilt with the same stones and capped by a block of granite, upon which the name of St. Piran has been cut in early Roman characters. The head of the saint was probably enshrined in the 2nd ch., since the will of Sir John Arundell of Trerice, dated about the time when that edifice was rebuilt, contains a bequest for providing the relic with a handsome niche. The present condition of the original structure is deplorable. The hand of curiosity has proved more ruthless than the sand. The N. and S. walls are the only portions left entire. The S. and E., which alone were pierced with doors and windows, have partly fallen to the ground, and the sand is again gathering round the ruin. The remains of a cell, in front of which were discovered the shells of mussels and limpets with fragments of pottery, are barely to be discerned about 100 yds. to the S.E. The proofs of the high antiquity of St. Piran's *Oratory*, as the building has been called, are the absence of a font, the baptistery being at a little distance from the ch.; the rudeness of the masonry, and the substitution of china-clay for lime; the diminutive size of the edifice; the scarcity of windows, and their structure; the dissimilarity of the arch to Saxon or Norman models; the insertion of the heads over the doorway, a peculiarity observable in many of the Celtic buildings in Ireland; and lastly, tradition, which has always pointed to the spot in which the lost ch. of St. Piran was ultimately found. To the S. of this ruin a solitary cross and a few stones mark the site of the 2nd ch. This old moorstone cross has the peculiarity of having the holes in the disk occupying the usual position of the limbs of the cross, thus making the solid stone into the shape of the cross of St. Andrew. The surface is here thinly spread with turf, and the sand is fixed, but it covers the floor of the building to a depth of 19 ft. In the N. and E. it may still be seen in its naked desolation, shifting with the wind, and traversing the hills in cloud-like masses. Around both churches the soil is whitened by human bones, their sacred precincts having been long used as a burial-ground. (The existing *Ch.* of Perranzabuloe, consec. in 1805, is said to have, in the nave, the piers, arches, and windows removed from this 2*nd* ch. The font is Norman.)

Perran Round (which may be visited on your road to Perran Porth) is situated by the side of the Truro road about 1½ m. N. of the church-town of Perranzabuloe, and, with the exception of the amphitheatre at Dorchester, is the most perfect relic of the kind in England. It consists of an area 130 ft. in diam., encircled by an earthen bank about 10 ft. high and 7 broad at the top, divided into 7 rows of steps for a standing audience, and it is conjectured was used by the ancient Britons either as a court of justice or a theatre for the exhibition of feats of agility and strength, such as wrestling, and by the Cornish of later days for the performance of *Miracle Plays*, a species of composition of which the 3 most remarkable specimens remaining were edited and translated by Mr. Edwin Norris in 1859 (see Introd.). The Round is capable of containing about 2000 spectators. A pit in the enclosure communicates by a trench with an oval recess in the bank, and this antiquaries pronounce to have been the "green-room," to which the actors retired.

St. Agnes' Beacon (called locally St. Ann's Beacon), alt. 621 ft., rises about 4 m. W. of Perranzabuloe, and is remarkable for a deposit of sands and clays, in some places 40 ft. in thickness, occurring at an elevation of from 300 to 400 ft. above the present sea-level. Sir H. De la Beche is inclined to consider it a remnant of some super-cretaceous deposit. The clay is extensively employed by the miners, who throughout Cornwall use a lump of this substance for a candlestick. During the French war a signal guard was stationed at the summit of this hill, on the look-out for invaders, and ready to arouse the country by a bonfire. Tin-lodes may be traced along the sea-front.

The *cliff-scenery* between Perran Porth and the Beacon is highly interesting. Guarded by immense rocks of *killas*—the local term for clay-slate—the coast seems to defy the impetuosity of the sea itself. There is, however, no part of Cornwall where the destructive influence of the waves is so well illustrated. The slate is in a ruinous condition, and presents a perfect chaos of crags and chasms. At the *Cligga Head*, 1 m. W. of Perran Porth, bands of a hard and decomposed granite alternate. An elvan issues from them, and may be seen on the cliff at several points until it strikes inland a short distance W. of Trevaunance Porth.

St. Agnes is a tin-mining district, and distinguished as the birthplace of the painter *Opie* (his real name was *Hoppie*), who was the son of the village carpenter. Many of his productions may be found in the mansions of the Cornish gentry; and the house in which he was born, 1761, is still standing, 2 m. from the church-town, on the road to Perran Porth. It is called *Harmony Cot*, and is now occupied by a relation of the artist. Opie's genius was first noticed by Dr. Wolcott (Peter Pindar), when residing at Truro. St. Agnes' Ch. has been rebuilt from the plans of Mr. Wm. White, and is worth a visit. A small ch. by the same architect has been built at *Mithian*.

Trevaunance Porth is a wild cove under the E. side of St. Agnes' Beacon. Repeated attempts having been made to construct a pier at this exposed place, a company of gentlemen (1794) erected the present structure, which is of granite, and cost 10,000*l*. 2 m. from the shore are *the Man and his Man*, a couple of the most conspicuous rocks on the N. coast of Cornwall. The whimsical name is doubtless a corruption of *maen* or *mên*, a stone.

ROUTE 24.

PLYMOUTH (RAME HEAD) TO FALMOUTH, BY LOOE, FOWEY, AND ST. AUSTELL (THE SOUTH COAST).

Steamers run from Plymouth to Falmouth and Penzance many times a week. The coast of Cornwall is well seen from them; but they touch at Mevagissey only between Plymouth and Falmouth. The places of interest on the coast are best seen by following the road described in the present route, or by visiting them from the chief stations on the railway—Liskeard (for Looe), Lostwithiel (for Fowey), St. Austell (for Mevagissey and Veryan Bay), and Truro (for the creeks of the Falmouth river).

The road crosses the *Hamoaze* by ferry to *Torpoint*, as in Rte. 23. From Torpoint the traveller can proceed to Looe either by the very hilly carriage-road, 18 m., or by a bridle-road, about 14 m., through *Antony* and *Lower Tregantle*, and near the cliffs of *Whitesand Bay*. [At Tregantle the most important of the western defences of Plymouth has been constructed. A peninsula is formed by the Lynher river (which runs to the Hamoaze), the neck of which from the river to Whitsand Bay is about 2 m. in breadth. Across this, 2 new forts have been completed—Screasdon on the river, and Tregantle by the sea. The latter, 400 ft. above the sea-level, faces Devonport Dockyard, distant about 6000 yds. The guns (100) mounted here are of the largest range and heaviest metal, and command every conceivable approach to the harbour. The keep, an immense mass of masonry, stands between the battery and the barracks. The ground between the fort and the sea has been levelled so as to form an incline, which, in case of attack, would be swept by guns in the recesses of the fort. Screasdon Fort, about 1½ m. distant, mounts 40 guns and mortars.] The carriage-road is that to Liskeard as far as the head of the Lynher estuary, which terminates at the picturesque hamlet of *Polbathick*, 8½ m. from Torpoint and 1 m. from *St. Germans*. From the pretty valley beyond Polbathick the Looe road branches off on the l., ascending through a wooded coomb to very high ground, and then descending abruptly to the retired village of *Hessenford* (*Inn:* Cornish Arms), most delightfully situated in a deep and wooded *bottom*, on a stream which flows from the Bodmin moors by St. Cleer. From this point the road again climbs a long fatiguing hill, and passes for some distance over elevated land to its junction with the road from Liskeard to Looe. There it turns toward the sea, commanding on the rt. a view of the woods of *Morval House* (John Francis Buller, Esq.), and soon ascends to the ch. of St. Martin, near the summit of the ridge which shelters the romantic town and inlet of Looe (see *post*).

The bridle-road from Torpoint passes through *Antony* to *Lower Tregantle* about 4 m. In the cliff near the hamlet of *Higher Tregantle*, a short distance E., is a cavern called *Lugger's Cave* or *Sharrow Grot*. It was excavated by a lieutenant in the navy of the name of Lugger, who, during the American War, being stationed near the spot, and sorely troubled by the gout, undertook the work as a means of cure. The cavern in itself possesses no particular interest, but it commands a delightful view over the broken shore and azure waters of the bay. About 3 m. from this cave is the well-known promontory of the

Rame Head (Ruim, Brit., a headland. This was the Brit. name of the Isle of Thanet), which, projecting into the Channel from *Maker Heights* (402 ft. above the sea), constitutes the S.E. point of the county, and the termination of a semicircular range of cliffs which sweep eastward from Looe along the margin of Whitesand Bay. These cliffs here bend to the N., girding the shore of Plymouth Sound. The headland is crowned with the ruin of a chapel, and commands a view of the Cornish coast as far W. as the Lizard. The solitary lighthouse on the Eddystone (DEVON, Rte. 7) rises from the distant waves, and the woods of Mount Edgcumbe from the adjoining hills. The tower of *Maker Church* is a conspicuous object in the neighbourhood, and the view *from* it is unrivalled. This building contains several monuments to the Edgcumbes and other families, and from its commanding position was employed during the French war as a signal station communicating with Mount Wise at Devonport. It is 2 m. from Devonport. When *Dodman and Rame Head meet*, is a West Country proverb denoting an impossibility. Dodman is the W. point of Veryan Bay.

The desecrated chapel of St. Juliet (S. Julitta, mother of St. Cyrus) at Inceworth, in Maker parish, has beautiful Dec. details. There is an undercroft used as a stable.

E. on the shore of the Sound lie the villages of *Kingsand* and *Cawsand*, separated by a gutter, and at one time noted places for smuggling. *Cawsand Bay*, being sheltered by the Rame Head from westerly gales, was used as the principal anchorage previous to the construction of the Breakwater. From these villages there ranges towards Redding Point a porphyritic rock, which Sir H. De la Beche is inclined to refer to the era of the lower part of the new red sandstone, a formation prevailing in the E. of Devon. It throws out veins into the grauwacke, some of which are traversed by the same lines of lamination as the latter rock, a circumstance which would seem to throw some light upon the date of the lamination of the grauwacke.

Whitesand Bay, so called from the whiteness of the sand, abounds in beautiful and romantic coast scenery, but is justly dreaded by sailors as the scene of many a fatal disaster. The beach and cliff afford abundant matter for the naturalist. From Lower Tregantle the distance to Looe is about 10 m., and the traveller can proceed for some way along the *Batten Cliffs* by a bridle-path.

18 m. from Torpoint.—*Looe.* (*Inns:* Ship Hotel; Swan Inn.) This fishing-town, divided by the estuary of the same name into E. and W. Looe, is a small place romantically situated in a deep recess, the acclivities above it being hung with gardens, in which the myrtle, hydrangea, and geranium flourish the year round in the open air. It is an old-fashioned town, which has descended to us from the time of Edward I. It is intersected by narrow lanes, and, before the new road was made along the water-side, was approached from the eastward by so steep a path that travellers were in fear of being precipitated upon the roofs. It presents a strange jumble of old crazy walls and projecting gables, some of the little tenements being ornamented externally with wooden stairs leading to a doorway in the upper story. The estuary, confined by lofty hills, was

long spanned by an antique narrow bridge of 15 arches of as many shapes and sizes; but that picturesque structure has been replaced by one less interesting, although more commodious. The towns (ancient boroughs) of East and West Looe are quite worth a short visit from those in search of the picturesque. The streets remind one of the small towns on the shore of the Mediterranean, except that those are filthy while these of Looe are very clean. Near the "Church end" at East Looe there yet remains the pillory, one of the *very* few in England. The ch. tower is picturesque, but the main building is modern, of the worst date. The little chapel of West Looe, dedicated to St. Nicholas, has (1862) been rescued from desecration and restored to the Church by the liberality of Colonel Somers Cocks. It presents a pretty ch.-like aspect on a very humble scale. Until lately it served as the *town-hall*, and was used by strolling players! The view from the sea-side presents a dark array of sombre cliffs, and a rocky islet 170 ft. high, which, once crowned by a chapel to St. George, is now used as a station by the coast-guard. Some delightful excursions can be made in the vicinity of Looe, such as a walk along the coast to *Talland* and *Polperro*, or in the opposite direction to the shore of *Whitesand Bay*.

That to the *Inlet of Trelawne Mill* is one of the most worthy the stranger's attention, and may be easily accomplished in a boat. This inlet opens into the Looe river immediately above the bridge, and furnishes perhaps the most beautiful scene of the kind in Cornwall—the shelving hills being steep and lofty, and literally covered with trees from the water's edge to the summit. The rt. bank belongs to *Trelawne* (that is, Fox's Place — Sir J. S. Trelawny, Bart., an ancient seat of this family), and the l. to *Trenant Park*, formerly the property of Mr. Henry Hope, the author of 'Anastasius,' but now of Wm. Peel, Esq. Trelawne is a fine old house. (The south wing, which was in complete disrepair, has been rebuilt (1862) in very good style, by Sir John Trelawny.) "The chapel is of the 15th century, with a good open timber roof restored. The windows are plain late Perp., the rest all modern or modernized. The tower and 2 doorways of the hall are of the 15th or early 16th; the hall itself is modernized: the passage through remains, with the doorways at each end. The battlement on the hall, and another small square turret at the opposite end, and a good Perp. buttress between the windows, should be noticed. . . This house is said by Lysons to have been built by Lord Bonville, temp. Hen. VI."—*J. H. P.* Here are many valuable pictures, some by *Sir Godfrey Kneller*. Among them is an original portrait of Bp. Atterbury, who was chaplain to Bp. Trelawny, and another of Queen Eliz. when young — a gift of that princess to Sir Jonathan Trelawny, who was related to the royal family, and purchased this estate from the crown. At the head of the inlet, on the wooded heights, are remains of a circular encampment connected with a rampart or raised bank, which extended from this point through Lanreath to the large earthwork on Bury Down, isolating a tract of country on the coast. Some suppose this line of defence to have been thrown up by the Danes, but it is more probably an ancient line of demarkation between Saxons and Britons. At Lanreath, in Borlase's time, it was 7 ft. high and 20 ft. wide. It proceeds in a straight line, up and down hill indifferently, for at least 7 miles, and is popularly called the *Giant's Hedge*. Another interesting relic in the valley of Trelawny is *St. Nun's, St. Ninnie's,* or *Piskies' Well*. It is on the rt. bank of the river, and has been recently restored.

Route 24.—*Looe.—Polperro.* Sect. II.

The visitor to Looe should also proceed by boat or road up the course of the estuary, as far as the lock, to which point the winding shores present a waving sheet of foliage. He will notice in this excursion on the l. bank, about 1 m. from Looe, an inlet which is confined by a causeway: it has the appearance of a wood-encircled lake, and is bordered by the demesne of *Morval House*, an ancient mansion, seat of J. F. Buller, Esq., and in 1755 the birthplace of *Judge Buller*. In earlier times it had been a possession of the Glynns. The ramble may be extended with advantage by the side of the canal to the village of *Sandplace*, 2¼ m. from Looe, where the scenery deserves particular notice. From this village a road ascends the opposite bank to the village of *Duloe*, near which are the remains of an ancient circle of stones (Rte. 23); and from Duloe *St. Keyne's Well* is not above 2 m. distant. If the traveller should wish to walk from Looe to Liskeard, the path by the canal, 9 m. (a common course), is to be preferred to the carriage-road. From Moorswater down the valley to Looe there is now a railway to convey ore and granite to be shipped.

From the harbour of Looe there is a considerable export of copper-ore and granite, and during the season the pilchard-fishery is actively pursued. The remains of fossil trees have been found beneath the shore at a place called *Millendreath*, 1 m. E.

The parish ch., *St. Martin's*, stands on high ground above E. Looe, and for 34 years was the living of the Rev. *Jonathan Toup*, editor of Longinus. There is a Norm. door in St. Martin's Church, nearly buried by a modern porch. The font is curious, of Norm. character. The ch. of *Pelynt*, 4 m. N.W., contains monuments and effigies of the Achyms, Bullers, and Trelawnys, and the pastoral staff of Sir Jonathan Trelawny, one of the 7 bishops committed to the Tower by James II., and in whose behalf the Cornish miners were ready to march to London to the ringing burden of their song—

"And shall they scorn Tre, Pol, and Pen?
  And shall Trelawny die?
Here's twenty thousand Cornish men
  Will know the reason why."

The staff is now of wood, gilt. Its copper ornaments were struck by lightning some years since, and partially fused.

Pelynt Church was restored and beautified (?) by Sir Jonathan Trelawny so completely, that it is one of the ugliest in Cornwall. The tower is Dec.

Proceeding from Looe towards Fowey—

2 m. *Talland*, in a little bay closely invested by hills. The ch. (with an E. Eng. east end) stands detached from its tower, and contains monuments of old Cornish families. A charming path pursues a winding course along the cliffs.

1¾ m. *Polperro* (*Inn:* the Ship). a fishing village in a situation eminently romantic, nestling, as it were, on the rocky shore and ledges of an inlet, which enters among the hills through a fissure in a dark coast of transition slate. It is an ancient place, mentioned by Leland as "a fishar towne with a peere." The bluffs which rise around it are supposed by a learned geologist to exhibit a striking example of the action of a mighty torrent upon the strata of the earth, and at the mouth of the harbour they have the appearance of having been once united. The fossils formerly known as "Cornish Ichthyolites," but now termed "Polperro Sponges," were discovered some years ago by Mr. Couch of this town in the cliffs E. and W. of Polperro. Under the signal station they occur in the greatest abundance, and may be found as far W. as Pencarrow Head. It is a curious circumstance that the rocks to which these remains are confined underlie towards the land, whilst the rest of the southern coast of Cornwall underlies towards the sea. This inversion of the strata is first seen in Pottledler Bay, opposite Looe Island, and may be traced W. beyond Fowey Haven, and for 2 or 3 m. inland. Above the village are remains of an ancient chapel of St. Peter. The road from Polperro leads through a deep valley to high ground, where *Lansallos ch.*, a sea-mark, will be observed on the l. A short distance further, rt. is the ch. of *Lanteglos*, mainly Dec. with a Perp. tower. The font is E. Eng. There are *brasses* for Thomas Mohun, 1440; and John Mohun and wife, died 1508, of the "sweating sickness." The church, which is worth a visit, is quickly subsiding into ruin from utter neglect. The road then descends to Fowey Harbour at Bodinnick Ferry.

7 *Fowey (Inn:* the Ship), delightfully situated near the mouth of a broad estuary navigable for 6 m. towards Lostwithiel. It extends along the rt. bank nearly a mile, under its sheltering hills, and opposite to the village of *Polruan*, i. e. "the Pool of St. Rumon." *Fowey Haven* is one of the most commodious harbours in the county, and admits vessels of large size at all times of the tide. On each shore are the ruins of square forts, built in the reign of Edw. IV., and from which a chain was formerly stretched across the water as a protection to the town. The schistose cliffs of Polruan are included among the red and variegated slates of De la Beche, and are mingled with calcareous beds containing zoophytes, associated with encrinites and shells.

Fowey, in the early days of English history, was one of the principal seaports of the kingdom, and during the crusades many vessels were here fitted out for the Holy Land. An old windmill, situated on the heights above the town, is mentioned in 1296 as a well-known sea-mark; and as windmills are believed to have been introduced into England from Palestine, this venerable relic was probably built by returned crusaders. In the reign of Edw. III. Fowey contributed to the fleet intended for the blockade of Calais no less than 47 ships and 770 men—a larger armament than was provided by any other town in the kingdom except Yarmouth. In subsequent reigns the *Fowey gallants*, as the seamen of this place were termed, carried out a system of plunder upon the coast of Normandy, and committed such havoc, that the French several times fitted out an expedition against the town. In the reign of Henry VI. they effected a landing under cover of the night, and having set fire to the town destroyed a number of the inhabitants. Those who had time to escape hastily sheltered in Treffry House (the original of Place House), and so assailed the Frenchmen in their turn as to compel them to retreat to their ships. In the reign of Edw. IV. the seamen of Fowey were accused of piracy, their vessels were taken from them and given to their rivals of Dartmouth—a reverse of fortune from which the town never recovered. The inhabitants, however, on various subsequent occasions sustained their character for bravery, and in the reign of Charles II. preserved a fleet of merchantmen from capture by assailing a Dutch line-of-battle ship with the guns of their little towers. The principal defence of Fowey in those times was *St. Catherine's Fort*, erected by the townspeople in the reign of Hen. VIII., and crowning a magnificent pile of rocks at the mouth of the harbour. At the present day this ancient stronghold is much dilapidated, and better calculated to take a prominent place in a traveller's sketch than the repulse of an enemy. In the civil war Fowey was the scene of an important event. The army of the Earl

[*Dev. & Corn.*]

of Essex here surrendered to the King, their commander escaping by sea to Plymouth (1644). In 1846 Her Majesty and P. Albert landed at Fowey when cruizing on the Cornish coast. The visit is commemorated by an obelisk of Luxulian granite, 23 ft. in height, erected 1858.

The shores of the estuary for a long distance above the town are well wooded, and a trip by water to Lostwithiel is deservedly a favourite excursion. One branch flows to *St. Veep* (3 m. from Fowey; the ch., Dec. and Perp., has been well restored), near which is *St. Cadoc*, the seat of the Wymonds. Further up the river, on the W. bank, is *Penquite*, corruption from Pen *coed*, i. e. head of the wood (T. Graham, Esq.); and on the E. bank the ch. of *St. Winnow*, remarkable for the beauty of its position. A window in this building, after a design by the artist H. Stacey Marks, represents the Angel and the Marys at the Tomb. There is also a very excellent window filled with glass of 15th centy., sadly in want of re-leading.

There are some excellent houses in Fowey, specimens of 14th cent. work. The *ch.* is a fine edifice, chiefly of the 14th centy., with a handsome tower, an ornamented oak ceiling, and a pulpit of the 15th centy. The N. aisle is said to date from 1336, and the rest of the building from 1456. In the S. aisle is a monument to John Treffry, of which Polwhele remarks,—"This was put up during the lifetime of Mr. Treffry by his direction. He was a whimsical kind of man. He had his grave dug, and lay down and swore in it, to show the sexton a novelty."

Place House, the residence of the late Joseph T. Treffry, Esq., and now of the Rev. E. J. T., stands immediately above Fowey, and is well known in the county for its antiquity, and for its restoration. The old building, according to Mr. Treffry (who contributed an account of *Place* to the Report of the Royal Institution of Cornwall for 1840), was once called *Cun Court*, the *Chief's Court*, and, in digging the foundation for the new buildings, several bodies, of which some were in armour, and other relics of an ancient burying-place, were discovered. The name by which the mansion is at present known is said by Pryce to be the Cornish word *plás*, a palace. As a castle Place House dates from the reign of Hen. VI., but the tower described by Leland has been destroyed, and no part of the building is now earlier than the reign of Henry VII. Of that period there are 2 remarkably fine bay windows, covered with shallow panelling of the richest description, and in the finest preservation. The stone appears to have been scraped during the restoration; but the work is original, and contains several shields of arms, temp. Hen. VII. Another window in imitation of these is temp. Eliz., and has shields of the form in use at that period, quite different from the others. The old hall also exists, but is now turned into the kitchen; the original porch is preserved in a singular manner under the modern tower; and being lined with polished porphyry (raised in a quarry belonging to the proprietor), is now called the "Porphyry hall." Some other parts are temp. Eliz. (1575). Place is well worth seeing. Besides the Porphyry Hall, the house is ornamented with granite and elvan, and contains a number of curiosities, among which is a fine original portrait of *Hugh Peters*, the Puritan chaplain of Cromwell, and a native of Fowey.

The late Mr. J. T. Treffry, by whom Place House was restored and enlarged, deserves the notice of every writer on Cornwall, as one of the most extraordinary men of his time, and as the projector and author of magnificent works in this neighbourhood. Born in the parish of St. Germans, his paternal name was Austen, but in 1838, when sheriff of Cornwall, he assumed, by virtue of a royal warrant, the name of Treffry, having become the representative of that ancient family. Gifted with uncommon enterprise and talent, and with almost unlimited means at his command, he employed his energy and capital in advancing the interests of those around him, in effecting improvements and in planning and executing the most colossal and useful works. At one and the same time he was a shipowner, a merchant, a farmer of upwards of 1000 acres, a silver-lead smelter, and the sole proprietor or principal shareholder of some of the largest and richest mines in the county. He diverted a river from its course to the use of machinery, and was the first to bring a canal to a mine for the purpose of conveying the ore to his own ports. He constructed from his own purse, and after his own designs, a breakwater, the harbours of Par and Pentowan, and the magnificent granite viaduct near St. Blazey; and at the period of his demise was engaged in connecting the north and south coasts of the county by a railway. Mr. Treffry died at Place House, at the age of 67, on the 29th of January, 1850.

At *Polruan*, on the shore opposite Fowey, are some remains (a chapel and guardhouse) of *Hall House*, which was garrisoned in the Civil War; and the ruins of *St. Saviour's chapel* or baptistery, and a stone cross — a group similar to the dilapidated shrine and well of St. Cleer, near Liskeard. A delightful promenade, called *Hall Walk*, runs along the water-side. The botanist in this neighbourhood may notice *Anchusa sempervirens*, or evergreen alkanet, in the lanes.

Menabilly, the seat of the Rashleighs, celebrated for its grotto and collection of minerals, is delightfully situated upon the promontory of the *Greber Head*, about 2 m. W. of Fowey. You may either walk to the grotto by the coast, or proceed by road to the E. entrance of the park, and there visit the *Longstone*, an ancient British monument of the Roman era, originally erected over the remains of one Carausius, the son of Cunimorus. It stands by the roadside near the gate (at Castle Dour), and the inscription is still in part legible. At the top of the Longstone is a mortice as if to tenon a small cross and a ⊤-shaped cross incised at the back.

"The cabinet of minerals is principally composed of Cornish specimens, and its chief excellence consists in the splendour and variety of the oxide of tin, fluors, malachite, and sulphuret of copper. Among the most remarkable specimens of tin are large octahedrons, with and without truncations; the crystal described by Klaproth as of the rarest occurrence, viz. the four-sided prism, with a four-sided pyramid at each extremity; a group of four-sided pyramids covered with a thin coating of calcedony; wood-tin, forming a vein in a matrix of quartz; tin crystals, having a coating of black hæmatite; and sulphuret of tin, an exceedingly rare mineral. The collection also contains several blocks of tin, as prepared by the Jews for commerce during the early working of the Cornish mines, among which is a fraudulent one, consisting of a mass of stone disguised by a thin coating of metal. Of other minerals the following specimens deserve particular notice, viz. yellow copper-ore with opal; the triple sulphuret of copper, antimony, and lead in various forms; ruby copper in cubes; quartz containing globules of water; the hydrargyllite or wavelite in a plumose form, accompanied by apatite in a matrix of

Route 24.—*Mevagissey.* Sect. II.

quartz; topazes of considerable lustre; green fluor in crystals of 24 sides; a beautiful cube of fluor, the surface of which reflects a delicate green hue, but when held to the light exhibits an octahedral nucleus of a purple colour; a superb octahedron of gold; and a mass of stalactitical arragonite from the grotto of Antiparos." Before quitting Menabilly the stranger should visit the grotto erected near the sea-shore. It is constructed in the form of an octagon, with the finest marbles and serpentine, interspersed with crystals, shells, and pebbles. Two of the sides are occupied by the door and a window, and the remaining six form receptacles for minerals. Four of these are filled with specimens of the Cornish ores, and two with fossils, polished agates, and jaspers; while the intermediate spaces are ornamented with shells, coralloids, and other curious substances. The roof is hung with stalactites of singular beauty. In this elegant grotto are preserved two links of a chain which were found by some fishermen in Fowey Haven in the year 1776, and are supposed to have formed a part of the chain which was once stretched across the harbour from tower to tower in times of danger. Among the specimens there is one of calcedony deserving particular notice for its magnitude and beauty. The centre of the grotto is occupied by a table inlaid with 32 polished specimens of Cornish granite. In addition to the cabinet of minerals Menabilly contains a rich collection of drawings. On his return to Fowey the traveller may visit the village of *Polkerris*, a wild fishing cove situated to the N. of the park.

Other interesting excursions may be made from this town, viz. to *Carcluze tin-mine* near St. Austell, and to the great copper-mines of *Fowey Consols* and *Par Consols*, the *Valley of Carnears*, the *Treffry Viaduct*, and the harbour of *Par* near St. Blazey (see Rte. 23). 2½ m. on the road to Lostwithiel is a small encampment called *Castle Dour.*

Proceeding on our road from Fowey, we skirt Tywardreth or St. Blazey Bay, and reach
St. Austell (Rte. 23). From here you may visit

Mevagissey. (*Inn:* the Ship.) This fishing-town, 5 m. S. of St. Austell, and noted for dirt and pilchards, derives its name from two saints, St. Mevan and St. Issey. It is situated in a hilly district upon the shore of a beautiful bay, which, bounded on the N. by the *Black Head* (alt. 153 ft.), on the S. by *Chapel Point*, commands a view of the coast as far as the Rame Head: The harbour is capacious, with a depth of 18 ft. within the pier at high-water spring tides, and of 12 during the neaps. There has long existed a jealousy between the fishermen of this place and their neighbours of *Gorran Haven*, a village 3 m. S. Mevagissey Ch., which contains a very curious font of Norm. character, and probable date, has lost its tower, and the men of Gorran affirm that the inhabitants sold their bells to pay the cost of pulling down the tower; a joke which in Mevagissey is retorted by asking, "Who cut up their own seine?" This is in allusion to a story that some years ago the fishermen of Gorran and Mevagissey, having enclosed a shoal of pilchards in their respective seines, anchored the nets for the night and returned home, when the Gorran men went out a little before daylight and destroyed, as they thought, the net belonging to their rivals; but the tide had drifted and altered the relative position of the two seines, so that they had, indeed, cut their own to pieces. There are several old monuments in the ch. In 1849 Mevagissey was so severely visited by the cholera, that the fishermen, with their families, embarked in their boats and sought safety in Fowey

Haven. One good resulted—a thorough cleansing of the town; the inhabitants encamping on the neighbouring fields while the necessary operations were being effected. A delightful road runs near the cliffs from Mevagissey to *Portmellin* (i. e. yellow port), a fishing-cove distant about 1 m. S. Here are remains of a double entrenchment, and a mound called *Castle Hill*; and in the neighbourhood a farmhouse, once part of a splendid mansion, which belonged to an old Cornish family named Bodrigan. A rock on the coast near Chapel Point (the S. horn of Mevagissey Bay) still bears the name. It is called *Bodrigan's Leap*, from a tradition that Sir Henry Bodrigan, having been convicted of treason in the reign of Henry VII., here sprang down the cliff when flying from his neighbours Edgcumbe and Trevanion, who were endeavouring to take him. He is said to have been so little injured by the fall as to have gained a vessel sailing near the shore, and to have escaped into France. The mansion of the Trevanions once stood in the parish of St. Michael Carhayes, N.W. of the Deadman Head. A Gothic building, by the architect of Buckingham Palace, now occupies the site, and the only thing to interest the antiquary in the present *Castle of Carhayes* is a stone sculptured with the royal arms (temp. Henry VIII.), which is fixed on the wall of the entrance hall. The parish ch. is hung with the rusty helmets, swords, and gauntlets of the old family of Trevanion, including a sword wielded by Sir Hugh Trevanion in the battle of Bosworth Field.

Gorran is 2 m. from Mevagissey. The tower of the church dates from 1606, and the body of the building contains a monument to Richard Edgcumbe of Bodrigan, 1656.

The *Dodman*, i. e. Dod maen, "stone of position," from its being one of the most conspicuous headlands on the S. coast, is associated with a grander headland in the Cornish proverb, "When Rame Head and Dodman meet." This, says Fuller, has come to pass, for they have met in the possession of the same owner, Sir Pierce Edgcumbe, who enjoyed the one in his own right, and the other in right of his wife. It is a wild and remote point, 379 ft. above the sea.

The cliffs of *Veryan Bay*, W. of the Deadman, afford an excellent section of various grauwacke rocks, associated with trap and conglomerates, as the coast-line cuts the strike of the beds, which is S.W.

On the cliffs W. of *Penare Head* (338 ft. above the sea) are *Giant Tregeagle's Quoits*, a number of huge blocks of quartz rock. (Penare Head has some serpentine rocks cropping from it.) It would be passing strange in Cornwall if the presence of such striking objects were not accounted for by a legend. Accordingly we hear that giant Tregeagle—the melancholy monster who frequents Dozmare Pool—hurled them to this locality from the N. coast. On the shore there is a cavern called *Tregeagle's Hole*, and in the immediate vicinity of the headland an enormous mound known as *Veryan* or *Carn Beacon* (372 ft. in circumf., and 370 ft. above the sea), which by popular accounts is the burial-place of Gerennius, a king of Cornwall. This traditional monarch is said to have been here interred about the year 589, with his crown, and weapons, and *golden boat with silver oars*: accordingly, in 1855, when the barrow was opened, the proceedings were watched with considerable interest. But the visions of the golden boat were not to be realised. The ashes of the old king were found, enclosed within a rude stone chest, or kistvaen—but nothing more than ashes. When the search had been completed these relics were replaced, and the excavation in the barrow filled in.

The name of Gerennius is still preserved in that of the village of *Gerrans* (8 m. from Tregony), where an earthwork called *Dingerein*, N. of the ch., and communicating with the shore by an underground passage termed the *Mermaid's Hole*, is pointed out as the remains of his palace. The peninsula W. of Gerrans is called *Roseland*, (Rhòsland = moorland).

You may find upon the shore on the eastern side of *Gerrans Bay* a remarkably fine example of *a raised beach*, composed of pebbles cemented together by oxide of iron.

(For St. Antony's Head, Falmouth Harbour, the various creeks of the Fal river, and for Falmouth itself, see Rte. 26).

ROUTE 25.

PLYMOUTH TO BUDE HAVEN, BY SALTASH, CALLINGTON, LAUNCESTON, AND STRATTON (THE COAST FROM BUDE TO MORWENSTOW).

(An easier way of reaching Bude Haven from Plymouth is to go to Tavistock by railway, and thence by coach to Launceston. The present route, however, from Plymouth to Launceston, has many points of interest.)

The tourist may proceed to Saltash either by boat up the Tamar; by the turnpike-road on the l. bank of the river, crossing by the steam-ferry to Saltash; or by the railway, crossing the Albert Bridge. The distance, in either case, is about 5 m.

For *Saltash*, see Rte. 23. For the excursion up the Tamar, see DEVONSHIRE, Rte. 7. Many of the points there indicated are described in the present route.

Proceeding from Saltash toward Callington, 2 m. rt. is the Ch. of *Botus Fleming*, Perp., but containing in the N. aisle the monument of a crusader, Stephen le Fleming, who accompanied Rd. I. to the Holy Land, and is said to have built the first church here. The nave piers *may* be E. E., as the font certainly is. *Moditonham*, in this parish, was in 1689 the residence of the Earl of Bath, governor of Pendennis and Plymouth Castles. He treated here with Will. III.'s commissioner for the surrender of the two fortresses.

[The old *Ch. of Landulph*, on rt. bank of the river (2 m. from Saltash by water), and opposite the mouth of the Tavy, is remarkable for containing the tomb of *Theodore Palæologus*, a descendant of the emperors of Byzantium. The following is the inscription on the monument :—
"Here lyeth the body of Theodoro Paleologus of Pesaro in Italye, descended from ye Imperyall lyne of ye last Christian Emperors of Greece, being the sonne of Camilio, ye sone of Prosper, the sonne of Theodoro, the sonne of Iohn, ye sonne of Thomas, second brother to Constantine Paleologus, the 8th of that name, and last of y^t lyne y^t raygned in Constantinople, untill subdewed by the Turkes, who married with Mary ye daughter of William Balls of Hadlye in Souffolke Gent, & had issue 5 children, Theodoro, Iohn, Ferdinando, Maria, & Dorothy, and departed this life at Clyfton ye 21th of January, 1636." Some years ago the vault was opened and the lid of the oaken coffin raised, when the body was found sufficiently perfect to show that it exceeded the common stature, and that the face had been furnished with a long white beard. The ch. itself is of no great interest.

Some trifling remains of *Clyfton*, which was a manorhouse of the Courtenays, may be seen on the point opposite Hall's Hole.]

Proceeding on our route, we pass over high land commanding in places beautiful views down the winding Tamar and over the misty regions of Dartmoor.

About 5 m. from Saltash and 1 m. rt. of the road is *Pentillie Castle* (A. Coryton, Esq.), a modern building erected from designs by the late Mr. Wilkins, and situated most delightfully upon the steep shore of the Tamar. A finely-wooded hill, called Mount Ararat, rising N. of the castle, is crowned by a tower of which a strange tale is told in connection with Sir James Tillie, one of the former possessors of this estate, who died in 1712. It is said that this individual expressed a desire that after death he should be placed in this building, seated on a chair in his customary dress, and before a table furnished with the appliances of drinking and smoking. It is further said that he was buried according to his wish as regards the locality, but in a coffin. The castle is furnished with great elegance, and in the hall are a painted window (a fine specimen of old German glass, turned inside out by the carelessness of those who placed it) and a statue of Sir James Tillie, the size of life.

6 m. *St. Mellion.*—The ch. (dedicated to St. Melanius, Bp. of Rennes, d. 490—originally Dec., but much altered, restored 1862,) contains some monuments with effigies of the Corytons, baronets of Newton Park in the 17th cent., while their helmets, spurs, swords, gauntlets, and pennons hang from the roof. Against the N. wall is a good *brass* for Peter Coryton, d. 1505, wife and children. The mansion of *Newton* is still standing, and about 3 m. to the l. In a farmhouse rt. of the road is a fragment of *Crocadon House*, once the residence of a family named Trevisa, one of whom, John Trevisa, chaplain to Lord Berkeley, translated the Bible, the 'Acts of King Arthur,' and Higden's 'Polychronicon.' He died 1470, æt. 86. This family failed in 1690, when Crocadon was purchased by the Corytons.

1 m. *Viverdon Down.*— The traveller will find in its vicinity a road to the rt., which—(passing the Ch. of St. Dominick, in which is a good 17th cent. monument with effigies of Sir Anthony Rouse and his son. Halton, in this parish, was their residence, and here lived John Rouse, Speaker of Cromwell's Little Parliament, "the old illiterate Jew of Eton," as the Cavaliers called him. He was the chief author of the metrical version of the Psalms now used in the Scottish Kirk)—in about 3 m. will bring him to

Cothele, i. e. "Coet-heyle," the woods on the river (Earl of Mount Edgcumbe, now the residence of the Countess Dowager), a most interesting old mansion, begun by Sir Rd. Edgcumbe, temp. Hen. VII., carried on slowly through the reign of Hen. VIII., and not completed before that of Eliz. The ancient fittings and furniture, as well as the granite walls, are in excellent preservation. It is an embattled structure, built round a quadrangle, and situated above an ancient wood of oak, elm, and chesnut, sloping to the Tamar. (A Spanish chesnut in the wood is probably the largest in England, being 26 ft. in circumference. It is now decaying.) The hall is hung with the trophies of war and the chace,— coats of mail, arms of various kinds, and the horns of the stag,—while a figure in complete armour adorns the wall at the upper end. The timber roof is of the time of Hen. VIII. A chair has the date 1627, and much of the furniture in the house corresponds with this. The other apartments are extremely interesting, especially to the antiquary, since they contain a store of antique furniture, and many curious appliances of the luxury of bygone days. All the rooms are hung with tapestry, which is lifted to give an entrance; and the hearths, intended for wood alone, are furnished with grotesque figures or andirons for the support of the logs. The cabinets should be closely examined for their delicate carving. The dining-room, at the end of the hall, joins the *chapel*, which has a triptych over the altar, a screen and stall-desks, temp. Hen. VIII. The decorations of the altar are worth inspecting. There is a small window near the altar, opening to a closet from a bedroom. From the other end of the dining-room a staircase leads to bedrooms in which is furniture temp. Eliz. and Jas. I., including some curious mirrors (one of polished steel), with frames worked in needlework. The drawing-room, on the first-floor of the W. tower, has ebony chairs, temp. Eliz. Above this room are small bedrooms: one called Queen Anne's; another said to be that in which Charles II. slept, with the furniture as left by him—(the bed is of James I.'s reign.) Cothele belonged to a family of that name previous to the reign of Edw. III., when it passed by marriage to an ancestor of the Earl of Mount Edgcumbe. The house has been honoured more than once by the presence of royalty. Charles II. resided in it for several days. In 1789 it was visited by Geo. III. and his queen; and recently by her Majesty Queen Victoria and Prince Albert. The scenery on the Tamar below Cothele is extremely beautiful. The wood overhangs the river in clustering masses, and at the bend of the stream becomes wild and tangled in a verdant hollow called *Danescombe*. At another spot a bold rock projecting from the foliage throws a gloomier shadow upon the water. This is crowned by a small chapel, and connected with the following legend:— In the reign of Richard III., Sir Richard Edgcumbe being suspected of favouring the claims of Richmond, a party of armed men was despatched to apprehend him. He escaped, however, from his house into the wood, closely followed by his pursuers, and, having gained the summit of this rock, his cap fell into the water as he was clambering down the rocks to conceal himself. The soldiers soon arrived on the spot, and, upon seeing the cap floating on the river, imagined that Edgcumbe had drowned himself, and so gave over the pursuit. Sir Richard afterwards crossed into France, and, returning upon the death of the king, erected this chapel in grateful remembrance of his escape. The chapel contains windows of stained glass, two 15th cent. paintings, a monument of Sir Richard Edgcumbe, a gilt crucifix, and the image of a bishop in his pontificals. Cothele is in the vicinity of the *Morwell Rocks*, and other interesting scenes on the Tamar. (See DEVON, Rte. 7.) The botanist may procure *Melittis grandiflora*, a plant rather local than rare, in the neighbourhood. *Melittis Melissophyllum*, an uncommon species, is also found in the county.

Returning to Viverdon Down, after proceeding 2½ m. the traveller arrives at a small patch of uncultivated land. If on foot or on horseback he can here diverge from the road and visit one of the "lions" of Callington in his way to that town. For this purpose, at the further boundary-hedge turn to the right over the common towards a narrow lane which, crossing another at right angles, leads direct to a farm-house. Just below the farmyard is

Dupath Well, a pellucid spring, which, once the resort of pilgrims, overflows a trough, and, entering the open archway of a small chapel, spreads itself over the floor, and passes out below a window at the opposite end. The little chapel is a complete specimen of the *baptisteries* anciently so common in Cornwall (see *Introd.*). It has a most venerable appearance, and is built entirely of granite which is grey and worn by age. The roof is constructed of enormous slabs, hung with fern and supported in the interior by an arch, dividing the nave and chancel. The building is crowned by an ornamented bellcot. This well, according to a legend, was once the scene of a fierce combat between two noble Saxons, rivals in a lady's affections—Colan, a youth and the favoured suitor, and Gotlieb (?), a man of more advanced years. The duel terminated in the death of Gotlieb; but Colan had received a wound which, aggravated by his impatience to wed the lady of his affections, eventually proved mortal. The story has been told as a metrical legend by the Rev. R. S. Hawker, rector of Morwenstow.

1 m. *Callington* (*Inn:* Golding's Hotel), a dreary town, disfranchised by the Reform Bill (Horace Walpole sat for Callington during his father's last administration), and now containing about 1700 Inhab., chiefly occupied in mining. King Arthur, says tradition, had a palace here, when the place was called " Killywick." The *Church* is now the sole lion. It is a daughter ch. to South Hill, and was rebuilt by Sir Nich. Assheton, who died in 1465. It has been thoroughly restored (1861), J. P. St. Aubyn, archit. The walls are of granite, with a good W. tower, on the buttresses of which are the evangelistic symbols. In the chancel is the fine *brass* of the founder or rebuilder, Sir Nicholas Assheton and wife. Sir Nicholas, who was one of the "Justices of the King's Bench," wears a coif and long furred robe. On the N. side of the chancel is the tomb with alabaster effigy of Sir Robt. Willoughby, first Lord Willoughby de Broke—died 1502. He is in armour, bareheaded (as usual at this period), and wears the collar, badge, and mantle of the Garter. On the soles of the feet are the figures of 2 monks telling their beads, an unique example. This first Lord W., who died steward of the Duchy of Cornwall, was a sharer in the victory of Bosworth. The font is of Norm. character. In the churchyard is a canopied cross, worth notice. Callington is in a great measure supported by the mines in the neighbourhood, and is situated immediately under

Kit Hill, alt. 1067 ft., an outlying eminence of granite, and summit of *Hingston Down*, which stretches eastward to the Tamar, and before the reign of Hen. III. was the place of meeting of the Cornish tinners, who assembled here every 7th or 8th year to confer with their brethren of Devon. In 835 it was the scene of the defeat of the Danes and Britons by Egbert; of which great and decisive battle the tumuli which occur on the down may be traces. Kit Hill, from its isolated position, intermediate between the moors of Bodmin and Dartmoor (about 16 m. apart), and in full view of the windings of the Tamar and distant Channel, commands perhaps the most impressive and beautiful view in Cornwall. Upon the summit is the ruin of a windmill, which, erected upon that exposed spot to work a mine, was destroyed by the violence of the wind; while the mine was abandoned in consequence of the great expense attending its excavation in a hard granite. Kit Hill, like all barren ground in a populous neighbourhood, has a dreary aspect. Its sides are covered with rubbish, and the summit is pierced by a number of shafts, which render caution most necessary in those who ascend to it. " The country people," says Carew, " have a bye-word that

'Hengsten Down well ywrought
Is worth London town dear ybought,'

which grew from a store of tynne, in former times there digged up."

Dupath Well (see *ante*) is about 1 m. from this town, and the following are the directions for finding it. Pursue the Tavistock road about ¼ m. to the open down. Here, at a signpost on the rt., strike over the grass to a lane trending in that direction. Pursue this lane ½ m.; then turn down the lane on the l. which leads to a farmhouse. Adjoining and below this house is the well. The traveller is there also in the vicinity of *Cothele*.

[*Liskeard* (Rte. 23) is 8 m. from Callington, and the road to it one of the most hilly in Cornwall. Midway is *St. Ive*, of which the ch. deserves special notice, as one of the few good examples of Dec. in Cornwall. The E. window, with canopied niches at the sides, is fine. There is a large 16th cent. monument to John Wrey and wife. There is a good tower. The ch. was founded by the Knights Templars, who had a preceptory at Trebigh in the parish. There are some remains of Dec. stained glass in St. Ive's Ch. (St. Ive can hardly be "St. John of Jerusalem," as has been asserted, but the Breton saint—

"Sanctns Ivo erat Brito
Advocatus, sed non latro
Res miranda populo.")

In the Dec. church of *Quethiock*, 1 m. from St. Ive, is a fine *brass* to Roger Kingdon (d. 1371) and wife. The tower (Dec.) is very singular. The second stage rises from and crowns a western gable, like a gigantic bell-turret. The staircase only reaches to the base of the second stage, where it terminates in a small gable on the S. front of the tower.

Gunnislake, a village in the heart of this mining district, is 5½ m. on the road to Tavistock. On the heights above it is the tin-mine of *Drake-walls* (rt. side of the road above the village), particularly worth visiting, as one of the lodes, traversed by a cross-course, is open to the day. Here also has been introduced an important process for separating wolfram (tungstate of iron) from the tin-ore, and which was invented by Mr. Oxland, of this mine. The *Morwell Rocks* (DEVON, Rte. 7) are seen to great advantage from Gunnislake; and a slender water-wheel, suspended above the river, will strike the traveller's attention, from the singularity of its position among woods and beetling crags. It belongs to a mine called *Chimney Rock*. The Tamar is spanned by the picturesque structure of *New Bridge*, above which its shores, receding, form a wooded basin, which is crowned by the engine of *Huel Sophia*.]

The road from Callington to Launceston crosses the foot of Kit Hill, having the *Holmbush* and *Redmoor* copper-mines respectively rt. and l.

[After passing the Redmore mine, a road branches l. to South Hill (2 m.), where is a good Dec. church —the mother ch. of Callington— ded. to S. Sampson of Dol. The rude Norm. font is worth notice. The Ch. of *Linkenhorne*, 1 m. beyond, is Perp., with a very fine tower, said to be the highest in Cornwall except Probus. The caps. of the nave piers are embattled, and finely sculptured with varying details. This ch. was rebuilt by Sir Henry Trecarrell, temp. Henry VIII. (the rebuilder of Launceston ch.). He was lord of the manor. The chancel is modern and very bad. There is an Elizabethan house (now a farm) at *Browda* in this parish, and a circular entrenchment on the estate, which, says the local legend, must never be broken by the plough, or the owner will die.]

2½ m. l. *Whiteford House* (Sir John Call, Bart.).

½ m. *Stoke Climsland*. (The church, late Dec., has been well restored.) A road on rt. leads over the Tamar by *Horse Bridge* 2½ m.

1½ m. The traveller here passes the *Inny*, which flows down a pleasant vale towards the Tamar.

½ m. The *Sportsman's Arms*, and half-way-house between Callington and Launceston. rt., distant about 1 m., the *Carthamartha Rocks*, a fine wild scene of limestone cliff, "bursting from the slopes," and overlooking an amphitheatre of wood. Below and far beyond stretches the valley of the Tamar. A lane opposite the inn, and then a field-path, lead direct to this charming point of view.

1¼ m. l. *Lezant*, with a granite ch., containing monuments of the Trefusis family. The ch. is Perp.; there are some good cradle roofs. 1½ W. of it is the ivied ruin of *Trecarrel* (Rte. 21); and 1 m. farther W., on the opposite side of the Inny, a small circular earthwork called *Round Bury*.

⅞ m. rt. *Hexworthy House*, E. Prideaux, Esq., and a road to *Greystone Bridge*, one of the most ancient structures on the Tamar. Beyond it is the old Tudor manor-house of *Bradstone* (DEVON, Rte. 6), and S. of it *Endsleigh* (Duke of Bedford), so renowned for its romantic beauty.

The geologist should be informed that near *Landue Mill*, to the l. of the road, the carbonaceous deposits rest in an unconformable position on the grauwacke.

1 m. rt. *Lawhitton*, where the small ch. has been restored.

2 m. *Launceston* (Rte. 21).

1 m. rt. *Werrington*, a seat of the Duke of Northumberland; l. *St. Stephen's Down*.

14 m. *Stratton* (*Inn:* the Tree), a poor town lying among hills, about a mile from the coast, but of considerable antiquity, the name being evidence of its Roman origin. The Saxons, it is well known, called the Roman roads *streets*, and the towns which were situated upon them *street-towns*, or *strettons*, and "in this instance," says Borlase, "as in many others, corruption in speech has jostled out the E and put an A in its place." The name occurs in Somerset, in Gloucestershire, and, indeed, in many parts of England, on the lines of the old Roman ways. The *ch.* is Perp., and contains the black marble tomb of Sir John Arundell, of Trerice (1561), his 2 wives and 13 children, whose effigies are represented on *brasses*. The hilly country of this neighbourhood—though rich and well cultivated—has somewhat a wild and bare appearance; but your landlord at Stratton will tell you that there is timber to be found in it. Thus his inn is the *Tree*, he himself an *Ash*, his farm-bailiff a *Wood*, his neighbours *Ivy* and *Oak*, and the farm of the latter at *Bush*.

There are two objects of particular interest in the vicinity of Stratton—*Stamford Hill*, and the *inclined plane* on *the Bude Canal*. The former lies immediately N. of the town, and was the scene of the battle of Stamford Hill, in which the forces of the Parliament were defeated by the Royalists. By Clarendon's account it was towards the middle of May, 1643, when the Earl of Stamford marched into Cornwall with an army of 1400 horse and 5400 foot, and a park of artillery consisting of 13 pieces of brass ordnance and a mortar, and encamped near Stratton, on a lofty hill, steep on all sides, while he despatched a body of 1200 horse, under Sir George Chudleigh, to surprise Bodmin. The king's forces, not amounting to half this number, were at the same time quartered near Launceston, under Sir Ralph Hopton and Sir Beville Grenville, who, though far inferior in the strength and equipment of their troops, resolved to give the enemy battle, and with that purpose marched, on Monday the 15th, with 2400 foot and 500 horse, upon Stratton, although "so destitute of provisions, that the best officers had but a biscuit a man." The next morning by daybreak, this force, being arranged in 4 divisions, advanced to the attack on different sides of the hill, the horse standing aloof as a reserve. For several hours the battle was waged with varying success, when the royalists, having reduced their supply of powder to 4 barrels, determined upon advancing to the summit of the hill before they fired another shot. With this intention they steadily pushed forward, and being charged by Major-General Chudleigh near the top of the hill, that officer was taken prisoner, and the enemy recoiled. The Royalists now pushed their advantage, and rushing with fresh spirit on the Roundheads, succeeded in throwing them into disorder, when, the Earl of Stamford giving the signal of defeat by galloping from the field, the panic became general, and the Parliamentary troops fled on all sides. They left about 200 men dead on the field, and their camp and ammunition in the hands of the victors. Stamford Hill bears to this day the marks of the battle. It is crowned by the remains of a tumulus, upon which, turned up by the plough, lie the bleached bones of the combatants. The summit is of small girth, and the ground slopes steeply from it to the S. and E.; but on the W., and especially on the N. side, the position might be more easily assailed. A monument erected on the hill, in commemoration of the battle, was destroyed many years ago, but the inscription in white characters on a black wooden tablet, and to the following effect, was preserved, and is now fixed on the wall of the Tree Inn. "In this place ye army of the rebells under ye command of ye Earl of Stamford received a signal overthrow by the valor of Sir Bevill Grenville and ye Cornish army, on Tuesday, the 16th of May, 1643." Stamford Hill is further interesting as commanding a fine view, in which Roughtor and Brown Willy are conspicuous though distant objects.

The *inclined plane of the Bude Canal*, which the stranger should visit, is on Hobbacott Down, 1½ m. from Stratton, and just to the rt. of the Holsworthy road. It is an ingenious substitute for a chain of locks, and consists of a steep roadway, about 900 ft. in length, which is furnished with two lines of rails dipping at each end into the canal, and traversed by an endless chain. The barges, which are provided with small iron wheels, and generally loaded with sand, are raised or lowered on this roadway by being attached to the chain, which is set in motion by two enormous buckets, each 8 ft. in diam., alternately filled with water, and working in wells 225 ft. in depth. As soon as the descending bucket has reached the bottom of the well, it strikes upon a stake which raises a plug, when the water runs out in one minute, and finds its way through an adit to the canal below. This bucket is then in readiness to be raised by the other, which, having been filled with water, descends in its turn. In case of any accident happening to the machinery, the water can at any time be emptied in one minute through valves with which a chain communicates; this chain being ingeniously made to wind and unwind as the buckets ascend and descend, so as to be always of the proper length. A steam-engine is also at hand should the buckets become unserviceable. This canal extends from Bude to Launceston, sending off a branch to Holsworthy, and the barges climb from one level to another by 7 of these inclined planes. One is situated at *Marhamchurch*, 1 m. from Stratton, but this is worked by a common waterwheel. Marhamchurch, ded. to St. Morwenna, is Perp., and has some good bench-ends.

½ m. from Stratton towards Marhamchurch, in the orchard of a farm called *Binhamy*, is a quadrangular moat overgrown with briers, marking the site of a manor-house or castle, in which, it is said, lived one

Ranulph de Blanchminster, of whom many strange legends are current in the parish. Tradition represents him as an eccentric individual, who lived retired from the world in his castle, and protected from intrusion by a drawbridge, which was generally raised. After his death, which occurred, it is said, without a person to witness it, a will was found bequeathing a large amount of property to the poor of the parish, who have now annually 80*l*. divided amongst them as the interest of this fund. The country-people call him "old Blowmanger," and entertain a superstitious dread of the spot where he dwelt; and this has partly originated in the circumstance of hares having been started from the moat, which always, as it happened, escaped the dogs. It was therefore concluded that the spirit of Blanchminster haunted the spot in the shape of this animal. The effigy of Blanchminster may be seen in the church.

1½ m. S. of Stratton is the pretty village of *Launcells*, and *Launcells House*, seat of G. B. Kingdon, Esq. The ch. (Perp., with granite arches and very good carved bench-ends) contains a monument, dated 1644, to John Chamond, one of the former possessors of this mansion. In the parish is *Morton*, a farm belonging to Mr. Kingdon, and of interest as an ancient possession of Robert de Moritune or "Morton," Earl of Cornwall, the half-brother of William the Conqueror.

At *Week St. Mary*, 7 m., commonly called St. Mary Week, is the ruin of a chantry, founded by one Dame Percival about the beginning of the 14th centy. The history of this person is curious as connected with her maiden-name, *Bonaventura*. She is said to have been a labourer's daughter, who, one day tending sheep upon the moor, engaged the attention of a London merchant who happened to be passing. Pleased with her appearance, he begged her of her parents and carried her to London as a servant, and after the lapse of a few years, at the death of his wife, made her the mistress of his house, and, dying himself shortly afterwards, bequeathed to her a large amount of property. She then married a person of the name of Gall, whom she also survived; when Sir John Percival, Lord Mayor of London, became her 3rd husband. The constitution of a London citizen was, however, no match for that of a "wilding" from the moors; and accordingly the mayor died while life was yet vigorous in Dame Percival. The lady, however, was by this time contented with her experience as a wife, and, retiring to her native village, devoted the remainder of her days to acts of charity. In these her 3 husbands were not forgotten, and for the benefit of their souls she founded and endowed this chantry, which at the period of the dissolution shared the fate of the monasteries. *Week* is a Saxon word, and signifies a place of residence.

Jacobstow, pronounced Dewstow, about 8 m. S. of Stratton, was the birthplace of *Degory Wheare*, 1573, author of a Life of Camden and other works. Adjoining it is *Berry Court*, a mansion of the olden time, now a farmhouse.

1½ m. *Bude Haven* (*Inn:* Falcon Hotel), a small but growing watering-place on a grand and curious coast. It commands delightful sea-views and is begirt by unfrequented hills. The *haven* consists of the mouth of the Bude Canal, opening to a shallow bay, the sand of which has been blown inland by the N.W. winds, and is heaped to some distance in arid dunes. In the midst of these hillocks, and opposite to the hotel, is the house of Mr. Gurney, the inventor of the Bude Light. The bay is sheltered from the heaviest seas by an embankment, which, constructed in a similar manner to the Plymouth Breakwater, connects a rock, called the *Chapel Rock*, with the shore. At low water this bay is a scene of considerable bustle, as it supplies the neighbouring parts of Devon and Cornwall with sea-sand, which is used as manure and carried up the country in such amazing quantities that 4000 horse-loads have been taken from the shore in one day. The conveyance of this sand is calculated to cost 30,000*l.* per annum, and forms the principal commerce on the Bude and Launceston Canal and its branch to Holsworthy.

The vast and picturesque *sea-cliffs* in this part of Cornwall are a great attraction to Bude. The strata belonging to the carbonaceous formation dip at right angles to the shore, and for this reason, as offering but a feeble resistance to the waves, are in a ruinous condition. The bands of strata are also so narrow and distinctly marked as to give a ribboned appearance to the cliffs, and are everywhere varied by the most irregular contortions.

Compass Point, on the W. side of the haven, commands an excellent view of this rugged coast, and is crowned with an octagonal tower, a temple of the winds, the sides of which are turned to the 8 cardinal points. At the foot of this tower is a seat from which a very singular ridge projects into the sea, since it resembles a wall, the surfaces being smooth and precipitous. A striking cliff in the neighbourhood is *Beacon Hill*, ½ m. W., presenting a sheer precipice of about 300 ft.: but the points most calculated to delight and astonish the traveller are the amazing headlands of *Hennacliff*, N. of Bude, alt. 450 ft., and the *Dizard*, the western boundary of *Widemouth Bay*, alt. 550 ft.

Kilkhampton Ch., an ancient structure, built by one of the Granvilles, and celebrated as the scene of Hervey's ' Meditations among the Tombs,' is situated 5 m. from Bude, the road to it being up-hill the greater part of that distance. There is much interesting Norman work in the ch., the finest portion being the S. door, with shafts and bands and beak-head and zigzag mouldings; a small arch, ornamented with the arms of the Granville family, over a doorway on the same side of the ch., should also be noticed; and in the interior of the building an ancient pulpit and font, carved seats, and the costly monuments of the Granvilles. Among them is one to the memory of Sir Beville Grenville, the hero of Stamford Hill, who was killed at the battle of Lansdown in 1643. The coffins of the Earls of Bath are deposited in a vault under the E. end of the S. aisle, where, says Hervey, " they lie ranged in mournful order, in a sort of silent pomp." They are partly covered with copper-plates bearing the arms and titles of their occupants. The church was admirably restored (1860) by Lord John Thynne, under the superintendence of Mr. G. G. Scott. The Grenvilles—who trace their descent from Rollo Duke of Normandy—were long seated at *Stow*, a magnificent mansion above the neighbouring village of Comb. John, 3rd son of Sir Beville Grenville, rebuilt it 1680. He had been created, 1661, Earl of Bath, a title which became extinct on the early death of his grandson, 1711. Stow then descended to his sister, widow of George Lord Carteret, created Countess Granville, and through her it came to the present possessor, Lord John Thynne. The house was dismantled 1720, and a moated site is at this day the only vestige of it. The corner of the wood, at which Sir Beville appeared to his wife after his death on Lansdowne field, is still pointed out. (Pictures of Stow in its old grandeur will be found in Kingsley's ' Westward Ho.') A small manor-house, facing the sea, in a very exposed situation, has been built for the present possessor by Mr. G. G. Scott.

Comb Valley is the name of a picturesque *bottom*, commencing just N. of Kilkhampton and opening to the sea between lofty cliffs; and farther N. the country towards the hamlet of *Morwenstow* is here and there furrowed by deep hollows, which are prettily wooded. The coast in the neighbourhood is everywhere magnificent, and at *Stanbury Creek* "exhibits a fine example of the curvatures and contortions of rocks, the strata being heaped on each other apparently in utter confusion, dipping towards every point of the compass and at various degrees of inclination." In the parish of Kilkhampton is a curious old manorhouse called *Aldercombe*, belonging to Sir G. Stuckley. It is 17th cent., and a very good specimen of the gentleman's house of that period.

Morwenstow is 4 m. N.W. of Kilkhampton, and 7 m. from Stratton, on a height bounded by cliffs 420 ft. above the sea; and, though a poor village in itself, contains a splendid old church, of great interest to the ecclesiologist. It is chiefly Norman, and the S. door and elaborately sculptured caps and arches of the nave are well worthy of notice. There are besides a Norm. font, an elaborate screen, and costly monuments to old Cornish families now extinct. The ch. contains a curious old *pitchpipe*. The porch is covered with short ferns (not the true Maidenhair, but *Asplenium trichomanes*); and in the ch.-yard, through the drifting spray, are discerned memorials, including the graves of 3 entire crews of ships lost here, which simply tell their tale, but bear affecting testimony to the perils of the neighbouring shore. One is a battered boat, resting above the remains of those who perished in her; and another the broken oars, which have been formed into a rude cross. Morwenstow is the rectory of the Rev. R. S. Hawker, who, in a volume of very beautiful poems, has thrown a wild interest into 'Echoes from Old Cornwall.' The picturesque rectory adjoins the church, and above the cliffs in front is the well of St. Morwenna, the patroness. She was the daughter of an Irish king, who cured by her prayers a son of King Egbert. He built for her the monastery of Pollesworth, in Warwickshire, where she trained St. Edith, St. Osyth, and others.

3 m. from Kilkhampton, due E., is a reservoir for the supply of the Bude Canal. It covers 70 acres.

About 3 m. N.E. of Kilkhampton the country rises in bleak and elevated hills, which are divided into furzy crofts and rush-covered swamps. Upon these, near the border of the county, the Hartland road passes close to *Wooley Barrows* (rt.), ¼ m. S. of which rise the two rivers *Tamar* and *Torridge*. They drain from a dreary bog down opposite sides of the hill, and their waters are soon a great way apart; the one river hastening southward in its course of 59 m. to Plymouth; the other trending northward, to run nearly an equal distance (53 m.) before it reaches the sea below Bideford.

ROUTE 26.

TRURO TO FALMOUTH, BY PENRYN. (FALMOUTH HARBOUR AND INLETS.)

(This is a short line in connection with the Cornwall Rly. The distance is performed in half-an-hour.)

The Rly. (11¾ m.) is carried over the Penwether Viaduct, 173 yds. long and 84 high, ¾ m. from Truro, and through a tunnel in the slate, 484 yds., at Sparnick. Viaduct at Ringwall; also at Carnon, 264 yds. long.

About 2 m. from Truro, l., is *Killiow* (*i. e.* the secluded place, or place of refuge), seat of Mrs. Daubuz. It was the old residence of the Gwatkins. In the house is a collection of ancient pictures. The (new) adjoining church of *Kea*, more like a riding-school than a church in appearance, contains a very fine font of the Norm. character so common in Cornwall. Here are also a chalice and paten which belonged to Cardinal René d'Amboise. The mineral ochre used in the preparation of paint and in staining paper is procured in this parish.

1½ m. l. *Killiganoon*, seat of the late Admiral Spry.

A little farther rt. is *Carnon*. The traveller will observe that the valley is everywhere furrowed by mining operations. The *Carnon Tin Stream-works*, which for the present are abandoned, were here conducted on a large scale, and in a very spirited manner, the water having been actually banked from the works, which were carried on for some distance in the bed of the estuary. The space of ground thus streamed exceeded a mile in length, by 300 yards in width. In this the tin stratum, which varied in thickness from a few inches to 12 feet, was found at a depth of from 40 to 50 feet below the surface, under accumulations of marine and river detritus, consisting of mud, sand, and silt. One of these beds contained the trunks of trees, and the horns and bones of deer; and in the tin-ground grains of gold and pieces of wood-tin were occasionally discovered. In the village of Carnon are extensive works for the preparation of arsenic from arsenical pyrites.

The *Great Adit*, which, passing from mine to mine through the Redruth and Gwennap districts, is calculated, with its branches, to pursue a subterranean course of nearly 30 m., discharges its waters, sometimes to the amount of 2000 cub. ft. in a minute, through Carnon valley into Restronguet Creek.

4 m. from Truro is *Perranwell Stat. Perran Arworthal*, or *Perran Wharf*, is a village romantically situated in a deep bottom or dell, at the head of *Restronguet Creek*, which is here joined by the *Kennal*, a small stream rising near *Carnmenellis*, and working 39 water-wheels in its course of 5½ m. This dell presents a delightful contrast to the rough hills in the neighbourhood. It is densely clothed with trees, through which protrude the harsh features of the county, rugged rocks, but here mantled with mosses and creepers. A large *iron-foundry* harmonises with this picturesque scene. The *Ch.* is a small building dedicated to St. Piran, the patron of tinners; and near it gushes forth the little *Well*

of St. Piran. The woods above this valley belong to *Carclew* (*i. e.* "grey rock"), the seat of Sir C. Lemon, Bart., late M.P. for W. Cornwall, distinguished as a patron of science, and president of more than one learned society in this county. The park is of great extent, full of deer, and quite a forest of fine timber. The botanist may notice. growing under the trees, *Erica ciliaris* (a ciliated variety of *Erica tetralix*, which is found wild nowhere but in this neighbourhood), a heath confined to the extreme S. of the kingdom, and rare except on this estate. He will be delighted with the gardens, so richly are they stored with curious plants. For many years Sir Charles Lemon has cultivated a collection of exotic trees and shrubs, and, as the climate is peculiar, the result of his experiments is highly interesting. The magnificent collection of rhododendrons is alone worth a visit. Rhododendron arboreum, from the Himalayas, here really becomes a tree. Here are fine specimens of the *Lucombe oak* (Lucombe was gardener at Carclew), an accidental hybrid between the cork-tree (*Q. suber*) and the Turkey oak. There are also, in the gardens at Carclew, a number of hybrids between other oaks. Of the genus pinus the most remarkable are the Indian, Mexican, and Californian kinds, well showing how favourable the Cornish climate is to the growth of coniferæ. Loudon, in his Encyclopædia, describes many plants flourishing at Carclew as either quite irregular or in a state of growth not to be seen in other places.

8¼ m. *Penryn Stat.* (*Inn*: King's Arms). (Collegewood Viaduct is 100 ft. high, and 320 yds. long.) This old borough and market-town is pleasantly situated on the declivity of a hill, at the head of a branch of Falmouth Harbour, and opposite the pretty ch. of *St. Gluvias*, embosomed in trees. It is in a warm sheltered valley, richly fertile, and particularly productive in early vegetables. These with granite form the exports of the place.

The chief objects of curiosity are the *Tolmén* (Rte. 28), 4 m. distant, rt. of the road to Constantine through Mabe, and the *granite-quarries* in the parishes of *Mabe* and *Constantine*. The most important of these works are about 2 m. from Penryn on each side of the old road leading to Helston. Penryn granite has been long known for its fine grain, and is the material of which Waterloo Bridge and the Docks at Chatham are constructed. Nearly 20,000 tons have been shipped here in the course of the year, but as the supply is regulated by the demand it necessarily varies much. Before export the stone is approximately valued at 1*s.* 9*d.* per cubic foot. Beryls have been found in a quarry between Falmouth and the Tolmên. The geologist may observe slate altered by the proximity of granite in the cutting of the road on the ascent from Penryn towards Constantine; and the botanist *Antirrhinum repens* (or creeping snap-dragon), a very rare plant, in the neighbouring hedges.

Some small streams descend from the high land W. of the town, and one, falling in a cascade and turning a water-wheel, deserves notice as originating a picturesque scene. A very beautiful view of Falmouth Harbour, and St. Gluvias ch. and glebe, is commanded from *Treleaver Hill*, on the road to Roscrow, and about ½ m. from Penryn. *Enys* (J. S. Enys, Esq.), the seat of the Enyses from a very ancient time, is situated rt. of the road to Carclew and Perran Wharf. Its grounds contain a wych elm of enormous size.

3 m. *Falmouth*. The *stat.* is close to Pendennis Castle, and is approached by a bridge. (*Inns*: Pearce's Royal Hotel; Selley's Green Bank Hotel.) This town, seated on the shore of

one of the finest harbours in the kingdom, derives its principal interest from the beauty of its position, as it mainly consists of one long narrow street, of a mean appearance, straggling along the side of the water. Of late years, however, Falmouth, like other towns, has been extended and improved, and there are now at either end of it, and on the heights above the shore, handsome and commodious dwellings, which command an uninterrupted view of the estuary. Falmouth (Pop. in 1861, 5709) suffered much from a fire in 1862 which destroyed a considerable portion of the town. But the oldest part of Falmouth is of a comparatively modern date. In the reign of Elizabeth Sir Walter Raleigh visited the harbour on his return from the coast of Guinea, and found but one solitary house, in addition to a mansion called Arwenack, the seat of the ancient family of Killigrew, standing upon the site of the present town. Sir Walter was struck with the advantages of this noble estuary, and on his return to London made a representation to the council on the subject. Public notice being thus drawn to the spot, there soon collected on the shore a village, which, at first called *Smithike*, and then by the singular name of *Penny-come-quick* (obviously a corruption of a Cornish name from *Pen, Coomb,* and *Ick*), gradually rose into importance, when, in 1652, by act of parliament, the custom-house was removed to it from Penryn, and it became the centre of a busy trade. In 1660 a royal proclamation declared that henceforward its name should be *Falmouth;* and in 1661 it was invested by charter with all the dignities of a corporate town. The buildings are ranged along the heights and shore of the western side of the harbour, which terminates in a bluff point bounding the entrance of the haven, and crowned by the grey walls of *Pendennis* (Pen *Dinas*, head of the fort?) *Castle,* 198 feet above the sea. A circular tower, erected in the reign of Henry VIII., and now the residence of the lieut.-governor, is the most ancient part of this fortress, which was strengthened and enlarged in the reign of Elizabeth. Occupying a considerable area, the castle is fortified on the N.E. and N.W. by bastions and connecting curtains. The defences on the other sides have been constructed in conformity with the shape of the ground. It is further protected by outlying batteries, and is well furnished with barracks and magazines. In 1644 Pendennis afforded shelter to the queen, Henrietta Maria, when embarking for France; and in 1646 to Prince Charles, who hence sailed to Scilly. Soon after his departure the place was invested by the forces of the Parliament, and its gallant governor, John Arundell of Trerice, began that stubborn defence by which he so highly distinguished himself. Although in his 87th year, he held the castle for 6 months against the utmost efforts of the enemy; and when at length hunger had compelled him to capitulate, he had the satisfaction of knowing that the royal standard had floated longer on Pendennis than on any other fort in England. The ramparts command a view of extreme beauty, in which the stranger may contrast the rugged coast of Falmouth Bay, bounded on the W. by *Rosemullion Head* and the *Manacles* (i.e. "maen-eglos," "church-stone"), with the clustering houses and tranquil scene of the harbour. On his return to the town he may make a circuit by a lane on the l. and the heights of Falmouth. In the fields adjoining this lane are remains of the earthworks thrown up during the siege; and at a little distance to the rt. the ancient seat of the Killigrews, *Arwenack*, now the property of Lord Wodehouse. An obelisk in the grounds of this estate commemorates the visit of Sir Walter Raleigh.

The *Royal Cornwall Polytechnic Society* meets annually at Falmouth. It was the first institution of the kind established in England, and was founded in 1833 for the encouragement of the sciences, art, and industry. It originated in the exertions of a lady—Miss A. M. Fox, of Grove Hill; the Queen is the patron, Sir Chas. Lemon the president. The Hall contains some portraits, including those of Sir Humphry Davy and Richard Carew, author of the 'Survey of Cornwall,' and several busts of eminent persons connected with the county, viz. of the Prince of Wales, Lord de Dunstanville, Davies Gilbert, Sir H. de la Beche, Sir Charles Lemon, Mr. Adams the astronomer, and Dr. Paris, the founder of the Royal Geological Society of Cornwall and biographer of Davy. The Society has published about 20 vols. of Transactions, and at the annual exhibition in the autumn the principal gentry of the county assemble, when papers are read, models and works of art displayed, and prizes awarded to the most deserving.

The climate of this town is remarkable for equability and mildness, in proof of which exotic plants flourish the year round in the open air. Mr. Fox, of Grove Hill, obtained the Banksian medal for *acclimatising* upwards of 200 foreign plants. Orange and lemon trees are grown against the garden walls, and yield an abundant return of fruit.

Grove Hill (G. T. Fox, Esq.) contains some valuable paintings, including — *Titian*, Portrait of Ignatius Loyola; *Ann. Carracci*, The Syro-Phœnician Woman; *Bassano*, Jacob at the Well; and specimens of *L. da Vinci, Correggio, Claude*, and *G. Poussin*.

Tregedna, seat of Joshua Fox, W. of the town (and contiguous to *Pengerrick*, Robert Were Fox), is also decorated with valuable paintings. Here are — *Titian*, "Filia Roberti Strozzi, Nobilis Florentini;" *Vandyke*, a Dead Christ; *A. del Sarto*, a Holy Family; and works by *Raffaelle, Sassoferrato, Morland*, &c. Another fine collection may be seen at *Gyllyngdune*, the seat of the rector, the Rev. Wm. John Coope. This is the largest house and one of the prettiest spots in the neighbourhood, and commands a most beautiful view of the harbour and its castle and the blue expanse of sea. Among the pictures are works by *Rembrandt, Carlo Dolce, Wouvermans, Backhuysen, Vandevelde, Bassano*, and other eminent masters. The singular name means *William's Height*, and is connected with that of the seat below —*Gyllanvaes, William's Grave*, which, according to tradition, is so called as the burial-place of Prince William, son of King Henry, drowned on the passage from Normandy.

Falmouth Harbour is the principal attraction to the traveller searching for scenes of natural beauty. Its winding shores, everywhere penetrated by deep and wooded inlets, afford many a subject for the exercise of the pencil. It has been celebrated from a remote period for its extent and commodiousness. Leland speaks of it as "a haven very notable and famous, and in a manner the most principal of all Britayne;" and Carew observes that "a hundred sail of vessels may anchor in it, and not one see the mast of another." Its entrance, about 1 m. wide, is defended by the castles of Pendennis and Mawes. In the middle of the passage lies the *Black Rock*, an obstruction of little import, as, though covered by the tide, its situation is marked by a beacon, and there is on either side of it a broad and deep channel. The sea, having entered through this opening, immediately expands into a basin, so capacious, that, during the French war, buoys were laid down in it for 16 sail of the line, and in 1815 a fleet of 300 vessels, including several of large size, took shelter within it, and rode out a gale without a casualty. The centre of this basin is called the *Carrick Roadstead*, while the name of *Falmouth Harbour*, properly speaking, exclusively attaches to that part of the estuary which borders the town. The haven, however, extends as far as the entrance of the Truro River, a distance of 4 m., and in a sheet of water 1 m. in its average breadth, but opposite Falmouth expanded to 2 m. Its shores are penetrated by the following inlets, which form supplementary harbours, completely land-locked. An arm of the sea, which runs northward of the town to Penryn. On its shore, opposite Falmouth, is the village of *Flushing*, reputed the warmest place in Cornwall. This shore terminates in *Trefusis Point*, a pretty object from Falmouth, crowned, as it is, by trees, which embosom an ancient mansion of the same name, belonging to Lord Clinton, but tenanted by a farmer. In 1814 this rocky point was the scene of a disastrous shipwreck. In a furious gale of wind the 'Queen' transport, laden with invalids from the Peninsula, was driven from her anchors and dashed upon it. The wounded men had little chance of escaping, and as many as 195 perished. 140 bodies were found, and buried in the churchyards of Mylor, Budock, and Gluvias. The next inlet, in proceeding N. up the harbour, is *Mylor Creek*, a winding piece of water, extending to the woods of *Enys* (J. S. Enys, Esq.). At its mouth, in *Mylor Pool*, a favourite anchorage with vessels of small tonnage, the stranger will notice a hulk, lying as a coal depôt off the little dockyard of Mylor, and in view of an old antagonist, in as forlorn a condition, stationed off St. Just Pool, on the opposite side of the harbour. These two melancholy objects are the *Astræa* and *l' Aurore* frigates, which once, as English and French, were engaged in a deadly conflict, which terminated in the capture of the Frenchman.

The hull of the Aurora is worth looking at for the beauty of its lines. The parish of *Mylor* is known to botanists as affording many of the varieties of the English heaths. The *church* stands near the water, and, originally Norm., was altered in the Perp. period, but retains its Norm. character. The N. doorway (Norm.) is peculiar, and deserves notice. The building contains a handsome monument with an effigy to one of the Trefusis family, and in the churchyard are 2 fine yew-trees. To this inlet succeeds *Restronguet Creek*, running into the land for 3 m. to *Perran Wharf*, where it is bordered by the woods of *Carclew* (Sir Chas. Lemon, Bart.). Upon the shore is the busy port and rising town of *Devoran*, from which a railroad has been carried to the mining district of Redruth; and near Devoran the church of *St. Feock* (4 m. from Falmouth or Truro), interesting for its ancient *cross*, and as the church in which service was last performed in the Cornish language. *Pill Creek*, penetrating N.W. about 1¼ m., is the next in order, the body of Falmouth Harbour terminating a short distance beyond it, at the entrance of the river *Fal*, or, as it is now commonly called, the *Truro River*. Here the mansion and park of *Trelissic* (Hon. Mrs. Gilbert) bound the vista of promontories and bays which indent the shores of the estuary. The Truro River, winding a serpentine course, and branching into numerous ramifications, affords a variety of pleasing scenes. At *Tregothnan* (the place of the "twisting brook") (Viscount Falmouth) it is joined by the river *Fal*, which, rising near Hensbarrow, flows by Grampound, and meets the tide a mile below Tregony. Returning to Falmouth, along the eastern side of the harbour, we skirt an unbroken shore, until within 1¾ m. of St. Mawes Castle, where the hills are penetrated by *St. Just's Creek*. In this there is a secluded bay worth visiting, where the water washes the walls of the churchyard of St. Just (in Roseland). At the mouth of the creek is the station of the Lazaretto, and, in its vicinity, *St. Just's Pool*, in which vessels perform quarantine. The next inlet, although mentioned the last, is one of some importance, extending about 3 m., almost to the shore of Gerran's Bay, and constituting, for a distance of ¾ m. from its mouth, the *Harbour of St. Mawes*. Upon the N. side of the entrance stands the *castle*, a fortress of inferior size to Pendennis, but erected abont the same time (1542). The town of *St. Mawes* is inhabited principally by fishermen and pilots, and built along the N. shore. This creek is bounded on the S. by *St. Anthony's Head*, which, with its lighthouse, projects into the sea at the mouth of Falmouth Harbour, and in its vicinity is the small *Church of St. Anthony* (E. English, with a Norman S. doorway), containing a monument by *Westmacott* to the memory of Adm. Sir Richard Spry. It is a beautiful little structure, the best and most complete example of E. E. in Cornwall, and has been restored by Sir S. T. Spry. Adjoining it is *Place House*, one of his seats, occupying the site of the Augustine priory of St. Anthony, founded 1124, by Warlewast, Bp. of Exeter.

Among other objects of interest in the neighbourhood of Falmouth may be specified some rugged masses of granite, covered with numerous rock basins, in *Budock Bottom*, about 1 m. W.: and the *Swan Pool* (1 m. W.), separated from the shore, like the Loe Pool, near Helston, by a bar of sand. Near this sheet of water the geologist may find a mass of porphyry enclosing rhombic crystals of quartz. To those desirous of studying certain grauwacke rocks, called by De la Beche *the red and variegated slates*, the coast between the Swan Pool and Pendennis Castle will afford a good field for such an object. A *raised beach*, from 9 to 12 ft. above the present level of the sea, extends about 4 m. between Falmouth and the Helford River. Near Pendennis Castle it is associated with rocks which have been worn by the sea, although now elevated beyond its reach.

The stranger may also visit the *Mabe granite-quarries* (see Penryn), and the singular rock called the *Tolmén* or *Muentol*, i. e. Hole Stone (Rte. 28), situated in the parish of Constantine, about 1½ m. from Mabe, and 4 from Falmouth.

The botanist will observe the rare plant *Viola hirta*, or hairy violet, in the neighbourhood.

ROUTE 27.

TRURO TO PENZANCE, BY REDRUTH (PORTREATH, CARNBREA), CAMBORNE, AND HAYLE (LELANT, LUDGVAN), MOUNT'S BAY, MADRON.

(*West Cornwall Railway*, or road.)

The traveller can proceed from Truro to Penzance by the *West Cornwall Railway*, a journey of 27½ m., generally accomplished in about 1½ hrs. This line—the last link of the iron road from London — traverses the centre of the great mining-field, passing in a cutting through the busy scenes of *Carn-brea*, *Tin Croft*, *Stray Park*, &c., and under their stages of timber. Beyond Guincar-road Stat. it crosses, on a viaduct,

Penpons Bottom, a pretty scene, with the village 1. and a new ch. rt. It descends to Hayle by an incline, about 3 m. long, of 1 in 70, which has superseded the formidable hill on which the trains were raised and lowered by a stationary engine. The old line will be seen on the rt. To pursue our course by the road:—

5 m. *Chacewater*, an increasing village, inhabited principally by miners. The rly., which has a *station* at this place, here mounts its stilts, striding across the valley on piles of wood.

2 m. *Scorrier Gate* (*Rly. Stat.*). 1. *Scorrier House*, a seat of George Williams, Esq. (2 m. from Redruth), known for containing a valuable cabinet of minerals, principally Cornish, including several large pieces of Cornish gold. Among the more remarkable specimens are the red oxide and arseniate of copper, uranite, blende, native and ruby silver, the muriate of that metal, and the arseniate of lead. In the grounds are remains of an encampment. Scorrier was the scene of Mr. Williams's celebrated dream of the murder of Mr. Percival. Rt. the old highway from Bodmin, which here joins the comparatively new road by Truro.

2 m. *Redruth* (*Rly. Stat.*) (*Inns* : Tabbs' Hotel; London Inn), where the station is on a hill, and the rly. on a lofty viaduct. This mining town is situated in the heart of that famous district comprised by the 5 parishes of *Illogan*, *Camborne*, *St. Agnes*, *Redruth*, and *Gwennap*. The country around it is dreary enough, bare of vegetation, and strewn with rubbish, but it affords the richest field for mineralogical inquiry that is to be found in any country. Antiquaries have conjectured that Redruth is one of the most ancient towns in the kingdom, deriving its name from *Tre-Druith*, the *Druid's town*. But there can be no doubt it originated in later times, indeed subsequently to the division of the county into parishes, and that, built around a chapel dedicated to St. Uny, it was christened in Cornish as *Tretrot*, signifying *the house on the bed of the river*. Copper is the chief produce of this great mining-field, and the following are the principal mines: the *Consolidated Mines* in Gwennap, the *United Mines* in the same parish, and *Huel Buller*, *Huel Basset*, *S. Huel Francis*, *Huel Seton*, and the *Carnbrea Mines* in Illogan. The largest steam-engines are on the *United Mines*, *Tresavean*, and the *Consolidated Mines*. (Tresavean mine was the first in Cornwall to work a man engine, to lower and raise the men going and returning from their work.) The *ch.*, a mile distant, under Carn-brea Hill, contains a monument by *Chantrey*, to William Davey, Esq. The town has an *Institution for the Promotion of Useful Knowledge*, in union with the Society of Arts in London.

Dolcoath (about 2 m. W., nearer the *Camborne* stat. than Redruth), long celebrated for its rich copper-ores, is often visited by strangers, as it is so situated on a hill (370 ft. above the sea) that the spectator can obtain a panoramic view of the machinery by which it is worked. The bustle of the scene is truly surprising : steam-engines, horse-whims, and stamping-mills are everywhere in motion, labourers are employed in separating, dressing, and carrying the ore; and a stream of water hurries from one busy spot to another, giving an impetus to huge wheels, and performing other duties on the surface, and then diving underground, where at a depth of 150 ft. it again turns an overshot wheel of 50 ft. diam. Dolcoath is upwards of 1400 ft. deep, and in 1815 was considered the first mine in Cornwall. It produced in that year copper-ore which was sold for 66,839*l.*, a larger amount than was returned by any other mine. In

1810 it yielded silver to the value of 2000*l.* *Cook's Kitchen*, another rich copper-mine, is separated from Dolcoath by a cross-course, which has so *heaved* the lodes, that many which have been worked with great profit in the former mine cannot be discovered in the latter.

The *Consolidated* and *United Mines* are about 3 m. E. of Redruth, just S. of St. Day, and 1 m. N. of the church-town of Gwennap. The Consol. M. are worked as one concern, and have held the first place in the Cornish group since the year 1822, from which time they have annually yielded more copper than any other mine. The surface of this gigantic work is about 2 m. long; the *sump*, or bottom of the mine, is 1740 ft. below the surface, or, in other words, at a depth equal to 5 times the height of St. Paul's; the levels, with their ramifications, have been calculated to extend a distance of 63 m. On the Consolidated and United Mines, which adjoin each other, there are about 8 large pumping engines, with cylinders ranging from 65 to 90 inch diam.; an equal number of engines with 30-inch cylinders, for raising the ore and for other work on the surface; a water-wheel of 48 ft. diameter, for pumping; another of 40 ft. for driving machinery; and several smaller wheels for stamping. This group of mines is excavated in slate. In 1836 the Consol. M. produced ore of the value of 145,717*l.*, while the total expenses for the year amounted to 102,007*l.* The church-town of *St. Day* (locally St. Dye; nothing is known of the saint) is built upon an eminence, and so commands a view of the wonderful region in its vicinity. To the S. are the 2 iron tramroads, which serve as arteries to the mining district; the one for the conveyance of timber, &c., from Devoran, the other for the transport of the copper-ore to the little harbour of Portreath, where it is shipped for the smelting-houses at Swansea. The parish of Gwennap, over which the eye ranges from this height, is said to have yielded from a given space more mineral wealth than any other spot in the Old World.

Tresavean (2¼ m. from Redruth, and rt. of the road to Gwennap) and the *United Mines* are convenient for the traveller to descend, should he be desirous of so gloomy an adventure, as in these a machine called the man-engine has been introduced, which renders a visit to the lowest depths of the mine a matter of the greatest ease. It consists of 2 wooden rods, descending from the top to the bottom of the shaft, and fitted with platforms at equal distances. By the means of a steam-engine these rods are alternately lifted and depressed, so that the miner or visitor, by stepping from one platform to another, is carried up or down the shaft without fatigue. Tresavean is one of the richest and driest copper-mines in the county; it is more than the third of a mile (350 fath.) in depth, and the lower levels are excavated in granite. *Trebowling Hill*, S.E. of it, is crowned by a small earthwork.

Gwennap Pit (about 1 m. from Redruth, and l. of the Falmouth road), an excavation in the hillside of *Carn Marth* (alt. 757 ft.), is celebrated as the scene of Wesley's preaching to the miners, and so shaped that the voice of a single speaker can be distinctly heard in it by a very numerous audience. It is called, by way of pre-eminence, *The Pit,* and is still used by the Wesleyans in the celebration of their anniversary on Whit-Monday, when, if the weather should be fine, there are always from 20,000 to 30,000 persons present. Wesley deserves all honour for the good he effected among the miners and fishermen of Cornwall, who, before his coming, were certainly not remarkable for sobriety or good conduct. It is said that they seldom uttered a prayer, except to solicit the special providence of a shipwreck; and that the county was then known as *West Barbary*. The changes, however, which Wesley brought about by his preaching were equally rapid and universal, and his doctrines became the belief and practice of the community. The members of this persuasion are now decreasing in their numbers. In 1844 the Wesleyans in Cornwall amounted to 21,642, but in 1854 only to 16,430.

On the hill opposite Carn Marth is an old entrenchment, occupying about an acre. The church-town of *Gwennap* is 3 m. from Redruth, and inhabited principally by persons connected with the mines. Near it are *Penjreep* (John M. Williams, Esq.), a delightful seat midway between Redruth and Penryn; *Burncoose* (late Mrs. Williams); and *Trevince*, property of the Beauchamps, occupied by George Williams, Esq., of Scorrier House, Carhays Castle, and Lanerth. The gardens are well worthy of a visit. Here camellias of all shades flourish in the open air throughout the year. The tower of Gwennap Ch. stands apart from the rest of the building.

Carn Menelez or *Carnmenellis*—i. e. "stony rocks," from the broken rocks scattered on the surface—(alt. 822 ft.), 3½ m. and l. of the road to Helston, is the highest hill in the granitic district between Redruth and Stithians.

Plauquarj, a small village N. of Redruth, deserves notice for its name, which originated in an ancient *plân an quare*, i. e. *plain for play*, or *round*, once in its vicinity, but now destroyed. Many villages and parishes have a spot so called, the old wrestling-place, &c., of the neighbourhood.

Portreath, or *Basset's Cove*, is a picturesque little place (3½ m. N.W.), of which a large proportion of the copper-ore is shipped for Swansea, where it is smelted. The cliffs here are huge and sombre, and the valley opening to the sea a good specimen of a Cornish *bottom*, the verdure of its woods agreeably contrasting with the desolation of the country about Redruth. The harbour is connected with the mines by a railway, and protected by batteries on the adjacent heights.

Castle Carn-brea (alt. 740 ft.), a rocky eminence S.W., derives interest from its fanciful description by Borlase, the author of the 'Antiquities of Cornwall.' This antiquary regarded Carn-brea as the principal seat of Druidic worship in the West of England, and beheld in its weather-worn, fantastic rocks, all the monuments of that worship. Here he discerned the sacred circle, the stone idol, the pool of lustration, and the seat of judgment; but it is perhaps needless to say that all traces of such remains, if they ever existed, have long since disappeared. The logan stone and rock-basin are, however, found in every granitic country, and are the forms which granite will invariably assume when exposed for long periods to the abrading influence of the weather. At the E. end of the hill, in the midst of some rocks, is a small *castle*, occupying the site of one supposed to have been erected by the Britons, and to have originated the name of the neighbouring parish of Illogan; the Cornish words *huq gan* signifying the *white tower*, and *luq gan the tower on the downs*. (Illogan, however, may be *Llogain*, a "glittering," from the micaceous glitter of its granite.) The structure is ancient, but has been enlarged of late years, and coated with plaster. It is built upon several masses of granite, which, lying apart, are connected by arches. The rooms are small, the floors uneven from being laid on sloping surfaces, and the walls pierced with small square apertures like those of Tintagel. A short distance to the W. are the remains of a circular fortification called the *Old Castle*, and on the summit of the hill a column erected to the memory of the late Lord de Dunstanville, which commands a very extraordinary view over the mining-field. The country people tell some marvellous tales of Carn-breá; among others, that a giant of mighty bone lies buried beneath it; and a block of granite, indented into 5 nearly equal parts, is pointed out as the hand of the Goliath, which, protruding through the surface, has been converted into stone. This hill is also the fabled scene of a combat between his satanic majesty and a troop of saints, in which Lucifer was tumbled from the heights; the rocky boulders having been on this occasion the "seated hills," which were loosened from their foundation and used as missiles.

Proceeding on our route—
2½ m. *Poole.*—Observe a beautiful chapel, in excellent taste, erected at the western end of the village, by the late Lady Basset, at a cost of 2000*l.* It is built in the Norman style, of porphyry, with granite quoins. From the road beyond this place the traveller will observe to the rt. *Tehidy*, the seat of the Bassets. The park extends over 700 acres, and is mentioned by Leland as reaching, in his time, to the foot of Carnbrea. The mansion contains some fine pictures, notably two *Gainsboroughs*. There are also portraits by *Vandyke*, *Kneller*, *Lely*, and *Reynolds*. The monuments of the family are in the neighbouring ch. of *Illogan* (2 m. from Redruth).

There is a small *Rly. Stat.* at *Poole*, between Redruth and—

1 m. *Camborne* (*Inn:* Tyack's Hotel ; Commercial), a thriving town, surrounded by mines. Dolcoath, N. Roskear, S. Francis, may be visited from this. The *Ch.* (restored 1862), a large, but very low Perp. structure of granite, contains a carved pulpit of wood, and memorials of the family of Pendarves. Observe also the capitals of the pillars of the¹ aisle. On the exterior of the

ch. is an ancient stone, placed in that position by the late Lord de Dunstanville, and bearing the following rather ungrammatical inscription:—
" Leuint jusit hæc altare pro animâ suâ." The stone is flat, and probably at one time covered an altar in a neighbouring chantry.

The localities worth notice near this town are—

Pendarves, 1 m. S., the seat of the late Edward William Wynne Pendarves, who represented this county in Parl. for a period of more than 30 years. Pendarves was entirely his creation. He converted a moor into the park, planted the woods, and built the mansion, which is of granite. On the W. side a charming terrace-walk commands the range of hills in the Land's-End district. On the S. side the windows look upon a wild moorland hill, called *Carwinnen Carn.* The rooms contain pictures by *Opie* and other masters, and a valuable cabinet of minerals, including a nugget of native gold. At the foot of *Carwinnen Carn,* in a cornfield, is *Carwinnen Cromlech,* or *Pendarves Quoit,* a monument which is seen from the house; and on an eminence in the park, a handsome chapel, erected 1842, by subscription, to which Mr. Pendarves liberally contributed. It contains an old font, and occupies the site of an ancient chapel, among the ruins of which the workmen discovered an inscribed and curiously sculptured tablet of granite. Adjoining the chapel are a clergyman's house, school - house, and schoolmaster's house, erected by Mr. Pendarves, and constructed, like the chapel, of porphyry and granite. The *Silver Well,* in their vicinity, deserves mention for its poetical name.

Clowance (*Clow-nans,* the "grey dingle"—*nan* is a small valley with water running through it). 3 m. W. of Pendarves, the seat of the family of St. Aubyn, anciently St. Albyn, who came over with the Conqueror,

[*Dev. & Corn.*]

and were originally seated at Alfoxton, co. Somerset. They acquired Clowance by marriage late in the 14th cent. It is a delightful seclusion, embowered in trees, among which may be observed a number of Cornish elms, remarkable for the small size of their leaves. The house, which has been lately rebuilt, contains some genuine pictures, including a fine cattle-piece by *Paul Potter*; specimens of *P. Wouvermans, Berghem, Ruysdael, Teniers, Sir Peter Lely*, and *Wilson*; and family portraits by *Sir Joshua Reynolds*. This collection was made about 100 years ago by an ancestor of the Rev. H. Molesworth St. Aubyn, the present proprietor. The park is 5 m. in circumference, and the gardens and hothouses richly stored with curious plants. Adjoining Clowance, on the road from Camborne, is a village which rejoices in the name of *Praze an Beeble* — probably a corruption of "Prase an Pobl," the thicket or brushwood of the people—i. e. common land. E. is the church-town of *Crowan*, with a ch. interesting for the St. Aubyn monuments; and about ½ m. S. of Crowan a rude pile of rocks, which once supported a logan stone, called *Mên Amber*, a name often occurring, and said by Stukeley to signify, in a general sense, an altar. (It is however most probably "mên ambol," the "rounded" stone.) The Mên Amber still lies on the spot, but was thrown off its balance by a detachment of Cromwell's soldiers, who are said to have been sent for that purpose from Pendennis Castle. *Crowan Beacon* is 850 ft. above the sea, and commands a fine view.

Hell's Mouth (about 3 m. N.W. of Camborne), a gloomy gap in the cliffs, which are of considerable altitude, and as black as night. A walk along the coast to Portreath (4 m.) is interesting, and the seal is often to be observed basking on the rocky shore. A *Cliff Castle* may be noticed by Tehidy.

Proceeding on our route from Camborne:—

Between Godrevy Point and Hayle the coast is desolated with sand, which has overwhelmed a number of houses, and long threatened the ch. and village of *Gwithian* with a similar fate. The walls of buildings have been frequently exposed by the shifting of its unstable hillocks, but the sand is now fixed by the growth of the arundo arenaria, which was planted with that object. A few years ago a very interesting discovery was made in the vicinity of Gwithian church. A farmer digging into the sand found the remains of a little chapel which had been evidently buried for ages. They were of the rudest construction, and very similar to those of the oratory of St. Piran discovered among the towans of Perranzabuloe. There was likewise a baptistery, and around the building a graveyard, and numerous human skeletons were disinterred. (St. Gwithian was one of the many Irish preachers in Cornwall during the 5th cent. He is said to have been martyred by Tewdor, the chief of this district.) The geologist may find, at the mouth of the Gwithian river, about 2½ m. from Hayle, and also on the shore opposite Godrevy Island, a *recent formation* of a peculiar character. He may, at these spots, actually detect Nature at work changing sand into a compact stone, of which several houses in the neighbourhood are constructed. This fact was first investigated by Dr. Paris, when residing at Penzance (see vol. i. Trans. of the Roy. Geol. Soc. of Cornwall). The rocks in the vicinity of this formation are *greenstone* and *clay-slate*, which appear to alternate. He can also obtain evidence respecting the up-raising of the shore in an ancient beach near Gwithian, resting on a cliff of grauwacke, from 35 to 40 ft. above the present level of the sea. Another excellent section of a raised beach may be seen near Godrevy Farm.

(There is a small railway stat. at Gwinear, and one at Hayle.)

6 m. Hayle (Cornish, "the river") (Inns: White Hart Hotel; Steam Packet Hotel, on the shore of Phillack Creek). The traveller here enters the *Land's End district*, which, bounded by an imaginary line drawn from Hayle on the N. to Cuddan Point on the S. coast, extends 13 m. in length, and 5 or 6 in breadth. Nine-tenths of its surface consist of granite. Hayle has no pretensions as a town. It consists chiefly of mean cottages, a few poor shops, an inn, and a shabby rly. viaduct, and over all whitewash and coal-dust seem to struggle for the mastery. It is, however, a busy port, and the coast in the neighbourhood is most beautiful. Hayle was formerly celebrated for its *copper-house* for smelting the ore; but it is now found a cheaper method to carry the copper to the coal at Swansea, and the speculation has, on that account, been abandoned. The *scoria* or *slag* was run into moulds for building purposes as it issued from the furnace. Some of the houses and hedges are partly constructed of this vitreous material, and, since there are interstices between the stones, it has been facetiously said that in Cornwall the walls are built of glass, and that you may distinctly see through them. The town has since acquired celebrity from Mr. Harvey's 2 *Iron Foundries*, in which the largest cylinders are cast, not only for the Cornish mines, but for exportation. A few years ago a ponderous work of this description was sent from Hayle to Holland, for the drainage of the Lake of Haarlem, made by Mr. H. Harvey, who is one of the most enterprising men of business in Cornwall, and ranks among the chief makers of steam-engines in the kingdom. The moulds in which the iron is cast are made of sand. Tin is smelted in the works of Williams and Co., adjoining the town. Near the western end of the Hayle viaduct (adjoining the station) is an *inscribed stone* 6 feet long, found in 1843 in one of the sides of the moat of a cliff castle at Carnsew. A grave, filled with a mixture of sand, charcoal, and ashes, was found N. of it.

Hayle furnishes London with early spring brocoli and other vegetables, which are sent by up per rail, by the ton.

The sea at Hayle forms an estuary, flowing over an immense area, which is dry at low-water, and weak in places called *quicks*. There is a bar at the mouth, impassable in certain states of the tide, but its further accumulation is held in check. About 60 years ago Phillack Creek was converted into a back-water, and this has effected such a considerable reduction in the sand, that vessels of 200 tons can now enter the harbour. The river rises near Crowan, and for 3 m. runs sluggishly on the ocean level. The towans of Phillack intercept the view of St. Ives bay, and its island *Godrevy*, on which a lighthouse was erected 1858 by the Trinity Board. It is to warn the mariner of *The Stones*, a most dangerous reef of sunken rocks, extending from the island a mile or more to sea, and on which hundreds of vessels have been wrecked. The 'Nile,' an iron screw-steamer of 700 tons, belonging to the Irish Steam Company, was lost here in thick and tempestuous weather, Dec. 1854. Not a soul was saved, and, doubtless, the vessel, after striking, foundered in the deep water, which is 12 or 14 fathoms. The beacon was first lighted March, 1859. Its lantern is 120 ft. above the level of high water, and the light revolves, exhibiting a flash every 10 seconds. It is on the dioptric principle, and can be seen in fine weather at a distance of 16 m. In 1649, on the day on which Charles I. was executed, a vessel bound for France, and having on board the wardrobe and other property of the king, was wrecked on Godrevy Island, with a loss of about 60 lives.

There are several mines in the neighbourhood. *Huel Alfred*, about 1½ m. S.E., has been remarkable for the large size of its lodes, and has yielded several rare minerals, as stalactitic, swimming, and cubic quartz; carbonate and phosphate of lead; stalactitic, botryoidal, and investing chalcedony, &c. *Huel Herland* (about 1 m. E. of Huel Alfred) was originally opened as a silver-mine, and has produced specimens of native vitreous, and black oxide of silver, and silver-ore, of the value of 8000l. The lodes of the Herland Mines are very different from those of Huel Alfred, being small and numerous, but they contain a very rich ore. Huel Herland is close to

Gwinear, the ch. of which is ancient, and a conspicuous object on the hills. Near the village are the farmhouses of *Lanyon* and *Rosewarne*; the former in olden times the seat of the Lanyons, of whom was Capt. Lanyon, the companion of Cook in his voyages round the world; the latter, once the property of the "Great Arundells," of Lanherne, who built the N. aisle of the ch.; and this contains the marble monument of Eliz. Arundell.

The ch. of *Phillack*—lately rebuilt, save the tower—is conspicuous to the N. of Hayle, and exemplifies in a very striking manner the encroachment of the sand from the shore, since it is overhung by *towans* (Cornish for sandhills) which seem to threaten it with destruction. In the churchyard is an inscribed stone which has not been deciphered, and in the wall of the church-porch a small stone with the Christian monogram. Both were found in the walls of the old church.

The view of St. Ives and its bay from the mouth of Hayle river is exceedingly beautiful. The sandy shore, girded by cliffs, sweeps along the margin of the sea in a crescent of some miles, and terminates to the W. at Battery Point, and to the E. at the promontory opposite the island rock of Godrevy. It will probably tempt the stranger to make an excursion to the town. (For St. Ives see Rte. 29, Exc. 2.)

Leaving Hayle for Penzance, the road traverses an embankment 1040 ft. long, completed in 1826, at a cost of 7200l. The Hayle river is here expanded to an inlet, which was formerly impassable at high water, when the traveller had to go round by St. Erth. To the l. are the mansion and grounds of *Carnsew*, and on the road leading to the house the *inscribed stone*, found in 1843, and already noticed. On crossing the embankment the traveller will notice the pretty village of

Lelant on the opposite shore. The fuchsia, hydrangea, and myrtle flourish in its cottage gardens the year round. Near the sea the parish is covered with sand, which is continually being blown up the cliffs from the beach; and there is a tradition that beneath it lies the castle of Theodorick, a "rough and ready" king of Cornwall, who decapitated many of those Irish saints who crossed the sea to preach the Gospel to the Cornish. In the church (N. side of nave) is a Norm. arch, the only Norm. relic in the district. Adjoining it is a fine sharp-pointed arch of the 13th cent. The granite pyramid on the top of the hill was erected in 1782, by a Mr. Knill, for his own place of burial. He died and was buried in London; but left 10l. a year, part of which was to be given to 10 girls, not above 10 years old, who, every fifth year, on St. James's day, were to dance near the pyramid (see Rte. 28, Exc. 2, St. Ives). *Trecroben Hill*, alt. 550 ft. (properly *Tre-crum-ben*, the *crooked hill*), and a most picturesque eminence, rises behind Lelant from the woods of *Trevethoe*, a seat of the family of Praed. *Trecroben Castle* consists of a single wall (with gate-

CORNWALL. *Route 27.—St. Erth.—Ludgvan.—Penzance.* 203

ways) of large stones and earth, enclosing the hill-top. On this estate are extensive plantations of the pinaster, a tree introduced into Cornwall by the father of the late proprietor, and found capable of sustaining the fury of westerly gales. The geologist should know that upon the eastern side of Trecroben Hill there are some good examples of schorl-rock and schorlaceous granite. There is a *railway stat.* at *St. Ives Road.*

1 m. *St.Erth* (pronounced St.Eerth), a village once known for its *coppermills*, which, abandoned at the same time as the *copper-house* at Hayle, are now, following the fortunes of that establishment, used for rolling and hammering iron. St. Erth Bridge is evidently of very great age, and is said to be 500 years old. Near it stands the ch., and in the centre of the village, on the hill, an ancient cross rudely sculptured with a figure of the Saviour. S., on a pathway to Marazion, are the woods of *Trewinnard*, now a farmhouse, the property of Heywood Hawkins, Esq., but formerly a residence of Sir Christopher Hawkins, Bart. Much of the tapestry still remains in this old house, in a high state of preservation; and at the stables the rickety ruin of a gilded coach of primitive construction, which, it is said, caused no little ferment among the natives when it appeared with its four coal-black steeds at the churchyard gate of St. Erth, as it was the first carriage introduced into the county. *Tredrea*, also in this parish, was the seat of the late Davies Gilbert, Esq., president of the Royal Society. *Railway stat.* at *Marazion Road*, and

4 m. rt. *Ludgvan.*—The churchyard commands a charming view, and the ch. is interesting to Cornishmen for containing the mortal remains of *Dr. Borlase*, author of the 'Antiquities and Natural History of Cornwall,' and for 52 years rector of this parish. He died in 1772. " Pope," says Dr. Paris, " in thanking him for a beautiful Cornish diamond, remarked that it had been placed in his grotto in a situation where it resembled the donor, 'in the shade, but shining.' "—*Memoir of Dr. Maton.* There is an E. Eng. font in the ch.; and a well here has the property (says tradition) of preserving from the halter all who are baptized with its water. Hence a Ludgvan man has never been hanged. In this parish is situated the estate of *Varfell*, which the ancestors of Sir H. Davy had long possessed, and upon which he had resided in his earlier days. In the church there are tablets of the family, one of which bears a date as far back as 1635. *St. Michael's Mount* and its beautiful bay here open to the view, and the road soon reaches the *Eastern Green*, and passing along the shore by the side of the rly. enters

3 *Penzance*, a municipal borough containing 9500 Inhab. (*Inns:* Queen's Hotel, on the Esplanade, commanding a fine view of Mount's Bay, the newest and largest; Union Hotel; Western Hotel; Three Tuns.) The traveller will probably make this town head-quarters for some days, as there is much to be seen in the immediate neighbourhood, and all the curiosities of the Land's End district are within the compass of a ride. Penzance derives its name—the *Holy Headland*—from a chapel dedicated to St. Anthony, which formerly stood on the point adjoining the pier. It was one of the coinage towns from the reign of Charles II. to 1838, when the tin dues were abolished. It is now of considerable commercial importance, and particularly celebrated for early vegetables. In 1858 it exported potatoes of the value of 20,000*l*. During February, March, and April, many tons of brocoli go up to London daily by train. If the brocoli makes 1*d.* a head, it is calculated that the produce of an acre of land is worth

£40 a year. Young potatoes and fish are sent also in large quantities. Its market supplies an extensive district with groceries and butcher's meat, and with pork, poultry, and fish, which are both abundant and cheap. By the means of numerous steam-vessels it has constant communication with Bristol, Plymouth, and London.

The position of Penzance on the beautiful Mount's Bay is universally admired. The vegetation in the neighbouring valleys has quite a southern luxuriance. On the higher ground rocky carns and wild furze-crofts contrast with cultivation, and give a charm to the landscape. To the N. are extensive moors, where you may range at will over the hills; and along the shore of the Atlantic, one of the grandest coasts in the kingdom. In 1595 Penzance suffered from the exposure of its situation, when a party of Spaniards, having landed at Mousehole, after destroying that village together with Newlyn, advanced to this town, and meeting with no opposition laid it in ashes. According to Carew, the inhabitants were infatuated by a prediction in the Cornish language, to the effect that a period would arrive when

"Strangers would land on the rocks of Merlin,
Who would burn Paul's church, Penzance, and Newlyn;"

and that, when the prophecy had been fulfilled, they found courage to assemble on the beach and thus intimate to the Spaniards that any farther aggression would be resisted. Accordingly, it is said, the marauders spread their sails to the breeze and left the coast. In 1646 Penzance was again a sufferer by the chances of war, when it was sacked by Fairfax. It is distinguished as the birthplace of *Lord Exmouth*, of *Davies Gilbert*, and of *Sir Humphry Davy*, the eminent philosopher, who has merited the grateful remembrance of his countrymen by his invention of the *safety-lamp* for coal-mines, and who bequeathed 100*l*. to the grammar-school of his native town on condition that the boys were allowed an annual holiday on his birthday. The house in which Davy was born stands a little below the market-place, on the rt. as you enter the town. It has received a new front, but is otherwise the same. The house in which he passed his apprenticeship as an apothecary with Mr. Tonkin (see Dr. Paris's memoir) was removed to make way for the Town Hall. (A tower is erecting here as a monument to this great "illustration" of Penzance; archit. Salter and Perrow. It will command the whole range of Mount's Bay, and may be used as an observatory.) Another "worthy" of Penzance, to be classed with the immortal Dolly —"the last who jabbered Cornish" —was the famous fishwoman *Mary Kalynack*, who, in 1851, at the age of 84, walked from the Land's End to London to see the Great Exhibition, and to pay her respects personally to the Lord Mayor and Lady Mayoress.

The following are the principal buildings, &c.:—

The Pier. Its northern arm was reconstructed 1745-72, and rests upon a large vein of felspar porphyry, which may be seen at low water. Its eastern arm was an addition in 1845. It abuts upon the *Railway terminus*, and on a cyclopean granite wall which protects the line from the sea. On the rising ground opposite is a *battery*, completed 1858. The *Battery Rocks* to the W. of the pier are of greenstone. These trappean rocks in the vicinity of Penzance are particularly interesting on account of the contemporaneous manner in which they are associated with argillaceous slate.

The *Esplanade* is one of the very best in the W. of England, and has a delightful view towards the land as well as towards the sea. At one end of it are the *Royal Baths*, at the other, the coast-guard station, and a Russian 36-pounder gun from Bomarsund. Beyond is a large factory in which ornamental articles are made from the serpentine of the Lizard.

The *Town Hall* and *Corn Market*, forming a modern granite building with Ionic tetrastyle portico. The whole is surmounted by a dome, within which is the collection of the *Penrith Nat. Hist. Soc.*, consisting chiefly of birds. This museum is open on Tuesdays, Thursdays, and Saturdays from 12 to 3. Besides Nat. Hist. it contains some antiquities found in the neighbourhood. At the corner of Alverton-street and North-street, on the wall of a shop, is the ancient *market-cross*, which formerly stood detached.

Below the Town Hall are the fish-stalls. A market has been built for their reception in Princess-street, but, as the fish-women assert a prescriptive right to this locality, they remain here. The business is entirely conducted by women, who were formerly distinguished by a flat beaver hat called the "Mount's Bay" hat. This, however, has been superseded by the bonnet, a person known as "the Queen" having been the last to wear it. They bring their fish to market in the *cowel*—a basket universally used here by the women, and in which they carry great weights. It is supported on the back, and by a band passed around the forehead, and in this position bears some resemblance to the *cowl* of a monk, from which the name is absurdly said to have been derived. Among the curiosities of the market the stranger will remark the *conger eel*, a fish of formidable appearance—a kind of sea-serpent—which the poorer people cook in their favourite piés, and consider "main good eating."

The *Chapel of St. Paul*, a modern structure, built in 1835 by the Rev. Henry Batten, at a cost of 5000*l*. It is wholly of granite, and in the E. Eng. style. It has transepts; a pulpit in one granite block; an altar-rail and steps of the same material; the windows are filled with excellent stained glass by Willement, and the organ is disposed of out of sight E. of the S. transept. The altar-rail is a very curious piece of granite-cutting from the solid stone. The gate into the sacrarium is also of solid granite. The roof is open and the main beams gilt. The effect of the whole is not successful.

The *Roman Catholic Chapel of St. Mary* (Rosevean Row) is of granite, and in the Dec. style.

The *Royal Geological Society of Cornwall* (North Parade), which now ranks among the most distinguished institutions in the kingdom, was founded in Feb. 1814 by the late Dr. Paris, President of the College of Physicians, but at that time residing in Penzance. The advantages of such a society in a country like Cornwall had long been apparent, and a perusal of its first volume of Transactions (date 1817) will show by what valuable inventions it at once secured the gratitude and support of the county. About the year 1817 it was the means of introducing into the mines a safety tamping-bar, so ingeniously contrived that it could be used with perfect security; and this instrument immediately caused so marked a diminution in the annual amount of accidents as to attract the notice of the Prince Regent, who at that time became the patron of the society. The institution has now reached a high place in public estimation. The Queen is the patron, and Augustus Smith, Esq., M.P., the president. The *Museum* — for which, however, the accommodation is very inadequate—contains a valuable collection of minerals, principally Cornish, consisting of several thousand specimens. Observe as unusually fine those of calcedony, sodalite, haüyne, petalite, colophronite, vesuvian, carbonate of lead, specular iron, arseniate of iron, the oxide, carbonate, arseniate, and phosphate of copper, native gold from the tin stream-works, arsenical pyrites, uranite, uran ochre, and native nickel. Several models and series of specimens illustrate the mining operations, and the rocks and veins of the county, including every variety of Cornish granite. Here also may be seen Mr. Peach's unique collection of Cornish fossils, including the "Polperro Sponges," at first called ichthyolites, discovered by Mr. Couch, the curator of this society; several interesting casts, the bones of a whale taken from the Pentewan stream-works, and a splendid slab of sandstone imprinted with the foot-marks of the chirotherium from Cheshire. This is placed conspicuously at the entrance. In the principal room, in which the meetings of the Society are held, are prints of Sir Humphry Davy and Dr. Paris, and a bust of Sir Charles Lemon.

Penzance contains another fine collection of minerals, made by the late Joseph Carne, Esq., F.R.S., author of many valuable papers in the Transactions of the R. Geol. Soc. of Cornw., and now the property of his daughter. It has also a Nat. Hist. and Antiq. Soc., established in 1839; an Agric. Soc.; a Cottager's Garden Soc.; an Institute and a Lit. Inst.; a Public Library containing about 10,000 vols.; and, in the possession of E. H. Rodd, Esq., one of the family of Trebartha Hall, near Launceston, and an excellent ornithologist, *a museum of native birds*, probably the most complete and valuable private collection in the county. *Lavin's Museum*, Chapel-street, is the store of an experienced dealer in Cornish minerals.

On the 23rd and 28th of June a curious custom is observed in this town—the celebration of the *eves of St. John and St. Peter*. At sunset the people assemble in the streets and kindle a number of tar-barrels, erected on the quay and on other conspicuous places, and aid the illumination with blazing torches as long as mopsticks, which they whirl round their heads. Bonfires are also lighted at Mousehole, Newlyn, Marazion, and the Mount, and the bay glows with a girdle of flame. Then follows the ancient game of *Thread-the-needle*. Lads and lasses join hands, and run furiously through the streets, vociferating, "An eye—an eye—an eye!" "At length they suddenly stop, and the two last of the string, elevating their clasped hands, form an *eye* to this enormous *needle*, through which the *thread* of populace runs, and thus they continue to repeat the game until weariness dissolves the union." On the following day the festivities assume a different character, and idling with music on the water (called "having a pen'orth of sea") succeeds to the riot of the previous evening. With respect to the origin of this curious custom, the summer solstice has been celebrated throughout all ages by the lighting up of fires, and the Penzance festival on the 23rd is doubtless a remnant of that most ancient idolatry, the *worship of the sun*. The same custom is kept up in Norway (and in many parts of Germany) on Midsummer's Eve.

In the vicinity of Penzance charming walks lead over the hills in every direction, and surprise the stranger by the suddenness with which they unfold the most delicious prospects; the effect of which is considerably heightened by the southern brilliancy and purity of the air, and the varied colours of the sea, which receives every tint from the clouds that float over it. But before conducting the visitor to the best points of view, we must give a short sketch of the

Mount's Bay, so famed for its beauty and temperate skies. It is an expanse of azure sea contained within the headlands of Tol Pedn Penwith (W.) and the Lizard (E.), although the name more commonly attaches to that portion which is included between Mousehole (W.) and Cuddan Point (E.). It is justly celebrated for a mild and equable climate, and its seasons have been aptly compared to the neap tides, which neither ebb nor flow with energy. Winter is here deprived of its terrors, and summer is never oppressive; and for these reasons a residence at Penzance is so often prescribed to persons suffering under pulmonary complaints. Its principal feature is the romantic Mount of St. Michael, but its shores are also highly picturesque, and noted for the marked evidence they afford of the encroachment of the sea. A part of the *Western Green*—now a bare sandy beach—was described in the reign of Charles II. as 36 acres of pasturage; and at no very distant period the grandfather of the present vicar of Madron received tithe for land which was situated under the cliff at Penzance. The shore called the *Eastern Green*, between Penzance and Marazion, has been sensibly wasted within the last 50 years, and it is considered that the removal of the sand for manure has been the chief cause of the diminution, the action of the wind and sea upon the flat coast of a bay having in general a contrary effect. Tradition points to a time when dry land extended over that portion of the bay which would be within a line drawn from Cuddan Point to Mousehole, and represents it as having been covered with wood and submerged by the sea at a distant period. Florence of Worcester and the Saxon Chronicle mention an inundation of the ocean in 1099, and it is remarkable that beneath the sand of the bay a deposit of black vegetable mould, filled with the detritus of leaves, nuts, and branches, and containing the roots and trunks of large trees, and remains of the red deer, elk, &c., may be traced seaward as far as the ebb will allow. De Luc has attributed the inundation to a subsidence of the land, and the circumstance of ripe nuts and leaves remaining together would seem to point to the autumn as the time of year in which it must have occurred. From the neighbouring hills the views of the bay are most delightful, particularly from Madron, from Rose Hill, and from the field beyond Castle Horneck. The agricultural traveller should be informed that a belt of 1000 acres of land in the vicinity of Penzance is characterised by a singular fertility (its annual rental is 10,000*l*.), attributed to the decomposition of the greenstone which abounds in the soil. It is celebrated for its early vegetables, such as brocoli and the kidney potato, which are grown for the London markets.

Mount's Bay is further interesting as one of the principal stations of the pilchard fishery, affording accommodation to a fleet of 150 or 200 boats, of which nine-tenths are for drift-net fishing, and average from 20 to 22 tons burden. Few spectacles are more pleasing than that which is so often presented by this beautiful bay, when its fishing fleet has assembled, equipped and ready for sea, or, with hull and sail illumined by a setting sun, is leaving the shore in a line extending seaward as far as the eye can reach. A Mount's Bay fishing boat of 15 tons, called "The Mystery," sailed from Penzance to Sydney a few years since, with a crew of 5 men, calling at the Cape of Good Hope for water and provisions. She was decked over for the voyage.

With respect to the *climate* of the Mount's Bay, the following is a comparison of the mean temperature of the seasons in Penzance and London.

Seasons.	Penzance.	London.
Spring	49·66	48·76
Summer	60·50	62·32
Autumn	53·83	51·35
Winter	44·66	39·12

Degrees of Fahr.

The mean range of daily temperature for the year at Penzance is 6·7°, in London 11°. Thus, for equability and warmth, the climate of western Cornwall is far superior to that of London, and its peculiarity in this respect is strikingly shown by its effect on vegetation. On Jan. 1, that is, in mid-winter, of 1851, there were no less than 58 plants in full blossom in the gardens and fields around Penzance. Among the garden flowers were the geranium, heart's-ease, sweet violet, hollyhock, sweet pea, mignonette, carnation, pink, auricula, anemone, narcissus, primrose, polyanthus, cowslip, stock, gillyflower, lupine, roses of various kinds, verbena, magnolia, fuchsia, and campanula. In the hedges were the dandelion, lesser periwinkle, hawkweed, herb Robert, dog violet, all-heal, white nettle, black knapweed, buttercup, daisy, ox-eye, and red robin.

Among the hills and valleys around Penzance are many charming *villas* and *seats*, which bear old Cornish names, and have been long occupied by Cornish families. The finest for position and extent of their woods are *Trengwainton* (literally "*Strong and lively*"), on the high land beyond Madron, for many years the seat of the late Sir Rose Price, Bart., and now occupied by Mrs. Davy; and *Kenegie*, above Gulval, lately purchased by William Coulson, Esq., the surgeon. One of the most venerable is *Trereife*, in a valley on the Land's End road, completely embowered among lofty elms; where there are a rookery and avenues. From the lawn there is a view which is perfectly unique. Through an opening in the foliage is seen a single block of *Tolcarne* (at Newlyn) and a blue patch of sea. Trereife was the seat of the late Rev. C. Val. Le Grice, and is now the property of his son Day Perry Le Grice, Esq. The house dates from the 17th cent., and is partly covered by a yew-tree trained against it. On the opposite side of the road are the *Trereife tin smelting works*, and on the hill beyond a wayside *cross*, known as *Trereife Cross*, and the entrance to *Trewidden*, Edward Bolitho, Esq.

To the N. of Penzance are *Treneere* and *York House*; further N. *Rosemorran*, and beyond Hea *Trevaylor*, seat of the Rev. W. Veale. On the road to Madron is *Nancealverne*, J. Scobell, Esq.; and further l. *Rosecadjehill*, an ancient residence of the Borlase family; *Rose Hill*, Louis Vigurs, Esq.; and *Castle Horneck*, Samuel Borlase, Esq., the last so named from an ancient entrenchment, *Kesingy Round*, which encircles an adjoining eminence. At the foot of Madron Hill is *Poltair House*; on the slope above the Western Green, *Lariggan* (Walter Borlase, Esq.); and at Chyandour the villas of the Bolithos, *Pendrea* and *Ponsondine*, the latter with a roof of thatch, and a pretty object among the trees.

The *walks* around Penzance are so numerous that we must leave to the visitor the pleasant task of discovering and exploring them for himself, or refer him to the excellent local 'Guide to Penzance,' by J. S. Courtney. They traverse the country in every direction, converging to the churches of Paul, Sancreed, Madron, and Gulval. We may, however, draw attention to the following points:—

The *valley of Tolcarne*, leading from Newlyn to Trereife. A yet prettier walk is the path which ascends to the rocks of Tolcarne, crosses a field to a clump of firs called *The Grove*, and thence runs to the Trereife and Penzance road. It commands a very beautiful view of Newlyn, Guavas Lake, and the hills which dip to the coast. The entrance to this path is at the mill by the bridge.

Love Lane, ascending from the

Western Green to *Alverton*, as the cottages W. of Penzance are called, a name derived from Alwardus the lord of the district in the time of Edw. the Confessor.

Lescaddock or *Lescudjack Castle*, remains of a circular encampment on the hill above Chyandour, and an excellent position for a view of the town and harbour. A lane, a little E. of the rly. station, leads up to it.

Gulval. The turning at Chyandour branches into 3 roads: that on the l., a narrow and pretty lane called *the Coomb*, runs to Treneere House and Ilea; that in the centre also to Hea, and to Zennor, Madron, &c.; that on the rt. to Gulval. The village is prettily situated in a deep, wooded valley, or dell. The ch. lies to the rt. on high ground, and has an ancient *cross* in the churchyard. To the N. of it are the granite rocks of *Gulval Carn*, a relic of the primeval moor, now islanded in fields, and overgrown with ivy and briers. It commands a beautiful prospect of Penzance and Mount's Bay, similar to that from Lescudjack, but more extensive. A path from the ch. towards Kenegie runs close to it. From the higher end of Gulval a lane on the l. leads through the elm-shadowed *Burlowena Bottom* to the Madron road. It passes through a stream, where an *inscribed monumental stone* which was long used as the footbridge is now fixed upright. The words are *Quenatavus Icdinui filius*, at least so says the antiquary, and the indentation of the letters may be seen.

Madron (the parish church-town). On leaving Penzance the road passes at the top of the hill; rt. an avenue to *Treneere*, and l. *York House*. Then on the rt. the new *Cemetery* and its chapels; and l. in the valley *Nancealverne*. The lane to Nancealverne also forms the approach to *Rosecadyehill*, *Ross Hill*, and *Castle Horneck*, and ends in a field-path to Madron ch., a pretty walk, with a wayside *cross* on the ascent of the hill. About ¼ m. beyond the cemetery a turning on the rt. leads to *Hea* (pronounced Hay), a village in a fertile valley, which was an uncultivated moor when *John Wesley* first came into Cornwall, and here preached to the assembled fishermen from a boulder of granite, now covered by the *Wesley Rock Chapel*. Wesley's last open-air sermon was delivered under an ash-tree, still standing, at Winchelsea, Sussex. From Ilea there is a road N. to Ding-Dong tin-mine, and to Zennor by Try Valley, passing *Trevaylor*. Continuing our walk, we ascend the steep hill to Madron (by a path through the adjoining fields), and open a most beautiful view of Mount's Bay. To the l. is *Poltair*. Madron *ch.*, an ancient pile, stands at an elevation of 350 ft. above the sea. The ch., which is of no great interest, contains a square font of Norman character, always covered with a white, fringed, linen napkin, a very old custom in this parish. In the piscina is placed a remarkable fragment of sculptured alabaster, representing archangels holding spears and shields. It is perhaps a portion of the reredos. There is a good late *brass* for John Clies (1623) and wife, and some very bad modern stained glass, and in the churchyard a mausoleum of the Price family, formerly of Trengwainton. In the hedge opposite the entrance is an ancient *cross*, rudely sculptured, which for ages occupied a position in the centre of the village, where the pedestal still remains, by the blacksmith's shop. About 1 m. to the N. are the ruins of the *Baptistery of Madron Well*, a spring once in great repute for its healing virtues, to which cripples resorted, and also love-sick lads and lasses, who dropped pins into the water and watched the bubbles for an omen of good or bad fortune. This little building was reduced to its present condition by Major Ceeley, one of Cromwell's officers. It has still remaining the old stone altar—a rough slab of granite with a small square hole in the centre and above it, on the top of the ruined wall, there is an old thorn-bush, covered with bits of rag fluttering in the wind, tied there as votive offerings. (Many holy wells in Ireland are decorated in a similar manner). Along the inside walls are stone seats. About 100 yards farther on in the marsh is a small clear well which feeds that of the baptistery. This is the true "wishing well." About the marsh may be found various cyperus, sphagnum, bog asphodel, bog pimpernel, and Cornish moneywort. The baptistery is situated on swampy ground in a secluded spot, but may be found by aid of the following direction. At the top of the town is the Penzance Union, and a path through the fields, l. to Trengwainton, and onward to a lane and a clump of firs. At these firs turn rt. through a gate into a furze-croft. At the lower end and extreme corner of this croft are the ruins. The roof is gone, but the 4 walls remain, and at one of the angles is the little *well*, or basin, which was filled by the water which still trickles past. The walk may be extended to *Lanyon Cromlech* (Rte. 29, Exc. 3), about 1 m. distant. From the fir-clump a lane (in which lies an ancient *cross* overturned) and a path up the hill will lead you direct to it. It comes in view at the top of the ascent (where you regain the road). You see it thrown out against the sky on the slope of a wild moor, which rises to a rocky crest called *Bosvavas Carn*. From the same spot another cromlech is in sight—*Mulfra Quoit* (Rte. 29, Exc. 3)—which may be clearly discerned on a distant hill to the N.E. After a walk to the cromlech you may return by the road, along the fir-covered heights of Trengwainton, and visit *Trengwainton C rn*, a beautiful point of view, 100 yds. rt., through a gate which you will pass on descending the hill.

Castell-an-Dinas (Rte. 29, Exc. 2) (the moorland hill to the N.E.), in a position intermediate between the two Channels, and commanding a superb panorama. The summit, 735 ft. above the sea, is crowned by an earthwork and ruined tower, occupying the site of an ancient *hill-castle*.

For longer excursions from Penzance see Rte. 29.

ROUTE 28.

TRURO TO PENZANCE, BY HELSTON AND MARAZION.—THE LIZARD. THE COAST FROM HELSTON TO PENZANCE.

For this route, as far as Perran Arworthal and Carclew, see Rte. 26. The tourist may either proceed to Penryn (Rte. 26) and rejoin the Helston road at the 12th milestone from Truro, or he may take the shorter and more direct turnpike, passing rt., 10 m. from Truro, *Stithians*.

Near the junction of this road with that from Penryn the traveller will find rt. a celebrated rock called the *Tolmên*, *Maentol*, or *Holed Stone*, a block of granite, shaped like an egg, and raised aloft conspicuously on a barren hill 690 ft. above the sea. Its dimensions are, length 33 ft., depth 15 ft., and greatest breadth 19 ft.

This enormous block has been regarded by some antiquaries (without the least real ground) as an idol of the Druids, and Borlase attributes its spheroidal figure to the handiwork of that priesthood, referring to the circumstance of its major axis pointing N. and S. as a proof that it was raised to its present position by mechanical means. At the present day the elements are considered to have been the only agents employed in rounding blocks of granite, although it is not improbable that such imposing masses as the Tolmên were regarded in remote times with a feeling of superstition, as, indeed, they are at present. This rock, which is also called the *Cornish Pebble*, is supported by the points of others, so that there is a hole beneath it through which a person can crawl,—and to creep through such orifices on certain days of the year was long regarded as a specific for rheumatism and similar maladies (see Introd.). Hence the name of Tolmên, or the Holed Stone. "A pebble," again, is a technical term of the miner, who applies it to any mass of solid rock which may obstruct him when excavating such ground as disintegrated granite. The upper surface of the Tolmên is pitted with numerous circular basins formed by the action of the weather. The entire mass is far more striking than that of the Logan Rock (Rte. 29, Exc. 5), which it greatly exceeds in size, the Logan being estimated at 65 tons, the Tolmên 8 or 10 times as many. In the neighbourhood are the *Mabe quarries*, and the country for some distance round the Tolmên is covered with surface-granite and roughened by carns. One of these is likened to the head of a man, surmounted by an old-fashioned wig (a common form, vide "heads" of Drs. Johnson and Syntax at the Land's End), and a spring of water gushes from the summit of another.

18 m. from Truro, *Helston*. (*Inns:* Angel, good; Star.) This old town is pleasantly situated on a hill, and above a pretty valley opening to the sea. In Domesday it is called *Henliston*, and in other old records *Hellas*, and the following legend attributes the origin of the name to a block of granite, which for many years lay in the yard of the Angel Inn, but in 1783, when the assembly-room was erected, was broken up and used as part of the building materials. This stone, says the legend, was originally placed at the mouth of Hell, from which it was one day carried away by the devil, as he issued forth in a frolicsome mood on an excursion into Cornwall. There he traversed the county, playing with his pebble: but it chanced that St. Michael (the guardian saint of Helston, and who figures conspicuously in the town arms) crossed his path; a combat immediately ensued, and the devil, being worsted, dropped the *Hell's Stone* in his flight. It is added that the inhabitants were spectators, and instituted the

Furry-day in commemoration of the event. This is a festival which from time immemorial has been annually held in this town on the 8th of May, and has been traced by antiquaries to so high a source as the Roman Floralia. Polwhele, however, derives the name from the Cornish word *fear*, a *fair* or *holiday*, and suggests that it may have been instituted in honour of a victory obtained over the Saxons. This however is doubtful. Others suggest its connexion with *forrior* (Corn.), a thief, from the green *spoils* brought home from the woods. The day is still celebrated, although not with all the strictness of former times, when any person who could be detected at work was instantly seized, placed astride upon a pole, and then hurried to the river, when, if he did not commute his punishment by a fine, he was constrained to leap the stream at a wide place, in which he was sure to fall into the water. The morning is ushered in by the merry-pealing bells, and at about 9 o'clock the people assemble at the Grammar-school and demand a prescriptive holiday. After this they collect contributions to defray the expense of the revels, and then proceed into the fields, when they are said to *fade* into the country (*fade* being an old English word for *go*). About noon they return, carrying flowers and branches, and from this time until dusk dance hand-in-hand through the streets, and *in and out of the different houses*, preceded by a fiddler playing an ancient air called the *furry-tune*. They also occasionally chant in chorus a traditional song, of which the first lines run—

" Robin Hood and Little John they both are
gone to fair O,
And we will to the merry green wood to see
what they do there O;
And for to chase the buck and doe, with
Halan to sing merry O."

The higher classes of the inhabitants assist in these rites, and in the evening repair to the ball-room, where, with the assistance of the neighbouring families, they prolong the festivities to a late hour of the night. The Furry tune may be regarded as a county air, and is heard at all seasons in Penzance and other Cornish towns. It will be found, with the words, in *Chappell's* 'National English Airs.

Helston is an ancient place, and had formerly a castle which is mentioned by William of Worcester as a ruin in the reign of Edw. IV. The Bowling-green at the W. end of the principal street is supposed to have been its site. There is nothing worth particular notice in the town, but in general it is the starting-point for an excursion to the *Lizard*, and the neighbourhood can boast some pretty scenery.

A favourite walk is to the *Loe Pool* —i. e. " *Lake* Pool"—(½ m. to the head of the lake, 2 m. to the bar at the lower end), the largest sheet of water in the county. A stream called the *Cober* (from *cobra*, an old word signifying serpentine or sinuous), rising near Carnmenellis (alt. 822 ft.), and flowing by Helston, meanders towards the sea. This stream, being obstructed at the shore by a bar of small pebbles, has spread over the lower part of the valley and formed a lake about 7 m. in circumference. During the summer the water gradually filters through the barrier; but in wet seasons it cannot pass off with a rapidity equal to its influx, and then it frequently rises 10 ft. above its usual level, and accumulates so as to stop the mills which are situated upon the tributary streams. When this occurs the corporation, according to an ancient custom, present the lord of the manor with a leathern purse, containing three halfpence, and solicit permission to open the bar. This being of course granted, the mayor of Helston engages workmen for the purpose, and, a small trench being cut in the sand, the pent-up waters rapidly enlarge it, and ultimately sweep the entire obstruction into the sea. The spectacle is really a fine one. The rush of the emancipated element, the conflux of the waves and the contents of the lake, and the numerous cascades and eddies, often glistening in the beams of the moon, altogether form a scene of singular wildness and beauty, whilst the roar of the troubled water lends its aid to impress the mind of the beholder. The bar thus removed for a time is in a few days thrown up as before. In 1807 the Anson, a 40-gun ship, was wrecked upon it, with the loss of its gallant commander, Capt. Lydiard, and about 60 of the crew. As a bank which separates the Lucrine Lake from the sea was supposed to be the work of Hercules, so legendary lore has attributed the origin of the Loe Bar to Tregeagle, of whom so many stories are told in the county. This mythical giant was, however, a veritable person, a steward to Lord Robartes of Lanhydrock during the Parliamentary wars, who tyrannised over the poor, and rendered himself so generally unpopular as to acquire a title to the posthumous notoriety which he now enjoys. In relation to the Loe Bar he is reported to have received a certain sum of money from a tenant, and to have died before he had entered it in the receipt-book. His successor, ignorant of the transaction, applied for the money, and, on the tenant's refusing a second payment, instituted proceedings against him. At the trial, however, the supposed debtor, having contrived to raise the spirit of Tregeagle, brought this singular witness into court, and by its evidence established the fact of the previous payment. The proceedings were thus terminated: but a fresh difficulty arose; the ghost remained behind in the court, and the defendant, being requested to dismiss it, replied, that, since he had been at the trouble of bringing the witness, the task devolved on those who had driven him to that expedient. To dispose of Tregeagle became now a matter for grave consideration, and it was resolved that some impracticable task should be given him as an employment. He was accordingly sentenced to remove the sand from a certain cove to another, from which the sea was always sure to return it, and whilst employed in this labour it is said that he accidentally dropped a sackful at the mouth of the river, in consequence of which the bar and the pool were immediately formed. The lake is a pretty object, embosomed in trees, and abounds with a peculiar trout and other fresh-water fish. On its shingly banks the botanist may find *Corrigiola littoralis*, or *strapwort*, a rare plant. The woods of *Penrose*, a seat once belonging to the Penroses, but now to the family of Rogers, and lately to the Rev. Canon R., are the principal ornament of the Loe Valley, and afford a delightful walk from the bar to Helston. At one spot the park wall returns a remarkable echo, by which, in serene weather, a sound is repeated six or seven times. On the opposite side of the lake is *Nansloe House*, the seat of the Robinsons.

The village of *St. John's*, ¼ m. W. of Helston, is named after a Hospital of St. John which once dignified the locality. Some architectural relics have been discovered on the site.

———

S. of the town lies the district of the *Lizard*, sometimes denominated the Cornish Chersonese. Its old name was *Meneage* (menêg, stony). Its length, from the northern boundary to the Lizard, is 10 m.; and its greatest breadth does not exceed 10 m. There are 12 parish churches in it. It is, says Norden (temp. Eliz.), "a frutefull and plentifull place for people, corne, fleshe, fishe, tynn, and copper." At present it is almost wholly agricultural. The district is remarkable for containing a large area of *serpentine*, a rare and beautiful rock of an eruptive character, which has derived its name from the supposed resemblance of its streaks and colours to those of a serpent's skin, and which constitutes, with *diallage*, half the district under consideration. Serpentine contains a large share of magnesia (it is a silicate of magnesia), and for this reason the soil upon it is poor and ungrateful, but characterised by the growth of the *Erica vagans*(Cornish heath), the rarest and most beautiful of the English heaths. The only place in which *Erica vagans* is known to grow elsewhere is a small district on the west coast of Portugal; the same is the case with *Sibthorpia Europæa* (Cornish moneywort.) The Lizard district would be comprehended within a line drawn from the mouth of the Helford river E. to the Loe Bar W., and, when viewed from the granite ridge near Constantine, presents the appearance of a bald and dreary table-land elevated a considerable height above the sea, and from the neighbourhood of Penzance its surface appears so exactly horizontal as to resemble an artificial terrace. In a picturesque point of view the interior of the district possesses little interest, but the coast is both grand and curious. It has been pleasantly described by the Rev. C. A. Johns, in a little work entitled 'A Week at the Lizard,' pub. by the Soc. for promoting Christ. Knowl. 1848.

Visitors to Helston commonly content themselves with an excursion in this direction to the *Lizard Point*, distant by the direct road about 11 m., diverging from that road to the far-famed *Kinance Cove*, which they contrive to reach at low water, and returning home by the *Frying-pan* at Cadgewith. Those who are able will, however, do well to devote some days to the examination of the coast between Mullion Cove and the Black Head; but if limited as to time, you should depart from the usual lazy course by walking along the cliffs from Kinance Cove, or, if possible, from Mullion Cove, to the Lizard Lights, and from the Lizard Lights to Cadgewith, sending on your horse or carriage to await you at that village. If unequal to this, you should at least walk the short distance (2 m.) from Kinance to the Lizard Point by the cliffs. Those who can content themselves with the common excursion should refer to the heads *Kinance Cove*, *Lizard Point*, and *Cadgewith* in the following description. At a distance of about 6 m. from Helston they will enter the area of serpentine, and behold this rock protruding through the turf in sharp ridges. It constitutes the basis of *Goonhilly Down*, a bare waste which derives its name (*goon*, a down; *huller*, to hunt) from the circumstance of its having been once famous for a breed of small horses.

The traveller will observe that the boundary of the serpentine is very clearly defined by the growth of the *Erica vagans*; for so essential would a magnesian soil appear for the production of this beautiful plant, that not a single specimen is to be found beyond the line which defines the limit of the serpentine. (*Erica vagans* is lilac, flesh-coloured, and white; its chief distinction is having all the anthers arranged around the bell inside, instead of being clustered in the centre of the flower.) It will be also seen that the cottages are built of serpentine.

Commencing a survey of the coast at the western termination of that long shingly beach which extends from Porthleven to the fishing village of *Gunwalloe*, the traveller will pass the precipitous *Halzaphron* (i.e. Western Sea) *Cliffs*, and reach the *Ch. of Gunwalloe*—a lonely and picturesque 15th cent. structure, of no great architectural interest, continually sprinkled with the spray of the sea, and having a detached belfry built on solid rock against a steep ascent W. of the ch.; the rock forms a portion of the W., N., and S. walls. Many shipwrecks have occurred here; and the ch. is said to have been an offering from a survivor, who vowed he would build it where the sounds of prayer and praise should blend with the voice of the waves from which he had escaped. The ch. is ded. to St. Winwaloe, who lived here as a hermit, and died 529, Abbot of Landeveneck in Brittany.

[2 m. inland from Gunwalloe is the ch. of St. Cury or St. Corantyne, died 401, who was, says tradition, consecrated bishop of Cornwall by St. Martin, and converted all the district. The S. doorway is Norm., the ch. itself mainly late Dec. A remarkable *hagioscope* is formed at the junction of the chancel and transept "by a large chamfer of the angle, supported by a detached shaft and arches to small responds of similar character." There are similar hagioscopes at Landewednack and St. Mawgan (see *post*); and others occur in Somersetshire and in Bosherston church, Pembrokeshire. Either this ch. or that of Menheniot in East Cornwall (both ded. to St. Corantyn) was the first in which the Liturgy was read in English. In the churchyard is a monolithic cross, 9 ft. high.]

From Gunwalloe we reach
1½ m. *Poljew*, a sandy cove, where the coast assumes a character of grandeur. A short distance from Poljew is

1 m. *Bellurian Cove*, known to geologists for its conglomerate, which, containing fragments of grauwacke limestone, appears to support the hornblende slate. The descent to it commands a striking view of *Mullion Island*, which is about a mile in circumf., and bears a whimsical resemblance to the figure of a huge animal crouching in the sea. The passage between this island and the mainland is called *the Gap*. The cliffs to the l. are crowned by the *Cathedral*, a pinnacled group of rocks, to which the stranger should climb for a prospect over the Mount's Bay. He can then descend to that romantic recess

1 m. *Mullion Cove*, or *Porthmellin*, which should be visited at low water, as the shore is adorned by picturesque rocks, and a chink in the cliff, a little way to the l., is accessible from the land when the tide is out, and will admit the adventurous explorer to one of the finest serpentine caverns in the district. "It is a striking object," says Mr. Johns, "when seen externally, yet the view from within it is yet more so—impenetrable gloom above—brilliant light streaming in through the fissures, but revealing nothing behind —the smoothest of all possible sands —little pools of crystal water, so still that not even a sunbeam is seen to dance on them—richly dark rocks, so polished as to reflect the light with a splendour scarcely to be endured—the blue sea with its curled edging of snow-white lace, and, in the distance, St. Michael's Mount, the fabled tower in the bay." A mile inland of the spot is *Pradannck Cross*, a time-honoured memorial about 5 ft. high; and a mile up the valley from the cove the village of *Mullion*, with its venerable Perp. ch., the tower of which dates from 1500, and has a curious sculpture of the Crucifixion over the W. window. The fragments of stained glass were collected and placed in the E. chancel window in 1840. The bench-ends are chiefly original, and are the best in their carving in the W. of Cornwall. The figures in front of the altar formed part of the roodscreen. The ch. is ded. to St. Melanus, died 617. Proceeding again along the brow of the cliffs, the traveller will observe below him the *Mullion Gull Rock* detached from the shore; and then visit in succession the grand promontory of *Pradanack Head*, and *Vellan Point*, from which the cliffs sink to a sheltered recess called

3 m. *Gue-graze*, but better known by the name of the *Soap Rock*. This is situated in the ravine leading down to the cove, and consists of serpentine traversed by large veins of *steatite*, a dull white substance, which, being unctuous to the touch, has originated the name. Steatite is considered by some to be felspar, by others serpentine itself in a state of decomposition. It has been employed in the potteries, and largely quarried at this spot, but at the present day its extraction is no longer profitable, as the china-clay of St. Austell and other parts of the county answers the same purpose and is prepared at a much less expense. It is soft when first taken from its matrix, gradually hardening on exposure to the air, but it never loses that peculiar *soapy* feel by which it is

characterised. The botanist may find that rare plant *Genista pilosa*, or hairy green-weed, in this valley.

Just S. of Gue-graze is a sheer precipice of 250 ft., pierced at the base by a cavern called *Pigeon's Hugo* (pron. *oujo*. In the Land's End district the same word is pron. fûgo and fûgan. All are the same with Welsh, *Ogof*, a cave), accessible only from the water and during the finest weather. *The Horse*, a narrow ridge slanting to the sea, is the next feature of interest; and then the bold headland of *the Rill*, commanding a superb prospect over the Mount's Bay and of the clustered rocks of Kinance Cove. On its summit is the *Apron-string*, a heap of stones which the country people aver were brought to this spot by the Devil. He came hither, they say, with an apron full of stones to build a bridge across the Channel for the convenience of smugglers, and was hurrying with his load to the edge of the cliff, when his apron-string broke, the stones were thrown to the ground, and in despair he abandoned his enterprise. ½ m. from the Rill is the far celebrated

1 m. *Kinance* (Ky-nans, *i.e.* dogsbrook) *Cove*, one of the "wonders" of the Cornish coast. A steep descent leads the traveller to the shore among wild and shaggy rocks, where, in the scene which opens before him, he may find realised some of the glowing fancies of a fairyland. The rocks appear as if they had been purposely grouped; and by their dark but varied colours pleasingly contrast with the light tints of the sandy beach and azure sea. The predominant colour of the serpentine is an olive green, but this is diversified by waving lines of red and purple, while many of the rocks are encrusted by the yellow lichen, or seamed by veins of steatite. The fragments into which the cliffs have been dissevered are pierced by caverns which are beautifully polished by the waves, and the beach is strewed with gorgeous pebbles. From the centre of the cove rises a natural pillar, but the most prominent object in the scene is a pyramidal rock which, insulated at high-water, is called *Asparagus Island*, as the habitat of *Asparagus officinalis*. At a certain state of the tide it exhibits a curious phenomenon. A deep chasm, whimsically denominated the *Devil's Bellows*, pierces the island, and from this at intervals a column of water is violently projected, its passage through the chasm being indicated by a rumbling noise like thunder. "This singular effect is produced by the air, which, disengaged from the waves as they are dashed into the aperture, and confined by the perpetual entrance of the sea, becomes highly compressed, and is driven from chamber to chamber until forced together with a column of water through the opposite opening." When the water has thus been blown through the bellows the traveller may communicate with the presiding spirit of the place by holding his letter open before an orifice known as *the Post-office*. But he must not expect that it will be courteously received. The invisible postman—an inward current of air—will rudely tear it from his hand, and, unless he be prompt and active in his movements, such an answer will be thrown in his teeth as may effectually incapacitate him from further efforts at good fellowship. The caverns of the shore are, however, so named, that it is impossible to consider the Genius of Kinance as an uncivilized savage, for they are respectively called the *Parlour*, the *Drawing-room*, and the *Kitchen*. Travellers possessed of common activity will find it an easy matter to climb to the top of Asparagus Island, from which, on the seaward side, they may have the pleasure of looking down the *Devil's Throat*, a hideous rocky chasm filled with froth and foam, and at intervals sending forth

a dismal sound as the waves burst into its cavernous recesses. Those who come hither direct from Helston should make an effort to reach the summit of the Rill, and should also, as previously stated, walk from Kinance to the lighthouses (2 m.) by the cliff. The geologist may observe among the rocks at Kinance a brown diallage, jade, compact felspar or saussurite, asbestus, and a vein of granite descending the cliff in the manner of a dike. The botanist will notice on the shore asparagus, carrot, chamomile, eryngo, sea-kale, beet, and fennel; and on the heights *Geranium sanguineum*, or blood-red crane's-bill (local), sea convolvulus, spring and autumn squills, ivy-leaved campanula, and butcher's broom. To be fully explored the cove should be visited about the time of low water, as the caverns are flooded by the tide.

Kinance is held in undivided moieties by a number of proprietors, and is now of some commercial value, the serpentine being an object of trade. It is manufactured into tables, pillars, and various ornamental articles, at Penzance and Truro, the stone for the purpose being mostly taken from the beach.

Proceeding again on our route along the coast, we ascend at once to the *Tor Balk*, or *Tar Box*, an excellent point of view for Kinance Cove; and then cross a hollow to the *Yellow Carn*, a precipice 200 ft. high, separated by the sea from an insulated rock called *Innis Vean*—i. e. little island. Beyond it we soon reach a remarkable spot known as *Holestrow*, where the face of the cliff has lately fallen in ruins, which are based among huge blocks of serpentine and smaller *débris*, affording excellent specimens of a convenient size for the pocket. To Holestrow succeeds *Caerthillian*, a ravine chiselled by a stream which flows through it to the sea, and of interest as the point where the *mica slate* of the Lizard rises from beneath the serpentine, and further remarkable for its botanical rarities, such as *Lotus hispidus, Trifolium bocconi, T. mollinerii,* and *T. strictum;* the three species of trefoil, according to Mr. Johns, being peculiar to this part of Cornwall and of England. From Caerthillian a walk of some 20 min. will bring the wanderer to the

Old Lizard Head, where he will rest awhile to admire the view; and then proceed by *Pistol Meadow*, containing the graves of a number of persons drowned in the wreck of a transport about a century ago, and so named from the fire-arms which were washed ashore on that melancholy occasion, to the sandy cove and fishing-village of *Polpeer.* Here the cliffs are worn into numerous caverns, but there is one about 100 yds. W. of the cove which deserves particular notice, as, being situated at an angle of the coast, and having two entrances, one on each side of the point, two different rockframed views are commanded from the interior. Mr. Johns describes it as a deep and lofty cavern, apparently lined with the richest purple velvet, and entered through a chink in the sombre cliff. It is perhaps unnecessary to say that it can be reached from the shore only when the tide is out. From Polpeer the traveller will ascend to the lighthouses on the

2 m. *Lizard Point,* the *Ocrinum* of Ptolemy, and the most southerly promontory of England, and generally the first land made by ships upon entering the Channel. The two large and substantially built lighthouses, the bases of which are 186 ft. above the sea, were erected in 1792, by Thomas Fannereau, Esq., under the direction of the Trinity House, and were worked by coal fires up to the year 1813. These beacons display two lights, to distinguish the Lizard from Scilly, known to mariners by one, and from Guernsey, which

exhibits three. Notwithstanding, however, the brilliant illumination which is hence thrown for miles over the sea, ships, embayed in thick weather between the Lizard and Tol Pedn Penwith, are frequently lost in the vicinity of this headland, and the cliffs are of such a character that it is almost impossible to render from them the slightest assistance. The fields near the point are based upon hornblende and talco-micaceous slate, and the traveller who has journeyed hither by the road from Helston will be struck by the contrast between the fertility of this patch and the barrenness which has accompanied him over the serpentine. It forcibly illustrates the value of a soil derived from the decomposition of hornblende. A single acre of this land is commonly rented by the year for 4*l*., and, sown with barley, has produced the extraordinary crop of 90 bushels, the average produce in England being 35½ bushels. The botanist, at certain seasons, may find in the neighbourhood the rare plants *Scilla autumnalis*, or autumnal squill, and *Herniaria glabra*, or rupture-wort. The name *Lizard* has been variously explained by etymologists: some consider that it originated in the shape of the land, as seen from the Channel, or from the variegated colouring of the serpentine cliffs; others derive it from the Cornish word *Liazherd*, signifying a projecting headland. Mr. Edwin Norris, no bad authority, makes it identical with the Welsh "Ilidiart," a *gate*. *Llydaw*, the Welsh name of Armorica, has in the same manner been changed in Cornish to Lezou.

The point below the lighthouses is prolonged at low water to a columnar rock called *the Bumble*, which at other times is insulated. On the E. the land slopes to a bay, and in this direction, near the edge of the cliff, is the *Lion's Den*, a circular chasm which was formed in the month of February, 1847, and has much interested geologists as explaining the origin of similar cavities, such as the Frying-pan at Cadgewith. The strata of this county contain *lodes* or *veins* of a material either softer or harder than the rock which encloses them, and it is evident that at this spot the cliff was traversed by a portion of stone which readily yielded to the assault of the billows, as a cavern, called the *Daw's Hugo*, had been excavated at its base. This softer stone probably cropped out at the surface near the edge of the cliff, where the roof of the cavern at length gave way, and formed this remarkable chasm, which is now entered by the sea through an archway at high water, and in rough weather bears, like the Frying-pan at Cadgewith, no fanciful resemblance to a huge boiling caldron. If the tide will allow it, you should descend to the shore and enter the cavern, for, says Mr. Collins in his 'Notes in Cornwall,' "the effect of the two streams of light pouring into the Daw's Hugo from two opposite directions, and falling together in cross directions on the black rugged walls of the cave, and the beautiful marine ferns growing from them, is supernaturally striking and grand."

From the Lizard the visitor is recommended to walk by the cliffs to Cadgewith, as the road from the village of *Lizard Town* is uninteresting. (At Lizard Town, however, Skewes's Hotel is clean and very comfortable; and there is also a clean and moderate little *Inn*, Three Tuns— Mr. Lyne, the landlord, is a good guide to Land's End, &c.) The distance is about 3 m.

Beyond the Lion's Den he will find the romantic cove and bay of *Househole*, terminated by *Penolver*, the grandest headland to the E. of the Lizard; and then a recess in cliffs which are surmounted by slopes of turf, forming the *Amphitheatre of Belidden*. This is supposed by some antiquaries to have been used as a temple by the ancient Britons, the Druidical rites being performed on Penolver, in view of the assembled multitude. (Such speculations as these may be noticed, but with the addition that they are utterly without foundation.) E. of Belidden is *the Chair*, a rock most conveniently placed for the foot-weary pedestrian, as it commands a beautiful view of the coast towards the Lizard. Beyond the Chair are the *Beast*, or *Bass Point*, and the *Hot Point*, where the coast sweeps to the northward, displaying that fine bay which terminates at the Black Head, and opening to view the distant points of the Dodmèn and Rame Head. After passing a cove called *Kilkobben*, the traveller will reach *Parnvose* or *Lizard Cove*, the harbour of the parish. About ½ m. up the valley is the village of *Landewednack*, where the last Cornish sermon, according to Borlase, was preached in 1678. It is the most southerly ch. in England. The chancel (restored by the present rector) and transept are Dec. The S. porch, unusually for Cornwall, has a groined stone roof. The inner doorway is Norm., complete in itself, with a Perp. doorway constructed within it. The peculiar hagioscope of S. Cury (see *ante*) and S. Mawgan (see *post*) also occurs here. The pulpit is of serpentine; and there are many tombstones of polished serpentine in the chyard. A part of the ch.-yard, enclosed by a rail, contains the graves of a number of persons who died of the plague in 1645. The sea view from the top of the tower is very fine. The antiquary may find between the ch. and Lizard Town an old granite *cross*; and the botanist, in the vicinity of the village, *Alisma ranunculoides*, a local plant.

Those who are fond of exploring the lonely caverns of a rocky shore should take boat at Parnvose, and thus pursue their journey to Cadgewith, as the *Raven's Hugo* and *Dolor Hugo* are situated between these points. The latter is a grand and solemn cavern, with a gorgeous portal of serpentine, and in all states of the tide is filled with the sea, which, entering it with hoarse murmurs, disappears in its gloomy recesses. The *Balk of Landewednack* is the most remarkable cliff between Parnvose and

2½ *Cadgewith, i.e.* "the upper field fort" (*Inn*: Star), a romantic fishing-village in a pretty valley, but principally known for that singular pit, or amphitheatre, called the *Devil's Frying-pan*, the area of which is nearly 2 acres, and the sides 200 ft. high. At the top of the flood the sea enters it through an arch which opens to the shore, where an apparent passage of hornblende slate into serpentine may be seen. Near Cadgewith are the villages of *Grade* and *Ruan Minor*. (St. Ruan is a corruption of St. Rumon, a rather common saint in Cornwall, there being SS. Ruan Major and Minor, Polruan near Fowey, and Ruan Langhorne in Roseland. The village of Ruan Minor is pointed out as the place of his oratory, and his well is still shown there. In the ch. of St. Ruan Major (2 m. inland) are two narrow openings at the junction of the nave and chancel side arcades, and immediately adjoining the screen piers—the use of which is unknown. A similar arrangement is found at St. Mullion, and in one or two other W. Cornish churches. The tower (date 1400) is "black and white"—built of blocks of serpentine and coarse granite.) Grade Church contains monuments and brasses of the Eriseys, who lived in *Erisey House*, built in 1620, in the form of an E. It is said that, when one of the Eriseys was dancing at Whitehall, he danced his cap off his head, but with a kick of his foot kicked it on again. King James II., who was present, said, "Melikes that active gentleman much, but not the name of Erisey (heresy)." Since that dance the name has been Erisey. ½ m. N.E.

of Grade Church is *St. Ruan's Well*, an ancient baptistery, with an arched granite entrance. ½ m. E. of Cadgewith the grand rocks of *Innis Head* may tempt the wanderer to a supplementary stroll. The usual course, however, is to return from Cadgewith direct to Helston; but those who should be desirous of completing a survey of the Lizard district will find references below to localities which deserve attention.

First, the romantic *Valley of Poltesco*, about 2 m. E., is well worth exploring by all who are fond of wild and rocky scenery. *Calleon Cove* is its termination on the shore. *Kennack Cove*, further E., is a pretty cove with a sandy beach; and the *Black Head*, a bare and gloomy promontory, but remarkable for the beauty of its serpentine. This rock beyond Cadgewith assumes a dark green colour, and constitutes the coast round the Black Head to

Coverack Cove (about 6 m. from Cadgewith), to the geologist a very interesting spot, since the great mass of serpentine is here succeeded by a beautiful rock, which continues along the shore as far as the *Manacles*, and predominates in the interior through the greater part of the parish of St. Keverne. It appears to have compact felspar for its base, in which are embedded crystals both of diallage and hornblende. At Coverack, between the pier and the rivulet, veins of the latter mineral may be seen traversing the serpentine; and here also you may obtain specimens of striated felspar of a violet colour, and, below high-water mark, pieces of diallage metalloide 6 or 8 inches in length. The village is exceedingly picturesque, and in its vicinity is "a little mill, the smallest you ever saw, kept jogging by a tiny rill." On the high ground of *Crousa* (Cross) *Down*, N.W., upon which are the large masses of diallage rock called the *Brothers of Grugith* (*i. e.* "of the heath"), occurs an isolated patch of quartz gravel, about ½ m. square, respecting the date of which geologists have been considerably puzzled. The *Manacles* are rocks well known and dreaded by all coasters. The name is a corruption of "Maen eglos," *i. e.* church stone.

About 2 m. N.E. of Crousa Down lies the church-town of *St. Keverne*. Search for ore has been frequently made in this parish, but hitherto without success. The country-people have a saying that *no metal will run within the sound of St. Keverne's bells*, and account for it by a legend that their patron saint, having been treated with disrespect by the inhabitants, denounced a curse upon the parish. However, a belt of land situated between the church and Coverack Cove possesses such extraordinary fertility that it has been called *the Garden of Cornwall*. Its richness is attributed to the decomposition of hornblende, diallage, and felspar. *Charles Incledon*, the singer, was a native of St. Keverne. The ch., which is the largest in the W. of Cornwall, is mainly Perp. (parts of the N. aisle are E. Eng.). Many original bench-ends remain. The oak from which they are made is traditionally said to have been grown on Crousa Down, now a wilderness of rocks. The geologist will find schistose greenstone, cut by veins of diallage, on the shore at *Porthoustock*; a bed of serpentine, which has the appearance of having been thrust up violently among the hornblende slates, between *Dranna Point* and *Porthalla*, N. of St. Keverne; and a pudding-stone, or conglomerate, composed of rounded fragments of slate, in which veins of quartz are visible, near the *Dennis Creek*, S. of St. Anthony. In the sea off St. Keverne lie those dangerous rocks called the *Manacles* (see *ante*), in May, 1855, the scene of the shipwreck of the emigrant ship "John," with the loss of 191 lives.

At the *Nare Point*, 1 m. S.E. of St. Anthony, occurs a grauwacke conglomerate of peculiar interest, since it encloses fragments of hornblende, but affords no trace of serpentine or diallage, although these rocks occur in mass near the point; a circumstance which seems to show that the hornblende is an older formation than the serpentine. The headland is pierced by a remarkable cavern, the roof of which is formed by an ancient beach.

St. Anthony in Meneage (i. e. *stony district*), at the mouth of the Helford river. The church of St. Anthony is situated on the shore at the base of a promontory called *Dinas*, and at high water is but little elevated above the surface of the sea. It originated, according to a legend, in the following manner: some persons of rank sailing from Normandy to England were overtaken by a storm, when they made a vow to St. Anthony to build him a church if he would guide the ship into a place of safety. The saint acceded to their supplication and conducted the vessel into Gillan Harbour, and the passengers, mindful of their promise, erected the church upon the spot where they landed. The small size of this parish favours the idea that it was severed from Manaccan on some occasion of this kind. *Great* and *Little Dinas* are two ancient entrenchments commanding the entrance of the river, and were occupied as military posts during the civil war of Charles. The latter was taken by Fairfax in 1646, but is now a rabbit warren. The *Helford River*, about 1 m. wide at the mouth, branches into picturesque creeks, which penetrate the country in various directions. It is said by Carew to have been in former days much frequented by pirates, " whose guilty breasts," he adds, " with an eye in their backs, look warily how they may go out again."

On its shore, by Manaccan, is *Bosahan House*, T. Grylls, Esq. *Manaccan*, i.e. "the Monks," 1½ m., has become celebrated by the discovery of titanium in its vicinity. The mineral which contained this metal was found in the stream of Tregonwell Mill, and was a titaniferous iron, which has been since called Manacchanite, or Gregorite after the name of its discoverer, the late Rev. William Gregor. Manaccan *Ch.* is E. Eng. (chancel and transept—the chancel roof is perhaps original, and should be noticed). The S. doorway is E. Norm., and one of the best examples in Cornwall. Out of the S. wall of the nave grows a large fig-tree—the diameter of the trunk being about 10 inches. Manaccan is also known in Cornwall as having been the residence of the *Rev. R. Polwhele*, author of a history of the county, who for several years was rector of this and the adjoining parish of St. Anthony. *Tremayne*, an old house in the parish of St. Martin, once belonged to Captain Wallis, who discovered Otaheite, and was born near Camelford. From this old seat the family of Tremayne of Heligan took their name. (Tremayne means "town place," or "dwelling near *the stone*," i. e. some remarkable stone.) It has been recently purchased by Sir R. R. Vyvyan.

St. Mawgan in Meneage, 3 m., where there is a stone cross, some 1500 years old, with the inscription *Cnegumi fil. Enans*. *Trelowarren*, the seat of Sir R. R. Vyvyan, Bart., lies to the S. of this village. The house, a castellated building of the same date as many others in the county (circ. 1620-40), contains pictures by Vandyke and *Kneller*, and was probably erected early in the 17th centy. One of the pictures by Vandyke is a portrait of Charles I., which was presented to the Vyvyans by Charles II. as a mark of gratitude for their services during the civil war. A chapel is attached to the mansion. At a place called *Gear* or *Caer*, ½ m. N. of Trelowarren, you may find a circular camp of about 14 acres, which commands the river, and is in a line with 2 smaller entrenchments. From the downs in the neighbourhood of Mawgan a fine view may be obtained over the adjacent districts. Mawgan is 4 m. from Helston. In the *church* (Dec. chancel and transept, the rest later) is a hagioscope of the same character as those at Landewednack and St. Cury, but differing in detail. The Perp. tower, battlemented and pinnacled, and much enriched with shields, is the finest in this part of the country. In the S. transept are some ancient effigies of the Carminowes (temp. Edw. I.?), who claimed descent from K. Arthur, and were formerly seated on the banks of the Loe Pool. (The family of Carminowe was probably at one time the most important in the county. All Boconnoc, Lanhydrock, and Glynn in the eastern division, and Tregothnan and Loe Pool in the west, belonged to them. A portion of their house at Lanhydrock, called "Col-madoc," now a cottage, still remains; and their name is kept there by a cross-road, yet called Carminowe Cross.) In the N. aisle is a monument to Sir Richard Vyvyan (1696), and the sword which he loyally wielded in the Rebellion. The encampment of Gear has its legend of that period. A Mr. Bogans, of St. Keverne, having posted himself on the spot in military array, was deserted by his men when the enemy approached, and forced to fly in hot haste to the coast for concealment. His adventure is remembered to this day as *The Gear Rout*.

Proceeding on our route from Helston towards Marazion—

1½ A road on the l. leads to *Porthleven*, a small seaport situated in the centre of the Mount's Bay, and about 1½ m. W. of the Loe Bar. The harbour has been constructed at a great expense, and, from its position on a wild dangerous coast, would be of extreme value if more easy of access. In tempestuous weather, however, when such a refuge is required, it is scarcely possible to enter it, since the mouth is narrow, and the sea sets into it with extreme violence. The geologist will find much to interest him in the rugged shore of this neighbourhood, especially some fine sections of trap dikes cutting the slate. At *Trewavas Head*, W. of Porthleven (Trewavas, *i. e.* "dwelling of the mole," "shaped like a mole-hill"), granite, extending from Tregonning and Godolphin Hill, abuts upon the sea in magnificent cliffs. On this imposing headland are the remains of a forsaken mine, formerly worked under the sea; a columnar pile of granite called the *Bishop Rock*; and a *raised beach*, associated with rocks worn smooth by the waves, though now far above their reach.

1 m. *Breage* (pronounced Brague), said to have been founded by St. Breaca, an Irish saint. 1½ m. N.E. of it is the tin-mine of *Huel Vor* (i. e. *great work*), at one time considered the richest tin-mine in the county. Lodes have been here found of the unusual width of 30 ft., and so rich withal as to reward the adventurers with a clear profit of 10,000*l*. in 3 months. The old workings extend for more than a mile and a quarter under-ground. The ch. is interesting as containing the remains of *Mrs. Godolphin*, the "dearest friend" of John Evelyn, who has "consecrated her worthy life to posterity." (Evelyn's 'Life of Mrs. Godolphin' has been edited by the Bp. of Oxford.) In this neighbourhood an insulated mass of granite, separated by a channel of slate from the granitic district of Wendron and Crowan, constitutes the striking eminences of *Tregonning* (properly Tregonan)

Hill (596 feet) and *Godolphin Hill* (495 feet), which rise from bases desolated by the miner. The former is crowned by the earth-works of a hill-castle, and shelters from westerly gales the old mansion of *Godolphin*, which is situated below it on the eastern side. This is a quadrangular building of granite, studded with windows, and fronted by a handsome portico. It formerly belonged to the family of Godolphin, which became extinct in 1785, and is now the property of the Duke of Leeds and occupied as a farmhouse. It is a venerable object, grey with age, but is closely beset by mining works. The minister of Queen Anne, connected by marriage with the great Duke of Marlborough, was the most eminent of the Godolphin family. Part of this hill is worked for china-clay, which is shipped at St. Michael's Mount and Porthleven. These quarries were the first to be opened in this country, and they supplied the clay with which the earliest Plymouth china was made. The northern side of Tregounning has been lately brought under the plough. Godolphin Hill is the site of *Huel Vor*, or the *Great Work* tinmine. Various etymologies have been proposed for the name of Godolphin: "Godawth," half-melted, dissolved, in allusion to the soft granite or kaolin, and "goon," a down; or "Godawth" and "gwyp," white; or "Coed," woods, and "alcan," tin. Neither of these seems entirely satisfactory.

2 m. rt. the village of *Germoe*, founded, according to tradition, by Germochus, a king of Ireland, who is said to have landed at Hayle in the year 460. The traveller should notice on the N. side of the churchyard a singular structure, popularly known as *St. Germoe's Chair*, and said to have been built by the Millitons of Pengersick. It is a stone seat, placed in a recess, which is ornamented with pointed arches, pil-

[*Dev. & Corn.*]

lars, and the rude sculpture of a human head. About 1 m. l. of the road, in a bottom near the coast, stands *Pengersick Castle*, consisting of two towers (temp. Hen. VIII.), which were once united to a castellated edifice. The larger is built in three stories, and the other contains a winding flight of stairs which lead to the summit of the tower. The walls, which are loopholed, are lined with a wainscoting, decorated with carving, and inscribed with several quaint pieces of poetry, illustrated by paintings, much defaced, but still intelligible. On one of the panels, under a rude representation of water dropping from a rock, with the title "Perseverance," is the following poetical effusion :—

"What thing is harder than the rock?
What softer is than water cleere?
Yet wyll the same with often droppe
The hard rock perce, as doth a spere;
Even so, nothing so hard to attayne,
But may be hadd with labour and payne."

A paraphrase of the well-known lines of Ovid,—

"Quid magis est saxo durum, quid mollius unda?
Dura tamen molli saxa cavantur aquâ."

The following lines illustrate another picture, representing a blind man carrying a lame man on his back:

" The one nedith the other ys helpe.
The lame, wyche lacketh for to goo,
Is borne upon the blinde ys back,
So mutually, between them twoo,
The one suppileth the other's lack;
The blinde to laime doth lend ys might,
The laime to blinde doth yeld his sight."

Pengersick, or *Pen-giveras-ike*, signifies the *head ward of the cove*. According to tradition it was built in the reign of Henry VIII., by a merchant, who, as the story goes, acquired so large a fortune at sea, that, when he loaded an ass with his gold, the weight of it broke the poor animal's back. At the latter end of this monarch's reign it is said to have been purchased by a Mr. Milliton, who, having slain a man privately,

P

immured himself in this castle to escape the consequences of his crime. The botanist may find *Silene Anglica*, or English catch-fly, in the neighbouring corn-fields.

At *Sidney Cove*, below the castle, a mine has been recently opened, and christened by Mr. Fred. Hill of Helston by the good historic name of *Sidney Godolphin*. Further W., between Pengersick and Cuddan Point, is

Prussia Cove, so named from a smuggler, who here constructed and mounted in the cliff a formidable battery; but, to disguise and favour his real occupation, acted as landlord at an adjoining public-house, called the King of Prussia. At length Carter, for such was his name, came to blows with the authorities, and, unmasking his guns, fired into the Fairy sloop of war, which thereupon sent its boats against the battery, and destroyed it. In the time of Carter, about 1780, the smuggler was regarded almost in the light of a merchant, and such was the latitude allowed him by law, that no goods could be seized above high-water mark. Immediately W. of this bay is the romantic recess called *Bessie's Cove*.

400 yds. beyond Pengersick lane end, in a field called *Tremenkeverne*, l. of the road, lie several large blocks of an iron gritstone known by the same name, and connected with the following legend. In the olden time, when saints were rife in Cornwall, St. Just of the Land's End paid a visit to St. Keverne, who, residing near the Lizard, entertained him hospitably for several days. After St. Just's departure, however, St. Keverne missed sundry pieces of plate, and, suspecting the honesty of his late guest, hastened after him to ascertain the correctness of his surmises. Upon passing over Crousa Down the idea of resistance flashed across his mind, and he forthwith pocketed three large stones, each weighing about a quarter of a ton, and thus armed continued the pursuit. He overtook his saintly brother at a short distance from Breage, and immediately charged him with the robbery. St. Just feigned great astonishment at so serious an accusation, high words ensued, and from words the disputants soon came to blows. St. Keverne, however, so plied his pocket ammunition, that the affray was shortly terminated by the flight of St. Just, who, making the most of his heels, disburdened himself as he ran of the missing articles. The fight being thus satisfactorily concluded, St. Keverne had no further need of his cumbersome weapons, and accordingly left them on the ground, where they remain to this day, unquestionable monuments of saintly prowess. It is a curious circumstance that the sienitic rock, of which the boulders are composed, and which is called iron-stone from its excessive hardness, is foreign to this district, whilst blocks of it are scattered over Crousa Down in the greatest abundance. Possibly these boulders were ice-borne from the North.

At *Cuddan* (i. e. dark, gloomy) *Point* the geologist will find trappean rocks associated with argillaceous slate in a manner that would lead the observer to assign them a contemporaneous origin. The dark headland bears some resemblance to the promontory of the Start.

E. of Cuddan Point, a short ½ m., is Bessie's Cove, a rocky recess, and home of fishermen—a very romantic spot. A fisherman's cottage stands above the precipice, and below are caverns, over which hang branches of the tamarisk. The largest cave has lately been filled up, since it threatened to undermine the cottage. Through it the fishermen used to draw up their gear from the shore, and by its means in the winter they procured a number of starlings and other birds, which had sheltered in it to hybernate. When the mouth of the cavern was closed by seaweed they stretched a net over the aperture above, and thus entrapped the birds, as many as 500 of which have thus been taken at once.

Acton Castle is situated upon the cliffs W. of Cuddan Point. The locality is wild and unsheltered, and the castle commands a prospect of extraordinary beauty. It was erected as a marine residence by the late John Stackhouse, Esq., and was for some years occupied by the late Admiral Praed.

rt. a lane to *Goldsithney*, a village (on the Camborne and Marazion road) distinguished for its annual fair on Aug. 5, and for a beautiful view of the Mount and Mount's Bay, which first greet the traveller from the Goldsithney hills. l. a lane to *Perran-uthnoe* (i. e. Perran the elevated or "highest"), on the coast between Cuddan Point and Marazion. Near it is a rocky recess in which a Cornish legend lands an ancestor of the Trevelyans, who, according to the story, was swept into the sea with the fabled Lyonesse and its 140 churches, and was borne to this cove by the marvellous swimming of his horse.

After passing Perran-uthnoe, and ½ m. from Marazion, there is a very fine view from the high ground with *Huel Halamanning* on the rt., where a road branches off for Truro and Redruth. From this point all the hills of the Land's End lie in view, and the eye ranges from Mousehole and Paul Ch. to Knill's Monument at St. Ives. In the far W. rises Chapel Carnbrea, and N. the sandy towans glitter in the sun. Between this point and the turnpike we obtain one of the best views of Michael's Mount in connection with the distant coast and Penzance. On the shore are the *Mount's Bay Mine*, and a rich tract of land on which the "Market Jew" turnips are grown. We now enter *Marazion*, from which *St.*

Michael's Mount is to be visited (for both places, see Rte. 29, Exc. 1); and 3 m. further, *Penzance* (see Rte. 27).

ROUTE 29.

EXCURSIONS FROM PENZANCE.

1. Penzance to St. Michael's Mount.
2. Penzance to St. Ives, by the old road over Castell-an-Dinas, returning by the N. coast through Zennor.
3. Penzance to the Gurnard's Head, returning by Morvah and Madron, visiting Chywoon Castle, the Holed Stone, Lanyon Quoit, and Trengwainton Cairn. (For pedestrians over Carn Gulva, by the Mên Scryffen, Boskednan Circle, the Holed Stone, and Lanyon).
4. Penzance to St. Just, Cape Cornwall, Botallack Mine, &c., by Sancreed, returning by Newbridge.
5. Penzance to the Land's End, returning by the Logan Rock, and Buryan.
6. Penzance to Lamorna Cove, returning by Mousehole and Newlyn.
7. The Scilly Islands.

The following excursions all radiate from Penzance as a centre, like the sticks of a fan, avoiding as much as possible travelling twice over the same road. A tolerable coast road, however, runs nearly round the peninsula from St. Ives by the Gurnard's Head, Morvah, Pendeen, St. Just, Land's End, and the Logan Rock. Taking this road, ladies would scarcely find sufficient sleeping accommodation, except at the Land's End, or St. Just. The "rougher sex," if not too exacting, might do so at any of the above places, except Gurnard's Head. The cliff scenery is by far the finest thing in the district;

P 2

but it must be remembered that by this road nothing is seen except what is on the coast.

1. *Penzance to St. Michael's Mount:* 3 m. by road, 2 m. by water; or by train to Marazion Road Stat., 1 m. from the Mount. *By going at low tide the necessity of having a boat will be avoided.*

The road to St. Michael's Mount leaves Penzance by its suburb *Chyandour,*—Chy-an-dour, *i.e.,* "house by the water"—in which are the smelting-house and tannery of the Messrs. Bolitho. It crosses *Chyandour Brook,* which descends in a muddy stream from *Ding-Dong* tin-mine. It then starts fairly for Marazion, in view of the bay and its fabled Mount, and runs by the side of the rly. along the margin of the shore called the Eastern Green. On the l. are the range of hills on which Gulval and Ludgvan are situated, and a low tract of boggy land called *the Marsh,* a part of which was drained about 60 years ago, by Dr. Moyle of Marazion, who was presented for his enterprise with the gold medal of the Soc. of Arts. This marsh, consisting mainly of a bed of peat from 3 to 8 ft. thick, covers a bed of sea-sand 12 ft. deep, and below that a so-called "submarine forest"—oaks and hazel prostrate, and lying in all directions. A similar "forest" extends W. of Penzance for some distance. On the Eastern Green the botanist may find some rare plants, viz. *Panicum dactylum, Alisma damasonium,* and *Santolina maritima;* and in the marshes l. of the road, *Illecebrum verticillatum, Exacum filiforme,* and an uncommon variety of *Senecio Jacobæa.* He may also observe several plants of a local character, viz. *Neottia spiralis* (*Lady's Tresses*), *Euphorbia peplus,* and *E. paralias* or *Sea Spurge,* on the green; *Alisma ranunculoides,*

Drosera longifolia, and *Scutellaria minor* in the marshes. On the beach he may find *Bulimus acutus,* a shell almost peculiar to our S.W. counties. The road passes along the shore to *Marazion,* or *Market-Jew,* a name still applied to it by the country people (*Inn,* the Star), a town in ancient times supported by the pilgrims who resorted to the shrine of St. Michael. Marazion is generally said to have been named by the Jews, who had here their market for tin, and called this their place of rest, "Mara-Zion," the "Bitter-Zion." The name is, however, in all probability from "marghas," "maras," a *market. Ion* and *iou* are both plural terminations; so that "marghasion," and "marghas-iou," both signify the "markets," and afford satisfactory etymologies for both "Marazion" and "Market-Jew." That Marazion was a very ancient smelting place for tin is proved by the discovery, in 1849, of the fragments of a bronze furnace within a rude building of unhewn stones near the western boundary of the town. (See Edmonds' 'Land End District,' *J. R. Smith,* 1862.) The town was pillaged by the French in the reign of Hen. VIII., and again by the Cornish rebels in that of Edward VI., and owing to the suppression of the priory, and the growing importance of Penzance, it never recovered its former prosperity. The chapel here was built in 1861. The geologist will find between this place and the Greeb Point, at low water, the back of a *fault* well displayed. It may be remarked that Marazion is known for the production of a delicious species of turnip. A causeway 400 yds. long, but flooded 8 hrs. out of the 12 by the tide, runs from the beach to

St. Michael's Mount, skirting on the rt. an insulated mass of greenstone, resting on clay slate, called the *Chapel Rock,* which some suppose to have been once crowned with a chapel, in which the pilgrim performed an initiatory exercise; but there are no traces of such a building, and the rock was probably so named from its vicinity to the shrine of St. Michael. At the base of the Mount lies a fishing-town of 80 houses, furnished with a harbour capable of admitting vessels of 500 tons, and visited in 1846 by the Queen and P. Albert; an event commemorated by a metal tablet in the wall of the E. pier, and by a brass footstep marking the spot on which her Majesty placed her foot on landing. From this village the hill rises abruptly to a height of 195 ft., its margin of sea being about 1 m. in circumf. On the W. side the rock scenery is of a romantic description; and a descent should be made to the water's edge. There are steps in the sea wall (and a raised beach adjoining), and at low tide you may scramble round to another flight on the E. side. The geologist will observe that the granite is vertically divided, and that the intermediate spaces are filled principally with quartz, but they also contain wolfram, oxide of tin, topazes, apatite, schorl, a kind of tin pyrites, and other minerals. The body of the hill is of granite, but its northern base of slate; and from this circumstance, as exhibiting various phenomena at the junction of these formations, this rock of St. Michael has excited more geological controversy than any mountain of the world. The structure which has attached to it such importance is to be seen on its water-worn margin—on the N.W., where 2 irregular patches of granite are bedded in the slate, and on the S.E., where veins of quartz traverse both the granite and the slate. It supported the old hypothesis of the contemporaneous origin of these formations, but is now explained as the result of the following series of events:—1. The granite was violently projected through the slate in a state of fusion. 2. The adjoining slate was dissevered by the heat, and the fluid granite pressed into the fissures, and both the granite and slate, as they gradually cooled, were rent by contraction. 3. The partings were afterwards filled by mineral substances. The botanist may find the *Tamarisk*, *Asplenium marinum* and *lanceolatum*, and *Inula Helenium*.

The visitor ascends to the castle on the summit by a rocky path, at the foot of which is a draw-well about 6 fath. deep, and a little way up a tank called the *Giant's Well*. Higher, the approach is commanded by a cross-wall with embrasures, terminated by a picturesque ruin which once served the purpose of a sentry-box; remains which have an ancient appearance, but have been built since the use of gunpowder. Beyond this defence the stranger finds himself upon a platform armed with 2 batteries, the cannon bearing the shield of St. Aubyn. An open flight of steps leads to a small saluting battery of brass guns, and to the portal of the castle. The principal rooms are the hall and the chapel. The *hall* was the refectory of the monks, and is now called the *Chevy Chase Room*, because surrounded by a cornice representing the chace of the boar, stag, bull, fox, ostrich, hare, and rabbit. At the upper end of this apartment are the royal arms and date 1660; at the lower the escutcheon of St. Aubyn. The door is old and of Perp. date; the oaken roof in the style of that of Crosby Hall, with a heavy pendent, out of proportion, hanging from the centre, was added in 1826, and cannot be admired. Here are a Glastonbury chair, which is at least as authentic a relic as that formerly at Strawberry Hill; another chair of dark wood, richly carved, with a bas-relief representing Susanna and the Elders; a curious large corner chair; and a clock, said to have come from Godolphin House when that mansion was dismantled. The chapel is of Perp. date, with a tower on the N. side. The windows are Ear. Perp., except the E. window, which is modern. The stalls were put up in 1804. The chandelier deserves notice; the centre part represents St. Michael, surmounted by the Virgin and Child. During the repairs a low Gothic doorway was discovered in the S. wall: it was closed by masonry, and had been concealed by a platform, but, upon being opened, revealed a flight of steps leading to a vault, in which were found the bones of a large man, but no traces of a coffin; a mysterious circumstance which gave rise to many conjectures as to the fate of the individual who had been here immured. From the chapel a staircase leads to the top of the *tower*, which should be ascended for the sake of the prospect, and also for a view of the stone lantern on its S.W. angle. This tower, dating from the early part of the 15th centy., is the most ancient portion of the building, and the loftiest. Its summit is 250 ft. above the sands. The lantern is popularly called *St. Michael's Chair*, since it will just allow of one person sitting down in it; but this, a common feat, is not devoid of risk, as the lantern projects, and it requires a dexterous movement of the body to return to the tower. Ladies, however, not unfrequently find courage for the adventure, as there is a conceit that the husband or wife who first obtains a seat in this chair will thereby gain the ascendency in domestic affairs. It was undoubtedly a stone lantern or beacon, by which the fishermen were guided to their port in the winter; the grooves for the glass, and holes for the bars, remaining distinct. (The will of Sir John Arundell, 1433, gives 13s. 4d. to the light of St. Michael in the Mount, and the same sum "operi cancellarie ibidem faciende." A similar light-house existed on the top of the chapel of St. Nicholas at Ilfracombe.) The dwelling-rooms are principally remarkable for the wild views they command, and for their retirement, which is alone disturbed by the deep murmur of the sea, or the noise of the howling wind. The drawing-rooms, erected by the late Sir John St. Aubyn upon the site of the ancient convent, are surrounded by an elevated and broad terrace with an open granite parapet, and contain some family portraits, besides a very pretty picture by *Opie* of his niece Miss Burns, and another by the same artist of Dolly Peutreath. At the E. end of the building is a handsome *cross*, and on the S. side a garden. The abominable Roman cement with which the walls are desecrated was part of the " decoration " of 1826.

With respect to the natural, ecclesiastical, and military history of this interesting spot, the following brief particulars must suffice. Its old Cornish name, according to Carew, was *Curaclowse in Cowse*, "carreg cleug in coes," the *Grey Rock in the Wood;* and seems to favour the tradition that at a remote period the Mount was clothed with trees and situated some distance from the sea. This is further corroborated by a charter of Edward the Confessor, in which the rock is mentioned as *nigh* the sea, and by the statement of William of Worcester, who informs us that it was "originally enclosed within a very thick wood, distant from the ocean six miles, affording the finest shelter to wild beasts." With respect to the catastrophe which is supposed to have inundated this shore, see Rte. 27, *Penzance*. At a very early time this romantic eminence was consecrated to religion. Old legends assert that the archangel St. Michael appeared to some hermits upon one of its crags; and tradition, pointing to a large rock on the western side, as the spot where this vision was seen, has given it the appellation of *St. Michael's Chair*, a name erroneously transferred to the lantern on the tower.

Milton in his 'Lycidas,' has alluded to this apparition in the following lines :—

" Or whether thou, to our moist vows deny'd,
Sleep'st by the fable of Bellerus old,
Where the great vision of the guarded Mount
Looks toward Namancos and Bayona's hold,
Look homeward, angel, now, and melt with ruth,
And, O ye dolphins, waft the hapless youth."

We have notices of the Mount having been a hallowed spot long before Edward the Confessor granted it to St. Michael in Normandy, and there is a legend that in the 5th centy. St. Keyne, a damsel of royal birth, came here on a pilgrimage to the shrine of its tutelary saint. At the Conquest, Edward's monastery fell to the share of Robert Earl of Mortain, who bore the Standard of St. Michael in the Norman host, and who confirmed a grant which had already been made by the Confessor, bestowing St. Michael's Mount in Cornwall on the Great Benedictine House of St. Michael "in periculo maris" on the opposite coast of Normandy. The Cornish St. Michael's was at first a mere cell; but afterwards obtained a distinct corporate character, and had a convent, a seal, and a perpetual prior. (See *Oliver's* ' Monast. Diocesis Exon.' There is no evidence whatever for the assertion made by Nichols and others, that the monks here were Gilbertines, whose rules permitted nuns under the same roof.) The rock and buildings here are on a small scale compared to those of St. Michael's in Normandy ; but it is probable that the resemblance of the two rocks suggested the donation by Edward the Confessor.

Both Mounts were fortresses as well as religious houses ; both contained garrisons as well as convents ; and it is remarkable that the same tradition of extensive lands and forests submerged by the sea, is current of both. The priory here (as a distinct corporation) was not taken possession of under the acts for suppressing alien priories, temp. Hen. IV. and V. ; but under the authority of parliament it was transferred by Hen. V. to the new monastery of Sion, to which it belonged until the Dissolution. After that period the families of Arundell of Lanherne, Millitou, Harris, Cecil, and Basset, became successively its proprietors, and about the year 1660 it was sold to the St. Aubyns.

The military annals of the Mount commence with King Richard's captivity, when Henry de la Pomeroy gained possion of the place, and reduced it to the service of John, who was aspiring to his brother's throne. Upon the return of the king, however, the garrison surrendered, and, according to the tradition, Pomeroy, in despair, caused himself to be bled to death. In the reign of Edward IV. the Earl of Oxford and some companions, having fled from the field of Barnet, approached the Mount under the disguise of pilgrims, and, thus effecting an entrance, prepared to defend themselves to the last extremity. They repulsed several attacks by the sheriff of the county, Sir John Arundell, who was slain on the sands and buried in the Mount Church, and they resisted so manfully as to obtain a pardon. In the reign of Henry VII. Lady Catherine Gordon, the wife of Perkin Warbeck, here found a temporary asylum, from which she was taken by Lord Daubeny, and delivered to the king. Again, during the Cornish riots (Edward VI.), the Mount attracted the notice of the country, when its Governor, Humphrey Arundell of Lanherne, having joined the rebels, it was taken by a party for the king, but retaken by the rebels, who, passing the sands at low water, stormed the base of the hill, and then the summit, by carrying trusses of hay before them to deaden the shot. They were, however, eventually driven out, and their leader paid the penalty of his treason on the scaffold. The last event of a military nature which occurred at the Mount was its reduction by the parliamentary troops under Colonel Hammond. Upon this occasion the garrison made a stout defence under the command of Sir Francis Basset, and upon capitulation obtained permission to retire to the Isles of Scilly. For the antiquary the Mount of St. Michael possesses additional interest as having been considered the *Iktis* of Diod. Siculus, to which the Greek merchants traded for tin. This, however, is at least doubtful; and if the island can be identified at all, Wight (Vectis) seems to have the best claim. But it is probable that the 'Ictis' of Diodorus represents more than one insulated "emporium" for tin. (See *Introd.* for some remarks on this subject, and on the supposed intercourse of the Phœnicians with Cornwall.)

2. *Penzance to St. Ives by the old road over Castell-an-Dinas, returning by the N. coast through Zennor.*

There are three ways of going to St. Ives. (a) By train to *St. Ives-road Station*, distant 4 m. from St. Ives. (No conveyances, public or private, are to be obtained at the station. Omnibuses run between Hayle and St. Ives from some of the trains.) (b) By the new turnpike road through Lelant, following very much the line of the railway as far as St. Ives-road Station. By this road St. Ives is about 10 m. from Penzance. (c) By the old road over Castell-an-Dinas, which, though rough and hilly, is by far the most beautiful, and amply repays the traveller for any inconvenience arising from the badness of the road. It leaves Penzance by its eastern entrance, passes through Chyandour, and turns immediately to the left at the back of *Ponsandane*, R. F. Boli-tho, Esq.; and *Pendré*, J. St. Aubyn, Esq., M.P. Turning off from the Zennor road, we enter the village of Gulval. The ch. (restored 1857) is ½ m. to the eastward, and is remarkable for the great inclination (northward) of its chancel. In the churchyard is a cross of the usual Cornish type. St. Gulwal was Bp. of St. Malo (?) in the 6th centy. From Gulval village commences a long climb of 2 m. over the shoulder of Castell-an-Dinas.

The entrance on the left, soon after leaving Gulval, is *Kenegie*, formerly the seat of a younger branch of the Harris family of Hague, near Lifton, in Devon (many of whose monuments are in Gulval ch.), but now belonging to W. Coulson, Esq., the eminent surgeon. The views of Mount Bay, during the whole of the ascent, are most beautiful. At the nearest point to the top of *Castell-an-Dinas* there is a footpath on l., leading up to it across three or four fields, about 10 minutes' walk. The carriage must be left in the road. We are now 735 ft. above the sea, in a position intermediate between the two channels, and commanding a superb panorama. On a clear day to the eastward, between Trink and Trecrobben Hills, the lighthouse on Trevose Head can be seen. Inland from it Roughtor and Brown Willy are said to be visible, but are not easily made out by persons unacquainted with the country. The round hill on the cliff short of Trevose is St. Agnes Beacon. Beneath us, still to the E., is the great mining field of Redruth and Camborne, with its numerous population dotted in white houses about it. Above it is Carn Brê, with the Dunstanville pillar on it.

To the S. is the expanse of Mount's Bay from Mousehole to the Lizard, with Penzance and the Mount almost at our feet.

To the W. Burgan Tower rises conspicuously, and the high hills of Sancreed Beacon and Chapel Carn

Brô, which overlooks the Land's End; while to the N., over Towednack, a small patch of the Bristol Channel can be seen between the hills.

The summit of Castell-an-Dinas is crowned with a circular fortification, similar to the one at Chûn (see next Exc.), but not so perfect; in the centre of it there is a modern watch-tower or " folly," probably built with stones taken from the walls of the old camp. The castle consisted originally of 2 very thick concentric stone walls, with a space of about 30 ft. between them. Beyond these walls, at a distance of about 40 ft., was an external vallum of earth and stones; and without again is another strong wall toward the west, reaching nearly half round the castle. In Borlase's time there were many circular enclosures within the central area, each about 7 yds. diam., formed by walls only 2 or 3 ft. high. (*Edmonds's 'Land's End District.'*) Between the camp and the road, close to the footpath, is a modern grave and monument of a gentleman who preferred this airy situation to the "snug lying" of a churchyard.

Returning to the carriage we soon descend to Naucledry, a small village in the valley, thence to Chypons. 1 m. l., as we rise the hill, is the ch. of *Towednack*. [This ch. is late, with the exception of an E. Eng. chancel arch — a rare feature in Cornish churches. The massive cornice and stringcourse of the low tower, " though plain, are very effective, and in harmony with the rugged desolation of the spot."—*E. Godwin.* The plaster of the internal walls encourages the growth of a rare alga, Oscillatoria cyanea. " It grows here abundantly, clothing the walls with a beautiful light sky-blue colour."—*Blight.*] The names of the farms between Chypons and Towednack are curious: Amalebria, Amalwidden, Amalveor, Biggletubben, Skelywadden, and Coldhar-

bour. Passing over the shoulder of Trink Hill, we approach *Halsetown*, a curious village of detached houses, apparently constructed for the purpose of manufacturing votes for the borough of St. Ives. The road passes through Halsetown, and enters St. Ives by its western entrance, the one the traveller will probably leave it by; we recommend him, therefore, to turn away to the right before reaching Halsetown, and by a winding lane to come out into the St. Ives and Lelant road, between Trevethow and Weal Providence, just above Carrack Gladdeu beach, where the Maidenhair fern grows. (See *post.*) The traveller will thus enter St. Ives from the S. " The slopes and banks between St. Ives and Lelant are very beautiful from the abundance of blue, red, and white varieties of columbine, *Aquilegia vulgaris*. Near St. Ives may be found *Statice Dodartii* and *Orobanche barbata.*"—*Blight's 'Week at Land's End.'*

The old rickety houses of St. Ives (*Inns:* Western Hotel; St. Ives Hotel) lie nestling on the very skirt of the sea, and with the blue of sky and ocean (the dim coast-line running up to Trevose Head, a distance of 30 m.), the green tints of the shallows, and the sparkle of the bright yellow sandy shore, altogether form a very pleasing picture. The traveller may gaze at this gem of western scenery with yet greater interest when he learns that it has been compared, as seen from this point, with a Greek village; and it must be admitted that " the charm of blended and intermingled land and sea, the breaking waves and changing brightness of the resounding ocean, amidst picturesque cliffs richly tinged with aërial hues," which have been said to characterise Grecian scenery, here lend their aid to complete the resemblance. A descent into the streets, or rather lanes, will, however, somewhat qualify his admiration, although in this respect

P 3

there is no want of resemblance to the Greek type. The town is the head-quarters of the pilchard fishermen (refer to Introduction), and therefore tainted with the effluvia of the cellars. Tradition assigns its foundation to St. Ia, the daughter of an Irish chieftain, and companion of St. Piran in his missionary expedition to Cornwall. According to the legend, St. Piran landed, about the year 460, at Pendinas, where Tewdor, the king of the country, had a palace, and Dinan, a lord of his court, at the request of St. Ia, built a church at the same place. As a fishing station, St. Ives is likewise patronised by St. Leonard, to whom there was once a chapel, of which remains may still be seen near the pier. It is now used for storing away fishing-tackle. The town of those early days stood on the promontory, where walls and other ruins have been found beneath the sand.

The *church* (Hen. V., VI.) stands close to the beach, and is sprinkled by the sea during gales of wind. It is built of granite, and contains a curious font, and according to tradition the bones of St. Ia.

A ch. at *Halsetown*, near St. Ives Consols, was opened 1858.

The *pier* was constructed in 1767, by Smeaton, the architect of the Eddystone lighthouse; and a *breakwater* was commenced 1816, but abandoned after an outlay of 5000*l*. It would have rendered the bay a secure anchorage, which is now exposed to the N. and E. The project, however, may yet be carried out, as the completion of the breakwater was recommended by a committee of the House of Commons in 1859, and the fitness of St. Ives for a harbour of refuge is under consideration. The harbours of Hayle, Portreath, and St. Agnes are within the jurisdiction of this port.

There are several mines in the vicinity of St. Ives. The *St. Ives Consols*, situated close to the town, is one of the largest tin concerns in the county, and remarkable for a lode of extraordinary size, which is known as the Carbona, and has been worked full 60 ft. in length, breadth, and height. The neighbourhood bristles with rugged rock-strewn hills, of which *Rosewall*, S.W., has a logan stone on its eastern summit. An eminence to the S., and 545 ft. above the sea, is crowned by a monument erected 1782, by one Knill, an eccentric bencher of Gray's Inn. This person originally intended it as a mausoleum for his remains, but he revoked this intention, and left his body by will to the anatomists of London. The structure consists of a granite pyramid, on one side of which is inscribed " Johannes Knill, 1782;" on another, " Resurgam;" and on a third, " I know that my Redeemer liveth." Knill died in 1811, leaving directions that, at the end of every 5 years, a matron and 10 maidens dressed in white should walk in procession, with music, from the market-house to this pyramid, around which they should dance, singing the 100th Psalm. He bequeathed for the purpose of perpetuating this custom some lands, which are vested in the officiating minister, the mayor, and the collector of the port of St. Ives. At the foot of the hill is *Tregenna*, the seat of H. Lewis Stephens, Esq. The house is a castellated building, erected in 1774, and commands the beautiful shore-scene of St. Ives Bay. Among the plants of this neighbourhood the botanist will notice *Exacum filiforme*, and the rare and elegant fern *Adiantum capillus Veneris*. This latter grows in a damp cave on Carrack Gladden beach, about half way between Hayle and St. Ives. The cave until lately was festooned and lined with Maidenhair; but the ferns have been, to a great extent, destroyed by the "natives," in order to increase the value of plants they have for sale. The cave might, and should, be closed by an iron grating. *Helix inoculosa* and *H. pisana*, or Banded-snail, both rare shells, and the latter confined in England to this locality, are to be found on the sandhills. St. Ives, which is the only parliamentary borough in this district, was incorporated 1639, mainly through the exertions of Francis Basset, of Tehidy, who, as M.P. for the borough, presented to the town the "loving cup" which graces the mayor's table at the meetings of the corporation. It is surmounted by the figure of a man in armour resting on the shield of the Bassets. It is of silver gilt, and bears the following inscription:—

"If any discord 'twixt my friends arise
Within the borough of beloved St. Ives,
It is desyred that this my cup of love
To everie one a peacemaker may prove;
Then I am blest to have given a legacie
So like my harte unto posteritie.
FRANCIS BASSET, 1640."

The town seal, the gift of James Praed of Trevethow, 1690, represents an ivy-branch. In 1647 St. Ives was ravaged by the plague, which swept away nearly a third of its inhabitants. It, however, escaped the cholera. It was the birthplace of *Jonathan Toup*, the editor of Longinus (year 1713).

The return journey to Penzance by Zennor is about 11 or 12 m. of hilly road, and will take nearly 2 hours. The road leaves St. Ives by its western entrance, and immediately commences a long steep ascent; the views, however, from which, seawards and eastwards, are exceedingly beautiful in clear bright weather. On reaching St. Ives Consols (the road goes through the middle of the mine), a road turns l. to Towednack and Halsetown (the road, indeed, from which we diverged before reaching the latter village). Our road still ascends: on l., *Trevalgan Hill*, a fine rough hill covered with granite boulders. A fine view backwards, from the highest point of the road, before it descends again, should be noticed. The road now winds along, having rough granite hills and furzy crofts on the l., a great expanse of sea ½ m. to the rt.; the cliffs of no great height, but an ugly neighbourhood for a ship in a storm.

The hill over *Zennor* is covered with remarkable horizontally divided masses of granite in many places, reminding one of the Cheesewring. Here, too, is *Zennor Quoit*, the finest cromlech in the district. It lies on an elevated plain, nearly ½ m. E. of Zennor ch., and consists of a double "kistvaen" (stone chest), with a covering slab which measures 18 ft. in length, 11 in breadth, and 48 in circumference. One end of this stone rests on the ground. It was supported by seven upright piers. The cromlech belongs to the same class as Arthur's Stone, in Gower, South Wales, which has nine supporters. In Borlase's time the heap of stones, 14 yds. in diameter, under which the whole structure was buried, almost reached the edge of the quoit or horizontal slab when resting on its supporters. It seems probable that this cromlech is the largest in the British islands. The road passes within 200 yds. of Zennor ch., plain, and of no great interest, said to have been dependent on St. Michael's Mount. It contains a font of the late Dec. period, and some remains of carved bench-ends, on one of which is the figure of a mermaid. On the further side of the ch. from us (towards the sea) is a small logan stone, 19 ft. long, 3 thick, called the "Giant's Rock." "It rocks admirably if any one stands upon it on the corner nearest the church."

A road rt. leads from here to the Gurnard's Head, about 2 m. distant, which, if pressed for time, can be combined with to-day's excursion (for description see the next excursion); otherwise our, and the best, road turns away over the hill to the l.; from the top of the hill the

Gurnard's Head can be seen and a view of both channels. The road from hence is not very interesting till near Penzance. It joins the direct road from Penzance to the Gurnard's Head, under Mulfra Quoit. For description, see the next Excursion.

From Zennor to Penzance is about 7 m.

3. *Penzance to the Gurnard's Head, returning by Morvah and Madron, visiting Chûn Castle, the Holed Stone, Lanyon Quoit, and Trengwainton Cairn. (For pedestrians over Carn Galva, by the Mên Scryffen, Boskednan Circle, the Holed Stone, and Lanyon.)*

The *Gurnard's Head*, or *Treryn Dinas*, is a promontory on the N. coast, about 7 m. from Penzance. The direct road leaves Penzance by its E. entrance, and turning immediately to the left at Chyandour, ascends the hill towards Trevailer, instead of turning rt. to Gulval village. A fine view of St. Michael's Mount immediately after the turning.

rt. *Bleu* (*i.e.* parish) *Bridge*, at the bottom of the steep hill next turning on rt., a picturesque spot, with some lofty elms. At the end of the bridge (which is a mere crossing-stone) is a granite block, 6 ft. high, with the inscription, "Quenatavus Iedinui filius."

Trevailer, the seat of the Rev. W. Veale : the road passes under a fine avenue of trees. We are now just on the junction of the granite and slate. In the bottom, on the rt. between this place and Chyandour, we have passed probably some of the most productive land in the neighbourhood of Penzance. With the exception of a granite quarry on rt. belonging to the Messrs. Freeman, there is little of interest till we come to the turning rt. to Zennor.

The high hill on l. is *Mulfra Quoit* (Mulfra is "a round bald hill"), the summit of which is crowned with another of those remarkable cromlechs (which seems to have stood originally on four uprights, like the Chûn cromlech) : the table-stone of this appears to have been pushed, or to have slipped off. There is a fine view of both channels from the top of the hill.

About 1 m. after passing Mulfra, and ¼ m. to the l., is a fallen cromlech, of the same plan as those of Mulfra and Chûn, but with the remarkable feature of a circular covering stone, diam. 4 ft. 10 in., and 5 in. thick. It is now lying on the ground. 500 yds. N. from this cromlech, and close to the village of *Bosphrennis*, is the most perfect specimen of a bee-hive hut remaining, probably in England. It consists of two chambers, one circular, 13 ft. diam.; the other, an oblong parallelogram, 9 ft. by 7, with a doorway 3 ft. 10 high, communicating with the outer chamber. In the end wall (8 ft. 6 in. high) of the square chamber is a window about 1 ft. high and 4 ft. from the ground. The principal entrance faces S.W.; and not far from it is a window (? opening) in the wall of the circular chamber, with lintel and jambs. Each course of stone was stepped over that beneath it. There are remains of other huts in the immediate vicinity, and traces of rude enclosures. More perfect examples may be seen in Ireland, where a square chamber adjoining a circular one is generally believed to indicate an oratory opening from a hermit's cell. The date of this hut at Bosphrennis is quite uncertain.

The direct road continues straight to the Gurnard's Head, or rather to the village of Trereen, where the carriage must be left: the headland itself being ¼ m. further across some fields, with one or two hedges to be climbed.

In preference to this road we venture to recommend travellers to follow the old St. Ives road from Penzance as far as a place marked "Badger's Cross" on the Ordnance map (for description, see previous Excursion 2), and to take the turning l., which will bring him out on the direct road, a little to the S. of Mulfra Quoit. He will thus be enabled to see the remains of the ancient British village of *Chysoyster* (the name signifies "heap-shaped," or "bee-hive" houses). It lies on the rt. of the road, near a farm of the same name. It seems to have once been enclosed by a wall or fortification of some kind, two tolerably perfect slopes or embankments existing on the W. side. Within this embankment are about a dozen dwellings; each oval-shaped, with a very thick and strong wall of uncemented stone, surrounding an open central area, to which there is only one entrance. In the thickness of this wall three or more oval apartments are formed, each faced internally with a wall of rough masonry, and each having a doorway between 2 and 3 ft. wide, leading into the central area. The walls inclined inward towards the top, till they either met, or left but a small space to be roofed over, which was probably done with a flat stone. [The "pounds" or villages on Dartmoor, and especially Grimspound (Devon., Rte. 13), should be compared ; Chysoyster, however, more nearly resembles the Irish "cloghauns." Similar remains in Cornwall are Bodennar Crellas in Sancreed (see *post*), Bosphrennis in Zennor (*ante*), and Bosullow (see *post*). (For some general remarks see *Introd.*) Between the "village" and Chysoyster farm is a so-called cave ; it may perhaps be doubted whether this is one of the habitations remaining perfect with its roof on, and its interior considerably filled up, or whether it is such a cave as that at Treewoofe (see Exc. 6). Like so many of the antiquities all over the world, the possessors have been too apt to look on the walls as a quarry of stones lying ready to hand.

The village lies about 3 fields in to the rt., ¼ m. N.W. of Chysoyster farm, partly in a field, partly in the croft, and can easily be found, although the walls are now much covered with turf, furze, and broom.

The *Gurnard's Head*, like the headland of the Logan rock, has evidently, at an early time, been fortified as a cliff-castle, and, projecting far into the waves, commands an excellent view of the neighbouring coast. E. and W. this huge barrier dives sheer down into deep water, so that the heaviest seas roll in unchecked and burst upon it with terrific violence. The background of the shore is also most interesting. Hills of rock and heather, sweeping round in the form of a crescent, terminated on one side by Carnminnis, on the other by Carn Galva, enclose a great terrace extending to the cliffs. On the isthmus connecting the Gurnard's Head with the mainland are the remains of a small chapel, with the altar-stone entire. There was a holy well close by. The Gurnard's Head exhibits to those who scramble along the base of it (a feat practicable at low water) a splendid section of the strata. It is composed of slaty felspar, hornblende, and greenstone. In its vicinity the romantic cliffs of *Zennor* (E.) run for nearly ½ m. on the junction-line of the granite and slate; and *Porthmeer Cove*, 1 m. W., is well known to geologists for the large size of the granite veins which there penetrate the slate. (For pedestrians see end of this Excursion.)

Returning to the carriage at Trereen, a picturesque road leads between the high lands of Carn Galva, &c., and the sea, on rt. through Morvah and Zennor mines to *Morvah*.

One of the most picturesque head-

Route 29.—*Chûn Castle.*

lands passed on rt. is Bosigran Castle, once fortified, like so many of the points in the W. Within it is a flat logan rock, containing several rock basins, and measuring several yards in circumference.

Shortly before reaching Morvah, our road turns up a sharp hill to the l. : on reaching the top a fine view of both channels is gained.

¾ m. rt. across the down, only accessible for pedestrians (the carriage had better be left at this point), is *Chywoon* (pronounced *Chûn*) castle (the name means *house on the down*), the most easterly of seven hill castles between this place and the Land's End, from which signals might be interchanged. The circle of the walls may be easily made out crowning the summit of the second hill S. of the road, just before it begins to descend towards Lanyon farm. It is similar in construction to Caer Bran Round (see next Exc.), but is by far the best example of a hill castle remaining in the West.

Three lines of wall exist, built of loose stones. The hand of the destroyer has been at work here too, and so many of the stones have been removed for building, that the circles are far less perfect than in Borlase's time, 100 years ago. The interior diameter, E. to W., is 125 ft., and N. to S., 110. Traces of divisions, or walls, exist in the interior, which Borlase supposes to have been huts or chambers for the shelter of the occupants of the castle. Within one of these is a well, with steps to go down to the water. The entrance, called "the iron gateway" (the walls crossing the ditches, and the arrangements for defending this gateway, should be noticed), faces W.S.W., pointing straight to

Chûn Quoit, a cromlech about 200 yards distant: a picturesque object, but smaller and less striking than Lanyon Quoit (vid. inf.). Its table-stone is 12½ ft. in length, by 11½ in width; a barrow of stones formerly surrounded it, as was the case with other cromlechs in Wales and Cornwall. The 3 parishes of Morvah, Madron, and St. Just, meet here.

At *Old Bosullow*, N. of the castle, on the slope of the hill, are some remains of a British village, similar in construction, but perhaps less perfect than those at Chysoyster. An ancient road leads from them to the castle. The side of the hill and the plain below are covered with small barrows.

At Bodennar, about ¾ m. S.E. of Chûn Castle, is a single dwelling called the Crelláãs (a corruption, it has been suggested, of *Cryglás*, a "green hillock," from its appearance, covered with turf and furze), which is worth notice. It consists of 2 circles, formed by rough strong walls, the larger circle (40 ft. from N. to S.) opening into the smaller (21 ft. from N. to S.) by a passage, 6 ft. wide, between 2 large slabs. The larger circle has 2 concentric walls, the space between which has been divided at intervals by traverse walls, one of which remains. Above the higher circle is a large green terrace.

Returning to the carriage, we descend the hill eastwards, till we come to a small stream, which crosses the road just W. of Lanyon farm. Hence a track to the l. across *Anguidal Down* leads to the *Mên-an-tol*, or *Holed Stone*, one of 3 stones which are disposed in a straight line. It is known locally as the "Crick Stone:" it being supposed that, if a person afflicted with a crick in the back crawls 9 times through the hole, and sleeps with a sixpence under his pillow, he will be cured. A similar stone exists in Constantine parish, possessing the same charm, if the ceremony is performed on Easter-day. Of the 3 stones the centre one is 4 ft. in diameter, and 1 thick : the hole itself is 1 ft. 3 in. in diameter. The stones are easily found, as no other upright stones are in the same croft. They lie nearly in a straight line between Lanyon farm-house and the western peak of Carn Galva, about ¼ m. W. of the stream, which crosses the road, and ⅛ m. in from it.

Mên Scryffen, or *Screpha*, the *Written Stone*, lies in a croft under Carn Galva, and *Gwn mên Screpha*, the *Down* of the *Written Stone*, about 1 m. N.E. of Lanyon. It is one of the most ancient sepulchral monuments in Cornwall, supposed to date from a period antecedent to the departure of the Romans from the country. It is about 8 ft. in length, and bears the inscription "Rialobran Cunoval Fil." It is stated by Mr. Lhuyd, whose researches formed the basis of Pryce's Cornish Dictionary, that the reading in British would be *Rhiwalhvran map Kynwal*, and that such names are not uncommon in old Welsh pedigrees. He also remarks that the neighbouring parish of *Gulval* is probably called after this *Kynwal*, as he has found many such instances in Wales. The Mên Scryffen for a long time lay prostrate on the moor, and was thrown down by a miner digging for treasure, who nearly lost his life by the fall of the huge mass. It has (1862) been raised, and is now a conspicuous object. The inscription can be easily read.

Between Mên Scriffen and Ding Dong mine is *Boskednan Circle*, or the *Nine Maidens*, a ring of stones, similar to those of Dawns Mên and Boscawen rise. The diameter is 66 ft. 8 stones stand erect, and one is nearly 8 ft. in height. 3 lie prostrate. The eye ranges over a vast extent of uncultivated country, and to the blue expanse of ocean. Directly N. rise the magnificent rocks of Carn Galva; to the S. is the mine of Ding Dong; to the E. is seen Mulfra Quoit on the crown of a barren height, some 2 m. away.

It must be remembered that to go to these two last objects and return will entail a walk of from 2 to 3 m. over rough ground. After leaving the holed stone it is perhaps better to make inquiries as to the position of the Mên Scryffen at a solitary house between the holed stone and Carn Galva. The house rejoices in the name of "Four Parishes," as Madron, Gulval, Morvah, and Zennor, meet there. Returning from Boskednan circle, and taking Lanyon for a landmark, it is better to come out at the top of the hill just E. of Lanyon, the carriage having been ordered to come there.

Here on the moor of *Boswaras* is the celebrated *Lanyon Quoit* (Lanyon is said to signify the "furzy enclosure"), a most lonely old monument, the effect of which is much enhanced by the wildness of the country. It is sometimes called the *Giant's Quoit*, and consists of a large table-stone 47 ft. in girth, 18½ in length, by 9 in width, pointing nearly N. and S., and supported by 3 rude pillars, which are inclined from the perpendicular. This stone, which is raised about 5 ft. from the ground, was upset some years ago, one of its supporters being split by lightning, but it was shortly afterwards replaced by means of the machinery which restored the Logan rock to its position. At all times this cromlech is grand and impressive: but it appears to the greatest advantage when looming from the sea-mist which so often envelops this part of the country. There is another cromlech in a field, ½ m. W. of Lanyon farm-house, nearly as large as the one described, with the table-stone resting on the ground, but otherwise uninjured. It was found in 1790 within a great tumulus of earth and stones, after nearly 100 cartloads had been removed.

1 m. a cart-track to the l. leads to *Ding Dong* mine, one of the oldest mines in the county: from this corner there is a fine view over Mount's Bay.

The road presently passes through the plantations belonging to Trengwainton (Lewis Stephens, Esq.), formerly the seat of the late Sir Rose Price, Bart. Observe the luxuriant undergrowth of rhododendrons. At the end of the plantation a gate rt. leads from the road to *Trengwainton Cairn*, a rough pile of rocks from which there is a grand view of Mounts Bay. It is popularly known as "Bull's View," probably a corruption of "Belle Vue." Near the footpath, 100 yds. W. of the gate, there is an old cross.

½ a cart-track leads to *Madron well* and *Baptistery* in a croft ½ m. E. of the road. See Rte. 27.

¼ *Madron Church-town* (see Rte. 27). Observe the view from the churchyard, and the fine old cross near the gate. The enormous stone edifice in the churchyard is the mausoleum of the Price family.

1½ *Penzance.*

Good walkers are strongly recommended on leaving Gurnard's Head to ascend Carn Galva, and crossing it to visit the *Mên Scryffen, Boskednan Circle, Lanyon Quoit*, and the *Mên an tol*, or holed stone, all described above. Coming out into the road followed above, near Lanyon, they can either return as described above (in which case the holed stone had better be visited before Lanyon Quoit), or, prolonging their walk, visit *Chûn Castle*. A farm marked on the Ordnance map as *Great Bosollow*, lies immediately at the E. foot of the hill, on which Chûn stands; from hence a capital footpath leads through various crofts, and across *Trengwainton Cairn* to Madron. The distances for a pedestrian would be approximately: Penzance to Gurnard's Head, 7 m. direct; Gurnard's Head to Lanyon, over Carn Galva, 4 m.; Lanyon to Chûn, 1½ m.; Chûn to Penzance, 6 m. *Carn Galva* is the finest hill in the Land's End district, being literally covered with granite, which crests it in a very beautiful manner.

Mr. Blight ('Week at the Land's End,' p. 21) states that "there is a logan stone near the summit of the most westerly crag of the range, easily got at, and easily moved." "The botanist may find here *Polypodium phegopteris, Hymenophyllum Wilsoni* and *Tunbridgense*, and *Sticta crocata*."—*Id.*

4. *Penzance to St. Just, Cape Cornwall, Botallack Mine, &c., by Sancreed, returning by Newbridge.*

The direct road to St. Just by Newbridge is about 7 m. There is little of interest on this road. The road by Sancreed is longer and more hilly, but possesses more interest, passing as it does through Sancreed church town, and near *Caer Bran*. For the first 3 m. from Penzance we follow the Land's End road as far as the village of *Driff* (for description see succeeding Excursion). At Driff our road turns away to the rt., and in about 1½ m. reaches

Sancreed, a picturesque little ch. (late 15th cent.), of no architectural interest) surrounded by trees. In the vestry are some panels of the old roodscreen, curious, though not very early. Observe a cross on the churchyard-wall near the gate; and a still finer one 7 ft. high in the churchyard itself, having on it among other emblems the lily of the Virgin, a rare emblem on these crosses. The dedication of this ch. is uncertain (perhaps Sancreed is equivalent to St. Faith). The road ascends soon after leaving the village, passing between Sancreed Beacon on rt., and

1 m. W. of the village, *Caer Bran* on l. The summit of this hill is crowned with the remains of an old castle, *Caer Bran Castle*, or *Round*, similar to that at Chûn. (Caer Brân in North Wales means "Crow's Rock." It may, however, also signify "King's Castle." Brân is Celtic for king or chief; hence the name Brennus, which occurs so frequently.)

Route 29.—St. Just.

The castle "consisted of a stone wall about 12 ft. thick; 2 ditches and an earthen embankment; and a circular building of stone appears to have stood in the centre. It is now little more than a heap of ruins, though its circular form may be distinctly traced."—*Blight.*

At the bottom of the hill on the western side are the remains of an old paved road. "Near *Cairn Uny,* close at hand, is a curious subterranean gallery, walled on the sides, and covered with flat slabs of granite; it is partly fallen in, and cannot easily be entered."—*Blight.* This is one of the remarkable caves of which the "Fogou" at Treewoofe (see Exc. 6) is the most perfect example. The Cairn Uny Cave was opened by a miner about the year 1860, who asserted that the floor "was well paved with large granite blocks, beneath which, in the centre, ran a narrow gutter or bolt, made, I imagine, for admitting the air into the inmost part of the building, from whence, after flowing back through the cave, it escaped by the cave's mouth—a mode of ventilation practised immemorially by the miners in this neighbourhood, when driving adits, or horizontal galleries, under ground."—*Edmonds's 'Land's End District.'* The higher end of the cave consisted of a circular floor 12 ft. in diam., covered with an overlapping roof or "bee hive" of granite. Between this hill and Chapel Carn Brê is another curious relic, namely, the ruins of a Baptistery dedicated to St. Euinus, and known by the name of *Chapel Uny.* It stands near a well, to the waters of which are attributed many wonderful qualities. No portions of the baptistery walls are standing; it is far less perfect than Madron chapel, a building probably of the same nature. St. Uny seems to have been an important saint in this country. Lelant and Redruth churches are dedicated to him. N.W. of the chapel is

The hill of *Bartiné* (usually translated *the hill of fires,* but query?) alt. 689 ft., the highest eminence in the vicinity of the Land's End. The hill across the hollow to the S. W. is *Chapel Carn Brê.* This, perhaps, is more easily ascended from the Land's End road. One of these hills, however, should be climbed for the sake of the prospect, which from the small girth of this part of the peninsula, includes a wonderful expanse of water. Three seas roll in sight, and the eye ranging round 28 points of the compass, reposes during the interval on their azure surface. The chapel which crowned the hill of Carn Brê has disappeared entirely. The mining field of St. Just, and the rough hill of *Carn Kenidjack* (alt. 640 ft.) to the N., present a dreary scene. From Chapel Carn Brê, Mount's Bay (E.) assumes the appearance of a lake, in which St. Michael's Mount is an island. On a clear day Scilly (W.) is perhaps better seen from these heights than from the Land's End itself.

Returning to the road, from which we have strayed too far, we pass on rt. *Bostrea,* a farm of about 500 acres, converted by Col. Scobell, of Nancealverne, from a howling wilderness into smiling pastures. Descending the hill, we have a glorious expanse of sea before us.

Rt. is *Balleswidden Mine,* one of the largest tin mines in Cornwall.

1¼ *St. Just Church-town* (in *Penwith.*)—the ch. is dedicated to St. Justus, the companion of Augustine — (Commercial Inn.) Omnibuses to and from Penzance daily; generally leaving St. Just in the morning, and Penzance in the afternoon. The ch. is a 16th centy. 'building on the foundation of an earlier one. The sculptured caps of the piers and the E. windows of the aisles should be noticed. The chancel was re-built in 1834. A cross found in an old chapel on Cape Cornwall was placed in it by the then vicar, the Rev. J.

Buller. There is also a monumental stone with the inscription, "SILVS HIC IACET," found during the re-building, and placed in the ch. Who this Silus was is not known; the question is discussed with a full account of the 'Church and Parish of St. Just,' by the late Rev. J. Buller, who published a book under that title. In the village near the Commercial Inn are the remains of an *amphitheatre* or *round,* "*plane an guiry,*" a "playing place," 126 ft. in diameter, originally with 6 tiers of stone steps, and till lately the scene of wrestling matches on Easter and Whit Mondays and Tuesdays. There are now no remains of the steps, and the amphitheatre itself is much filled up. It was here that "miracle plays" were performed in Cornish (see Introd.) "The bare granite plain of St. Just, in view of Cape Cornwall, and of the transparent sea which beats against that magnificent headland, would be a fit theatre for the exhibition of what in those days of simplicity would appear a serious presentation of the general history of the Creation, the Fall, and the Redemption of man, however it might be marred occasionally by passages of lighter or even of ludicrous character. The mighty gathering of people from many miles round, hardly showing like a crowd in that extended region, where nothing ever grows to limit the view on any side, with their booths or tents, absolutely necessary when so many people had to remain three days on the spot, would give a character to the assembly probably more like what we hear of the so-called religious revivals in America, than of anything witnessed in more sober Europe."—*Norris's* '*Ancient Cornish Drama,*' ii., p. 466. The last surviving relic of such performances—the miracle play at Ammergau—should also be compared. N. E. of St. Just is *Carn Kenidjack*, a hill with a remarkable pile of rocks on it, and directly S. of it a stone circle called the *Merry Maidens*.

Cape Cornwall is about 1 m. W. of St. Just. A footpath leads to it. The junction of the granite and slate here may be seen very well (see Gurnard's Head), especially on the beach to the N. E. in Porthleden Cove, below Boswedden Mine. On the isthmus connecting the cape with the land the ruins of an ancient chapel called St. Helen's Oratory are still to be seen in a field called Parc-an-chapel. From the top of the cape there is a fine view to the southward of the cliffs as far as the Land's End (for names, &c., see Land's End excursion). At the very point is the old engine-house now disused, once belonging to *Little Bounds*, a submarine mine. In part of these works, significantly called *Surcull's Lode*, the avarice of the miner has actually opened a communication with the sea, and the breach, which is covered every tide, is protected by a platform calked like the deck of a ship. The noise of the waves is distinctly heard in every part of the mine. In the 40-fath. level a curious crop of stalactites (specimens of which may be seen in the museum at Penzance) has been formed by the dripping of the water through the roof of the mine. The *Brisons*, or the *Sisters*, two dangerous rocks between 60 and 70 ft. in height, are situated about a mile off this headland. A reef nearer the shore is called *the Bridges. Carrickgloose Head* (the Hoar Rock), immediately S. of Cape Cornwall, should be visited, as it commands a most interesting view of the coast. In *Pornancon Cove*, just S. of it, is a fine example of a *raised beach*, 15 ft. above high-water mark. In the stormy winter of 1850-51 the Brisons were the scene of a remarkable shipwreck. Before daybreak of the 11th of Jan., during a gale from the S.W., the brig 'New Commercial,' bound from Liverpool to the Spanish Main, struck upon a ledge of rocks between the Great and Little

Brison, and, as the sea ran very high, went speedily to pieces. The crew, consisting of nine men, with one woman, the wife of the master, succeeded in landing upon the ledge; but the tide was rising, and their position became momentarily more perilous. At length a tremendous wave broke amongst them; the whole party were swept into the sea, and seven out of the ten sank at once to rise no more. Of the remaining three, one, a mulatto, reached a portion of the floating wreck, and by using a plank for a paddle, and a rag of canvass for a sail, contrived to keep clear of the broken water, and was eventually rescued by the Sennen fishermen. The other two, the master and his wife, were washed upon the Little Brison, where they gained a footing, and climbed above the reach of the waves. Whilst these poor people were thus struggling for their lives, efforts were being made for their rescue. Her Majesty's cutter 'Sylvia' was working gallantly round Land's End, and soon her boat was lowered, and a most dangerous attempt made to approach the Brisons, but the sea was so terrific, it was found impossible to get near them; and the night soon closed in wet and stormy. When day dawned on the morrow, the man and his wife were still seen upon the rock; and as the wind had slightly abated and changed in direction, another attempt was made for their rescue. Captain Davies, the officer of the coast-guard, provided a number of rockets, and, in company with other boats, pushed gallantly from the shore; but it was found impracticable to approach the fatal spot within 100 yds. The rockets, however, were promptly discharged, and at length a line fell in the desired direction across the Brison. The man tied it round the waist of his wife, and after some hesitation she plunged into the sea, whilst a succession of heavy breakers rolled over the rocks, perilling the safety of all. The rope was, however, drawn speedily into the boat; but the unfortunate woman, although she breathed when taken from the water, shortly afterwards expired. The man had sufficient strength to survive the immersion; he was dragged into one of the other boats, and, though greatly exhausted, finally recovered.

Botallack Mine, about 15 m. from St. Ives, and 2 from St. Just, lies 1½ m. N.N.E. of Cape Cornwall. It is an interesting walk for those who are not afraid of a scramble through the busy scene of *Boscedden Mine*, and up the steep ascent of *Kenidjack Castle*. Here some remains of an old fortification may still be traced; and at the Bunny Cliffs, a little S. of Botallack, some "*old men's workings*," as what are supposed to be the surface works of the ancient miners are generally called.

On the next headland is *Botallack Mine*. The traveller, having reached the main object of his excursion, must betake himself to the cliff, and rest awhile in admiration of the scene which is there unfolded, and which exhibits one of the most singular combinations of the power of art and the sublimity of nature that can be imagined. Gloomy precipices of slate, which have successfully defied the ocean itself, are here broken up by the operations of the miner, and are hung with all his complicated machinery. The *Crown Engine*, well known for the wild exposure of its position, was lowered down a cliff of 200 ft. to the ledge it now occupies, for the purpose of enabling the miner to penetrate beneath the bed of the Atlantic. The first level of this mine is 70 fath. from "grass," and extends upwards of 400 ft. under the sea, and the traveller who should venture to descend into its dreary recesses may be gratified by hearing the booming of the waves and the grating of the stones as they are rolled to and fro over his head. The lode, consisting of the grey and yellow sulphuret of copper, crops out in the Crown Rocks below the engine. The cliffs are composed of hornblende alternating with clay slate, and contain a store of curious minerals, as jasper, jaspery iron-ore, arseniate of iron, sulphuret of bismuth, peach-blossomed cobalt, specular iron-ore, hæmatitic iron, hydrous oxide of iron, veins of garnet rock (in the Crown Rocks), epidote, axinite, thallite, chlorite, tremolite, and a crystallised schorl. Beautiful specimens of arborescent native copper have been also found in them. There is now a large "diagonal shaft" or inclined plane called Boscawen shaft, which runs from just above the water's edge in an oblique direction out under the sea. By this means the mine is now worked at a cheaper rate, and is much better ventilated. Boscawen shaft was commenced in May, 1858, under the following circumstances:— A year or two previous, on driving the 185 fath. level N. of Wheal Button shaft, and about 300 fath. distant from it, the entire length of the level being under the sea, a vein of copper was discovered, which, from its dip corresponding with the deposit they were then working on, and the similarity of the strata, led the agents to suppose that they were on the head of another rich bunch of copper. They in a true miner-like manner commenced probing the ground, and having satisfied themselves, they, at a meeting of the adventurers, held on the 20th April, 1858, made the following remarks in their report:— "We now suggest the propriety of sinking a diagonal shaft from surface so as to reach the present end 160 fath. level. The shaft would have to be carried about 35 deg. from the horizontal line, and the distance will be about 360 fath. This we think can be done in as little time and less expense than sinking the present shaft, driving the level, and sinking wings for ventilation." This report was adopted, and the shaft forthwith was commenced, and from 20 to 50 men were employed in rising and sinking from the different levels to communicate the shaft from that time to the 22nd of March, 1862, on which day the first tram waggon laden with copper ore was drawn to the surface. This shaft is carried 8 ft. wide by 6 ft. in height, and although in some places it is very crooked and the angles very sharp, yet the same underlay of 35 deg. is continued throughout. The rails are laid on the most approved principle, and little or no motion is felt in ascending or descending in the waggon, which is capable of holding 6 or 8 men with comfort, and will hold nearly a ton of ore. The present length of the shaft is over 400 fath., or nearly $\frac{1}{2}$ a mile; and, although it has not been driven through much solid ground, its cost has been estimated at 10l. per fath., or 4,000l. Apart from the difficulties of sinking the shaft were the removing of the 24-in. cylinder engine, and building the house for its reception. Those who, some years ago, witnessed the lowering of the machine over the face of the rugged cliff, 150 ft. high, left with an impression that it could never again be removed; but a few months ago many who thus thought saw the huge boiler and beams drawn to the very top of the cliff, and again relowered to its new resting-place. It is a great satisfaction to know that throughout the whole of this great undertaking, either at the surface with the machinery or in the shaft, not a single accident has happened.

1 m. The *Levant Mine*, another of the submarine mines. The levels run under the sea for a distance of 40 fath., and to a point at which the roof is calculated to be not more than 10 ft. in thickness. To return from hence to Penzance by the road is nearly 3 m.

2 m. *Pendeen Cove.* The objects of curiosity here are the granite veins

penetrating the slate at the junctions of the two formations as we have seen at Cape Cornwall and the Gurnard's Head; and in a garden at the village of *Pendeen* a cave or excavation called *Pendeen Vau*, consisting of 3 passages, the two end ones branching off from the outermost. The sides incline inwards, and the cave is closed at the top with flat stones. The outer passage only can be explored at present. The others are closed by fallen stones. Such caves may have been places of concealment during the British period, but by whom they were first constructed is quite uncertain. (See a longer notice of them in Exc. 6—the cave at Treewoofe.) The old seat of *Pendeen* was the birthplace of *Dr. Borlase*, the antiquary. The house is now used as a farm-house; the family (in whose possession however it still is) having moved inland to *Castle Horneck*.

The traveller had better order his carriage to meet him at Pendeen village; he can then return to Penzance by the Morvah and Penzance road (see Excursion 3), or by the direct Pendeen and Penzance road, a distance of about 8 m. Ascending the hill we pass on rt. *Carn Kenidjack*, with its curious pile of rocks. The plain below is the " *Gump* " (Corn.—a level tract). Just beyond the summit we enter the direct St. Just and Penzance road, about 4 m. from Penzance. Descending the hill, 200 yds. rt. is an old Druidical circle (called Tregeseal Circle or the Nine Maidens) on the moor; and a furlong N.E. of the circle are two caves called " Giants' Graves," which may reward examination. At the bottom of the hill we pass the village of *Newbridge*. [A road here branches off to the rt.; and about ¼ m. beyond the junction is the village of *Truen*, on the hill above which is a " *round* " or circular enclosure, about 125 ft. diameter. " Near its centre a circular pavement of broad unhewn granite slabs, with small stones in the interstices, and about 10 ft. diameter, was discovered in 1845, and a few feet from it the upper and nether stones of a handmill." —*Edmonds's* ' *Land's End District.*'] Hence, with the exception of fine views of Mount's Bay, there is nothing of interest to Penzance. 2½ Treenethack Cross on rt.; the clump of trees on l. is *Lesingey Round*, an old fortification. Below us on rt. is *Trereiffe* (D. P. Le Grice, Esq.) ½ m. the Land's End-road is joined. Penzance.

It is thought that it will hardly be desired to explore the coast southward, between Cape Cornwall and the Land's End in this excursion, especially if Botallack shall have been descended. If, however, the traveller should return to St. Just, and desire to do so, he will find the names of the headlands, &c., given in the succeeding excursion. A good road also leads from St. Just to the Land's End; and if the traveller desires to see the intervening country, he can return to Penzance by this way. It is, however, the least interesting part of the district, and will not repay the trouble of going 4 extra m. The road joins the Penzance and Land's End-road about 7 m. from Penzance.

5. *Penzance to the Land's End, returning by the Logan Rock and Buryan.*

We venture to suggest, that it is better to go direct to the Land's End first. It is more probable that Scilly will be visible in the morning than with the afternoon sun in your eyes.

The Land's End is 10 m. from Penzance; the first 4 m. hilly. The miles are reckoned from Penzance. Leaving Penzance by the western entrance, we pass on rt. *Castle Horneck*, S. Borlase, Esq.; at the top of the hill rt. the direct road to St. Just turns off. Among the trees on rt. stands

1 m. *Trereiffe* (pronounced *Treeve*), D. P. Le Grice, Esq. The house is covered with a yew-tree, which has been trained all over it. Observe the 4 avenues at the junction of the 4 roads. The hedge by the road side is the habitat of several rare ferns, and of the *Sibthorpia Europæa*, a small plant found only, we believe, in Cornwall and Brittany. It was discovered and named by Ray about the year 1675. *Asplenium lanceolatum*, a rare fern out of this country, may be found in almost every hedge near Penzance.

1½ m. *Buryas Bridge*. Beyond rt. is *Trewidden*, E. Bolitho, Esq. Opposite the lodge an old cross.

2½ m. The village of *Driff*; on rt. the road to Sancreed (see Excursion 4); on l. a road leading to Paul, and Lamorna Cove; places, however, which are more accessible from Penzance by the S. road. Beyond Driff, in a field on l., are some upright stones, the remains of an ancient circle.

3¼ m. The road l. leads to Buryan, by which place we propose to return.

4 m. The road ascends *Tregonebris Hill*, remarkable for its musical name. On rt. a large upright stone; on l., at top of the hill, the *Nine Maidens*, a celebrated Druidic circle on the farm of *Boscawen-Un*. The original number of stones is uncertain. There is one upright in the middle of the circle. A Welsh triad ranks " Beiscawen in Danmonium " among the three "Gorsedds (places of judgment) of poetry" in Britain; and this Boscawen has been pointed out as the place meant. The circle is however probably sepulchral.

5½ m. *Crows an uru (the Cross by the wayside).* rt. a road to St. Just, l. to Buryan; rt. are the hills of *Bartinné* and Chapel Carn Brê. (See previous Excursion.) The latter is more accessible from this road than from Sancreed.

7 m. *Quakers' Burial-ground*, now disused. Observe a curious tomb to Phillis Ellis, 1677. We have now a magnificent sea-view before us, and rapidly descend to

9 m. *Sennen Church-town*, 387 ft. above the sea. *Inn:* the "first and last" inn in England is the first object that catches one's attention, being "the first" on coming from the W., and "the last" from the E. The proprietor has built another hotel, called the "Land's End or Point Hotel," on the Land's End itself, where very tolerable accommodation can be procured. It is, however, only open in summer, and is frequently full.

Sennen Church is a small weather-beaten building, calling for no special remark. (It is Perp., and contains a mutilated figure of the Blessed Virgin.) In the village just E. of the ch. is a large stone, on which 7 Saxon kings, who had come down by an excursion train to see the Land's End about the year 600, are reported to have dined. Merlin, says the local tradition, prophesied that many more kings shall one day dine here, and that great troubles shall follow.

10 m. *Land's End, Pedn an Laaz*, the *Furthest Land* —the "Penwithsteort," or " Penwithstart," of the Sax. Chron. (*i.e.* the "start" (Sax.) or "end" of Penwith, as the hundred is still called. Penwith (Celt.) signifies the "headland to the left"), the Bolerium of the ancients, and the most westerly point of England, is wholly composed of granite, darkened by the spray of the sea and the mists driven past it from the Atlantic. Its extreme point, which is pierced by a natural tunnel, is not above 60 ft. in height, but the cliffs rise on either hand to a much greater elevation, and below them, in gloomy recesses, lie huge rocks, rounded like pebbles and eternally buffeted, and the mouths of caverns in which the voice of the sea is never hushed. The view from

so commanding a point necessarily includes an expanse of ocean which, when the winds are abroad, presents a spectacle of grandeur which is truly sublime. The line of coast, as seen from this promontory, terminates N. with *Cape Cornwall* (alt. 230 ft.), and between that point and the Land's End is indented by *Whitesand Bay,* which affords a shelter to vessels when the winds are adverse in the Channel. It is said that this bay was the landing-place of Athelstan after his conquest of Scilly, of King Stephen in 1135, of King John when he returned from Ireland, and of Perkin Warbeck in his final attempt upon the crown in 1497. Some rare microscopic shells are to be found upon its sands, and on its western side, near Sennen Cove, a patch of slate enters the granite. Under the point of the Land's End is the *Pele* (a spire) *Rock;* out at sea N.N.W. the *Shark's Fin* ; to the S. the *Armed Knight,* cased in solid stone; and on the profile of Carn Kez *Dr. Johnson's Head,* a very whimsical resemblance, even to the wig. 1¼ m. from the shore the *Longships Lighthouse* rises from a cluster of rocks. It was erected in 1797 by a Mr. Smith, whose enterprise was rewarded by a toll to be levied upon shipping for a limited number of years. It is now under the jurisdiction of the Trinity House. The tower is built of granite, and the stones are trenailed in a similar manner to those of the Eddystone Lighthouse. The circumf. of the structure at the base is 62 ft., the height from the rock to the vane of the lantern 52 ft., and from the sea to the foot of the building 60 ft., and yet the lantern has been frequently shivered by the waves. The patch of slate which runs out from Sennen Cove constitutes the rock upon which the lighthouse stands, the rest of the cluster consisting of granite. At the edge of the precipice to the l. of the Land's End the mark of a horse-shoe imprinted on the turf was long cleared out from time to time to perpetuate the memory of a frightful incident which occurred on the spot. An officer, quartered at Falmouth, on a visit to Penzance, laid a wager that he would ride to the extreme point of the Land's End. He was attempting this rash and silly enterprise when the feather which at that time formed part of the military costume alarmed the horse, which commenced backing towards the precipice. The rider hastily alighted, but the bridle caught the buttons of his coat, and he was dragged to the very brink before his companions could disengage him. The horse rolled over the cliff and was dashed to pieces. In clear weather the *Islands of Scilly,* about 9 leagues distant, may be distinguished upon the western horizon. Their appearance under a setting sun is eminently beautiful, but they are more frequently visible in the light of a clear morning. There is a tradition that these islands were once connected with the mainland by a tract of country called the *Lyonesse*—that "sweet land of Lyonesse," where, according to the poet, fell the heroic King Arthur, when—

"All day long the noise of battle roll'd
Among the mountains by the winter sea."

Spenser has given us a glimpse of this legendary region, which he places on the confines of Fairyland; but the chroniclers enter into particulars, and tell us how it contained 140 parish churches, and was swept away by a sudden inundation. At the present day the sea which flows between Scilly and the mainland is known by the denomination of *Lethowsow,* or the *Lioness;* the race between the Longships and the Land's End being distinguished by that of *Gibben,* or the *Kettle's Bottom*—names which distinctly mark the character of this turbulent ocean. A dangerous rock of greenstone called the *Wolf* is situated 8 m. from the shore, and is geologically interesting for containing veins of white limestone. An attempt was once made to fix upon it the figure of an enormous wolf, which, constructed of copper, was made hollow within, that the mouth receiving the tempest should emit sounds to warn the mariner of his danger. The violence of the elements, however, frustrated the project.

It is an interesting but rough walk along the shore to Cape Cornwall and Botallack Mine, the latter of which is about 5 m. dist. Below are the old Cornish names of several striking points on this part of the coast.

Pedn Mên Dhu, the *Head of Black Rock*. The *Shark's Fin* lies between this headland and the Longships, and the *Irish Lady* rises from the waves at the foot of the cliffs. A very perfect specimen of a *cliff-castle* may be found between the Land's End and Pedn Mên Dhu. It is called *Maen Castle*.

Sennen Cove and its little village, boasting a pilchard-fishery and fish-cellars. Here the traveller has entered *Whitesand Bay*. Observe the junction of the granite and slate.

Carn Olva, the *Carn at the head of the Breach*: the breach being called *Vellan Dreath*, the *Mill in the Sand*. The origin of the name of this sandy hollow was ascertained a few years ago, when the remains of a *tin streamwork*, together with the skeleton and horns of a deer, and an oak with its branches and leaves, were discovered about 30 ft. beneath the surface. The shore scene here is of singular beauty.

Carn Towan, the *Carn in the Sand*.
Carn Barges, the *Kite's Carn*.
Carn Crease, the *Middle Carn*.
Carn Kei, the *Carn by the Hedge*.
Aire, the *Inner Point*, as inside Cape Cornwall. This headland is the northern boundary of Whitesand Bay.
Carn Venton, the *Carn near the Well*.

Carn Kreigle, the *Carn from whence to call or cry*; probably so named as a station of the *huers* in the pilchard-fishery.
Carn Mellyn, the *Yellow Carn*.
Polpry, the *Clay Pit*.
Carn Leskez, the *Carn of Light*, which was so called, says Borlase, from the Druid fires which were kindled on it. The lowermost carn is called
Carn e Wethan, the *Carn of Trees;* and here, remarks the same author, "an oak-tree is still (1769) to be seen growing among the clifts of the rocks."
Carn or *Carreg Glos*, the *Grey* or *Hoary Rock*—an appropriate name, on account of the quantity of moss and lichens with which the headland is covered.

Cape Cornwall. (See Excursion 4.) About 1 m. beyond it is *Botallack*, one of the most celebrated of the Cornish mines. (Excursion 4.)

In this excursion you should search along the shore for *raised beaches*, which are numerous, and very striking from the large size of their rounded stones.

To return to the Land's End. Unquestionably the finest cliff scenery in the W. of Cornwall lies between the Land's End and the Logan Rock; and unquestionably (as we think) the two finest points there are Pardenick Point and Tol Pedn Penwith. The only way to see it thoroughly is to walk along the cliff. The distance is about 6 m., and will require from 2 to 4 hours, according to the pace walked and the time spent looking at the scenery. Before leaving the Land's End, the carriage should be ordered to go to *Treen*, ½ m. from the Logan, and wait there. For those who are not good walkers, or who have not time to spare, we venture to suggest that they should be driven in their carriage as near *Pardenick Point* as they can, after leaving Sennen, and walk from thence to the Land's End. No carriages can approach within 1 m. of *Tol Pedn Penwith*; and if that is not too much, it can be taken in the way to the Logan after the horses are rested at the Land's End. The Penzance drivers know where to put one down at the nearest point.

From the Land's End to the village of *Treen*, by road, is about 4 m.

The following are the names of the most remarkable points and objects the pedestrian will meet on his walk along the cliff, starting from the Land's End:—

South Carn and *Dollar Rock*. The latter has derived its name from some dollars having been dredged up in its vicinity.

Carn Creis.

Carn Greeb. Several rocks called Guela or Guelaz (*easily seen or distinguished*) lie off this headland. They are sometimes called *High Seen*. The most striking of the group is the "*Armed Knight*,"

"huge and in a rock (of granite) arm'd,"

a pyramidal mass divided in such a manner by joints as to resemble a knight in armour.

Enys Dodnan, the *Island having soil upon it*. It is perforated by an archway.

Pardenick, or Pradenack (collection or "herd" of rocks). This is a headland of remarkable grandeur and beauty, and particularly excited the admiration of Turner, who sketched what the traveller will see by a downward glance from the summit. One might, indeed, imagine that giants of old had been here rearing columns in sport. The most striking group of rocks is called *Chair Ladder*. The cliff-scenery between Pardenick and Tol Pedn Penwith is the finest in Cornwall, and probably in Great Britain. To the W. is the Land's End Inn on Carn Kez.

Under Pardenick are

The Pludn, the *Pool*, a deep place, and

[*Dev. & Corn.*]

Mozrang Pool, the *Maid's Pool*. Adapted for bathing.

Zawn Reeth, the *Open* or *Free Cave*, so named from the colour of the granite. It is a wild and magnificent archway, noble in its dimensions, and well worth a visit, and the descent to it by the chine is quite practicable, though not very easy.

Carn Voel, the "Mounds" of Rocks, crowned by piles of rock, and below them is a beautiful slope of turf, commanding the coast eastward as far as Tol Pedn. The W. side is precipitous, slanting sheer to Zawn Reeth.

Zawn Pyg, *Cave resembling the beak of a bird*, and known also by a prettier name—*The Song of the Sea*. It is a dark tunnel, or chink, in a point of Pendower, through which the light streams and the waves roll with fine effect. Taking the cave for the eye, and the tongue of rock for the beak, the resemblance to a bird's head is obvious. A path—but a rugged one—leads along the steep side of the bay, passing some excavations where miners have broken ground in search of tin, but with no great success. On the W. is a picturesque crane at the edge of the cliff for raising sand from the beach. This is effected by an ingenious contrivance. The ascending bucket, loaded with a certain quantity of sand, is drawn up by the greater weight of the descending bucket, which is filled with water from a stream conducted to the spot with that object. In a mine near Merthyr Tydvil in South Wales the coal is raised to the surface by a similar contrivance.

Mill Bay, or *Nankissal* (valley of the bosom), a wild romantic scene. By the shore are the ruins of the mill.

Carn Pendower, *Carn at the head of the water*; i.e. of the streams which flow into Mill Bay.

Zawn Kellis or *Gellis*, *The Hidden Cavern*.

Q

Carn Barra (*a loaf*), *Carn* resembling *loaves*, but in which other freaks of form may be discerned; for instance, on the profile of the cliff the figure of a lady at her devotions, and on the slope above Por Loe the likeness of a grotesque human head and face.

Por Loe (Lake Port), a small rocky recess, where an Indiaman was wrecked some years ago.

Tol Pedn Penwith, the *Holed Headland in Penwith*. This promontory forms the western boundary of the Mount's Bay, and derives its name from the *Funnel Rock*, a deep well-like chasm, the bottom of which, opening to the sea, may be visited at low water. A person accustomed to cliffs may find his way down over the granite, which, by its roughness, affords a secure footing, and at any state of the tide you may, and should, descend to the level of the sea. You will then gain a magnificent view of the columns of weatherbeaten stone, which rudely resemble Gothic spires. *Carn Mellyn*, the *Yellow Carn*, in a golden coat of lichen, rises directly before you; beyond it is *Carn Brawse*, the *Great Carn*, and island rocks at its foot, and in the distance the Longships. 1 m. off the promontory a dark speck and a ring of foam mark the *Rundlestone* or *Runnel Stone*, a point of granite 4 yds. long by 2 in breadth rising from the deep sea. Two beacons on the headland indicate its position. But it is the cause of repeated and fatal disasters. In 1854, during a fog, a French brig and 2 English schooners were wrecked upon it one after the other. In 1855 the Trinity-House erected upon it, at considerable expense, an iron beacon, and mast, surmounted by a ball; but in a severe winter's gale of 1856 the whole fabric was washed away. Tol Pedn is well known to geologists as affording fine examples of granite veins in granite, and it likewise contains a quantity of black schorl,

which is distributed in patches, and generally occurs in crystals in a matrix of quartz.

Polostoc, the *Headland in the form of a cap* (the fisherman's cap). It is one of the grandest rocks on Tol Pedn. The granite has the appearance of sable drapery hanging in folds. Directly W. of it a monstrous figure (very striking indeed when the sun is low in the W.) seems to rest with its back against the cliff.

Porthgwarra, Port of Refuge, a romantic fishing station, at the mouth of a wild valley, where a roadway to the shore is formed by tunnels driven through a tongue of granite. It is famous for lobsters, which are caught on the Rundlestone.

Carn Scathe (*a boat*), i.e. a protecting carn for boats, is the E. point of the cove.

Pol Ledan, the *Broad Pool.*
Carn Vessacks, the *Outside Rock*, so called from a rock lying off the point.

St. Levan, a remote and lonely place, consisting of a ch. and a couple of cottages. The Church, though late Perp. (the transept may be rude E. Eng.), is well worth a visit, if only for its situation in a very pretty valley. The bench ends are good. Remark especially two, close to the entrance, representing jesters in cap and bells. In the porch is a curious square stonp. The moor stone rises from the long grass of the chyard, and the impression of desertion and solitude is enhanced by the solemn sound of the distant sea. There is a fine old *cross* in the chyard, and *lich-stones* and a small cross at the entrances. Near the edge of the cliff, and on the rt. bank of the stream, is the ruin of the ancient baptistery or well of St. Levan. "Tradition says that St. Levan spent some of his time at Bodillan, about ¾ m. distant; and the path thence through Rosepletha, which he took to Pedn-mên-an-mere, the 'stone headland by the sea,' to fish, is said to be still visible, being marked by a stronger vegetation."—*Blight*. He caught only one fish a day. But once, when his sister and her child came to visit him, after catching a chad, which he thought not dainty enough to entertain them, he threw it again into the sea. The same fish was caught 3 times: and at last the saint accepted it, cooked, and placed it before his guests, when the child was choked by the first mouthful, and St. Levan saw in the accident a punishment for his dissatisfaction with the fish which Providence had sent him. The chad is still called here " chack-cheeld " = choke-child.

Pedn Mean an Môr, the stone headland in the sea. At its foot is *Manach Point*, the *Monk's Point*, a pile of granite.

Porth Kernow (now spelled *Porthcurnow*), the "Port of Cornwall." The rocks are magnificent, and the sands formed entirely of curious shells. As many as 150 varieties have been found; but the abundance of certain species depends in a measure on the direction of the wind, which, to be favourable, should blow from the shore.

Por Selli, the *Cove of Eels* (*i. e.* conger eels).

Pedn Vounder (*a lane*), a narrow cove. The finest view of Castle Treryn is to be had from this spot. The Logan rock is seen on the second ridge of rocks inland. Off the cove is a ledge of rocks on which lance may be caught in numbers. This is an excellent bait for turbot.

Treryn Castle, or *Treryn Dinas*, the *Fighting Place*, a magnificent headland of granite, which by itself would amply repay any fatigue attendant on an excursion from Penzance; but besides the interest attaching to so vast and lonely a fabric reared by nature on the shore of the ocean, this promontory has claims on the attention of the traveller as the site of the celebrated *Logan Stone*, a block of granite weighing upwards of 60 tons (65·8 tons, Maculloch), but so nicely balanced that it may be made to oscillate on its point of support. In 1824, however, this rocking-stone was deprived of much of its former interest, when a Lieutenant Goldsmith, in command of a revenue cruiser—perhaps incited to the feat by the confident assertion of Borlase, that " it is morally impossible that any lever, or indeed any force, however applied in a mechanical way, can remove the Logan Rock from its present situation " — overturned it with the assistance of his boat's crew. It was a sailor-like but expensive frolic, as the Admiralty ordered the officer (who was nephew to the author of the 'Vicar of Wakefield') to replace the stone. This arduous duty was accomplished at the end of the same year, the Government, at the request of the late Mr. Davies Gilbert (who also subscribed most handsomely to the work), lending machinery, &c., for it. The village of Treen was supported by visitors to the Logan, but after the stone's overthrow it decayed, and was called "Goldsmith's deserted village." The rock basins in the granite are remarkable. They are said to have been used by the Druids in their religious ceremonies. However that may have been, (and there is not the slightest real ground for such a belief), the headland of Treryn is isolated by an entrenchment of earth and stones, forming a triple line of defence, of which the outer vallum is about 15 ft. high. Hence the prefix of *castle*. Most of the Cornish headlands are cut off from the mainland by a sort of scarp and breastwork. The "Black Head" in St. Austell parish is a good example. Others are to be traced on Ramehead, the Dodman, Cudden Point, and Tintagel. At Treryn Castle (besides the 3 lines of fortifications) this scarp occurs faced with stones, and has an entrance with granite

Q 2

posts. These "cliff castles" have been assigned to Britons, Romans, Saxons, Danes, and Irish; but it seems quite impossible to determine by whom they were originally constructed. Similar remains (of which Port Castle and Castle Feather in Wigtonshire are the most important) exist on the W. coast of Scotland. Passing through this ancient camp, we gain the promontory by a narrow isthmus, and scale it by a well-worn path. The best point of view is from the E. group of rocks, whence the Logan stone is well seen, and the *Castle-peak*, the summit of the pile. The granite, shaggy with *byssus* (old man's beard), is weathered into rhomboidal masses, and, assuming in places a porphyritic character, is marked by vivid colours. Some of the caverns rival those in serpentine for the brilliancy of their tints. The botanist may find the common thrift, wild carrot, Sedum telephium, Saxifraga stellaris, and Asplenium marinum, or sea spleenwort; the mineralogist crystals of felspar, veins of red felspar, and schorl, which is principally distributed among the *joints* of the granite. On the E. side are the recess called *Gunpen seez*, i. e. a crooked bay with a dry rock in it, and *Penberth Cove*; on the W. a beautiful bay which sweeps round to the valley of Porthcurnow, and the headland of Pedn Mean an Môr.

Many hours may be pleasantly passed here. Along the steeply shelving shore are numerous fine carns, and so clear is the water that the sands below it may be seen moving as the waves roll past. Cormorants cluster on the outlying rocks, and little companies of mullet and bass wander from cove to cove. In early spring the blue flowers of the *Scilla verna* are plentiful on the turf about the cliffs. (At St. Ives it varies with white and pink flowers.)

From the Logan rock a footpath leads due N. across some fields to the village of *Treen*, ½ m. distant,

where the carriage should be waiting at the small publichouse.

Leaving Treen by a steep descent, and equally steep ascent on the other side, the road passes through an uninteresting country, till we reach *St. Buryan*, now consisting of a ch. and a few wretched cottages, but once a place of note, and the seat of a college of Augustinian canons, said to have been founded by Athelstane after his conquest of Scilly, on the site of the oratory of St. Buriana, "a holy woman of Ireland," according to Leland. Remains of collegiate buildings were destroyed by Shrubshall, the iconoclastic governor of Pendennis Castle under Cromwell, but the supposed site is still called the "Sanctuary." The present ch. (date 15th centy., Henry VII.—but an early Norm. arch is built up on the N. side of the chancel, and the granite font is perhaps E. Eng.), probably the 3rd which has stood here, is of rather large size, with a nave, and N. and S. aisles. It is built of Ludgvan granite, a fine grained stone of a kind which no longer is found in Ludgvan, or the neighbourhood. The fine tower is 90 ft. high. The antiquities of the ch were, with few exceptions, destroyed in 1814, when the building was repaired: and particularly a fine rood screen, the loss of which is much to be deplored. A few of the fragments have been pieced together, and placed across the ch. in their original position. The carving is fine bold work, of grotesque figures and demons among foliage, grapes, &c. A door in the S. wall is the entrance to a staircase, which led to the roodloft. In the belfry, or tower, there is a curious coffin-shaped monument (13th centy.), which was found under the turf in the chyard, and bears an inscription in Norman French to the following effect:—

"Clarice, la femme Gheffrei de Bolleit, git ici: Deo de lalme eit merci: ke por le alme priont di lor de pardon averond."

"Clarice the wife of Geoffrey de Bolleit lies here: God on her soul have mercy: whoever shall pray for her soul shall have 10 days' pardon."

One of the bells, dated 1738, has the inscription, "*Virginis egregiæ vocor campana Mariæ*," a curious instance of post-reformation adoption. Near the porch is a cross raised on 5 steps.

Bolleit is the name of a farm still existing in this parish (see succeeding excursion). The traveller will remark the 2 time-worn crosses which stand, the one by the roadside, and the other elevated on steps in the churchyard, truly venerable objects with their rude sculpture and grey stones corroded by the saltladen air. (Small models of the latter cross are to be obtained at Mr. Prockter's shop in Penzance.) The Ch. is situated in a wild desolate position, 415 ft. above the sea, and commands from the summit of the tower a vast prospect over the Atlantic, extending in a westerly direction to the islands of Scilly, which are distinctly seen on a clear day. *Buryan*, with the parishes of St. Levan and Sennen, is a deanery, and a royal peculiar: *i.e.* held direct from the sovereign, and independent of the jurisdiction of the bishop of the diocese. The annual value of Buryan, in the gift of the Crown, is 1004*l*.

This parish was the birthplace of *William Noy*, attorney-general to Charles I., born 1577. 1 m. S.E. of the ch., on the estate of Borliven, are the remains of an ancient chapel.

Buryan is 6 m. from Penzance. The direct road joins the Penzance and Land's End road about 3½ m. from Penzance. There is nothing of much interest by the way. The traveller can return to Penzance from hence by Lamorna Cove, Paul, and Newlyn; but, as it is 2 or 3 m. longer, we prefer to subjoin a description of that side of the country in another excursion.

6. *Penzance to Lamorna Cove, returning by Mousehole and Newlyn.*

This is a much shorter excursion than many given above, and can be easily done in an afternoon. Lamorna is about 6 m. from Penzance. A most delightful road, or rather terrace, passes along the margin of the bay to this village, and between Newlyn and Mousehole commands such a view of Penzance, its curving shore and background of hills, as would be gained from a vessel coming in from sea. Between Penzance and Newlyn the stranger will observe the ruins of an engine-house, marking the locality of the once celebrated *Wherry Mine*. This was a work of an extraordinary character. Not only were the *levels* driven under the bay, but the shaft was actually sunk through the sea at a distance of 720 feet from the shore. The upper portion consisted of a caisson rising twelve feet from the surface of the water, and the pump-rod was conducted along a stage, or *wherry*, erected upon piles. So exposed were the works of this mine to the casualties of storms, that upon one occasion the platform was carried away by a ship driving ashore. The miners worked at a depth of 100 feet beneath the bay, the water drained through the roof, and the noise of the waves was distinctly heard in the levels. This bold adventure, which was the only mine ever known to have been sunk *in* the sea, was abandoned, 1798, on account of the great expense attending it; 3000*l*. worth of tin was, however, raised one year in the course of the summer. In 1836 it was again worked for a time, but at a heavy loss. Passing the bridge at the opening of the valley of Tolcarne, we enter *Street-an-Nowan* (*i. e.* New street), and *Newlyn*, situated at the foot of *Paul Hill*—a most formidable ascent, and at the bend of the bay which here forms the roadstead of *Gwavas Lake*, being well protected by the land from the prevalent winds.

It may be fairly questioned whether it is better to go or return by the under cliff road from Newlyn to Mousehole; but it is perhaps preferable to ascend Paul Hill, and return under the cliff. This latter road comes out half-way up Paul Hill, after a most tortuous and intricate course through Newlyn streets, or rather passages. This road should not be attempted, if the horses are liable to take fright at the sea, or at being driven near the edge of the cliff.

Having reached the top of Paul Hill, turn, or climb up on a hedge, to look back at the magnificent view. A lane l. leads to *Paul Ch.*, ½ m. distant, and Mousehole. If it be intended to walk along the cliff from Lamorna to Mousehole, it is better to diverge now to see the church. If intending to return to Mousehole in the carriage, it will be better to return to this point, and take Paul Ch. *en route.* The *Church* (Perp.) is of little architectural interest. There is, however, a curious small arch between the nave and N. aisle, constructed on a solid block of masonry, 3 ft. 6 in. above the floor. It is earlier than the rest, and may have been a hagioscope from the transept, retained when the nave was rebuilt. In the N. aisle is a monument to William Godolphin of Trewarveneth (1689), said to have been the last representative of that family; and a curious one to Stephen Hutchins, who gave to the ch. and almshouse, and "saw his desire upon his enemies." It has an old Cornish inscription, the only one now remaining, which is translated—

"Eternal life be his, whose loving care
Gave Paul an almshouse, and the church
repair."

The ch. is chiefly famous, however, for being the burying-place of old "Dolly Pentreath," reputed to be the lost person, who could speak the Cornish language. She died in 1778, at the age of 102. A monument has been lately erected to her memory on the churchyard wall facing the road, with the following inscription:—

"Here lieth interred Dorothy Pentreath, who died in 1778; said to have been the last person who conversed in the ancient Cornish language, the peculiar language of this county from the earliest records, till it expired in the 18th century in this parish of St. Paul. This stone is erected by the Prince Louis Lucien Bonaparte, in union with the Rev. John Garrett, vicar of St. Paul, June 1860. Honour thy father and thy mother, &c. *Ex.* xx. 12."

With a translation into Cornish:—

"Gura Perthi de Taz, Sta. de Mammal de Dythlow Bethens hyr war au tyr neb au Arleth de Dew Ryes deca. *Exod.* xx. 12."

A curious cross, of the usual Cornish type, is also on the churchyard wall. The following Irishism once existed in the ch. in the form of a notice: "The Spanger burnt this ch. in the year 1595." Tradition represents the porch as having escaped the conflagration in consequence of the direction of the wind; and this was confirmed some years ago, when, on making repairs, one of the wooden supporters was found charred at the end nearest the ch. There is a magnificent view from the tower.

Returning to the Buryan road, we soon reach a point which looks down on the beautiful valley leading up from Lamorna. On the opposite side of the valley, and in front of us, on an estate called *Treewoofe* (pronounced *Troore*) is a triple entrenchment, in which is a cave called the *Fogou* (Welsh, *Ogof*; a cavern). It is 36 ft. long, and about 6 ft. high; faced on each side with unhewn and uncemented stones, roofed in with long stone slabs, covered with thick turf. The breadth of the cave is about 5 ft. On the left hand, soon after entering, a narrow passage leads into a branch cave, of considerable extent, constructed in a similar manner. This may be much larger than is at present known, since the roof has fallen in and blocked the end. The entrance, at the S.W.

end, is, as well as the whole structure, almost entirely concealed by the furze which has grown over it. Similar caves exist at Pendeen in St. Just (Excursion 4); at Chapel Euny (Excursion 4); and probably at Chysoyster (Excursion 3). Others, which have never been properly examined, are said to be at Boscaswell in St. Just; at Bos-au-an in Constantine parish; at Rosemorran in Gulval; at Trelowarren in Mawgan; and at Tremenheer in Mullion. Similar caves exist in Scotland (near Aberdeen, and at Blairgowrie, where one has been turned up 100 yds. in length); and in Ireland, where they are almost always connected with "raths" or forts, sometimes within, sometimes outside the walls. In all these caves there are many chambers communicating one with another. They are probably places of concealment in disturbed times, rather than ordinary dwellings; and nothing has as yet been discovered which throws any certain light on their original constructors. In this cave of Treewoofe a party of Royalists are said to have successfully concealed themselves from the troopers of Fairfax.

¼ m. beyond Treewoofe, on the Buryan road, is the hamlet of *Bolleit* or *Boleigh* (pronounced with accent on the last syllable), the *Place of Slaughter*, or the *House of Blood*, traditionally the scene of the final overthrow of the Britons by Athelstan in the year 936. The *Pipers*, rt. of the road, are two large upright stones, 12 and 16 ft. in height, standing about a furlong apart, and perhaps mark the burial-place of those slain in this fight. They have received their present appellation from their vicinity to a stone circle called the Merry Maidens, but are also known as the *Giant's Grave*, a name which is certainly more appropriate, if we consider them as memorials of a place of sepulture. It may, however, have originated in their resemblance to the head and tail stones of a grave. Beyond Boleigh we pass the hamlet of *Newtown*. We are here on high ground, with a delightful view over the country, which is rendered beautiful by the wild valleys and the many crofts of furze, heather, and grey stones. A turn in the road brings us to a wayside *cross* and a solitary cottage. Immediately opposite, by the side of a gate, is a *holed stone*, and in a field l. of the road, on the estate of Rosemodris, a celebrated circle known as the *Dawns Mên*, the *Stone Dance* or *Dancing Stones*, and popularly as the *Merry Maidens*. This remarkable monument once consisted of 19 stones, 16 of which are now upright, and is supposed to have originated the name of the farm on which it is situated (Rosemodris—*i.e.* Rhôs modris—the moor of the circle, the old word *modris* or *moderenq* signifying *an orb, ring*, or *circle*). The whimsical title is said to be derived from a legend that these stones were once young women, who were thus transformed for dancing on the Sabbath. Lhuyd, however, has given a more rational view of its origin, and says that the stones " are so called of the common people, on no other account than that they are placed in a circular order and so make an area for dancing." A little distance to the W. is a large upright stone, similar to those at the Giant's Grave; and close at hand (as before mentioned) the holed stone to which the Druid priests are *supposed* (by Borlase) to have fastened their victims, while they went through the ceremonies preparatory to sacrifice. The circle stands on a hill-side in a lonely country, and is a most interesting relic of antiquity.

Lamorna Cove, formerly one of the most romantic spots on the coast, but now, being selected for the site of some granite works, it is little better than a mason's yard. It is curious that the granite on the E. side only is of sufficiently fine grain to be valuable; the W. side is much intersected by quartz veins.

1 m. W. of Lamorna is the headland of *Carn Boscawen*, remarkable for some rocks so placed as to form an archway, through which a person can pass. Their arrangement has been attributed by Borlase to the Druids, but is probably natural. *Boskenna*, C. D. Bevan, Esq., but the property of Thomas Paynter, Esq., is near this headland, and is as wild and secluded a place of residence as can well be imagined.

A good walker will require little longer time to walk to Mousehole, which is about 2 m., along the cliff, than a carriage will to return by the road. To the geologist the cliffs W. of Mousehole are extremely interesting on account of the granite veins, which there penetrate the slate at the junction of the two formations, becoming schorlaceous as they enter the slate.

Both Mousehole and Newlyn are colonies of fishermen, with narrow paved lanes, glistening with pilchard scales in the season—with external staircases, and picturesque interiors, of which glimpses are obtained through an open doorway or window. They will exceedingly delight artists who entertain "a proper sense of the value of dirt," and in this respect, indeed, may call to mind the semi-barbarous habitations of some foreign countries—such as Spain. The perfume of garlic fills the air, and other odours not so sweet hasten the step of the traveller. These arise from little enclosures which front every cottage-door. They are neatly bordered with stones or shells, and consist—not of a flower-bed, but of a dunghill, formed chiefly of the refuse of fish, in which the process of decay is hastened by the activity of many unhappy-looking fowls and pigs. It is a custom of the country, but how it can be tolerated passes comprehension. Mouse-hole is prettily placed at the mouth of a coomb. Though not the sweetest of places in one sense of the word, it offers pleasing subjects for the pencil, and we may draw attention to the rocky point by the pier as worthy of a sketch, in connexion with the thatched cottages and distance of Penzance. The pier is of singular construction, the granite stones being arranged vertically. Beyond it is a curious house, the *Keigwin Arms*, formerly residence of the Keigwins, a family known for John K., who assisted Lhuyd in his Cornish grammar, and was probably the last person thoroughly acquainted with the old language. Here, in 1595, when the Spaniards landed at Mousehole, lived Jenkin K., the squire of the place, whose death by a shot from one of the galleys caused a panic among the inhabitants, who had assembled to oppose the invaders. The cannon-ball by which he was killed is still preserved, and is kept in the cottage opposite this inn. The walls of the house were originally 4 ft. thick, and the timbers, so at least says "the oldest inhabitant," were grown in the forest which now lies submerged on the shore of Mount's Bay. Some 50 years ago, when smuggling was rife along this coast, and tubs of spirit were netted in preference to pilchards, the Mousehole people were by no means regarded as models of excellence from a moral point of view; but John Wesley and his followers effected a great change by their preaching, and, much to their credit, reclaimed the fishermen from their former reckless and disorderly habits. Drunkenness is now almost unknown in the place, and Sunday is reverenced by all as a sacred day. The fishermen have built for themselves an additional pier at a cost of 1400*l*., 1200*l*. of which was raised by their own joint bond, which they are now discharging by a yearly contribution from each boat. Mousehole was anciently called *Porth Enys*

(Enys, an island), from *St. Clement's Isle*, a rock of slaty felspar lying off the harbour, and on which there was once a chapel. By Mousehold Island the torpedo, or electric eel, is often caught of great size. The rare boar-fish is caught off the Runnel Stone. The present name of the village may excite the curiosity of the traveller. He will probably place little faith in the popular tradition that it has been derived from a cavern on the shore called the *Mouse Hole*; but the suggestion that it originated in the Cornish words *Môz-hêl*, or *Mouz-hel*, the Maids' Brook or River, deserves more attention. To the geologist the shore west of the village is interesting on account of the granite veins which penetrate the slate at the junction of the two formations, becoming schorlaceous as they enter the slate. The junction is about 100 ft. beyond the pier, the Mousehole about 400. It is a rough and difficult walk, but the cavern is often visited, even by ladies.

The road from hence to Newlyn, for about 2 m., follows the indentations of the cliff, affording magnificent views of the bay and its environs. From Newlyn it is possible to pass, in a light carriage, at low water from one end of the village to the other; but when the tide is in, the hill must be scaled through the narrow ways of Newlyn, till we emerge half way down Paul Hill on the main road to Penzance.

7. *The Scilly Islands.*

The Islands of Scilly are about 30 m. from the Land's End, and may be reached by steamer from Penzance. The inducements to this trip are the remote and wild position of these islands, the beauty and grandeur of the rock scenery, and some antiquities. Lodging-houses and good inns are to be found at St. Mary's. The group consists of about 40 islands bearing herbage, but only six are inhabited; the others, with a number of islets of rock, being tenanted by gulls and rabbits.

The names of those meriting notice by their size are—

		Acres.
St. Mary's	about	1600
Tresco	„	700
St. Martin's	„	550
St. Agnes	„	350
Bryher	„	300
Samson	„	80
St. Helen's	„	40
Annette	„	40
Jean	„	35
Great Ganniley	„	35
Arthur	„	30
Great and Little Ganniornic		10
Northwithial	„	8
Gweal	„	8
Little Ganniley	„	5

The islands of Scilly were known to the Greeks under the name of the *Cassiterides—Tin Islands*. Ausonius is the first writer who describes them as the *Sillinæ Insulæ*, and this appellation, now changed into Scilly, is differently said to be derived from *Silya*, the Cornish for *conger*, and *Sulléh*, a British word signifying *the rocks consecrated to the sun*. The latter derivation will be probably adopted by the traveller who has beheld these islands from the Land's End by sunset, when they appear as if they were embedded in the setting luminary; but the real etymology is most probably to be sought in a Cornish word signifying "divided," *i.e.* separated from the mainland. With respect to their history, they were occasionally used by the Romans as a place of banishment; and in the 10th centy. annexed to the English crown by Athelstan. In the great civil war they were long held for the king. In 1645, after the defeat of the royal cause in the West, they sheltered Prince Charles; but a hostile fleet having formed a cordon round the islands, the prince fled to

Jersey when the first opportunity occurred. The most memorable event of which these isles have been the scene was their fortification in 1649 by Sir John Grenville, the royalist who took so active a part in the restoration of Charles II. He converted these lonely rocks into a stronghold for privateers, and with these he swept the neighbouring seas, and so crippled the trade of the Channel that the Parliament at length fitted out a powerful fleet under Blake and Sir George Ayscue, and to this Grenville was forced to surrender June 1651. At an early period in our history the isles of Scilly belonged to the crown, but on the endowment of the Abbey of Tavistock were granted in part to that establishment, the remainder, in the reign of Edw. I., being held of the king at a rent of 300 puffins. They are now included in the Duchy of Cornwall, but how they became merged in it is not well understood. In the reign of Elizabeth they appear to have been divided among a number of proprietors, from whom they were bought up by the crown; and from that period to the year 1830 they were rented by the family of Godolphin. At present Augustus Smith, Esq., M.P. for Truro, is the lessee, or Lord Proprietor, of these lonely isles, and a most kind and beneficent ruler, continually studying the welfare of his subjects. The inhabitants, who are principally sailors, fishermen, and pilots, are a long-lived race, when spared by the boisterous sea which surrounds them; but the frequency with which this element demanded a victim, previously to recent improvements in their pilot and fishing craft, is denoted by a saying, that *for one who dies a natural death nine are drowned*. The chief produce of Scilly is an early potato, which within the last few years has given rise to a very flourishing trade, many tons of this vegetable being annually shipped to the markets of London and Bristol. The total Pop. in 1851 was 2627; in 1861, 2431.

The isles of Scilly are wholly composed of granite, and form an outlying member of that series of granitic highlands which extends through Cornwall to Dartmoor. They are traditionally said to have been once united to the mainland—as the other granite districts are with each other—by a tract of slate, which is mentioned by early writers under the name of the *Lyonesse*, and is said to have been overwhelmed by a sudden irruption of the ocean. The fisherman still points to the Seven Stones as "the City;" and it is not uninteresting to call to mind that about 50 years ago, during a violent storm, the seas threatened to form a junction between Hayle and Marazion, and thus to sever the next link in the chain. The granite of Scilly consists in general of a coarse-grained mixture of felspar, quartz, and mica, often stained by iron, and therefore of little economical value; but hornblende, schorl, and chlorite are in some localities found in it; and in Taylor's Island prisms of tourmaline occupying the place of the mica. As a feature of the scenery it is highly interesting. Its principal ingredient, the felspar, is often of a deep red colour, which beautifully contrasts with the tints of the sea; whilst the rocks of the coast, continually battered by storms, present impressive pictures of natural decay. In different places the granite will be found to vary in composition, structure, and condition. In Water-mill Bay, St. Mary's, it is seamed by numberless joints, which give it the appearance of a stratified rock; the caverns of Piper's Hole, in St. Mary's and Tresco, are roofed by a secondary or regenerate granite; Holy Vale, in St. Mary's, contains a china-clay, or decomposed granite; and the beach of Porth Hellick (Hillick, *i. e.* willows) is strewn with stones of a binary compound of quartz and felspar. The destruction of the felspar in these granite rocks has served to decorate the shore with the liberated quartz and mica. The southern beaches of Tresco are mainly composed of pure white quartz, and the sands of Permellin, near Hugh Town, streaked by curved lines of black mica. With respect to the climate and the botany, the mean temperature of the summer is 58°, of the winter 45°; the chief botanical feature the fern tribe, and in particular *Asplenium marinum*, or sea-spleenwort, which grows to an uncommon length in the damp caverns of the coast. The following rarer species are enumerated by Mr. North:—

Osmunda regalis	Royal or flowering fern.
Asplenium Adiantum nigrum	Black maidenhair.
A. Ruta muraria	Wall-rue fern.
A. lanceolatum	Hudson's spleenwort.
Aspidium Filix femina	Lady fern.
A. Filix mas	Male fern.
A. recurvum	Bree's fern.
A. dilatatum	Broad-shield fern.
A. spinulosum	A variety of the preceding.

All of these, including the *Asplenium marinum*, are to be found in many parts of Cornwall, particularly in the neighbourhood of Penzance. The botanist, as he rambles round the islands, may also notice the *Archill* (Rocella tinctoria), a lichen which yields a valuable red dye, and grows abundantly in Scilly. He will find the flora, as well as the topography, of these islands fully described in Mr. North's ' Week in the Isles of Scilly,' published by Rowe of Penzance, and Longman of London, in 1850. The geology forms the subject of a most interesting paper by Joseph Carne, Esq., printed in the Report of the R. Geol. Soc. of Cornw. for 1850.

St. Mary's (Pop. in 1861, 1532, circumf. about 9 m.) is the principal island, and *Hugh Town* its capital. (*Inns*: Mumford's and Bluoitt's.) Hugh Town is built on a sandy isthmus which connects a peninsula with St. Mary's. This peninsula is crowned by Star Castle, at an elevation of 110 ft. above the sea, and was probably the origin of the name of the town, as Borlase tells us that *heugh* signifies a high piece of land projecting into the water, and the word has that meaning in Scotland. The town has a pier, re-constructed in 1835-8, and an excellent harbour called *the Pool*, bounded N. by *Carn Morval*, and entered between the *Cow* and the *Calf* rocks. The most prominent and interesting building on the island is *Star Castle*, a fortress erected in the reign of Elizabeth, and probably so named from the star-like form of its walls, which project in eight salient angles. Over the entrance is the date 1593, and the letters E. R.; in the vicinity of the castle, *the Garrison*, with its batteries, park, and delightful promenade. At the E. end of the main street stands the *New Church*, built in 1835, and chiefly at the expense of the present Lord Proprietor. The *Old Church* (in which are some curious old monuments of the time of the Puritans—particularly one of the Governor of the island during the Commonwealth) is situated ¼ m. from the town, and, though partly a ruin, is still used for the burial service. In the New Church are memorials of those who perished with Sir Cloudesley Shovel in Oct. 1707. This was a melancholy disaster. A fleet, on its return from the siege of Toulon, came unexpectedly upon Scilly in thick and tempestuous weather. The admiral's ship, the Association, struck the *Gilstone Rock*, and went to pieces in a few minutes. The Eagle and Romney, line-of-battle ships, shared a similar fate, and only one man was saved out of these three ships. He was thrown upon a reef called the *Hellwethers*, where he was obliged to remain for some days before he could be rescued. The fireships Phœnix and Firebrand ran ashore; the Royal

Anne passed the *Trenemer Rock* so closely that it carried away her quarter gallery; and the St. George had even a narrower escape. She and the Association struck the Gilstone together, but the wave which stove in the one floated the other into deep water. 2000 persons perished on this memorable occasion.

In a walk round St. Mary's (keeping the sea on your rt.) the following points of interest will successively present themselves. — The bay of *S. Porcrasa.—Buzza Hill*, commanding a beautiful view. The curious name is rendered Bosow by Borlase, and is said to have been derived from a family so called. S. W. of the windmill you will observe a *barrow.* — *Dutchman's Carn*, and beneath it the *Bluff*, a bold rock in the sea. — *Peninnis Head*, a magnificent group of rocks, and by far the finest headland in the islands. Here you will particularly notice, on the higher ground, the *Kettle and Pans*, the largest rock-*basins* in the W. of England ; the *Monk's Cowl*, a mass of granite above an amphitheatre 100 ft. high ; the *Tooth Rock*, or *Elephant's Tusk*, S. of the Kettle and Pans, with a rock-*basin* on its vertical side, a puzzle to those antiquaries who maintain that such cavities were made by the Druids, and once held holy water ; *Pitt's Parlour*, a small recess under the Tooth Rock; and beneath the Parlour a deep cleft, into which the sea is perpetually plunging. Here, too, the geologist should observe the structure and the *weathering* of the granite. On the W. side of the headland the *joints* are so closely arranged as to resemble the cleavage of slate rock ; at Pitt's Parlour the granite has been divided into cubical blocks by the action of the weather in the vertical and horizontal joints; and at another place separated at the vertical joints alone, detached slabs having been formed, which stand on end, and are in some instances united by the centres.—*Piper's Hole*, a small cavern, containing a spring of fresh water, and roofed with regenerate granite, and which the islanders absurdly represent as passing under sea to Piper's Hole in Tresco. — The *Pulpit Rock*, a fine example of decomposition in the horizontal joints, with a *sounding-board* 47 ft. in length by 12 in breadth, to the top of which you should climb. Below, in the sea, is a lonely rock called *Carrick-stirne;* and on the high ground the *Tower*, used as a station in the trigonometrical survey, and 140 ft. above the level of mean water.—*Carn Lea*, the W. point of *Old Town Bay*, decorated with pillars of granite. At *Old Town* are some fragments of an ancient castle, and in the neighbourhood some remains of the *Old Church*. Ascend *Maypole Hill* for a view of *Holy Vale.* — *Tolmên Point*, the E. termination of Old Town Bay, and so called from a *tolmên*, or holed stone, upon it —*Porth Minick*, with a white quartzose beach and rocks of red granite.—*Blue Carn*, the S. point of the island, a wild group of tabular rocks, indented with basins. — The *Giant's Castle*, a carn anciently fortified as a cliff-castle. Here there are numerous rock-basins, and on the W. side of the promontory, near the edge of the cliff, a *logan stone*, 45 tons in weight, so exactly poised that a child can move it. N., several barrows on the neighbouring hill. — *Porth Hellick* (*i. e.* cove of willows), the bay in which the body of Sir Cloudesley Shovel was washed ashore. On the W. side is the *Drum Rock*, a reputed tolmên of the Druids, and on the beach some stones of a binary granite (quartz and felspar). On the S. E. side, *Dick's Carn*, a fine example of decomposition in the horizontal joints of the granite ; and S.E. of Dick's Carn the *Clapper Rocks*, on which may be found many of the largest and most curious rock-basins in the island, some formed on the vertical sides, and others on surfaces which are nearly in contact with upper rocks.

In Oct. 1840, Porth Hellick bay was the scene of an extraordinary escape from shipwreck, when the brig Nerina, of Dunkirk, drove into it keel uppermost. having been capsized in the Atlantic two days previously. During this interval four men and a boy, by crouching close to the keelson of the vessel, had contrived to keep their heads above water, though immersed to the waist, but, fearing that they would be suffocated for want of air, one worked incessantly for some time to make a hole in the roof. Fortunately this purpose, which would have sealed their fate, was prevented by the knife breaking. It is not the least remarkable part of the narrative that two pilot-boats on the afternoon of the second day fell in with the wreck and took it in tow for an hour, when, night approaching, and a heavy sea running, they were obliged to abandon it. Had it not been for this circumstance, the unfortunate Frenchmen entombed in this floating sepulchre would have been drifted by the current clear of the islands. S. of this bay, on Sallakee Hill, are two ancient *crosses*, now part of a stone hedge; and E., on the high ground, the *Giant's Chair*, from which, it is said, the arch-Druid was accustomed to watch the rising sun; and the *Sun Rock*, N. of which (¼ m.) are three large rock-basins in a cavity where a tool could by no possibility have been used. — *Deep Point*, the easternmost point of the island.—*Pellew's Redoubt*, named after Lord Exmouth, who, when Capt. Pellew, commanded at the Scilly Islands.—*Newquay*, on the S. side of *Watermill Bay*; and between it and the stream, which here flows to the sea, the *porphyritic beds of St. Mary's*, a mass of granite which has excited much discussion among geologists, as apparently displaying a distinct stratification. "The question at issue," says Mr. Carne, "is whether the apparent strata are joints, or whether the whole is of slaty structure."—*Pendrathen Quay*, and off the shore the *Crow Rock*, a mark for vessels entering Crow Sound.—*Inisidgen Point*, the N.E. extremity of the island, crowned by a stone-covered barrow, and interesting for its rocks. On this part of the island is the *Telegraph*, commanding a panoramic view, the top being 204 ft. above the sea; N.E. of it the *Longstone*, a rock-pillar 9 ft. high; N., *Bant's Carn*; and S. W. of this carn a barrow roofed with stones.— *Carn Morval*, N.E. of St. Mary's Pool, a point of view which should not be neglected. —*Porthloo Bay*, with two island rocks, the northernmost, *Taylor's Island*, remarkable for a beautiful variety of granite containing prisms of tourmaline in the place of the mica—*Permellin Bay* (formerly Porth Mellyn), where the beach is almost wholly composed of fine particles of quartz, and near low-water mark streaked by bands of black mica, which was once collected for writing sand. On the hill above the bay are *Harry's Walls*, the remains of a fortification commenced in the reign of Hen. VIII., but never finished; and an isolated rock which has been termed a Druidic idol. The W. point of this bay is *Carn Thomas*.

Having completed his survey of St. Mary's, the stranger will be ready to embark for the other islands, which will be now described in the order in which they naturally occur. They may be conveniently divided into 3 separate groups, each of which will be sufficient for one day's excursion. Thus, 1. St. Agnes, Annette, and the rocks further W., commonly known as the *Off Islands*; 2. Samson, Bryher, Tresco, and St. Helen's; 3. St. Martin's and the Eastern Islands.

St. Agnes (Pop. in 1861, 200) is separated from St. Mary's by St. Mary's Sound, and at high water, spring-tides, divided by the sea into two parts, that on the N.E. being termed the *Gugh*. Upon this there are several stone-covered barrows; near the centre a rock-pillar, 9 ft. in length, called the

Route 29.—*Islands of Scilly.* Sect. II.

Old Man cutting Turf; off the N.W. point the *Kittern*, deserving notice for its picturesque form; and at the S. extremity, between the Gugh and St. Agnes, the *Core*, in which the islanders often capture in a single night as many as 40,000 fish. In St. Agnes, properly so called, are several interesting points. Proceeding from the Gugh round the S. end of the island, the stranger will be delighted by the beautiful carns of granite, decked with emerald turf, adorning the slopes of the shore. Above St. Warna Bay he should notice the *Nag's Head*, an example of the fantastic effects produced by the abrasion of the prevailing winds. Beyond this bay is the carn of *Castlebeam*, and then *Cumberdril Point*, remarkable for its pointed rocks. In St. Nicholas or Priglis (Port Eglise) Bay stands the *ch.*, which some 40 years ago was erected to supply the place of a smaller building, which is said to have been built with salvage-money paid to the islanders for rescuing a French ship from the rocks in 1685. Beyond Priglis Bay is the *lighthouse*, 72 ft. high, commanding a beautiful view, and displaying a revolving light, which is seen by mariners in connection with the lights on the Seven Stones and Longships; and, lastly, S.E. of the lighthouse, on Wingletang Downs, the *Punchbowl Rock*, so called from its rock basin, which is nearly 4 ft. in diam.

Annette (uninhab.) is separated from St. Agnes by Smith's Sound, which contains the *Great Smith* and *Little Smith*. The leading feature of the island is *Annette Head*, its N.W. extremity. In a westerly direction the rapid tides surge and eddy among innumerable rocks, objects picturesque and pleasing to tourists wafted round them by a summer breeze, but as terrible when beheld white with foam and cataracts of raging water from the deck of some luckless vessel driving towards the land. They are the "dogs" of Scilly, and as fierce as those which howled around the monster of the Italian seas. S. of the island is the reef of the *Hellwethers*; S.W. of this reef, *Meledgan*, and beyond Meledgan *Gorregan*; W. of Gorregan, *Rosevean* and *Rosevear*; and S.W. of these the *Gilstone*, on which Sir Cloudesley Shovel was wrecked. N.W. of Rosevear *Great* and *Little Crebawethan*, memorable for the loss of the Douro, with all hands, in Jan. 1843; and between Crebawethan and Rosevear, *Jacky's Rock*, the scene of the destruction of the Thames steamer in 1841, when only 4 persons were saved out of 65. N. of Crebawethan are the *Gunner*, *Nundeeps*, and *Crim Rocks*, treacherous ledges, which have abruptly closed the career of many a gallant seaman; and W. of all the *Bishop Rock* (7 m. from H. Town), standing sentinel, as it were, to this formidable host, but at high water immersed to the chin. It is now crowned by a granite lighthouse, a triumph of the engineering skill and perseverance of Mr. Walker, who had previously attempted to build one of a different material. This was to have been formed of cast-iron columns, sunk in the rock, and stayed to each other by rods of wrought iron; and had been nearly completed in 1850, when it totally disappeared in a terrible gale which arose on the night of Feb. 5, simultaneously with an eruption of Vesuvius. The present structure was then planned, but it was the work of 2 years to lay the foundation stone. It was placed at the level of low water and on a sunken rock fully exposed to the restless roll of the Atlantic.

Samson. In his passage across the Road the voyager will observe the *Nut Rock*, the mark for the principal anchorage. On the W. side of Samson are several rugged islets, and, in particular, *Scilly*, which gives name to the whole archipelago. W. is *Mincarlo*; further W. *Maiden Bower*; N. of Mincarlo, *Scilly*, divided in two parts by a chasm; and S. of Mincarlo

Great and *Little Minalto*. Nearer the shore are *Gweal*, an islet of 8 acres, with a tenantry of gulls; and *Castle Bryher*, some 90 ft. high, a rock rising conspicuously above all the others. The only act incumbent on a visitor to Samson is to ascend to its highest point for the sake of the view; but those who delight in cliff-scenery will of course ramble round the island and peer into its numerous cavernous recesses.

Bryher (Pop. in 1861, 115), a wild and rugged island, derives its name from *bré*, an old Cornish word signifying a hill. Its highest lands are happily on the W. side, for they add much interest to the deep romantic bays which the stormy Atlantic has excavated on that side. On the S. is *Gweal*, to which you may walk dry-shod at low tides; on the N.W. a spring of fresh water on the shore; and N. the promontory of *Shipman Head*, one of the finest among the islands; it is about 60 ft. high, and separated from the mainland by a deep and fearful chasm, hedged in by precipices. The N.E. side of the island forms with Tresco the harbour of *New Grimsby*, whose leading features are a rock in mid-channel, called *Hangman's Isle*, and *Cromwell's Castle* on the opposite shore. Before you leave Bryher you should ascend *Watch Hill*.

Tresco (Pop. in 1861, 399), second only to St. Mary's in point of size, is the first island in dignity, being the residence of the Lord Proprietor, whose mansion occupies the site of the ancient *Abbey of Tresco*, which was founded as early as the 10th centy., and annexed to Tavistock Abbey in the reign of Hen. I. In front of the house is a delightful terrace, and above it a hill which commands a panoramic view of the islands. With Mr. Smith's permission the stranger should visit the gardens, which strikingly illustrate the genial and equable nature of the climate, and contain, in addition to their rich store of plants, some remains of the old *Abbey-ch.*, consisting of walls of granite and arches of a red arenaceous stone supposed to have been brought from Normandy, the whole mantled with geraniums. Here, too, are the *Abbey ponds*, covering 50 acres. These gardens are well worth a visit. The rocks are covered with large plants of the Cape Fig marigold, Mesembryanthemums of various colours, hedges of Geraniums above 6 ft. high, and amongst plants rare to find out of doors are the Camphor laurel and different species of Eurybia, Acacia lophantha, and the Peruvian Gunera scabra. The Norfolk Island pine, Araucaria excelsa, lived out for about 5 years, but died at last. Some large Aloes by the ruins of the abbey make a very striking feature; some 24-lb. round shot are also piled up here: they were discovered in removing the rubbish while clearing the ruins. And at the end of one of the walks is placed the old fire-basket by which the light at St. Agnes was exhibited. Ostriches run about the grounds, and their eggs are used by the inhabitants and visitors of the abbey. The golden oriole has been known to build its nest in these gardens. The road from the abbey to the village—which is, in part, called *Dolphin*, probably a corruption of Godolphin, after the name of the family who so long rented these islands—commands a beautiful view of Shipman's Head, and, on a stormy day, of the huge billows leaping its rocks. This headland is well seen, too, from *Charles's Castle*, a ruin on the W. side of the island, 155 ft. above the sea, and immediately over *Oliver Cromwell's Castle*, a circular tower with walls 12 ft. thick, and a battery of 9-pounders on its roof. At the N.E. point of the island is *Piper's Hole*, a deep cavern, whose recesses may be explored for a distance of 600 ft.; but a torch and a boat will be required, for the cavern contains a pool of fresh water which varies in size, but is often nearly 200 ft. across. The roof is extremely interesting. It is formed entirely of regenerate granite, and in this are imbedded large boulders of the original rock. There are other caverns in the vicinity of this Hole, and particularly the *Gun*, which contains a spring or *well* of fresh water. Off the N. side of Tresco lie *Northwithial*, and many picturesque rocks. *Menavawr* is, perhaps, the most beautiful of all the islets of Scilly (especially when seen from the N.), rising in three distinct peaks, 139 ft. above the sea. *Rounl Island* also presents an imposing group of carns. It is 18 ft. higher than Menavawr, and the chosen haunt of puffins. On the E. side of Tresco are the harbour of *Old Grimsby* and the battery of the *Old Blockhouse*; and off the S. side of the island a rock called the *Mare*, bearing some resemblance to the head and neck of a horse.

St. Helen's (called St. Elid's by Borlase) adjoins Tresco, and is an uncultivated island stocked with deer and goats, the only building upon it being the *Pest House*, which has seldom an occupant. You should make the circuit of this island. The rocks are fine, and on the N. side is a long and deep chasm, perpetually reverberating the dismal sound of the sea.

Tean, between St. Helen's and St. Martin's, is a warren of white rabbits, and principally remarkable for the beauty of its bays. You will notice a rock called *Penbrose* to the N. of it.

St. Martin's (185 Inhab. in 1861) has several points of interest. At its S.E. extremity are the *Higher Town*, *Cruther's Bay*, and *Cruther's Hill*, some 70 ft. above the sea; and on the S. and W. coasts *St. Martin's Flats*, which should be diligently searched for shells. At the W. end *Tinckler's Point*, bearing a so-called Druidic idol, and near it the remains of 2 sacred circles. On the N.W., *Pernagie Isle*, and *Plumb Island*, and the *Lion Rock*, all accessible from the land at low water. N., *St. Martin's Bay* and *White Island*, which is connected with St. Martin's at low tide, and has a deep cavern (or old tin-mine) on its E. side. E., *St. Martin's Head*, 160 ft. high, crowned by the *Day Mark*, and commanding the most beautiful and extraordinary sight in these seas—the whole cluster of those numberless, fantastic, many-coloured rocks which are known as the *Eastern Islands*. The most northerly of these is *Hanjague*, or the *Sugarloaf* (due E. of St. Martin's Head), rising abruptly to a height of 83 ft. from a depth of 25 fath.; the next to the N., *Nortor*, an islet of 3 acres, distinguished by as many rocky points. *Great Ganniley* is the largest of the group, 107 ft. high, and connected at low water with *Little Ganniley*, and with *Great* and *Little Inisvouls*. Near them is *Ragged Island*, of a wasted form; and S.W. *Menewethan*, a noble granite pile, 47 ft. above the mean level of the sea. *Great* and *Little Arthur* are further interesting for their ancient barrows, protected by slabs of granite; and *Great* and *Little Ganniornic* of some importance for their size. From the heights of these islands, or from St. Martin's Head, you will observe to the N. a line of foam, which marks the dangerous reef called the *Seven Stones*; this is situated about 9 m. from Scilly (13½ from Hugh Town), and is pointed out to mariners by a lightship.

(353)

INDEX.

ABBOTSHAM.

A.

Abbotsham Court, 170.
Acton Castle, 315.
Adams the astronomer, birthplace, 206.
Adit, the Great, 280.
Advent, 208, 212.
Affeton Barton, 164.
Agnes, St., 260. In Scilly, 349.
Agnes' Beacon, St., 260.
Aire, 336.
Alan, river, 212.
A-la-Ronde, 42.
Albert Bridge, 84, 210.
Aldercombe, 279.
Alphington, 53.
Alternun, 205.
Alverton, 299.
Alwington, 188.
Amalebria, 121.
Amalveor, 321.
Amal-widden, 121.
Amicombe Hill, 155.
Amphitheatres, 260, 308, 330.
Anchor Stone, 61.
Anguidal Down, 336.
Annery, 167.
Annette, 350. Head, 350.
Anstis Cove, 91.
Anthony, St., 285. In Méneage, St., 311.
Anthracite beds, 172.
Antiquities, xxiii.
Antony, 261. In East, 235. House, 84, 233.
Appledore, 171.
Apron-string, 306.
Archerton, 114.
Arish-mows, L
Arlington, 184. Court, 169.
Armed Knight, 335, 337.
Arthur, Great and Little, 352.
Arthur, King, birthplace, 217. Legends, 219, 229.
Arthur's Bed, 239. Cups and Saucers, 219. Grave, 212. Hall, 206. Hunting-Seat, 229.
Arwenack, 282.
Ashburton, 112.
Ashcombe, 110.
Ashe, 25.
Ash Hole, 97.

BEAM.

Ashley Combe, 178.
Ashton, 110.
Asparagus Island, 306.
Atherington, 166.
Austell, St., 250.
Austen's Engine, 249.
Austin's Bridge, 62, 116.
Auswell Tor, 111.
Avenues, Druidic, xxv, 66, 126, 128, 129, 140, 239.
Aveton Gifford, 157.
Avon valley, 157.
Awliscombe, 27.
Axe, river, 21, 25. Valley, 11.
Axminster, 23. Carpets, 23. Tradition, history, minster, 23. Excursions, 24.
—— to Exeter, by rail, 25. By road, 12.
Axmouth, 32.

B.

Babbacombe, 91.
Badcock, Samuel, birthplace, 164.
Badgery Water, 176.
Bagtor, 112.
Bairdown, 115. Man, 137. Tor, 137.
Bake, 234.
Balleswidden Mine, xlv, 329.
Bampton, 195.
—— to Holsworthy, 195.
Bantham, 107.
Bant's Carn, 349.
Barbrick Mill, 174.
Barclay, Alex., his prebend, 29.
Barle valley, 180. River, 196.
Barnstaple, 168. Stat., 168. Fair, 168.
Barons Down, 198.
Barricane, 187.
Barrow Down, 253.
Bartiné, 329.
Basil's Well, 205.
Basset's Cove, 288.
Bassett Park, 42.
Batten Cliffs, 262.
Beaches, ancient, xxii.
Beacon, the, 42, 101. Hill, 39, 244, 278.
Beam Mine, 251.

BLACKABROOK.

Beasands, 101.
Beast Point, 109.
Beckamoor Cross, 153.
Becky Fall, 121.
Bector Cross, 110.
Beechwood House, 66.
Beer, 34. Head, 33. Quarry, 34.
Beer Alston, 84. Ferrers, 153, 154.
Beggar's Island, 233.
Belidden Amphitheatre, 308.
Bellamine's Tor, 210.
Bellurian Cove, 105.
Belovely Beacon, 211.
Belstone, 45, 48. Cleave, 48. Tor, 48.
Bel Tor, 134.
Bendon, 34.
Benjie Tor, 114.
Benuet's Monastery, St., 210.
Berry Court, 277. Head, 90, 97. House, 15. Pound, 135. Tower, 243.
Berrynarbor, 184.
Berry Pomeroy Castle, 60.
Bessie's Cove, 314.
Bickington House, 169.
Bickleigh, 22, 86, 141. Bridge, 22, 143. Court, 22. Vale 86, 139, 142. Stat., 142.
Bicton, 40.
Bideford, 169. Bay, 189.
Bigadon, 116.
Bigbury, 157. Bay, 107.
Biggletubben, 321.
Binhamy, 276.
Birds, collections of, 52, 72, 86, 256, 295, 296. Of Dartmoor, 134.
Biscovey, 249.
Bishop Rock, in Scilly, 350. In Mount's Bay, 312.
Bishop's Court, 30.
Bishop's Nympton, 165.
Bishop's Tawton, 167.
Bishop's Teignton, 53.
Bishopstowe, 91.
Bitton House, 57.
Blachford, 66.
Blackadown, 162.
Blackaven, 48.
Blackabrook, 137, 139.

INDEX.

BLACKBOROUGH.

Blackborough Down, 27.
Blackbrook, the, 111.
Blackbury Castle, 19.
Black Down Hills, 2. Camp, 102.
Black Head, 268, 310.
Black Jack, xlv.
Black Pit, 215. Pits, 179.
Blackpool, 102.
Black Rock, 281.
Black Stone, 120, 121.
Black Tor, 119. Great, 47.
Blake, Adm., birthplace, 2.
Blanch-down Wood, 112.
Blank's Mill, 108.
Blazey, St., 247. Gate, 249.
Bleu Bridge, 124.
Blisland, 210.
Bloody Corner, 171.
Blow-holes, 228, 106.
Blue Anchor, 194.
Blue Carn, 148.
Boconnoc, 247. Cross, 245.
Bodennar, 126.
Bodley, Sir Thomas, birthplace, 7.
Bodmin, 210, 242. Moors, 205. Road stat., 210, 242.
Bodrigan's Leap, 260.
Bodruthan Steps, 228.
Bolbury Down, 107.
Bolerium (ancient), 134.
Bolham House, 21.
Bolleit, 141, 141.
Bolt Head, 106. Tail, 107.
Bone, Henry, birthplace, 256.
Boniface, St., birthplace, 161.
Boringdon House, 142.
Borlase, Dr., birthplace, 111. Grave, 291.
Bosahan House, 311.
Boscarne, 245.
Boscastle, 211.
Boscawen Un Circle, 134.
Boskednan Circle, 137.
Boskemna, 144.
Bosphrennis, 124.
Bossiney, 217. Hole, 217.
Bossington Hill, 177, 178, 195.
Bostrea, 129.
Boswavas Carn, 300. Moor, 127.
Boswedden Mine, 111.
Botallack Mine, 111.
Bottor Rock, 112, 121, 124.
Bottreaux, 214.
Botus Fleming, 270.
Boulder Ridge, 171.
Boulder-stones, 248.
Boundary-lines, xxvii.
Bounding, the right of, xxxv.
Bovey Brook, 122. Coal, 111. Heathfield, 111. House, 35. Tracey, 111.
Bovisand, 82.

BUCKISH.

Bow, 161.
Bowden, 184.
Bowerman's Nose, 122.
Bowethick Quarry, 220.
Braddoc Church, 247. Down, 242.
Braddons, 89.
Bradfield Hall, 4.
Bradley Manor-house, 58.
Bradmere Pool, 120.
Bradninch, 5. House, 5.
Bradstone Manor-house, 51, 151.
Brampford Speke, 161.
Branscombe, 35. Lace manufacture, 35. Mouth, 34.
Braunton, 187. Burrows, 188.
Bray Hill, 224.
Bray, Mrs., 149.
Breage, 112.
Brendon, 176. Valley, 176.
Brent Stat., 117.
Brent, South, 64, 116. Stat., 64. Tor, 51, 64, 111.
Brent Tor, North, 51.
Breock, St., 223. Downs, 226.
Breward, St., 207, 208.
Bridestow, 52.
Bridford, 110, 121.
Bridge, the longest in England, 56.
Bridgend, 159.
Bridgerule, 199.
Bridges, British, xxvii, 127, 129, 134, 137, 181.
Bridges rocks, 130.
Bridgewater, 2.
Brier Cave, 184.
Brisons rocks, 130.
Brixham, 96. Road Stat., 96.
Broadhembury, 27.
Broad Clyst stat., 31.
Broad Down, 19.
Broad Nymet, 161.
Broadoak Down, 242.
Brockedon, the Alpine traveller, where born, 59.
Brook House, 116.
Brookhill, 101.
Broomborough, 62.
Brothers of Grugith, 310.
Browda, 274.
Browne the poet, birthplace, 149.
Brown Gilly, 208. Willy, 206.
Brunenburgh, battle of, 21.
Brushford, 164.
Bryant, Jacob, birthplace, 69.
Bryher, 151.
Brynn, 245.
Brynsworthy, 169.
Buckfast Abbey, ruins of, 115. Modern, 116.
Buckfastleigh, 115.
Buckish Mill, 188.

CANN.

Buckland, 113. Abbey, 151. Beacon, 113. House, 113.
Buckland, Dr., birthplace, 24.
Buckland Brewer, 198. Monachorum, 151. On the Moor, 113. West, 165.
Budeaux, St., 86.
Bude Canal, 276. Haven, 277.
Budgell, Eustace, birthplace, 7.
Budleigh, East, 41. Salterton, 41.
Budock Bottom, 285.
Budocksheds, 87.
Buller, Judge, birthplace, 264.
Bull's Hole, 106.
Bulverton Hill, 38.
Bumble Rock, 308.
Burdon, 199.
Burlescombe, 1.
Burlowena, 299.
Burncoose, 288.
Burnham, 2.
Burning-house, xlii.
Burr Island, 107.
Bury, 161. Down, 242.
Buryan, St., 140.
Buryas Bridge, 134.
Butter Stone, 141.
Buzza Hill, 148.
Bystock, 42.

C.

Cad, Valley of, 143, 144. River, 143, 145.
Cadaford Bridge, 143.
Cadbury Castle, 22.
Cadgewith, 309.
Cadhay, 10.
Cadoc, St., 266.
Cadover Lane, 62. Hill, 62, 116.
Caer Bran Castle, 328.
Caerbillian, 307.
Cairns, 45, 65.
Cairn Uny, 139.
Calenick, 256.
Calleon Cove, 310.
Callington, 271.
Calliquolter Rock, 211.
Calstock, 84.
Camberdrill Point, 150.
Camborne, 289.
Camel, river, 208, 212. Flood of, 208. Valley, 208, 223.
Camelford, 212. Excursions from, 213.
Camps, xxvii.
Canal, Exeter ship, 19.
———, Grand Western, 20.
———, Tavistock, 149.
Cann Quarry, 143.

INDEX. 355

CANONTEIGN.

Canonteign House, 109, 117.
Canyke Castle, 244.
Cape Cornwall, 110.
Capstone Hill, 186.
Caradon Hill, 236. Mines, 236, 237.
Carbonaceous formation, xviii.
Carclaze Mine, 251.
Carclew, 256, 281, 284.
Cardinham Bury, 210.
Carew, Bamfylde Moore, birthplace, 22. Grave, 22.
Carhayes Castle, 269.
Carmears Valley, 248.
Carnanton, 226.
Carnbeuk, 215.
Carn Birges, 336.
—— Barra, 338.
—— Beacon, 269.
—— Boscawen, 344.
—— Brawse, 338.
—— Castlebean, 350.
—— Crease, 336.
—— Creis, 337.
—— Galva, 328.
—— Gloe, 336.
—— Greeb, 337.
—— Kei, 336.
—— Kenidjack, 329, 330, 331.
—— Kreigle, 336.
—— Lea, 348.
—— Leskez, 336.
—— Marth, 287.
—— Mellyn, 336.
—— Menelez, 288.
—— Morval, 347, 349.
—— Olva, 336.
—— Pendover, 337.
—— Scathe, 338.
—— Thomas, 339.
—— Top, 187.
—— Towan, 336.
—— Venton, 336.
—— Vessacks, 338.
—— Voel, 337.
—— e Wethan, 336.
Carn-brea, 288.
Carnmenellis, 280.
Carnon, 280.
Carns, xlix.
Carnsew, 292.
Carpenter, Nath., birthplace, 198.
Carpet manufacture, 23.
Carrick roadstead, 257, 284.
Carrickgloose Head, 330.
Carrickstarne, 348.
Carrington the poet, birthplace, 69.
Carters, the, 229.
Carthamartha Rocks, 204, 275.
Carvedras, 256.
Carwinnen Carn, 289. Cromlech, 289.

CIRCLES.

Cassiterides, ancient, 345.
Castell-an-Dinas, 211, 229, 300, 320.
Castle Bryher, 351. Carn-brea, 288. Dike, 109. Ditch, 55. Dour, 268. Hill, 24, 165. 269. Horneck, 298, 333. Kenyoe, 244. Rock, 175.
Castles, xxxii, xxxiii.
Catchfrench, 234, 235.
Catford's Lane, 197.
Catherine's Tor, St., 193.
Caton, 65.
Catwater, the, 85.
Caves, xxvii.
Cawsand, 262. Bay, 262. Beacon, 45, 47, 120, 156.
Chacewater, 286.
Chaddlewood, 67.
Chagford, 126.
Chair Ladder, 337.
Chair rock, 309.
Chalk-cliff, the last in England, 11.
Chalk formation, xxi.
Challacombe Down, 126.
Chamber Combe, 185.
Chapel Carn-bré, 29. Eumy, 329. Ford, 48. Point, 268. Rock, 278.
Chapman Barrows, 178.
Charles's Castle, 351.
Charlestown, 250.
Cheesewring, 175, 238.
Cheriton Bishop, 44. Cross, 44.
Cherrybridge, 174.
Cherrybrook, the, 131.
Chick, islet, 229.
Chimney Rock, 150, 175, 274.
China-clay works, 66, 144, 252.
Chinehead, 28.
Chineway Head, 39.
Chittaford Tor, 115.
Chittlehampton, 165.
Cholwich-town, 66.
Choughs, xlix.
Chnstow, 110, 117.
Chudleigh, 108. Rock, 109. Fort, 170.
Chulmleigh, 164.
Chun Castle, 326. Cromlech, 326.
Church architecture, xxviii.
Churchstow, 157.
Church-towns, L.
Churston Court, 98.
Chyandour, 316. Brook, 316.
Chysoyster, 325.
Chywoon Castle, 326.
Cider, xlvii.
Circles, Druidical, xxv, 45, 48, 66, 114, 123, 124, 126, 127, 128, 129, 134, 139, 140, 141, 144, 207, 237, 239, 264, 333, 334, 343.

COPLESTONE.]

Clapper Rocks, 348.
Classenwell Pool, 139, 146.
Clayhanger, 196.
Cleer, St., 240. Down, 240. Well, 239.
Cleeve Abbey, ruins, 194.
Clement's, St., 256. Isle, 345.
Clerk Rock, 55, 56.
Clether, St., 205.
Clicker Tor, 235, 237.
Cliff-castles, xxvii.
Clifford Bridge, 118.
Cligga Head, 260.
Climate, lvi. Of Dartmoor, 133.
Clocombe House, 24.
Clouted cream, xlvii.
Clovelly, 188. Court, 189. Cross, 191. Dikes, 191.
Clowance, 289.
Clyfton, 271.
Clyst, river, 43.
—— St. George, 43.
—— St. Mary, 43.
—— Heath, 43.
Coaxdon, 25.
Cob, xlvii.
Cober stream, 302.
Cockington, 94.
Cock's Tor, 141.
Coddon Hill, 169.
Coham, 199.
Coinage towns, xxxv, xliv.
Colan, 229.
Colcombe Castle, 25, 37.
Coldharbour, 321.
Coldrinick, 234, 235.
Coleridge the poet, birthplace, 28.
Coleridge, 164. House, 103.
Collacombe Barton, 150.
Colleton Barton, 164.
Collipriest, 21.
Columb Major, St., 226. Minor, St., 228. Porth, 228.
Colyford, 32.
Colyton, 36. Stat. 25.
Comb, 278. Valley, 279.
Combe, 198. Park, 179.
Combe Martin, 182. Silver-lead mines, 182. Bay, 181.
Combe-in-Teignbead, 57.
Combehead, 196.
Compass Point, 278.
Compton Castle, 94.
Consolidated Mines, xlv, 287.
Fowey, 249. Gwennap, 287. Par, 249.
Constantine, St., 225. Quarries, 281.
Conveyances from London, 2.
Cook's Kitchen, 287.
Coomb in Teignhead, 57.
Copiestone Cross, 163. Stat. 163.

COPLESTONE.

Coplestone oak, 85.
Copper, history, xxxvi.
Lodes, xxxvii. Mining, xxxviii. Ores, xxxvi.
Cormorants, xlix.
Cornish chough, xlix. Diamond, 222. Heath, 103. Language, lvii. Pebble, 201. Proverbs, 262, 269. Toasts, lii, lv.
Cornwall, Duchy of, lix.
Cornwood, 66.
Cornworthy Priory, 62.
Cory rivulet, 24, 25.
Coryton House, 24.
Cosdon, 45.
Cotford, 39.
Cothele, 271.
Cotley Camp, 117.
Cotmaton Hall, 40.
Council Barrow, 210.
Countesbury, 174.
Countess Weir, 19.
Court Hall, 19, 165. House, 165.
Courtlands, 42.
Coverack Cove, 110.
Cow and Calf Rocks, 347.
Cowel, the, 295.
Cowley, Hannah, birthplace, 20.
Cowsic, river, 137.
Crackington Cove, 215.
Cramber Tor, 140.
Cranbrook Castle, 118.
Cranmere Pool, 45, 47, 127, 129, 135.
Crannmore, 20.
Crantock, 229. Bay, 229.
Creacombe, 164.
Crebawethan, Great and Little, 350.
Crediton, 161. Trade, 161. Church, 161. Schools, 162.
Creedy Park, 161. River, 5, 22, 163. Vale, 161.
Creggan Moor, 249.
Crellas, 326.
Crick-stone, the, 326.
Crim Rock, 350.
Crip Tor, 118.
Crocadon House, 271.
Crockern Tor, 113, 135. Well, 44.
Cromlechs, xxiv, 44, 120, 127, 140, 141, 237, 289, 323, 324, 326, 326.
Crosses, xxxii, 45, 125, 130, 134, 141, 205, 210, 222, 225, 227, 228, 233, 256, 259, 267, 284, 295, 298, 299, 300, 305, 309, 318, 329, 334, 338, 341, 342, 343, 349.
Cross House, 167.
Crousa Down, 110.
Crow Rock, 349.

DEVIL.

Crowan, 290. Beacon, 290.
Crowndale, 147.
Crown Rocks, 331.
Crows an ura, 334.
Cruther's Bay, 352. Hill, 352.
Cuby, 253. Well, 237.
Cuddan Point, 314.
Cuddenbeak, 234.
Cudlipp-town, 152.
Culbone, 178, 195.
Cullompton, 4.
Culme river, 4, 5. Valley, 4.
Culmstock, 5.
Cumston Tor, 114.
Cury, St., 304.
Cut Hill, 113, 129.

D.

Daddy's Hole, 92.
Daignton Tunnel, 58.
Danes, 175.
Danescombe, 84, 272.
Dartington House, 61.
Dart-meet, 114.
Dartmoor, 110. Birds, 114. Bogs, 113. Climate, 113. Prison, 137. Soil, 113. Stables, 113. Tors, 131. Wild animals, 113.
Dartmoor, walk across, 135.
Dartmouth, 98. Antiquity, celebrities, 98. Historic associations, 99. Old houses, 99. Church, 100. Castle, 100. Excursions, 102.
Dart river, 59, 61, 94, 98, 111, 114, 137. Source, 47, 110, 111. Valley, 62.
——— rivulet, 22.
Davey's Engine, xl.
Davidstow, 212.
Davis, navigator, birthplace, 99.
Davy, Sir Humphry, birthplace, 294. Portrait, 283.
Dawlish, 54. Stat. 54.
Dawns Mên, 143.
Daw's Hugo, 308.
Day, St., 287.
Dazard Head, 278.
Dean Burn, Vale of, 63, 116.
Dean Court, 117. Prior, 63, 116.
Deep Point, 349.
Deer Park, 28.
Delabole Quarries, 220.
Delamore, 66.
Denbury Down, 88.
Dennabridge Pound, 137.
Dennis Creek, 110.
Denridge, 163.
Devil's Bellows, 306. Cheesewring, 275, 278. Frying-

DUNMEER.

pan, 309. Jump, 208. Lime-kiln, 191. Post-office, 306. Throat, 306.
Devil Tor, 137.
Devon Great Consols, 154.
Devonian system, xlv.
Devonport, 68, 76. Dockyard, 76. Excursions, 79. Gun Wharf, 77. Mount Wise, 78. Public buildings, 78. Steam-yard, 77.
Devonshire cream, xlvii. Proverbs, 20, 163. Lane, 112. Sand, 64.
Devoran, 284.
Dewerstone, 144.
D'Ewes, Sir Symonds, birthplace, 25.
Diallage-rock, xv.
Dick's Carn, 348.
Dinas Cove, 225. Great and Little, 111.
Ding Dong Mine, 327.
Dingerein, 230.
Ditchen Hills, 191.
Dittisham, 61.
Divining-rod, xliv.
Dodbrooke, 156.
Doddiscombleigh, 110, 117.
Dodman, 269.
Doe Tor, 50.
Dolbury, 23.
Dolcoath Mine, 286.
Dollar Rock, 117.
Dolor Hugo, 309.
Dolphin, 151.
Domestic architecture, xxiii.
Doones of Badgeworthy, 179.
Double Water, 152.
Doublebois, 242.
Downes, 161.
Down Head, 162.
Dowrish House, 163.
Dozmare Pool, 208.
Drake, Sir Francis, birthplace, 147. Portrait, 41. Legend of, 73.
Drake's Island, 79.
Drakewalls Mine, 274.
Dranna Point, 310.
Drewsteignton, 119. Loganstone, 119.
Dreynes, river, 240, 242.
Driff, 134.
Drift-net fishing, liii.
Druid's Altar, 326.
Drum Rock, 348.
Duchy of Cornwall, lix.
Duloe, 237, 264.
Dulverton, 196, 197.
Dumpdon Hill, 27.
Dunchideock, 108.
Dunkery Beacon, 177, 178.
Dunkeswell Abbey, 4, 27.
Dunmeer Bridge, 244. Castle, 244. Wood, 244.

INDEX. 357

DUNNING.

Dunning, John, birthplace, 112.
Dunscombe Cliff, 16.
Dunsford, 44, 110. Bridge, 117.
Dunsland, 199.
Dunster, 194.
Dupath Well, 272.
Duporth, 250.
Dutchman's Carn, 348.
Duty Point, 176.

E.

East Huel Rose, 255.
Eastern Islands, 352.
Eastlake the artist, birthplace, 69.
East Ottery Hill, 39.
Eddystone lighthouse, 87.
Edge, 15.
Egg Buckland, 86.
Eggesford, 164. Stat., 164.
Egloshayle, 223.
Elfordleigh, 67.
Elvans, xx, xlv.
Endellion, St., 222, 223.
Endsleigh, 151, 204, 275.
Enoder, St., 211.
Enodoc, St., 224.
Enys, 281, 284. Dodnan, 337. Porth, 344.
Erica ciliaris, 281. Vagans, 303, 304.
Erisey House, 309.
Erme Estuary, 65. Head, 65. Pound, 65. River, 64, 131.
Ermington, 65, 159.
Erth, 234. St., 293.
Escot House, 30.
Ewe, St. 253.
Exbridge, 197.
Exe, river, 5, 19, 22, 43, 44, 54, 196. Source, 180.
Exeter, 5. Origin, situation, history, 5. Former and present modes of reaching, 7. Eminent natives, 7. Streets, 8. Cathedral, 8. Episcopal palace, Deanery, churches, 14. Castle, 15. Public buildings, 16, 17. Nursery-grounds, 17. Excursions, 18. Ship canal, 19. Stats., 5, 31.
Exeter to Exmouth, 43.
—— to Launceston, 44.
—— to Plymouth, 53.
—— to Torquay, 88, 108.
—— to Ashburton, 111.
—— to Tavistock, 117
—— to Bideford, 160.
Exford, 181.
Exminster, 53.

FUR.

Exmoor, 178. Farms, 179.
Exmouth, Lord, birthplace, 294.
Exmouth, 42. Excursions, 42.
Exwick Hill, 18.

F.

Fairmile Hill, 40.
Fal river, 255, 284.
Fallapit House, 106.
Falmouth, 281. Harbour, 283.
Fardell, 66.
Farway Castle, 28.
Feniton, 31.
Fentonwoon, 212.
Feock, St., 284.
Fernworthy Circle, 129.
Filorey, 229.
Fingle Bridge, 118.
Fisheries, lii.
Fistral Bay, 229.
Fitzford, 148.
Fitz's Well, 46, 139.
Five Barrow Down, 245.
Fivelanes, 205.
Flavel, John, 103.
Fleet House, 65, 158.
Flitton oak, 165.
Flukan, xlv.
Flushing, 284.
Fly-fishing, lvi.
Fogou, 342.
Foliaton House, 62.
Foote the comedian, birthplace, 256.
Ford the dramatist, birthplace, 112.
Ford Abbey, 24.
Ford House, 58.
Fordlands, 18, 117.
Forrabury, 214.
Fortescue, Chancellor, birthplace, 168.
Four-hole Cross, 210.
Fowellscombe, 159.
Fowey, 265. Consols, 249. Haven, 265. River, 206, 240, 244. Well, 206. Valley, 247.
Fox Tor, 140.
Fraddon, 211.
Fremington House, 169. Stat., 169.
Frithelstock, 167.
Fuidge House, 44.
Fulford House, 44.
Funnel Rock, 338.
Furry-day, 301.
Fursbrook House, 24.
Fursdon House, 22.
Fur Tor, 139, 152.

GOSSAN.

G.

Gale, Theophilus, birthplace, 57.
Gallantry Bower, 189.
Galmpton, 98.
Gampen seez, 140.
Gandy, Wm., birthplace, 7.
Gannel estuary, 229.
Ganniley, Great and Little, 352.
Ganniomic, Great and Little, 352.
Garrah, 206.
Gates, Sir Thos., birthplace, 12.
Gear, 112.
Geological notice, xiv.
Geological Society of Cornwall, 295.
Germans, St., 233. River, 233.
Germoe, 311.
Gerrans, 270. Bay, 270.
Giant Tregeagle, 209, 211, 247, 269.
Giant's Castle, 348. Chair, 349. Grave, 143. Graves, 333. Hedge, 261. Quoit, 327. Rock, 132. Staff, 252. Well, 117.
Gibben, 335.
Gibbs, Sir Vicary, birthplace, 7.
Gidleigh, 128. Park, 127.
Gifford, Lord, birthplace, 7.
——, William, birthplace, 112.
Gilbert, Davies, birthplace, 294.
Gilbert, Sir Humphrey, birthplace, 98. His castle, 91.
Gilstone Rock, 347, 350.
Gittesham, 28.
Glanville, Sir John, birthplace, 149.
Glenthorne, 176.
Gluvias, St., 281.
Glynn, 244. Bridge, 244. Valley, 244.
Goat, Little and Great, 106.
Godolphin, 311. Hill, 311.
Godolphin, Mrs., grave, 312.
Godrevy, 291.
Gold found in Cornwall, xxxvii, 253. In Devon, 165.
Goldsithney, 315.
Golytha rock, 240.
Goodamoor, 66.
Goonhilly Down, 304.
Goose rock, 229.
Gorran, 269. Haven, 268.
Gorregan, 350.
Gosford House, 30.
Gossan, xlv.

INDEX.

GRADE.

Grade, 309.
Grampound, 251. Road stat., 251.
Granate Tor, 48.
Grand Western Canal, 20.
Grange, the, 4.
Granite, xix. Veins, xx. Works and quarries, 118.
Grauwacke, xv.
Gravesend, 84.
Great House, 17.
Great Stone, 226.
Greber Head, 267.
Greenaway's Foot, 186.
Greensand, xxi.
Greenstone, xv.
Greenway, 61, 98.
Grenofen, 143, 152. House, 146.
Grenville, Sir Beville, birthplace, 245.
Greystone Bridge, 275.
Grey Wethers, the, 129.
Grimspound, 121, 125.
Grimstone, 146.
Grove Hill, 283.
Growan, xlv, 111.
Grower Quarry, 215.
Gubbins' Land, 50.
Gue Graze, 105.
Gugh, 149.
Guile Bridge, 149.
Guinear road stat., 285.
Gulval, 299. Carn, 291.
Gumb, Daniel, birthplace and retreat, 238.
Gumb's Rocks, 238.
Gump, 111.
Gun, the, 152.
Gunner Rock, 150.
Gunnislake, 150, 274.
Gunwalloe, 304.
Gurnard's Head, 124, 125.
Gwavas Lake, 141.
Gweal, 151.
Gwennap, 288. Pit, 287.
Gwinear, 292.
Gwithian, 290.
Gwn mên Screpha, 127.
Gyllanvaen, 283.
Gyllyngdune, 283.

H

Haccombe Church, 88. House, 88.
Hadilon Down, 195.
Haine Castle, 52.
Halberton, 20.
Haldon Hills, 18, 42, 54, 55, 108. House, 108.
Half Stone, 219.
Halgaver, 244.
Hall House, 66, 267. Walk, 267.

HEMYOCK.

Hall's Hole, 84.
Hallsands, 101.
Hals, his residence, 255.
Halsetown, 121.
Halwyn, 224.
Halzaphron Cliffs, 304.
Hamilton Down, 125.
Hamoaze, 83, 211.
Ham Stone, 106.
Hanging Stone, 182.
Hangman Hills, 182. Isle, 151.
Hanjague Rock, 152.
Hankford, Sir Wm., birthplace, 167.
Hanna Hill, 11.
Hannon Valley, 208.
Hanter Gantick, 207.
Harberton, 62.
Harbertonford, 63.
Hare Tor, 52, 152, 155.
Harewood House, 84, 150.
Harford, 65.
Harlyn, 224.
Harpford Wood, 18.
Harrels, Thomas, birthplace, 256.
Harry's Walls, 149.
Hartland, 192. Abbey, 192.
Point, 191. Quay, 193. Tor, 135.
Hatherleigh, 198.
Haven Cliff, 12.
Hawksdown Hill, 25, 32, 11.
Hawkins, Sir John, birthplace, 69.
Hawk's Tor, 209, 239.
Haydon the artist, birthplace, 69.
Hayes Barton, 41. Wood, 41.
Hayle, 291. River, 292.
Hazel Tor, 111.
Hea, 299.
Headlands, xlix.
Heanton Court, 188. House, 167.
Heath's Court, 30.
Heavitree, 18.
Heddon china-clay works, 66.
Heddon's Mouth, 181.
Hele Stat., 5. Village, 186.
Helen's, St., 152.
Helesborough, 185, 186.
Helford river, 311.
Heligan, 250.
Hell's Mouth, 290.
Hellwethers, 147, 150.
Helmên, 249.
Helston, 301.
Heltor, 117, 121.
Hembury Fort, 27. Castle, 116.
Hemerdon Ball, 66. House, 67.
Hempstone Arundel, 63.
Hemyock Castle, 3.

HOUND.

Henbury Fort, 198.
Hengar House, 222.
Hennacliff, 278.
Hennock, 112.
Hennons, the, 57.
Henny Castle, 171.
Hensbarrow, 211, 253.
Heronry at Sharpham, 63.
At Pixton Park, 197.
Herrick the poet, his vicarage, 116. Grave, 116.
Hertford Bridge, 152.
Hervey, his curacy, 170.
Hessary Tor, 113, 137.
Hessenford, 261.
Hewas Mine, 253. Water, 251.
Hexworthy House, 275.
Heytor Rocks, 121. Quarry, 124. Town, 124.
High Cliff, 215. Peak, 37, 39.
Higher Combe, 197.
Highland House, 66.
Hill Bridge, 152.
Hill-Castles, xxvii.
Hillersdon House, 4.
Kingston Down, 273.
Hobby, the, 172, 188.
Hockworthy Court, 196.
Holbeton, 158.
Holcombe Rogus, 3.
Holed Stones, xxvi, 127, 100, 126, 141, 148.
Holestrow, 307.
Hollam House, 198.
Holloway Cross, 205.
Holmbush Mines, 274.
Holne, 114. Bridge, 113.
Moor, 113.
Holne Chace, 112, 113.
Holnicote, 178, 194.
Holstone Barrow, 182.
Holsworthy, 199.
Holy-street, 127.
Holy Vale, 148.
Holywell Bay, 229.
Honey Ditches, 33.
Honiton, 26. Lace, 26. Vale of, 26. Stat., 26.
Hood, Admiral, birthplace, 24.
Hooker, Rich., birthplace, 7.
Hooknor Tor, 126.
Hope, 107.
Hope's Nose, 90.
Hornblende-slate, xv.
Horner, stream, 194.
Horrabridge, 146.
Horse, the, 257.
Horse Bridge, 274.
Horsham Bay, 122. Steps, 122.
Horticultural Soc. of Cornwall, 256.
Hot Point, 309.
Hound's Pool, 116.

INDEX. 359

HOUNDTOR.
Houndtor, 121. Coomb, 121.
Household, Cove and Bay, 108.
Howard House, 164.
Howe, John, his residence, 167.
Hubba, his supposed grave, 171.
Hubblestone, 171.
Huckworthy Bridge, 141.
Hudscott, 103.
Huel Alfred, 294. Friendship, 52, 152. Garras, 255. Halamanning, 115. Herland, 292. Sophia, 274. Vor, 112.
Hugh Town, 347.
Hunstor, 119.
Hunter's Lodge, 28.
Hurlers, the, 219.
Hut-circles, xxvi, 45, 66, 114, 124, 126, 127, 129, 134, 139, 140, 141, 207, 239.

I.
Ide, vale of, 44.
Iktis, ancient, xxxiv, 73.
Ilford Bridges, 174.
Ilfracombe, 185. Harbour, lighthouse, 185. Church, baths, 186. Environs, 186.
Illogan, 289.
Ilsington, 112. Manor-house, 112.
Ince Castle, 211.
Incledon the singer, birthplace, 110.
Indian Queens, 211.
Ingsdon, 112.
Inisidgen Point, 349.
Inisvouls, Great and Little, 352.
Innis Head, 110. Vean, 307.
Inny river, 205, 275.
Inscribed Stones, xxviii, 66, 121, 291, 292, 299, 330.
Institution of Cornwall, 256.
Instow Quay, 169.
Irish Lady, 336.
Islands of Scilly, 345.
Isnioc Cross, 256.
Issey, St., 224. Beacon, 226.
Ive, St., 274.
Ives, St., 321. Consols, 322. Road stat. 293.
Ivy Bridge, 64. Stat. 64.

J.
Jackson, Wm., birthplace, 7.
Jacky's Rock, 350.
Jacobstow, 277.
Jamaica Inn, 206.

KINGSBRIDGE.
Jewel, Bishop of Salisbury, birthplace, 184.
Jews' Houses, xxxiv.
Johnson's Head, Dr., 335.
John's, St., 303. Cottage, 42. Eve, 296. Hill, 149. Lake, 84.
Jump, 154.
Junket, xlvii.
Just in Penwith, St., 329. In Roseland, St., 285. Creek, 284. Pool, 285.

K.
Kalynack, Mary, 294.
Karsdon quarry, 196.
Kea, 280.
Kelland, 163.
Kellan Head, 225.
Kelly, 153. House, 53. Rounds, 222.
Kenegie, 298, 330.
Kenidjack Castle, 331.
Kenn, 51.
Kennack Cove, 310.
Kennal, stream, 280.
Kennicott, Benj., birthplace, 59.
Kensey river, 202.
Kenton, 54.
Kent's Hole, 92.
Kentisbeare, 5.
Kentisbury, 184.
Kenwith Lodge, 172.
Kenwyn, 256.
Kenyoe Castle, 244.
Kestor Rock, 128.
Kettle and Pans, 348.
Kettle's Bottom, 335.
Keverne, St., 310.
Kew, St., 222.
Keyne's Well, St., 236, 264.
Kilby's, St., well, 237.
Kilkhampton, 199, 278.
Kilkobben cove, 309.
Killas, xvi, xlv.
Killbury, 222.
Killerton Park, 5.
Killigunoon, 256, 280.
Killiow, 256, 280.
Kilmarth Tor, 218.
Kilmington, 26.
Kilworthy, 150.
Kinance Cove, 306.
King Arthur, 217, 219, 229.
King, Lord Chancellor, birthplace, 7.
King's and Queen's Houses, 208.
King's Nympton Park, 165.
Kingsand, 262.
Kingsbridge, 156. Road Stat., 64, 156.
—— to Plymouth, 156.

LAVER.
King's Kerswell, 88. Nympton, 165. Teignton, 57, 110.
Kingswear, 101. Castle, 102.
King Tor, 118.
Kirkham's Hill, 95.
Kistvaens, xxvi, 45, 65, 114, 123, 134, 135, 146, 237, 323.
Kit Hill, 273.
Kitley, 160. Cavern, 160.
Kitt's Fall, 50.
Kittern, 350.
Kneeset Tor, Great, 155.
Knighton, 111.
Knight's Hayes, 21.
Knill, John, his monument, 322.
Knolie, farmhouse, 145.

L.
Ladock, 211.
Ladram Bay, 39.
Laira Bridge, 68, 85. Estuary, 68, 86. River, 142.
Lake, 48.
Lakehead Circle, 134.
Lambert, his prison, 79.
Lamerton, 153.
Lamorna Cove, 343. Valley, 342.
Lamorran, 254. Creek, 254.
Lander, Richard and John, the travellers, birthplace, 256.
Landewednack, 309.
Land's End, 314. District, 291.
Landue Mill, 275.
Landulph, 270.
Laneast, 206. Down, 212.
Langstone, 54, 55.
Language, old Cornish, lvii.
Lanherne Convent, 227.
Lanhydrock House, 246.
Lanivet, 210.
Lank, 207. River, 207. Down, 207. Rocks, 207.
Lanlivery, 245.
Lannacomb Mill, 104.
Lansalloe, 265.
Lanteglos, 212, 265.
Lantern Hill, 185, 186.
Lanyon, 292. Cromlech, 327.
Lapford Stat., 163.
Lariggan, 298.
Launcells, 199, 277. House, 277.
Launceston, 201. Castle, 202. Churches, 203. Environs, 204. Historical notice, 205.
Launceston to Truro, 201, 212.
Laver, 184.

LAWHITTON.

Lawhitton, 275.
Lawrence, St., 244.
Laywell House, 98. Spring, 96.
Leawood House, 52.
Lee Abbey, 176. Bay, 176. Valley, 186.
Leigh House, 164.
Lelant, 292.
Lemon rivulet, 57.
Lerrin river, 247.
Lescaddock Castle, 299.
Lesingey Round, 111.
Lesnewth, 216.
Lethltor, 146.
Lethowsow, 115.
Levan, St., 118.
Levant Mine, 132.
Lew, North, 198.
Lezant, 275.
Lich-stones, 212, 118.
Lidford, 48. Castle, 49. Bridge, 49. Cascade, 50. Law, 49. Tor, 137.
Lifton, 53. Park, 53.
Limestones, xvi.
Linkenhorne, 274.
Links Tor, Great, 47.
Lint's Tor, 152.
Lion Rock, 152.
Lion's Den, 108.
Liskeard, 236. Excursions, 236-242.
Lithwell Chapel, 55, 57.
Little Bounds Mine, 110.
Littleham, 42.
Livermead, 95.
Livery Dole, 19.
Lizard Cove, 109. District, 303. Point, 304, 307. Town, 308.
Loddiswell, 157.
Loe Pool, 302.
Logan Rock, 339.
Logan Stones, xxvi, 119, 122, 124, 125, 207, 290, 322, 319, 348.
London to Exeter, 2, 21.
—— to Tiverton and Crediton, 20.
Longaford Tor, 135.
Longator, 114.
Longbridge, 142, 216.
Longships lighthouse, 335.
Longstone, 146. The, 128, 232, 267, 349.
Looe, 236, 262. Valley, 242.
Lostwithiel, 245.
Lover's Leap, 113, 186.
Loyes, St., 18.
Lucombe oak, 281.
Ludgvan, 293.
Lugger's Cave, 261.
Lundy Island, 190.
Lupton House, 97.
Luscombe, 55.

MAWGAN.

Lustleigh Cleave, 121. Valley, 121.
Luxulian, 248. Quarries, 248.
Lyd, river, 50.
Lyme Regis, 11.
—— to Exeter, 11.
Lympstone, 44.
Lyn torrents, 172. Cliff, 173, 174. River, 174, 181.
Lynbridge, 174.
Lyndale, 174.
Lyndridge, 57.
Lynher Creek, 84, 232, 233, 215. Estuary, 261.
Lynmouth, 172. Foreland, 174.
—— to Hartland, 172.
Lynton, 172. Cottage, 174.
Lyonesse, 11, 346.

M.

Mabe quarries, 281, 285, 301.
Mabyn, St., 222.
Madron, 299, 338. Well, 299.
Maen Castle, 336.
Maentol, 300.
Maiden Bower, 150.
Maidencombe, 57, 94.
Maisonette, 61.
Maker, 262. Heights, 262.
Mulpas, 257.
Mambead, 54.
Manaccan, 311.
Manach Point, 339.
Manacles, 282, 310.
Man and his man, 260.
Manaton, 122.
Manor House, 28.
Manstone, 38.
Marazion, 316. Road stat., 293.
Mare Rock, 152.
Marhamchurch, 276.
Maristowe, 151.
Market-Jew, 316.
Marlborough, 157. Duke of, where born, 25.
Maridon, 94.
Marley House, 117.
Marsh, the, 316.
Marsland, 193.
Martin's, St., 152. Flats, 152. Bay, 152. Head, 152.
Martyn the missionary, birthplace, 256.
Marwood, 169. Family of, 26.
Mary Church, St., 93.
Mary's, Scilly, St., 347.
Mary Tavy, 151. Rock, 152.
Mawes, St., 285. Castle, 285.
Mawgan, St., 227. In Ménéage, 311. Porth, 227, 228. Vale, 227.

MINVER.

Maypole Hill, 348.
Meachard, 215.
Meadfoot Cove, 92.
Meavy, 145. Vale, 145. Oak, 145.
Mediæval remains, xxviii.
Medrose, 220.
Meldon Quarry, 46.
Meledgan, 350.
Mellion, St., 271.
Membury, 25.
Menability, 267.
Menacuddle Well, 250.
Menavawr, 352.
Mên Amber, 290. An-tol, 326. Scryffen, 327.
Menewetban, 352.
Menheniot, 215.
Mermaid's Hole, 270.
Merrivale Bridge, 140.
Merry Maidens, 330, 343.
Merryn, St., 224.
Merther, 255.
Merton, 166.
Mevagissey, 268.
Mew, river, 143.
Mewstone, 79, 106.
Mica slate, xiv.
Michael Carhayes, St., 269. Of Halstock, St., 48. Penkivel, St., 257.
Michael's Mount, St., 293, 316. Chair, 217, 318.
Michaelstow, 222. Beacon, 222.
Milber Down, 88.
Milford valley, 193.
Millaton, 52.
Mill Bay, 74, 106, 337.
Millbrook, 84.
Millendreath, 264.
Mill-hill quarries, 154.
Mill Mouth, 190.
Milton Abbot, 151.
Minalto, Great and Little, 351.
Mincarlo, 350.
Minchead, 194.
Mines, xxxiii. Articles consumed in, xlv. Bounding, xxxv. Descent of, xl. Dressing the ore, xlii. History, xxxiii. How managed, xliv. How worked, xxxviii. Levels, xxxviii. Lodes, xxxvii. Miners, xli, xliv. Sale of the ore, xliii. Shaft, xxxviii. Shoding, xxxvii. Smelting the ore, xliii. Steam engines, xxxix. Stannary laws, xxxv. Stream-works, xli. Submarine mines, xli. Temperature, xxxix.
Minster, 216.
Minver, St., 225.

MIRACLE.

Miracle plays, 260.
Mis Tor, Great, 52, 118, 152.
   Little, 118. Pan, 118.
Mitchell, 211.
Mithian, 260.
Modbury, 102, 107, 157.
Moditonham, 84, 270.
Mole river, source, 164.
Mole's Chamber, 179.
Molland, 198.
Molton, North, 165. South, 164. Ridge, 182.
Monk, Duke of Albemarle, birthplace, 167.
Monkleigh, 167.
Monk's Cowl, 148.
Moorswater, 216, 242.
Morchard Bishops, 163. Road Stat., 161.
Moreton Hampstead, 120. House, 170.
Morice, Sir Wm., birthplace, 7.
Moridunum of Antoninus, 27, 11, 19.
Morisco's Castle, 191.
Morleigh, 102.
Morley china-clay works, 66.
Morte Stone, 187.
Morthoe, 186.
Morton, 277.
Morton's Leam, 19.
Morvah, 325.
Morval House, 261, 264.
Morwellham, 84.
Morwell House, 151. Rocks, 84, 150, 272.
Morwenstow, 279.
Mothecomb, 158.
Moult, the, 105.
Mount Batten, 82. Boone, 64. Tavy, 150.
Mount Edgcumbe, 79, 82.
Mount's Bay, 297. Climate, 297.
Mousehole, 344.
Mozrang Pool, 337.
Mulfra, 324. Quoit, 324.
Mullion, 305. Cove, 305. Island, 305.
Mundic, xlv.
Musbury, 25, 34.
Mylor, 284. Creek, 284. Pool, 284.

N.

Nag's Head, 150.
Nancealverne, 298.
Nankissal, 337.
Nansloe House, 301.
Nanswhyden, 227.
Nare Point, 311.
Neot, St., church, 240. Miracles, 240, 241.

[Dev. & Corn.]

OLD.

Netherton Hall, 28.
Nethway House, 98.
New Bridge, 114, 150, 274, 311.
Newcomen, birthplace, 99.
Newenham Abbey, 24.
New Grimsby, 351.
New Ground, 98.
Newhouse, 134.
Newlyn, 211. Near Penzance, 341.
Newnham Park, 67.
Newquay, in Cornwall, 228. In Scilly, 349.
Newton, 57. Ferrers, 159. House, 161, 271. Poppleford, 39. Stat., 57.
Newton St. Cyres Stat., 161.
Newtown, 343.
Newt's Down, 21.
Nighton's Keive, St., 216.
Nine Maidens, 226, 327, 333, 334.
Nine Stones, 48.
No Man's Land, 226.
Northam, 171. Burrows, 171.
North Brentor, 51.
Northcote the artist, birthplace, 69.
North Hall, 124. Lew, 198.
Northwithial, 352.
Nortor, 152.
Noss, 159.
Nottar Bridge, 334.
Noy, attorney-general, birthplace, 341. Residence, 227.
Nundeeps Rock, 350.
Nut Rock, 350.
Nutcrackers Logan-stone, 122, 124.
Nutwell Court, 43.
Nymet Tracy, 161.

O.

Oare Hill, 177. Water, 176.
Ockley, Simon, birthplace, 7.
Ocrinum (ancient), 307.
Off Islands, 349.
Offwell House, 28.
Ogwell Rocks, 58.
Okehampton, 45. Castle, 46. Park, 46.
Okelands, 46.
Okement, river, 45, 46. Source of E., 47. Valley of E., 48. Source of W., 130, 155.
Oldaport, 158.
Oldbarrow Camp, 177, 195.
Old Blockhouse, 352.
Old Bosullow, 326.
Old Crinnis mine, 249.
Old Grimsby, 352.

PENDEEN.

Olditch Court, 24.
Old Lizard Head, 307.
Old Man cutting Turf, 350.
Old Man and his Children, 106.
Old Town, 348. Bay, 348.
Oliver Cromwell's Castle, 351. Convention-room, 28.
Opie, birthplace, 260.
Orange, prince of, his landing, 90 ; scene of his first council, 96.
Oratories, xxx, 257, 259, 225.
Orcomb Point, 42.
Oreston quarries, 85.
Orleigh Court, 170.
Other Half Stone, 239.
Otter river, 27, 28, 40, 41.
Otterton, 40.
Ottery Park, 153. St. Mary, 28. Road stat., 28.
Oxton House, 54.

P.

Packsaddle Bridge, 115.
Padstow, 223. Harbour, 224.
Paignton, 95.
Par, 249. Consols, 249.
Paracombe, 181.
Parallelelitha, xxv.
Pardenick, 337.
Park Hill, 89. House, 245.
Parkham, 188.
Parliament Lane, 96.
Parnvose, 309.
Parrett, river, 25.
Parson Rock, 55, 56.
Paul, 342. Hill, 341.
Payhembury, 31.
Peak House, 40.
Peamore House, 53.
Peartree, headland, 104.
Peat bogs, xlix.
Pebble Ridge, 171.
Pedn an Laaz, 334.
Pedn mean an Mor, 339.
Pedn mên dhu, 336.
Pedn Vounder, 339.
Pele Rock, 335.
Pellew's Redout, 349.
Pelyn House, 247.
Pelynt, 264.
Penair, 255, 256.
Penare Head, xvii, 269.
Pen Beacon, 66.
Penberth Cove, 340.
Penbrose, 352.
Pencalenick, 255, 256.
Pencarrow, 221, 244. Head xvii.
Pencoose Castle, 251.
Pendarves, 289. Quoit, 289.
Pendeen, 333. Cove, 333. Vau, 333.

R

PENDENNIS.

Pendennis Castle, 281.
Pendrathen Quay, 149.
Pendrê, 130.
Pendrea, 298.
Pengelly, 221.
Pengerrick, 281.
Pengersick Castle, 211.
Pengreep, 288.
Penhale Point, 229.
Penhargate Castle, 244.
Peninnis Head, 281.
Penkinna Head, 215.
Pennance, 253.
Penn slate-quarry, 114.
Pennsylvania, 18.
Penny-come-quick, 282.
Penolver, 108.
Penpons Bottom, 286.
Penquite, 266.
Penrice, 250. - -
Penrose, 101.
Penryn, 281.
Penshell, 66.
Pentillie Castle, 271.
Pentire Point, 225, 229.
Pentreath, Dolly, 142.
Pentewan stone, xx.
Pentowan, 251.
Penwether Viaduct, 280.
Penzance, 293. History, 293.
  Notabilities, 294. Principal buildings, &c., 294, 295.
  Museums, 295, 296. Curious custom, 296. Environs, 296-300. Excursions from, 315-352.
Penzance to St. Michael's Mount, 216.
—— to St. Ives, 130.
—— to the Gurnard's Head, 324.
—— to St. Just, &c., 338.
—— to the Land's End, 333.
—— to Lamorna Cove, 341.
Permellin Bay, 349.
Pernagie Isle, 352.
Perran Arworthal, 280.
Perran Porth, 257. Round, 260. Wharf, 280, 284.
Perran-uthnoe, 215.
Perranwell Stat., 280.
Perran-zabuloe, 257. Old church of, 257.
Perridge Camp, 117.
Peter Pindar, birthplace, 157. School, 216.
Peter Tavy, 152.
Peter's Eve, St., 296.
Peters, Hugh, birthplace, 266. Portrait, 266.
Petherick, Little, 224.
Petit Tor, 93.
Petton, 196.
Peverell's Cross, 210.
Pewtor, 151.

POLPERRO.

Phillack, 292.
Pidley, 161.
Pigeon's Hugo, 106.
Pilchard fishery, lii, 297. King, lili.
Pill Creek, 284.
Pillars, Stone, xxv, 127, 137, 140, 141, 149.
Pilton, 169. House, 169.
Pin Beacon, 39.
Pindar Lodge, 157.
Pinhoe, 18.
Pinney landslips, 31.
Pipers, the, 343. Hole, 346, 348, 351.
Piran, St., 258. Oratory, 257. Well, 280.
Piskie's Well, 261.
Pistol Meadow, 307.
Pitt's Parlour, 148.
Pixies, 145. House, 145. Parlour, 109.
Pixton Park, 196, 197.
Place House, 109, 224, 266, 285.
Planguary, 288.
Plâns an guare, 288, 310.
Pludn, 137.
Plumb Island, 152.
Plym Bridge, 142. Head, 65, 145, 146. River, 184, 142, 141.
Plymouth, 68. Athenæum, 69. Bovisand, 82. Breakwater, 79. Churches, 72. Citadel, 71. Dockyard, 76. Excursions, 79. History, 68. Hoe, 71. Leet, 74. Mill Bay, 74. Mount Batten, 82. Public Library, 69. Sound, 79. Sutton Pool, 71.
Plymouth to Tavistock, 142.
—— to Modbury and Kingsbridge, 156.
—— to Truro, 230.
—— to Falmouth, 261.
—— to Bude Haven, 230.
Plympton Earl, 67. St. Mary, 66. Stat., 66. House, 67.
Plymstock, 159.
Plymtree, 5.
Point-in-view, 42.
Polbathick, 261.
Pole, Sir Wm., the antiquary, grave, 36.
Polgooth, 253.
Pollew, 305.
Polkerris, 268.
Pollard, Sir Lewis, birthplace, 165.
Pol Ledan, 338.
Polmear, 250.
Polostoc, 338.
Polpeer, 307.
Polperro, 264.

PRIGLIS.

Polpry, 116.
Polruan, 265, 267.
Polsloe Priory, 18.
Poltair, 299. House, 298.
Poltesco, Valley of, 110.
Poltimore House, 5, 18.
Polwhele, birthplace, 256. Residence, 311. House, 255, 256.
Polytechnic Society of Cornwall, 281.
Ponsandane, 120.
Ponsondine, 298.
Poole, 101, 289. Court, 244.
Pooling granite, xlix.
Poor Man's Endeavour, 208.
Porch House, 38.
Porcrass, 348.
Porlock, 177, 195.
Por Loe, 118.
Pornanvon Cove, 110.
Por Selli, 339.
Port Eliot, 274. Gavorne, 221. Isaac, 225. Issyk, 222. William, 230.
Porthalla, 110.
Porthcurnow, 339.
Porth Enys, 344.
Porthgwarra, 338.
Porth Hellick, 336, 338.
Porth Hern, 217.
Porthledan Cove, 110.
Porthleven, 112.
Porthloo Bay, 349.
Porthmeer Cove, 325.
Porthmellin, 269.
Porth Minick, 348.
Porthoustock, 110.
Porthqueen, 225.
Portledge, 170.
Portlemouth, 105.
Portmellin, 269.
Portreath, 288.
Portsmouth Arms Stat., 165.
Posbury Hill, 162.
Post Bridge, 114.
Potato Market, a British village so called, 141.
Potheridge, 166.
Pounds, xxvi, 45, 122, 125, 134, 135, 137, 140, 141, 144, 240.
Pound Scawens, 110.
Poulston, 53.
Powderham Castle, 18, 53. Church, 54.
Pradanack Cross, 305. Head, 305.
Prawle Point, 104.
Praze-an-Beeble, 290.
Prestonbury Castle, 118.
Prideaux, 248. Warren, 248. Humphrey, birthplace, 224. School, 236.
Pridhamsleigh, 115.
Priglis Bay, 350.

INDEX. 363

PRINCE.
Prince Albert Mine, 165.
Prince, John, birthplace, 24.
His living, 60.
Prince's Town, 113, 137.
Quarries, 138.
Probus, 254.
Prout the artist, birthplace, 69.
Proverbs, of Devon, 163. Of Cornwall, 262, 269.
Prussia Cove, 314.
Puckie Stone, 127.
Pulpit Rock, 148.
Punchbowl Rock, 150.
Puslinch, 160.
Pynes House, 5, 161.

Q.
Quakers' Burial-ground, 334.
Quethiock, 274.

R.
Radford, 82.
Ragged Island, 152.
Railway, Great Western, 2, 20. S. Western, 21, 43. N. Devon, 44, 160. S. Devon, 51, 88. Dartmouth and Torbay, 95. Plymouth and Dartmoor, 138. S. Devon and Tavistock, 142. W. Cornwall, 230.
Raised beaches, xxii, 90, 172, 224, 270, 285, 312, 330, 336.
Raleigh House, 169.
Raleigh, Sir Walter, birthplace, 41. His first cigar, 102. Residence, 28.
Ralph's Hole, 107.
Rame Head, 262.
Ramillies Cove, 107.
Rattery, 61.
Rattle Brook, 155.
Raven's Hugo, 309.
Raven Rock, 152.
Red Deer, 198.
Redford, 155.
Red Moor, 247.
Redmoor mines, 274.
Redruth, 286.
Red Sandstone, New, xxi. Old, xiv.
Resingy Round, 298.
Resparvell Down, 215.
Restormel Castle, 246. House, 246. Mine, 246.
Restronguet Creek, 280, 284.
Resugga Castle, 253.
Revelstoke, 158.

SAND.
Reynolds, Sir Joshua, portrait, 22. Birthplace, 67.
Rialton, 228. Priory, 228.
Ridgeway, 68.
Rill, the, 106.
Ring Castle, 180.
Ringrone, 105.
Rippon Tor, 111, 124.
Road into Cornwall, ancient, 220.
Roborough Down, 154. Stone, xx, 84.
Roche, 211. Rocks, 211, 229.
Rock basins, xxvi, 128, 138, 207, 248, 249. Idols, 101. Pillars, 127, 137, 140, 141.
Rockham, 186.
Rolls Tor, 119.
Roman remains, xxviii.
Roncumbe Gate, 39.
Rose, 258.
Rosecadgehill, 298.
Rose Hill, 298.
Roscarrock House, 223.
Roseland, 270.
Rosemorran, 298.
Rosemullion Head, 282.
Rosevean, 150.
Rosevear, 150.
Rosewall, 322.
Rosewarne, 292.
Rotten Pits, 107.
Rougemont Castle, 15. Lodge, 15.
Roughtor, 206. Copper-mine, 206.
Round Bury, 275.
Round Island, 152.
Rounds, 288, 328, 330, 333.
Roundy Pound, 128.
Rowdon Wood, 150.
Rowe the dramatist, birthplace, 153.
Ruan Lanlhorne, 254. Minor, 309.
Ruan's Well, St., 310.
Rugged Jack, 175.
Rugglestone, 125.
Rundlestone, 138.

S.
Sadborough House, 24.
Salcombe, 105. Harbour, 105. Castle, 106. Regis, 36. Down, 36. Hill, 38.
Salston House, 30.
Saltash, 84, 211. Viaduct, 230.
Saltram, 68, 86.
Sampford Courtenay, 163. Peverell, 3. Spiney, 153.
Samson, 150.
Sancreed, 328.
Sand, 39.

SIMONSBATH.
Sandford, 162.
Sandhills, xxiii.
Sandplace, 264.
Sandridge, 61, 95.
Sawmill Cove, 106.
Saxon's Burrow, 185.
Schorl-rock, xix.
Scilly, Islands of, 345. Islet, 350.
Scob Hill, 179.
Scorhill Circle, 128.
Scorrier Gate stat., 286. House, 286.
Scythe-stone quarries, 2.
Sea-beaches, ancient, xxii.
Seacombe House, 24.
Seaton, 25, 31.
Sector House, 24.
Seine-fishing, liv.
Sennen church-town, 334. Cove, 336.
Serpentine, xv.
Seven Stones, 346, 352. Tors, 186.
Shabicombe, 108.
Shaldon, 56.
Sharkham Point, 97.
Shark's Fin, 335.
Sharpham, 61. Lodge, 62, 63.
Sharpitor, 65, 114, 119, 238.
Sharp Point Tor, 238.
Sharrow Grot, 261.
Shaugh, 143. Bridge, 143. Beacon, 144.
Sheafhayne House, 28.
Shebbeare, John, birthplace, 172.
Sheepstor, 139, 145.
Shellands, 152.
Shell Top, 6.
Shelstone Pound, 45.
Shercombe, 182.
Sheviock, 235.
Shillingford, 108.
Shillingham, 233.
Shipman Head, 351.
Shobrook, 163. Park, 22, 161.
Shovel, Sir Cloudesley, death of, 347.
Shute, 25. House, 25, 37.
Sid, river, 37, 40.
Sidbury, 38. Hill, 38. Castle, 39.
Sidenham, Humphrey, birthplace, 198.
Sidford, 38.
Sidmouth, 37. Environs and Excursions, 38, 39. Vale, 36.
Sidney Cove, 314.
Sidney Godolphin Mine, 314.
Silver-lead mines, 182.
Silver Well, 289.
Silverton Park, 21.
Simonsbath, 180.

R 2

SISTERS.

Sisters rocks, 110.
Sittaford Tor, 129.
Skat Tor, 108, 121.
Skeleton tours, vii.
Skelywadden, 321.
Slade, 66.
Slapton, 101. Lea, 101. Sands, 102.
Slate-quarries, 114, 154.
Slaughter Bridge, 213.
Sloven's Bridge, 211.
Small Hanger china-clay works, 66.
Smallmouth, 184.
Smelting-furnaces, xxxiii.
Smith, Great and Little, 150.
Smithike, 282.
Soap Rock, 105.
Sound, the, 79.
Sounding Gate, 115.
Sourton Down, 52.
South Brent, 64. Beacon, 64.
South Carn, 137.
South Down, 15.
South Hams, xlix.
South Molton, 164.
South Zeal, 156.
Sowton, 10.
Span Head, 178.
Spar, xiv.
Spinsters' Rock, 45, 119.
Spitchwick, 111.
Sportsman's Arms, 204, 275.
Spreyton, 44.
Sprydoncote, 5.
Staddon Heights, 82.
Stair Hole, 106.
Stamford Hill, 275.
Stanborough Camp, 102.
Stanbury Creek, 279.
Stannary Court, xxxiv, 245. Laws, xxxv. Parliaments, xxxv, 135. Prisons, xxxv, 49, 245.
Stannaton Down, 152.
Stapletor, 139.
Star Castle, 147.
Starcross, 54. Stat., 54.
Start Point, 101.
Staverton Bridge, 62.
Steam-bridge, 211.
Steatite, xv, 105.
Stedcombe House, 32, 34.
Steeperton Tor, 156.
Steeple Cove, 106.
Stephen's, St., in Brannel, 252. Down, 275.
Stepper Point, 224.
Stevenstone House, 167.
Sticklepath, 45.
Stockeridge, 195.
Stockleigh Pomeroy, 22.
Stoke, 79. Climsland, 274. Fleming, 102. Gabriel, 63, 95. Point, 158.
Stokeley House, 101.

TAWTON.

Stokenham, 101.
Stone avenues, xxv, 66, 116, 128, 129, 140, 239. Hedges, xlvi. Pillars, xxv.
Stone Dance, 141.
Stonehouse, 68, 75. Marine Barracks, 76. Naval Hospital, 76. Victualling-yard, 75.
Stones, the, 291.¹
Stonyford, 222.
Stoodleigh Court, 196.
Stothard, where he died, 154.
Stover Lodge, 112. Canal, 124.
Stow, 278.
Stratton, 275.
Stream-works, xii.
Street, 102.
Street-an-Nowan, 141.
Strete Raleigh Manor House, 21.
Submarine forests, xxii, 90.
Summercourt, 211.
Sun Rock, 148.
Sutton Pool, 71.
Swan Pool, 285.
Swimbridge, 169.
Sydenham, 150. Mount, 197. South, 151.
Symonsborough, 3.
Syward's Cross, 140.

T.

Talland, 264.
Tamar river, 51, 79, 81, 87, 151, 199, 211, 213, 275. Source, 279. Silver-lead mine, 153.
Tamerton Creek, 84. Follot, 85.
Tane, St., 212.
Taphouse, West, 245, 255.
Tapley Park, 169.
Tar Balk, 107.
Taunton, 2. Vale of, 3.
—— to Lynmouth and Lynton, 191.
Tavistock, 146. Abbey, 147. Church, 148. Eminent natives, 149. Excursions, 149-154.
Tavistock to South Zeal, 155.
Tavy Cleave, 52, 152. River, 84, 85, 146, 149, 151, 152. Source, 47, 110, 131. Vale, 52, 142, 146, 152.
Taw river, 45, 165, 168, 169, 171, 188. Source, 47, 110, 111. Marsh, 45. Vale, 167.
Tawstock Court, 167.
Tawton, Bishop's, 167. South, 45.

TORQUAY.

Taylor's Island, 149.
Tean, 152.
Teath, St., 222.
Tehidy, 289.
Teigncoomb, 128.
Teignmouth, 56. Excursions, 57. Stat., 56.
Teign river, 56, 57, 109, 117, 127. Source, 110, 131. Valley, 108, 110.
Temperature of Devon and Cornwall, lvii.
Temple, 210. Tor, 210.
Termolum of Romans, 165.
Tertiary deposits, xxii.
Thankes, 84, 211.
Thatcher Rock, 90.
Theodore Palæologus, tomb, 270.
Thomas's, St., stat., 53.
Thorn, 16.
Thorncombe, 24.
Three-barrow Tor, 65.
Throwleigh, 45, 128.
Thurlestone, 107.
Tideford, 234.
Timberscombe, 197.
Timewell House, 196.
Tin, grain, xli. History, xxxiii. Islands, xxxiv, 345. Lodes, xxxvii. Mining, xxxviii. Ores, xxxvi. White, xliii.
Tinckler's Point, 152.
Tintagel, 217. Castle, 217. Church, 220. Head, 217.
Titanium, where first discovered, 311.
Tiverton, 20. Junction, 3. Castle, church, 20. Almshouses, grammar-school, manufactures, 21.
Tober, 206.
Tolcarne, valley, 298.
Tolch Gate, 1.
Tolmên, the, 281, 285, 300.
Tolmên Point, 148.
Tolmêns, xxvi, 127, 281, 285, 300, 341, 348.
Tol Pedn Penwith, 118.
Toogood, Micaiah, birthplace, 24.
Tooth Rock, 148.
Topsham, 41, 51.
Tor Abbey, 90. Moham, 89. Stat., 88. Wood Mine, 48.
Torbay, 90. Fishery, 96. Landing-place of the Prince of Orange, 90.
Torcross, 101.
Torpoint, 84, 231.
Torquay, 89. Excursions, 92. Stat., 88.
—— to Brixham and Dartmouth, 95.

INDEX. 365

TORRIDGE.

Torridge Canal, 167. River, 169, 170, 171, 199. Source, 279. Valley, 167, 170.
Torrington, 166.
Tors, 131.
Tor's Steps, 181, 198.
Totnes, 58. Castle, 59. Church, 60. Library, excursions, 60. Stat., 58.
—— to Plymouth, 159.
Toup, Rev. Jonathan, birthplace, 323. His living, 264.
Towan Head, 229.
Towans, xxiii, 292.
Towednack, 121.
Tracey House, 27.
Track-lines, 125.
Trackways, xxvii, 65, 124, 125, 134, 135.
Trappean rocks, xv.
Traveller's View, xlv.
Trawl-fishing, lii.
Trebawith Strand, 220.
Trebartha Hall, 204.
Trebowling Hill, 287.
Trecarrel, 204.
Trecroben Hill, 292.
Tredrea, 291.
Tre-Druith, 286.
Treen, 117, 119, 140.
Treenethack Cross, 111.
Treewoofe, 142.
Treffry, Mr. J. T., birthplace, 267. Residence, 266.
Treffry Viaduct, 248.
Trefusis, 284.
Tregantle, Lower, 261. Higher, 261.
Tregeagle, Giant, 209, 211, 247, 269.
Tregeagle's Hole, 269. Quoits, 253, 269.
Tregear Bottom, 245.
Tregedna, 283.
Tregenna, 122.
Tregeseal Circle, 111.
Tregolls, 255, 256.
Tregonebris Hill, 114.
Tregony, 253.
Tregonning Hill, 312.
Tregoss Moors, 210, 211.
Trogothnan, 255, 256, 257, 284.
Tregrehan, 249.
Trelaune, 255.
Trelawne, 261. Mill, Inlet of, 261.
Trelawny, Bishop, 264.
Treleaver Hill, 281.
Trelissic, 257, 284.
Trelowarren, 111.
Trematon Castle, 232. Law, 233.
Tremayne, 311.
Tremenkoverne, 314.

UPTON.

Trenant Park, 261.
Treneere, 298.
Trenemer Rock, 148.
Trengwainton, 298, 300. Carn, 100, 128.
Trentishoe, 181. Barrow, 182.
Trereife, 298, 333, 334.
Trerice, 211, 229.
Treryn, 119. Castle, 119.
Tresavean Mine, 287.
Tresawsen, 255.
Tresco, 351. Abbey, 351.
Tresilian Bridge, 255. Creek, 256.
Trethill, 235.
Trevalgan Hill, 121.
Trevaunance Porth, 260.
Trevaller, 324.
Trevaylor, 298.
Treveddoe tin stream-work, 209.
Trevena, 217.
Treverbyn Vean, 242.
Trevethow, 292.
Trevethy Stone, 237.
Trevince, 288.
Trevorder, 209.
Trevose Head, 225.
Trewan, 226.
Trewartha Tor, 239.
Trewarthenick, 254.
Trewavas Head, 312.
Trewidden, 298, 334.
Trewinnard, 293.
Trewint, 205.
Trewithen, 254.
Trink Hill, 121.
Tristford, 62.
Troove, 342.
Trowlsworthy Tor, 144.
Truen, 311.
Truro, 211, 255. River, 255, 257, 284.
Truro to Falmouth, 280.
—— to Penzance, 285, 300.
Try Valley, 299.
Tudy, St., 221.
Two Barrows Hill, 206.
Two Bridges, 135.
Two Waters Foot, 240.

U.

Uffculme, 4.
Ugborough, 159. Beacon, 159. Castle, 159.
Ugbrooke Park, 109.
Umberleigh Bridge, 165, 198. Stat., 165.
United Mines, 287.
Upcott, 169.
Uplyme, 24.
Upton, 97. Lodge, 98.

WELLINGTON.

V.

Vale Down, 48.
Valley of Rocks, 174. Cornish, 217.
Varfell, 293.
Vectis, ancient, xxxiv.
Veep, St., 266.
Vellan Dreath, 116. Point, 105.
Venn House, 153.
Veryan Bay, 269. Beacon, 269.
Vincent Pits, 107.
Virtuous Lady Mine and Cave, 152.
Vitifer Mine, 125.
Viverdon Down, 271.
Vivian, Lord, birthplace, 256.
Vixen Tor, 141.

W.

Waddeton Court, 61, 95.
Wadebridge, 222.
Waidon Hill, 89.
Walk across Dartmoor, 155.
Walkham river, 139, 141, 146, 152. Valley of, 141, 146, 152.
Walkhampton, 146.
Walla brook, 127, 128, 150.
Wallis, Captain, birthplace, 212. Residence, 111.
Walreddon House, 150.
Warbstow Barrow, 212.
Ward Bridge, 153.
Warfleet, 100.
Warleggan, 209, 242.
Warleigh, 84, 85, 87, 151. Tor, 85.
Warren, the, 42, 54.
Watch Hill, 151.
Watchet, 194.
Watcombe, 57, 94.
Watergate Bay, 229.
Watermill Bay, 149.
Watermouth, 184.
Watern Tor, 129, 130. Oak, 155.
Waters' Meet, 174.
Wattle Down, 18.
Watton Court, 61, 95.
Wear Gifford, 167. Manor-house, 170. Oak, 170.
Webburn, river, 113.
Week St. Mary, 277.
Weir House, 43. Head, 83, 84, 143, 150.
Welcombe, 193.
Wellington, 2.
Wellington Monument, 2.
Wellington's Sarcophagus, 248.

WEMBURY.

Wembury, 159.
Wemworthy, 164.
Wenford Bridge, 245.
Wenn, 245.
Werrington Park, 204, 275.
Wesley, the scene of his preaching, 287, 144. Where he first preached in Cornwall, 299.
Wesley's Rock, 299.
West Allington, 157.
West Down Beacon, 41.
Western Beacon, 64, 65.
Weston Mouth, 16.
—— Super-Mare, 2.
Weycroft Bridge, 25.
Wheare, Digory, birthplace, 277.
Wherry Mine, 147.
Whetstone quarries, 1, 27.
Whimple stat., 31.
Whispering Stone, 249.
Whitaker the antiquary, his rectory, 254. Grave, 254.
Whitchurch, 146. Down, 151.
White ale, 105, 156.
Whiteball Tunnel, 2.
White Cliff, 11.
White Island, 152.
White Stone, 108, 117, 121.
White Tor, 115.
Whiteford House, 274.
Whitehorse Hill, 130.
Whitepebble Bay, 186.
Whiterock, 115.
Whitesand Bay, 261, 262, 335, 336.

WOOLEY.

Whiteway House, 109.
Whyddon Park, 119, 129.
Widdecombe, 103. In the Moor, 124.
Widemouth Bay, 278.
Widey Court, 87.
Widworthy, 26. Court House, 26.
Wild Tor, 156.
Willapark Head, 214. Point, 215, 217.
William's Height, 283. Grave, 283.
Wilsey Down, 212.
Winnow, St., 266.
Winsford, 181.
Winslade House, 43.
Winstow, the, L
Wiscombe Park, 37.
Wistman's Wood, 135.
Witheby, 40.
Withiel, 245.
Withycombe, 42.
Withypool, 180.
Wolcott, Dr, birthplace, 157. School, 216.
Wolf Rock, 335.
Wolford Lodge, 4.
Wonham, 196.
Woodborough, 58.
Woodbury Castle, 39, 102. Common, 42. Hill, 39. Road stat., 43.
Woodford Bridge, 199.
Woodville, 106.
Woolacombe, 186.
Woolbrook Glen, 40.
Wooley Barrows, 279.

ZENNOR.

Wooston Castle, 118.
Worlington, 164.
Worth, 21.
Worthyvale, 213.
Wray Barton, 121.
Written Stone, 127. Down of the, 127.

Y.

Yalden the poet, birthplace, 7.
Yardbury, 17.
Yart, river, 25.
Yartor, 114.
Yealm, 159. Bridge, 160. Cavern, 160. Estuary, 159. Head, 65. River, 66, 111.
Yealmpton, 160.
Yellow Carn, 307.
Yeo Vale, 170.
Yeoford Stat., 163.
Yes Tor, 46, 113.
York House, 298.
Youlston Park, 169.

Z.

Zawn Kellis, 337.
Zawn Pyg, 337.
Zawn Reeth, 337.
Zeal, South, 156.
Zennor, 123. Quoit, 123.

THE END.

LONDON: PRINTED BY W. CLOWES AND SONS, STAMFORD STREET, AND CHARING CROSS.

MURRAY'S HANDBOOK ADVERTISER.
1869.

The best Advertising Medium for all who are desirous of attracting the attention of English and American Tourists in all parts of the world.

Annual Circulation, 15,000.

Advertisements must be received by the 20th April, and are inserted at the rate of £5 for a page and 50s. for half a page.

INDEX TO THE ADVERTISEMENTS.

	Page
AIX LES BAINS—Grand Hôtel de l'Europe	64
AMSTERDAM—Brack's Hotel	32
AMPHION—Bains d'Amphion	43
ANDERMATT—Nagel-Donazians, Naturalist	60
ANTWERP—Hôtel St. Antoine	38
Hôtel de l'Europe	40
Hôtel de la Paix	42
Hôtel du Grand Labourer	64
ATHENS—Hôtel des Etrangers	48
BADEN-BADEN—Victoria Hotel	37
BARCELONA—Hôtel de Quatre Nations	46
BELLAGIO—Great Britain Hotel	40
BERLIN—Hôtel Royal	22
Hôtel d'Angleterre	30
BERNE—Heller's Musical Boxes	31
BIARRITZ—Hôtel de France	28
BOLOGNA—Hôtel d'Italie	50
BONN—Golden Star Hotel	24
BREISGAU—Hôtel d'Allemande	46
BORDEAUX—Hôtel des Princes	42
BRIENZ—Grossmann's Wood Sculpt.	6
BRUSSELS—Hôtel de Belle Vue	64
Grand Hôtel de Saxe	45
CADENABBIA—Hôtel de Belle Vue	46
CHAUMONT—Hôtel de Chaumont	37
COLOGNE—Farina's Eau de Cologne	2
Jacobi's Cigars	12
CONSTANTINOPLE—Hôtel d'Angleterre	64
DIEPPE—Hôtel des Bains	45
Hôtel Royal	46
DIJON—Hôtel du Jura	32
DRESDEN—Hôtel de Saxe	44
ENGADINE—Baths of St. Moritz	42
ENGELBERG—Hôtel Titlis	11
FLORENCE—Aglietti & Sons, Artists	10
Bianchini's Mosaic	6
Brizzi's Musical Establishment	25
Costa and Conti, Artists	12
Hôtel de la Paix	14
Montelatici's Mosaics	14
Romanelli, Sculptor	26
FRANKFORT—Tacchi's Glass Warehouse	
Roman Emperor Hotel	20
Böhler's Manufactory of Staghorn	51
FREIBURG—Hôtel Sommer	37
GENEVA—Baker, Chemist	14
Brémond, Musical Boxes	26
Grand Hôtel, Beau Rivage	22
Grivaz, Jeweller	7
Hôtel de la Couronne	25
Hôtel du Lac	19
Hôtel de la Paix	2
Hôtel de l'Ecu	
Hôtel de la Metropole	32
Journal des Etrangers	65
Ladies' Boarding School	64
Lacroix, Watchmaker	20

	Page
GENEVA—Moulinié, Watchmaker	32
Manchain, Wood Carvings	60
Pension des Alpes	33
Tissot and Co., Watchmakers	65
GENOA—Grand Hôtel d'Italie	65
Hôtel des Quatre Nations	60
HANOVER—Union Hotel	35
HEIDELBERG—Court of Baden Hotel	36
Hôtel de l'Europe	43
Prince Charles Hotel	44
HOMBOURG—Hôtel Victoria	42
Hôtel des Quatre Saisons	40
INTERLACHEN—Hôtel de Belle Vue	47
Hôtel Jungfrau	47
INTERLAKEN—Hôtel Belvedere	37
LAUSANNE—Hôtel Beau Rivage	42
Hôtel Belvedere	
Hôtel Gibbon	35
Hôtel Richemont	
LUCERNE—Hôtel d'Angleterre	28
Hôtel Beau Rivage	42
Hôtel Belle Vue	37
Hôtel Schweizerhof	32
Swan Hotel	30
LUCERNE — Grand Hôtel Bonne-Maison	30
LUGANO—Hôtel du Parc	47
MARSEILLES — Grand Hôtel de Marseilles	22
Grand Hôtel Noailles	
MAYENCE—Hôtel d'Angleterre	19
MENTONE—Hôtel de la Méditerranée	48
MILAN—Hôtel Cavour	47
Grand Hôtel de Milan	41
MUNICH — Wimmer's Gallery of Fine Arts	7
NAPLES—Civalleri, Agent	18
Hôtel du Louvre	20
Hôtel d'Angleterre	20
NICE—Baker, Chemist	
Hôtel Chauvain	36
NUREMBERG—Hôtel de Baviere	14
Red Horse Hotel	45
PARIS—Hôtel des Deux Mondes	30
Galignani's Guide	26
PISA—Andreoni, Sculptor	6
PRAGUE—Hofmann's Glass Manufactory	10
RAGAZ—Hôtel Tamina	19
ROME—Baker, Chemist	14
Shea, House Agent	13
ROTTERDAM—Kramers, Bookseller	26
SCHAFFHAUSEN—Hôtel Schweizerhof	41
SEVILLE—Hôtel de Londres	46
STOCKHOLM—Blanch's Café	53
TURIN—Grand Hôtel de l'Europe	31
VENICE—Grand Hôtel Victoria	54
Ponti, Optician	12
VEVAY—Hôtel Monnet	53

	Page
VICHY—Grand Hôtel du Parc	44
Grand Hôtel Velay	44
VIENNA—Lobmeyr's Glass Manufactory	10
Neuhoefer, Optician	42
VILLENEUVE—Hôtel Byron	2
WIESBADEN—Black Bear Hotel	48
Four Seasons Hotel	42
WILDBAD—Hôtel Klumpp	41
LONDON.	
Agents—M'Cracken	3-5
— Olivier and Co.	16, 17
— Carr and Co.	62, 63
Archaeology, Handbook of	60
Athenaeum	55
Atlas and the Morts	58
Books and Maps	59
Brown and Polson's Patent Flour	23
Bubbles from the Brunnen	15
Birmingham—Western Hotel	67
Cary's Telescope	7
Chubb's Locks and Safes	16
Continental Express Agency	21
Couriers and Servants	65
Foreign Books	33
Gillot's Pens	57
Handbook of Travel Talk	66
Heal's Furniture and Bedsteads	61
Highlands of Turkey	58
Lee and Carter's Guide Depôt	54, 66
London and Westminster Bank	22
Maddie's Library	28
National Provincial Bank	52
Nile and Its Banks	29
Norway	47
Parr's Life Pills	42
Passport Agency—Adams	21
Passport Agency—Dorrell	55
Passport Agency—Goodman	67
Passport Agency—Stanford	22
Pompeii and Its History	60
Portmanteaus—Allan's	27
Railway—South-Western	28
Thresher's Essentials for Travelling	13
Winter in America	58
LYNTON— Valley of Rocks Hotel	42
OXFORD— Spiers' Ornamental Manufactures	26
PENZANCE— Mount's Bay House and Hotel	53
IRELAND.	
PORTRUSH— Antrim Arms Hotel	22

SWITZERLAND.—Geneva.

GRAND HOTEL DE LA PAIX.

J. KOHLER, PROPRIETOR.

FIRST-CLASS HOTEL.

FROM THE TWENTY BALCONIES ADORNING THIS HOTEL THE MOST SPLENDID PANORAMIC VIEW IN THE WHOLE OF SWITZERLAND MAY BE HAD.

GENEVA. (SWITZERLAND.)

HÔTEL DE L'ECU.

New Proprietor, GUSTAVE WOLFF.

Same Proprietor of Hôtel Byron, near Villeneuve.

THIS unrivalled and admirably conducted Hotel has long enjoyed an extensive and high reputation among Travellers. Situated in the finest part of the town, and facing the lake, it commands a beautiful view of the environs. Its accommodation is of so superior a character, that tourists will find it a highly desirable place of residence or of temporary sojourn. Table-d'Hôte at 1 o'clock, 4 fr.; at 5 o'clock, 4 fr. Arrangements made with families during the winter months at very reasonable charges. New Reading and Smoking Rooms.

VILLENEUVE.

HÔTEL BYRON,

NEAR TO THE CASTLE OF CHILLON.

New Proprietor, GUSTAVE WOLFF.

Same Proprietor as of the Hôtel de l'Ecu at Geneva.

FIRST-CLASS HOTEL, offering every comfort for an agreeable residence; surrounded by a vast Park and a beautiful Garden, and admirably situated for excursions to the mountains. Reading, Billiard, and Smoking Rooms. Reduced prices for a prolonged stay. Horses and Carriages. Breakfast; Table-d'Hôte. Private Dinners at any hour. English spoken. Landing place for Steamers. Telegraph Bureau.

LONDON, May 1, 1869.
MESSRS. J. & R. M^cCRACKEN,
38, QUEEN STREET, CANNON STREET, E.C.,

AGENTS, BY APPOINTMENT, TO THE ROYAL ACADEMY, NATIONAL GALLERY,
AND GOVERNMENT DEPARTMENT OF SCIENCE AND ART,

GENERAL AND FOREIGN AGENTS,

WINE MERCHANTS,
Agents for Bouvier's Neuchatel Champagne,

AND

AGENTS GENERALLY FOR THE RECEPTION AND SHIPMENT OF WORKS OF
ART, BAGGAGE, &C.,

FROM AND TO ALL PARTS OF THE WORLD,

Avail themselves of this opportunity to return their sincere thanks to the Nobility and Gentry for the patronage hitherto conferred on them, and hope to be honoured with a continuance of their favours. Their charges are framed with a due regard to economy, and the same care and attention will be bestowed as heretofore upon all packages passing through their hands.

J. and R. McC. have the advantage of

DRY AND SPACIOUS WAREHOUSES,

Where Works of Art and all descriptions of Property can be kept during the Owners' absence, at most moderate rates of rent.

Parties favouring J. and R. M^cC. with their Consignments are requested to be particular in having the Bills of Lading sent to them DIRECT by Post, and also to forward their Keys with the Packages, as, although the contents may be free of Duty, all Packages are still EXAMINED by the Customs immediately on arrival. Packages sent by Steamers or otherwise to Southampton and Liverpool also attended to; but all Letters of Advice and Bills of Lading to be addressed to 38, QUEEN STREET, as above.

MESSRS. J. AND R. M^cCRACKEN
ARE THE APPOINTED AGENTS IN ENGLAND OF MR. J. M. FARINA,
Gegenüber dem Julichs Platz, Cologne,

FOR HIS

CELEBRATED EAU DE COLOGNE.

MESSRS. J. AND R. M^CCRACKEN'S

PRINCIPAL CORRESPONDENTS.

ALEXANDRIA..... The Egyptian Commercial and Trading Company—late BRIGGS & Co.
ALICANTE .... Mr. P. R. DAHLANDER.
ANCONA .... Messrs. MOORE, MORELLET, & Co.
ANTWERP .... { Messrs. F. MACK & Co.
{ Mr. P. VAN ZEEBROECK, Picture Dealer, &c., Rue des Récollets, 2076.
ATHENS, PIRÆUS
BADEN BADEN ... { Messrs. STUFFER & BINDER. Mr. F. PELIKAN's Successor, C. RASCH.
{ Messrs. MELLERD FRERES. Mr. H. ULLRICH.
BAD EMS......... Messrs. BECKER & JUNG. Mr. H. W. THIEL.
BAGNERES DE BI-
GORRE (Hautes { Mr. LÉON GÉRUZET, Marble Works.
Pyrénées).........
BASLE .... { Messrs. JEAN PREISWERK & FILS. Mr. JEAN THOMMEN, Fils.
{ Mr. J. FREY.
BERLIN .... { Messrs. SCHOCKLER Brothers.
{ Mr. LION M. COHN, Comm^{re}. Expéditeur.
BERNE .... Messrs. A. BAUER & Co.
BEYROUT .... Mr. HENRY HEALD.
BOLOGNA .... Messrs. RENOLI, BUGGIO, & Co. Sig. L. MENL.
{ Mr. GREMAILLY Fils Ainé.
BORDEAUX .... { Mr. LÉON GÉRUZET, 44, Allées de Tourny.
{ Messrs. RIVIERE & Co., Place du Palais, 4.
BOULOGNE S. M... Messrs. MORY & Co. Messrs. L. J. VOGUE & Co.
CALAIS........... Messrs. L. J. VOGUE & Co.
CALCUTTA........ Messrs. GILLANDERS, ARBUTHNOT, & Co.
CANNES.......... Mr. TAYLOR.
CARLSBAD .... Mr. THOMAS WOLF, Glass Manufacturer.
CARRARA......... Sig. F. BIENAIMÉ, Sculptor.
CATANIA .... Messrs. JEANS & Co.
CIVITA VECCHIA. Messrs. LOWE BROTHERS, British Vice-Consulate.
COLOGNE......... { Mr. J. M. FARINA, gegenüber dem Julichs Platz.
{ Messrs. G^{me}. TILMES & Co.
CONSTANCE....... Mr. FRED. HOZ.
CONSTANTINOPLE Mr. ALFRED C. LAUGHTON. Messrs. C. S. HANSON & Co.
COPENHAGEN.\... Messrs. H. J. BING & SON.
CORFU .... Mr. J. W. TAYLOR.
DRESDEN .... { Messrs. H. W. BASSENGE & Co. Mr. E. ARNOLD, Printseller. The
{ Director of the Royal Porcelain Manufactory Depôt. Mr. E.
{ RICHTER, 4, Neumarkt. Messrs. SEEGER & MAESER. [Madame
{ HELENA WOLFSOHN, Schössergasse, No. 5. Mr. MORITZ MEYER,
{ Moritz Strasse.
FLORENCE........ { Messrs. FRENCH & Co. Sig. LUIGI RAMACCI. Messrs. Emm^{le}. FENZI
{ & Co. Messrs. MAQUAY and PAKENHAM. Mr. E. GOODBAN.
{ Messrs. NESTI, CIARDI, & Co. Mr. ANT^o. DI LUIGI PIACENTI.
{ Mr. T. BIANCHINI, Mosaic Worker. Messrs. P. BAZZANTI & FIG.,
{ Sculptors, Lungo l'Arno. Sig. CARLO NOCCIOLI.
FRANKFORT O. M. { Mr. P. A. TACCHI's Successor, Glass Manufacturer, Zeil D, 44.
{ Messrs. BING, Jun., & Co. Mr. F. BÖHLER, Zeil D, 17.
{ Messrs. SACHS and HOCHHEIMER, Wine Merchants.
FRANZENSBAD.... Mr. C. J. HOFMANN.
GENEVA .... Mr. AUGst. SNELL. Mr. G. EIDENBENZ.
GENOA .... { Messrs. GRANET, BROWN, & Co.
{ Messrs. G. VIGBOLD & FIG^l. Mr. A. MOSSA, Croce di Malte.
GHENT .... { Messrs. DE BUYEEE FRERES, Dealers in Antiquities, Marché au
{ Beurre, No. 21.
GIBRALTAR ...... Messrs. ARCHBOLD, JOHNSTON, & POWERS. Messrs. TURNER & Co.
HAMBURG .... Messrs. J. P. JENSEN & Co. Messrs. SCHÖRMER & TEICHMANN.
HAVRE .... Messrs. LOUKDIN, Père, Fils jeune, and G. CAPRON.
HEIDELBERG .... Mr. PH. ZIMMERMANN.
HONFLEUR ...... Mr. J. WAGNER.

1869.   MURRAY'S HANDBOOK ADVERTISER.   5

MᶜCRACKEN'S LIST OF CORRESPONDENTS—continued.

INTERLACKEN .... Mr. J. GROSSMANN. Messrs. IMER, TAEMP & Co. Mr. C. H. SCHUH.
JERUSALEM ...... Messrs. E. F. SPITTLER & Co.
LAUSANNE .... Mr. DUBOIS RENOU, Fils.
LEGHORN .... { Messrs. ALEX. MACBEAN & Co. Messrs. MAQUAY & PAKENHAM.
                   Messrs. THOMAS PATE & SONS. Mr. M. RISTORI.
LEIPZIG .... Mr. J. E. OEHLSCHLAGER's Successor.
LISBON .... Mr. E. BOURGARD.
LUCERNE .... Messrs. F. KNORR & Fils.
MADRAS .... Messrs. BINNY & Co.
MALAGA .... Mr. GEORGE HODGSON.
MALTA .... { Mr. EMANUEL ZAMMIT. Messrs. Jos. DARMANIN & SONS, 45, Strada
                    Levante, Mosaic Workers. Mr. FORTUNATO TESTA, 92, Strada Sta
                    Lucia.
MANNHEIM .... Messrs. EYSSEN & CLAUS.
MARIENBAD .... Mr. J. T. ADLER, Glass Manufacturer.
MARSEILLES ...... { Messrs. CLAUDE CLERC & Co. Messrs. HORACE BOUCHET & Co.
                    Mr. PHILIORET, 7, Place du Théâtre.
MAYENCE .... Mr. G. L. KAYSER, Expediteur.
MENTONE .... Mr. PALMARO, Mr. JEAN ORENGO Fils.
MESSINA .... Messrs. CAILLER, WALKER, & Co.
MILAN .... { Mr. G. B. BUFFET, Piazzale di S. Sepolcro, No. 3176.
                    Messrs. FRATELLI BRAMBILLA. Messrs. ULRICH & Co.
MONTREAL .... Messrs. THOMPSON, MURRAY, & Co.
MUNICH .... { Messrs. WIMMER & Co., Printsellers, Brienner Strasse, 3. Messrs.
                    BLEICHER and ANDREIS.
NAPLES .... Messrs. IGGULDEN & Co. Messrs. W. J. TURNER & Co.
NEW YORK .... Messrs. AUSTIN, BALDWIN, & Co.
NICE .... { Messrs. A. LACROIX & Co., British Consulate. Messrs. M. & N.
                    GIORDAN. Mr. H. ULLRICH. M.M. MIGNON FRÈRES, 9, Rue Paradis.
NUREMBERG .... { Mr. JOHN CONRAD CNOPF, Banker and Forwarding Agent.
                    Mr. A. PICKERT, Dealer in Antiquities. Mr. MAX PICKERT.
OSTEND .... Messrs. BACH & Co. Messrs. MACK and Co.
PARIS .... Mr. L. CHENUE, Packer, Rue Croix Petits Champs, No. 24.
PAU .... Mr. J. MUSGRAVE CLAY. Mr. BRGEROT.
PISA .... Messrs. HUGUET & VAN LINT, Sculptors in Alabaster and Marble.
PRAGUE .... { Mr. W. HOFMANN, Glass Manufacturer, Blauern Stern.
                    Mr. A. V. LEBEDA, Gun Maker.
QUEBEC .... Messrs. FORSYTH & PEMBERTON.
ROME .... { Messrs. PLOWDEN, CHOLMELEY, & Co. Messrs. ALEX. MACBEAN & Co.
                    Messrs. FREEBORN & Co. Messrs. MAQUAY, PAKENHAM, & HOOKER.
                    Messrs. SPADA, FLAMINI, & Co. Messrs. FURSE BROS. & Co.
                    Mr. LUIGI BRANCHINI, at the English College. Mr. J. P. SHEA.
                    Messrs. WELBY, Bros.
ROTTERDAM .... Messrs. PRESTON & Co. Messrs. C. HEMMANN & Co.
SANREMO .... M. M. ASQUASCIATI FRERES.
SCHAFFHAUSEN .... Mr. FRED HOZ.
SEVILLE .... Mr. JULIAN B. WILLIAMS, British Vice-Consulate. M. J. A. BAILLY.
SMYRNA .... Messrs. HANSON & Co.
ST. PETERSBURG .. Messrs. THOMSON, BONAR, & Co. Mr. C. KRUGER.
THOUNE .... Mr. A. H. J. WALD, Bazaar. Mr. N. BUZBERGER.
TRIESTE .... Messrs. MOORE & Co.
TURIN .... Messrs. J. A. LACHAISE & FERRERO, Rue de l'Arsenal, No. 4.
VENICE .... { Mr. L. BOVARDI, Campo S. Fantino, No. 2000, russo.
                    Messrs. FRERES SCHIELIN. Mr. ANTONIO ZEN. Mr. C. PONTI.
                    Messrs. S. & A. BLUMENTHAL & Co.
VEVEY .... Mr. JULES GETAZ FILS.
VIENNA .... { Mr. H. ULLRICH, Glass Manufacturer, am Lugeck, No. 3.
                    Messrs. J. & L. LOBMEYER, Glass Manufacturers, 940, Kärnthner
VOLTERRA .... Sig. OTTO SOLAINI.   [Strasse.
WALDSHUTT .... Mr. FRED. HOZ.
ZURICH .... Mr. HONEGGER-FÜGLI.

FLORENCE.

TELEMACO DI G. BIANCHINI,
MANUFACTURER OF TABLES AND LADIES' ORNAMENTS
OF FLORENTINE MOSAIC,
LUNG' ARNO NUOVO, 1, AND BORG' OGNISSANTI, 2,

INVITES the English Nobility and Gentry to visit his Establishment, where may always be seen numerous specimens of this celebrated and beautiful Manufacture, in every description of Rare and Precious Stones. Orders for Tables and other Ornaments executed to any Design.

T. BIANCHINI's Correspondents in England are Messrs. J. & R. M'CRACKEN, 38, Queen Street, Cannon Street, E.C., London.

BRIENZ—INTERLACKEN.

J. GROSSMANN,
SCULPTOR IN WOOD, AND MANUFACTURER OF SWISS
WOOD MODELS AND ORNAMENTS,

AT INTERLACKEN.

HIS WAREHOUSE is situated between the Belvedere Hotel and Schweizerhof, where he keeps the largest and best assortment of the above objects to be found in Switzerland. He undertakes to forward Goods to England and elsewhere.

Correspondents in England, Messrs. J. & R. McCRACKEN, 38, Queen Street, Cannon Street, E.C., London.

PISA.

GIUSEPPE ANDREONI,
Sculptor in Alabaster and Objects of Fine Art,

NO. 872, VIA SANTA MARIA;

WHERE

A GREAT ASSORTMENT OF FINE ARTS, SCULPTURE, &c.,
CAN BE SEEN.

GENEVA.

F. GRIVAZ,
MANUFACTURING JEWELLER,
No. 10, GRAND QUAI.

Only Proprietor of the celebrated Grotto de Topazes discovered in August, 1868, in the Mountains de Galenstock, Canton d' Uri.

An immense choice of Jewels in the first taste will be found here, and all the Oriental Stones mounted and unmounted.

This house was founded in 1837, and is highly recommended by the numerous travellers who have visited it.

CARY'S IMPROVED POCKET TOURIST'S TELESCOPE.
(See '*Murray's Handbook*.')

MANUFACTURER of all descriptions of Mathematical, Surveying, and Optical Instruments, for the use of Naval and Military Officers, &c. Also the new Binocular Reconnoitring Field Glass, in Aluminium of exceeding lightness and durability, so highly spoken of by officers and other gentlemen: from 7*l*. 7*s*.; ordinary metal from 2*l*. 10*s*. Cary's improved Achromatic Microscope, with two sets of choice lenses, capable of defining the severe test objects; from 4*l*. 4*s*. Travelling Spectacles of all kinds.

* Mathematical and Optical Instrument Maker to the Admiralty, Trinity House, Royal Military College, Sandhurst, Royal Geographical Society, Christ's Hospital, Trinity House, King's College, &c.; and Optician to the Royal London Ophthalmic Hospital.

GOULD & PORTER, Successors to CARY,
181, STRAND, LONDON.
Established upwards of a Century.

MUNICH.

WIMMER & CO.,
GALLERY OF FINE ARTS.
3, BRIENNER STREET,

Invite the Nobility and Gentry to visit their GALLERY OF FINE ARTS, containing an Extensive Collection of

MODERN PAINTINGS
by the best Munich Artists,

PAINTINGS ON PORCELAIN AND ON GLASS,
also a large Assortment of

PHOTOGRAPHS,
including the complete Collections of the various Public Galleries.

Correspondents in England, Messrs. J. & R. M'CRACKEN, 38, Queen Street, Cannon Street, E.C., London.

Correspondents in the United States, Messrs. KELLER & LINGG, 97, Reade Street, New York.

FRANKFORT.

P. A. TACCHI'S SUCCESSOR,

ZEIL, No. 44,

BOHEMIAN FANCY GLASS AND CRYSTAL WAREHOUSE.

P. A. TACCHI'S SUCCESSOR, MANUFACTURER OF BOHEMIAN GLASS, begs to acquaint the Public that he has always an extensive Assortment in the Newest and most Elegant Designs of

ORNAMENTAL CUT, ENGRAVED, GILT, & PAINTED GLASS,

BOTH WHITE AND COLOURED,

In Dessert Services, Chandeliers, Candelabras, Articles for the Table and Toilet, and every possible variety of objects in this beautiful branch of manufacture. He solicits, and will endeavour to merit, a continuance of the favours of the Public, which he has enjoyed in so high a degree during a considerable number of years,

P. A. TACCHI'S SUCCESSOR has a BRANCH ESTABLISHMENT during the Summer Season at

WIESBADEN, in the Old Colonnade,

Where will always be found an extensive Selection of the newest Articles from his Frankfort Establishment.

Visitors to Frankfort should not fail to pay a visit to the Show Rooms of Mr. P. A. TACCHI'S SUCCESSOR.

His Correspondents in England, to whom he undertakes to forward Purchases made of him, are Messrs. J. & R. M'CRACKEN, 38, Queen Street, Cannon Street, E.C., London.

COLOGNE ON THE RHINE.

JOHANN MARIA FARINA,
GEGENÜBER DEM JÜLICH'S PLATZ

(Opposite the Jülich's Place),

PURVEYOR TO H. M. QUEEN VICTORIA;
TO H. R. H. THE PRINCE OF WALES;
TO H. M. THE KING OF PRUSSIA; THE EMPEROR OF RUSSIA;
THE EMPEROR OF FRANCE;
THE KING OF DENMARK, ETC. ETC.,

OF THE

ONLY GENUINE EAU DE COLOGNE,

Which obtained the only Prize Medal awarded to Eau de Cologne at the Paris Exhibition of 1867.

THE frequency of mistakes, which are sometimes accidental, but for the most part the result of deception practised by interested individuals, induces me to request the attention of English travellers to the following statement:—

The favourable reputation which my Eau de Cologne has acquired, since its invention by my ancestor in the year 1709, has induced many people to imitate it; and in order to be able to sell their spurious article more easily, and under pretext that it was genuine, they procured themselves a firm of *Farina*, by entering into partnership with persons of my names which is a very common one in Italy.

Persons who wish to purchase *the genuine and original Eau de Cologne* ought to be particular to see that the labels and the bottles have not only my name, *Johann Maria Farina*, but also the additional words, *gegenüber dem Jülich's Plats* (that is, opposite the Julich's Place), without addition of any number.

Travellers visiting Cologne, and intending to buy my genuine article, are cautioned against being led astray by cabmen, guides, commissioners, and other parties, who offer their services to them. I therefore beg to state that my manufacture and shop are in the same house, situated *opposite* the Julich's Place, and nowhere else. It happens too, frequently, that the said persons conduct the uninstructed strangers to shops of one of the fictitious firms, where, notwithstanding assertion to the contrary, they are remunerated with nearly the half part of the price paid by the purchaser, who, of course, must pay indirectly this remuneration by a high price and a bad article.

Another kind of imposition is practised in almost every hotel in Cologne, where waiters, commissioners, &c., offer to strangers Eau de Cologne, pretending that it is the genuine one, and that I delivered it to them for the purpose of selling it for my account.

The only certain way to get in Cologne my genuine article is to buy it personally at my house, *opposite the Jülich's Place*, forming the corner of the two streets, Unter Goldschmidt and Oben Marspforten, No. 23, and having in the front six balconies, of which the three bear my name and firm, *Johann Maria Farina*, Gegenüber Dem Julichs Platz.

The excellence of *my* manufacture has been put beyond all doubt by the fact that the Jurors of the Great Exhibitions in London, 1851 and 1862, awarded to me the Prize Medal; that I obtained honourable mention at the Great Exhibition in Paris, 1855; and received the only Prize Medal awarded to Eau de Cologne at the Paris Exhibition of 1867, and in Oporto 1865.

COLOGNE, *January*, 1869.

JOHANN MARIA FARINA,
GEGENÜBER DEM JÜLICH'S PLATZ.

⁎ *My Agency in London is at* MESSRS. J. & R. M'CRACKEN, 38, *Queen Street, Cannon Street, E.C.*

PRAGUE.

WILLIAM HOFMANN,
BOHEMIAN GLASS MANUFACTURER,
TO HIS MAJESTY THE EMPEROR OF AUSTRIA,
HOTEL BLUE STAR,

RECOMMENDS his great assortment of Glass Ware, from his own Manufactories in Bohemia. The choicest Articles in every Colour, Shape, and Description, are sold, at the same moderate prices, at his Establishments.
Correspondents in London, Messrs. J. and R. M'CRACKEN, 38, Queen Street, Cannon Street, E.C. *Goods forwarded direct to England, America, &c.*

FLORENCE.

JOHN AGLIETTI AND SONS,
ARTISTS,
GROUND FLOOR, No. 15, VIA MAGGIO,

HAVE a large Collection of Ancient and Modern Original Paintings, and also Copies from the most celebrated Masters.
Copies, Carved Frames, Gilt or Plain, made to order, and forwarded with despatch to all parts of the world.
Correspondents in England, Messrs. J. and R. M'CRACKEN, of No. 38, Queen Street, Cannon Street, E.C., London.

VIENNA.

The most extensive Warehouse for Bohemian White and Coloured Crystal Glass.

J. & L. LOBMEYR,
GLASS MANUFACTURERS,
No. 13, KÄRNTHNERSTRASSE.

ALL kinds of Bohemian White and Coloured Crystal Glass; Table, Dessert, and other Services; Vases, Candelabras, Chandeliers, Looking-glasses; Articles of Luxury, in Crystal Glass, mounted in Bronze, and in Carved Wood. They obtained the Prize Medal at the International Exhibitions of 1862 and 1867.
The prices are fixed at very moderate and reasonable charges.—The English language is spoken.
Their Correspondents in England, Messrs. J. and R. M'CRACKEN, No. 38, Queen Street, Cannon Street, E.C., London, will transmit all orders with the greatest care and attention.

ENGELBERG.

HOTEL ET PENSION TITLIS.

CATLAIN, Proprietor.

THIS new Hotel is fitted out with every comfort; containing 80 Beds, Ladies' Sitting-room, Reading, Billiard, and Smoking-rooms. English, French, and German Newspapers. English Services every Sunday.

The best starting-place for ascending Mount Titlis (18 miles); good guides, tariff 10 francs; the same as at Engstlen (see Berlepsch). Very nice excursions on the glaciers of Uri-Rothstock, Schlossberg, and Grasseu.

HOTEL ET PENSION DE L'ANGE,
BELONGING TO THE SAME PROPRIETOR.

Excellent Second-class Hotel. Clean and well-furnished Rooms at moderate prices. Warm and Cold Baths.

FLORENCE.

GRAND HÔTEL ROYAL de la PAIX,

LUNG' ARNO NUOVO AND PIAZZA MANIN.

Commanding a View of Bello Sguardo.

Patronized by the Royal Family and H.R.H. the Crown Prince of Prussia in 1868.

It contains one of the largest and handsomest Dining-rooms in Italy, constructed for the use of Balls, Banquets, and Concerts. Table d'hôte in the same, at 5 francs, the Wine included.

Rooms for Single Tourists, from 2 francs upwards. Large and small Apartments for Families.

Omnibus at every Train. All the Servants speak English.

Open all the Year round.

A. DE SALVI, *Sole Proprietor and Manager.*

FLORENCE.

MESSRS. COSTA & CONTI,
ARTISTS,
No. 8, VIA ROMANA,

Opposite the Museum of Natural History (Specola), and near the Pitti Gallery.

Messrs. COSTA and CONTI keep the largest collection in Florence of original Ancient and Modern Pictures, as well as Copies of all the most celebrated Masters.

N.B.—English spoken.

Correspondents in England, Messrs. J. and R. M'CRACKEN, 38, Queen Street, Cannon Street E.C., London.

COLOGNE ON THE RHINE—HAVANNA CIGARS.

A. G. JACOBI,
15, Fitzengraben, Cologne.

MESSRS. MAHLER BROTHERS AND CO., 7, Mincing-Lane, London, most respectfully beg to draw the attention of the English nobility and gentry to Mr. A. G. JACOBI'S well assorted Depôt of real fine Havanna Cigars of choice brands, imported *viâ* London Docks direct from Havanna, at reasonable prices. Orders to all parts of Germany, &c., promptly attended to by A. G. JACOBI, Wholesale Department, 15, Filzengraben.

Retail at Bruckenstrape, 5 c, in the centre of the town, between "Disch Hotel" and the Glass Passage.

VENICE.

CARLO PONTI,
OPTICIAN AND PHOTOGRAPHER,

WHO gained the Prize Medal at the International Exhibition of 1862, and whose House is acknowledged to be the first of its kind in the City, has opened a new and large Establishment in Piazza di San Marco, Procuratie Nuove, in addition to that which he keeps in the Riva dei Schiavoni, No. 4180, near the Albergo Reale Danieli.

The Optical Instrument invented by him, and known under the name of the

ALETOSCOPE, or MEGALETOSCOPE,

has undergone such improvements as to render it (according to the judgment of intelligent persons) the most perfect thing of its kind, both for its simple construction and magnificent optical effects.

Correspondents in London, Messrs. J. and R. M'CRACKEN, 38, Queen Street, Cannon Street, E.C.

ROME.

J. P. SHEA,
ENGLISH HOUSE-AGENT,
FORWARDING AGENT
TO H.R.H. THE PRINCE OF WALES,
11, PIAZZA DI SPAGNA.

At this Office persons applying for
Large or Small Furnished Apartments
invariably obtain correct and unbiassed information on all matters connected with
Lodging-Houses, Boarding-Houses,
and
Household Management,
while
Low and Fixed Charges
for practical services offer safe and satisfactory assistance to Proprietor and Tenant, as testified by the increasing confidence of English and American Travellers since the opening of the establishment in 1852.

Plans and Lists of Apartments sent by Post
to persons who wish to secure accommodation, or avoid inconvenience at the approach of Carnival or the Holy Week.

AS CUSTOM-HOUSE AGENT,
MR. SHEA clears and warehouses
Baggage and other effects
for travellers who, to avoid the expense of quick transit, send their things by sea or luggage-train, directed to his care.

He also superintends the
Packing of Works of Art and other Property
intrusted to his care, and the forwarding of the same to England, &c.; and being Agent for Messrs. Burns and McIvers' Italian line of steamers, can offer facilities on the freight of packages between Italy and England.

CORRESPONDENTS—
LONDON.................Messrs. J. & R. M'CRACKEN, 38, Queen Street, Cannon Street, E.C.
Messrs. CHAS. CARR & CO,. 14, Bishopsgate Street Within.
LIVERPOOL ....Messrs. STAVELEY & STARR, 9, Chapel Street.
Messrs. JAS. MOSS & CO., 78, Tower Buildings.
FOLKESTONE ....Mr. FAULKNER.
BOULOGNE S.M.......Mr. BERNARD, 18, Quai des Paquebots.
PARIS ....Messrs. L'HERBETTE, KANE, & CO., 8, Place de la Bourse.
MARSEILLES ....Messrs. GIRAUD FRERES, 44, Rue Sainte.
FLORENCE ....Messrs. HASKARD & SON.
NEW YORK ....Messrs. AUSTIN, BALDWIN, & CO., 72, Broadway.
BOSTON...................Messrs. WELLS, FARGO, & CO.

GENEVA.
NO. 2, PLACE DES BERGUES.

GEO. BAKER,
ENGLISH CHEMIST AND DRUGGIST,
PRESCRIPTIONS CAREFULLY PREPARED.
ALL KINDS OF PATENT MEDICINES & PERFUMERY.

Homœopathic Preparations. Soda and Saratoga Water.

Medicines and Preparations forwarded with the greatest despatch and safety to all parts of Switzerland by Post.

ROME.
17 & 18, VIA DELLA MERCEDE.

GEO. BAKER,
ENGLISH CHEMIST, GENEVA,

INFORMS the Inhabitants and Visitors of Rome that he has opened an Establishment at the above address, for the supply of English specialities and goods adapted for the use of Families at prices far inferior to those hitherto charged in Rome.

NICE.

PHARMACIE DANIEL ET Cie.
QUAI MASSENA.

GEO. BAKER,
ENGLISH CHEMIST OF GENEVA,

INFORMS the Visitors and Residents of Nice, that he has succeeded to the above old established and justly renowned Pharmacy, and that having associated with him Mr. GEORGE BUSBY, who for nine years past has been Assistant Manager of it, he hopes by careful attention and a moderate Scale of Charges, not only to maintain, but to extend, its ancient and well deserved reputation.

VISITORS TO NAPLES.

GENERAL AGENCY & COMMISSION OFFICE of the BRITISH LIBRARY

(*Established in 1837 by Mrs. Dorant*),

DIRECTED BY

GEORGE CIVALLERI,
Palazzo Friozzi, No. 267, Riviera di Chiaja.

WORKS OF ART, GOODS, AND LUGGAGE

forwarded to and received from all parts of the world, and warehoused at moderate charges of rent.

BANK BILLS, CIRCULAR NOTES, AND LETTERS OF CREDIT
cashed free of commission.

COUNTRY WINES OF EVERY DESCRIPTION,
both in Bottle and in Cask, for exportation, at reduced prices.

FOREIGN WINES, ENGLISH BEERS, TEAS, &c., IMPORTED.

Agency Business of every description attended to; also the PURCHASE of LANDS, HOUSES, or VILLAS for the account of Foreigners.

Correspondents in London—Messrs. OLIVIER & CO., 37, Finsbury Square.

FLORENCE.
12, LUNG' ARNO NUOVO.

MONTELATICI BROTHERS,
Manufacturers of Florentine Mosaics.
ASSORTMENT OF CASKETS AND ALBUMS.

COMMISSIONS AND EXPORTATION.

NASSAU.	ESSENTIALS
Seventh Edition, with Illustrations, Post 8vo., 7s. 6d.	FOR **TRAVELLING.**
BUBBLES FROM THE BRUNNEN OF NASSAU. By an OLD MAN.	Thresher's India Tweed Suits. Thresher's Kashmir Flannel Shirts. Thresher's Kashmir Woollen Socks. Thresher's Coloured Flannel Shirts. Thresher's Travelling Bags.
JOHN MURRAY, Albemarle Street.	SOLD ONLY BY **THRESHER & GLENNY,** NEXT DOOR TO SOMERSET HOUSE, STRAND.

VISITORS TO THE CONTINENT.

OLIVIER & CO.,
37, Finsbury Square, London,

(MR. OLIVIER ESTABLISHED IN 1830,)

COMMISSION MERCHANTS AND GENERAL AGENTS

For Shipment and Reception of Goods to and from all Parts of the World, and **IMPORTERS OF WINES,** *&c.*

OLIVIER & CO. have the honour to inform
VISITORS TO THE CONTINENT
that they undertake to receive and pass through the Customhouse in London, Liverpool, Southampton, &c.,

WORKS of ART, BAGGAGE, and PROPERTY of EVERY DESCRIPTION,
which are attended to on arrival

with the utmost Care in Examination and Removal,
under their own personal superintendence. They beg to call particular attention to

their Moderate Charges,
which have given universal satisfaction.

Many Travellers having expressed a desire to know in anticipation to what expenses their Purchases are liable on arrival in England, the following

Rates of Charges on the Reception of Packages

may be relied upon, for Landing from the Ship, Clearing, Delivery in London, and Agency:—

On Trunks of Baggage. . . . . about 9s. each.
On Cases of Works of Art, &c., of moderate size and value . about 15s. „
„ „ „ of larger „ „ 20s. to 25s. „

On very large Cases of valuable Statuary, Pictures, &c., on which an estimate cannot well be given, the charges will depend on the care and trouble required. When several cases are sent together the charges are less on each case.

OLIVIER & CO. undertake the
FORWARDING OF PACKAGES OF EVERY KIND
to the Continent, to the care of their Correspondents, where they can remain, if required, until the arrival of the owners.

Also

THE EXECUTION OF ORDERS FOR THE PURCHASE OF GOODS
of all kinds, which, from their long experience as Commission Merchants, they are enabled to buy on the most advantageous terms.

Residents on the Continent will find this a convenient means of ordering anything they may require from London.

N.B.—The keys of locked Packages should always be sent to OLIVIER & CARR, as everything, although free of duty, must be examined by the Customs on arrival.

INSURANCES EFFECTED, and Agency Business of every description attended to.

OLIVIER & CO.'S principal Correspondents are—

At Aix-la-Chapelle	Messrs. A. SOUHEUR and CO.
,, Alexandria	Mr. J. W. BROWNE.
,, Antwerp	Mr. F. VERELLEN BEERNAERT.
	Messrs. VLEUGELS and GUFFANTI.
,, Basle	Mr. J. J. FREY.
,, Bologna	Messrs. ANTONIO MAZZETTI and CO.
,, Bordeaux	Messrs. H. and O. BEYERMAN and CO., Wine Growers.
,, Boulogne	{Messrs. L. BRANLY and CO., 81, Rue Napoleon. {Messrs. L. I. VOGUE and Co.
,, Brussels	Mr. G. LUYCKX, 24, Rue des Fabriques.
	Mr. L. STEIN, 22, Montagne de la Cour.
,, Calais	Messrs. L. I. VOGUE and CO.
,, Cologne	Messrs. C. H. VAN ZUTPHEN and CO.
	Messrs. G. TILMES and CO.
,, Constantinople	Messrs. VALSAMACHY and CO., Galata.
,, Dresden	Messrs. KRAETSCHMER and CO.
,, Florence	Messrs. HASKARD and SON, 4, Borgo SS. Apostoli.
	Messrs. W. H. WOOD and CO.
,, Frankfort	Mr. MARTIN BECKER, 5, Bleidenstrasse.
	Mr. MORITZ B. GOLDSCHMIDT, Banker.
,, Geneva	Messrs. JOLIMAY and CO.
,, Genoa	Messrs. G. B. PRATOLONGO and CO.
	Messrs. P. CAUVIN, DIAMANTI, and COSTA.
,, Hamburg	Messrs. JULIUS WÜSTENFELD and CO.
,, Havre	Messrs. CHR. EGLIN and MARING.
,, Interlaken	Messrs. RITSCHARD and BURKI.
,, Leipzig	Messrs. GERHARD and HEY.
,, Leghorn	Messrs. HENDERSON BROTHERS.
,, Malta	Messrs. ROSE & CO.
,, Marseilles	Messrs. GIRAUD FRÈRES.
	Messrs. HORACE BOUCHET and CO.
,, Milan	Messrs. GIO. CURTI & FIGº.
,, Munich	Messrs. GUTLEBEN and WEIDERT.
,, Naples	{Mr. G. CIVALLERI, 267, Riviera di Chiaja. {Messrs. CERULLI & CO., 5, Vico Satriano a Chiaia. [le Port.
,, Nice	Messrs. LES FILS DE CH. GIORDAN, Quai Lunel, 14 (sur
,, Ostend	Mr. J. DUCLOS ASSANDRI. [Martin, 43.
,, Paris	Messrs. LANGLOIS FILS FRÈRES, Rue des Marais St.
	M. HECTOR L'HERBIER, 18, Rue de la Douane.
,, Pau	Mr. BERGEROT.
,, Prague	Mr. J. J. SEIDL, Hibernergasse, No. 1000.
,, Rome	Mr. J. P. SHEA, 11, Piazza di Spagna.
	Mr. A. TOMBINI, 23, Place St. Louis des Français.
,, Rotterdam	Mr. J. A. HOUWENS; Messrs. P. A. VAN ES and CO.
,, Trieste	Messrs. MARTIN FRÈRES.
,, Turin	Mr. CHIABODO PIETRO, Via Dora Grossa, 13.
,, Venice	Mr. HENRY DECOPPET. Mr. Fco TOLOMEI DI Fco
,, Vienna	Mr. ANTON POKORNY, Stadt Sonnenfelsgasse, 2.

Any other houses will also forward goods to O. & C. on receiving instructions to do so. Travellers are requested always to give particular directions that their Packages are **consigned direct** to OLIVIER & CO., 37, FINSBURY SQUARE.

PRICES OF WINES IMPORTED BY
OLIVIER AND CO.,
AGENTS TO GROWERS.

—o—

	per doz. duty paid.
Claret, Shipped by F. Beyerman, Bordeaux	18s., 24s., 30s., 36s., to 120s
Burgundy ,, Dumoulin ainé, Savigny-sous-Beaune	24s., 28s., 36s., to 84s
Hock & Moselle, Jodocius Frères & Co., Coblentz	21s., 30s., 36s., to 120s.
,, Sparkling, ,,	48s. to 60s
Champagne	46s. to 72s
Marsala, in Qr. Casks, from £11; lHds. £21	26s. to 30s.
Sherries, Pale, Gold, or Brown, in Qr. Casks, £15 to £35, delivered	42s. to 60s

CLARET, BURGUNDY, and HOCK, in the Wood, at Growers' Prices.

Detailed Price Lists may be had of O. & C., 37, *Finsbury Square.*

C

CHUBB'S LOCKS and SAFES.

Paris Exhibition, 1867, SILVER PRIZE MEDAL.
Dublin International Exhibition, 1865, PRIZE MEDAL AWARDED.

CHUBB & SON,
BY APPOINTMENTS,
MAKERS TO THE QUEEN, AND TO H.R.H. THE PRINCE OF WALES.

CHUBB'S PATENT DETECTOR LOCKS, the most secure from picklocks and false keys, are strong, simple, and durable, and made of all sizes and for every purpose to which a Lock can be applied.

Trunks, Portmanteaus, Travelling Bags, Dressing Cases, Writing Desks, &c., fitted with only the usual common and utterly insecure Locks, can have the place of these supplied by CHUBB'S PATENT without alteration or injury.

TRAVELLERS' LOCK-PROTECTORS and PORTABLE SCUTCHEON LOCKS for securing Doors that may be found fastened only by common Locks.

CHUBB & SON have always in stock a variety of Writing and Despatch Boxes in Morocco or Russia Leather and japanned Tin; the latter being particularly recommended for lightness, room, durability, and freedom from damage by insects or hot climates.

Best Black Enamelled Leather Travelling Bags of various sizes, all with Chubb's Patent Locks. Cash, Deed, and Paper Boxes of all dimensions.

CHUBB'S PATENT SAFES are constructed in the very best manner, of the strongest wrought iron, fitted with CHUBB's PATENT DRILL-PREVENTIVE and their GUNPOWDER-PROOF STEEL-PLATED LOCKS, are the most secure from fire and burglary, and form the most complete safeguard for Books, Papers, Deeds, Jewels, Plate, and other valuable property.

CHUBB & SON have also strong wrought-iron Safes, *without* fire-resisting lining, but equally secure in all other respects, intended for holding plate where protection from fire is not an object, and affording much more room inside than the Patent Safes. They are recommended specially in place of the ordinary wooden cases for plate, which may so easily be broken open.

BUENOS AYRES GOVERNMENT CERTIFICATE.
TRANSLATION.

We, the undersigned, at the request of Messrs. JAS. C. THOMPSON & Co., certify that the IRON SAFES of Messrs. CHUBB & SON, London, of which these gentlemen are Agents, were exposed for several hours to the Fire that took place in the offices of the National Government on the evening of the 26th instant; that in our presence they were easily opened with their respective keys; that the moneys and important documents they contained were found in perfect order, and that those Safes are now in use in the National Treasury Office.—Buenos Ayres 31st July, 1867.

(Signed)   J. M. DRAGO, Treasurer of the National Government.
JOSE TOMAS ROJO.
JUAN M. ALVAREZ.   A true copy—A. M. BELL.

Complete Illustrated Priced Lists of Chubb's Locks, Boxes, Safes, and other Manufactures, gratis and post-free.

CHUBB and SON, Makers to the Bank of England,
57, St. Paul's Churchyard, London, E.C.

RAGAZ LES BAINS,

Canton de St. Gall.

HÔTEL TAMINA PENSION FOR FAMILIES.

This FIRST-CLASS HÔTEL is recommended to all English and American Families for its great comfort.

Hot and Cold Baths and Mineral Waters in the Hôtel.

It is very well situated for all kinds of Excursions.

Pension from 15th September to 1st June.

For information, and to engage rooms, apply to Mr. JAKLE, Directeur of the Hôtel.

GENEVA.

HÔTEL DU LAC.

Splendid view on the Lake and the Mountains; opposite the Steamers. Especially recommended to families. Very reasonable prices.

TABLE D'HÔTE AT 12, 5, and 7 O'CLOCK.

H. SPAHLINGER, PROPRIETOR.

MAYENCE.

HÔTEL D'ANGLETERRE.

HENRY SPECHT, Wine Merchant and Grower.

This **first-rate** and **excellent Hotel** (combining every English comfort), situated in front of the Bridge, is the nearest Hotel to the **Steamboats** and close to the **Railway Stations.** From its Balconies and Rooms are Picturesque Views of the Rhine and Mountains. *Galignani*, *Times*, and *Illustrated News* taken in. The Table-d'Hôte is renowned for its excellence, and for its **Genuine Rhenish Wines** and **Sparkling Hock,** which Mr. Specht exports to England at **Wholesale Prices.**

NAPLES.

HÔTEL DU LOUVRE,
Kept by R. DONZELLI.

THIS new Hotel is beautifully situated on the Chiaja, enjoying at once a full and splendid view of the bay and of the Villa Nazionale. It is fitted up in a luxurious style, combining elegance and comfort, and possesses all modern improvements of a first-rate establishment.

HÔTEL D'ANGLETERRE,

Kept by the same Proprietor, also situated in front of the Villa Nazionale, is well known and highly recommended for its cleanliness, the excellence of its Cuisine, and great attention paid to Travellers.

LACROIX and FALCONNET,
J. LACROIX, SUCCESSOR,
WARRANTED WATCH MANUFACTURER,
2, BEL-AIR, 1st Floor, GENEVA.

FRANKFORT O. M.

MR. C. A. LÖHR,
PROPRIETOR OF
THE ROMAN EMPEROR HOTEL,
Begs to recommend his House to English Travellers.

THIS large and well-situated Establishment is conducted under the immediate superintendence of the Proprietor, and newly furnished with every comfort, and a new splendid Dining-room.

The "ROMAN EMPEROR" is often honoured by Royal Families and other high personages. The following have lately honoured this Hotel—
H.M. THE KING AND QUEEN OF WURTEMBERG.
H.M. THE QUEEN OF HOLLAND.
B.R.H. THE CROWN PRINCE AND PRINCESS OLGA OF WURTEMBERG.
H.I.H. THE ARCHDUKE OF AUSTRIA. &c. &c. &c.

Table-d'hôte at 1, 1fl. 30kr.　　　Breakfast, 42kr.
　　" 　　" 　5, 2fl.　　　　　　Tea, 42kr.
Bed Rooms, from 1fl. to 3fl.

PASSPORT AGENCY OFFICE,
LONDON, 59, FLEET STREET, E. C.

Regulations gratis for obtaining Foreign Office Passports.

COUNTRY or LONDON Residents, who desire to avoid trouble, can, by forwarding a Banker's Application, or Certificate of Identity, have a PASSPORT obtained and viséd. Country Residents, by this arrangement, are saved the trouble of a personal attendance, as the Passport can be forwarded to them by Post (*en Regle*).
Fee obtaining Passport, 1s. 6d.; Visas, 1s. each.
Passports carefully Mounted and Cased, and Names lettered thereon in Gold.
Passport Cases from 1s. 6d. to 6s. each.
Every Requisite for Travellers.

THE LATEST EDITIONS OF MURRAY'S HANDBOOKS.
BRADSHAW'S BRITISH and CONTINENTAL GUIDES and HANDBOOKS to France, Belgium, Switzerland, Italy, Spain and Portugal, Normandy, Brittany, Tyrol, Paris, London, &c.
BRADSHAW'S DIARY AND TRAVELLER'S COMPANION.
BRADSHAW'S COMPLETE PHRASE BOOKS, French, Italian, Spanish, and German. 1s. each.
BRADSHAW'S Overland and Through Route Guide to India, China, and Australia, 5s.
BRADSHAW'S Handbook to the Bombay Presidency and the North-West Provinces, Madras, and Bengal, 10s. each.
KELLAR'S, LEUTHOLD'S, and ZIEGLER'S Maps of Switzerland. MAYR'S MAP OF THE TYROL. Original Editions.
Knapsacks, Rugs, Waterproof Coats, Door-fasteners, Handbags, Portmanteaus, Straps, Soap, Compasses, Drinking Cups, &c.
HARPER'S HANDBOOK to Europe and the East. Phrase Books and Dictionaries.
BLACK'S GUIDES to England, Ireland, Wales, and Scotland.
Works on Health-Resorts, Climates, and Waters. By EDWIN LEE, M.D.

Experienced Couriers engaged upon application.
W. J. ADAMS (BRADSHAW'S BRITISH AND CONTINENTAL GUIDE OFFICE),
LONDON, 59, FLEET STREET, E.C.
OFFICE HOURS 8 TO 7. SATURDAYS 8 TO 3.

THE CONTINENTAL DAILY PARCELS EXPRESS (established 1849), SOLE AGENTS for ENGLAND of the Belgian Government Railway and North German Postal Confederation, and Correspondents of the Northern of France Railway, CONVEY by MAIL STEAMERS EVERY NIGHT (Sunday excepted), viâ DOVER, CALAIS, and OSTEND, Samples, Parcels, and Packages of all kinds between ENGLAND and all parts of the CONTINENT, at Through rates, including all charges *except Duties and Entries.*

Homeward Parcels should be booked as follows:—
IN ALL GERMANY.—At any Post Office of the North German Confederation, or in connection therewith.
BELGIUM.—At the State Railway Stations; or at the Office of the Agents in Ostend, DE RIDDER, 54, Rue St. Joseph; Brussels, CROOT, 90 bis, Montague de la Cour.
HOLLAND.—In the principal Towns. VAN GEND and LOOS.
FRANCE.—Paris: PRITCHARD, Agent of the Peninsular and Oriental Steam Co., 4, Rue Rossini. From the Provinces, Parcels should be sent under cover, with advice, to Mr. PRITCHARD.
Outward to the Continent.—Parcels received at the Agencies in most of the large provincial towns, of which a printed list with tables of rates and full instructions to senders, may be had GRATIS, at

Chief Office: 53, GRACECHURCH STREET,
D. N. BRIDGE, *Manager*, to whom all communications should be addressed.

N.B.—Amount of Invoices and out charges collected on delivery of parcels in Belgium, Holland, and Germany; and persons wishing to obtain goods of any kind from the Continent can have them sent through this Express "CONTRE REMBOURSEMENT," *i.e.* Payment on delivery.

London, 1st May, 1869.

Stanford's Foreign Office Passport Agency,
6 & 7, CHARING CROSS, LONDON, S.W.

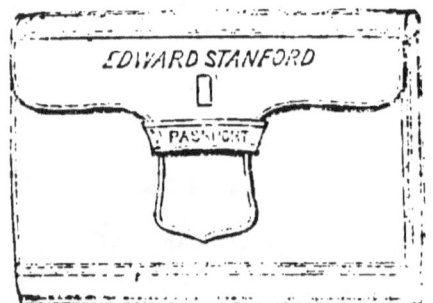

Passports (which are good for life) mounted on Muslin or Silk, in Roan, Morocco, or Russia Case, with the name of the Owner lettered on the outside, thus preventing injury or loss, as well as lessening the delay in examination abroad.

For further particulars, including the Forms of Application, Cost of Passport, Visas, &c. &c., see **Stanford's Passport Circular,** which will be forwarded per post on receipt of One Stamp.

STANFORD'S TOURIST'S CATALOGUE,

Containing Title, Price, &c., of the Best GUIDE BOOKS, MAPS, CONVERSATION BOOKS, DICTIONARIES, &c. &c., published in the United Kingdom, the Continent, and America, Gratis on application, or free per post for One Stamp.

LONDON: EDWARD STANFORD, 6 & 7, CHARING CROSS, S.W.,

Agent for the Sale of the Ordnance Maps, Geological Survey Maps, and Admiralty Charts.

GENÈVE.

GRAND HÔTEL BEAU RIVAGE.

THIS first-rate, splendid Hotel has the advantage of being the most pleasantly situated in Genève, on the Quai du Mont Blanc, near the English Church, in front of the Steamboat Landing, and very near the Railway Station. From the Garden and two delightful Terraces, and from each window of the Hôtel, Mont Blanc, the Lake, and the Town, can be seen in their fullest extent. Charges moderate. Table-l'Hôte three times a day. Is the resort of the first English and American Families.

MAYER & KUNZ, Proprietors.

First-rate House, containing about one hundred large Apartments and Saloons for Families, having been lately enlarged.

ENGLISH SPOKEN AND ENGLISH NEWSPAPERS KEPT.

BERLIN.

HÔTEL ROYAL.
Proprietor: Mr. FRIEDRICH LANGE,

UNTER DEN LINDEN, No. 3, and corner of Wilhelm Street.

Situated in the most beautiful part of the town, near the Royal Theatres, the Museum, the Hotels of the Ministry and Ambassadors. Waterworks and Baths in the Hotel. Carriages. Dinners and suppers at any hour. Good English cuisine, and French restaurant in elegant saloons looking over the Promenade. Prompt attendance and moderate prices.

BROWN & POLSON'S
PATENT CORN FLOUR

Paisley, Manchester, Dublin, & London.

The LANCET states—"This is Superior to anything of the kind known."

The First Manufactured in the United Kingdom and France.

This favourite article of Diet is especially suitable for

PUDDINGS, CUSTARDS, BLANCMANGES,

and, being very light and of easy digestibility, it is recommended for

BREAKFASTS, SUPPERS, &c.,

for which it is easily prepared, requiring only to be boiled with milk for eight minutes.

It is preferred for all the purposes to which the best Arrowroot is applicable, and prepared in the same manner.

For various purposes, such as to thicken Soups, Sauces, Beef-tea, &c., it is invaluable, and extensively used in all parts of the world.

CAUTION.—To obtain extra profit by the sale, other kinds are sometimes substituted instead of BROWN and POLSON'S.

BONN ON THE RHINE.

MR. SCHMITZ,
PROPRIETOR OF THE GOLDEN STAR HOTEL,

BEGS leave to recommend his Hotel to English Travellers. The apartments are furnished throughout in the English style; the rooms are carpeted; and the attendance, as well as the kitchen and the wine-cellar, is well provided. MR. SCHMITZ begs to add that at no first-rate Hotel on the Rhine will be found more moderate charges and more cleanliness.

The STAR HOTEL has been honoured by the visits of the following Members of the English Royal Family :—

1857. Oct. 16 { H. R. H. the Prince of WALES, accompanied by General Sir W. CODRINGTON, Colonel PONSONBY, Sir Frederic STANLEY, Dr. ARMSTRONG, Rev. F. C. TARVER, Mr. GIBBS, etc.

1857. Aug. 20 { H. R. H. the Prince of WALES and his Suite paying a visit *at the Golden Star Hotel* to His Majesty the King of the BELGIANS.

1857. Aug. 8 — H. R. H. the Prince of WALES and his Suite.

1857. July 29 { T. R. H. the Duchess of CAMBRIDGE and Princess MARY of CAMBRIDGE, accompanied by the Baron KNESEBECK and Suite.

1857. July 29 { H. R. H. the Prince of WALES paying a visit *at the Golden Star Hotel* to T. R. H. the Duchess of CAMBRIDGE and Princess MARY of CAMBRIDGE.

1857. July 15 { H. R. H. the Prince of WALES, accompanied by the Right Honourable C. GREY, General MAJOR, Colonel PONSONBY, Sir Frederic STANLEY, Dr. ARMSTRONG, Rev. F. C. TARVER, Mr. GIBBS, etc.

1856. Nov. { H. R. H. Prince ALFRED of GREAT BRITAIN, accompanied by Lieutenant-General Sir Frederick STOVIN and Lieutenant COWELL.

1846. June 18 { H. M. ADELAIDE, QUEEN DOWAGER OF GREAT BRITAIN, accompanied by His Highness Prince EDWARD of SAXE WEIMAR, Lord and Lady BARINGTON, Sir DAVID DAVIES, M.D., Rev. J. R. WOOD, M.A., Captain TAYLOR, &c. &c., honoured the above establishment with a THREE DAYS' VISIT.

1818. May — H. R. H. the Duke of CAMBRIDGE and Suite.

1825. March and Sept. { H. R. H. the Duke and Duchess of CLARENCE (King WILLIAM IV. and Queen ADELAIDE) and Suite.

1834. July { H. M. QUEEN ADELAIDE, accompanied by the Earl and Countess of ERROL, Earl and Countess of DENBIGH, Earl and Countess HOWE, &c.

1836. Aug. — H. R. H. the Duchess of GLOUCESTER and Suite.

1837. July — H. R. H. the Duchess of CAMBRIDGE and Suite.

1839. Nov. — H. R. H. the Prince GEORGE of CAMBRIDGE and Suite.

— Nov. { H. R. H. Prince ALBERT of SAXE COBURG GOTHA, accompanied by Prince ERNEST of SAXE COBURG GOTHA, and their Suite.

1840. { H. R. H. the Duchess of CAMBRIDGE, accompanied by the Princess AUGUSTA of CAMBRIDGE, and their Suite.

1841. { H. R. H. the Duchess of KENT and Suite, accompanied by H. S. H. the Prince of LEININGEN.

1841. — H. R. H. the Duchess of CAMBRIDGE and Suite.

— — H. R. H. Princess CAROLINA of CAMBRIDGE.

1844. — H. R. H. the Duchess of CAMBRIDGE and Suite.

— — H. R. H. Princess MARY of CAMBRIDGE.

1845. June { H. R. H. the Duchess of KENT and Suite, accompanied by H. S. H. the Prince of LEININGEN.

1847. July { T. R. H. the Duke and Duchess of CAMBRIDGE, with their Family and Suite.

MUDIE'S SELECT LIBRARY.

BOOKS FOR ALL READERS.

FIRST-CLASS SUBSCRIPTION
FOR A CONSTANT SUCCESSION OF THE NEWEST BOOKS,
One Guinea per Annum,
COMMENCING AT ANY DATE.
BOOK SOCIETIES SUPPLIED ON LIBERAL TERMS.

CHEAP BOOKS.—NOTICE.
FIFTEEN THOUSAND VOLUMES OF
BOUND BOOKS FOR PRESENTS AND PRIZES.
CONSISTING CHIEFLY OF
WORKS OF THE BEST AUTHORS,
AND MORE THAN ONE HUNDRED THOUSAND VOLUMES
of Surplus Copies of other Popular Books of the Past Season,
ARE NOW ON SALE AT GREATLY REDUCED PRICES.

Catalogues postage free on Application.

MUDIE'S SELECT LIBRARY, New Oxford Street, London.
CITY OFFICE—4, King Street, Cheapside.

GENEVA.

HÔTEL DE LA COURONNE.
PROPRIETOR, Mr. F. BAUR.

THIS ESTABLISHMENT, of the first Rank, completely newly furnished throughout, situated in front of the magnificent Pont du Mont Blanc, the National Monument, the Steam-boat landing, and the English Garden, enjoys a most extended view of Lac Leman and Mont Blanc.
Every attention paid to the comfort and wishes of Families and Gentlemen. Active attendance, good cuisine and cellar. English and American newspapers. Tables-d'Hôte 3 times a day. Omnibus from the Hotel to every Train.

FLORENCE.

BRIZZI AND NICCOLAI'S
Musical Establishment.

PIANOFORTES, OF THE BEST MAKERS,
FOR SALE AND ON HIRE.

GENERAL DEPOT FOR WIND-INSTRUMENTS.
Italian and Foreign Music.
Musical Lending Library.

PIAZZA MADONNA,	BRANCH HOUSE (Music Depôt)
PALAZZO ALDOBRANDINI.	12, VIA CERRETANI.

FLORENCE.

P. ROMANELLI,
Sculptor, Pupil of and Successor to the late Professor Bartolini, has opened a Gallery,

Lung' Arno Guicciardini, No. 7.

The intelligent amateur will find there a Collection of Statues, both originals and copies, artistically executed.

PRINCIPAL WORKS:—The Son of William Tell; the Young Franklin; the Young Washington; the Young Whittington; the Young Napoleon; the Young Moses; Garibaldi.

OXFORD.

SPIERS AND SON,
102 & 103, HIGH STREET,

Respectfully invite TOURISTS to VISIT their Extensive Warehouses for Useful and Ornamental Manufactures, suitable for Presents and remembrances of Oxford. Copies of every published Guide-Book and Map of the City and neighbourhood kept in stock. Also Photographs, Views, &c. Inventors and Manufacturers of the celebrated "Oxford Cyclopean Washstands." Information relative to Oxford afforded to strangers visiting their establishments.

GENEVA MUSICAL BOXES.

B. A. BRÉMOND, MANUFACTURER.
Prize Medal, Paris Exhibition, 1867.

WHOLESALE.   RETAIL.   EXPORTATION.

7, RUE PRADIER, GENEVA, SWITZERLAND.

LUCERNE.

ENGLISCHER HOF.—HOTEL d'ANGLETERRE.
Proprietor—JEAN REBER.

THIS First-rate Establishment, very well recommended by the best class of Travellers, is situated close to the Steamers' Landing-place, and vis-à-vis the Railway Stations, on the loveliest position of the Lake, with superb views of the Rigi, Pilatus, Alps, and Glaciers; contains several Saloons, 62 comfortable Rooms, Smoking and Reading Rooms, where are French and English newspapers.

Charge for Rooms per diem, 1fr. 50c. to 3fr.

Table d'Hote, at 1 . . . 3fr.
      ,,   ,,   4·30 . . 4fr.
      ,,   ,,   7·30 . . 3fr.

The 'Times,' 'Galignani,' 'l'Indépendance,' the 'Bund,' and other German, French, and American papers are taken for the Reading Room.

GALIGNANI'S
NEW PARIS GUIDE.

Compiled from the best authorities, revised and verified by personal inspection, and arranged on an entirely new plan, with Map and Plates. Royal 18mo. 10s. 6d. bound; or with Map only, 7s. 6d. bound.

London : SIMPKIN, MARSHALL, & CO.

ROTTERDAM.

H. A. KRAMERS,
Importer of Foreign Books.

Mr. MURRAY's 'Handbooks for Travellers, BRADSHAW's Monthly Railway Guides, BAEDEKER's 'Reisehandbücher,' and HENDSCHEL's 'Telegraph,' always in Stock.

English, French, and German Books imported Weekly, and a great variety of New Books kept in Store.

47, GELDERSCHE KADE.

1868. MURRAY'S HANDBOOK ADVERTISER. 27

By Appointment to H.R.H. The Prince of Wales.

ALLEN'S PORTMANTEAUS
37, WEST STRAND, LONDON, W.C.
ILLUSTRATED CATALOGUES of 500 ARTICLES Post Free.

ALLEN'S PATENT BAG.   ALLEN'S PATENT DESPATCH-BOX DESK.   ALLEN'S PATENT Quadruple Portmanteau.

SOLID LEATHER DRESSING-CASE.   ALLEN'S NEW DRESSING BAG.   RAILWAY PORTMANTEAU.

ALLEN'S DRESSING BAG.   ALLEN'S SOLID MAHOGANY DRESSING-CASE.   LADY'S WARDROBE PORTMANTEAU.

ALSO

Allen's Barrack Furniture Catalogue, for Officers joining, Post Free.

PRIZE MEDAL AWARDED, 1862,

FOR GENERAL EXCELLENCE.

IRELAND.

ANTRIM ARMS HOTEL,
PORTRUSH.

THIS Hotel is beautifully situated, having an uninterrupted view of the ATLANTIC OCEAN, the GIANT'S CAUSEWAY, the SKERRIES, and LOUGH FOYLE.

It contains upwards of 100 Apartments,
Principally facing the Sea.

A NOBLE COFFEE-ROOM,
with Drawing-Room attached, equally available for Ladies and Gentlemen.

Table-d'Hôte daily during the Season.
Cuisine and Wines First-Class.   Terms moderate.   French spoken.

Billiard and Smoking Rooms.

THE SEA BATHS,
Recently rebuilt on the Hotel Grounds, by Mr. BROWN, will be found to contain every modern improvement. Separate Apartments for Ladies and Gentlemen. Hot, Cold, Shower, and Douche Baths. The Superintendents in each Department being people of experience, visitors to the Baths may depend on every attention.

Extensive Posting and Livery Establishment in connection with the Hotel.
A Vehicle to the Giant's Causeway and back daily during the Season.

Visitors to the Hotel are respectfully requested to be particular in inquiring for the ANTRIM ARMS HOTEL Omnibus. It attends all Steamers and Trains, for the conveyance of Passengers to the Hotel free.

J. BROWN, PROPRIETOR.

Portrush is the nearest Railway Station to the Giant's Causeway.

London and South-Western Railway.
LONDON STATION, WATERLOO BRIDGE.

The Cheap and Picturesque Route to

PARIS, ROUEN, HONFLEUR, AND CAEN,
Viâ SOUTHAMPTON and HAVRE.

Every Monday, Wednesday, and Friday, the last Train from London at 9 p.m. for the Southampton Docks, alongside the Steamer.

Fares throughout (London and Paris)—FIRST CLASS, **33/0**; SECOND CLASS, **22/0**.
Return Tickets (available for one month)—FIRST CLASS, **50/**; SECOND CLASS, **36/**.

JERSEY, GUERNSEY, AND ST. MALO,
MAIL SERVICE,
Viâ SOUTHAMPTON—The favourite Route.
Every Monday, Wednesday, and Friday.

Fares throughout (London and Jersey or Guernsey)—**32/0** FIRST; **23/0** SECOND CLASS.
Return Tickets (available for One Month)—**48/0** FIRST; or **38/0** SECOND CLASS.

The Last Train from London in time for the Steamers leaves at 9 p.m. for the Southampton Docks, alongside the Steamer.

For further information apply to Mr. De Voulle, 3, Place Vendôme, Paris.—Mr. Langstaff, 47, Grand Quai, Havre.—Mr. Enault, Honfleur.—Mr. E. D. Le Couteur, Jersey.—Mr. Spencer, Guernsey.—Captain Gaudin, St. Malo.—Or to Mr. E. K. COKER, Steam Packet Superintendent, Southampton.

MARSEILLES.

GRAND HÔTEL DE MARSEILLE.

Canebière Prolongée; Rue de Noailles, 26.

THE NEAREST HOTEL TO THE RAILWAY STATION.

WITH A SPLENDID VIEW.

Two Hundred Bed-Rooms, from 2 francs and upwards; Reading-Room, and elegant Drawing-Rooms. Baths and Carriages in the Hotel.
The Hotel is under the same Management as the

GRAND HÔTEL DES COLONIES.

Travellers are informed that they will always find at the Railway Station Omnibuses belonging to the Hotel, on the arrival of every Train.

THE LONDON and WESTMINSTER BANK issues Circular Notes of £10, £25, and £50 each, for the use of Travellers, payable in the principal Towns on the Continent of Europe, also in Asia, Africa, and North and South America. No expense whatever is incurred, and when cashed no charge is made for commission. Letters of Credit are also granted on the same places. They may be obtained at the City Office in Lothbury, or at any of the Branches, viz.:

Westminster Branch	,,	1, St. James's Square.
Bloomsbury	,,	214, High Holborn.
Southwark	,,	3, Wellington Street, Borough.
Eastern	,,	130, High Street, Whitechapel.
Marylebone	,,	4, Stratford Place, Oxford Street.
Temple Bar	,,	217, Strand.
Lambeth	,,	89 & 91, Westminster Bridge Road.

May 1, 1869.   WM. EWINGS, General Manager.

ATTRACTIONS OF THE NILE.

Now Ready, with Woodcuts, 2 vols., post 8vo., 18s.

THE NILE AND ITS BANKS: a JOURNAL of TRAVELS in EGYPT and NUBIA, showing their Attractions to the Archæologist, Naturalist, and General Tourist. By Rev. A. C. SMITH.

JOHN MURRAY, ALBEMARLE STREET.

PARIS.

HÔTEL DES DEUX MONDES ET D'ANGLETERRE,

8, RUE D'ANTIN,

Near the New Avenue Napoleon III., Tuileries, Place Vendôme, and the Boulevards.

THIS magnificent first-class Hotel, recently constructed and elegantly furnished in the newest and most fashionable style, surrounded by gardens, justifies the preference accorded to it by Families and Gentlemen for the splendour and comfort of its Apartments, its excellent *Cuisine*, and the care and attention shown to all who honour the Hotel with their patronage.

LARGE AND SMALL APARTMENTS, AND SINGLE ROOMS, AT MODERATE CHARGES.

PRIVATE RESTAURANT.

SPLENDID COFFEE-ROOMS, SALOONS, READING AND SMOKING ROOMS.

LETTER-BOX. INTERPRETERS.

HORSES, ELEGANT CARRIAGES, OMNIBUSES FOR THE RAILWAYS.

BERNE (Switzerland).
MUSICAL BOXES,
WOOD CARVINGS, &c.,
OF
J. H. HELLER AT BERNE.

Mr. J. H. HELLER of Berne, Manufacturer of the celebrated Swiss **MUSICAL BOXES** with all the latest improvements, and Inventor of the greatest part of Articles with Music, Purveyor to several Courts, &c., begs to invite the Nobility and Gentry of England, travelling in Switzerland, to visit his well-known Establishment at Berne, where will be found the largest and richest Assortment of his celebrated **MUSICAL BOXES**, playing from 4 to 84 airs, with or without Chimes, Drums, Castagnettes, Celestial Voices, Mandolines, Expressives, &c.; also Swiss Chalettes, Nécessaires, Photographic Albums, Glove-boxes, Work-tables and Boxes, Writing-stands, Letter-weights, Cigar-cases, Cigar-holder, Snuff-boxes, &c., all with Music; Chairs playing when sitting on them, &c. Further, an extensive Assortment of Swiss **SCULPTURES IN WOOD**, Cuckoo-clocks, Drawing-room Clocks, Tables, Chairs, &c., as well as every possible variety of objects in this important and beautiful branch of Manufacture unattained by any other house!

Mr. Heller's Correspondent and Sole Agent for Great Britain, Ireland, and the Colonies, is

Mr. F. W. HEINTZ, 102, London Wall, E.C.,
To whom he forwards, exclusively, Purchases made of him.

Mr. F. W. HEINTZ, Commission Merchant and Agent, will be happy to receive, deliver, or forward all Articles intrusted to his care. Musical Boxes, Wood Carvings, &c., in particular; which are, on arrival, attended to with the utmost care in examination and removal under his own personal superintendence.

Mr. F. W. HEINTZ undertakes the forwarding of Packages of every kind to the Continent, also the execution of orders for the purchase of Goods of all kinds on the most advantageous terms.

F. W. HEINTZ, 102, London Wall, London, Sole Agent to J. M. FARINA, opposite the Altenmarkt, No. 54, at Cologne, for his celebrated Eau de Cologne, which gained the Prize Medal awarded for excellent quality at the London Exhibition, 1862.

GENEVA.

HÔTEL DE LA MÉTROPOLE,

Directed by Mr. CHARLES ALDINGER, formerly the well-known
Proprietor of the Hotel de la Couronne, and now the
Proprietor of the Hotel de la Metropole.

THIS large and excellent Establishment, situated in the most favourable quarter of the town, facing the Pont du Mont Blanc, with the English Garden in front, which is well provided with flowers and shrubs, and shady seats, and goes down to the edge of the lake.

From the rooms in front there is a very fine view of the lake, and from those at the back the snow-capped summit of Mont Blanc is seen in the distance; and from an Observatory at the top of the house, of very easy access, both can be seen, and a very extended view of the surrounding country.

It contains 200 most elegantly furnished Bed and Sitting Rooms in every variety, and the Proprietor himself superintends all the arrangements.

A Reading Room, with all English, American, French, and German newspapers, and a spacious Coffee and Smoking Room are in the Hotel; in short, every comfort Visitors can expect in a first-class Hotel is at their disposition.

The House, by its good ventilation, is exceedingly cool in summer; and in winter is heated by large stoves. Charges are very moderate, and pension during the winter. Table-d'hôte 3 times a day. Omnibus from the Hotel 3 times a day.

Private Carriages and Cabs always ready.

DIJON.

HÔTEL DU JURA.

MR. DAVID, Proprietor.

THIS Hotel, which has been considerably enlarged, is a first-class house, and the nearest to the Railway Station. Contains five Salons, sixty Bed-rooms *en suite*, for families, Drawing-room, Smoking-room. Table-d'hôte; Private Service. Carriages for Drives; Omnibus to all the Trains. French, English, and German Papers. English and German spoken. Bureau de Change in the Hotel, where English Bank Notes can be exchanged. A first-rate cellar of the finest Burgundy Wines.

There is a Church of England Service in the Hotel. Visitors taken *en pension* at reduced Prices from the 18th November to 15th May.

FOREIGN BOOKS AT FOREIGN PRICES.

TRAVELLERS may save expense and trouble by purchasing Foreign Books in England at the same prices at which they are published in Germany or France.

WILLIAMS & NORGATE

have published the following CATALOGUES of their Stock :—

1. CLASSICAL CATALOGUE.
2. THEOLOGICAL CATALOGUE.
3. FRENCH CATALOGUE.
4. GERMAN CATALOGUE.
5. EUROPEAN LINGUISTIC CATALOGUE.
6. ORIENTAL CATALOGUE.
7. ITALIAN CATALOGUE.
8. SPANISH CATALOGUE.
9. ART-CATALOGUE. Art, Architecture, Painting, Illustrated Books.
10. NATURAL HISTORY CATALOGUE. Zoology, Botany, Geology, Chemistry, Mathematics, &c.
11. MEDICAL CATALOGUE. Medicine, Surgery, and the Dependent Sciences.
12. SCHOOL CATALOGUE. Elementary Books, Maps, &c.
13. FOREIGN BOOK CIRCULARS. New Books, and New Purchases.
14. SCIENTIFIC-BOOK CIRCULARS. New Books and Recent Purchases.

ANY CATALOGUE SENT POST-FREE FOR ONE STAMP.

WILLIAMS & NORGATE, Importers of Foreign Books,
14, HENRIETTA STREET, COVENT GARDEN, LONDON, and
20, SOUTH FREDERICK STREET, EDINBURGH.

GENEVA.

MOULINIÉ AND LEGRANDROY'S
WATCHMAKING ESTABLISHMENT,
28, QUAI DES BERGUES, GENEVA, AND 99, STRAND, LONDON.

THIS respectable firm, established in 1809, obtained a first-class Medal at the London Exhibition, 1862, and supplies Chronometers, Repeaters, and all kinds of plain or ornamental Watches for Ladies and Gentlemen at the most moderate prices.—Jewellery and Musical Boxes.—English spoken.—Speciality of Self-winding Watches.

GENEVA.
Rue des Alpes 5, First Floor.—Rue des Alpes 5, First Floor.

PENSION DES ALPES,
FAMILY BOARDING HOUSE.

Splendid view over the Lake and Mont Blanc—Furnished Apartments and elegant Sitting-rooms for Private Families—Comfortable House. Entrance Rue des Alpes, and through the Square.

Rooms to the South, very comfortable for the Winter.

TURIN.

GRAND HÔTEL DE L'EUROPE.

PROPRIETORS—
MESSRS. BORATTI AND CASALEGGIO.

Situated, Place du Château, opposite the King's Palace.

THIS unrivalled and admirably conducted Hotel has been entirely refurnished with every comfort, and in the very best taste, and thus peculiarly recommends itself to the notice of English travellers.

EXCELLENT TABLE-D'HÔTE at 5½ o'clock. Without Wine, 4 fr.; Dinner in Apartments, 6 fr.; Breakfast, with Tea or Coffee and Eggs, 2 fr.

REDUCED TERMS FOR A LENGTHENED STAY.

Interpreters speaking all the European Languages.

CHARGES MODERATE.

THE TIMES NEWSPAPER.

An Omnibus from the Hotel will be found at every Train.

N.B.—Alterations and embellishments have been carried out in this Hotel which renders it one of the handsomest and most comfortable in Turin; such as a noble marble staircase, a private staircase for servants, electric bells in all rooms, wooden door to grand entrance to deaden the sound in the Hôtel, new carpets, &c. &c.

VEVAY (Switzerland).

HÔTEL MONNET,
Dit des 3 Couronnes.

Messrs. SCHOTT & CO., Proprietors, and Successors to Mr. Monnet.

THIS Large and First-class Establishment, situated close to the Lake, affords superior accommodation for Families and Gentlemen. It is extensively patronised for its comfort and cleanliness. Persons remaining some time will find this a most desirable Residence; and from October 15 to June 1 they can live here moderately *en pension*.

HANOVER.

UNION HOTEL.

THIS old-established and highly recommended First-class Hotel has been considerably enlarged and elegantly furnished this spring by the new Proprietor. The new dining salon, and a new coffee room, where a great choice of newspapers are kept, call forth the admiration of every visitor. The situation of the Hotel near the Railroad-station and the Theatre, its fine rooms, capital Table-d'hôte and excellent wines, added to the attention and civility displayed to all visitors, have made it deservedly popular.

Persons residing for a week or longer are taken on moderate terms, especially in winter.

LAUSANNE.

Hôtel Gibbon: Mr. Ritter, Proprietor.

THIS First-class Hotel, highly recommended in every respect, is situated in the best part of the town, and commands the finest and most extensive views of the Lake, the Alps, and the splendid scenery around Lausanne. The terraced garden adjoining the salle-à-manger is unsurpassed by any in the neighbourhood, and was the favourite residence of Gibbon, who wrote here his History of Rome. From the extensive Garden, which is tastefully laid out and attached to the Hotel, the view is most grand and romantic. In fact, this house will be found to give very superior accommodation, and to offer to travellers a highly desirable place of residence or of temporary sojourn.

Pension at Reduced Prices during the Winter.

LAUSANNE.

Hôtel Richemont: kept by Fritz Ritter.

THIS Hotel is of the first order, worthy of the highest recommendations, and in a situation of surpassing beauty. It is surrounded by gardens and promenades, and possesses the advantage of having three fronts facing the Alps. Reduced prices for protracted stay, and Pension during Winter season.

HEIDELBERG.
COURT OF BADEN HOTEL.
(BADISCHER HOF).
MR. L. BIERINGER, PROPRIETOR,

THIS first-rate Establishment, situated in the centre of the town, at an equally convenient distance from the Railway Station and Castle, possesses the advantages of a beautiful garden, and is particularly renowned for its superior accommodation, excellent table, genuine Wines, cleanliness, and moderate charges. The English Church and Post-office are close by. Reading-room which is supplied with English and American Newspapers. Mr. L. BIERINGER, the Proprietor, who speaks English, as well as his attendants, is anxious to make travellers as comfortable as possible. Most advantageous arrangements are made for board and residence during the winter months.—(See "*Murray*," page 531.)

LUCHON (BAGNÈRES DE), PYRENEES.

Grand Hôtel Bonne-Maison et de Londres,
Mr. VIDAL, Jun., Proprietor.

SITUATED opposite the Thermal Establishment or Bath-rooms. This favourite and first-rate Hotel affords extensive accommodation of the best description for a large number of visitors. It is delightfully situated, and will be found most comfortable for Families or Gentlemen.

NICE.

ALPES MARITIMES—FRANCE.

GRAND HOTEL CHAUVAIN.

THE largest and nicest Hotel of the town, situated all South, much frequented by the English nobility and most of the Americans coming to Nice. Newly enlarged by the addition of a splendid "Atrium," magnificent Ball and Concert-rooms, very fine Salons for Reception, and Reading-rooms—the best Table d'Hôte of Nice. Charges moderate.

MR. P. CHAUVAIN FILS, Proprietor.

BADEN-BADEN.

VICTORIA HOTEL.
Proprietor, Mr. FRANZ GROSHOLZ.

THIS is one of the finest built and best furnished First-class Hotels, situated on the new Promenade, near the Kursaal and Theatre; it commands the most charming views in Baden. It is reputed to be one of the best Hotels in Germany. The Table and Wines are excellent, with prompt attendance and great civility. Prices very moderate. English and other Journals.

LAUSANNE.

HOTEL BELVÉDÈRE.
AT THE CORNER OF THE PROMENADE OF MONTBENON.
KEPT BY MR. X. ROY,

WHO has resided for many years in England. This Hotel is charmingly situated; being elevated, it commands one of the finest and most beautiful views of the Lake and Alps; Garden with Terrace and Baths. Arrangements made for long stays and *pension* during the winter season. Omnibus at every train and steamer.

CHAUMONT (near Neuchatel, Switzerland.)

HOTEL AND PENSION DE CHAUMONT,
C. RITZMANN, Proprietor.

THIS Hotel, exceedingly well situated for an extensive view of the magnificent Panorama of the Alps and the surrounding scenery, contains large and small Apartments, Saloons, Dining Rooms, Billiard and Reading Rooms. Private Suites of Rooms for Families. Bath Rooms. New milk and whey supplied on the premises. Leading country and foreign Newspapers. Telegraph Station and Post-office here. Moderate charges.

LUCERNE.

HÔTEL BELLE VUE.

NEW and magnificent Establishment, unrivalled in Switzerland as much for its fine situation as for the luxury and comfort of Apartments and Parlours. Specially recommended to English and American families. Open all the year. Moderate charges.

FREIBURG in Bresgau, Duchy of Baden.

HÔTEL SOMMER, Zahringer Hof,

NEWLY built, opposite the Station; finest view of the Black Forest and the Vosges; most comfortable and best house there. Baths in the Hotel.
Proprietor, Mr. G. H. SOMMER.

ANTWERP.

HÔTEL ST. ANTOINE,
PLACE VERTE,
OPPOSITE THE CATHEDRAL.

THIS Excellent first-class Hotel, which enjoys the well-merited favour of Families and Tourists, has been repurchased by its old and well-known Proprietor, Mr. SCHMITT-SPAENHOVEN; who, with his Partner, will do everything in their power to render the visit of all persons who may honour them with their patronage as agreeable and comfortable as possible.

BIARRITZ.

HÔTEL DE FRANCE,
And the magnificent Maison Garderes.

PROPRIETOR, MR. GARDERES.

THESE two first-class Establishments are delightfully situated on the Beach, in front of the Imperial Château, the Baths, and in the centre of the Promenades. They are furnished in a most superior style, with every comfort and convenience that can be desired by English or American Travellers. Moderate charges. The Proprietor speaks English.

Carriages for Excursions in the Pyrenees and Spain.

Table-d'hôte. 'The Times' newspaper.

LUGERNE.

HÔTEL SCHWEIZERHOF.

HAUSER BROTHERS, Proprietors.

THE LARGEST HOTEL IN SWITZERLAND.

Best Situation on the Quay, with splendid view of the celebrated panorama of the Lake and Mountains.

THE high reputation which this establishment enjoys among Travellers, and especially English and American families, is the best and strongest assurance of its superior arrangement and comfort. Its new immense Dining-Room, with adjoining Garden, Salon, and large Parlour, attract the attention of every Visitor.

Reduced Prices (Pension) are made for longer visits in the early and later parts of the Season.

BERLIN.

HÔTEL D'ANGLETERRE,
2, PLACE AN DER BAUACADEMIE, 2.

SITUATED IN THE FINEST AND MOST ELEGANT PART OF THE TOWN,
Next to the Royal Palaces, Museums, and Theatres.

Single travellers and large families can be accommodated with entire suites of Apartments, consisting of splendid Saloons, airy Bedrooms, &c., all furnished and carpeted in the best English style. First-rate Table-d'Hôte, Baths, Equipages, Guides. *Times* and *Galignani's Messenger* taken in. Residence of Her British Majesty's Messengers.

R. SIEBELIST, Proprietor.

AMSTERDAM.

BRACK'S DOELEN HOTEL—Situated in the Centre of the Town, and most convenient for Visitors on pleasure or business. It commands a splendid view of the Quays, &c.; and, being conducted on a liberal scale, it is patronised by the highest classes of society in Holland. It is also much frequented by English Travellers for the comfort and first-rate accommodation it affords, as well as for the invariable civility shown to visitors. Carriages for hire. Table-d'hôte at half-past 4, or dinner à la carte.

LUCERNE.

SWAN HOTEL.—This Hotel, in the very best situation, enjoys a high character. Mr. HÆFELI, the Proprietor, has made in the later years a great many improvements, and does his utmost to offer to his visitors a comfortable home. An elegant new Ladies' Drawing-room, besides a Reading-room and Smoking-room. Cold, Warm, and Shower Baths.

MARSEILLES.
GRAND HOTEL NOAILLES,
RUE NOAILLES, CANNEBIÈRE PROLONGÉE.

THIS splendid establishment, the largest, most important, and most recent in Marseilles, must be reckoned in the first rank of European Hotels, from its admirable position, from its splendid furniture, the number of its bed-rooms and sitting-rooms, the excellence of its cuisine, its cleanliness, and strict attention paid to travellers.

It is the only Hotel in the Rue Noailles which possesses a beautiful Garden full south, with 12 private Dining-rooms, and a magnificent Salle à Manger capable of accommodating 200 persons; Drawing-room, Reading-room, Smoking-room, &c. Baths in the Hotel, private Carriages, Omnibus of Hotel at the Station, Tariff.—Chambers elegantly furnished on all floors, from 3 francs on the entresol; 5 francs 1st floor; 4 francs 2nd floor; 3 francs on the 3rd floor; 2 francs on 4th floor. Table-d'hote richly ornamented and served with all the delicacies of the season, 4 francs; ½ bottle of burgundy, 1 franc. Meals served à la carte either in the bed or sitting-rooms at very moderate prices. Dinners at fixed prices at all hours from 5 francs. Arrangements can be made to include a good Bed-room Breakfast, Dinner at table-d'hôte, lights, and service, from 9 francs per day, according to the Floor. Omnibus at the Station, 1 franc without luggage, 1½ franc with luggage.

ANTWERP.
HÔTEL DE L'EUROPE,
Next to the Post Office.
THE MOST AGREEABLE SITUATION IN THE TOWN.
Formerly Hotel du Parc.

THIS Hotel has been rebuilt, a magnificent *Salle à manger* added, as well as many Bed and Sitting Rooms, entirely new furnished and redecorated; and the present Proprietor spares no exertion to render it one of the most popular hotels on the Continent. Excellent Table-d'Hôte. Hot and Cold Baths. Stabling and Coach-House. English and French Newspapers.

ANTWERP.
HÔTEL DE LA PAIX.

IN the centre of the town, in close proximity to the Cathedral, the Exchange, Theatres, &c. This Hotel, formerly the HOTEL DES PAYS BAS, has been entirely rebuilt and newly furnished. No pains will be spared by the present Proprietors to render it worthy of the patronage of the travelling public. First-class Table-d'Hôte. Choice Cellar of Wines. English and Foreign Newspapers.

LAKE OF COMO, BELLAGIO.
GREAT BRITAIN HOTEL.

LARGE and Small Apartments, Reading, Billiard, and Smoking Rooms, Baths in the Hotel and on the Lake. Divine Service according to the Established Church throughout the year. This Hotel is beautifully situated, enjoying at once a full and splendid view of the Lake and of the villas Melzi, Serbelloni, and Sommariva.

The Hotel, having been recently enlarged, will afford every possible comfort to strangers during their stay on the Lake. Telegraph office in the Hotel.

Proprietor: A. MELLA.

MILAN.

GRAND HÔTEL DE MILAN.—This Hotel contains Two Hundred Rooms for Single Persons or Families, furnished with the greatest care. Table-d'hôte, Breakfast, Lunch, Dinner, &c., private, at fixed prices, or à la carte, at any hour. Choice Wines. A comfortable ascending Saloon conveys visitors to each floor. Mr. CAMILLE GAVOTTO, the new Manager, who has already introduced a great many excellent improvements, will spare no pains to render it more and more deserving the patronage of English travellers. Large and fine Music Saloon, with Piano, for ladies. Reading-room, Smoking-room, Foreign Newspapers, &c.

SWITZERLAND.

FALLS OF THE RHINE, near SCHAFFHAUSEN.

HÔTEL SCHWEIZERHOF
(formerly Hotel Weber).

THIS large and justly renowned first-class Establishment is under the personal management of the proprietor, Mr. WEGENSTEIN, who spares no pains to render it agreeable and comfortable. Charmingly situated opposite the celebrated Falls of the Rhine and surrounded by a beautiful garden, with shaded walks. The apartments command splendid views of the glaciers and the beautiful scenery around. The air is very salubrious and healthy, the temperature regulated by the "Rhine Fall Breeze." Boarders taken by the week. Grayling and trout fishing. Croquet ground. Billiard and smoking-rooms. Ladies' Sitting-room. Reading-room, with "Times," "Galignani," "Punch," "Illustrated," "New York Herald," etc., etc.

On Sundays, English Divine Service in the house.

WILDBAD.

Hôtel Klumpp, formerly Hôtel de l'Ours,

MR. W. KLUMPP, PROPRIETOR.

THIS First-class Hotel, containing 36 Salons and 170 Bed-rooms, a separate Breakfast, a very extensive and elegant Dining-room, new Reading and Conversation as well as Smoking Salons, with an artificial Garden over the river, is situated opposite the Bath and Conversation House, and in the immediate vicinity of the Promenade.

It is celebrated for its elegant and comfortable apartments, good cuisine and cellar, and deserves its wide-spread reputation as an excellent hotel. Table-d'hôte at One and Five o'clock. Breakfasts and Suppers à la carte.

EXCHANGE OFFICE.

Correspondent of the principal Banking-houses of London for the payment of Circular Notes and Letters of Credit.

Omnibus of the Hotel to and from each train. Elegant private carriages, when required.

WIESBADEN.

FOUR SEASONS HOTEL & BATHS.
PROPRIETOR, DR. ZAIS.

THIS First-Class Establishment, equal to any on the Rhine, is in the best and most delightful situation in the Great Square, opposite the Kursaal, the Theatre, the Promenades; close to the Boiling Spring and the new English Chapel.

This Hotel is the largest in the place, containing a great choice of

SPLENDID AND COMFORTABLE APARTMENTS,

for Families and Single Travellers; exquisite Cuisine and first-class Wines, combined with attentive service and moderate charges.

TABLE D'HÔTE at 1 and 5 p.m., and PRIVATE DINNERS.

Numerous comfortable Bathing Cabinets, supplied with Hot, Mineral, and Sweet Waters.

LUCERNE.

HÔTEL BEAU RIVAGE.
PROPRIETOR—MR. ED. STRUB.

THIS newly-established Hotel is fitted up with every comfort, and recommends itself by its magnificent view on the Rigi, Pilatus, &c. Beautiful Gardens. Pleasure Boats. Private Saloons for Ladies and families. Smoking-rooms. Baths. Variety of Newspapers. Most scrupulous attendance. Moderate prices. (Reduced prices for protracted visits.) Omnibus at the Railway Station.

NEAR TO LAUSANNE.
HÔTEL BEAU RIVAGE.
SITUATED IN ONE OF THE MOST BEAUTIFUL SPOTS OF THE LAKE OF GENEVA.

DIRECTEUR, RUFENACHT.

HOMBOURG.

HÔTEL VICTORIA, close to the Springs and the Kursaal, is one of the finest and best situated Hotels. A new Dining Saloon, with a suite of Rooms with a fine view over the Taunus, have been recently added to the Hotel. The Proprietor, M. GUSTAVE WEIGAND, who has been for many years in first-class Hotels in London, offers to English travellers a good house, with every comfort. Excellent Table-d'hôte and good Wines, at moderate charges. Sponge Baths. N.B.—All kinds of Wines are exported to any part of England, particularly his excellent Sparkling Wines (nice and dry, which are expressly prepared for England), called Victoria Sparkling Moselle and Hock.

ENGADINE, GRISONS, SWITZERLAND.
BATHS OF ST. MORITZ.

Railway to Coire and Como. Daily Diligences to and from Coire, Chiavenna, and Colico (Lake of Como).

THESE BATHS, the highest in Europe, are open from 15th June to 15th September. The waters (acidulous-chalybeate) are superior in their beneficial effects, combined with the bracing mountain air, to the similar and celebrated waters of Schwalbach, Pyrmont, Spa, &c., in all disorders characterised by a want of tone. The comfort and excellence of the Hotel Bathing and Drinking Arrangements are well known and universally admitted. The spacious Boarding-houses have a covered communication with the steam-heated Baths and Springs. Church Service; saloons; telegraph. Good causeway and frequent carriage communication with the neighbouring village of ST. MORITZ, which has also abundant and comfortable accommodation. Romantic scenery. Magnificent tours in all directions of the Alpine Valley, renowned for its sublime beauty, rich with glaciers and lakes.

Perfect, durable, and unaltered conservation of the bottled waters in cases of 15 or 30 quarts (carriage free to Coire) at 10fr. and 18fr.; 25 or 50 pints, 13fr. and 23fr.

For a description of the Baths, see 'The Principal Baths of Switzerland and Savoy, by Edwin Lee, M.D., London.'

Applications for rooms to be addressed, as much beforehand as possible, to the Director of the Hotel, and for bottled Waters to the Director of the Water Department.

London Dépôts—
W. SCHACHT, English and Foreign Chemist, 6, Finsbury Place South, E.C., etc., etc.

HEIDELBERG.
HÔTEL DE L'EUROPE.

THIS new, magnificent, first-rate Establishment, surrounded by private and public gardens, with the view of the Castle, and the very best situation in Heidelberg, enjoys already an European reputation.

READING ROOM,
With English and American Papers.

Reduced prices for protracted stay, and for the Winter Season.

HÆFELI-GUJER, Proprietor.

HEIDELBERG.
PRINCE CHARLES HOTEL.
(In the Market Place, nearest to the Castle.)
WITH THE BEST VIEW OF THE RUINS.

THIS first-class Family Hotel, patronised by their Royal Highnesses the Prince and Princess of Wales and Prince Alfred, is without question the largest and best situated Establishment in the town for families and individuals who visit the celebrated Castle, or making a longer stay, being near all the attractive points, and at the foot of the Castle. It contains large and small apartments of all descriptions; its rooms are light, airy, cheerful, and truly comfortable; and the Hotel is conducted on the most liberal scale under the personal superintendence of the Proprietor, Mr. C. H. SOMMER.
Superior Table-d'hôte at 1 P.M. and 5 P.M. Warm Baths in the Hotel. Reading-room supplied with London 'Times,' and 'Galignani's Messenger.' Two Dining-rooms (in one of them no smoking allowed). Fresh trout in the pond. Prices moderate. English spoken.

NUREMBERG.

HÔTEL DE BAVIERE
(BAYERISCHER HOF).

THIS old-established, first-class, and best situated Hotel, in the centre of the town, close to the river, contains suites of apartments and single rooms, all elegantly furnished in the new style. It is patronised by the most distinguished families. English Divine Service during the season. Foreign newspapers, Carriages in the Hotel. Omnibus to and from each train. Moderate and fixed prices.

VICHY-LES-BAINS.

GRAND HÔTEL DU PARC,
PROPRIETOR, MR. GERMOT,
Opposite the Baths and the Park.

AS in Paris and London, Vichy has its Grand Hotel. The Grand Hotel du Parc of Vichy, for comfort, elegance, and convenience, is equal to any of the large Hotels of Paris or London. Omnibus and Carriages at the Station.

Separate Suites of Apartments for Families.

DRESDEN.

GRAND HÔTEL DE SAXE.

THIS celebrated First-class Hôtel, kept by Mrs. DORN and her SONS, has been recently enlarged and embellished. It contains 150 Front Rooms, with 200 Beds, and is situated in the centre of the town, at the New Square, in the immediate vicinity of all the curiosities. Table-d'Hôte at one and four o'clock, in the splendid dining-hall first-floor. Carriages, Baths, Reading and Smoking Room. Arrangements for the winter.

DIEPPE.

HÔTEL ROYAL,
FACING THE BEACH,
Close to the Bathing Establishment and the Parade.

IT IS ONE OF THE MOST PLEASANTLY SITUATED HOTELS IN DIEPPE, commanding a beautiful and extensive View of the Sea.

Families and Gentlemen visiting Dieppe will find at this Establishment elegant Large and Small Apartments, and the best of accommodation, at very reasonable prices.

The Refreshments, &c., are of the best quality.

In fact, this Hotel fully bears out and deserves the favourable opinion expressed of it in Murray's and other Guide Books.

Table-d'Hôte and Private Dinners.

NUREMBERG.

RED HORSE HOTEL
(Rothes Ross),
PROPRIETOR: M. P. GALIMBERTI.

THIS excellent old-established Hotel, situated in one of the best quarters of the town, is well adapted for Tourists and Families making a visit to Nuremberg of some duration, and who will find every conceivable comfort and convenience. Table-d'Hôte at 1 P.M., and Private Dinners at all hours. The Establishment will be found well worthy of the renown and patronage it has enjoyed from English travellers of the highest rank during many years.

DIEPPE.

HÔTEL DES BAINS
(MORGAN),

FACING the Sea and Baths, of the Highest Class, quiet, thoroughly recommendable. A large private House also on the beach for Families.

BRUXELLES.

THE GRAND HÔTEL DE SAXE, RUE NEUVE, 77 and 79, is admirably situated close to the Boulevards and Theatres, and is the nearest Hotel to the Railway Stations. The Hotel is considerably enlarged, and has a new Jitning-room which will contain 300 persons. Fixed prices:—Plain Breakfast, 1¼ franc; Dinner at the Table-d'hôte, 3¼ francs; Bedrooms, from 2 to 4 francs; Service, 1 franc; Sitting-rooms, 3 to 12 francs; Steaks or Cutlets, 1¼ franc. Travellers must beware of coachmen and conductors of omnibuses who endeavour to drive them to some other hotel.

CADENABBIA.

HOTEL DE BELLE VUE.

FIRST-RATE HOTEL, situated on the western bank of the Lake of Como, opposite Bellagio. Its position is delightful for its beautiful views and fine shady walks along the shore, the whole length of the lake, shaded from the north winds.

CADENABBIA, already favourably known, is rising into repute for the salubrity of the climate. *It has the sun all day long in Winter.*

English comforts; moderate and fixed charges. Divine service in the Hotel. Telegraph Office.

N.B.—The best landing-place is the pier just opposite the Hotel.

BARCELONA.

GRAND HOTEL DES QUATRE NATIONS.
IN THE RAMBLA.
KEPT BY MESSRS. FORTIS & CO.

THIS is a first-rate Establishment, advantageously situated close to the Post-office and the Theatre, with a southern aspect, and newly decorated. Table d'hôte; private service; large and small apartments; many fire-places; baths; reading-rooms; Spanish and foreign newspapers. Carriages of every description. Omnibus at the Railway Stations. Interpreters. Moderate terms.

FREIBURG in Breisgau, Duchy of Baden.

DEUTSCHER HOF. HOTEL D'ALLEMAGNE.
EXCELLENT HOTEL & PENSION. MODERATE CHARGES.

MR. REHFUS, the Proprietor, speaks English fluently, and willingly gives best information about journeys to the Black Forest and Switzerland.

HOMBURG.

HOTEL DES QUATRE SAISONS.
MR. SCHLOTTERBECK, PROPRIETOR.

THIS Hotel is of the first class, and enjoys a well-merited reputation. It is situated near the Sources and the Cursaal. Excellent Table-d'Hôte and Wines; the Proprietor is a large dealer in Wines; and endeavours to make the stay of his patrons as comfortable and pleasant as possible.

VICHY-LES-BAINS.

GRAND HOTEL VELAY BORTELET.
Opposite the Baths and the Park.

THIS Establishment, of the first-class, is particularly recommended to distinguished visitors, as being the most comfortable of the locality. One Hundred Rooms, and Salons, are on the first floor. Large and fine Garden, with great trees and flowers.

SEVILLE (SPAIN).

HOTEL DE LONDRES.—This highly-recommended Hotel is situated on the Plaza Nueva, the most central and beautiful part of this delightful city. Travellers will find here every accommodation for families and single gentlemen. Splendid dining-room, fine sitting-rooms, clean bed-rooms, and excellent attendance. French and English newspapers. Baths, carriages, &c. English, French, and Italian spoken.

MILAN.
Hôtel Cavour, Place Cavour,
Just opposite the Public Gardens.
KEPT BY J. SUARDI AND CO.

THIS first-rate Hotel is fitted up with every modern appliance, and situated in the finest part of Milan. It commands a fine view of the Promenade near to the Station, the Grand Theatre, the National Museum, and the Protestant Church. Excellent Table-d'hôte. Charges very moderate. Baths on each floor. A Smoking and a Reading Room supplied with foreign newspapers.

Omnibus of the Hotel at the arrival of all trains.

Manager—G. VALLETTA.

INTERLACHEN.
HOTEL DE BELLE VUE,
KEPT BY MR. HERMANN RIMPS.

EXCELLENT Second-class Hotel, very well situated, containing a branch "Pension Felsenegg," with a fine Garden attached to it. Boarders taken in, per day 5½ francs during the months of May, June, September, October; and 6½ francs per day during the months of July and August. English, French, and German Newspapers. Omnibuses; Private Carriages, and Saddle Horses. English spoken.

INTERLAKEN.
Hotel and Pension Jungfrau.
Proprietor, MR. F. SEILER.

THIS excellent Hotel is situated on the finest Promenade, and is surrounded with a large and beautiful garden, from which an extensive view is to be had all over the Glaciers. English travellers will find at this Hotel large and small well-furnished apartments and rooms for families and single tourists. Moderate charges.

NORWAY.

This day, 3rd Edition, small 8vo., 6s.

A SUMMER AND WINTER IN NORWAY.
BY LADY DI BEAUCLERK.
With Illustrations by the Author.
JOHN MURRAY, ALBEMARLE STREET.

LUGANO, SWITZERLAND.
HOTEL ET BELVEDERE DU PARC.
KEPT BY A. BEHA.

THIS first-class HOTEL contains 150 Sleeping-Rooms and Saloons, all elegantly furnished; "Salons de réunion; an English chapel; and one of the most beautiful Gardens in the country. The Hotel is very agreeably situated for the two seasons. During the winter the Hall and landings are warmed. Great improvements have been made since last year, by the addition of new Public Rooms, and numerous Apartments for Families, with every comfort desirable.

AMPHION (Haute-Savoie).

BAINS D'AMPHION.

THE ONLY BATH ESTABLISHMENT REALLY SITUATED ON THE BORDERS OF THE LAKE OF GENEVA, NEAR EVIAN.

THE Alkaline Waters of Amphion are of the same nature as those of Evian (according to the official analysis made of them); and are recommended to Invalids suffering from all kinds of diseases where Alkaline Waters are required. The ferruginous waters of Amphion, enjoying an ancient celebrity, are also strongly recommended in cases requiring the use of tonics. Three fine Hotels connected with the Establishment. Baths of all descriptions. Good attendance. Magnificent Park and Garden. Splendid view. Billiard and Conversation Rooms. Telegraphic Station. Steamboats, &c.

Persons remaining in the said Hotels have the free use of Baths, Saloons, Promenades, &c.

WIESBADEN.
BLACK BEAR HÔTEL AND BATHS.
OTTO FREYSAG, Proprietor.

SCRUPULOUS CLEANLINESS, ATTENTIVE SERVICE, AND MODERATE CHARGES.

Central Situation—Close to the Mineral Springs, the Theatre, the Conversation House, and the Charming Promenades. Contains 140 Rooms and Saloons, elegantly furnished; 60 neatly fitted-up Bathing Cabinets, spacious Dining-Rooms, and Ladies' Parlour. *Table d'Hôte at 1 and 5 o'clock, and Private Dinners.*

Exquisite Wines. English, French, and German Papers. Visitors Boarded during the Winter Months.

ATHENS.
GRAND HÔTEL DES ETRANGERS,
Near the Royal Palace.

IN the most delightful situation, opposite the Royal Gardens, near the Palace. The best Hotel in Athens. Moderate Prices; good attendance. All Languages spoken.

MENTON.

HÔTEL DE LA MÉDITERRANÉE, Avenue Victor Emmanuel.
—This new and first-rate Hotel is situated full South, with view of the Sea. Families will find it a most desirable residence for its comfort and cleanliness. "Salon de Conversation." Reading-room, with English and Foreign papers. The Servants speak English and other languages. N.B.—The English Church is in the garden.

THOUSANDS AND TENS OF THOUSANDS DIE OF DISEASE,

produced in the first instance by neglect. The stomach is the most important organ, and is at the same time, from numerous causes, most frequently disordered, and thus begins more than half the ailments and troubles to which humanity is subjected: it is, therefore, most important to pay constant attention to the state of the stomach and bowels: and there is no medicine has such deserved repute as

for preserving regularity, and, consequently, ensuring long life.

VIENNA.
FOR OPTICAL INSTRUMENTS, OPERA GLASSES, &c.
THE ESTABLISHMENT OF
JOS. NEUHOEFER (LATE CH. GROSS & Co.),
1149, KOHLMARKT, VIENNA.

Manufacturer of Double Opera Glasses with six, eight, and twelve lenses, own invention and newest construction, to be used for the theatre, travelling, and the field, Telescopes for the Army and Navy, Racing Glasses, and all other kinds of Optical and Mathematical Instruments.

LYNTON, NORTH DEVON.
THE VALLEY OF ROCKS HOTEL.
JOHN CROOK, PROPRIETOR.

This First-class Hotel combines with Moderate Charges all necessary means for the accommodation and comfort of Families and Tourists. The Private Sitting Rooms range in a long front, overlooking the Sea, and looking into the Private Grounds of the Hotel. Here the visitor commands extensive and uninterrupted views of the Bristol Channel, the Welsh Coast, and the Valleys of the East and West Lynn, &c. The Hotel is also most conveniently situate as a centre for the visiting of all the places of interest in the district.

LADIES' AND GENTLEMEN'S COFFEE ROOMS.
Good Post Horses and Carriages of various descriptions are kept.
Coaches during the season to Ilfracombe, Barnstaple, and the West Somerset Railway.

BORDEAUX.
HOTEL DES PRINCES ET DE LA PAIX.
GRÉMAILLY FILS AINÉ, PROPRIETOR.

This is an Hotel of the first rank, in the centre of the town, facing the Grand Theatre and the Prefecture.

Excellent Table-d'hôte at Six. Restaurant and Private Dinners at moderate prices. The *Times* newspaper.

Correspondents in London—Messrs. J. & R. MCCRACKEN, 38, Queen Street, Cannon Street, E.C.

N.B.—The various types of the MÉDOC WINES may be tasted in this Hotel.

BOLOGNA.

HOTEL D'ITALIE.

THIS Hotel of the first order, in the centre of the town, is well known by its excellent service and the courteousness of the Proprietors, Messrs. AMBROSOLI and NICOLA.

The reconstruction of the Hotel has enabled the Proprietors to establish separate Rooms and complete Suites of Apartments for Single Travellers as well as for Families.

The Table, the excellence of which is well known, is served at all hours of the day à *prix fixe* or *à la carte*.

An Omnibus attends regularly the arrivals and departures of the trains.

An Interpreter and every desirable information are at the disposal of Travellers and the Families who may honour this Hotel with their confidence.

GENOA.

HÔTEL DES QUATRE NATIONS.

CEVASCO BROTHERS, Proprietors.

THIS Hotel can be strongly recommended: it is in one of the best situations in Genoa, and travellers will find there very good rooms, moderate charges, cleanliness, excellent Table-d'hôte, as well as private service, with great attention and civility; the comfort of visitors being consulted.

English spoken by the Proprietor.

FRANKFORT O. M.

FRIEDRICH BÖHLER,
ZEIL, No. 54,

NEXT DOOR TO THE POST OFFICE.

PRIZE MEDAL, LONDON. 1862.

MANUFACTORY OF
CARVED STAGHORN AND IVORY ORNAMENTS,

CARVED WOOD WORK (Vieuxchêne) Furniture & Fancy Objects,

Clocks, Lamps, Bronzes, China, Fancy Articles of every Description.

SPECIALITIES OF GERMAN ARTICLES.

Vienna Bronzes, Marquetry, Leather and Meerschaum Goods, Travelling Articles, Toilette Requisites, etc., etc.

SUPERIOR COPIES OF THE ARIADNE BY DANNICKER.

Genuine Eau de Cologne of Jean Marie Farina, opposite the Jülichsplatz.

FIXED PRICES.

The Agents in London are Messrs. J. and R. McCracken, 38, Queen Street, Cannon Street West.

THE
NATIONAL PROVINCIAL BANK OF ENGLAND

ESTABLISHED IN THE YEAR 1833.

Head Office—BISHOPSGATE STREET, corner of THREADNEEDLE STREET.
St. James' Branch—14, WATERLOO PLACE, PALL MALL.
St. Marylebone „   28, BAKER STREET.
Islington   „ 173, UPPER STREET.

Capital.

SUBSCRIBED CAPITAL	£2,100,000	0 0
PAID-UP CAPITAL	1,080,000	0 0
RESERVE FUND	259,706	3 2
No. of SHAREHOLDERS	2,266.	

Directors.

Right Hon. Lord ERNEST AUGUSTUS CHARLES BRUDENELL BRUCE, M.P., 17. St. George's Place, Hyde Park Corner, S.W.
JOHN OLIVER HANSON, Esq., Great Winchester Street, and 4, Dorset Square.
JOHN KINGSTON, Esq., 6, Crosby Square.
HENRY M'CILLERY, Esq., 18, Leadenhall Street.
WILLIAM JAMES MAXWELL, Esq., Richmond, Surrey, S.W.
HENRY PAULL, Esq., M.P., 33, Devonshire Place, Portland Place, W.

Sir JAMES SIBBALD DAVID SCOTT, Bart., 30. Hyde Park Square.
RICHARD BLANEY WADE, Esq., 58, Upper Seymour Street, Portman Square, W.
Hon. ELIOT THOMAS YORKE, 124, Park Street, Grosvenor Square, W.
DUNCAN MACDONALD, Esq., Weybank Lodge, Guildford, Surrey, and 21, Birchin Lane.
GEORGE HANBURY FIELD, Esq., Oakfield, Kent.
ALEX. ROBERTSON, Esq., 20, Grafton Street, Berkeley Square, W., and the College, Elgin, N.B.

The National Provincial Bank of England, having numerous branches in England and Wales, as well as agents and correspondents at home and abroad, affords great facilities to parties transacting Banking business with it in London. Customers keeping accounts with the Bank in town may have moneys paid to their credit at its various branches, and remitted free of charge.

Current accounts conducted at the Head Office and Metropolitan Branches on the usual terms of London Banks.

Deposits at interest received in London of sums of 10l. and upwards, for which receipts are granted, called "Deposit Receipts;" and interest allowed according to the value of money from time to time advertised by the Bank in the newspapers.

The Agency of Country and Foreign Banks, whether Joint Stock or Private, is undertaken.

Purchases and Sales effected in all British and Foreign Stocks; and Dividends, Annuities, &c., received for customers.

Circular Notes and Letters of Credit are issued for the use of Travellers on the Continent and elsewhere.

The Officers of the Bank are bound to secrecy as regards the transactions of its customers.

Copies of the last Annual Report of the Bank, Lists of Shareholders, Branches, Agents, and Correspondents, may be had on application at the Head Office, and at any of the Bank's Branches.

By order of the Directors,

E. ATKINSON,   } Joint
WM. HOLT,   } General Managers.

PENZANCE, CORNWALL.

MOUNT'S BAY HOUSE,

ESPLANADE, PENZANCE, CORNWALL,
Has been erected and fitted up expressly as a
SEASIDE
FAMILY HOTEL & SUPERIOR LODGING-HOUSE.

NO expense or labour has been spared by the Proprietor. The house is furnished in the most modern style, is well supplied with *Hot and Cold Baths*, and replete with every accommodation suitable for Tourists to West Cornwall.

All the Drawing Rooms command an *uninterrupted* and *unsurpassed* view of that
'Beauteous gem set in the silver sea,'
St. Michael's Mount, and the whole of the magnificent Bay.

Invalids will find in Mount's Bay House the comforts of a home, while the beauty and salubrity of the situation, and its nearness to the charming walks on the sea-shore, render it a healthy and delightful residence.

Suites of apartments for families of distinction.

Choice Wines and Ales.   Post Horses and Carriages.   Charges moderate.

E. LAVIN, PROPRIETOR.

STOCKHOLM.

BLANCH'S CAFÉ.

PROPRIETOR - MR. TH. BLANCH.

THIS new, magnificent, first-rate Establishment is situated in the centre of the Town, in the *Kungstradgarden* (Place of Charles XIII.)

CONCERT EVERY DAY.

READING ROOM, WITH THE BEST ENGLISH, FRENCH, GERMAN, AND SWEDISH PERIODICALS.

VENICE.

GRAND HOTEL VICTORIA.

(Formerly REGINA D'INGHILTERRA.)

ROBERT ETZENSBERGER, Manager.

THE largest and finest Hotel in Venice, most conveniently situated near the Piazza S. Marco and the principal Theatres. 180 Bed-rooms, Private Sitting-rooms, Reading-room, with Piano, Billiard-room, and Smoking-room. Baths of every description, great comfort and cleanliness. Service on the Swiss system. Charges more moderate than in any other first-class Hotel.

Arrangements for Pension.

English spoken by all the Servants.

CONSTANTINOPLE.

HÔTEL D'ANGLETERRE.

JAMES MISSIRIE, Proprietor.

THIS long-established and well-known Hotel, situated in the GRAND RUE DE PERA, commanding a magnificent view of the UNRIVALLED BOSPHORUS, is replete with every comfort and convenience for the Accommodation of Families and Tourists.

A Select Table d'Hôte.

In consequence of the largely increasing number of Visitors to the OTTOMAN CAPITAL, from the facility with which it can now be reached from all parts of Europe, and Passengers who select this agreeable Route to and from INDIA and the EAST, it is requested that Families desirous of securing Rooms telegraph or write in anticipation. Every attention will be paid to instructions thus transmitted.

CAREFULLY SELECTED INTERPRETERS FOR ALL LANGUAGES.

The Attendants and Boats of the Hotel await the arrival of the Steamers.

1869.   MURRAY'S HANDBOOK ADVERTISER.   55

TO CONTINENTAL TRAVELLERS.
DORRELL & SON'S
PASSPORT AGENCY,
15, CHARING CROSS, S.W.

Every Information given respecting Travelling on the Continent.

French and Italian spoken, and Correspondence carried on in either Language.

BRITISH SUBJECTS visiting the Continent will save trouble and expense by obtaining their Passports through the above Agency. No personal attendance is required, and country residents may have their Passports forwarded through the post. A 'PASSPORT PROSPECTUS,' containing every particular in detail, by post, on application.

Passports Mounted, and enclosed in Cases, with the name of the bearer impressed in gold on the outside; thus affording security against injury or loss, and preventing delay in the frequent examination of the passport when travelling.

Fee, Obtaining Passport, 1s.; Visas, 1s. each.   Cases, 1s. 6d. to 5s. each.

THE LATEST EDITIONS OF MURRAY'S HANDBOOKS.

English and Foreign Stationery, Dialogue Books, Couriers' Bags, Pocketbooks and Purses of every description, Travelling Inkstands, and a variety of other Articles useful for Travellers.

THE ATHENÆUM.

EVERY SATURDAY, OF ANY BOOKSELLER OR NEWS AGENT,

PRICE THREEPENCE.

Each Half-Yearly Volume complete in itself, with Title-Page and Index.

THE ATHENÆUM
JOURNAL OF ENGLISH AND FOREIGN LITERATURE, SCIENCE, AND THE FINE ARTS.

CONTAINS:—REVIEWS of every important New Book—REPORTS of the Learned Societies—AUTHENTIC ACCOUNTS of Scientific Voyages and Expeditions—FOREIGN CORRESPONDENCE on Subjects relating to Literature, Science, and Art—CRITICISMS ON ART, MUSIC, AND THE DRAMA—BIOGRAPHICAL NOTICES of distinguished Men—ORIGINAL PAPERS AND POEMS—WEEKLY GOSSIP.

THE ATHENÆUM is so conducted that the reader, however distant, is, in respect to Literature, Science, and Art, on an equality in point of information with the best-informed circles of the Metropolis.

Subscription for Twelve Months, 13s.; Six Months, 6s. 6d. If required to be sent by Post, the Postage extra.

Office for Advertisements—
20, WELLINGTON STREET, STRAND, LONDON, W.C.

COURIERS AND TRAVELLING SERVANTS.

THE ORIGINAL AGENCY

ESTABLISHED 1832.

440, WEST STRAND, LONDON, W.C.

Patronized by the Nobility and General Travelling Public.

GENTLEMEN and Families going abroad are respectfully informed that Couriers and Travelling Servants for all Countries, and of the highest character and experience, may as heretofore always be engaged at the above Agency, where none are recommended again who have not given entire satisfaction to their previous employers, thus ensuring to parties about to travel who may honour the agency with their patronage, the greatest amount of usefulness, civility, and respect from those whom they may employ through it.

MURRAY'S AND ALL THE OTHER GUIDES,

MAPS, DICTIONARIES, DIALOGUES, GRAMMARS, &c.,

For All Countries.

PORTMANTEAUX, HAT-CASES, AND ALL SORTS OF TRAVELLING BAGS,

And all the Requisites for Travellers, are kept on sale at

LEE & CARTERS

ORIGINAL GUIDE AND TRAVELLERS' DEPÔT,

440, WEST STRAND, LONDON, W.C.

(*nearly opposite the Charing Cross Railway*),

WHERE ALL INFORMATION ABOUT PASSPORTS, ROUTES ETC. CAN ALWAYS BE OBTAINED.

BY ROYAL  COMMAND.

JOSEPH GILLOTT'S
CELEBRATED
STEEL PENS.

Sold by all Dealers throughout the World.

Every Packet bears the Fac-simile of his Signature,

RECENT TRAVELS.

REMINISCENCES OF ATHENS AND THE MOREA:

Extract from a Journal of Travels in Greece. By the late Earl of CARNARVON, Author of 'Portugal and Gallicia.' With Map, Crown 8vo., 7s 6d.

RESEARCHES IN THE HIGHLANDS OF TURKEY,

Including Visits to Mounts Ida, Athos, Olympus, and Pelion, and to the Mirdite Albanians, and other remote Tribes; with Notes on the Ballads, Tales, and Classical Superstitions of the Modern Greek. By Rev. HENRY FANSHAWE TOZER, M.A., F.R.G.S., Tutor and late Fellow of Exeter College, Oxford. With Map and Illustrations, 2 vols., crown 8vo., 24s.

LAST WINTER IN THE UNITED STATES.

Being Table Talk collected during a Tour through the late Southern Confederation, the Far West, the Rocky Mountains, &c. &c. By F. BARHAM ZINCKE, Chaplain in Ordinary to the Queen. Post 8vo., 10s. 6d.

JOHN MURRAY, ALBEMARLE STREET.

GENEVA.
L. TISSOT and CO., Watch Manufacturers,
19, RUE DU RHONE, GENEVA.
CHRONOMETERS AND WATCHES OF HIGH ACCURACY.

GENEVA.
JOURNAL DES ÉTRANGERS.

GIVING a List of Strangers travelling to Geneva, Lausanne, Fribourg, Montreux, Vevey, and the rest of Switzerland.

Advertising Agency, VÉRÉSOFF and GARRIGUES, Place Bel Air, Geneva.

BOOKS AND MAPS FOR TRAVELLERS.

Travels in Bashan and the Central Caucasas, including
Ascents of Kazbek and Elbruz and a Visit to Ararat and Tabriz. By DOUGLAS W.
FRESHFIELD, Esq. In One Volume, with Maps and Illustrations. [*Now Ready.*

Cadore, or Titian's Country. By JOSIAH GILBERT, one of
the Authors of the 'Dolomite Mountains, or Excursions through Tyrol, Carinthia, Carniola, and Friuli.' In One Volume, with numerous Illustrations and a Facsimile of
Titian's Original Design for his Picture of the Battle of Cadore. [*Nearly Ready.*

The Alpine Guide. By JOHN BALL, M.R.I.A., late President
of the Alpine Club. With Maps, Panoramas of Summits, and other Illustrations. Three
Parts or Volumes, post 8vo. :—

Guide to the Eastern Alps, price 10s. 6d.

Guide to the Western Alps, including Mont Blanc, Monte
Rosa, Zermatt, &c., price 6s. 6d.

Guide to the Central Alps, including all the Oberland
District, price 7s. 6d.

Introduction on Alpine Travelling in general and on
the Geology of the Alps. Price One Shilling. Each of the Three Volumes or Parts of
the *Alpine Guide* may be had with this INTRODUCTION prefixed, price One Shilling extra.

Map of the Valpelline, the Val Tournanche, and the
Southern Valleys of the Chain of MONTE ROSA, from an actual Survey in 1865–1866.
By A. ADAMS-REILLY, F.R.G.S., M.A.C. In Chromo-lithography, on extra stout Drawing
Paper, 25 inches by 14 inches, price 6s. To be had also mounted on CANVAS, folded and
jointed, for POCKET OR KNAPSACK, price 7s. 6d.

Map of the Chain of Mont Blanc, from an Actual
Survey in 1863–1864. By A. ADAMS-REILLY, F.R.G.S., M.A.C. In Chromo-lithography
on extra stout Drawing Paper 28 inches by 17 inches, price 10s. To be had also mounted
on CANVAS, in a folding case, price 12s. 6d.

Guide to the Pyrenees, for the Use of Mountaineers. By
CHARLES PACKE. Second Edition, corrected; with Frontispiece and Map, and an
APPENDIX. Crown 8vo., price 7s. 6d.

Pictures in Tyrol and Elsewhere, from a Family Sketch-
Book. By the Author of 'A Voyage en Zigzag, &c.' Second Edition, revised; with 62
Lithographic Plates of Illustrations, containing 113 Sketches. Small quarto, price 21s.

Roma Sotteranea; or, an Account of the Roman Cata-
combs, and especially of the Cemetery of St. Callixtus. Compiled from the Works of
Commendatore G. B. DE ROSSI, with the consent of the Author, by the Rev. J. S.
NORTHCOTE, D.D., and the Rev. W. R. BROWNLOW. With numerous Engravings on
Wood, 10 Lithographs, 10 Plates in Chromo-lithography, and an Atlas of Plans, all
executed in Rome under the Author's superintendence for this Translation. In One
Volume, 8vo. [*Nearly ready*

LONDON: LONGMANS, GREEN & CO., PATERNOSTER ROW.

HANDBOOK OF ARCHÆOLOGY.

8vo., Illustrated, bound in half roan, 15s.,

TRAVELLERS' ART COMPANION
TO THE
MUSEUMS AND ANCIENT REMAINS OF ITALY, GREECE and EGYPT.

By HODDER M. WESTROPP.

'So convenient and attractive a volume ought to tempt travellers to systematize their impressions, and not be contented to ramble through temples and galleries without carrying away any better result than an ignorant succession of images hastily impressed on the retina, and destined to vanish as quickly as they came. Mr. Westropp has condensed into a small space an immense mass of useful information about architecture, sculpture, paintings, and gems, so that his book is a complete encyclopædia of ancient art.'—*Pall Mall Gazette.*

BELL AND DALDY.

Second Edition, 8vo., price 14s.,

POMPEII:
ITS HISTORY, BUILDINGS, AND ANTIQUITIES.
AN ACCOUNT OF THE CITY,
With a full Description of the Remains and of the Recent Excavations, and also an Itinerary for Visitors.

EDITED BY T. H. DYER, LL.D.

Illustrated with nearly 300 Wood Engravings, a large Map and a Plan of the Forum.

BELL AND DALDY.

ANDERMATT, ST. GOTTHARDT.

HERR NAGEL-DONAZIANS

Has for disposal the choicest Animals, Birds, Eggs, Minerals and Plants of this rich district.

Single specimens or characteristic collections may be had, and the greatest attention will be given to foreign orders. A few old and rare pictures.

GENEVA.

A. MAUCHAIN, 32 Grand Quai.

MANUFACTURER OF SWISS WOOD CARVINGS,
ALSO A VERY LARGE CHOICE OF ALL KINDS OF MUSICAL SURPRISES IN CARVED WOODS.

4 MEDALS.

THE FURNISHING OF BED-ROOMS.

HEAL & SON have observed for some time that it would be advantageous to their Customers to see a much larger selection of Bed-room Furniture than is usually displayed, and that to judge properly of the style and effect of the different descriptions of Furniture, it is necessary that each description should be placed in a separate room. They have therefore erected large and additional Show-rooms, by which they are enabled not only to extend their show of Iron, Brass, and Wood Bedsteads, and Bed-room Furniture, beyond what they believe has ever been attempted, but also to provide several small rooms for the purpose of keeping complete suites of Bed-room Furniture in the different styles.

Japanned Deal Goods may be seen in complete suites of five or six different colours, some of them light and ornamental, and others of a plainer decription. Suites of Stained Deal Gothic Furniture, Polished Deal, Oak, and Walnut, are also set apart in separate rooms, so that customers are able to see the effect as it would appear in their own rooms.

The Stock of Mahogany Goods for the better Bed-rooms, and Japanned Goods for plain and Servants' use, is very greatly increased, the whole forming as complete an assortment of Bed-room Furniture as they think can possibly be desired.

HEAL AND SON'S

ILLUSTRATED CATALOGUE OF

BEDSTEADS, BEDDING, & BED-ROOM FURNITURE,

SENT FREE BY POST.

196, 197, 198, TOTTENHAM COURT ROAD.

VISITORS TO THE CONTINENT.

CHARLES CARR & CO.,
14, BISHOPSGATE STREET WITHIN, LONDON, E.C.
(*Mr. CARR, late of the Firm of OLIVIER & CARR*),

COMMISSION AND MERCHANTS,
Agents for Shipment and Reception of Goods to and from all Parts of the World,

WINE MERCHANTS, &c.

CHARLES CARR & CO., have the honour to inform
VISITORS TO THE CONTINENT,
that they undertake to receive and pass through the Custom House
WORKS of Art, BAGGAGE, and PROPERTY of EVERY DESCRIPTION;
which are attended to on arrival
with the utmost Care in Examination and Removal,
under their Personal Superintendence, and at
very Moderate Charges,
of which the following may be taken as a guide:—

Landing from the Ship, Clearing, Delivery in London, and Agency—
On Trunks of Baggage . . . . about 9s. each.
On Cases of Works of Art, of moderate size and value . about 15s.
On Large and Valuable Cases, according to care and trouble required.
On several Cases sent together, the charges are less on each.

CHARLES CARR & CO. undertake the
FORWARDING OF PACKAGES OF EVERY KIND
to the care of their Correspondents, where they can remain, if required, until the arrival of the owners. Also

THE EXECUTION of ORDERS for the PURCHASE of GOODS,
which from their knowledge of all the markets they are enabled to buy on the most advantageous terms.

N.B.—Keys of all locked Packages should always be sent, as everything, although free of duty, must be examined by the Customs on arrival.

INSURANCES EFFECTED, AND AGENCY BUSINESS OF EVERY DESCRIPTION ATTENDED TO.

Mr. C. CARR having had many years' experience in all the above branches of business, can with confidence assure those who will kindly favour him with their support, that their interests will be well cared for in the hands of his firm.

CHAS. CARR & CO.'S principal Correspondents are—

At Aix-la-Chapelle	Messrs. A. SOUHER and CO.
" Alexandria	Mr. J. W. BROWNE.
" Antwerp	Mr. F. VERELLEN BEERNAERT.
	Messrs. VLEUGELS and GUFFANTI.
" Basle	Mr. J. J. FREY.
" Bologna	Messrs. ANTONIO MAZZETTI and CO.
" Bordeaux	Messrs. ALBRECHT et FILS.
" Boulogne	Messrs. L. BRANLY and CO., 81, Rue Napoleon.
" Brussels	Mr. G. LUYCKX, 24, Rue des Fabriques.
" Calais	Messrs. L. J. VOGUE and CO.
" Cologne	Messrs. C. H. VAN ZUTPHEN and CO.
	Messrs. G. TILMES and CO.
" Constantinople	Messrs. VALSAMACHY and CO.
" Dresden	Messrs. KRAETSCHMER and CO.
" Florence	Messrs. HASKARD and SON, 4, Borgo SS. Apostoli.
" Frankfort	Mr. MARTIN BECKER, 5, Bleidenstrasse.
" Geneva	Messrs. JOLIMAY and CO.
" Genoa	Messrs. G. B. PRATOLONGO and CO.
	Messrs. P. CAUVIN, DIAMANTI, and COSTA.
" Hamburg	Messrs. JULIUS WUSTENFELD and CO.
" Havre	Messrs. CHR. EGLIN and MARING.
" Interlacken	Messrs. RITSCHARD and BURKI.
" Leipzig	Messrs. GERHARD and HEY.
" Leghorn	Messrs. HENDERSON BROTHERS.
" Malta	Messrs. ROSE and CO.
" Marseilles	Messrs. GIRAUD FRERES.
	Messrs. HORACE BOUCHET and CO.
" Milan	Mr. G. POSSENTI.
" Munich	Messrs. GUTLEBEN and WEIDERT.
" Naples	Messrs. CERULLI and CO.; Mr. G. CIVALLERI.
" Nice	Messrs. M. and N. GIORDAN, Quai Lunel, 14 (sur le Port)
" Ostend	Mr. J. DUCLOS ASSANDRI.
" Paris	M. HECTOR L'HERBIER, 18, Rue de la Douane.
" Pau	Mr. BERGEROT.
" Prague	Mr. J. J. SEIDL, Hibernergasse, No. 1000.
" Rome	Mr. J. P. SHEA, 11, Piazza di Spagna.
	Mr. A. TOMBINI.
" Rotterdam	Mr. J. A. HOUWENS; Messrs. P. A. VAN ES and CO.
" Trieste	Messrs. MARTIN FRERES.
" Turin	Mr. CHIABODO PIETRO, Via Dora Grossa, 13.
" Venice	Mr. HENRY DECOPPET, Mr. F∞ TOLOMEI DI F∞
" Vienna	Mr. ANTON POKORNY, Stadt Sonnenfelsgasse, 2.

Any other houses will also forward goods to C. C. & Co., on receiving instructions to do so. Travellers are requested always to give particular directions that their Packages are consigned direct to CHAS. CARR & CO., 14, Bishopsgate Street Within, London, E.C.

CHAS. CARR & CO. beg to call attention to their

WINES

IMPORTED BY THEMSELVES DIRECT FROM THE GROWERS.

Per doz.

CLARET—Medoc	15s.	or 14s. per half hhds. of 12 dozen.		
"	24s.	or 21s.	ditto	ditto
Margaux	28s.	or 25s.	ditto	ditto
St. Julian	30s.	or 27s.	ditto	ditto
Finer qualities	36s. to 126s.			
BURGUNDY—Beaune	24s. to 30s.			
Volnay	36s. to 54s.			
Superior qualities	60s. and upwards.			
Chablis	30s. to 54s.			
HOCK and MOSELLE	21s. to 120s.			
CHAMPAGNE—Sparkling Hock and Moselle.	42s. to 72s.			
SHERRIES	36s. to 60s. In Quarter Casks 15l. to 35l.			
MARSALA	26s. to 30s.			

AND OTHER WINES.

Detailed Price Lists may be had at C. C. & Co.'s Office.

BRUSSELS.

HÔTEL DE BELLE VUE.

Proprietor, Mr. EDWARD DREMEL.

THIS magnificent Hotel, in offering to the Visitor every kind of comfort and accommodation, has the great advantage of being situated adjoining

THE PALACE OF THE KING,

and facing

THE PLACE ROYALE AND THE PARK.

It contains numerous large and small Apartments, as well as single Rooms.

Table-d'Hôte, richly served. Choice Wines.

SMOKING ROOM.

READING ROOM, with the best Belgian, English, French, German, and American Daily Papers and Periodicals.

Terraces, with Splendid View overlooking the Park.

ARRANGEMENTS MADE FOR THE WINTER.

Mr. DREMEL, the new Proprietor of this Hotel, hopes to justify the confidence placed in him, by a carefully arranged system of prompt and civil attendance, combined with moderate charges.

PASSPORT AGENCY AND GUIDE DEPÔT.

C. GOODMAN,

(LATE LEIGH & CO.,)

ESTABLISHED HALF-A-CENTURY,

407, STRAND, W.C.

(THREE DOORS EAST OF THE ADELPHI THEATRE.)

British Subjects about to Travel on the Continent, by forwarding a Banker's Application through this Agency, can obtain the Foreign Office Passport with the necessary Visas, by which means they will avoid trouble and loss of time.

PASSPORT CIRCULAR GRATIS.

Passport Cases, including Mounting on Muslin and Names lettered thereon, from 2s. 6d. to 5s.

THE LATEST EDITIONS OF MURRAY'S HANDBOOKS.

Baedeker's Guide in English and German; Blaik's Guides for Home Tours, Keller's and Loutchard's Maps of Switzerland. Panoramas of the Rhine, Switzerland, and Rome. Dictionaries, Phrase Books, Interpreters, Writing Cases, Couriers' Bags, Journals, Soup Boxes, Wallets, and every requisite for Travellers.

GENOA.

GRAND HÔTEL D'ITALIE.

THIS magnificent Establishment, formerly the RAGGIO PALACE, continues to retain the first place among all houses of this description in this city by its exceptional and central position, as well as by the extent of its accommodation and its cleanliness.

With the view of preserving the same reputation, the Proprietor has established agreeable salons de reunion, music, reading, and smoking, having a superb view of the Gulf. The prices are very moderate.

Excellent Table-d'Hôte at 4 francs. Comfortable Rooms at 2 francs.

For persons who remain some time in the Hotel arrangements are made on reduced terms.

Omnibuses and Carriages to meet every Train.

F

AIX LES BAINS.
GRAND HOTEL DE L'EUROPE.
PROPRIETOR, J. BERNASCON.

First-class house—admirably situated near the Casino, the Baths, and the English Church. This Hotel is strongly recommended to Travellers for the comfort of its arrangements. Good gardens with a beautiful view of the Lake and Mountains. Large and small apartments for Families at moderate prices, and a Chalet in the garden for Families who may prefer being out of the Hotel. Excellent Table d'Hôte. Carriages for hire, and an omnibus belonging to the Hotel to meet every train.

BOARDING SCHOOL FOR YOUNG LADIES.
SUPERINTENDED BY MADLLE. BRONN.
2 MOLARD, GENEVA, 2 MOLARD.

LESSONS GIVEN BY THE BEST MASTERS. AND SOJOURN IN THE COUNTRY DURING THE HOLIDAYS.

Small 8vo., 3s. 6d.
HANDBOOK OF TRAVEL TALK.
IN FOUR LANGUAGES.
JOHN MURRAY, ALBEMARLE STREET.

ANTWERP.

HÔTEL DU GRAND LABOUREUR,
PLACE DE MEIR, 26.

This old-established and highly-recommended Hotel, which has been considerably enlarged, is situated in the finest and healthiest square of the city of Antwerp; its cleanliness and the excellency of the Table-d'Hote and Wines, added to the attention and civility shown to all visitors, have made it deservedly popular.

HOT AND COLD BATHS.
ENGLISH AND FRENCH NEWSPAPERS.

BIRMINGHAM.

THE

NEW GREAT WESTERN HOTEL

(Snow Hill Station)

IS NOW OPEN.

THE ORIGINAL GUIDE & TRAVELLERS' DEPÔT,

Passport and Couriers' Agency,

NEARLY OPPOSITE THE CHARING CROSS RAILWAY.

ESTABLISHED 1832.

LEE'S POLYGLOT
WASHING BOOKS
(To save the trouble of translating Washing Bills)
For Ladies or Gentlemen,
IN
English & French.
English & German.
English & Italian.
English & Spanish.
English & Portuguese.

SPONGE BAGS.

METALLIC SOAP BOXES.

Waterproof Coats.

KNAPSACKS.

FLASKS.

Railway Rugs,
STRAPS,

Courier Bags.

MONEY BAGS and BELTS.

PURSES,
WALLETS,
SOVEREIGN AND
NAPOLEON CASES.

TRAVELLING
TELESCOPES,
Compasses,
and Spectacles.

PASSPORTS
Procured, mounted on linen, and inserted in morocco cases, stamped with coronet or name, at the shortest notice, and forwarded by Post. Visas obtained and information given.

The latest editions of MURRAY'S HANDBOOKS kept in the original binding, and in limp leather, more convenient for the pocket, at 2s. a volume extra.

TRUSTWORTHY COURIERS and TRAVELLING SERVANTS can be engaged at

LEE & CARTER'S,
440, WEST STRAND, W.C.

TWO DOORS WEST OF THE LOWTHER ARCADE,
Where an extensive collection of

GUIDES, HANDBOOKS, MAPS,
Dictionaries, Dialogues,
GRAMMARS, INTERPRETERS,
WORD AND PHRASE BOOKS,

In most of the Continental Languages, and every article necessary for home and foreign travel, is kept in great variety.

PORTMANTEAUX, HAT-CASES,
CARPET BAGS, FITTED BAGS,
PORTABLE BATHS,
SPONGE,
Air Cushions, Dressing & Writing Cases,
CAMP STOOLS,
LUNCHEON BASKETS, LEG-RESTS,
&c. &c. &c.

MOORE'S
GERMAN INTERPRETER.
With the exact pronunciation in English in a separate column. 5s. in cloth, or 6s. in leather.

MANUSCRIPT & ACCOUNT BOOKS.

Metallic and other Pocket Books.

Luggage Labels.

DOOR FASTENERS.

Patent Inkstands and Light Boxes.

ELASTIC BANDS.

Foreign Paper, Envelopes, &c.

POCKET PEN
AND
Pencil Holders.

KELLER'S AND LEUTHOLD'S
MAPS
OF
SWITZERLAND.

STUDER'S
MONTE ROSA.

MAYR'S
TYROL.

www.ingramcontent.com/pod-product-compliance
Lightning Source LLC
Chambersburg PA
CBHW021416300426
44114CB00010B/523